S0-BYE-067

LEADERSHIP
Enhancing the Lessons of Experience

LEADERSHIP
Enhancing the Lessons of Experience

Richard L. Hughes, Robert C. Ginnett,
and Gordon J. Curphy

IRWIN
Homewood, IL 60430
Boston, MA 02116

Senior sponsoring editor:	Kurt L. Strand
Editorial coordinator:	Lisa Brennan
Marketing manager:	Kurt Messersmith
Project editor:	Waivah Clement
Production manager:	Diane Palmer
Designer:	Jeanne M. Rivera
Art coordinator:	Mark Malloy
Compositor:	Precision Typographers
Typeface:	10/12 Palatino
Printer:	R. R. Donnelley & Sons Company

Library of Congress Cataloging-in-Publication Data

Hughes, Richard L.
    Leadership : enhancing the lessons of experience / Richard L.
Hughes, Robert C. Ginnett, and Gordon J. Curphy.
        p.   cm.
    Includes index.
    ISBN 0-256-10278-3
    1. Leadership.   I. Ginnett, Robert C.   II. Curphy, Gordon J.
III. Title.
HM141.H78   1993
303.3′4—dc20   92-32730

Printed in the United States of America

  2 3 4 5 6 7 8 9 0 DOC 0 9 8 7 6 5 4 3

We dedicate this book to our families,

Georgeann, Anne, Amy, and Sarah

Sherry, Laura, and Brad

Dianne and Chelsea

Foreword

Often the only difference between chaos and a smoothly functioning operation is leadership; this book is about that difference.

The authors are psychologists; therefore the book has a distinctly psychological tone. You, as a reader, are going to be asked to think about leadership the way psychologists do. There is much here about psychological tests and surveys, about studies done in psychological laboratories, and about psychological analyses of good (and poor) leadership. You will often run across common psychological concepts in these pages, such as personality, values, attitudes, perceptions, and self-esteem plus some not-so-common ''jargon-y'' phrases like double-loop learning, expectancy theory, and perceived inequity. This is not the same kind of book that would be written by coaches, sales managers, economists, political scientists, or generals.

Be not dismayed. Because these authors are also teachers with a good eye and ear for what students find interesting, they write clearly and cleanly, and they have also included a host of entertaining, stimulating snapshots on leadership: cartoons, quotes, anecdotal highlights, and personal glimpses from a wide range of intriguing people, each offered as an illustration of some scholarly point.

Also, because the authors are, or have been at one time or another, together or singly, not only psychologists and teachers but also children, students, Boy Scouts, parents, professors (at the U.S. Air Force Academy), Air Force officers, pilots, church members, athletes, administrators, insatiable readers, and convivial raconteurs, their stories and examples are drawn from a wide range of personal sources, and their anecdotes ring true.

As psychologists and scholars, they have reviewed here a wide range of psychological studies, other scientific inquiries, personal reflections of leaders, and philosophic writings on the topic of leadership. In distilling this material, they have drawn many practical conclusions useful for current and potential leaders. There are suggestions here for goal setting, for running meetings, for negotiating, for managing conflict within groups, and for handling your own personal stress, to mention just a few.

All leaders, no matter what their age and station, can find some useful tips here, ranging over subjects such as body language, keeping a journal, and how to relax under tension.

In several ways the authors have tried to help you, the reader, feel what it would be like "to be in charge." For example, they have posed quandaries such as the following: You are in a leadership position with a budget provided by an outside funding source. You believe strongly in, say, Topic A, and have taken a strong, visible public stance on that topic. The head of your funding source takes you aside and says, "We disagree with your stance on Topic A. Please tone down your public statements, or we will have to take another look at your budget for next year."

What would you do? Quit? Speak up and lose your budget? Tone down your public statements and feel dishonest? No easy answer, and not an unusual situation for a leader to be in. Sooner or later, every leader has to confront just how much outside interference he or she will tolerate in order to be able to carry out programs that they believe in.

The authors emphasize the value of experience in leadership development, a conclusion I thoroughly agree with. Virtually every leader who makes it to the top of whatever pyramid they happen to be climbing does so by building on earlier experiences. The successful leaders are those who learn from these earlier experiences, by reflecting on and analyzing them to help solve larger future challenges.

In this vein, let me make a suggestion. Actually, let me assign you some homework. (I know, I know, this is a peculiar approach in a book Foreword but stay with me, I have a point.)

YOUR ASSIGNMENT: To gain some useful leadership experience, persuade eight people to do some notable activity together for at least two hours that they would not otherwise do without your intervention. Your only restriction is that you cannot tell them why you are doing this.

It can be any eight people: friends, family, teammates, club members, neighbors, students, working colleagues. It can be any activity, except that it should be something more substantial than watching television, eating, going to a movie, or just sitting around talking. It could be a roller-skating party, an organized debate, a songfest, a long hike, a visit to a museum, or volunteer work such as picking up litter or visiting a nursing home.

If you will take it upon yourself to make something happen in the world that would not have otherwise happened without you, you will be engaging in an act of leadership with all of its attendant barriers, burdens, and pleasures, and you will quickly learn the relevance of many of the topics that the authors discuss in this book. In fact, if you try the eight-person-two-hour experience first and read this book later, you will have a much better understanding of how complicated an act of leadership can be. You will learn about the difficulties of developing a vision ("now that we are together, what are we going to do?'"), of motivating others, of setting agendas and timetables, of securing resources, of the need for follow-through. You may even learn about "loneliness at the top." However, if you are successful, you will also experience the thrill that comes from successful leadership. One person *can* make a difference by enriching the lives of others, if only for a few hours. And for all of the frustrations and complexities of leadership, the tingling satisfaction that comes from success can become almost addictive. The capacity for making things happen can become its own motivation. With an early success, even if it is only with eight people for two hours, you may well be on your way to a leadership future.

The authors believe that leadership development involves reflecting on one's own experiences. Reading this book in the context of your own leadership experience can aid in that process. Their book is comprehensive, scholarly, stimulating, entertaining, and relevant for anyone who wishes to better understand the dynamics of leadership, and to improve their own personal performance.

David P. Campbell

Preface

Sitting down to write the preface for this book, we realized how much we had learned in the process. As a result, the finished product is very different from our original idea. This seems appropriate since changing through learning and experience is what this book is really about.

We decided to write this book after teaching leadership courses for a number of years. We began to feel that the books we were using had some real shortcomings. Most books took on the subject of leadership as if it were a compound in organic chemistry. They said leadership could only be understood by analyzing it. These texts contained nearly every research study ever conducted. While this approach may be ideal for doctoral students looking for hypotheses to test, it usually left undergraduates a little cold. As David Campbell often says, ''Listening to a psychologist talk about leadership is like listening to a physicist talk about rainbows. When they're done, you'll know a lot more about the subject but somehow the magic is gone.''

We began to look for books that still had some of the magic in them, and were able to find them in a variety of places. We found that magic in biographies and autobiographies of great leaders, and in novels that portrayed characters with leadership qualities. While these books were inspiring and challenging, they didn't offer any theory to explain the experiences they related. In the absence of theory, students had difficulty applying what they learned to real life experiences.

Furthermore, neither the existing texts nor biographies and novels helped students to develop leadership skills. Instead, developing these skills was left to the athletic field, student government, or summer jobs. Unfortunately, the link between the experience and the leadership lesson was frequently missed. As teachers we found that when students made a connection between their experiences and classroom lessons, learning was remarkable. We realized that we had to somehow use education to accelerate learning from experience. We wanted a book based on theory, including some skill-building material, but with some of the magic still in it.

Like most people who have taught courses or presented training programs on leadership, we have often been asked, ''Do you really think a course can make you a better leader?'' That question usually springs from an assumption the questioner makes about leadership development. One assumption might be that one is either a good leader or not; that *leadership doesn't develop at all.* A different assumption that might prompt the same question is that *leadership develops, but through experience, not through academic study.* As we have tried to articulate more fully in the text, we agree with the idea that leadership develops significantly through experience. However, we disagree with the implication that academic study is therefore essentially irrelevant to leadership development. We hope this text will heighten the student's interest in the field of leadership and make her a more sophisticated observer and active learner. Do we agree people develop as leaders primarily through their "real life" experiences? Yes, but we also believe this text can help students learn more from their subsequent experiences (even after the course is over) than they otherwise might have. Understanding is most likely to develop out of an interest in the field and its relevance to each student's personal and professional development. Toward that end, we have tried to make the text personally relevant, readable, and interesting as well as scholarly.

The initial reviews helped us to determine that teachers wanted a lot more references and research findings than we had included. Subsequent reviewer comments revealed that more detailed research was still needed. The text already had a solid experiential foundation. On the advice of reviewers, we reinforced it with detailed research. We commiserated and cajoled each other through the edits and re-edits. But mostly, we improved from our experiences and so, we hope, did this book. We believe that it is much better than what we had originally intended. We designed the text to meet the needs of both teachers and students, and we sincerely hope it accelerates your learning and application in leadership.

Our primary audience is undergraduates, though we believe the book could be useful in other contexts such as professional schools or leadership training programs. Even at the undergraduate level it could be used in several distinctly different contexts. In addition to courses on leadership, the book could also be used to support leadership development efforts in various student affairs activities or specialized professional programs at the undergraduate level.

We have written the book for the general student. We wanted it to serve as a "stand alone" introduction to the subject of leadership which made no assumptions about a student's previous coursework. To meet that objective, we drew upon three different "literatures." One of these was the research base of empirical studies concerning leadership emergence and effectiveness. We strongly believe students of leadership should be familiar with relevant research from such social science disciplines as psychology and organizational behavior. But most existing treatments of this literature seemed intended for audiences already interested in rigorous research on leadership. We have presented a fair summary of this research literature without being exhaustively comprehensive or overemphasizing methodological issues.

The second type of "literature" we have tried to include is what we consider high-interest anecdotes, stories, or findings. These are materials we believe most people find intrinsically interesting. This material generally appears as textual examples or in the feature we call *Highlights*. We have tried to use this material synergistically with the more abstract literature. We hope such material brings "color" and heightened interest to the research literature, allowing the concepts from the latter to offer new ways of thinking about the former.

The third "literature" we have included is that of leadership skills. We have aspired to teach students more than leadership as a field of study. We will achieve this by helping them become better leaders themselves. Hence our attention in this text to skills such as communicating, active listening, giving feedback, resolving conflicts, encouraging creativity, and setting goals. We disagree with "recipes" of effective leadership. Instead we believe students should be encouraged to formulate their own ideas and opinions and draw their own conclusions. Therefore, we mentioned relevant research findings in these skill sections as much as possible without interfering with the clearly more-applied nature of these sections or chapters.

FEATURES

We believe the very structure of the book is one of its unique features and strengths. In Part I we address different aspects of the view "leadership is a process, not a position." These include: looking at how leadership develops, how it is measured or assessed, how it is an art as well as a science, and how leadership is related to other concepts such as power and influence. Also in Part I we propose a simple framework for conceptualizing leadership. This framework or model (it is *not* a theory)—The Leader, The Followers, and The Situation—provides the structure for the rest of the text, and it does so on two different levels. First of all it provides the structure for the remaining major sections of the book, Parts II–V. Part II addresses the leader, Part III addresses the followers, Part IV addresses the situation, and Part V addresses the interactions and contingencies among these major elements of leadership more comprehensively and systematically than in any preceding part. In general, Part V deals with the more comprehensive theories of leadership.

On the second level, this framework functions as a graphic "Lens" within chapters for viewing the concepts or ideas within that chapter. In doing so, it also provides a common mechanism for integrating material from different chapters or research domains. It becomes, for example, a heuristic tool for looking at similarities and differences across different theories of leadership.

Another key feature is the *Highlights*, many of which accompany each chapter. As noted above, these typically involve interesting illustrations related to the textual material. The *Highlights* come in many forms. They include personal anecdotes by or about leaders in their own words, those of biographers, or even (in one case) a fable. The *Highlights* also serve to focus attention on studies of special interest or relevance which may not have fit readily into the main text (e.g., the series on personality and the presidency in Chapter Seven). They also provide vivid example of concepts in the text. One special category of *Highlight,* leadership quotes, begins every chapter. We believe they stimulate student interest in reading the chapter and can themselves be the topics of engaging class discussion.

This text is also unique because it contains a number of pedagogical features which are found in other types of textbooks, but not generally in leadership books. Key Terms and Concepts appear in boldface throughout the text and are also listed at the end of each chapter. Each chapter is followed by a summary, several thought provoking discussion questions, and suggested readings. These readings represent many different genres of leadership literature for anyone wishing to delve further into some of the issues raised in that chapter.

We strongly believe that the leadership process cannot be described adequately without representing both genders, and we have tried to do this as equally as possible. Women leaders are featured in some detail in several examples in the text and in *Highlights* focusing on "women in leadership." These describe particular women leaders and factors affecting women in leadership roles. We would feel rewarded if the book played any constructive part in increasing openness and acceptance of women in nontraditional leadership roles.

Finally, supplementing the text itself is an Instructor's Manual that includes an extended outline of every chapter, test items of varying types, exercises or activities for each chapter, and masters for overheads.

Acknowledgments

There are many people who have shared their thoughts, criticisms, words of encouragement, and energy in helping us on this project and, more generally, influencing our thinking about leadership and teaching about leadership.

From the Air Force Academy faculty (at one time or another), we would like to thank Bill Clover, Dave Porter, Tom McCloy, Bill Rosenbach, Jeff Austin, Fred Harburg, Bob Gregory, John Anderson, and Chip Wood. We are also especially indebted to Andy Stricker, Laurel Mellott, Terri Newcomb, Sheila Rhett, and Dawn Anthony for their generous technical assistance and undying patience in helping us prepare the manuscript.

From the Center for Creative Leadership we would like to thank Henry Browning, David Campbell, Dianne Nilsen, Pete DeLisle, Glenn Hallam, Roberta Kraus, Peter Neary, Gary Rhodes, Walt Tornow, Jodi Kassover-Taylor, and Walt Ulmer.

We also deeply appreciate the enthusiastic encouragement and professional guidance of Karen Johnson, Kurt Strand, and Lisa Brennan at Richard D. Irwin.

There are also a few more personal acknowledgments we would like to make. RCG would like to thank Richard Hackman of Harvard University and Barbara Kanki of NASA Ames Research Center for their support in ongoing research on leadership and team effectiveness.

GJC would like to thank Jack and Jeanette Curphy, Jim Hansen, Dennis Mailloux, Barnie Barnes, John Campbell, Marv Dunnette, Fred Fiedler, Bernie Bass, Gary Yukl, Bob House, John Matchefts, Randy Bolen, Dan Smith, and Bob and Joyce Hogan.

Richard Hughes
Robert Ginnett
Gordon Curphy

Contents in Brief

Contents

PART

I

LEADERSHIP IS A PROCESS, NOT A POSITION

I f any single idea is central to this book, it is that leadership is a process, not a position. The entire first part, in fact, explores that idea. One is not a leader—except perhaps in name only—merely because one holds a title or position. Leadership involves something happening as a result of the interaction between a leader and followers.

We believe that better leadership is something everyone shares responsibility for (Chapter One) and that each of us can become better leaders by profiting most fully from our experiences (Chapter Two). At the same time, becoming a better leader is not just a matter of following certain rules; there is an art to leadership as well as a science (Chapter Three). There *is* a science of the study of leadership, however, and developing leaders can benefit from an understanding of how leadership is investigated empirically (Chapter Four). That is not to say studying leadership is simple. Both the study and practice of leadership involve complex interactions among the leader, the followers, and the particular situation they find themselves in (Chapter Five). The most fundamental way to understand leadership, though, is as a process involving various aspects of power and influence tactics (Chapter Six).

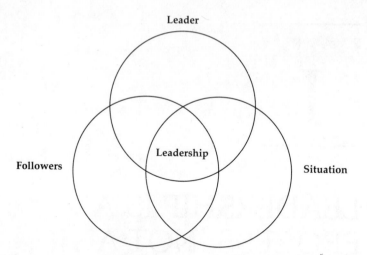

Chapter One

Leadership Is Everyone's Business

INTRODUCTION

I n the spring of 1972, an airplane flew across the Andes mountains carrying its crew and 40 passengers. Most of the passengers were members of an amateur Uruguayan rugby team en route to a game in Chile. The plane never arrived. It crashed in snow-covered mountains, breaking into several pieces on impact. The main part of the fuselage slid like a toboggan down a steep valley, finally coming to rest in waist-deep snow. Although a number of people died immediately or within a day of the impact, the picture for the 28 survivors was not much better. The fuselage initially offered little protection from the extreme cold, food supplies were scant, and a number of passengers had serious injuries from the crash. Over the next few days, several of the passengers became psychotic and several others died from their injuries. Those passengers who were relatively uninjured set out to do what they could to improve their chances of survival.

HIGHLIGHT 1–1

Leadership Quotes, Chapter One

The halls of fame are open wide and they are always full. Some go in by the door called "pushed" and some by the door called "pull."

Stanley Baldwin

Stow this talk. Care killed a cat. Fetch ahead for the doubloons.

Long John Silver, in Robert Louis
Stevenson's *Treasure Island*

Progress always involves risks. You can't steal second base and keep your foot on first.

Frederick B. Wilcox

If you miss seven balls out of ten, you're batting three hundred and that's good enough for the Hall of Fame. You can't score if you keep the bat on your shoulder.

Walter B. Wriston

If you want some ham, you gotta go into the smokehouse.

Huey Long

He who would eat the fruit must climb the tree.

Scottish Proverb

Lives of great men all remind us
We can make our lives sublime,
And, departing, leave behind us
Footprints on the sands of time.

Henry Wadsworth Longfellow

Several worked on "weatherproofing" the wreckage, others found ways to get water, and those with medical training took care of the injured. Although shaken from the crash, the survivors initially were confident they would be found. These feelings gradually gave way to despair, as search and rescue teams failed to find the wreckage. With the passing of several weeks and no sign of rescue in sight, the remaining passengers decided to mount several expeditions to determine the best way to escape. The most physically fit were chosen to go on the expeditions, as the thin mountain air and the deep snow made the trips extremely taxing. The results of the trips were both frustrating and demoralizing; the expeditionaries determined they were in the middle of the Andes mountains, and walking out to find help was believed to be impossible. Just when the survivors thought nothing worse could possibly happen, an avalanche hit the wreckage and killed several more of them.

The remaining survivors concluded they would not be rescued and their only hope was for someone to leave the wreckage and find help. Three of the fittest passengers were chosen for the final expedition, and everyone else's work was directed toward improving the expedition's chances of success. The three expeditionaries were given more food and were exempted from routine survival activities; the rest spent most of their energies securing supplies for the trip. Two months after the plane crash, the expeditionaries set out on their final attempt to find help. After hiking for 10 days through some of the most rugged terrain in the world, the expeditionaries stumbled across a group of Chilean peasants tending cattle. One of the expeditionaries stated, ''I come from a plane that fell in the mountains. I am Uruguayan. . . .'' Eventually, 14 other survivors were rescued.

When the full account of their survival became known, it was not without controversy. It had required extreme and unsettling measures; the survivors had lived only by eating the flesh of their deceased comrades. Nonetheless, their story is one of the most moving survival dramas of all time, magnificently told by Piers Paul Read in *Alive* (1974). It is a story of tragedy and courage, and it is a story of leadership.

Perhaps a story of survival in the Andes is so far removed from everyday experience that it does not seem to hold any relevant lessons about leadership for you personally. But consider for a moment some of the basic issues the Andes survivors faced; for example, tension between individual and group goals, dealing with the different needs and personalities of group members, and keeping hope alive in the face of adversity. These issues are not so very different from those facing many groups we're a part of. We can also look at the Andes experience for examples of the emergence of informal leaders in groups. Before the flight, a boy named Parrado was awkward and shy, a ''second-stringer'' both athletically and socially. Nonetheless, this unlikely hero became the best loved and most respected among the survivors for his courage, optimism, fairness, and emotional support. Persuasiveness in group decision making also was an important part of leadership among the Andes survivors. During the difficult discussions preceding the agonizing decision to survive on the flesh of their deceased comrades, one of the rugby players made his reasoning clear: ''I know that if my dead body could help you stay alive, then I would want you to use it. In fact, if I do die and you don't eat me, then I'll come back from wherever I am and give you a good kick in the ass'' (Read, 1974, p. 77).

WHAT IS LEADERSHIP?

The story on the preceding page provides vivid examples of many of the phenomena examined by leadership researchers. However, you may find it surprising that leadership researchers disagree considerably over what does and does not constitute leadership. Most of this disagreement stems from the fact that leadership is a complex phenomenon involving the leader, the followers, and the situation. Some leadership researchers have focused on the personality, physical traits, or behaviors of the leader; others have studied the relationships between leaders and followers; still others have studied how aspects of the situation affect the ways leaders act. Some have extended the latter viewpoint so far as to suggest there is no such thing as leadership; they argue that organizational successes and failures often get falsely attributed to the leader, but the situation often has a much greater impact on how the organization functions than does any individual, including the leader (Meindl & Ehrlich, 1987).

Perhaps the best way for you to begin to understand the complexities of leadership is to see some of the ways leadership has been defined. Leadership researchers have defined leadership as follows:

- The creative and directive force of morale (Munson, 1921).
- The process by which an agent induces a subordinate to behave in a desired manner (Bennis, 1959).
- The presence of a particular influence relationship between two or more persons (Hollander & Julian, 1969).
- Directing and coordinating the work of group members (Fiedler, 1967).
- An interpersonal relation in which others comply because they want to, not because they have to (Merton, 1969).
- Transforming followers, creating visions of the goals that may be attained, and articulating for the followers the ways to attain those goals (Bass, 1985; Tichy & Devanna, 1986).
- The process of influencing an organized group toward accomplishing its goals (Roach & Behling, 1984).
- Actions that focus resources to create desirable opportunities (Campbell, 1991).

As you can see, these definitions differ in many ways and have resulted in different researchers exploring very different aspects of leadership. For example, if we were to apply these definitions to the survival scenario described earlier, researchers adopting Munson's definition would focus on the behaviors Parrado used to keep up the morale of the survivors; researchers adopting Fiedler's definition would focus on the behaviors Parrado used to direct the survivors' activities in support of the final expedition; and researchers using Roach and Behling's definition would examine how Parrado managed to con-

vince the group to stage and support the final expedition. Each group of researchers would focus on a different aspect of leadership, and each would tell a
different story regarding the leader, the followers, and the situation.

Although such a large number of leadership definitions may seem confusing,
it is important to understand that there is no single "correct" definition. The various definitions can help us appreciate the multitude of factors that affect leadership, as well as different perspectives from which to view it. For example, in Bennis's definition, the word *subordinate* seems to confine leadership to downward
influence in hierarchical relationships; it seems to exclude informal leadership.
Fiedler's definition emphasizes the directing and controlling aspects of leadership, and thereby may deemphasize emotional aspects of leadership. The emphasis Merton placed on subordinates "wanting to" comply with a leader's
wishes seems to exclude coercion of any kind as a leadership tool. Further, it becomes problematic to identify ways in which a leader's actions are "really" leadership if subordinates voluntarily comply when a leader with considerable potential coercive power merely asks others to do something without explicitly
threatening them. Similarly, Campbell used the phrase *desirable opportunities* precisely to distinguish between leadership and tyranny.

All considered, we believe the definition provided by Roach and Behling
(1984) to be a fairly comprehensive and helpful one. Therefore, this book also
defines leadership as "the process of influencing an organized group toward
accomplishing its goals" (Roach & Behling, 1984). One aspect of this definition
is particularly worth noting: Leadership is a social influence process shared
among *all* members of a group. Leadership is not restricted to the influence exerted by someone in a particular position or role; followers are part of the leadership process, too.

Leadership and Followership

In recent years, observers have emphasized the relatedness of leadership and
followership. For example, Burns (1978) observed that since leadership by its
nature is collective, the idea of "one-man leadership" is a contradiction in
terms. Similarly, Gardner (1990) observed that team leaders cannot "fly solo"
and must share the leadership task with the whole leadership team. Leadership and followership are linked concepts (Heller & Van Til, 1983). The view
one has of leadership inevitably implies a view of followership, and vice versa,
just as *left* only has meaning in the context of *right*.

Another way to put it is that leader-follower relationships are not a one-way
street. Superiors influence subordinates, but subordinates also influence superiors. At best, they both do so through their expertise, innovative ideas, moral
integrity, encouragement, loyalty, and so on. Some superiors have viewed
subordinates as adversaries to be controlled, but it increasingly seems fruitful

FIGURE 1–1
The Leadership/Followership Möbius Strip

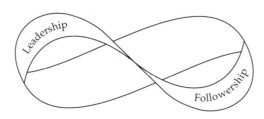

(and necessary) to view subordinates as allies who can be developed and empowered and thereby contribute more to the whole organization. Sharing the leadership task with followers as fully as possible and encouraging their individual initiative and responsibility are even consistent with Western cultural, democratic ideals.

Thus, the question *What is leadership?* cannot be separated from the question *What is followership?* There is no simple line dividing them; they merge. The relationship between leadership and followership can be represented by borrowing a concept from topographical mathematics: the Möbius strip. You are probably familiar with the curious properties of the Möbius strip: When a strip of paper is twisted and connected in the manner depicted in Figure 1–1, it proves to have only one side. You can prove this to yourself by putting a pencil to any point on the strip and tracing continuously. Your pencil will cover the entire strip (i.e., both "sides"), eventually returning to the point at which you started. In order to demonstrate the relevance of this curiosity to leadership, cut a strip of paper. On one side write *leadership,* and on the other side write *followership.* Then twist the strip and connect the two ends in the manner of the figure. You will have created a leadership/followership Möbius strip wherein the two concepts merge one into the other, just as leadership and followership can become indistinguishable in organizations (adapted from Macrorie, 1984).

This does not mean leadership and followership are the same thing. When top-level executives were asked to list qualities they most look for and admire in leaders and followers, the lists were similar but not identical (Kouzes & Posner, 1987). Ideal leaders were characterized as honest, competent, forward looking, and inspiring; ideal followers were described as honest, competent, dependent, and cooperative. The differences could become critical in certain situations, as when a forward-looking and inspiring subordinate perceives a significant conflict between his own goals or ethics and those of his superiors. Such a situation could become a crisis for the individual and the organization, demanding choice between leading and following.

HIGHLIGHT 1–2

Women and Leadership I, A Few Women Leaders throughout History

69 B.C.   Cleopatra, Queen of Egypt is born and ascends the throne at age 17.

1429   Joan of Arc is finally granted an audience with Charles the Dauphin of France and subsequently captains the army at the siege of Orleans.

1492   Queen Isabella of Spain finances Columbus's voyage to the new world.

1558–1603   England's Queen Elizabeth I establishes England as a dominant sea power and defeats the Spanish Armada.

1638   Religious dissident Anne Hutchinson leads schismatic group from Massachusetts Bay Colony into wilderness and establishes Rhode Island.

1775–1781   Catherine the Great of Russia adopts an "Armed Neutrality" policy, which undermines the British blockade of the colonies during the American Revolution.

1803–1806   Sacajawea leads the Lewis and Clark expedition.

1837   Educator Mary Lyons founds Mount Holyoke Female Seminary (later Mount Holyoke College), the first American college exclusively for women.

1843   Dorothea Dix reports to Massachusetts legislature on treatment of criminally insane resulting in a significant reform of American mental institutions.

1849   Harriet Tubman escapes from slavery and becomes one of the most successful "conductors" on the Underground Railroad. She helps more than 300 slaves to freedom.

1854   Florence Nightingale, the founder of modern nursing, organizes a unit of women nurses to serve in the Crimean War.

1869   Susan B. Anthony elected president of the National American Woman Suffrage Association.

1900   Carry Nation gains fame destroying saloons as head of the American Temperance Movement.

1919   Mary Pickford becomes the first top-level female executive of a major film studio by helping found United Artists with her husband, Douglas Fairbanks, Sr.

HIGHLIGHT 1–2 *(concluded)*

1940	Margaret Chase Smith is the first woman elected to Congress; she later becomes first woman elected to the U.S. Senate (1948).
1966	National Organization of Women (NOW) founded by Betty Friedan.
1969	Golda Meir elected prime minister of Israel.
1979	Mother Teresa receives Nobel Prize for her three decades of work leading the Congregation of Missions of Charity in Calcutta, India.
1979	Margaret Thatcher becomes the United Kingdom's first female prime minister and the first prime minister this century to win two consecutive terms. She held office for 11 years.
1981	Jeane Kirkpatrick appointed U.S. ambassador to the United Nations.
1981	Sandra Day O'Connor appointed to the U.S. Supreme Court.
1988	Benazir Bhutto elected first female prime minister of Pakistan.
1990	Although women won three governorships (Texas, Oregon, and Kansas) and the mayorship of Washington, D.C., women still compose only 7 percent of all elected offices.

Source: Adapted from the *Colorado Education Association Journal,* February–March 1991. Based on original work by the Arts and Entertainment Network.

Leadership on Stages Large and Small

Do you consider yourself a leader? Do you want to make a difference? Do you believe you can? To some of us these may be intimidating questions because leaders seem like a remote group of specially gifted, talented, or ambitious individuals. George Washington and Thomas Jefferson were both featured in a book about the 100 most influential people of all time, but there was not a 20th-century American on the list (Hart, 1978). It is easy to feel humble about our ability to make a difference in the world if we compare ourselves to historical leaders like these or to contemporary world-class leaders, such as presidents, statesmen, business leaders, and so on (see Highlight 1–2 for a listing of women leaders from several stages). However, we believe that we must appreciate the role we all can play in helping every activity and every group we are a part of to be more effective. Our definition of leadership makes no mention of the size or the organizational level of the group being led, and we believe there are ample opportunities for all of us to be leaders and to make a difference.

Thus, we need leaders on the smaller stages of life as well as on the world stage. The following are examples of leadership on the small stage, where individuals influenced and helped their respective groups attain their goals.

• An elderly woman led an entire community's effort to organize an advocacy and support group for parents of mentally ill adult children and provide sheltered living arrangements for these people. She helped these families while also serving an invaluable role in educating state legislators and social agencies about the needs of this neglected constituency. There had been numerous parents with mentally ill children in this community before, but none had had the idea or took the initiative to organize among themselves. As a result of this woman's leadership, many adults live and work in more humane conditions than they did before.

• A seasoned air force sergeant took two young, "green" enlistees under her wing after they both coincidentally reported for duty on the same day. She taught them the ropes at work and took pride as they matured. One of them performed so well that he went on to be commissioned as an officer. Unfortunately, the sergeant discovered the other pilfering cash from the unit gift fund. Though it pained her to do so, the sergeant took action for the enlistee to be discharged from the service. Leadership involves significant intrinsic rewards such as seeing others blossom under your tutelage, but with its rewards also goes the responsibility to enforce standards of conduct.

• The office manager for a large advertising agency directed its entire administrative staff, most of whom worked in the reception area. His engaging personality and concern for others made everyone feel important. Morale in the office was high, and many important customers credit their positive "first impression" of the whole agency on the congeniality and positive climate among the office staff. Leaders set the tone for the organization, and followers often model the behaviors displayed by the leader. This leader helped create an office mood of optimism and supportiveness that reached outward to everyone who visited.

These examples are representative of the opportunities every one of us has to be a leader. To paraphrase John Fitzgerald Kennedy, we all can make a difference and each of us should try. However, this book is more than an exhortation for each of us to play a more active leadership role on the various stages of our lives. It is a review of what is known about leadership from available research, a review we hope is presented in a way that will foster leadership development. We are all more likely to make the kind of difference we want if we understand what leadership is and what it is not, how you "get" it, and what improves it (see Highlight 1–3 for a contrasting view of how much of a difference leaders really make).

We also believe many aspects of leadership can be best understood if we do not limit our focus to the seemingly larger-than-life scale of great and famous leaders (see Highlight 1–4). Leadership is a complex process, and sometimes we can be blinded by the personal distance between ourselves and the leaders

---

HIGHLIGHT 1–3

The Romance of Leadership

This text is predicated on the idea that leaders can make a difference. Interestingly, though, while people in the business world generally agree, not all scholars do.

People in the business world attribute much of a company's success or failure to its leadership. One study counted the number of articles appearing in *The Wall Street Journal* that dealt with leadership and found nearly 10 percent of the articles about representative target companies addressed that company's leadership. Furthermore, there was a significant positive relationship between company performance and the number of articles about its leadership; the more a company's leadership was emphasized in *The Wall Street Journal*, the better the company was doing. This might mean the more a company takes leadership seriously (as reflected by the emphasis in *The Wall Street Journal*), the better it does.

However, the authors were skeptical about the real utility of leadership as a concept. They suggested leadership is merely a romanticized notion, an obsession people want and need to believe in. Belief in the potency of leadership may be a sort of cultural myth, which has utility primarily insofar as it affects how people create meaning about causal events in complex social systems. The behavior of leaders, the authors contend, does not account for very much of the variance in an organization's performance. Nonetheless, people seem strongly committed to a sort of basic faith that individual leaders shape organizational destiny for good or ill.

Source: J. R. Meindl, S. B. Ehrlich, and J. M. Dukerich, "The Romance of Leadership." *Administrative Science Quarterly* 30, 1985, pp. 78–102.

---

we read about in the news or in history books. We may not see their leadership accurately for the brightness of their lights. Neither can we accurately assess the subtleties of their personal interactions with others, subtleties often fundamental to their leadership, for good or ill. Therefore, this book will offer examples of leadership by regular people in everyday contexts as well as examples of more famous leaders.

THE PURPOSE OF THIS BOOK

In his seminal article about the state of leadership research, Campbell (1977) stated that leadership researchers needed to pay a lot more attention to the ultimate consumers of their work—leadership practitioners. Most people would find it extremely difficult to distill the myriad findings from leadership research into a coherent set of ideas that would help them become better leaders. Similar

---

HIGHLIGHT 1–4

Lights, Camera, Action!

The director's role is probably the most critical one in the production of any motion picture. Being a director means wearing many hats: visionary, encourager, taskmaster, coach, and numerous others.

What kind of person becomes a movie director? Take the case of Matty Rich, whose major credit is *Straight out of Brooklyn*. Rich is just 20 years old, but he is one of the talented young directors following Spike Lee's lead in making passionate and pointed films about life in the inner city. Rich grew up in Brooklyn watching drugs and crime infect the lives of people close to him. Not liking what he saw, he declared war with his weapon of choice—a camera. "I was angry that everybody around me got destroyed, and I wanted to show that everyday struggle."

Despite his youth, Rich has years of experience in his trade. He began reading books about filmmaking a decade ago. Then, when he was 17, he gambled that those years of study had prepared him well. He got $16,000 in cash advances from relatives' credit cards to finance supplies and a small film crew. Then, out of money, he made an appeal for help over a local black radio station. It worked; Rich collected $77,000 from contributors. He completed his movie, then fortunate breaks led to its screening at a major film festival. Now several studios are pursuing him. "It's kind of weird when you're 19 and you're being wooed . . . If I hadn't done this movie, I'd be just another black kid on the street with a gold tooth and a funny haircut."

Source: R. Corliss (1991), "Boyz of New Black City." *Time*, June 17, pp. 64–68.

---

sentiments were echoed by Mintzberg (1982), who complained that most research about leadership is uninterpretable by people in real leadership roles. It seems that most leadership research is written primarily for other leadership researchers, and the only people to really benefit from such efforts are the researchers themselves.

We agree with both Campbell (1977) and Mintzberg (1982) in that most of the leadership research is uninterpretable to the leadership practitioner and does little directly to help people become better leaders. This does not mean, however, that leadership research is of little value to the leadership practitioner. Leadership practitioners might benefit from what researchers have discovered about leadership if the findings were written for a less research-oriented audience. Thus, one purpose of this book is to serve as a sort of interpretive guide for leadership research. It describes and critically evaluates a number of leadership theories and research articles, and also offers practical advice on how to be a better leader. This book is designed to fill the gap between the books that provide excellent summaries of the leadership research but little practical advice on how to be a better leader and those that are not based on theory or research but instead are little more than the author's personal opinions on how to be a better leader. (Most of the books in the self-help section of your local bookstore probably fit into the latter category.)

A book's purpose also must be understood in terms of its intended audience. Both Campbell (1977) and Mintzberg (1982) would probably argue that a leadership book's value is contingent on how well it is matched to the needs of its audience. This book is somewhat limited in focus and is not intended to be all things to all leaders. It may not be as suitable for general officers as it is for military cadets, for senior pastors as it is for seminary students, for school superintendents as it is for teaching interns. It is a book for young leaders or leaders-to-be still relatively early in their maturation and development. But we do not see that as a good reason to exclude examples of higher levels of leadership (any more than we would suggest that higher-level leaders could not benefit from the contents of this book). We believe it is developmentally helpful to be aware that leaders at different levels face different sorts of problems. We also believe it is helpful to be aware that leaders even at the highest levels do face some of the same challenges we all do. Young leaders will develop more fully not only if they appreciate and master the tasks appropriate to their immediate responsibilities but also if they appreciate that differing concerns might be most salient to other leaders in other situations. In a fundamental sense, a restrictive reliance on materials having direct applicability to a specific audience may become blinders to broader issues. This is not to say the young foreman should master the responsibilities of the plant manager. However, it may help the young foreman in his own role if he appreciates some of the constraints and challenges facing his bosses. Therefore, this book will describe not only the dilemmas facing the novice leader or the leader-to-be but also some of the problems facing senior leaders.

MYTHS THAT HINDER LEADERSHIP DEVELOPMENT

Few things pose a greater obstacle to leadership development than certain unsubstantiated and self-limiting beliefs about leadership. Therefore, before we begin examining what leadership and leadership development are in more detail, we will consider what they are not. We will examine several beliefs (we call them myths) that stand in the way of fully understanding and developing leadership.

Myth: Good Leadership Is All Common Sense

At face value, one myth says one needs only common sense to be a good leader. It also implies, however, that most if not all of the studies of leadership reported in scholarly journals and books only confirm what anyone with common sense already knows.

The problem, of course, is with the ambiguous term *common sense.* It implies a common body of practical knowledge about life that virtually any reasonable person with moderate experience has acquired. A simple experiment, however, may convince you that common sense may be less common than you think. Ask a few friends or acquaintances whether the old folk wisdom ''Absense makes the heart grow fonder'' is true or false. Most will say it is true. After that ask a different group whether the old folk wisdom ''Out of sight, out of mind'' is true or false. Most of that group will answer true as well, even though the two proverbs are contradictory.

A similar thing sometimes happens when people hear about the results of studies concerning human behavior. On hearing the results, people may say, ''Who needed a study to learn that? I knew it all the time.'' However, several experiments by Slovic and Fischoff (1977) and Wood (1979) showed that events were much more surprising when subjects had to guess the outcome of an experiment than when subjects were told the outcome. What seems obvious after you know the results and what you (or anyone else) would have predicted beforehand are not the same thing. Hindsight is always 20/20.

The point might become clearer with a specific example you may now try. Read the following paragraph:

> After World War II, the U.S. Army spent enormous sums of money on studies only to reach conclusions that, many believed, should have been apparent at the outset. One, for example, was that southern soldiers were better able to stand the climate in the hot South Sea islands than northern soldiers were.

This sounds reasonable, but there is just one problem; the statement above is exactly contrary to the actual findings. Southerners were no better than Northerners in adapting to tropical climates (Lazarsfeld, 1949). Common sense can often play tricks on us.

Put a little differently, one of the challenges of understanding leadership may well be to know when common sense applies and when it does not. Do leaders need to act confidently? Of course. But they also need to be humble enough to recognize that others' views are useful, too. Do leaders need to persevere when times get tough? Yes. But they also need to recognize when times change and a new direction is called for. If leadership were nothing more than common sense, then there should be few, if any, problems in the workplace. However, we venture to guess you have noticed problems between leaders and followers. Effective leadership must be something more than just common sense.

Myth: Leaders Are Born, Not Made

People differ in a number of ways—such as by their energy level, drive, intelligence, and emotionalism—and recent research indicates that many cognitive abilities and personality traits are at least partly innate (McGue & Bouchard, 1990; Tellegen, Lykken, Bouchard, Wilcox, Segal, & Rich, 1988). Thus, certain natural talents or characteristics may give some people advantages over others when these people are influencing individuals to accomplish group goals. Furthermore, the stability of many cognitive abilities and personality traits over time make it easy to conclude that people do not change (i.e., are not "made"). However, it is also true that the environment plays a crucial role in the development of cognitive abilities and personality traits. Thus, one's environment can help to build or suppress one's natural talents or abilities, depending on the richness of experiences the environment provides and one's ability and desire to learn from experience.

A good example of being able to profit from one's experiences can be seen in Lech Walesa. Lech Walesa emerged from the ranks of workers in the Gdansk shipyards to become the leader of the solidarity movement in Poland. He went on to use what he had learned as a leader in both the shipyard and the Solidarity movement to become prime minister of Poland and to play a major role in challenging the Soviet Union and ultimately changing the nature of East-West relations. Similarly, taking advantage of leadership opportunities on the smaller stage can help prepare you for the bigger stages of life. People can grow as leaders in the face of challenge and the forge of experience.

Myth: The Only School You Learn Leadership from Is the School of Hard Knocks

Some people skeptically question whether leadership can develop through formal study, believing instead it can only be acquired through actual experience. It is a mistake, however, to think of formal study and learning from experience as mutually exclusive or antagonistic. In fact, they complement each other. Rather than ask whether leadership develops from formal study or from real-life experience, it is better to ask *what kind* of study will help students learn to discern critical lessons about leadership from their own experience. Approaching the issue in such a way recognizes the critical role of experience in leadership development, but it also admits that certain kinds of study and training can improve a person's ability to discern critical lessons about leadership from experience. It can, in other words, help accelerate the process of learning from experience.

We would argue that one of the advantages of formally studying leadership is that formal study provides students with a variety of ways of examining a particular leadership situation. By studying the different ways researchers have defined and examined leadership, students can use these definitions and theories to better understand what is going on in any leadership situation. For example, earlier in this chapter we used three different leadership definitions as a framework for describing or analyzing the situation facing Parrado and the remaining survivors of the plane crash, and each definition focused on a different aspect of leadership. These frameworks can similarly be applied to better understand the experiences one has as both a leader and a follower. We think it is very difficult for leaders, particularly novice leaders, to examine leadership situations from multiple perspectives, but we also believe developing this skill can help you become a better leader. *Being able to analyze your experiences from multiple perspectives may be the greatest single contribution a formal course in leadership can give you.*

AN OVERVIEW OF THIS BOOK

In order to fill the gaps between leadership research and practice, this book will critically review the major theories of leadership as well as provide practical advice about improving leadership practice. Before reviewing the major theories, however, the next five chapters of the book describe how (*a*) leadership develops through experience; (*b*) leadership is both an art and a science; (*c*) leadership researchers have measured leadership; (*d*) leadership is an interaction between the leader, the followers, and the situation; and (*e*) power and influence affect leader-follower relationships. The remainder of the book uses the leader-follower interaction model described in Chapter Five as a framework for organizing and discussing various theories and research findings related to leadership. The chapters in Part II discuss the theories and research concerning the leader: how good and bad leaders differ in intelligence, personality traits, attitudes, values, and preferences. Another chapter in Part II describes the types of behaviors leaders exhibit and provides leaders and leaders-to-be with practical advice on how to improve communication, listening, assertiveness, and feedback skills. Part III primarily focuses on the followers; it summarizes the research and provides practical advice on such topics as motivating subordinates, using delegation, and administering punishment. Part IV examines how the situation affects the leadership process. Part V examines several theories of leadership that predict systematic relationships among the leader, the followers, and the situation.

SUMMARY

This chapter contains just a few simple points. First, although many definitions of leadership exist, we define leadership as the process of influencing others toward achieving group goals. Second, leadership and followership are equally important. Leadership does not occur without followers, and good leaders are also good followers. Third, leadership is everyone's business and everyone's responsibility. Finally, learning certain conceptual frameworks for thinking about leadership can be helpful in making your own on-the-job experiences a particularly valuable part of your leadership development. Thinking about leadership can help you become a better leader than you are right now.

DISCUSSION QUESTIONS

1. We say leadership involves influencing organized groups toward goals. Do you see any disadvantages to restricting the definition to organized groups?
2. How would *you* define leadership?
3. Are some people the "leader type" and others *not* the "leader type"? If so, what in your judgment distinguishes them?
4. Identify several "common-sense" notions about leadership that, to you, are patently self-evident.

SUGGESTED READINGS

Bennis, W. and B. Nanus. *Leaders: The Strategies for Taking Charge.* New York: Harper & Row, 1985.

Kouzes, J. M. and B. Z. Posner. *The Leadership Challenge.* San Francisco: Jossey-Bass, 1987.

Nixon, R. *Leaders.* New York: Warner Books, 1982.

Chapter Two

Leadership Is Developed through Education and Experience

INTRODUCTION

I n Chapter One, we discussed the importance of using multiple perspectives to analyze various leadership situations. Moreover, we argued that it is relatively difficult for leaders to develop this method of analysis on their own and that formal education is one of the best ways to develop multiple perspectives on leadership. Given the importance of formal education and experience in leadership development, this chapter reviews some of the ways you can better learn about leadership (see also Highlight 2–1). As an overview, we begin this chapter by describing a general model that describes how we learn from experience. Next, we describe how perceptions can affect a leader's interpretation of and actions in response to a particular leadership situation and why reflection is important to leadership development. In addition, this chapter reveals how the people you work with and the task itself can help you become a better leader, and reviews some of the typical content and pedagogy found in many formal leadership education programs. Finally, we discuss how to evaluate and choose between the many different kinds of leadership programs available.

THE ACTION-OBSERVATION-REFLECTION MODEL

Consider for a moment what a young person might learn from spending a year working in two very different environments: as a staff assistant in the U.S. Congress or as a carpenter on a house construction crew. Each activity has a rich store of leadership lessons there for the taking. Working in Congress, for example, would provide opportunities to observe political leaders both onstage in the public eye and backstage in more private moments. It would provide opportunities to see members of Congress interacting with different constituencies, to see them in political defeat and political victory, and to see a range of leadership styles. A young person could also learn a lot by working on a building crew as it turned plans and materials into the reality of a finished house: watching the coordination with subcontractors, watching skilled craftsmen train younger ones, watching the leader's reactions to problems and delays, watching the leader set standards and assure quality work. At the same time, a person could work in either environment and *not* grow much if he or she is not disposed to. Making the most of experience is key to developing one's leadership ability. In other words, leadership development depends not just on the kinds of experiences one has but also on how one uses them to foster growth. One study of successful executives found one key quality that characterized them was an ''extraordinary tenacity'' in extracting something worthwhile from their experience and in seeking experiences rich in opportunities for growth'' (McCall, Lombardo, & Morrison, 1988, p. 122).

But how does one do that? Is someone really more likely to ''get'' the lessons of experience by ''looking'' for them? Why is it not enough just to ''be there''? Experiential learning theorists, such as Kolb (1983), believe people learn more from their experiences when they spend time thinking about them. Extending these ideas to leadership, the **action-observation-reflection model** depicted in Figure 2–1 shows that leadership development is enhanced when the experi-

HIGHLIGHT 2–1

Leadership Quotes, Chapter Two

It's not what we don't know that hurts, it's what we know that ain't so.

Will Rogers

An educated man can experience more in a day than an uneducated man in a lifetime.

Seneca

I took a great deal o' pains with his education, sir; let him run the streets when he was very young, and shift for his-self. It's the only way to make a boy sharp, sir.

Charles Dickens, *Pickwick Papers*

Common sense is the collection of prejudices acquired by age 18.

Einstein

What would a man be wise, let him drink of the river
That bears on its bosom the record of time;
A message to him every wave can deliver.
To teach him to creep till he knows how to climb.

John Boyle O'Reilly

Teach a highly educated person that it is not a disgrace to fail and that he must analyze every failure to find its cause. He must learn how to fail intelligently, for failing is one of the greatest arts in the world.

Charles F. Kettering

Tell me and I'll forget; show me and I may remember; involve me and I'll understand.

Chinese proverb

Anyone who stops learning is old, whether at 20 or 80. Anyone who keeps learning stays young. The greatest thing in life is to keep your mind young.

Henry Ford

Leadership and learning are indispensable to each other.

John F. Kennedy

FIGURE 2–1
The Spiral of Experience

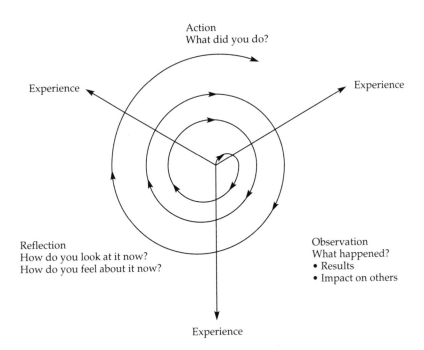

Action
What did you do?

Experience

Experience

Reflection
How do you look at it now?
How do you feel about it now?

Observation
What happened?
• Results
• Impact on others

Experience

ence involves three different processes: action, observation, and reflection. If a person acts but does not observe the consequences of her actions or reflect on their significance and meaning, then it makes little sense to say she has learned from an experience. Because some people neither observe the consequences of their actions nor reflect on how they could change their actions to become better leaders, leadership development through experience may be better understood as the growth resulting from repeated movements through all three stages rather than merely in terms of some objective dimension like time (e.g., how long one has been on the job). We believe the most productive way to develop as a leader is to travel along the **spiral of experience** depicted in Figure 2–1 (see also Highlight 2–2).

Perhaps an example will clarify how the spiral of experience pertains to leadership development. Steve, a popular member of his university's hockey team, had a reputation for being an aggressive player. Steve was a talented player who scored a lot of goals for his team, but he also spent a lot of time in the penalty box because of his aggressive play. During the course of the season, the head coach had warned Steve that his aggressive play and penalties were getting out of hand

HIGHLIGHT 2–2

Heroic Archetypes and Leadership

We got the idea of growth as a spiral of experience from Carol Pearson, who has identified several heroic archetypes in Western culture. These are cultural myths and images, abiding psychic patterns that help guide personal development, ego formation, and individuation. The several conceptions of heroism that follow are not just familiar literary conventions. According to Pearson, they reflect deep-seated beliefs about basic dimensions of character and human experience. Therefore, we might expect our idealized notions of leadership to be colored by these same themes and archetypes. Among the archetypes she discussed were these:

The Orphan: Rags-to-riches stories have always been popular. "Cinderella," *Oliver Twist,* and even the recent motion picture *Pretty Woman* reflect the basic theme. The Orphan is a good person struggling against seemingly insurmountable odds until finally being "rescued" by a benevolent protector.

The Wanderer: In fairy tales, Wanderers are held captive in some limiting confine by a powerful and wicked figure (e.g., a witch, a giant, or an ogre). To be free, the Wanderer must confront the villain (and the status quo), prevail against personal imprisonment, and escape. But Wanderers are not limited to fairy tales. The theme is reflected in any adventurous quest where the central character's identity is defined by individualistic opposition to prevailing norms.

The Martyr: Sacrifice for others is a universal theme. Fertility religions required sacrifices to assure the continuing cycle of nature, and sacrificial death and rebirth are central to Judaism and Christianity. Heroic martyrs like Jesus, Gandhi, Martin Luther King, Jr., and Mother Theresa endure hardship and give their lives, literally or figuratively, to others. Ennobling sacrifice is also apparent in the lives of individuals on smaller stages who devote their lives to helping others, and even in passing on life itself through the painful birth of every child.

The Warrior: To many of us, being a hero means being a Warrior. The Warrior's story is of good triumphing over evil and the difference one courageous person can make. Warriors are tough-minded, assertive, and action-oriented. Warriors prevail over others through will and through strength.

Growth as a Spiral toward Wholeness

One of Pearson's richest ideas is that personal growth can be conceptualized as a journey through all these heroic archetypes. They can be thought of as stages we pass through, each with lessons that contribute to ever more mature and complex identity and individuality. In addition, each archetype itself can be expressed in a range of forms from immature to mature. Each archetype can only be attained in its true fullness by also realizing the qualities of the others. That is why Pearson describes personal wholeness and integration in terms of a spiraling developmental process through all of the heroic archetypes.

HIGHLIGHT 2–2 *(continued)*

T. S. Eliot expressed a similar idea in his poem "Four Quartets":

We shall not cease from exploration
And the end of all our exploring
Will be to arrive where we started
And know the place for the first time. . . .

Perhaps leadership development also involves a spiraling growth toward wholeness. Perhaps the most complete leaders are those who have fully developed and integrated qualities of the seemingly disparate archetypes of Orphan and Wanderer, Martyr and Warrior.

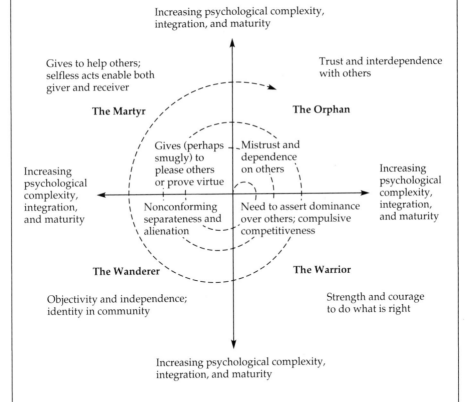

Source: C. S. Pearson, *The Hero Within!* (San Francisco: Harper Collins, 1986).

and were beginning to hurt the team. In a particularly close game, Steve received several unnecessary penalties, which the coach believed cost the team the game. The head coach privately told Steve he would not be playing the next two games because of the penalties he received in the last game. Although disappointed, Steve agreed with the coach's decision and told the coach he would try to stay out of the penalty box in the future. The next day, Steve noticed a prominent article about himself in the sports section of the local newspaper. Apparently, the head coach had discussed Steve's dilemma with a reporter, and the article resulted in a great deal of unwanted notoriety for Steve. The head coach had not told Steve that the story was going public, and as Steve reflected on what the coach had done, his disappointment soon turned to anger.

The action component in the spiral of experience examines the behaviors or actions that took place in the leadership situation; one action in this situation was Steve's aggressive play. The damage caused to the team falls into the observation component of the model, as it is the result of Steve's penalties. Steve's disappointment and promise to do better in the future fall into the reflection component of the model; being punished by missing the next two games made Steve realize he needed to change his behavior on the ice if he wanted to be part of the team in the future.

The action-observation-reflection model can also be used to understand leadership development from the head coach's perspective. The coach's decisions to bench Steve for the next two games and to tell the newspaper reporter about his conversation with Steve can be categorized as actions. The team's being shorthanded for two games and the notoriety Steve received from the article in the newspaper fall into the observation component of the model. Unfortunately, the notoriety Steve received about the newspaper article and Steve's subsequent anger never got back to the coach, and the coach never thought about handling the situation any differently. Because the coach did not go through the reflection component of the model, another newspaper article about the coach benching one of his players for a similar problem appeared several years later. The player who was benched this time also got angry when the results of his conversation with the coach went public. The consistent behavior of the head coach provides a good example of *not* learning from experience; if the coach had completed the spiral of experience, then he might not have gone public with the second discipline problem.

THE KEY ROLE OF PERCEPTION IN THE SPIRAL OF EXPERIENCE

It is clear that Steve and his coach perceived the same situation very differently and thus experienced it very differently. Experience is not just a matter of what events happen to you; it also depends on how you perceive those events. Perception affects all three components of the action-observation-reflection model and thus plays a very important role in what anyone will extract from a leadership course or from any leadership situation. Human beings are not passive recorders of experiences that "happen" to them; rather, people actively shape and construct their experiences. In order to better understand how perception affects experience, we will examine its role in each part of the action-observation-reflection model. We will begin with the stage that seems to correspond most directly with perception—the observation stage.

Perception and Observation

Observation and perception both deal with attending to events around us. Furthermore, both seem to take place spontaneously and effortlessly, so it is easy to regard them as passive processes. Our common mental images of the perceptual process reflect this implicit view. For example, it is a common misconception that the eye operates essentially like the film in a continuously running camera. The fallacy of this passive view of perception is that it assumes we attend to all aspects of a situation equally. We do not see everything that happens in a particular leadership situation, nor do we hear everything. Instead, we are selective in what we attend to and what we, in turn, perceive. One phenomenon that demonstrates this selectivity is called **perceptual set**. Perceptual sets can influence any of our senses, and they are the tendency or bias to perceive one thing and not another. Many factors can trigger a perceptual set, such as feelings, needs, prior experience, and expectations. Its role in distorting what one hears proved a costly lesson when a sympathetic airline pilot told his depressed copilot, "Cheer up!" The copilot thought the pilot had said "Gear up" and raised the wheels while the plane was still on the ground (Reason & Mycielska, 1982). Try your own ability to overcome perceptual set with the following exercise. Read through the narrative passage below several times:

FINISHED FILES ARE THE RE-
SULT OF YEARS OF SCIENTIF-
IC STUDY COMBINED WITH THE
EXPERIENCE OF MANY YEARS.

Make sure you have read it to yourself several times *before going any further*. Now, go back to the text and count the number of times the letter F appears.

How many did you count? Three? Four? Five? Six? Most people do not get the correct answer (six) the first time. The most frequent count is three; perhaps that was how many you saw. If you did not find six, go back and try it again. The most common error in this seemingly trivial task is overlooking the three times the word *of* appears. People easily overlook it because the word *of* has a *v* sound, not an *f* sound. Most people unconsciously make the task an auditory search task and listen for the sound of F rather than look for the shape of F;

hence, they find three *F*s rather than six. Listening for the sound constitutes a counterproductive perceptual set for this task, and having read the passage through several times before counting the *F*s only exaggerates this tendency. Another reason people overlook the word *of* in this passage is that the first task was to *read* the passage several times. Because most of us are fairly accomplished readers, we tend to ignore little words like *of*. It disappears from our perceptual set. Then, when we are asked to "count" the number of *F*s, we have already defined the passage as a reading task, so the word *of* is really not there for us to count.

There are strong parallels between the perceptual set example above and the perceptual sets that come into play when we are enrolled in a leadership course or observe a leadership situation. For example, your instructor for this class may dress unstylishly, and you may be prejudiced in thinking that poor dressers generally do not make good leaders. Because of your biases, you may discount or not attend to some things your instructor has to say about leadership. This is unfortunate, as your instructor's taste in clothes has little to do with his or her ability to teach (which is, after all, a kind of leadership).

A similar phenomenon takes place when one expects to find mostly negative things about another person (e.g., a problem employee). Such an expectation becomes a perceptual set to look for the negative and look past the positive things in the process. For example, if you do not believe women and/or minorities are as successful as white males in influencing others, then you may be biased to identify or remember only those instances where a woman or minority leader failed, and discount or forget those instances where women or minority members succeeded as leaders. Unfortunately, we all have similar biases, although we are usually unaware of them. Often, we only become aware of our perceptual sets when we spend time reflecting about the content of a leadership training program or a particular leadership situation.

Perception and Reflection

Perceptual sets influence what we attend to or do not attend to, what we observe or do not observe. In addition, perception also influences the next stage of the spiral of experience—reflection—since reflection deals with how we interpret our observations. Perception is inherently an interpretive or meaning-making activity. One important aspect of this deals with a process called **attribution**.

Attributions are the explanations we develop in our own minds for the behaviors or actions we attend to. For example, if you see Julie fail in an attempt to get others to form a study group, you are likely to attribute the cause of the failure to dispositional factors within Julie. In other words, you are likely to attribute the failure to form a study group to Julie's intelligence, personality, physical appearance, or some other factor. On the other hand, if you attempt to get others to form a study group and fail, you are more likely to blame factors in

"Just don't make any personal appearances until after the election."

The Saturday Evening Post Society

the situation (e.g., there was not enough time, or the others were not interested, or they would not be good to study with) for the failure. This tendency to overestimate the dispositional causes of behavior and underestimate the environmental causes when others fail is called the **fundamental attribution error** (Shaver, 1985). People prefer to explain others' behavior on the basis of personal attributions, even when obvious situational factors can fully account for the behavior. It is important to realize that the fundamental attribution error also comes into play when we or others succeed. However, in this case the dispositional and environmental attributions are reversed. If we succeed, then it is due to our intelligence, personality, or physical abilities; if others succeed, then we often attribute the cause to situational factors or to luck.

We hasten to note in concluding this section that reflection also involves ''higher'' functions like evaluation and judgment, not just perception and attribution. We will address these broader aspects of reflection, which are crucial to learning from experience, just ahead.

Perception and Action

We have seen ways perception influences both the observation and reflection stages in the spiral of experience. It also affects the actions we take. For example, Mitchell and his associates (Green & Mitchell, 1979; Mitchell, Green, & Wood, 1981; Mitchell & Wood, 1980) have examined how perceptions and biases affect supervisors' actions in response to poorly performing subordinates. In general, these researchers found that supervisors were biased toward making dispositional attributions about a subordinate's substandard performance and, as a result of these attributions, often recommended that punishment be used to remedy the performance deficit.

Another perceptual variable that can affect our actions is the **self-fulfilling prophecy**. The self-fulfilling prophecy occurs when our expectations or predictions play a causal role in bringing about the events we predict. It is not difficult to see how certain large-scale social phenomena may be affected this way. For example, economists' predictions of an economic downturn may, via the consequent decreased investor confidence, precipitate an economic crisis. But the self-fulfilling prophecy occurs at the interpersonal level, too. A person's expectations about another may influence how he acts toward her; and in reaction to his behavior she may act in a way that confirms his expectations (Jones, 1986). One typical interaction sequence is shown in Figure 2–2.

Some of the best evidence to support the effects of the self-fulfilling prophecy on leadership training was collected by Eden and Shani (1982). Eden and Shani conducted a field experiment where they told leadership instructors their students had either unknown, regular, or high command potential. However, the students' actual command potential was never assessed, and unbeknownst to the instructors, the students were actually randomly assigned to the unknown, regular, or high command potential conditions. Nevertheless, students in the high potential condition had significantly better objective test scores and attitudes than the students in the unknown or regular potential conditions, even though instructors simultaneously taught all three types of students. Somehow the students picked up on their instructor's expectations and responded accordingly. Thus, just having expectations (positive or negative) about others can subtly influence our actions, and these actions can, in turn, affect the way others behave.

REFLECTION AND LEADERSHIP DEVELOPMENT

Perhaps the most important yet most neglected component of the action-observation-reflection model is reflection. Reflection is important because it can provide leaders with a variety of insights about how to frame problems differently,

FIGURE 2–2

The Role of Expectations in Social Interaction

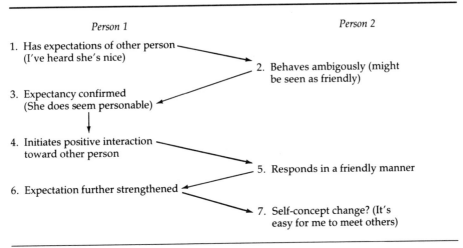

Source: Adapted from E. E. Jones, ''Interpreting Interpersonal Behavior: The Effects of Expectancies,'' *Science* 234, no. 3 (October 1986), p. 43. Used with permission.

look at situations from multiple perspectives, or better understand subordinates. However, most managers spend relatively little time on this activity, even though the time spent reflecting about leadership can be quite fruitful.

One reason the reflection component is often neglected may be time pressure at work. Leaders are usually very busy people working in pressure-filled situations and often do not have time to ponder all the possible consequences of their actions or reflect on how they could have accomplished a particular action better. In addition, some leaders may not be aware of the value of reflection in leadership development. Hopefully, this section will clarify the value of reflection, which can complement the emphasis throughout the remainder of the book of looking at leadership from different perspectives.

Single- and Double-Loop Learning

It is difficult for leaders to fundamentally change their leadership style without some kind of reflection on their part. Along these lines, Argyris (1976) described an intensive effort with a group of chief executive officers whereby highly successful leaders, through increased self-awareness, became even better. Argyris's model for conceptualizing this growth is applicable to any level of leader and is worth considering in more detail.

Argyris (1976) said that most people interact with others and the environment based on a belief system geared to manipulate or control others, and to minimize one's own emotionality and the negative feelings elicited from others. This belief system also tends to create defensive interpersonal relationships and limits risk taking. People "programmed" with this view of life (as most of us are, according to Argyris) produce group and organizational dynamics characterized by avoidance of conflict, mistrust, conformity, intergroup rivalry, misperceptions and miscommunications with others, ineffective problem solving, and poor decision making. Most important for our purposes here, it generates a certain kind of learning that Argyris called **single-loop learning**.

Single-loop learning describes a kind of learning between the individual and environment in which learners seek relatively little feedback that may significantly confront their fundamental ideas or actions. There is relatively little public testing of ideas against valid information. Consequently, an actor's belief system becomes self-sealing and self-fulfilling, and little time is spent reflecting about the beliefs. Argyris used the term *single-loop learning* because it operates somewhat like a thermostat; individuals learn only about subjects within the "comfort zone" of their belief systems. They might, for example, learn how well they are achieving a designated goal. They are far less likely, however, to question the validity of the goal or the values implicit in the situation, just as a thermostat does not question its temperature setting. That kind of self-confrontation would involve **double-loop learning**.

Double-loop learning involves a willingness to confront one's own views and an invitation to others to do so, too. It springs from an appreciation that openness to information and powersharing with others can lead to better recognition and definition of problems, improved communication, and increased decision-making effectiveness. Mastering double-loop learning can be thought of as learning how to learn. With considerable collective work, including the difficult task of working through personal blind spots, Argyris' group of leaders did move to this stage. In other words, through reflection they learned how to change their leadership styles by questioning their assumptions about others, their roles in the organization, and their underlying assumptions about the importance of their own goals and those of the organization.

Thinking Frames and Multiple Perspectives

Another way to conceptualize reflection in leadership development involves **thinking frames**, which refer to the tactics and strategies people use to organize their thinking and construe meaning to events (Perkins, 1986). Thinking frames are our mental tools, and they may or may not be useful, just as a hammer or saw may or may not be useful depending on the task at hand. In addition, just as a child with a hammer perceives the whole world in need of hammering, our thinking frames can also represent limits on the ways we can (conceptually) operate on our environment. Leadership development can be thought of as the process of developing more complex and differentiated frames for organizing one's thinking (and hence action) about leadership. Moreover, because some thinking frames are relatively subtle, their development may be better assisted through structured educational experiences. For example, most people would not have thought of the action-observation-reflection model on their own. The development of multiple frames, or perspectives, may be one of the greatest contributions a formal course in leadership can make to a leader's development. The overarching idea in discussing the different definitions and theories of leadership in this text is to help you to develop different frames or perspectives for interpreting leadership situations, which in turn may help you to better influence others to achieve organizational goals. Perhaps one key to leadership success is having a variety of tools to choose from and knowing when and where to use them. Hopefully, the theories and concepts described in this text will give you the tools, and by reflecting about your experiences as a leader, you should begin to gain some insight on when and where to use them.

LEADERSHIP DEVELOPMENT THROUGH EXPERIENCE

Although using the action-observation-reflection model will help you to make the most of your leadership experiences and mature into a better leader, it is also important to realize that some situations are developmentally richer than others. In this section, we will review two broad factors that make any given opportunity or experience potent in fostering managerial growth. These two developmental factors of a situation are the people you work with and the characteristics of the task itself (Kouzes & Posner, 1987; Lombardo & Eichinger, 1989). These two factors are important, as they provide more opportunities for a leader or a leader-to-be to apply the action-observation-reflection model and reflect on how to be a better leader.

The People You Work With

The people you associate with can stimulate development in many ways. Kouzes and Posner (1987) noted the diverse ways others nurture our growth:

> Other people have always been essential sources of guidance. We all remember the parent we looked to for advice and support; the special teacher who filled us with curiosity for our favorite subject; the neighbor who always let us watch, even take part in, the tinkering in the garage; the coach who believed that we had promise and

inspired us to give our best; the counselor who gave us valuable feedback about our behavior and its impact; the master artisan who instructed us in the fundamentals of a craft; or the first boss who taught us the ropes to skip and the hoops to jump (p. 286).

Others play an especially important role in personal and professional development at work, so we will focus attention there.

A boss, especially a very good or very bad one, can be a powerful catalyst for growth. Exceptional bosses are vivid examples of how to (or how not to) put values into action. However, bosses are not the only people who contribute to growth and development at work. Working with others who have different backgrounds, perspectives, or agendas can often be a growth experience. Working with problem subordinates can stimulate managerial growth, but so can the need to influence others over whom you have no direct authority or control. You may work on a project and report to a superior other than your own boss, or you may head a team of peers; such situations are particularly helpful in developing negotiation and other informal influence skills. Finally, different management skills are called on when you must make major changes to a group or project such as downsizing it, restructuring it, or starting it from scratch (Lombardo & Eichinger, 1989).

You can learn about effective and ineffective leadership by paying attention to the positive and negative models around you beyond your immediate boss. Watching others in leadership roles may suggest what to do as well as what not to do. Peers, especially, can be a great resource for developing one's effectiveness as a leader. In one program of peer coaching, school principals observed each other interacting in feedback conferences with their respective teachers and then met together afterward to share ideas about how well the conferences went (Gibble & Lawrence, 1987). Such principal-to-principal interaction is especially valuable in that it is rare for any supervisor to get feedback on his or her skill in providing feedback to subordinates. The principals praised their peer coaching as an extremely effective mechanism for enhancing their effectiveness as supervisors.

In an organization, you also can gain valuable perspectives and insights through close association with an experienced person willing to take you under his wing. Such an individual is often called a **mentor**, after the character in Greek mythology whom Odysseus trusted to run his household and see to his son's education when Odysseus went off to fight the Trojans. Now, 3,000 years later, Mentor's name is used to describe the process by which an older and more experienced person helps to socialize and encourage younger organizational colleagues (Wilson & Elman, 1990).

Generally. mentors are highly placed, powerful individuals who develop relatively long-lasting relationships with younger colleagues through which they help shape, mold, and further their protégés professional careers (Hunt &

Michael, 1983; Uecker & Dilla, 1985). Typically, the mentoring relationship is an informal one, though its value has encouraged some to recommend its use formally and systematically in organizations (Clutterbuck, 1982). In terms of value, both mentors and mentorees benefit from having this relationship. Mentors benefit by the greater influence they accrue by having former mentorees in various positions across the organization. Mentors also benefit by having a younger replacement ready to fill their position if they are promoted (Bass, 1990). The mentoree benefits from this relationship by gaining an influential ally and through the mentor's tutoring about the subtler aspects of organizational ethics, influence, and leadership. Having a mentor can also result in more career opportunities for the mentoree (Whitely, Dougherty, & Dreher, 1988; Zey, 1984), and the lack of mentors for women has been cited as one reason there are relatively few women in executive positions (Astin & Leland, 1991). Although some may advocate systematizing mentorship programs to improve the career opportunities for all employees, it remains to be seen whether a formalized program would preserve the essence and qualities of more informal, self-selected mentoring relationships (Rosenbach, 1989).

The Task Itself

In addition to the various sorts of relationships with other people, certain kinds of work-related tasks can also be particularly developmental. Tasks that are more developmental are often more complex and ambiguous than those one has faced before. In addition, leadership development can be enhanced if the environment one works in is changing, dynamic, uncontrollable, and unpredictable. The nature of the task may require new and creative solutions; old answers may not work anymore. Projects involving strategic planning and projections into an uncertain future can be quite challenging intellectually and can contribute to a leader's development (Lombardo & Eichinger, 1989).

Although we have emphasized the importance of applying the action-observation-reflection model to enhance one's learning from experience, the developmental value of challenging tasks in and of themselves cannot be denied. The best developmental opportunities are those that stretch individuals and allow them to test themselves against new and difficult tasks (Kouzes & Posner, 1987). Of course, the difficulty level of tasks and how much one will be stretched by doing them is meaningful mostly in the context of a given individual's maturity and experience. The following are the words of one college student who was in charge of the flag section of her school's marching band:

> I have 30 people under me broken into four sections. I am responsible for conducting our rehearsals, teaching flag routines, taking care of any problems, recruiting new members, and motivating my people. I do some of this through my four section lead-

ers, so I have to make sure they are doing their jobs properly. The biggest challenge of all this is keeping motivation high and making sure that everyone learns what they are supposed to and performs it well. It is really giving me a lot of experience in interacting with people.

Another student described his own best leadership experience in terms of his unique background as an instructor on his collegiate parachute team:

> During this period I learned a lot about what it takes to teach a person to jump out of an airplane successfully and injury free. The foremost concern and responsibility is the welfare of the student, so I had to be certain that they learned the procedures correctly, and be thoroughly convinced that they would be safe once out the door no matter what situation may arise. I was responsible for someone else's life.
>
> I had to be very patient and understanding many times when they would not grasp an idea or a procedure properly, spending a lot of time in certain areas until they were proficient. Other times I had to be stern and strict to emphasize certain emergency procedures and safety hazards in order to be sure they were aware of the seriousness of the situation. During this period I experienced everything that goes into leadership. I had to work with many people. Many of them were my peers, which makes things more difficult in some cases.

Feeling responsible for someone else's life certainly increases one's personal pressure, and it was partly this pressure that made this student-instructor's role such a valuable leadership experience. Whether or not a particular task is perceived as developmentally challenging and generates a high level of personal pressure depends on several factors. The most commonly cited developmental challenge mentioned by managers was a task where both success and failure were possible and would be obvious to others. The risk of possible failure is a strong incentive for managers to learn. Managers also mentioned deadlines, travel requirements, and longer hours as factors that, while adding to personal pressure, also contributed to professional growth (Lombardo & Eichinger, 1989).

One last aspect of leadership-developing tasks should be mentioned. Just as mentoring relationships fail to develop for all members, organizations may not provide the same developmental opportunities for all their members. In particular, there is a striking difference between large and small organizations in the opportunities they offer. This is apparent, for example, in the chances of having a significant responsibility in the school play in schools with either large or small student bodies. In small schools, virtually anyone who wants to have a significant part in putting on the play will be able to do so. In large schools, though, the number of students far exceeds the number of important functions; many motivated students will miss out on the chance to participate and grow from the experience. As John Gardner (1990) has pointed out, the sheer size and impersonalness of some of our organizations does not provide the soil in which a young person's leadership can grow.

Making the Most of Your Leadership Experiences

This section builds on the ideas previously introduced in this chapter by providing leadership practitioners with a few suggestions to enhance learning from experience (see Highlight 2–3 for a description of some executives who apparently did *not* learn enough from experience). It is based on the idea that learning must continue throughout life, beyond the completion of one's formal education.

> The end of extrinsically applied education should be the start of an education that is motivated intrinsically. At that point the goal of studying is no longer to make the grade, earn a diploma, and find a good job. Rather, it is to understand what is happening around one, to develop a personally meaningful sense of what one's experience is all about (Csikszentmihalyi, 1990, p. 142).

Leadership practitioners can enhance the learning value of their experiences by (*a*) creating opportunities to get feedback, (*b*) taking a 10 percent stretch, (*c*) learning from others, (*d*) keeping a journal of daily leadership events, and (*e*) having a developmental plan.

Creating opportunities to get feedback.   It may be difficult for leaders to get relevant feedback, particularly if they occupy powerful positions in an organization. Yet leaders often need feedback more than subordinates do. Leaders may not learn much from their leadership experiences if they get no feedback about how they are doing. Therefore, they may need to create opportunities to get feedback, especially with regard to feedback from those working for them.

First of all, leaders should not assume they have invited feedback merely by saying that they have an ''open-door'' policy. A mistake some bosses make is presuming that others perceive them as open to discussing things just because they say they are open to discussing things. How truly open a door is, clearly, is in the eye of the beholder. In that sense, the key to constructive dialogue (i.e., feedback) is not just expressing a policy but also being perceived as approachable and sincere in the offer.

Some of the most helpful information for developing your own leadership can come from asking for feedback from others about their perceptions of your behavior and its impact on your group's overall effectiveness. Some of the specific techniques leaders can use to systematically solicit feedback are described in more detail in Chapters Four and Nine. Leaders who take psychological tests and use periodic surveys or questionnaires will have greater access to feedback than leaders who fail to systematically solicit feedback from their followers. Unless leaders ask for feedback, they may not get it.

Taking a 10 percent stretch.   Learning always involves stretching. Learning involves taking risks and reaching beyond one's comfort zone. This is true of a toddler's first unsteady steps, a student's first serious confrontation with di-

HIGHLIGHT 2–3

Executive Derailment: Knocking Yourself Off the Track to Success

Some executives on an apparently clear track to the top never make it. They become derailed. Morgan McCall and Michael Lombardo, of the Center for Creative Leadership, studied executives who had fallen short of the levels of success predicted of them earlier in their careers. Typically, their derailments were the result of several factors, though insensitivity to others was the most frequent problem. Sometimes styles that served them well earlier became liabilities in new circumstances, and sometimes long-standing liabilities, previously outweighed by other aspects, eventually took their career toll. The 10 most common causes of derailment were the following:

An insensitive, abrasive, or bullying style.

Aloofness or arrogance.

Betrayal of personal trust.

Self-centered ambition.

Failure to constructively face an obvious problem.

Micromanagement.

Inability to select good subordinates.

Inability to take a long-term perspective.

Inability to adapt to a boss with a different style.

Overdependence on a ''sponsor'' or mentor.

How would you interpret these executives' derailments in terms of the action-observation-reflection model? Do you think the problem was in their actions? Their observation or awareness of the consequences of their actions? Or something else?

Source: M. W. McCall, Jr., and M. M. Lombardo, *Off the Track: Why and How Successful Executives Get Derailed* Tech. Rep., no. 21. (Greensboro, N C.: The Center for Creative Leadership, 1983.)

vergent worlds of thought, and leadership development. The phrase *10 percent stretch* conveys the idea of voluntary but determined efforts to improve leadership skills. It is analagous to physical exercise, though in this context stretching implies extending one's behavior, not muscles, just a bit beyond the comfort zone. Examples could include making a point to converse informally with everyone in the office at least once each day, seeking an opportunity to be chairman of a committee, or being quieter than usual at meetings (or more assertive, as the case may be). There is much to be gained from a commitment to such ongoing ''exercise'' for personal and leadership development.

Several positive outcomes are associated with leaders who regularly practice the 10 percent stretch. First, their apprehension about doing something new or different gradually decreases. Second, leaders will broaden their repertoire of leadership skills. Third, because of this increased repertoire, their effectiveness will likely increase. And finally, leaders regularly taking a 10 percent stretch will model something very valuable to others. Few things will send a better message to others about the importance of their own development than the example of how sincerely a leader takes his or her own development.

One final aspect of the 10 percent stretch is worth mentioning. One reason the phrase is so appealing is that it sounds like a measurable yet manageable change. Many people will not offer serious objection to trying a 10 percent change in some behavior, whereas they might well be resistant (and unsuccessful) if they construe a developmental goal as requiring fundamental change in their personality or interpersonal style. Despite its nonthreatening connotation, though, an actual 10 percent change in behavior can make an enormous difference in effectiveness. In many kinds of endeavor the difference between average performers and exceptional performers is 10 percent. In baseball, for example, many players hit .275, but only the best hit over .300—a difference of about 10 percent.

Learning from others.   Leaders learn from others, first of all, by recognizing they *can* learn from others and, importantly, from *any* others. That may seem self-evident, but in fact people often limit what and whom they pay attention to, and thus what they may learn from. For example, athletes may pay a lot of attention to how coaches handle leadership situations. However, they may fail to realize they could also learn a lot by watching the director of the school play and the band conductor. Leaders should not limit their learning by narrowly defining the sorts of people they pay attention to.

Similarly, leaders also can learn by asking questions and paying attention to everyday situations. An especially important time to ask questions is when leaders are new to a group or activity and have some responsibility for it. When possible, leaders should talk to the person who previously had the position in order to benefit from her insights, experience, and assessment of the situation. In addition, observant leaders are able to extract meaningful leadership lessons from everyday situations. Something as plain and ordinary as a high school car wash or the activities at a fast-food restaurant may offer an interesting leadership lesson. Leaders can learn a lot by actively observing how others react to and handle different challenges and situations, even very common ones.

Keeping a journal.   Another way leaders can ''mine'' experiences for their richness and preserve their learning is by keeping a journal (Csikszentmihalyi, 1990). Journals are similar to diaries, but they are not just accounts of a day's events. A journal should include entries that address some aspect of leaders or leadership. Journal entries may include comments about insightful or interesting quotes, anecdotes, newspaper articles, or even humorous cartoons about leadership. They may also include reflections on personal events, such as interactions with bosses, coaches, teachers, students, employees, players, teammates, roommates, and so on. Such entries can emphasize a good (or bad) way somebody handled something; a problem in the making; the differences between people in their reactions to situations; or people in the news, a book, or a film. Leaders should also use their journals to "think on paper" about leadership readings from textbooks or formal leadership programs or to describe examples from their own experience of a concept presented in a reading.

There are at least three good reasons for keeping a journal. First, the very process of writing increases the likelihood that leaders will be able to look at an event from a different perspective or feel differently about it. Putting an experience into words can be a step toward taking a more objective look at it. Second, leaders can (and should) reread earlier entries. Earlier entries provide an interesting and valuable autobiography of a leader's evolving thinking about leadership and about particular events in his or her life. Third, journal entries provide a repository of ideas that leaders may later want to use more formally for papers, pep talks, or speeches. As seen in Highlight 2–4, good journal entries provide leaders with a wealth of examples that they may use in speeches, presentations, and so on.

Having a developmental plan.   Leadership development almost certainly occurs in ways and on paths that are not completely anticipated or controlled. That is no reason, however, for leaders to avoid actively directing some aspects of their own development. A systematic plan outlining self-improvement goals and strategies will help leaders take advantage of opportunities they otherwise might overlook. Developing a systematic plan also will help leaders prioritize the importance of different goals so that their efforts can be put into areas with the greatest relative payoffs. Leaders who carefully choose which seminars and conferences to attend may help themselves maximize their contribution to their personal developmental goals. Leaders should look for opportunities on the job or in volunteer work for responsibilities that may further their growth. Leaders should recognize, however, that they may experience conflict—both internal and external—between doing more of what they already do well and stretching developmentally.

The following is an example of such a conflict. Suppose Sheila is an accountant who has just joined the board of a local charity. Because handling financial records is something many people do not enjoy, and because Sheila has a demonstrable knack and interest in it, others on the board may well ask her to become the treasurer. Almost certainly Sheila would do as good a job as anyone else on the board. But suppose Sheila's personal goals included develop-

---

HIGHLIGHT 2–4

Sample Journal Entries

I went skiing this weekend and saw the perfect example of a leader adapting her leadership style to her followers and situation. While putting on my skis I saw a ski instructor teaching little kids to ski. She did it using the game "red light, green light." The kids loved it, and seemed to be doing very well. Later that same day, as I was going to the lodge for lunch, she was teaching adults, and she did more demonstrating than talking. But when she talked she was always sure to encourage them so they did not feel intimidated when some little kid whizzed by. She would say to the adults that it's easier for children, or that smaller skis are easier. She made the children laugh and learn, and made the adults less self-conscious to help them learn too.

Today may not be a topic on exactly leadership, but I thought it would be interesting to discuss. I attended the football game this afternoon and could not help but notice our cheerleaders. I was just thinking of their name in general, and found them to be a good example (of leadership). Everyone gets rowdy at a football game, but without the direction of the cheerleaders there would be mayhem. They do a good job of getting the crowd organized and the adrenalin pumping (though of course the game is most important in that too!). It's just amazing to see them generate so much interest that all of the crowd gets into the cheering. We even chant their stupid-sounding cheers! You might not know any of them personally, but their enthusiasm invites you to try to be even louder than them. I must give the cheerleaders a round of applause.

I've been thinking about how I used to view/understand leadership, trying to find out how my present attitudes were developed. It's hard to remember past freshman year, even harder to go past high school. Overall, I think my father has been the single most important influence on my leadership development—long before I even realized it. Dad is a strong "Type A" person. He drives himself hard and demands a great deal from everyone around him, especially his family and especially his only son and oldest child. He was always pushing me to study, practice whatever sport I was involved in at the time, get ahead of everybody else in every way possible.

---

ing her public speaking skills. In such a case, doing what she does best (and what others want her to do) might stand in the way of growth in another area.

Sheila has several alternatives. She could refuse the job of treasurer because she has had her fill of accounting. Alternatively, she could accept the job of treasurer and look for yet another activity in which to develop her public speaking skills. Unfortunately, both of these options may present their own problems. Still another alternative would be to negotiate to expand the role of treasurer to allow greater opportunity to blend the role with her own developmental goals. For example, Sheila might choose to make regular oral reports to the board instead of submitting solely written reports. Additionally, she might take on a larger share of speaking at local service clubs for the purpose of public education about the charity and her own expert view of its needs with regard to fund raising and financial support. The point here is that leaders simply need to be deliberate in seeking opportunities to put their personal development plans into action. Leaders should exercise control over events to the extent they can; they should not let events exercise a counterproductive control over them.

A leader's first step in exercising control over his personal development is to identify what his goals actually are. The example above presumed Sheila already had identified public speaking as a skill she wanted to improve. But what if a leader is uncertain about what he needs to improve on? As described earlier, leaders should systematically collect information from a number of different sources. One place a leader can get information about where to improve is through a review of his or her current job performance, if that is applicable. Ideally, leaders will have had feedback sessions with their own superiors, which should help them identify areas of relative strength and weakness. Leaders should treat this feedback as a helpful perspective on their developmental needs. Leaders also should look at their interactions with peers as a source of ideas about what they might work on. Leaders should especially take notice if the same kind of problem comes up in their interactions with different individuals in separate situations. Leaders need to look at their own role in such instances as objectively as they can; there might be clues about what behavioral changes might facilitate better working relationships with others. Still another way to identify developmental objectives is to look ahead to what new skills are needed to function effectively at a higher level in the organization, or in a different role than the leader now has. Finally, leaders can use formal psychological tests and questionnaires to determine what their relative strengths and weaknesses as a leader may be.

On a concluding note, there is one activity leaders should put in their developmental plans whatever else might be included in them: a program of personal reading to broaden their perspectives on leadership. This reading can include the classics as well as contemporary fiction, biographies and autobiographies of successful leaders, essays on ethics and social responsibility, and assorted self-improvement books on various leadership and management issues. A vital part of leadership development is intellectual stimulation and reflection, and an active reading program is indispensable to that. Leaders might even want to join (or form) a discussion group that regularly meets to exchange ideas about a book everyone has read.

LEADERSHIP DEVELOPMENT THROUGH EDUCATION AND TRAINING

Although we believe experience plays a large role in leadership development, we believe formal education can play an important role, too. For example, Bray, Campbell, and Grant (1974); Howard (1986); and Wakabayashi and Graen (1984) all found that education level or academic performance in college was positively related to future managerial success. Furthermore, in a major review of the effectiveness of managerial training programs, Burke and Day (1986) found that educational programs generally had a positive effect on leadership development. Thus, formal education and training programs can help one become a better leader. However, it is important to note that these programs vary substantially in both content and pedagogy, and not all programs are appropriate for all leaders. The content of many leadership programs varies considerably, depending on the target audience; university-level courses generally provide a survey of the major leadership findings, programs for first-level supervisors often focus on how to train subordinates and give them feedback about their progress, and programs for senior executives often focus on strategic planning and public relations. Programs also vary in the extent to which they are based on well-established and professionally accepted practices and standards. Some leadership training programs represent little more than fads or popularized pseudoscience. In the following pages, we will review some of the more common educational and training techniques used to teach and develop leadership.

University Courses in Leadership

Spitzberg (1987) estimated that over 500 colleges or universities offer some type of leadership training program. Often these programs consist of extracurricular leadership activities run out of the student development office or are courses much like the one for which you are using this book. The extracurricular activities can vary greatly, but the leadership courses often have a high degree of overlap in both content and pedagogy. In terms of content, the topics covered in most leadership courses are similar to the subjects addressed in this book and include how personality traits, cognitive abilities, values, behaviors, motivation, group dynamics, communication, situational factors, and different theories of leadership can all be used to describe the leadership process. In addition, many universities offer specialized courses that focus primarily on historical, business, minority, or female leaders.

The techniques, or pedagogy, used to impart these different leadership concepts to students can vary greatly. Many courses use the standard lecture method, and Burke and Day (1986) found this method to be an effective way of imparting knowledge about leadership. Some courses also provide **individualized feedback** to students in the form of personality, intelligence, values, or interests test scores or leadership behavior ratings. A relatively new twist to individualized feedback is to have subjects compare the results of their personality or behavior self-ratings with those given to them by their peers (Curphy, 1991). **Case studies** consist of descriptions of various leadership situations (much like the description of Steve's situation earlier in the chapter) and are used as a vehicle for leadership discussions. **Role playing** is also a popular methodology. In role playing, participants are assigned "parts" to play (e.g., a supervisor and unmotivated subordinate) in a job-related scenario. Role playing has the advantage of letting trainees actually practice relevant skills and thus has greater transferability to the workplace than do didactic lectures or abstract discussions about leadership. **Simulations** and **games** are other methods of training. These are relatively structured activities designed to mirror some of the challenges or decisions commonly faced in the work environment. One of the better known leadership simulations is the Center for Creative Leadership's "Looking Glass" (McCall & Lombardo, 1982), in which participants play different leadership roles in a glass manufacturing plant. A newer approach to leadership development puts participants in relatively unfamiliar territory (e.g., outdoors rather than offices) and presents them physical, emotionally arousing, and often team-oriented challenges.

Leadership Training Programs

There are numerous leadership training programs aimed particularly toward leaders and supervisors in industry or public service. In many ways, these have strong parallels to both the content and techniques used in university-level courses on leadership. However, these programs are usually much shorter (typically less than a week), and the content tends to be more focused than that of a university course. The content of these programs also depends on the organizational level of the recipients; programs for first-level supervisors focus on developing supervisory skills such as training, monitoring, giving feedback, and conducting performance reviews with subordinates. Generally, these programs use lectures, case studies, and role-playing exercises to improve leadership skills.

The programs for midlevel managers often focus on improving interpersonal, oral communication, and written communication skills, as well as giving tips on time management, planning, and goal setting. These programs rely more heavily on individualized feedback, case studies, presentations, role playing, simulations, **in-basket exercises**, and **leaderless group discussions** as techniques to help leaders develop. In in-basket exercises, participants are given a limited amount of time to prioritize and respond to a number of notes, letters, and phone messages from a fictitious manager's in-basket. This technique is particularly useful in assessing and improving a manager's planning and time management skills. In leaderless group discussions, facilitators and observers rate participants on the degree of persuasiveness, leadership, followership, or conflict each member manifests in a group that has no appointed leader. These ratings are used to provide managers with feedback about their interpersonal and oral communication skills.

Leadership programs for senior executives and CEOs tend to focus on strategic planning, public relations, and interpersonal skills. Many times, the entire senior leadership of a company will go through a leadership program at the same time. One goal of such a group might be to learn how to develop a strategic plan for their organization. In order to improve public relations skills, some programs have CEOs undergo simulated, unannounced interviews with television reporters and receive feedback on how they could have done better.

Evaluating Leadership Development Programs

Although a number of leadership training programs are based on sound theory and research, some other programs have no basis in science and should be considered speculative at best. Still others are based on unwarranted and simplistic extensions of scientific findings. Perhaps the best way to guarantee that a leadership program will be useful to you or your organization is to adopt a systematic approach to leadership training. There is value in being an informed consumer, and this is just as true for investing one's time, energy, and money in leadership programs as it is for other products and services. To this end, Campbell (1988) has described a systematic model of training that can easily be adapted to leadership development programs. Some of the major steps in Campbell's (1988) model are (*a*) determining what needs to be learned, (*b*) determining the training objectives, (*c*) specifying the learning methods and media, and (*d*) evaluating the training outcomes. The following discussion is an adaptation of these steps in leadership development.

Although specifying what needs to be learned in a training program sounds straightforward enough, it is surprising how infrequently this step is actually taken with respect to leadership training. Instead, many organizations send employees to leadership training programs because (*a*) other companies are sending their employees (and maybe gaining some advantage), (*b*) the senior staff went to the training and liked it, or (*c*) the employees deserve a reward for their good work. Unfortunately, none of these is a particularly good reason for choosing a leadership training program. Better questions to ask involve the goals of the organization, the current level of leadership skills in the organization, and the gaps that need to be filled through training in order to accomplish the organization's goals. Systematically determining what leadership gaps need to be filled can be done by accomplishing a needs analysis. Although the details of a needs analysis are beyond the scope of this book, such an analysis will provide answers to the question *What needs to be learned?*

After determining what gaps need to be filled, the next step in Campbell's (1988) model is to determine the training objectives. In other words, what specific objectives does the training program hope to accomplish, and how do these objectives match up with the leadership gaps to be filled? If the training objectives are not tied to the gaps identified in the needs analysis, then the training will probably have little, if any, positive impact. In addition, if the training program does not offer any specific training objectives, then it will be difficult to evaluate whether or not the training was successful. Tying the training objectives to the gaps identified in the needs analysis is one way to ensure the training program is good for the organization and will be salient to the participants.

Another way to increase the salience of education and training programs is to integrate the material better with a person's ongoing work experience. That is the basis for an approach to management education called **action learning** (Margerison, 1988). Coca-Cola and TRW are two companies, among others, that have adopted such an action-oriented approach to management development (Berry, 1990; Clover, 1991). Coca-Cola did so, for example, because traditional management development programs often failed to ''add value'' to the company. The traditional management development programs did not help because they were not linked to the organization's actual challenges or problems, had objectives that stressed increases in awareness and understanding but did not build competence, and focused on individuals rather than teams or operating units. As an alternative, Coca Cola's new model for management development is attended by whole management teams analyzing current business issues. In general, relative to traditional management development programs, action learning is more work-based than classroom-based; more group-oriented than individual-oriented; more active than passive; and more action-based than knowledge-based (Margerison, 1988).

An overlooked component of Campbell's (1988) model of training is specifying the learning methods and media. Too often, companies buy leadership development programs for their employees because the program makes heavy use of interactive videodiscs, simulations, videotapes, and other types of high-tech training methods. Whether or not this high-tech-based training actually results in improved leadership training remains to be seen. The bottom line is that the needs of the organization and the training objectives determine the techniques to be used in training, rather than permitting the available techniques and equipment to determine the training content.

A final point to consider regarding leadership training involves evaluating the success or effectiveness of any training program. At a minimum, one should ask whether the training successfully accomplished all of the objectives. This again points out the importance of having clear objectives for any training program. According to Kirkpatrick (1967), reaction, learning, behavioral, and results criteria can all be used to evaluate a training program. Asking participants to subjectively rate a program's effectiveness exemplifies reaction criteria, and test scores (e.g., scores on a final exam) exemplify learning criteria. Either or both can be used to evaluate whether a leadership program accomplished its objectives. Determining whether leaders behaved or acted differently in the workplace after training exemplifies a behavioral criteria for evaluation, and the effect on a company's revenues exemplifies results criteria.

Although multiple criteria can and should be used to evaluate a training program, several additional points need to be considered. First, it is possible to get favorable reaction data but unfavorable learning, behavioral, and results data for a training program. Second, just because the impact of a leadership development program is not apparent using results criteria does not mean the program was unsuccessful. There are a number of factors that affect an organization's success, and some (such as market forces) may be relatively insensitive to a change in a leader's style. Finally, none of Kirkpatrick's four criteria really measure whether or not a leader has developed more thinking frames or perspectives as a result of the leadership training program. This may be the greatest contribution to leadership development a formal leadership course or program can make, yet none of the four criteria really tap this contribution. Recent developments in training evaluation and assessment are beginning to use more of a thinking frames or multiple perspectives approach to evaluate training (Kraiger, Ford, & Salas, 1992), and hopefully these advances will be applied to evaluating leadership development programs.

BUILDING YOUR LEADERSHIP SELF-IMAGE

This chapter has explored how leadership develops through experience and formal education. Before concluding, however, we should acknowledge that not everyone wants to be a leader or believes he can be. John Gardner (1965) has argued that many of our best and brightest young people actually have been immunized against and dissuaded from seeking leadership opportunities and responsibilities. Other young people, even if they want to be leaders, may not believe they have what it takes. Both groups, we believe, are selling themselves short.

To those who merely want to avoid the responsibilities of leadership, we encourage an openness of mind about leadership's importance and pervasiveness. We hope this book offers ways of thinking about leadership that make it at once more immediate, more relevant, and more interesting than it may have seemed before. To others, we encourage flexibility in self-image. Do not stay out of the leadership arena based on some global and self-defeating generalization such as "I am not the leader type." Experiment and take a few risks with different leadership roles. This will help you appreciate new facets of yourself as well as broaden your leadership self-image.

SUMMARY

This chapter reviews several major points regarding how leadership can be developed through both formal education and experience. One way to get more out of your leadership courses and experiences is through the application of the action-observation-reflection model. This model provides a framework for better understanding leadership situations. In addition, being aware of the role perception plays in leadership development is also important, as it affects what you observe, how you interpret your observations, and what actions you take as a leader. Finally, it is important to remember that both education and experience can contribute to your development as a leader by enhancing your ability to reflect and analyze leadership situations. Exposure to formal leadership education programs can help you to develop thinking frames or multiple perspectives to analyze leadership situations, and the people you work with and the task itself can also provide you with insights on how to be a better leader. However, what you gain from any leadership program or experience is a function of what you make of it. Successful leaders are those who have "an extraordinary tenacity in extracting something worthwhile from their experience and in seeking experiences rich in opportunities for growth" (McCall, Lombardo, & Morrison, 1988, p. 122). If you want to become a better leader, then you must seek challenges and try to get all you can from any leadership situation or opportunity.

KEY TERMS AND CONCEPTS

action-observation-reflection model   mentor

spiral of experience   individualized feedback

perceptual set   case studies

attribution   role playing

fundamental attribution error   simulations

self-fulfilling prophecy   games

single-loop learning   in-basket exercises

double-loop learning   leaderless group discussions

thinking frames   action learning

DISCUSSION QUESTIONS

1. Not all effective leaders seem to be reflective by nature. How do you reconcile that with the concept of the spiral of experience and its role in leadership development?

2. Explain how you can use knowledge about each of the following to enrich the benefits of your own present leadership experiences:
   a. The action-observation-reflection model.
   b. The people you interact and work with.
   c. The activities you're involve in.

3. Using the role of teacher as a specific instance of leadership, discuss how a teacher's perceptual set, expectations of students, and attributions may affect student motivation and performance. Do you think some teachers could become more effective by becoming more aware of these processes? Would that be true for leaders in general?

4. If you were to design the perfect leadership development experience for yourself, how would you do so and what would it include?. How would you know it was effective?

5. Do you think people have a need for growth and development?

6. One important aspect of learning from experience is observing the consequences of one's actions. Sometimes, however, the most significant consequences of a leader's actions do not occur for several years (e.g., the ultimate impact of certain personnel decisions or a strategic decision to change a product line). If that is so, then is there any way individuals can learn from the consequences of those actions in a way to modify their behavior? If consequences are so delayed, is there a danger they might draw the wrong lessons from their experiences?

SUGGESTED READINGS

Astin, H. S. and C. Leland. *Women of Influence, Women of Vision.* San Francisco: Jossey-Bass, 1991.

Bennis, W. *On Becoming a Leader.* Reading, Mass.: Addision-Wesley, 1989.

Erikson, E. *Gandhi's Truth.* New York: W. W. Norton, 1969.

Goldstein, I. L. *Training in Organizations: Needs Assessment, Development, and Evaluation.* 2nd ed. Monterey, Calif.: Brooks/Cole, 1986.

McCall, M. W.; M. M. Lombardo; and A. M. Morrison. *The Lessons of Experience.* Lexington, Mass.: Lexington Books, 1988.

Chapter Three

Leadership Is Both a Science and an Art

INTRODUCTION

I n many ways, the contents of this chapter build on the material covered in Chapter Two. Leadership as a science concerns the body of knowledge we have acquired about leadership through research. Enrolling in university-level courses and taking part in formal leadership training programs are ways you can build your own body of knowledge based on what others have discovered about leadership. At the same time, knowing what to do and knowing when or where to do it are often different things (see Highlight 3–1). The skill with which you apply different leadership techniques and the appropriateness of those techniques for a particular leadership situation may largely be a function of experience. The people you have worked with in the past (particularly mentors), as well as past tasks that involved high levels of personal pressure, can help you develop expertise regarding what to do in a particular leadership situation. Thus, the scientific and artistic aspects of leadership are not mutually exclusive, but rather interdependent. Having a better understanding of the sci-

---

HIGHLIGHT 3–1

Leadership Quotes, Chapter Three

Remember the difference between a boss and a leader: a boss says "Go!"—a leader says, "Let's go!"

E. M. Kelly

Never reveal all of yourself to other people; hold back something in reserve so that people are never quite sure if they really know you.

Michael Korda

A democracy cannot follow a leader unless he is dramatized. A man to be a hero must not content himself with heroic virtues and anonymous action. He must talk and explain as he acts—drama.

William Allen White

Nurture your mind with great thoughts. To believe in the heroic makes heroes.

Benjamin Disraeli

Any fool can keep a rule. God gave him a brain to know when to break the rule.

General Willard W. Scott

Never try to teach a pig to sing; it wastes your time and it annoys the pig.

Paul Dickson

---

ence of leadership can give you more perspectives for analyzing leadership situations, which may expand the range of actions you may take as a leader in response to a situation. Perhaps this interdependency was best epitomized with the action-observation-reflection model described in Chapter Two. The model is consistent with recent theories of adult learning, and applying this model to different leadership experiences can give you greater insight about your effectiveness as a leader.

As an overview, this chapter begins with a discussion of leadership as both a science and an art. Next, we describe some of the rational approaches to and emotional aspects of leadership. The rational approaches to leadership are techniques and theories that can be applied to a wide variety of leadership situations. Although these techniques can be effective, their effectiveness often is a function of the emotional factors in a leadership situation. Finally, this chapter concludes with a discussion about leaders and managers. Although many people distinguish between leadership and management, and between leaders and managers, the distinctions may not be very useful; individuals in supervisory positions perform many of the functions and roles traditionally associated with both leaders and managers.

LEADERSHIP IS A SCIENCE AND AN ART

Saying leadership is both a science and an art emphasizes the subject of leadership as a field of scholarly inquiry, as well as certain aspects of the practice of leadership. The scope of the science of leadership is reflected in the number of studies—approximately 8,000—cited in the most recent edition of an authoritative reference work, *Bass & Stogdill's Handbook of Leadership: Theory, Research, & Managerial Applications* (Bass, 1990). However, being an expert on leadership research is neither a necessary nor a sufficient condition for being a good leader. Some managers may be effective leaders without ever having taken a course or training program in leadership, and some scholars in the field of leadership may be relatively poor leaders themselves.

This is not to say that knowing something about leadership research is irrelevant to leadership effectiveness. Scholarship may not be a prerequisite for leadership effectiveness, but understanding some of the major research findings still can help individuals better analyze situations using a variety of perspectives. That, in turn, can give leaders insight about how to be more effective. Even so, because the skill in analyzing and responding to situations varies greatly across leaders, leadership will always remain partly an art as well as a science.

Leadership as a Science

In 1962, in a seminal book about the progression of science, Thomas Kuhn maintained there are two types of sciences—mature and immature. Mature sciences have answered many if not all of the major questions in their respective fields, and knowledge in them continues to accumulate gradually over time. An example of a mature science is the science of planetary motion. Scientists have discovered and verified the laws and theories governing the motion of the planets and have been able to develop mathematical formulas that can accurately predict planetary motion. Immature sciences, on the other hand, are characterized by the lack of consensus among scientists about even what major questions in the field are, much less the answers to them. Knowledge in immature sciences develops through fits and starts. During this stage, it may seem as though progress is not being made at all and that the phenomena in question are not even conducive to scientific study. The work of different scientists in the field may be based on radically different fundamental assumptions about the proper way to study the phenomena, and the cumulative record of such diverse work typically does not "add up" to science as we commonly understand it.

Leadership is an immature science, and the body of knowledge in the field of leadership has developed through a series of fits and starts. One of the earliest leadership theories was the "Great Man" theory (Stogdill, 1974). The Great Man theory maintained that leaders were distinguishable from followers in a number of different ways. Research efforts were focused on identifying the abilities and traits believed to separate leaders from followers, but for the most part these efforts failed to find conclusive evidence that leaders and followers were truly different.

Since the Great Man theory, research efforts have waxed and waned with respect to investigating things like the behaviors of leaders, how leaders need to modify their behaviors based on the followers and the situation, and the characteristics and effects of charismatic leaders. Although such efforts have helped us better understand the leadership process, the science of leadership has not yet produced laws and theories with the degree of precision found in the science of planetary motion. The failure to develop precision in the predicting of human behavior equivalent to the precision characteristic of certain other sciences may be frustrating, but it is important to bear in mind that people are much more complex than planets. It is relatively easy to predict where Mars will be in two days; it is more difficult to predict all the effects a leader's actions will have. With continued research, "laws of leadership" may someday be developed, but our current state of knowledge suggests that such a time is not near at hand.

Leadership as an Art

Just because we have failed to develop universal laws of leadership does not mean we know nothing about the topic. In reality, we do know quite a bit about the traits, abilities, and behaviors related to leadership effectiveness; the situational and follower characteristics that can affect a leader's behavior; and the effects of charismatic leaders. However, knowing about these findings and being able to effectively apply this knowledge are two different things. In many ways, the skillful application of leadership behaviors and techniques is much the same as the skillful application of brushstrokes by a master painter. Just as a master painter is not a mere copier, a "master" leader does not merely follow a set of rules or procedures (see, for example, Highlight 3–2). A similar argument holds even when we turn to a more scientific example—medicine. A physician may have mastered the facts and principles of medical science yet have a lousy bedside manner; she has mastered the science but not the art of medicine. By analogy, a person who mechanically copies another's leadership behavior without adapting it to his own personality and circumstance may come across as insincere (a "forgery") or stilted.

HIGHLIGHT 3–2

The Stateliness of Charles de Gaulle

> *Certain men have, one might almost say from birth, the quality of exuding authority, as though it were a liquid, though it is impossible to say precisely of what it consists.*

> Charles de Gaulle

In his fascinating book *Leaders,* former president Richard Nixon described the French president Charles de Gaulle as one of the great leaders he had met. Following are several aspects of de Gaulle's leadership based on Nixon's observations.

• *He conveyed stately dignity.* De Gaulle had a resolute bearing that conveyed distance and superiority to others. He was at ease with other heads of state but never informal with anyone, even close friends. His tall stature and imperious manner conveyed the message he was not a common man.

• *He was a masterful public speaker.* He had a deep, serene voice and a calm, self-assured manner. He used the French language grandly and eloquently. According to Nixon, "He spoke so articulately and with such precision that his message seemed to resonate apart from his words" (p. 59).

• *He played the part.* De Gaulle understood the role of theater in politics, and his meetings with the press (a thousand at a time!) were like audiences with royalty. He staged them in great and ornate halls, and he deftly crafted public statements that would be understood differently by different groups. In one sense, perhaps, this could be seen as a sort of falseness, but that may be too narrow a view. Nixon reflected on this aspect of de Gaulle's leadership: "General de Gaulle was a facade, but not a false one. Behind it was a man of incandescent intellect and a phenomenal discipline. The facade was like the ornamentation on a great cathedral, rather than the flimsy pretense of a Hollywood prop with nothing behind it" (p. 60).

Source: R. Nixon, *Leaders,* (New York: Warner Books, 1982).

RATIONAL AND EMOTIONAL ASPECTS OF LEADERSHIP

Leadership involves both the rational and emotional sides of human experience. Leadership includes actions and influences based on reason and logic as well those based on inspiration and passion. We do not want to cultivate leaders like Mr. Spock from the television series "*Star Trek,*" who wishes others would respond with logical predictability, as he does. Because people differ in their thoughts and feelings, hopes and dreams, need and fears, goals and ambitions, and strengths and weaknesses, leadership situations can be very complex. For example, if mistrust and antagonism existed between subordinates, then the leader might need to spend considerable time and energy dealing with the conflict. If the subordinates were very cohesive, then the leader could devote more time securing resources and providing guidance for goal accomplishment. Because people are both rational and emotional, leaders can use rational techniques and/or emotional appeals in order to influence followers, but they must also weigh the rational and emotional consequences of their actions. It follows that ignoring either side of human nature would give us an incomplete understanding of leadership.

Perhaps some further clarification of the rational and emotional sides of human nature is in order. A convenient place to start is the activity you are involved in right now—reading a textbook. Our usual mode for learning is rational. The material covered in textbooks, academic instruction, and writing in general are all predominantly rational in nature. The content in books and lectures tends to be factual, informative, and conceptual, and students probably learn best when their own emotional state is relatively calm.

Unfortunately, a view of learning built only on rational processes ignores a large and more complicated part of human nature. For example, students are sometimes too aroused to process complex conceptual material effectively. If you were trying to read this material while in an emotionally charged state (e.g., you have just had an argument with your boyfriend or girlfriend), chances are you would be having some difficulty keeping your attention focused; your mind might wander, and you might not remember what was in the paragraph you had just finished. Your feelings would be getting in the way of your attempts to process information rationally. At the same time, your emotions could be motivating you to take other actions (call him or her, call someone else, take a walk, etc.). The following are two other experiences you may have had that further show the power of emotions in our lives:

> Imagine yourself on the expressway in a busy city during a hot summer afternoon rush hour. You and hundreds of others are crawling forward in the right lane, approaching your exit, which has been clearly marked for the last several miles. After 15 minutes, you had to turn your air conditioner off since the engine was beginning to overheat. Finally, after another 10 minutes in oppressive heat, the exit sign is in sight. As you inch toward the off ramp, some ''idiot'' from the center lane (with his windows up and his air conditioner on high) tries to pull in front of you. How do you feel?

> Think back to the first time you were away from home. Do you remember the feeling of emptiness we usually call homesickness? Although being homesick is seldom fatal, the feelings associated with it in the short term can be quite debilitating.

Our emotional experiences can be both personal and intense, as these examples illustrate. They also illustrate how emotions may influence one's behavior, either positively or negatively. In rush-hour traffic, for example, angry drivers can be downright dangerous. And although feeling homesick is relatively common, it can interfere with doing more constructive things. Similarly, the study and practice of leadership must take into consideration the role feelings play in behavior. A leader who ignores the power of emotions and yells in a belittling way at a subordinate in front of others may never know the high price he or she pays in terms of lost loyalty and lowered performance. Human nature is both emotional and rational, and our understanding of leadership must address both. We shall look first at rational approaches to leadership.

Rational Approaches to Leadership

Much of the research literature on leadership is devoted to rational approaches to leadership, and these efforts certainly can enhance leader effectiveness. Two examples of the rational approach, goal setting and decision making, are described below.

Goal setting.   A substantial amount of research has been done on the impact of goal setting on team and group performance (see Locke & Latham, 1984, 1990; Locke, Shaw, Saari, & Latham, 1981). Goal-setting theory is rational because it is a systematic, rule-based approach to influencing behavior. To enhance motivation, goals must be challenging but attainable, clear and specific, measurable, and time-phased. A sales manager who sets a goal of immediately tripling sales may have little impact at all if others perceive the goal as totally unrealistic. On the other hand, one who merely asks her sales force to ''do a little better'' has offered a goal that is neither challenging nor specific. An example of a goal that met the criteria above was President John Kennedy's national goal of putting a man on the moon and returning him safely by the end of the 1960s. It met the four criteria and focused the efforts of thousands of scientists and engineers toward accomplishing it. Goal setting will be discussed more extensively later in this text. For now, just note that the approach takes advantage of our rational nature by providing explicit rules that help leaders progress toward distant objectives through manageable small steps.

Decision making.   Few aspects of leadership are more vital than making decisions. Whether a fraternity president is selecting a theme for an upcoming party or a general manager is introducing a new product to the marketplace, leadership and decision making go hand in hand. The decision-making process has been the subject of considerable study, and some aspects of decision making have been formalized into written procedures. One approach, called the Vroom-Yetton model (Vroom & Yetton, 1973), can be used to illustrate how a leader can use a rational method in deciding whether or how to use subordinate inputs in reaching certain decisions. According to this model (which will be presented in more detail in Chapter Fifteen), there are some situations in which leaders should seek input from their subordinates and other situations in which they should not. Furthermore, sometimes it is better to seek input privately from subordinates, whereas at other times it is better to have subordinates meet and discuss various options collectively with the leader. A number of factors determine which approach is preferable, including whether the subordinates have access to relevant information and whether their satisfaction and acceptance of the decision is critical to its successful implementation. This model does not give leaders specific answers to their problems, but it does tell them how much participation subordinates should have in the decision-making process.

One advantage of rational approaches is that leaders with different personalities can use them effectively. Goal setting involves a set of rules to be followed that are essentially transferable from situation to situation and leader to leader. An analogy here might be following directions for cooking a particular dish; if one follows the recipe, the meal should turn out all right. However, just as good cooks modify recipes in order to create more exciting dishes, good leaders will modify the prescriptions of the rational approaches in order to be more effective. Often these modifications are based on a leader's understanding of the emotional aspects of a leadership situation. Leaders may set more difficult goals or may disregard or modify the systematic decision-making rules of the Vroom-Yetton model when subordinates are in an emotionally charged state. Moreover, some leaders, particularly those seen as charismatic, seem to have the ability to create emotionally charged subordinates. These leaders have an energizing impact on others that cannot be put into a formula or prescription for others to copy. They seem to generate a sort of electricity that gets stronger around others, just as a comedian's jokes may seem more contagiously funny when you are not alone. Effects like these underscore the need to also examine the emotional aspects of leadership.

Emotional Aspects of Leadership

Emotions play an important role in leadership because they affect the perceptions and actions of both leaders and followers. For example, consider the concepts of perceptual sets, attributions, and self-fulfilling prophecies described in Chapter Two. A leader may have a negative perceptual set about a particular subordinate due to the subordinate's poor performance in the past. This negative perceptual set may effectively focus the leader's attention on only those activities or tasks the subordinate does poorly; the leader may not attend to or remember those activities the subordinate does well. Due to this negative perceptual set, the leader may be biased toward making internal attributions about the subordinate's performance. These internal attributions may, in turn, cause the leader to use punishment in order to correct the subordinate's performance deficit. The leader may also make a disparaging remark to the subordinate about his or her skills and abilities, which could become a self-fulfilling prophecy for the subordinate.

This same series of events could also be applied to followers' perceptions and actions. If followers perceived a leader as performing poorly, then they could develop a negative perceptual set about him. This negative set would focus the followers' attention on those tasks in which the leader failed, and the followers might make internal attributions about the underlying causes for these failures. Although followers are not in a position to punish the leader directly, they could engage in various counterproductive work behaviors (e.g., absenteeism, malingering, or insubordination), which could eventually result in the dismissal of the leader. Their perceptions of the leader might also lead to discouragement about how well the leader can represent them or help them succeed. Such doubts could reduce the followers' level of effort.

One example of this process may be evident in some of the "classic" skits from the television show "Saturday Night Live." A recurring skit involved Chevy Chase impersonating President Gerald Ford clumsily tripping over himself or falling down. It seems to have been based on one or two incidents where President Ford actually was caught on camera at just such an embarrassing moment. Through repeated and caricaturized enactments on television, however, President Ford may well have become widely perceived as the "clumsy" president. This is ironic and probably unjustified in that he was a varsity athlete in college and one of the fittest and most athletic individuals ever to hold the office of president. We can only speculate whether the repeated portrayal of him as physically clumsy may have generalized in voters' minds to more substantive aspects of his leadership. Could the caricaturized portrayals naturally have led to attributions about him, thus undermining voters' confidence in him as a president?

Emotions also can play a positive role in leadership. For example, emotions played a key role in the civil rights movement led by Dr. Martin Luther King, Jr. Many of the people in the civil rights movement had a particularly strong positive perceptual set regarding Dr. King and believed that Dr. King's vision of the future and strength of character were the primary reasons why the civil rights movement was successful (i.e., they made a positive internal attribution about the success of Dr. King). These internal attributions in turn caused people to act, and these actions eventually developed into a self-fulfilling prophecy for many of the participants. The excitement generated by some leaders can cause others to put forth extra effort for them.

A common thread running through both the negative and positive emotion examples just described, and through the whole cloth of leadership, is that leadership involves groups. The group may be as small as two people (e.g., you and the leader, or you and the follower), or it may be huge in number; further, the group members may be in close proximity or may be separated by considerable distances. In no case, though, is there leadership apart from a group. Individual accomplishment is not leadership. Leadership is a group phenomenon involving interactions between a leader and followers.

This point is worth emphasizing because at times groups themselves can cause irrational and emotional behavior. As an example, consider how people act during sporting events. If you have ever played a sport yourself, then you are aware of the effect of the team as it "gets psyched." The most emotional members of the team are often the informal team leaders and are also the ones who play with the greatest intensity. Emotions also influence the behavior of spectators. Most of us have seen examples of how a crowd of fans can encourage nonrational behavior, such as throwing one's hands in the air as the "wave" goes by. The heightened emotional intensity and lowered inhibitions of crowds can result in irrational behaviors by members of a group.

Most of us can cite extreme examples where individuals seemed to lose their normal behavioral limits as a result of the influence of groups. Riots are a prime case. One of the authors of this text happened to observe the riots in Washington, D.C., following the assassination of Dr. Martin Luther King, Jr. Caught up in the swell of the group as it moved along the streets in the northwest section of the city, he saw individuals coming out of a record store with armfuls of phonograph records, only to note when a pile was dropped that they were often taking 30 copies of the same album.

Some leaders are able to arouse followers' emotions and energize groups into collective action. Aroused feelings, however, can be used either positively or negatively, constructively or destructively. Some leaders have been able to inspire others to deeds of great purpose and courage. On the other hand, as images of Adolph Hitler's mass rallies or present-day angry mobs attest, group frenzy can readily become group mindlessness.

In understanding this emotional aspect of leadership, we should not ignore the extent to which people enjoy sharing intense feelings. Is that not part of the appeal of mass events like sports events, rock concerts, political rallies, and religious revivals? Performers from many different callings have become adept at arousing strong feelings in their audiences. They are even aided in that effort by the fact a group's emotional arousal can also be a somewhat self-reinforcing process. For one thing, emotional responsiveness can be somewhat "contagious." For another, increasing emotionalism may contribute to decreasing critical evaluation of a message's content. Thus, leaders whose style may prompt an audience's heightened affective levels may find an attendant "benefit" of less critical evaluation of their persuasive messages.

The mere presence of a group (without heightened emotional levels) can also cause people to act differently than when they are alone. For example, in airline cockpit crews, there are clear lines of authority from the captain down to the first officer (second in command) and so on. So strong are the norms surrounding the authority of the captain that some first officers will not take the airplane from the captain *even in the event of impending disaster.* Foushee (1984) reported a study wherein airline captains in simulator training intentionally feigned incapacitation so that the response of the rest of the crew could be observed. The feigned incapacitations occurred at a predetermined point during the plane's final approach in landing, and the simulation involved conditions of poor weather and visibility. Approximately 25 percent of the first officers in these simulated flights allowed the plane to crash. For some reason, the first officers did not take control even when it was clear the captain was allowing the aircraft to deviate from the parameters of a safe approach. This example demonstrates how group dynamics can influence the behavior of group members, even when emotional levels are not high.

Although groups themselves can cause followers to have heightened emotional levels and to behave irrationally, leaders can also have these same effects on followers. For example, emotional appeals by the Reverend Jim Jones resulted in approximately 800 of his followers volitionally committing suicide. Why do some leaders have substantial emotional effects on followers, and how can we study these emotional influences? One way to study the emotional impact of leaders on their followers is to use the methodological techniques developed by House and his associates (House, Woycke, & Fodor, 1988). These authors trained undergraduates to code the biographies of presidential cabinet members for affect (words that describe emotion). Then political scientists were asked to rate the presidents along the dimension of "greatness as a leader." The authors found a remarkably high relationship between the two factors; the great presidents were ones who inspired more feelings in their cabinet members (or at least in their biographers). The researchers also determined whether these affective statements represented positive or negative feelings. Surprisingly, affect was present in both positive and negative directions! Apparently, presidents who stir emotions do so both positively and negatively even within the same followers; they develop a sort of love-hate relationship felt by those near them.

It should be apparent from the examples throughout this section that leadership involves followers' feelings and nonrational behavior as well as rational behavior. Leaders need to consider *both* the rational and emotional consequences of their actions. Although it may not be traditional to discuss emotions in a book on leadership, it seems essential to consider the impact of emotions if we are to grasp the full spectrum of the topic.

Leadership and Management

Some people think of leadership as a more emotional process than management. After all, leaders have been characterized by terms such as *charismatic* and *inspiring*, but one rarely hears of a charismatic or inspiring manager. Management has more of a connotation of being rational, a process more involved with the head than the heart. Management is associated in many peoples' minds with words like *efficiency, planning, paperwork, procedures, regulations, con-*

trol, and *consistency.* Leadership is more associated with words like *risk taking, dynamic, creativity, change,* and *vision.* However, we believe this distinction between leaders and managers may be more a function of our implicit theories of leaders and managers than of what actually happens in real work settings. Individuals can be seen as charismatic and charming or as planful and controlling whether or not they happen to be called *leaders* or *managers.* In many ways, the differences between being perceived as a leader or as a manager are a function of the specific responsibilities of a given role and how the person in that role chooses to fulfill those responsibilities. Still, the connotations of the words *leader* and *manager* are often so loaded with stereotyped biases that it will be useful to explore these concepts, and the related ones of leadership and management, a little further. In this section, we will review some of the functions typically ascribed to leaders and managers and also the view put forth by some that being a leader or manager (job titles aside) reflects a characterological predisposition—that leaders and managers really are different types of people. We conclude this section with comments about the importance of being able to perform both leadership and management functions in order to be successful.

The Functions of Leaders and Managers

Bass (1990) wrote, "Leaders manage and managers lead, but the two activities are not synonymous" (p. 383). According to classical management theorists, the purpose of management is to keep complex human systems running optimally in line with established criteria. Thus, managers traditionally have been thought to perform the planning, investigating, coordinating, organizing, and controlling functions in an organization (Davis, 1942; MacKenzie, 1969; Mahoney, Jerdee, & Carroll, 1965; Urwick, 1952). Management theorists have paid relatively little attention to the face-to-face interactions managers have with followers in order to accomplish organizational goals. These face-to-face interactions with followers are generally seen as leadership functions; leaders focus more on resolving conflicts in groups, providing emotional support to group members, maintaining group cohesiveness and satisfaction, and working with group members to set group goals (Bales, 1958; Bass, 1990; Mann, 1965).

In actuality, however, it appears that leaders perform many of the activities traditionally assigned as management functions and vice versa. For example, it is difficult to see how managers could set policies, coordinate activities, or control work-unit or team activities without having face-to-face interactions with others. The idea that leadership and management essentially involve many of the same activities may best be seen in Figure 3–1, which shows leadership and management as two overlapping functions. Although some of the functions performed by leaders and managers may be somewhat unique, the degree of overlap is quite extensive. Focusing only on the areas of nonoverlap (i.e., the

FIGURE 3–1
Leadership and Management Overlap

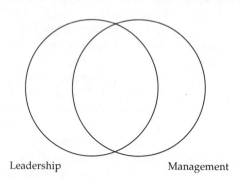

Leadership   Management

differences between leadership and management) does not provide a very realistic picture of the functions people actually perform in management or leadership positions. A more comprehensive understanding of the functions performed by leaders and managers must involve focusing on the large area of overlap depicted in Figure 3–1, not just on the distinctions.

However, just because leaders and managers can and do perform functions traditionally associated with the other does not mean they always will. The degree to which a leader performs management functions may depend on both the nature of the job and the individual. As people move up an organizational hierarchy, planning, organizing, and controlling functions often take on relatively more importance. Although the degree of follower participation in these activities can vary greatly, the amount of follower participation is often at the discretion of the supervisor. Some supervisors may encourage a high level of follower involvement; others may not. Similarly, some individuals in traditional management positions may interact with followers extensively in order to motivate them to achieve organizational goals. Simply put, the job itself may dictate to some extent the relative amount of time spent on traditional management or leadership functions, but people can and often do vary greatly on the way they fulfill their assigned responsibilities.

Gardner (1986, 1990) looked at the differences between leadership and management as a matter of degree. He pointed out how some managers think in longer terms, attend to broader organizational and environmental issues, extend influence beyond bureaucratic boundaries, understand more intuitively than others the nonrational and unconscious elements of influence, cope more skillfully with conflicting constituencies, and accept and foster organizational change and growth more than others. In this view, leadership is not a label or rigid categorization, but rather a function of one's breadth of perspective and nature of influence. Others see leadership as inherently a value-choosing, and thus a value-laden, activity; leaders are thought to *do the right things*, whereas managers are thought to *do things right* (Bennis, 1985; Zaleznik, 1983). Furthermore, leaders may function independent of formal organizations, whereas managers function within defined organizational roles.

Another way to think about leadership and management is to consider them complementary functions; organizations need both functions performed well in order to be successful. For example, consider again the civil rights movement. Dr. Martin Luther King, Jr., gave life and direction to the civil rights movement in America. He gave dignity and hope of freer participation in our national life to people who before had little reason to expect it. He inspired the world with his vision and eloquence, and changed the way we live together. America is a different nation today because of him. Was Dr. Martin Luther King, Jr., a leader? Of course. Was he a manager? Somehow that does not seem to fit, but the civil rights movement may have failed if it had not been for the managerial talents of his supporting staff. Leadership and management complement each other, and both are needed for organizational success.

Are Leaders and Managers Different Kinds of People?

As noted earlier, Bennis (1985) characterized managers as people who do things right and leaders as people who do the right things. This is just one among many distinctions Bennis makes between leaders and managers. The following are several more (Bennis, 1989):

- Managers administer; leaders innovate.
- Managers maintain; leaders develop.
- Managers control; leaders inspire.
- Managers have a short-term view; leaders, a long-term view.
- Managers ask how and when; leaders ask what and why.
- Managers imitate; leaders originate.
- Managers accept the status quo; leaders challenge it.

According to Zaleznik (1974, 1983), these differences between leaders and managers reflect fundamentally different personality types. The point is not merely that managerial roles emphasize tasks like administration and control whereas leadership roles emphasize tasks like innovation and inspiration. Zaleznik (1974, 1983) says leaders and managers are basically different kinds of people. He says some people are managers *by nature;* other people are leaders *by nature.* More specifically, leaders and managers differ in their views of means and ends, their sense of identity, and the way they relate to others. Leaders are interested in determining what the ends are, have a profound sense of separateness, and have extremely close relationships with followers. Managers are interested in the means to achieve ends, are much more in harmony with and at home in their environment, and try to maintain a sense of equity and objectivity in procedures and decisions; as a result, managers tend to have relatively superficial levels of emotional involvement with subordinates.

There are profound practical implications for organizational leaders if Zaleznik's (1974, 1983) analysis is correct. If leaders and managers are different personality types, and if personality is very difficult to change, then it would be extremely inefficient, maybe a waste of time, to try to teach management skills to individuals who are leaders by nature, or to try to teach leadership skills to individuals who are managers by nature. Nevertheless, Zaleznik (1983) himself notes executives themselves often reject his dichotomy. Perhaps this rejection comes from the recognition that their responsibilities demand a wider breadth of competencies than his analysis recommends. The challenges groups and organizations face require both management and leadership, and it does not seem likely or practical in the future that individuals will be selected or assigned to such simplistic and mutually exclusive roles as leader *or* manager. As described earlier, leaders perform many of the functions traditionally assigned to managers, and managers perform many functions traditionally assigned to leaders. Thus, we do not find a simple dichotomous classification very useful. Managers and leaders are largely one and the same; most of the differences stem from the responsibilities of the job itself and the manner in which individuals choose to fulfill them.

SUMMARY

Leadership is both a science and an art. Because leadership is an immature science, researchers are still struggling to find out what the important questions in leadership are; we are far from finding answers to them. However, even those individuals with extensive knowledge of the leadership research may be poor leaders. Knowing what to do is not the same as knowing when, where, and how to do it. The art of leadership concerns the skill of understanding leadership situations and influencing others to accomplish group goals. Formal leadership education may give individuals the skills to better understand leadership situations, and mentorships and experience may give individuals the skills to better influence others. Leaders must also weigh both rational and emotional considerations when attempting to influence others. Leadership sometimes can be accomplished through relatively rational, explicit, rule-based methods of assessing situations and determining actions. Nevertheless, there is also an emotional side of human nature that must be acknowledged. Leaders are often most effective when they affect people at both the emotional level and the rational level. The idea of leadership as a whole-person process can also be applied to the distinction often made between leaders and managers. Although leadership and management can be distinguished as separate functions, a more comprehensive picture of supervisory positions could be made by examining the overlapping functions of leaders and managers.

DISCUSSION QUESTIONS

1. Does every successful leader have a valid theory of leadership?
2. Would you consider it a greater compliment for someone to call you a good manager or a good leader? Why? Do you believe you can be both?
3. Think of further examples of both rational and emotional aspects of leadership.
4. Do you believe leadership can be studied scientifically? Why or why not?
5. To the extent leadership is an art, what methods come to mind for improving one's art as a leader?

SUGGESTED READINGS

Bass, B. M. *Bass & Stogdill's Handbook of Leadership: Theory, Research & Managerial Applications.* 3rd ed. New York: Free Press, 1990.

Vaill, P. B. *Managing as a Performing Art: New Ideas for a World of Chaotic Change.* San Francisco: Jossey-Bass, 1989.

Yukl, G. A., and D. D. Van Fleet. "Theory and Research on Leadership in Organizations." In *Handbook of Industrial and Organizational Psychology.* Vol. 3. eds. M. D. Dunnette and L. M. Hough. Palo Alto, Calif.: Consulting Psychologists Press, 1992.

Zaleznik, A. "Managers and Leaders: Are They Different?" *Harvard Business Review* 55, no.5 (1977), pp. 67–78.

Chapter Four

Assessing Leadership and Measuring Its Effects

INTRODUCTION

B ecause this chapter is about assessing leadership, it seems appropriate to begin with an example from research. The research in this case deals with leadership in commercial airline crews. Many airline crews consist of three positions with very distinct responsibilities. The aircraft captain is the final authority for all decisions regarding the aircraft and is ultimately responsible for the safety of the passengers and crew. The copilot helps the captain fly the aircraft, and the flight engineer is primarily responsible for the aircraft's preflight inspections and operation of systems (e.g., electrical, hydraulic, fuel, communication, etc.). Because airline crews must work together as a coordinated team in order to successfully complete a flight, one of the authors (Ginnett, 1988) of this text studied factors affecting crew coordination. As a part of this project, he flew with a number of different airline crews and recorded conversations between crew members. The following is an excerpt of an interview between a first officer and the researcher:

Researcher:

Are all the captains you fly with pretty much the same?

Aircrew member:

Oh no. Some guys are the greatest guys in the world to fly with. I mean they may not have the greatest hands in the world but that doesn't matter. When you fly with them, you feel like you can work together to get the job done. You really want to do a good job for them. Some other captains are just the opposite . . . you just can't stand to work with them. That doesn't mean you'll do anything that's unsafe or dangerous but you won't go out of your way to keep him or her out of trouble either. So you'll just sit back and do what you have to and just hope he or she screws up.

Researcher:

How can you tell which kind of captain you're working with?

Aircrew member:

Oh, you can tell.

Researcher:

How?

Aircrew member:

I don't know how you tell but it doesn't take very long. Just a couple of minutes and you'll know.

The above conversation details many of the main points in this chapter. Although it was the airline pilot's personal opinion that it was relatively easy to recognize good captains, scientists use more systematic ways to assess leadership, which in this case is precisely the project Ginnett undertook. Scientists use these more systematic techniques because personal opinions can vary substantially across individuals. Furthermore, personal opinions do not add systematically to our collective understanding of leadership. For example, that some people believe punishment will cause work-unit performance to increase and others believe punishment will cause work-unit performance to decrease does not tell us anything about the true impact of punishment on performance. Additionally, because of the perceptual biases discussed in Chapter Two, individuals holding these opposite views nonetheless may easily recall situations that confirm their own opinions and refute the opinions of others. When issues like this are left merely to personal opinion, there often is no logical way for the difference to be resolved. A more constructive approach is to systematically study the effects of punishment on performance.

What does the scientific evidence say about the effects of punishment on performance? Actually, there is no clear-cut verdict. Although most people probably accept the need to punish certain extreme kinds of misconduct, there seems to have been growing sentiment over several decades that punishment has numerous drawbacks and should be used cautiously. However, recent findings by Schnacke (1986) indicated that punishment can cause an increase in work-unit performance. By systematically testing the effects of punishment under controlled conditions, this study helps determine whether or not punishment actually has a positive or negative effect on work-unit performance and adds to the body of knowledge of leadership.

If leadership researchers do not rely on personal opinions to determine which traits, abilities, or behaviors are necessary for effective leadership, then just how do they assess leaders? Generally speaking, leadership researchers have used observations, interviews, and paper-and-pencil measures to assess leadership empirically. For example, leadership researchers could interview airline captains about their leadership styles, administer personality tests to captains to see what types of personality traits they possessed, or observe captains giving orders and interacting with other crew members. Each of these techniques would give a different perspective about each captain and the type of leader he or she may be.

Assessing leadership and measuring its effects are not the same thing, however. Using the example above, leadership researchers may choose to measure the effects of the captain's behaviors by recording the level of effort and coordination of the crew members, asking crew members how satisfied they are with the captain, or recording the proportion of times the captain's plane has taken off or landed on time. Just as the different assessment techniques provide different perspectives of the captain, the different measures used to assess the effects of the captain's leadership style can also yield different and sometimes conflicting results. A captain who is extremely disliked by his or her crew may have a perfect on-time takeoff and landing record, and a well-liked and respected captain may have a poor on-time takeoff and landing record. Which leader is more effective? Obviously, the answer to this question depends partly on the measure or measures being used to judge the leader's effectiveness. And, perhaps not quite so obviously, there are still other relevant measures of leadership effectiveness besides these.

We need to stress that this book is not intended to be a guide for conducting leadership research; it is a guide to help leadership students and budding practitioners be better leaders. The material in this chapter is provided for two reasons. First, because the findings of leadership research will be emphasized throughout the book, it will be helpful for you to be familiar with the ways leadership and its effects are typically measured. Second, it may be helpful for you as a leadership practitioner to be aware of the limitations of personal opinions as the primary basis for assessing leadership effectiveness. Understanding that leadership effectiveness can be measured in multiple ways will, we hope, encourage you to pay attention to alternative indicators of leadership impact (also see Highlight 4–1).

As an overview, this chapter first reviews the five major techniques that leadership researchers have used to assess leadership. Although researchers can use any of these five techniques, the specific one used often depends on which aspect of the leadership process a researcher wishes to examine, and there are pros and cons for each technique. Later, the chapter reviews and evaluates the types of outcomes used to measure leadership effects. As described earlier, these measures may yield very different results concerning leadership effectiveness. Finally, the chapter concludes with a description and evaluation of the common methodologies used to understand the relationships between leaders' traits or behaviors and various leadership criteria.

ASSESSING LEADERSHIP

There are many factors to consider when assessing leadership, but two of the most important are the researcher's own definition of leadership and the general assessment technique used. The following is a more complete discussion of the relationship between leadership definitions and leadership assessment.

The Importance of Leadership Definitions

By far the most important factor influencing which aspects of the leadership process will be the focus in any study is the individual researcher's own definition or theory of leadership. As described in Chapter One, there are many different theories and definitions of leadership. This has led leadership researchers to examine, for example, the traits and behaviors of leaders (Komacki, 1986; Lord, Devader, & Allinger, 1986; Stogdill, 1974; Zaccaro, Foti, & Kenny, 1991); the reactions and perceptions of followers (Bass & Yammarino, 1988; Curphy, 1991); the tactics leaders and followers use to influence each other (Hinkin & Schreisheim, 1989; Yukl & Falbe, 1991; Yukl, Lepsinger, & Lucia, 1992); and the situational factors affecting leadership behaviors (Fiedler, 1967; Gibson, 1992; Hersey & Blanchard, 1969; Kerr & Jermier, 1978). Because some assessment techniques are better suited to studying certain aspects of leadership than are others, the definitions and theories being studied may largely determine the assessment techniques used in a leadership study.

For example, it may be relatively difficult to accurately assess a leader's personality by interviewing different subordinates. Instead, a researcher may either have the leader complete a personality test or have subordinates complete personality tests on the leader to more accurately assess the traits possessed by the leader. Moreover, because different personality tests measure somewhat

---

HIGHLIGHT 4–1

Leadership Quotes, Chapter Four

As you go through life, brother
Whatever be your goal,
Keep your eye on the doughnut
And not upon the hole.

Mayflower coffee shop slogan

You have to set the tone and pace, define objectives and strategies, demonstrate through personal example what you expect from others.

Stanley Gault

If you're worried about that last at-bat, you're going to be miserable, you're only going to get depressed; but if you put a picture in your mind that you're going to get a base hit off him the next time, now how do you feel? I try to put positive pictures into the minds of my players.

Tommy Lasorda

Half the CEOs of the world are below average.

David Campbell

Trust men and they will be true to you; treat them greatly and they will show themselves to be great.

Ralph Waldo Emerson

---

different traits, the definition or theory of leadership underlying the research might even dictate which personality test will be best for a given study.

Different assessment techniques also can be used to investigate the same phenomenon. For example, Curtis, Smith, and Smoll (1979) used trained observers, interviews, and questionnaires to assess the leadership behaviors of Little League coaches. Because such diverse measures typically portray leaders in different lights, this study led to a broader understanding of coaching through the use of a combination of assessment techniques.

Methods Used to Assess Leadership

Many different techniques are used to assess leadership, but the five most common are the critical incidents technique, interviews, observations, paper-and-pencil measures, and assessment centers. The **critical incidents technique**

(Flanagan, 1951) consists of having followers, peers, and/or superiors describe a set of incidents where a leader did either a particularly good or bad job. The following is an example of a critical incident from an undergraduate student:

> The mid-term exam for our statistics class was to take place on the 15th of February. On the 9th of February, Dave convinced the rest of the members of the class that the best way to prepare for the exam was to share the studying burden. Dave's idea was to have each of us prepare study notes for one class lesson and to bring enough copies for the rest of the class on February 13th, which was the last class meeting before the midterm. On the 13th, everyone had completed their assignments except Dave, who had instead spent the weekend watching movies and generally goofing off. The rest of us thought we had been used by Dave, and none of us studied with him for the final exam.

This excerpt exemplifies how the critical incidents technique can highlight a number of important behavioral and situational details. For example, this critical incident describes the important characteristics of the situation (an upcoming midterm exam), the way in which Dave behaved (both to organize the group and his later lack of effort), and the results of Dave's behavior (group alienation and a lack of trust in Dave). There are, however, several problems with the technique. First, it can take a lot of time and effort to gather critical incidents for a particular leader. Second, because the specifics of incidents can vary dramatically across leaders, they often are not directly comparable. For example, the incidents for one leader may deal with his planning and organizational skills, whereas those for another leader may be related to her ability to motivate others to get the job done. It is nearly impossible to compare sets of incidents—and thus the leaders—without some common metric or standard, so this technique is generally not used to assess leaders directly. It is often used, however, as a preliminary stage in the development of more common leadership assessment methods such as questionnaires or interviews.

Both structured and unstructured interviews are used frequently in leadership assessment. In **structured interviews**, the interviewer asks the leader a predetermined set of questions, whereas in **unstructured interviews** the interviewer does not follow a predetermined set of questions (Saal & Knight, 1988). In an unstructured format, the interviewer has the latitude to allow the interview to proceed in whatever direction seems appropriate. The researcher–aircrew member conversation at the beginning of this chapter is an excerpt from an unstructured interview. Although unstructured interviews can provide interesting insights into the leadership process, it is difficult to compare the results of interviews with different leaders. Structured interviews, with their common set of questions, usually make it much easier to compare different leaders' attitudes and feelings.

Some problems are shared by both structured and unstructured interviews. Interviews of both sorts are time-consuming, which typically limits the number of individuals who can be interviewed in any study. Also, beyond the question of how many leaders can be interviewed is the question of which leaders should be interviewed. Some authors, such as Tichy and Devanna (1986), Bennis and Nanus (1985), and Astin and Leland (1991) conducted interviews only with individuals they perceived to be successful leaders. Because these studies included no interviews with unsuccessful leaders to serve as a comparison, it is impossible to discern whether successful leaders are really doing anything differently (or, more pertinently, are saying anything differently) than unsuccessful leaders; by interviewing only successful leaders, these studies limit the confidence we have in using interviews as a basis for gaining insight about effective leadership. The latter problem is not limited to interviews, but can affect all of the technques used to assess leadership. It is important to *keep the size and representativeness of the sample in mind* whenever reading the results of leadership research.

Observation is another common technique used to assess leaders. Like interviews, observation also can be structured or unstructured. With the former, observers are trained to categorize different behaviors into a predetermined set of dimensions. For example, the observers in the Little League study had to categorize the different behaviors manifested by the coaches into 12 categories such as technical instruction, punishment, goal setting, and positive reward (Curtis, Smith, & Smoll, 1979). Mintzberg (1973), on the other hand, used unstructured observations to record the activities of five executives over a one-month period. Mintzberg used only a stopwatch and notepad to record all the different activities his subjects performed. After collecting the data, Mintzberg then categorized the activities the managers performed into 10 different leadership roles, such as negotiator, leader, figurehead, or disturbance handler. Thus, the biggest difference between structured and unstructured observation is not so much that one involves categorizing behavior and the other does not; rather, they differ with regard to when behaviors are categorized. With structured observation the behavior dimensions are predetermined, but with unstructured observation the dimensions are developed after data are collected.

Observations can provide detailed information about what leaders actually do, but several cautions are in order when observations are used to assess leadership. First, as with interviews, observations take considerable time and effort, and so the number of leaders actually assessed tends to be small. Second, recording and categorizing behaviors via structured observations is not as simple as it sounds (Martinko & Gardner, 1985). For example, if a leader asks a subordinate to develop a plan for introducing a new product into the marketplace, should the leader's behavior be categorized as motivating subordinates, developing subordinates, or as planning? Such problems can make it relatively costly to train observers to have a high level of agreement when categorizing behaviors. Third, it is important to recognize that observations measure only overt behavior. This assessment technique cannot measure the cognitive activities, such as problem solving or strategy development, that are an important aspect of leadership and management. Despite such cautions, however, observation is a viable technique for assessing what managers actually do, and we agree with Campbell (1977) that more leadership studies should use this technique.

Paper-and-pencil measures are by far the most prevalent method for assessing leaders. There are several different kinds of paper-and-pencil measures, including personality inventories, intelligence tests, preference inventories, and questionnaires. The first three will be discussed in more detail in Chapters Seven and Eight. Questionnaires typically are used to assess the behaviors or skills manifest by leaders, the emotional effects of leaders on followers, or the influence tactics used by leaders. For example, the Managerial Behavior Survey is a 115-item inventory that assesses 23 different behavioral dimensions of leadership such as goal setting, inspiration, problem solving, and training (Charters & Pitner, 1986). Another is the Leadership Behavior Description Questionnaire (LBDQ-XII), which can be used to collect information on 12 behavioral dimensions such as emphasis on production, influence with superiors, and consideration toward subordinates (Stogdill, 1959). The Influence Behavior Questionnaire (Yukl, Lepsinger, & Lucia, 1992) explores how managers influence others through such ways as inspiration, ingratiation, or coercion.

Two aspects of questionnaires need to be considered a bit further. First, different questionnaires measure different leadership processes. For example, the LBDQ-XII (Stogdill, 1959) does not measure the same aspects of leadership as the Influence Behavior Questionnaire (Yukl, Lepsinger, & Lucia, 1992). There may be relatively little overlap in the processes measured by two different questionnaires. This does not mean questionnaires have little value, but rather that leadership is a complex phenomenon and that questionnaires in research are often tailored to examine only certain aspects of it. Second, researchers often get different pictures of a leader's behavior depending on *who* completes the questionnaire. Suppose you wanted to assess a professor's leadership in one of your courses. Even if you use the same questionnaire, you might get different impressions depending on whether you examined the department chairperson's ratings, the instructor's self-ratings, or students' ratings. With research results, it is helpful to keep in mind who completed any questionnaires and whether or not similar results would have been obtained if a different group had provided the ratings.

Assessment centers probably represent the most sophisticated method for assessing leadership (or at least leadership potential). The historical underpinnings of assessment centers lie in Europe, where they were used in the 1920s to select officers for the German military (Simoneit, 1944) and civil servants and foreign service officers for the British government (Garforth, 1945). In the United States, assessment centers were first used to select special agents and spies for the Office of Strategic Services, now known as the Central Intelligence

Agency (Murray & MacKinnon, 1946). The purpose of modern-day assessment centers is to assess and identify leadership potential. To this end, all the techniques previously discussed in this section are used. Over the course of several days, subjects attending an assessment center are interviewed and observed during a series of challenging exercises or realistic problem scenarios where critical incidents of good and bad leadership behavior are noted. They also make oral presentations, write letters and reports in the context of the scenarios, and complete a number of questionnaires, personality inventories, and intelligence tests. Because assessment centers do a pretty good job of assessing leadership potential (Gaugler, Rosenthal, Thornton, & Benson, 1987; Hunter & Hunter, 1984), it is entirely possible that someday you may participate in one, particularly if you are trying to get a job with a large corporation.

Concluding Thoughts about Leadership Assessment

Although the techniques described in this section are useful for assessing different aspects of leadership, each technique has particular advantages and disadvantages. Assessment centers are probably the most complete way to assess leadership, as they use a variety of techniques to converge on a subject's leadership potential. Similarly, research studies that employ several different techniques probably provide more complete assessments of leaders than do studies only employing a single technique. When examining results of leadership research, practitioners need to think critically about the way a researcher defines and assesses leadership, as well as about the size and representativeness of the sample, in order to be well-informed consumers of the leadership literature.

MEASURING THE EFFECTS OF LEADERSHIP

Just as various techniques are used to assess leaders' traits, skills, abilities, and behaviors, there also are various ways to measure the effects of these characteristics on subordinates, the work unit, and so on. The material in this section describes common measures of leadership effectiveness and their respective strengths and limitations.

The Nature of Criteria

Before describing different measures of leadership effectiveness, it is important to describe what a criterion is and what its properties are. A **criterion** is a "measure for judging the effectiveness of persons, organizations, treatments, or predictors of behavior" (Smith, 1976, p. 745). Criteria for evaluating the effectiveness of the academic or formal leadership training courses discussed in

FIGURE 4–1
Characteristics of Criteria

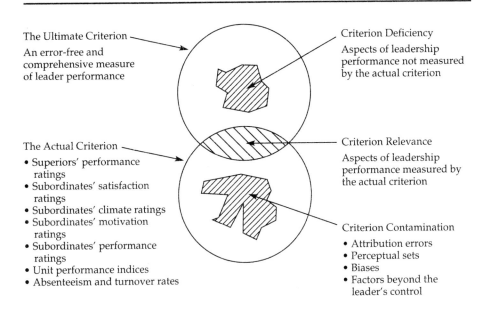

The Ultimate Criterion

An error-free and comprehensive measure of leader performance

Criterion Deficiency

Aspects of leadership performance not measured by the actual criterion

The Actual Criterion

- Superiors' performance ratings
- Subordinates' satisfaction ratings
- Subordinates' climate ratings
- Subordinates' motivation ratings
- Subordinates' performance ratings
- Unit performance indices
- Absenteeism and turnover rates

Criterion Relevance

Aspects of leadership performance measured by the actual criterion

Criterion Contamination

- Attribution errors
- Perceptual sets
- Biases
- Factors beyond the leader's control

Chapter Two might be students' midterm test performance, ratings of the course or program, or performance on the job after taking the course. Criteria for judging leadership effectiveness can range from superiors' performance ratings of the leader, to subordinates' satisfaction and morale ratings, to more objective measures of work-unit performance.

It will help you understand the advantages and disadvantages of different criteria of leadership better if we spend a little time examining certain characteristics of criteria. Figure 4–1 depicts the two basic types of criteria, the **ultimate criterion** and the **actual criterion**. The ultimate criterion is the most comprehensive and error-free standard by which to judge a leader's performance; it always should be kept in mind when selecting or designing an actual criterion for measuring leadership effectiveness. The actual criterion (or criteria) consists of the measures actually used to evaluate a leader's performance, such as superiors' performance ratings of the leader, subordinates' satisfaction or organizational climate ratings, or various performance indices that show how the leader's work unit did.

Unfortunately, none of the actual criteria are completely comprehensive, nor are they error-free measures of a leader's performance. Although the best actual criteria are those that have a high degree of **criterion relevance** (i.e., they are good measures of the ultimate criterion), all actual criteria suffer from some degree of **criterion deficiency** and **criterion contamination**. A measure of leadership effectiveness is said to suffer from criterion deficiency if it does not measure all aspects of a leader's actual performance. On the other hand, criteria such as absenteeism and turnover rates suffer from criterion contamination since working conditions, market conditions, and pay may not be under the control of the leader and yet can play a substantial role in these rates. All actual criteria suffer from some degree of both criterion contamination and criterion deficiency. Because different actual criteria measure different aspects of the ultimate criterion but also have different factors contributing to criterion contamination and deficiency, it is probably wise for leadership practitioners, as well as researchers, to use a variety of criteria to assess leadership effectiveness.

Criteria of Successful and Unsuccessful Leadership

Numerous actual criteria can be used to judge successful and unsuccessful leaders (see, for example, Highlights 4–2 and 4–3). Some of the more commonly used criteria include a superior's effectiveness or promotion ratings, subordinates' ratings of their job satisfaction and morale or of their leader's effectiveness, and various work-unit performance indices. Again, all these criteria have varying degrees of criterion relevance, contamination, and deficiency. We will discuss each of these in further detail below.

Superiors' effectiveness and performance ratings.   One way to judge a leader's success is in terms of her performance appraisals. Most performance appraisals are accomplished by a leader's superior and include ratings of performance on several relevant dimensions, as well as a recommendation (or not) for promotion. For example, Bass and Yammarino (1988) used superiors' overall performance ratings and promotion recommendations as criteria for judging the leadership effectiveness of navy surface fleet officers.

Although performance appraisals often have a high degree of criterion relevance, they also can have varying amounts of criterion deficiency and contamination. Often, companies use a standardized set of dimensions to assess leader performance, and some of the more important activities a leader may perform in a particular job may not be rated when a generic performance appraisal form is used (i.e., the form has criterion deficiency). For example, performance ratings of every supervisor in some large organization (maybe a number in the hundreds or even thousands) may be made on the following standard dimensions: judgment, communication, leadership, organizational skills, and job knowledge. Such generic dimensions do not necessarily capture the more salient and significant leadership activities of particular supervisors or leaders. In addition, friendships, perceptual sets, and attribution errors are forms of criterion contamination that can bias superiors' ratings of a leader's true performance.

HIGHLIGHT 4–2

What Makes a Good (or Bad) School Principal, I

Criteria of leadership effectiveness help you identify instances of poor leadership as well as instances of good leadership. Read the following description of a principal, written by a teacher from the same school, and then try to identify what *general* criteria this teacher was using in her very negative evaluation.

> In a staff meeting, the principal, a former football coach, was advising us on the procedure if a kid was caught smoking in the bathroom. He was asked what to do in the case of marijuana. He stated, ''There was no marijuana at Smithville Middle School.'' He went on to say he wouldn't even know what it smelled like. Several of us offered to educate him, and suggested he walk through the south stairwell after third lunch. He never did take our advice, and in the three years I taught there we never dealt with a kid under the influence of marijuana on an official basis. I did get to know the schedule of a few of my students and established a warning system with the shop teacher to keep certain students away from band saws and drills on certain days.
>
> Staff meetings were held infrequently (about three a year), and departmental meetings were nonexistent. The building had been built with an open classroom architectural concept, but no in-servicing was done to provide teachers with the methodology to develop curriculum and classes within that concept. Instead, bookcases were installed blocking out ventilation and light to try to keep the classrooms isolated. ''Do your own thing'' was the operational motto. This included the alcoholic teacher with the bottle in the locked file cabinet, the principal who was only seen when doing evaluations (of teachers) or when granting personal leave, and the homosexual who kept his private life very private until we had a staff party at his house. It was only when it was too late did we learn that one of the English teachers had an inoperable brain tumor which accounted for her rather bizarre disorientation at times.
>
> This principal did little to adjust class size to make teaching possible. He did not even acknowledge a teacher giving up lunch and planning time in order to split two large classes into smaller ones. Nor did he show any compassion when that same teacher succumbed to mononucleosis. He still didn't figure out that the problem was the numbers and the schedule when the sub had to call in sick! He avoided anything personal such as illness or injury. He was more concerned with order and discipline. He yelled at a teacher in front of the class because the children were not sitting in chairs. The name of the game in that setting was containment first, education second.

Subordinates' ratings of satisfaction, organizational climate, morale, motivation, and leadership effectiveness. Another way to judge leadership success is to examine how subordinates feel about the leader. Subordinates may be relatively satisfied or dissatisfied, may be motivated or unmotivated, or may believe their leader is relatively effective or ineffective. In addition, subordinates may perceive their work unit as being very cohesive, or they may feel the members of their work unit are untrustworthy and undependable. Like superiors' ratings of the leader, subordinates' ratings also suffer from criterion contamination due to friendships, attribution errors, or perceptual sets. Moreover, many factors beyond the leader's control may affect subordinates' overall satis-

---

HIGHLIGHT 4–3

What Makes a Good (or Bad) School Principal, II

It is becoming increasingly clear that good schools are led by good principals. It is also clear that criteria exist to help you tell a really good principal from an average or poor one. That there are, in other words, specific dimensions of school leadership by which a principal's effectiveness can be assessed. In Highlight 4–2, we asked what criteria of effective school leadership were reflected in a teacher's caustic evaluation of a former principal. See if your answers to that question are similar to the list below. Effective principals

Communicate a vision of school goals and priorities to students, teachers, and the community.

Build parent and community support for the school.

Assure a safe, secure, and orderly school setting.

Build a school climate and culture conducive to learning.

Develop a curriculum and instructional objectives related to school goals.

Are instructional experts sought out by their staffs.

Obtain needed teaching resources for their staffs.

Monitor teacher, student, and school performance.

Are visible presences in their schools.

Sources:

R. E. Blum, J. A. Butler, and N. L. Olson, "Leadership for Excellence: Research-Based Training for Principals." *Educational Leadership* 45 vol.1, 1987, pp. 25–29;

R. Brandt, "On Leadership and Student Achievement: A Conversation with Richard Andrews." *Educational Leadership* 45 Vol.1, 1987, pp. 9–16; and

M. Sashkin, and G. Huddle, "Recruit Top Principals." *School Administrator* 45 Vol.2, 1988, pp. 8–15.

---

faction ratings, such as the company's pay, fringe benefits, or vacation policies. Although having satisfied subordinates is a goal all leaders should strive to reach, it is important to note that there is often little, if any, relationship between satisfaction and performance, which means that increasing subordinates' satisfaction may have little or no bearing on subordinates' performance (Iaffaldano & Muchinsky, 1985).

Fostering a sense of motivation, cohesiveness, cooperation, and morale among unit members is another goal toward which most leaders will strive, yet several cautions may be in order when using subordinates' motivation and climate ratings to judge a leader's effectiveness. For one thing, some subordinates may be relatively unmotivated toward work no matter what the leader does. For example, it may be relatively difficult for a leader to motivate assembly-line workers, given the inherent boredom of many assembly-line jobs. For another, success in instilling a strong sense of motivation and cohesiveness in subordinates does not guarantee effective performance. It often is also necessary, for example, to ensure that subordinates are adequately trained and have the necessary equipment and resources to do the job. Without training and equipment, subordinates' performance still might be relatively low even if the subordinates are motivated. In addition, subordinates may be performing at a low level yet rate their leader as being relatively effective because he or she does not make them work very hard. Conversely, some subordinates may rate the leader as relatively ineffective if he or she does make them work hard.

Unit performance indices.   Unit performance indices are also frequently used as a way to measure a leader's effectiveness. There are a vast number of unit performance indices, such as unit sales, the number of products produced, the number of defective products returned, the number of on-time deliveries, the number of days an assembly line has run at full capacity, the dollar amount of charitable contributions collected, a team's win-loss record, or an airline company's safety record. Like the other actual criteria described earlier, each of these has varying degrees of criterion relevance, contamination, and deficiency. The biggest problem with such measures is that they often suffer from a high degree of criterion contamination. For example, many different factors can affect yearly sales figures for the manager of a car dealership. These can include having an inventory of lower-quality cars or trying to sell cars during difficult economic times. Conceivably, a sales manager could do "all the right things" yet still sell fewer cars from one year to the next, primarily due to circumstances beyond his or her control. Conversely, a sales manager may make a number of mistakes and still sell a greater number of cars due to a decrease in interest rates and the release of a hot-selling car. Leadership practitioners need to remember that unit performance indices often are affected by several factors, only one of which is the leader's behavior or actions. Moreover, many of these factors affect unit performance indices to a greater extent than does a leader's behavior, and some indices may be relatively insensitive to a leader's behavior. It is important to estimate how much a leader's behavior might affect a particular unit performance index before using that index to judge the leader's effectiveness.

Concluding Thoughts about Leadership Criteria

We propose that leadership practitioners think critically about the criteria they use to judge their own and other leaders' effectiveness. Each of the actual criteria above has some degree of criterion relevance, and often different criteria

HIGHLIGHT 4–4

The Leadership Secrets of Attila the Hun

Most people think of Attila the Hun as a cruel and ruthless leader. Wess Roberts, however, paints a very different (if speculative) picture, based on the idea that Attila succeeded in overcoming some major leadership challenges, including forging barbaric hordes into a nation and winning military victories against apparently superior forces. The following are some of Roberts's suggestions concerning a chieftain's responsibilities:

- Chieftains and leaders are responsible for establishing the atmosphere in which they lead.
- By their actions, not their words, do leaders establish the morale, integrity, and sense of justice of their subordinate commanders. They cannot say one thing and do another.
- Leaders must establish a high spirit of mutual trust among subordinates and with their peers and superiors.
- Leaders must attach value to high standards of performance and have no tolerance for the uncommitted.
- Leaders must expect continual improvement in their subordinates based on new knowledge and experiences.
- Chieftains must teach their Huns what is expected of them. Otherwise, Huns will probably do something not expected of them.
- Chieftains must inspect their Huns frequently.
- Chieftains make great personal sacrifice for the good of their Huns.
- Chieftains must not favor themselves over their Huns when supplies are short.

Notice how we could use different ways to assess a chieftain's effectiveness. We could use organizational climate surveys to measure "atmosphere" and mutual trust, we could measure actual performance against a standard, we could objectively assess the quality and content of the chieftain training courses, or we could even conduct observations of modeling behavior used by leaders.

Source: W. Roberts, *Leadership Secrets of Attila the Hun.* (New York: Warner Books, 1985), pp. 61–63. Used with permission.

will measure different aspects of a leader's true performance. However, each of these criteria also has some degree of criterion contamination and deficiency as well. We recommend that leaders seek out and use multiple criteria in order to get a more accurate picture of their overall effectiveness (see Highlight 4–4). Moreover, by having a better understanding of the different factors that can affect each of these criteria, leaders can better decide which they may want to use as yardsticks in their own improvement efforts. For example, a leader may perform relatively poorly on several unit performance indices yet also realize that performance on these indices is both relatively insensitive to his or her behavior and largely a function of, say, local economic conditions or inadequate resources. Leaders instead may choose to focus on improving their effectiveness in terms of criteria more sensitive to their actions, such as improving subordinates' perceptions of motivation, climate, or satisfaction.

METHODOLOGIES USED TO STUDY LEADERSHIP

Although this chapter has described the techniques used by leadership researchers to assess leaders and measure their effectiveness, we have not yet described the methodologies used to show that there is a relationship between a leader's assessed traits or observed behaviors and various criteria of leadership effectiveness. Three of the most common techniques used to demonstrate relationships between the results of different assessment techniques and leadership effectiveness criteria are case studies, correlational studies, and experiments. These common methodologies are described in greater detail below.

Case Studies

Case studies consist of an in-depth analysis of a particular leader's activities in a particular situation or series of situations. A common form of the case study is the biography. Biographies usually provide detailed descriptions of the various situations facing the leader, the actions taken in response to these situations, and the results of the leader's actions. Case studies can provide leadership practitioners with valuable ideas on what to do in different leadership situations, particularly if the situations facing the practitioner are similar to those described in a biography. However, there is no objective way to determine whether the actions taken actually had the results described in a case study. Often factors beyond the leader's actions have a greater role in determining outcomes. Because of these problems, caution should always be used when trying to apply lessons discerned from a case study or biography; they may not fit your particular leadership style or may not apply to your leadership situation. Nevertheless, case studies often provide interesting and valuable reading, and offer leadership practitioners alternative perspectives for analyzing leadership situations.

Correlational Studies

Correlational studies are used to determine the statistical relationship between leaders' traits, mental abilities, or behaviors and various measures of leadership effectiveness such as subordinates' satisfaction or climate ratings. An example of a correlational study would be to identify some group of leaders (e.g., fire station chiefs in a large urban area), collect their scores on a mental ability test (e.g., an intelligence test), and also collect satisfaction ratings from their respective subordinates (e.g., their firemen). A **correlation coefficient** would then be calculated using these two sets of scores. Correlation coefficients can range between +1.00 and −1.00. If the correlation coefficient were close to +1.00, then it would indicate that leaders with the highest IQs also have the most satisfied subordinates and that leaders with the lowest IQs have the least satisfied subordinates. A correlation coefficient of −1.00 would signify a perfect inverse relationship between these two sets of scores (i.e., leaders with the highest IQs have the least satisfied subordinates). If the correlation coefficient were zero, then we could conclude a leader's mental abilities and subordinates' satisfaction ratings were unrelated. In real life, sets of data like these are rarely, if ever, perfectly correlated, and correlation coefficients between +1.00 and −1.00 reflect degrees of statistical relationship between the sets; the greater the absolute value of the coefficient, the stronger the relationship.

Correlational studies are among the most common methods used to study leadership. Both the ease of data collection and the ability of correlational studies to illuminate relationships between leader characteristics and effectiveness measures are two major advantages of these studies. However, they have one major drawback. It is usually very difficult to make causal inferences based on correlational data. For example, the researchers in the Little League study described earlier discovered a modest negative relationship between a coach's punitive behaviors and the number of games the team won (Curtis, Smith, & Smoll, 1979). In other words, the more a coach used punishment, the fewer games his Little League team won. Some people may conclude that a coach's use of punishment caused the team to lose more games, but an equally plausible alternative put forth by the researchers was that the losing teams had less talent, and thus their coaches had many more opportunities to use punishment than did the coaches of the winning teams. The team's relative lack of talent, not the coach's use of punishment, may have been the primary reason for the team's poor performance. Leadership practitioners should be aware that the existence of a statistical relationship between two variables does not necessarily mean there is a cause-and-effect relationship between them. In fact, some of the most common erroneous reasoning from research results involves inferring causal relationships between variables when only a correlational relationship has been established.

Experiments

Experiments allow researchers to make **causal inferences** about leadership, and experimental designs are often based on the results of earlier correlational studies. Experiments generally consist of both **independent** and **dependent**

variables. The independent variable is what the researcher manipulates or varies to test the hypothesis; it causes change in the dependent variable. In leadership research, the dependent variable is usually an actual criterion used to measure leadership effectiveness, such as work-unit performance or subordinates' satisfaction ratings.

A description of a "laboratory" experiment on leadership may help make the distinction between independent and dependent variables a bit clearer. Howell and Frost (1988) were interested in determining whether charismatic leaders caused subordinates to perform at a higher level than supportive or directive leaders. These researchers trained two actresses to manifest charismatic, directive, or supportive leadership styles. Thus, the style of leadership exhibited by the actress-leader for different groups of subordinates was the independent variable in this experiment. The dependent variable was subordinates' performance, which in this case was measured by the number of memos subordinates successfully completed during a 45-minute in-basket exercise. As you can see, the researchers manipulated or changed the independent variable (the actresses' leadership styles varied across different groups of subordinates), but they merely recorded the subordinates' performance on the dependent variable (the number of memos successfully completed).

Although experiments allow us to make causal inferences about leadership, experiments have drawbacks of their own. One is that the effects obtained in many laboratory experiments are stronger than the effects obtained when the same experiments are conducted in organizations. This is primarily due to the fact that laboratory experiments are run under tightly controlled conditions, whereas experiments in organizations cannot be so tightly controlled. Extraneous influences often minimize or distort the effects of the independent variable on the dependent variable when the experiment is conducted in an organizational setting. Another problem concerns the subjects used in many laboratory experiments. Many times, college undergraduates are used as subjects in leadership experiments, and these individuals may have little leadership or followership experience. For such reasons it becomes legitimate to ask how much the results of any particular laboratory experiment can be generalized to actual organizations.

Maxims and Theories of Leadership

Although correlational studies and experiments have several noteworthy problems, they generally differ from case studies in one important way. Almost all correlational studies and experiments are conducted in order to test theories, whereas case studies are usually not conducted to test theories (though they can be). Instead, leaders in case studies usually articulate their personal views of leadership as principles or **maxims** other leaders should emulate (see, for example, Highlights 4–5 and 4–6). These views are prescriptive in that they tell leaders

---

HIGHLIGHT 4–5

One Person's View of 20 Leadership Fundamentals

1. Trust is vital.
2. A leader should be a good teacher and communicator.
3. A leader should rarely be a problem solver.
4. A leader must have stamina.
5. A leader must manage time well and use it effectively.
6. A leader must have technical competence.
7. Leaders must not condone incompetence.
8. Leaders must take care of their people.
9. Leaders must provide vision.
10. Leaders must subordinate their ambitions and egos to the goals of the unit or the institution that they lead.
11. Leaders must know how to run meetings.
12. A leader must be a motivator.
13. Leaders must be visible and approachable.
14. Leaders should have a sense of humor.
15. Leaders must be decisive, but patiently decisive.
16. Leaders should be introspective.
17. Leaders should be reliable.
18. Leaders should be open-minded.
19. Leaders should establish and maintain high standards of dignity.
20. Leaders should exude integrity.

Source: P. M. Smith, *Taking Charge* (Garden City, N.Y.: Avery Publishing Group, 1988), pp. 1–10.

---

what to do. They usually are not based, however, on anything other than one person's opinion. It is important to be mindful of the difference between such prescriptive approaches to leadership and empirical approaches to understanding leadership. The latter are represented by data-based studies and theories reported in this book. Although both approaches have legitimate purposes, it is vital to understand the differences between them.

Theories are central to scientific research. They provide frameworks for conceptualizing relationships between variables and guiding research toward a fuller understanding of phenomena. The essence of theories of leadership,

HIGHLIGHT 4–6

One Person's View of the Biggest Mistakes Managers Make

1. Failing to keep abreast of developments in your own field.
2. Confining yourself to your own specialty.
3. Refusing to seek higher responsibility or take responsibility for your own actions.
4. Failing to make sound and timely decisions.
5. Neglecting to conduct personal inspections properly.
6. Failing to make sure the job is understood, supervised, and accomplished.
7. Wasting time on details or work that belongs to others.
8. Refusing to assess your own performance realistically.
9. Accepting the minimum instead of going for the maximum.
10. Using your management position for personal gain.
11. Failing to tell the truth or to always keep your word.
12. Not setting the personal example for your people to follow.
13. Trying to be liked rather than respected.
14. Failing to give cooperation to your employees.
15. Failing to ask your subordinates for their advice and help.
16. Failing to develop a sense of responsibility in your subordinates.
17. Emphasizing rules rather than skill.
18. Failing to keep your criticism constructive.
19. Not paying attention to employee gripes and complaints.
20. Failing to keep your people informed.
21. Failing to treat your subordinates as individuals.
22. Refusing to train an assistant to take your place.

Source: J. K. Van Fleet, *The 22 Biggest Mistakes Managers Make* (West Nyack, N.Y.: Parker, 1973), pp. 9–17.

then, is to provide a reasonably coherent conceptual structure of how critical variables interact, involving ideas that can be put to the test and revised as new data accumulate. Simply put, theories of leadership involve testable ideas, whereas prescriptive approaches to leadership involve no such intended testability. Although both prescriptions of leadership and leadership theories are useful for understanding leadership situations, in general only leadership theories add to the body of knowledge concerning the science of leadership and help in the development of universal laws of leadership.

SUMMARY

The leadership practitioner should understand a number of different points after reading this chapter. First, leadership practitioners should be able to make the distinction between the techniques used to assess leadership and the criteria used to measure leadership effectiveness. Second, leadership practitioners should be familiar with the limitations of the different leadership assessment techniques and recognize that a more comprehensive picture of a leader's traits, behaviors, or skills can be made if multiple assessment techniques are used. Third, leadership practitioners should be aware that all of the actual criteria they could use to judge their effectiveness suffer from varying degrees of criterion contamination and deficiency and that they should seek out and use multiple criteria to assess their effectiveness. Fourth, by having a more sophisticated understanding of the factors that can affect the actual criteria, leadership practitioners should be better able to discern which criteria are the most sensitive to their actions and which criteria are affected more by external factors. Finally, leadership practitioners should understand that experiments and correlational studies are generally conducted to test theories and improve our body of knowledge regarding leadership, whereas the maxims found in many case studies are generally only prescriptive in nature.

KEY TERMS

critical incidents technique   criterion contamination
structured interviews   case studies
unstructured interviews   correlational studies
observation   correlation coefficient
paper-and-pencil measures   experiments
assessment centers   causal inference
ultimate criterion   independent variable
actual criteria   dependent variable
criterion relevance   maxims
criterion deficiency

DISCUSSION QUESTIONS

1. How do you react to the phrase *measuring leadership*? What positive and negative connotations does it have for you?
2. In what ways might leadership practitioners and leadership researchers interact for mutual benefit with regard to assessing leadership and its effects?

3. What are some of the actual criteria used to judge a coach's performance? A teacher's? A student's? What sources of contamination might detract from their criterion relevance?

4. Compare and contrast the empirical approach to studying effective leadership with trying to distill the essence of leadership from the maxims of effective leaders.

5. How do the "22 biggest mistakes" in Highlight 4–6 compare to the qualities of managers described in Highlight 2–3.

SUGGESTED READINGS

Arter, J. A. *Assessing Leadership and Managerial Behavior.* Washington, D.C.: Office of Educational Research and Improvement, U.S. Department of Education, 1990.

Borman, W. C. "Job Behavior, Performance, and Effectiveness." In *Handbook of Industrial & Organizational Psychology* 2. ed. M. D. Dunnet and L. M. Hough. Palo Alto, Calif.: Consulting Psychologists Press, 1991.

Clark, K. E., and M. B. Clark. *Measuring Leadership.* West Orange, N.J.: Leadership Library of America, 1990.

Clark, K. E.; M. B. Clark; and D. P. Campbell. *Impact of Leadership.* Greensboro, North Carolina: Center for Creative Leadership, 1992.

Chapter Five

Leadership Involves an Interaction between the Leader, the Followers, and the Situation

INTRODUCTION

In Chapter One, we defined leadership as the process of influencing an organized group toward accomplishing its goals. In this chapter, we will expand on this definition by introducing and describing a three-factor framework of the leadership process. We find this framework to be a useful heuristic for both analyzing various leadership situations and for organizing various leadership theories and supporting research. Therefore, the remainder of this chapter is devoted to providing an overview of the framework, and many of the remaining chapters of this book are devoted to describing each component of the framework in more detail.

LOOKING AT LEADERSHIP THROUGH SEVERAL LENSES

In attempting to understand leadership, scholars understandably have spent much of their energy studying successful and unsuccessful leaders in government, business, athletics, and the military. Sometimes scholars have done this systematically by studying good leaders as a group (see Bennis & Nanus, 1985; Astin & Leland, 1991), and sometimes they have done this more subjectively, drawing lessons about leadership from the behavior or character of an individual leader such as Martin Luther King, Jr., Lee Iacocca, or Golda Meir. The latter approach is similar to drawing conclusions about leadership from observing individuals in one's own life, whether it be a high school coach, a mother or father, or one's boss. It may seem that studying the characteristics of effective leaders is the best way to learn about leadership, but such an approach tells only part of the story. Consider the following two examples.

• A senior minister was told by one of the church's wealthiest and consistently most generous members that he should not preach any more pro-choice sermons on abortion. The man's contributions were the main reason a special mission project for the city's disadvantaged youth had been funded, and we might wonder whether the minister's church leadership would be influenced by this outside pressure. Would he be a bad leader if he succumbed to this pressure and still advocated what his conscience dictated? What if it meant the loss of a valuable youth program?

• An earthy and flamboyant general with an extraordinary record as an inspiring and courageous combat leader is assigned to a major diplomatic position where he will be judged by entirely different standards than he was before. Perhaps he will meet the challenges of the new post, perhaps not. If he does not, do we consider him less of a leader? In fact, this general performed rather poorly in his new position partly because he did not change his behavior; earthiness and flamboyance are not considered appropriate behavior for those working in diplomatic settings. This illustrates how a person may be an effective leader in one situation but a poor one somewhere else if the leader does not adapt to the changed environment.

Although we can learn about leadership by looking at leaders, the preceding two examples suggest the picture provided by studying only leaders provides a limited view of the leadership process. These two examples underscore how leadership depends on other factors, including the situation, not just the leader's qualities or characteristics. Leadership is more than just the kind of person the leader is or the things the leader does. Leadership is the process of influencing others toward the achievement of group goals, not just a person or position (also see Highlight 5–1).

HIGHLIGHT 5–1

Leadership Quotes, Chapter Five

All men have some weak points and the more vigorous and brilliant a person may be, the more strongly these weak points stand out. It is highly desirable, even essential, therefore, for the more influential members of a general's staff not be too much like the general.

Major General Hugo Baron von Freytag-Loringhoven

A leader is best
When people barely know that he exists
Not so good when people obey and acclaim him,
Worst of all when they despise him.
''Fail to honor people,
They fail to honor you;''
But of a good leader, who talks little,
When his work is done, his aim fulfilled,
They will all say, ''We did this ourselves.''

Lao Tzu

You've got to give loyalty down, if you want loyalty up.

Donald T. Regan

If you act like an ass, don't get insulted if people ride you.

Yiddish Proverb

Little things affect little minds.

Benjamin Disraeli

The crowd will follow a leader who marches twenty steps in advance; but if he is a thousand steps in front of them, they do not see and do not follow him.

Georg Brandes

The following is another example. Ruth Randall was a former school superintendent who rose to become the commissioner of education for the State of Minnesota. Ruth Randall was perceived to be extremely charismatic by the students, parents, and staff in her school district, and her leadership actions helped pull the school system through a major financial crisis. However, when Ruth Randall took over at the Department of Education, she was perceived to be uncharismatic and relatively ineffective by her subordinates (Roberts & Bradley, 1988). Roberts and Bradley claimed these dramatic differences in perceptions and impact were due to differences in both the situation and the followers; as a person Ruth Randall had changed little between being school superintendent and being the commissioner of education. This example points out the importance of looking beyond the individual qualities of a leader if we are to better understand the leadership process. The leader is a critical element, perhaps the most important element of leadership, but there is more to leadership than the leader. The followers and the situation also play key roles in the leadership process.

The example provided in the preceding paragraph illustrates the advantages of using different lenses through which to view the leadership process. If we use only leaders as the lens for understanding leadership, then we get a very limited view of the leadership process. We can expand our view of the leadership process by adding two other complementary lenses: the followers and the situation. However, using only the followers or the situation as a lens also would give us an equally limited view of the leadership process. For example, focusing solely on the values, traits, and experiences of the followers in the school district would not really tell us how or why Ruth Randall's actions helped to pull the district out of serious financial difficulties. Similarly, examining only the stresses, constraints, and resources of the position would say little about how or why Ruth Randall had relatively less impact as the commissioner of education. In other words, the clearest picture of the leadership process occurs only when we use all three lenses to understand it.

The Interactional Framework for Analyzing Leadership

Perhaps the first researcher formally to recognize the importance of the leader, follower, and situation in the leadership process was Fred Fiedler (1967). Fiedler used these three components to develop his contingency model of leadership, a theory of leadership that will be discussed in more detail in Chapter Fifteen. Although we recognize Fiedler's contributions, we owe perhaps even more to Hollander's (1978) transactional approach to leadership. We call our approach the **interactional framework**.

There are several aspects of this derivative of Hollander's (1978) approach that are worthy of additional comment. First, as seen in Figure 5–1, the framework depicts leadership as a function of three elements—the leader, the followers, and the situation. Second, a particular leadership scenario can be examined using each level of analysis separately. Although this is a useful way to understand the leadership process, we can have an even better understanding of the process if we also examine the interactions among the three elements, or lenses, represented by the overlapping areas in the figure. For example, we can better understand the leadership process if we not only look at the leaders and the followers but also examine how leaders and followers affect each other in the leadership process. Similarly, we can examine the leader and the situation separately, but

FIGURE 5–1

An Interactional Framework for Analyzing Leadership

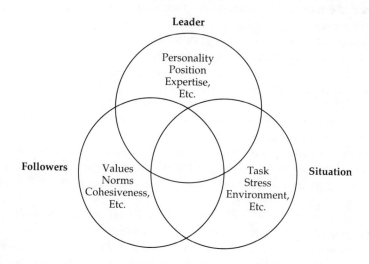

we can gain even further understanding of the leadership process by looking at how the situation can constrain or facilitate a leader's actions and how the leader can change different aspects of the situation in order to be more effective. Thus, a final important aspect of the model is that leadership is the result of a complex set of interactions between the leader, the followers, and the situation. These complex interactions may be why broad generalizations about leadership are problematic; there are many factors that influence the leadership process.

Because the interactional framework can help you better analyze the leadership process and because it plays such an important role throughout the rest of this book, we will illustrate its use and review each of the three elements of the model with an example.

A Case Study of Leadership in Social Services

Although the nation's economy was doing fairly well in the 1980s, these were not good economic times for the people in northern Minnesota. The major industries in the area, timber and steel, were in decline. Furthermore, persistent labor-management problems in several of the smaller industries resulted in a series of strikes, and these strikes eventually caused many of these industries to cease operations in Minnesota and relocate in other states. The lack of work and general malaise of the economy caused a number of social problems. Large numbers of people were seeking unemployment benefits, were having drinking problems, or were getting divorced. The county social services agency was responsible for dealing with many of the problems generated by the region's economic woes.

The social services agency was responsible for providing unemployed workers with general assistance, ensuring that child-support benefits were being provided, and providing retraining assistance to help unemployed workers find work in other vocations. To meet these ends, the agency was divided into three divisions. Each division consisted of six to eight workers and a supervisor, and each supervisor reported to the director of social services. The director of social services was responsible for ensuring that all of the services provided by the agency were properly administered and that the agency ran smoothly. The director of social services was appointed by and accountable to the county's board of commissioners.

In the mid-1980s, Jane rose from being a division supervisor to being appointed by the county board to become the director of social services. The mid-1980s were particularly stressful times for the agency, as the county's high levels of unemployment resulted in substantially increased caseloads for the workers in all three divisions. In addition, a state-mandated initiative was requiring all of the divisions in the agency to use computers to track caseloads, and few of the workers had any computer skills. Jane did not handle her new responsibilities very well, as her first (and perhaps only) priority as the director was to ensure her job security. She accomplished this by denying her workers access to the county commissioners during her weekly meetings with the board and by having all of the commissioners over to her house for dinner and drinks after each meeting. Jane's primary concern was to keep the board happy, and the best way to keep the board happy was to insulate them from the problems within the agency. However, the agency's caseloads had reached record levels, no additional personnel were hired to handle the increased work, and a computer implementation initiative was causing even more stress among the caseworkers. The increased caseloads resulted in sloppy record keeping, and one of the workers was eventually fired for embezzling over $10,000 of government funds. Jane left the agency when the details of the embezzlement and the other problems within the agency became public.

Given the lack of leadership and the high levels of stress and confusion during Jane's tenure, many of the workers within the agency felt that any new director would be an improvement. Although Bob was not from Minnesota, many of the caseworkers had high expectations for him when he was hired as the new director of social services. Bob assessed the situation and eventually set down a number of fairly strict guidelines for the agency. For example, caseworkers were no longer able to make or have personal phone calls during work hours, use county cars for personal business, or be absent from work unless on official business or on vacation. To help ensure that his guidelines were being followed, Bob cultivated a close relationship with one or two workers from each division. He used these contacts to find out what was going on in each division and to get information about the personal lives of each person in the agency.

After several months, it became apparent that Bob did not adhere to the guidelines he had set for the rest of the agency. Bob often was absent from work and used a county car to commute to and from work (which he did not allow others to do). In addition, it became apparent that someone was telling Bob about matters said in confidence during union meetings, division meetings, or client-caseworker meetings, and he would often take various personnel actions based on this information. Needless to say, the level of trust within the agency was at an all-time low. Eventually, Bob was dismissed because of the large number of caseworker complaints and his misuse of county resources.

Now let us go on to look in turn at each of the lenses of leadership in our framework, referring back at times to leadership in the social services agency.

THE LEADER

A number of different personality traits (Stogdill, 1948, 1974; Cleveland, 1985); cognitive abilities (Lord, DeVader, & Allinger, 1986); skills (Kanter, 1983); and values (Baltzell, 1980) have been found to differentiate leaders from followers or effective from ineffective leaders, and we can gain considerable insight into the leadership situation at the social services agency by examining Jane's and Bob's characteristics and skills. Neither Bob nor Jane really valued the agency's role in helping the unemployed and disadvantaged in the county. Instead, Jane's primary concern was to stay in her job as along as possible. Jane was a fairly intelligent individual who knew that she would lose her job if the agency's problems became known to the county commissioners. As an extrovert, Jane used her preferences for parties and her strong interpersonal skills to build solid relationships with each of the county commissioners so that she could easily discount those problems that did become public. Bob's primary concern was to do as little as possible but still maintain strict control of the agency. Bob was not as intelligent and was more introverted than Jane, but he could turn on the charm when he wanted to. Bob used his charm to cultivate several ''informants'' in each division so that he could keep tabs on the activities of his employees, thus enhancing his control of the agency.

Temperament, by which we mean whether the leader is generally calm or is prone to emotional outbursts, is another example of how personality can affect leadership. Leaders who have calm dispositions and do not attack or belittle others for bringing bad news are more likely to get complete and timely information from subordinates than are bosses who have explosive tempers and a reputation for killing the messenger. For example, Jane did not like to hear about the agency's problems, because she believed they could jeopardize her relationship with the county commissioners. If problems were brought to

Jane's attention, she would then either discount the information, publicly belittle the whistleblower, or give the whistleblower extra work. Eventually, none of the caseworkers would tell Jane about problems within the agency. Although both Bob and Jane were eventually dismissed, their differences in values, personality traits, temperament, and cognitive abilities resulted in two very different leadership situations within the agency.

Another important aspect of the leader is how he or she achieved leader status. Leaders who are appointed by superiors may have less credibility with subordinates and less loyalty from them than leaders who are elected by or emerge by consensus from the ranks of followers. Often, emergent or elected officials are better able to influence a group toward goal achievement because of the power conferred to them by their followers. However, both elected and emergent leaders need to be sensitive to their constituencies if they wish to remain in power. For example, several of the county commissioners failed to be reelected when the details of their relationships with the director and the problems at the agency became public.

Another variable is the leader's experience or history in a particular organization. For example, leaders promoted from within an organization, by virtue of being familiar with its culture and policies, may be ready to "hit the job running." For example, Jane was promoted from within and immediately set out to solidify her relationship with the county commissioners. In addition, leaders selected from within an organization are typically better known by others in the organization than are leaders selected from the outside. That is likely to affect, for better or worse, the latitude others in the organization are willing to give the leader; if the leader is widely respected for a history of accomplishment, then she may be given more latitude than a newcomer whose track record is less well known. On the other hand, many people tend to give new leaders a fair chance to succeed, and newcomers to an organization often take time to learn the organization's informal rules, norms, and "ropes" before they make any radical or potentially controversial decisions. For example, Bob spent time assessing the situation before he implemented his new guidelines for the agency.

A leader's legitimacy also may be affected by the extent to which followers participated in the leader's selection. When followers have had a say in the selection or election of a leader they tend to have a heightened sense of psychological identification with her, but they also may have higher expectations and make more demands on her (Hollander & Offermann, 1990). We also might wonder what kind of support a leader has from his own boss. If followers sense their boss has a lot of influence with the higher-ups (as in Jane's case), then subordinates may be reluctant to take their complaints to higher levels. On the other hand, if the boss has little influence with higher-ups, subordinates may be more likely to make complaints to these levels (as in Bob's case).

The foregoing examples highlight the sorts of insights one can gain about leadership by focusing on the individual leader as a level of analysis. Still an-

---

HIGHLIGHT 5–2

Women and Leadership, II: Changing Work Roles

John Naisbitt has called the 1990s the decade of women in leadership, and there is no question that women will play an increasingly significant part in both leadership and followership roles in the future. In the first place, in terms of sheer numbers women already are a large and indispensable element of contemporary work life. It is simply erroneous to think of women as a minority in the work force. In fact, as many women in their 20s and 30s work as men; and while just 75 percent of men work, nearly 80 percent of women with no children under 18 do.

Furthermore, women not only comprise a major portion of the work force but also are assuming an increasingly significant place as leaders in it, and this will affect the nature of leadership and followership for everyone. Women are reaching a critical mass in all of the white-collar professions. For example, the percentage of women physicians has doubled in the past two decades. They account for one third of the M.B.A. degrees and 40 percent of the law degrees awarded. They are advancing fastest in cutting-edge industries like computers and software, where in some cases women comprise nearly one third of a company's management force. And women are starting their own small businesses at a faster rate than men. Some have argued that thus far this century, corporations have been based on a bureaucratic and authoritarian organizational model compatible with male psychology and that different structures and leadership styles necessarily will evolve as women assume an increasingly large role in corporate leadership. Whether and how men and women differ in their leadership and followership styles are open issues, but it is certain that women's roles in both arenas will only grow.

Sources: J. Naisbitt, and P. Aburdene, *Re-inventing the Corporation* (New York: Warner Books, 1985); and *Megatrends 2000* (New York: William Morrow, 1990).

---

other aspect of this level of analysis is reflected in Highlight 5–2. Even if we were to examine the individual leader completely, however, our understanding of the leadership process would be incomplete. Understanding leadership involves knowing about followers as well as about leaders.

THE FOLLOWERS

Followers are part of the leadership equation, too, though their role has not always been appreciated. For example, one can look at history and be struck by the contributions of extraordinary individual leaders. Even the major reviews of the leadership literature show that researchers have paid relatively little attention to the roles followers play in the leadership process (see Bass, 1981, 1990; Stogdill, 1974). However, we know that the followers' expectations (Sutton & Woodman, 1989); personality traits (Burke, 1965); maturity levels (Moore, 1976); levels of competence (Scandura, Graen, & Novak, 1986); and levels and types of motivation (Sales, Levanoni, & Saleh, 1984) can affect the leadership process (also see Highlight 5–3).

We can use the caseworkers at the social services agency to highlight how followers constitute a separate yet necessary focus for understanding leadership. As one illustration, consider how subordinates' values and interests could affect the leadership process. Many of the caseworkers were dedicated to providing the best services possible to the disadvantaged, whereas others were primarily concerned with keeping Bob and Jane happy; still another was so concerned with keeping himself happy that he embezzled large sums of money from the government. The workers' skill levels also varied greatly; some workers were expert with computers, while others did not even know how to turn one on. In addition, some were more experienced in the agency than others, some were extroverted and others were introverted, and some had a strong work ethic while others did not. There were many other ways the workers differed, and these differences all have implications for leadership.

Another important variable is the nature of followers' work motivation. Workers who share a leader's goals and values, and who feel intrinsically rewarded for performing a job well, might be more likely to work extra hours on a time-critical project than those whose motivation is solely monetary (assuming overtime money is unavailable). For example, several workers in the child support division often stayed late to learn the computer tracking system, whereas others worked only because it paid the bills and were not about to put in unpaid overtime. Followers' feelings about each other also affect the leadership process. Followers who form a cohesive and closely knit unit create different leadership opportunities and challenges than those among whom conflict, dissension, and strife exist. The workers in the three divisions were pretty cohesive when Jane was the director, but in this case the cohesiveness was the result of Jane's incompetence and her public belittling of fellow co-workers. The opposite was true in Bob's case. The level of dissension among the workers was quite high, due to his cultivation of informants in each of the divisions. In both Jane's and Bob's cases, their ability to influence workers toward accomplishing group goals was fairly limited due to the relationships that had developed among the workers.

Even the number of followers reporting to a single leader can have significant implications. For example, a store manager who has three clerks working for him can spend more time with each of them (or on other things) than can a store manager responsible for eight clerks and a separate delivery service;

HIGHLIGHT 5–3

Women and Leadership, III: Adjusting to New Roles

Women are rapidly moving into leadership roles that previously had been occupied only by men. Such change, exciting and positive if also overdue, is accompanied by inevitable adjustments. The following is one contemporary woman's account of how it feels to be a trailblazer, a woman leader in a traditionally male-dominated field: the ministry.

"What do you do, Nancy?" the innocent, yet bold, six-year-old asked.

"I am a minister, Jason."

"You're not a ministerette?"

"No, just a minister, Jason. It doesn't matter if you are a girl or a boy . . . it is the same word."

"Oh," Jason replied. "I've never heard of that."

Jason is not alone. And his company is not only those in his age range. To most adults, youths, and children alike, a minister is a man. For anyone who is a pastor, a priest, a rabbi, or who is titled as "clergy," it is virtually assumed that person is male.

I am a woman and I am a minister. I could put those in reverse order, but I was indeed a woman first, and almost everyone I know uses the gender-then-title order: "Our lady minister," "Woman pastor," "Female clergy." Despite our seminaries and theological schools having an average female population of one third, and despite the fact some Protestant denominations began ordaining women over 30 years ago, it seems strange that I am still a novelty to the average American. Yet, I am reminded of that constantly.

"Here is your change, Father, . . . Sister, . . . Mother, . . ." the awkward-feeling store clerk responds to the woman in a clerical collar.

Part of the problem lies in the limitations of language, but even more, the problem lies in the limitations we place on ourselves and on those around us. Like it or not, clergy is not a traditional role for women. For most folks, there is really no good reason to restrict the ministry to males, only those seven words we hear all too often: "We have always done it that way." In being a minister, and in being female, I am breaking tradition. Not only am I breaking into a traditionally "man's" world; I am breaking out of a traditionally "female" world. And like so many women in nontraditional roles, I at times try to fill too many shoes. One of my greatest frustrations is the assumption that because I am female, I must be more sensitive, more caring, more concerned about cooking and our home, etc., than my husband. Those assumptions are almost as bad as those which assume I cannot be a good preacher because I am an alto and not a bass. Why can not people accept me as a minister, as a human being—with all the talents, personality quirks, faults, gifts, and eccentricities thereof?

From one of my first days wearing a clerical collar, and leaving our inner-city apartment to drive to my suburban church, I experienced first the stare, then the double-take. I have to deal with the fact that some people will never accept me as they would accept a male minister. I have to deal with the fact that I am asked for identification at local hospitals (when I am not wearing the clerical collar) because I "do not look like a minister."

I am breaking the norm, personifying progress in women's rights; I am doing not only what I want, but what I feel called to do. And I am not letting my gender, not to mention societal norms, get in the way.

"I'll be blunt, coach. I'm having a problem with this 'take a lap' thing of yours . . . "

chairing a task force with 5 members is a different leadership activity than chairing a task force with 18 members. Still other relevant variables include followers' trust in the leader and their confidence (or not) that he or she is interested in their well-being.

The preceding examples illustrate just a few ways in which followers comprise an important complementary level of analysis for understanding leadership. Such examples should point out how leadership must be understood in the context of a particular group of followers as well as in terms of an individual leader. Now, more than ever before, understanding followers is central to understanding leadership. That is because the leader-follower relationship is in a period of dynamic change (Lippitt, 1982). One reason for this changing relationship is an increasing pressure on all kinds of organizations to function with reduced resources. Another reason is a trend toward greater power sharing and decentralized authority in organizations, which in turn creates greater interdependence among organizational subunits and increased need for collaboration among them. Furthermore, the nature of problems faced by many organizations is becoming so complex that more and more people are required to solve them.

These trends suggest several different ways in which followers can take on new leadership roles and responsibilities in the future. For one thing, followers can become much more proactive in their stance toward organizational problems. When facing the discrepancy between the way things are in an organization and the way they could or should be, followers can play an active and constructive role collaborating with leaders in solving problems. In general, making organizations better is a task that needs to be "owned" by followers as well as by leaders. An extreme example of follower "ownership" of an organizational problem occurred in the social services agency. In this case, the workers at the social services agency recognized that the directors were the problem and took steps to ensure that their complaints were heard by the county commissioners.

In addition to helping to solve organizational problems, followers can better contribute to the leadership process by becoming better skilled at "influencing upward." Because followers are often at the level where many organizational problems occur, they can provide leaders with relevant information so that good solutions are implemented. Although it is true that some leaders need to become better listeners, it is also true that many followers need training in expressing ideas to superiors more clearly and positively. Still another way followers can assume a greater share of the leadership challenge in the future is by staying flexible and open to opportunities. The future portends more change, not less, and followers who face change with positive anticipation and an openness to self-development will be particularly valued and rewarded.

Thus, to an ever increasing degree, leadership must be understood in terms of both leader variables and follower variables, as well as the interactions

BIZARRO   by DAN PIRARO

Chronicle Features

among them. But even that is not enough. In addition to understanding the leader and the followers, we must also understand the particular situations in which leaders and followers find themselves.

THE SITUATION

The situation is the third critical part of the leadership equation. Even if we knew all we could know about a given leader and a given set of followers, leadership makes sense only in the context of how the leader and followers interact in a given situation (see, for example, Highlight 5–4). Consider the situation

HIGHLIGHT 5–4

Berkeley in the 1960s

The 1960s were a period of dissent and conflict, and perhaps even today no place epitomizes the decade more than Berkeley, California. But Berkeley did not always have a radical reputation.

The Berkeley campus of the huge University of California system had not always been a center of student protest and large-scale demonstrations. For a long time, it had been relatively sedate and conservative, even if also quite large; more than 20,000 students attended Berkeley in 1960. Campus leaders were clean-cut students who belonged to fraternities and sororities. Berkeley changed, however, in the fall of 1964 when a relatively small number of students launched what became known as the Free Speech Movement. Subsequent protests at other campuses across the country, and later globally, are traceable to the Free Speech Movement at Berkeley. One of its leaders was Mario Savio.

The sources of conflict and radicalism at Berkeley were many, including civil rights and the Vietnam War. But protest in Berkeley first erupted over the issue of whether students could solicit donations and distribute political materials near campus. That students could not solicit donations or distribute materials on campus had been settled earlier; they could not. In response to having been ordered off campus, however, some student groups set up card tables just off campus, between the university's impressive Sproul Plaza and Berkeley's Telegraph Avenue, with its exciting and bohemian milieu of bookstores and coffeehouses.

Perhaps because their appearance so near the campus offended university officials—the student workers were rarely dressed or groomed in the clean-cut image favored by conservative administrators—even this activity eventually was prohibited. Outraged, a few students defiantly set up tables back in Sproul Plaza, right in the heart of the campus. Disturbed at this open rebuke to its authority, the university directed police to arrest one of the disobedient students. It was October 1, 1964, the birth of the Free Speech Movement.

Presumably, university officials believed this show of force on their part would dishearten the band of student protesters and break them up. As the arrested student got into the awaiting police car, however, someone shouted, "Sit down!" and hundreds of other students immediately did just that. They sat down on the plaza right where they were, effectively blocking the car's movement. The police and administration had never before confronted such massive defiance, and for 32 hours the car stayed put (with the "prisoner," Jack Weinberg, inside) while demonstrators used its roof as a podium from which to speak to the crowd. One who climbed up to speak several times, and who clearly had a gift for energizing the crowd, was Mario Savio. In many ways, the Free Speech Movement, which

HIGHLIGHT 5–4 *(concluded)*

pitted a rigid university bureaucracy against increasing numbers of alienated students, became a confrontation between just two people: Mario Savio and the university's brilliant but aloof president, Clark Kerr. It was not, however, a fair fight.

As W. J. Rorabaugh has observed, Kerr didn't stand a chance. The student activists were prepared for war, and Kerr wasn't. He was out of touch with the sentiments of increasing numbers of students, sentiments that in part were a direct result of the university's continuing neglect of undergraduate education at the expense of graduate study and government-sponsored research.

The students, on the other hand, had a clear objective—the freedom to be politically active on campus (i.e., free speech). Furthermore, many were politically experienced, seasoned by their participation in civil rights marches in the South. They understood the politics of protest, crowd psychology, the importance of the media, and how to maintain spirit and discipline in their own ranks. Thus, many ingredients for a successful social movement were present. All that was needed was a spark to ignite them and a leader to channel them.

Mario Savio was not a typical undergraduate. His commitment to social reform already was deep, and his experiences were broad. Raised in a devout Catholic family, he had worked in rural Mexico for a church relief organization and had taught in a school for black children in Mississippi. He was proud, cocky, and defiant. It was his ability to articulate his rage, however, that set Savio apart. He could give words and reason to the frustration and anger others were only feeling. Interestingly, Savio was a very different person in private than in public. In private, he seemed cold, hesitant, and self-doubting, but in front of a crowd he could be inspiring.

He may have been at his best at a protest rally in December 1964. Here is what it was like to be in Berkeley in the 60s, listening to a new kind of student leader, one giving voice to the sense of powerlessness and frustration with modern life, which would be a common theme in student revolts throughout the rest of the decade:

> There is a time when the operation of the machine becomes so odious, makes you so sick at heart, that you can't take part; you can't even passively take part, and you've got to put your bodies upon the gears and upon the wheels, upon the levers, upon all the apparatus and you've got to make it stop. And you've got to indicate to the people who run it, to the people that own it, that unless you're free, the machines will be prevented from working at all (Rorabaugh, p. 31).

Earlier that year, Savio had written, "I'm tired of reading history. Now I want to make it." He did. Try to analyze the emergence of Mario Savio in terms of the interactional framework.

Source: W. J. Rorabaugh, *Berkeley at War* (New York: Oxford University Press, 1989).

surrounding the social services agency. Record numbers of people were seeking unemployment benefits, and the stress of unemployment caused many families to break up. Because of the higher divorce rates and the record levels of unemployment, pressure was put on the child-support division to find additional benefits for those single mothers whose ex-husbands could no longer afford to make their child-support payments. In addition, there seemed to be no immediate end in sight for the economic downturn. The steel and timber industries had huge stockpiles of materials to deplete before they would hire back the workers they had laid off, and many of the smaller industries had left the area due to labor disputes. Furthermore, the state had mandated that the agency implement a computer-based system for tracking cases. How would you, as the director of the social services agency, act in this situation? Would the actions you take be different if the local economy were booming or if the computer tracking system were already up and running before you took over? In all likelihood, the actions you would take would differ from one situation to the next, yet neither you as the leader nor your followers would have changed.

The situation may be the most ambiguous aspect of the leadership framework since it involves more than just the kinds of environmental variables illustrated above. You can also look at the situation in the narrower context within which the leader and followers work. For example, because of the embezzlement situation, the agency was audited more frequently by the state. State audits were never fun, and they often added stress to a crisis situation. When being audited, both Bob and Jane came across as directors who were extremely concerned for the welfare of their subordinates and for the county's unemployed. However, when an audit was not being conducted, both Bob and Jane showed little regard for either constituency. Thus, a change in the leaders' and followers' work context resulted in a substantial change in the way the leaders acted. Overall, the nature of the task, the economic environment, the work setting, the presence of a crisis, the lack of resources, and the presence of formal rules and regulations are but a few of the situational variables that can affect the leadership process.

THERE IS NO SIMPLE RECIPE FOR EFFECTIVE LEADERSHIP

As noted above, it is important to understand how the three domains of leadership interact—how the leader, the followers, and the situation are all part of the leadership process. Understanding their interaction is necessary before you can draw valid conclusions from the leadership you observe around you. When you see a leader's behavior (even when it may appear obviously effective or ineffective to you), you should not automatically conclude something good or bad about the leader, or what is the right way or wrong way leaders should act. You need to think about the effectiveness of *that* behavior in *that* context with *those* followers (see, for example, Highlight 5–5).

As obvious as the above sounds, we often ignore it. Too frequently, we just look at the leader's behavior and conclude that he or she is a good leader or bad leader apart from the context. For example, suppose you observe a leader soliciting advice from subordinates. Obviously, it seems unreasonable to conclude that good leaders always ask for advice or that leaders who do not frequently ask for advice are not such good leaders. The appropriateness of seeking input from subordinates depends on many factors, such as the nature of the problem or the subordinates' familiarity with the problem. It may be that the subordinates have a lot more experience with this particular problem, and soliciting their input is the correct action to take in this situation.

Consider another example. Suppose you hear that a leader disapproved a subordinate's request to take time off to attend to family matters. Was this bad leadership because the leader did not appear to be "taking care of her people"? Was it good leadership because she did not let personal matters interfere with the mission? Again, you cannot make an intelligent decision about the leader's actions by just looking at the behavior itself. You must always assess leadership in the context of the leader, the followers, and the situation.

The following statements about leaders, followers, and the situation make the above points a bit more systematically.

- *A leader may need to respond to various followers differently in the same situation.* For example, as the director of social services, you would probably need to use different strategies and behaviors to motivate those subordinates with and without prior computer skills in order to get everyone up to speed on the new computer-based tracking system.

- *A leader may need to respond to the same follower differently in different situations.* Consider the individual who was caught embezzling funds from the agency. As the director you may have sought the individual's input on certain issues prior to the discovery, but after the discovery you would have taken punitive legal actions against the individual.

- *Followers may respond to various leaders quite differently.* For example, Bob managed to cultivate several trusted subordinates in the social services agency. However, these same subordinates shared a common dislike for Jane.

- *Followers may respond to each other differently with different leaders.* Consider the degree of cohesiveness and trust among the workers during Bob and Jane's tenure. The workers rallied together in the face of a common enemy when Jane was the director. However, Bob was successful in creating a climate of distrust and internal dissension during his tenure. Hopefully, you will be able to create a climate of cooperativeness and trust because of the positive actions you take as a leader, not because the followers are rallying against you.

- *Two leaders may have different perceptions of the same followers or situations.* For example, Bob saw several subordinates as potential informants, and Jane saw

HIGHLIGHT 5–5

Vince Lombardi Was My Father

Vince Lombardi was one of the greatest football coaches in history. His son, also named Vince Lombardi, is a speaker and consultant on leadership who lives in Bellevue, Washington. Here are a few of the son's reflections on his father's leadership. In reading them, think about coach Lombardi's leadership in terms of our interactional framework.

> *Contrary to the opinion of many people, leaders are not born. Leaders are made, and they are made by effort and hard work.*

Vincent T. Lombardi

Vision

The essence of leadership is vision. Good leaders have a clear, precise vision of what they want for the people they lead. That is my opinion from the vantage point of observing an outstanding leader, my father, Vince Lombardi.

It is generally conceded that my father was one of the great coaches of the modern football era. Yet Vince Lombardi waited until he was 47 years old to become a head coach. Because of the long wait, when he finally became head coach of the Green Bay Packers, he knew precisely what he wanted and he knew exactly how he was going to obtain it.

My father went to Green Bay in 1959, and in 1960 the Packers played for the World Championship. They lost that game, but they never lost another championship game. In the next seven years they won five world championships, three in a row, including the first two Super Bowls.

Mental toughness

If vision is the essence of leadership, then mental toughness is the one quality that every leader must possess. Vision without mental toughness is nothing more than a good idea. For a leader, mental toughness is holding on to that picture of excellence they have for their people when everyone around them is saying: "Who are you to think you can do that, no one like you has ever done that before?"

Motivation

Vince Lombardi was a consummate motivator. Many times with his players it was "My way or the highway," or "If you can't get the job done I'll find someone who can." They tell the story of the sportswriter interviewing some Packer players and asking "What is it about Coach Lombardi that makes you so successful?" One of the players thought for a moment and replied, "He treats us all alike, he treats us all the same—like dogs." Coach Lombardi, however, knew that approach would not produce lasting motivation. So after he gained the players' attention with "do it or else," he would focus on the profitability of the task at hand. All good leaders paint great pictures for themselves and the people around them of the rewards for successfully completing the job before them.

An example of this involved Jerry Kramer, an All-Pro guard for many years. Jerry was sitting in front of his locker after an especially poor practice wondering if it was time to move on to a different occupation. My father walked by, sized up the situation, tousled Jerry's hair, and told him "Son, some day you're going to be one of the greatest guards in football." Jerry Kramer never had to be pushed again. He was recently named to the all-time Super Bowl team.

HIGHLIGHT 5–5 *(concluded)*

A winning attitude

Vince Lombardi's teams were not a loose collection of individuals. The whole was bigger than the sum of the parts on the Green Bay Packers. Lombardi's teams had trust for one another, they respected one another and they were committed to one another. These elements—trust, respect, and commitment—give a team a winning attitude! When the Green Bay Packers stepped on the field, they didn't hope to win, they expected to win! In their minds they never lost a game. Once in awhile they just ran out of time.

There is a corollary to a winning attitude. Leaders can transform a winning attitude into a winning tradition. When new people join the organization, the veterans, the old hands, pass the winning attitude on to the rookies. Either by word or example they show the new arrivals "This is how we do things. Around here we expect to win." With a winning tradition, the organization does not succeed just this year; it does not win once in awhile. With a winning tradition you win time after time, year after year after year.

Leaders embodying the quality of mental toughness, projecting a precise picture of the goals to be achieved and motivating constructively, build within their people trust, respect, and commitment. The result is a winning tradition, where the organization does not simply attain their goals, they *maintain* their goals—the mark of true leadership.

Source: Personal communication from Vince Lombardi.

---

the same subordinates as troublemakers and would publicly belittle them when they told her about the problems within the agency. Similarly, Jane viewed keeping the county commissioners ignorant of the agency's problems as the key to success; Bob saw maintaining control of the workers as the key issue.

Conclusion: Drawing Lessons from Experience

All of the above leads to one conclusion: The right behavior in one situation is not necessarily the right behavior in another situation. However, it does not follow that any behavior is appropriate in any situation. Although we may not be able to agree on the one best behavior in a given situation, we often can agree on some clearly inappropriate behaviors. Saying that the right behavior for a leader depends on the situation is not the same thing as saying it does not matter what the leader does. It merely recognizes the complexity among leaders, followers, and situations. This recognition is a helpful first step in drawing meaningful lessons about leadership from experience.

SUMMARY

Leadership is a process in which leaders and followers interact dynamically in a particular situation or environment. Leadership is a broader concept than that of leaders, and the study of leadership must involve more than just the study of leaders as individuals. The study of leadership must also include two other areas: the followers and the situation. In addition, the interactive nature of these three domains has become increasingly important in recent years and can help us to better understand the changing nature of leader-follower relationships and the increasingly greater complexity of situations leaders and followers face. Because of this complexity, now, more than ever before, effective leadership cannot be boiled down to a simple and constant recipe. It *is* still true, however, that good leadership makes a difference; and it can be enhanced through greater awareness of the important factors influencing the leadership process.

KEY TERM AND CONCEPT

interactional framework

DISCUSSION QUESTIONS

1. According to the interactional model, effective leader behavior depends on many variables. It follows there is no simple prescription for effective leader behavior. Does this mean effective leadership is merely a matter of opinion or subjective preference?

2. Generally, leaders get most of the credit for a group's or organization's success. Do you believe this is warranted or fair?

3. What are some of the other characteristics of leaders, followers, and situations you could add to those listed in Figure 5–1?

SUGGESTED READINGS

Hollander, E. *Leadership Dynamics: A Practical Guide to Effective Relationships.* New York: Free Press, 1978.

Lansing, A. *Endurance.* New York: Avon Books, 1959.

Chapter Six

Power, Influence, and Influence Tactics

INTRODUCTION

One cannot understand leadership without understanding the concepts of power, influence, and influence tactics. Many people use these concepts synonymously (Bass, 1990), but it may be useful to distinguish among power, influence, and influence tactics. **Power** has been defined as the capacity to produce effects on others (House, 1984) or the potential to influence (Bass, 1990). **Influence** can be defined as the change in a target agent's attitudes, values, beliefs, or behaviors as the result of influence tactics. **Influence tactics** refer to one person's actual behaviors designed to change another person's attitudes, beliefs, values, or behaviors. Although power, influence, and influence tactics are typically examined from the leader's perspective, it is important to remember that followers can also wield a considerable amount of power and influence, and that followers also use a variety of influence tactics to change the

attitudes, values, beliefs, and behaviors of their leaders. Leadership practitioners can improve their effectiveness by reflecting on the types of power they and
their followers have and the types of influence tactics that they may use or that
may be used on them (also see Highlight 6–1).

As an overview, this chapter first elaborates on the distinctions between
power, influence, and influence tactics. Next, the interactional framework detailed in Chapter Five is used to describe the different conceptualizations of
power and influence. More specifically, this chapter uses the model to analyze
French and Raven's (1959) five social bases of power. In addition, this chapter
examines those theories of power that focus primarily on the leader, the relationship between leaders and followers, and the characteristics of the situation
that can enhance or inhibit the exercise of power (i.e., influence). The chapter
concludes with a description of influence tactics often used by leaders and followers and an explanation of how various situational factors and power bases
can affect the choice of tactic.

DISTINCTIONS BETWEEN POWER, INFLUENCE, AND INFLUENCE TACTICS

Some of the earliest descriptions of and prescriptions for leaders concerned the
use of power. Shakespeare's plays were concerned with the acquisition and
failing of power (Hill, 1985), and Machiavelli's *The Prince* has been described as
the "classic handbook on power politics" (Donno, 1966). Current scholars
have also emphasized the need to conceptualize leadership as a power phenomenon (Gardner, 1986; Hinkin & Schriesheim, 1989). Power may be the single most important concept in all the social sciences (Burns, 1978), though
scholars today disagree on precisely how to define power or influence.

As described earlier, power is the capacity to produce effects on others
(House, 1984) or the potential to influence others (Bass, 1990). It is important to
note that this capacity or potential to influence is a function of the leader, the
followers, and the situation. Leaders have the potential to change their followers' behaviors and attitudes. However, followers also have the potential to
change the behaviors or attitudes of their leader. Characteristics of the situation
can also affect the capacity of a leader to influence his or her followers and vice
versa. For example, leaders who can reward and punish followers may have a
greater capacity to influence followers than those leaders who cannot use rewards or punishments. Similarly, a leader's potential to influence his or her
followers may be substantially diminished by certain characteristics of the followers and the situation, as when the former belong to a strong, active union.

Several other aspects of power also are worth noting. Gardner (1986) made
an important point about the exercise of power and its effects. He stated that
"power does not need to be exercised in order to have its effect—as any hold-

---

HIGHLIGHT 6–1

Leadership Quotes, Chapter Six

You do not lead by hitting people over the head—that's assault, not leadership.

Dwight D. Eisenhower

He who has great power should use it lightly.

Seneca

Don't threaten. I know it's done by some of our people, but I don't go for it. If people are running scared, they're not going to make the right decisions. They'll make decisions to please the boss rather than recommend what has to be done.

Charles Pilliod

And when we think we lead, we are most led.

Lord Byron

All forms of tampering with human beings, getting at them, shaping them against their will to your own pattern, all thought control and conditioning, is, therefore, a denial of that in men which makes them men and their values ultimate.

A. A. Berle, Jr.

The true leader must submerge himself in the fountain of the people.

V. I. Lenin

---

up man can tell you'' (Gardner, 1986, p. 5). Thus, merely having the capacity to exert influence can often bring about intended effects, even though the leader may not take any action to influence his or her followers. For example, some months after the end of his term, Eisenhower was asked if leaving the White House had affected his golf game. ''Yes,'' he replied, ''a lot more people beat me now.'' Alternatively, power represents an inference or attribution made on the basis of an agent's observable acts of influence (Schriesheim & Hinkin, 1990). Power is never directly observed but rather attributed to others on the basis of the sorts of influence tactics they use and on their outcomes.

Whereas power is the capacity to cause change, influence is the degree of actual change in a target person's attitudes, values, beliefs, or behaviors. Influence can be measured by the behaviors or attitudes manifest by followers as the result of a leader's influence tactics. For example, a leader may ask a follower to accomplish a particular task, and whether or not the task is accomplished is partly a function of the leader's request. (The follower's ability and skill as well as access to the necessary equipment and resources are also important factors.) The criterion variables described in Chapter Four—such as subordinates' satisfaction or motivation, group cohesiveness and climate, or unit performance indices—can be used to measure the effectiveness of leaders' influence attempts. The degree to which leaders can change the level of satisfaction, motivation, or cohesiveness among followers is a function of the amount of power available to both leaders and followers. On the one hand, leaders with relatively high amounts of power can cause fairly substantial changes in subordinates' attitudes and behaviors; for example, a new and respected leader who uses rewards and punishments judiciously may cause a dramatic change in followers' perceptions about organizational climate and the amount of time followers spend manifesting work-related behaviors. On the other hand, the amount of power followers have in work situations can also vary dramatically, and in some situations particular followers may exert relatively more influence over the rest of the group than the leader does. For example, a follower with a high level of knowledge and experience may have more influence on the attitudes, opinions, and behaviors of the rest of the followers than a brand-new leader may have. Thus, the amount of change in the attitudes or behaviors of the targets of influence is a function of the agent's capacity to exert influence and the targets' capacity to resist this influence.

Leaders and followers typically use a variety of tactics to influence each other's attitudes or behaviors (see Highlight 6–2 for a description of some nonverbal power cues common to humans). Influence tactics are the overt behaviors exhibited by one person to influence another. They range from emotional appeals, to the exchange of favors, to threats. The particular tactic used in a leadership situation is probably a function of the power possessed by both parties. Individuals with a relatively large amount of power may successfully employ a wider variety of influence tactics than those individuals with little power. For example, a well-respected leader could make an emotional appeal, a rational appeal, a personal appeal, a legitimate request, or a threat to try to modify a follower's behavior. The follower in this situation may only be able to use ingratiation or personal appeals in order to change the leader's attitude or behavior.

At the same time, because the formal leader is not always the person who possesses the most power in a leadership situation, followers often can use a wider variety of influence tactics than the leader to modify the attitudes and behaviors of others. This would be the case if a new leader were brought into an organization in which one of his or her subordinates was extremely well liked and respected. In this situation, the subordinate may be able to make personal appeals, emotional appeals, or even threats to change the attitudes or behaviors of the leader, whereas the new leader may be limited to making only legitimate requests to change the attitudes and behaviors of the followers.

HIGHLIGHT 6–2

Gestures of Power and Dominance

We can often get "clues" about relative power just by paying attention to behaviors between two people. There are a number of nonverbal cues we might want to pay attention to.

The phrase *pecking order* refers to the status differential between members of a group. It reminds us that many aspects of human social organization have roots, or at least parallels, in the behavior of other species. The animal kingdom presents diverse and fascinating examples of stylized behaviors by which one member of a species shows its relative dominance or submissiveness to another. There is adaptive significance to such behavioral mechanisms since they tend to minimize actual physical struggle and maintain a stable social order. For example, lower-ranking baboons step aside to let a higher-status male pass; they become nervous if he stares at them. The highest-status male can choose where he wants to sleep and whom he wants to mate with. Baboons "know their place." As with humans, rank has its privileges.

Our own stylized power rituals are usually so second-nature we aren't conscious of them. Yet there is a "dance" of power relations among humans just as among other animals. The following are some of the ways power is expressed nonverbally in humans.

Staring. In American society, it is disrespectful for a person of lower status to stare at a superior, though superiors are not bound by a similar restriction. Children, for example, are taught not to stare at parents. And it's an interesting comment on the power relationship between sexes that women are more likely to avert their gaze from men than vice versa.

Pointing. Children are also taught it's not nice to point. However, adults rarely correct each other for pointing because more than mere etiquette, pointing seems to be a behavior that is acceptable for high-status figures or those attempting to assert dominance. An angry boss may point an index finger accusingly at an employee; few employees who wanted to keep their jobs would respond in kind. The same restrictions apply to frowning.

Touching. Invading another person's space by touching the person without invitation is acceptable when one is of superior status but not when one is of subordinate status. It's acceptable, for example, for bosses or teachers to put a hand on an employee's or student's shoulder, but not vice versa. The disparity also applies to socioeconomic status; someone with higher socioeconomic status is more likely to touch a person of lower socioeconomic status than vice versa.

Interrupting. Virtually all of us have interrupted others, and we have all been interrupted ourselves. Again, however, the issue is who was interrupting whom? Higher power or status persons interrupt; lower power or status persons are interrupted. A vast difference in frequency of behaviors also exists between the sexes in American society. Men interrupt much more frequently than women do.

Source: D. A. Karp, and W. C. Yoels, *Symbols, Selves, and Society* (New York: Lippincott, 1979).

FIGURE 6–1

Sources of Leader Power in the Leader-Followers-Situation Framework

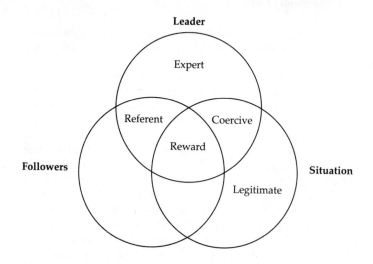

POWER AND LEADERSHIP

We began this chapter by noting how understanding power is essential to understanding leadership. Several perspectives and theories have been developed to explain the acquisition and exercise of power, and we believe it is heuristically useful to organize discussion of them in terms of the interactional framework described in Chapter Five. First, we will examine five bases of social power; second, theories that focus on the leader's motives; third, approaches that emphasize the relationship between leaders and followers; and finally, situational aspects of power.

A Taxonomy of Social Power

French and Raven (1959) identified five sources, or bases, of power by which an individual can potentially influence others. As seen in Figure 6–1, these five sources include one that is primarily a function of the leader; one that is a function of the relationship between leaders and followers; one primarily a function of the leader and the situation; one primarily a function of the situation; and finally, one that involves aspects of all three elements. The five bases of power in Figure 6–1 are organized from the leader's perspective, yet it is important to note that followers also have varying amounts of power they can use to resist a leader's influence attempts. Because both leaders and followers can use all five bases of power to influence each other, this section describes the bases of power from both the leader's and followers' perspectives. Understanding these bases of power from both perspectives can help leadership practitioners be more effective, because these bases can be used (a) to help determine why subordinates and superiors may successfully resist different influence attempts and (b) to improve the potential amount of influence leadership practitioners can have with subordinates and superiors. The following is a more detailed discussion of French and Raven's (1959) five bases of social power.

Expert power.   Expert power is the power of knowledge. Some people are able to influence others through their relative expertise in particular areas. A surgeon may wield considerable influence in a hospital because others are dependent on her knowledge, skill, and judgment, even though she may not have any formal authority over them. A mechanic may be influential among his peers because he is widely recognized as the best in the city. A longtime employee may be influential because his "corporate memory" provides a useful historical perspective to newer personnel. Legislators who are expert in the intricacies of parliamentary procedure, athletes who have played in championship games before, and soldiers who have been in combat before are valued for the "lessons learned" and wisdom they can share with others.

Because expert power is a function of the amount of knowledge one possesses relative to the rest of the members of the group, it is possible for followers to have considerably more expert power than leaders in certain situations. For example, new leaders often possess less knowledge of the jobs and tasks performed in a particular work unit than the followers do, and in this case the followers can potentially wield considerable influence when decisions are made regarding work procedures, new equipment, or the hiring of additional workers. Probably the best advice for leaders in this situation is to ask a lot of questions and perhaps seek additional training to help fill this knowledge gap. So long as different followers have considerably greater amounts of expert power, it will be difficult for a leader to influence the work unit on the basis of expert power alone.

Referent power.   One way to counteract the problems stemming from a lack of expertise is to build strong interpersonal ties with subordinates. Referent power refers to the potential influence one has due to the strength of the relationship between the leader and the followers. When people admire a leader and see her as a role model, we say she has referent power. For example, students may respond positively to advice or requests from teachers who are well liked and respected, while the same students might be unresponsive to less popular teachers. This relative degree of responsiveness is primarily a function of the strength of the relationship between the students and the different teachers. We knew one young lieutenant who had enormous referent power with the military security guards working for him due to his selfless concern for them, evident in such habits as bringing them hot chocolate and homemade cookies on their late-night shifts. The guards, sometimes taken for granted by other superiors, understood and valued the extra effort and sacrifice this young supervisor put forth for them. When Buddy Ryan was fired as head coach of the Philadelphia Eagles football team, many of the players expressed fierce loyalty to him. One said, "We'd do things for Buddy that we wouldn't do for another coach. I'd sell my body for Buddy" (Associated Press, January 9, 1991). That is referent power.

It is important to note that the relationships between leaders and followers take time to develop and often limit the actions leaders may take in a particular leadership situation. For example, a leader who has developed a strong relationship with a follower may be reluctant to discipline the follower for poor work or chronic tardiness, as these actions could disrupt the nature of the relationship between the leader and the follower. Thus, referent power is a two-way street; the stronger the relationship, the more influence leaders and followers exert over each other. Moreover, just as it is possible for leaders to develop strong relationships with followers and, in turn, acquire more referent power, it is also possible for followers to develop strong relationships with other followers and acquire more referent power. Followers with relatively more referent power than their peers are often the spokespersons for their work units and generally have more latitude to deviate from work-unit norms. Followers with little referent power have little opportunity to deviate from group norms. For example, in an episode of the television show "The Simpsons," Homer Simpson was fired for wearing a pink shirt to work (everybody else at the Springfield nuclear power plant had always worn white shirts). Homer was fired partly because he "was not popular enough to be different."

Legitimate power.   Legitimate power depends on a person's organizational role. It can be thought of as one's formal or official authority. Some people make things happen because they have the power or authority to do so. The boss can assign projects; the coach can decide who plays; the colonel can order compliance with uniform standards; the teacher assigns the homework and awards the grades. Individuals with legitimate power exert influence through requests or demands deemed appropriate by virtue of their role and position. In other words, legitimate power means a leader has authority because he or she has been assigned a particular role in an organization (and the leader has this authority only as long as he or she occupies that position and operates within the proper bounds of that role).

It is important to note that legitimate authority and leadership are not the same thing. Holding a position and being a leader are not synonymous, despite the relatively common practice of calling position holders in bureaucracies the leaders. The head of an organization may be a true leader, but he also may not be. Effective leaders often intuitively realize they need more than legitimate power to be successful. Before he became president, Dwight Eisenhower com-

Reprinted with special permission of King Features Syndicate.

manded all Allied troops in Europe during World War II. In a meeting with his staff before the Normandy invasion, Eisenhower pulled a string across a table to make a point about leadership. He was demonstrating that just as you can pull a string, not push it, officers must lead soldiers and not "push" them from the rear.

It is also possible for followers to use their legitimate power to influence leaders. In these cases, followers can actively resist a leader's influence attempt by only doing work specifically prescribed in job descriptions, bureaucratic rules, or union policies. For example, many organizations have job descriptions that limit both the time spent at work and the types of tasks and activities performed. Similarly, bureaucratic rules and union policies can be invoked by followers to resist a leader's influence attempts. Often the leader will need to change the nature of his or her request or find another way to resolve the problem if these rules and policies are invoked by followers. If this is the case, then the followers will have successfully used legitimate power to influence their leader.

Reward power.   Reward power involves the potential to influence others due to one's control over desired resources. This can include the power to give raises, bonuses, and promotions; to grant tenure; to select people for special assignments or desirable activities; to distribute desired resources like computers, offices, parking places, or travel money; to intercede positively on another's behalf; to recognize with awards and praise; and so on. Many corporations use rewards extensively to motivate employees. At McDonald's, for example, there is great status accorded the "All-American Hamburger Maker," the cook who makes the fastest, highest-quality hamburgers in the country. At individual fast-food restaurants, managers may reward salespersons who handle the most customers during rush periods. Tupperware holds rallies for its salespeople. Almost everyone wins something, ranging from pins and badges to lucrative prizes for top performers (Peters & Waterman, 1982). Schools pick "teachers of the year" and professional athletes are rewarded by selection to all-star teams for their superior performance.

The potential to influence others through the ability to administer rewards is a joint function of the leader, the followers, and the situation. Leaders vary considerably in the types and frequency in which they mete out rewards, but the position they fill also helps to determine the frequency and types of rewards administered. For example, employees of the month at Kentucky Fried Chicken are not given new cars; the managers of these franchises do not have the resources to offer such awards. Similarly, leaders in other organizations are limited to some extent in the types and frequency in which they can administer awards. Nevertheless, leadership practitioners can enhance their reward power by spending some time reflecting on the followers and the situation. Often a number of alternative or innovative rewards can be created, and these rewards, along with ample doses of praise, can help a leader overcome the constraints his or her position puts on reward power.

Although using the power to administer rewards can be an effective way to change the attitudes and behaviors of others, there are several situations where a leader's use of reward power can be problematic. For example, the perception that a company's monetary bonus policy is handled equitably may be as important in motivating good work (or avoiding morale problems) as the amount of the bonus itself. Moreover, a superior may mistakenly assume that a particular reward is valued when it is not. This would be the case if a particular subordinate were publicly recognized for her good work when she actually dislikes public recognition. Leadership practitioners can avoid the latter problem by developing good relationships with subordinates and administering rewards that they, not the leader, value.

Another potential problem with reward power is that it may produce compliance but not other desirable outcomes like commitment (Yukl, 1989). In other words, subordinates may perform only at the level necessary to receive a reward and may not be willing to put forth the extra effort needed to make the organization better. An overemphasis on rewards as "payoff" for performance may also lead to resentment and feelings by workers of being manipulated, especially if it occurs in the context of relatively cold and distant superior-subordinate relationships. Extrinsic rewards like praise, compensation, promotion, privileges, and time off may not have the same effects on behavior as intrinsic rewards such as feelings of accomplishment, personal growth, and development. There is evidence under some conditions extrinsic rewards can even decrease intrinsic motivation toward a task and make the desired behavior less likely to persist when extrinsic rewards are not available (Deci, 1972; Ryan, Mims, & Koestner, 1983). Overemphasis on extrinsic rewards may instill an essentially contractual or economic relationship between superiors and subordinates, diluting important aspects of the relationship like mutual loyalty or shared commitment to higher ideals (Wakin, 1981).

All these cautions about reward power should not cloud its usefulness and effectiveness, which is very real. As noted previously, top organizations make extensive use of both tangible and symbolic rewards in motivating their workers. Furthermore, some of the most important rewards are readily available to all leaders—sincere praise and thanks to others for their loyalty and work. The bottom line is that leadership practitioners can enhance their ability to influence others based on reward power if they (*a*) determine what rewards are available, (*b*) determine what rewards are valued by their subordinates, and (*c*) establish clear policies for the equitable and consistent administration of rewards for good performance.

Finally, because reward power is partly determined by one's position in the organization, some people may believe followers have little, if any, reward power. This may not be the case. If followers have control over scarce resources, then they may use the administration of these resources as a way of getting leaders to act in the manner they want. Moreover, followers may reward their leader by putting out a high level of effort when they feel their leader is doing a good job, and they may put forth less effort when they feel their leader is doing a poor job. By modifying their level of effort, followers may in turn modify a leader's attitudes and behaviors. And when followers compliment their leader (e.g., for running a constructive meeting), it is no less an example of reward power than when a leader compliments a follower. Thus, leadership practitioners should be aware that followers can also use reward power to influence leaders.

Coercive power.   Coercive power, the opposite of reward power, is the potential to influence others through the administration of negative sanctions or the removal of positive events. In other words, it is the ability to control others through the fear of punishment or the loss of valued outcomes. Like reward power, coercive power is partly a function of the leader, but the situation often limits the coercive actions a leader can take. Examples of coercive power include policemen giving tickets for speeding, the army court-martialing AWOL soliders, a teacher detaining disruptive students after school, employers firing lazy workers, and parents spanking children (Klein, 1991). Even presidents resort to their coercive powers. Historian Arthur Schlesinger, Jr., for example, described Lyndon Johnson as having a ''devastating instinct for the weaknesses of others.'' Lyndon Johnson was familiar and comfortable with the use of coercion; he once told a White House staff member, ''Just you remember this. There's only two kinds at the White House. There's elephants and there's ants. And I'm the only elephant'' (Barnes, 1989).

Coercive power, like reward power, can be used appropriately or inappropriately. It is carried to its extreme in harsh and repressive totalitarian societies. One of the most tragic instances of coercive power was in the cult led by Jim Jones, which tragically and unbelievably self-exterminated in an incident known as the Jonestown massacre (Conway & Siegelman, 1979). Virtually all of the 912 who died there drank, at Jones's direction, from large vats of a flavored drink containing cyanide. The submissiveness and suicidal obedience of Jones's followers during the massacre was due largely to the long history of rule by fear Jones had practiced. For example, teenagers caught holding hands were beaten, and adults judged slacking in their work were forced to box for hours in marathon public matches against as many as three or four bigger and stronger opponents. Jim Jones ruled by fear, and his followers became self-destructively compliant.

Perhaps the preceding example is so extreme that we can dismiss its relevance to our own lives and leadership activities. On the other hand, it does provide dramatic reminder that reliance on coercive power has inherent limitations and drawbacks. This is not to say the willingness to use disciplinary sanctions is never necessary. Sometimes it is.

Informal coercion, as opposed to the threat of formal punishment, can also be used to change the attitudes and behaviors of others. Informal coercion is usually expressed implicitly, and often nonverbally, rather than explicitly. It may be the pressure employees feel to donate to the boss's favorite charity, or it may be his glare when they bring up an unpopular idea. One of the most common forms of coercion is simply a superior's temperamental outbursts. The intimidation of a leader's poorly controlled anger is usually, in its long-term effects, a dysfunctional style of behavior for leaders.

It is also possible for followers to use coercive power to influence their leader's behavior. For example, a leader may be hesitant to take disciplinary action against a large, emotionally unstable follower. Followers can threaten leaders with physical assaults, industrial sabotage, or work slowdowns and strikes, and these threats can serve to modify a leader's behavior. In all likelihood, followers will be more likely to use coercive power to change their leader's behavior if they have a relatively high amount of referent power with their fellow coworkers. This may be particularly true if threats of work slowdowns or strikes are used to influence a leader's behavior.

Concluding thoughts about French and Raven's power taxonomy.   There has been considerable research addressing French and Raven's (1959) taxonomy of power, and generally the findings indicate that leaders who relied primarily on referent and expert power had subordinates who were more motivated and satisfied, were absent less, and performed better (Yukl, 1981). However, Yukl (1981) and Podsakoff and Schriesheim (1985) have criticized these findings, and much of their criticism centers on the instrument used to assess a leader's bases of power. Recently, Hinkin and Schriesheim (1989) have developed an instrument that overcomes many of the criticisms, and future research should more clearly delineate the relationship between the five bases of power and various leadership effectiveness criteria.

Even though much research to date about the five bases of power may be flawed, three generalizations about power and influence still seem warranted. First, effective leaders typically take advantage of all their sources of power. They understand the relative advantages and disadvantages of the different power sources, and they selectively emphasize one or another depending on their particular objectives in a given situation. Second, whereas leaders in well-functioning organizations have strong influence over their subordinates, they are also open to being influenced by them. High degrees of reciprocal influence between leaders and followers characterize the most effective organizations (Yukl, 1989). Third, leaders vary in the extent to which they share power with subordinates. Some leaders seem to view their power as a fixed resource that, when shared with others (like cutting a pie into pieces), reduces their own portion. They see power in zero-sum terms. Other leaders see power as an expandable pie. They see the possibility of increasing a subordinate's power without reducing their own. Needless to say, which view a leader subscribes to can have a major impact on the leader's support for power-sharing activities like delegation and participative management. Support for them is also affected by the practice of holding leaders responsible for subordinates' decisions and actions as well as their own. It is, after all, the coach or manager who often gets fired when the team loses (Hollander & Offermann, 1990; Pfeffer, 1977).

Several additional approaches to conceptualizing power and leadership will be examined in the following sections. We have arranged their treatment somewhat along the lines of the interactional framework.

Leader Motives

People vary in their motivation to influence or control others. McClelland (1975) called this the **need for power**, and individuals with a high need for power derive psychological satisfaction from influencing others. They seek positions where they can influence others, and they are often involved concurrently in influencing people in many different organizations or decision-making bodies. In such activities they readily offer ideas, suggestions, and opinions, and also seek information they can use in influencing others. They are often astute at building trusting relationships and assessing power networks, though they can also be quite outspoken and forceful. They value the tangible signs of their authority and status as well as the more intangible indications of others' deference to them. Two different ways of expressing the need for power have been identified: **personalized power** and **socialized power**. Individuals who have a high need for personalized power are relatively selfish, impulsive, and uninhibited, and lacking in self-control. These individuals exercise power for their own self-centered needs, not for the good of the group or the organization. Socialized power, on the other hand, implies a more emotionally mature expression of the motive. Socialized power is exercised in the service of higher goals to others or organizations and often involves self-sacrifice toward those ends. It often involves an empowering rather than autocratic style of management and leadership.

Although the need for power has been measured using questionnaires and more traditional personality inventories, McClelland and his associates have used the Thematic Apperception Test (TAT) to assess need for power. The TAT is a **projective personality test** consisting of pictures such as a woman staring out a window or a boy holding a violin. Subjects are asked to make up a story about each picture, and the stories are then interpreted in terms of the strengths of various needs imputed to the characters, one of which is the need for power. Since the pictures are somewhat ambiguous, the sorts of needs projected onto the characters is presumed to reflect needs (perhaps at an unconscious level) of the storyteller. Stories concerned with influencing or controlling others would receive high scores for the need for power.

The need for power has been found to be positively related to various leadership effectiveness criteria. For example, McClelland and Boyatzis (1982) found the need for power to be positively related to success for nontechnical managers at AT&T, and Stahl (1983) found that the need for power was positively related to managers' performance ratings and promotion rates. In addition, Fodor (1987) reported that small groups of ROTC students were more likely to successfully solve a subarctic survival situation if their leader had a strong need for power. Although these findings appear promising, several cautions should be kept in mind. First, McClelland and Boyatzis (1982) also reported that the need for power was unrelated to the success of technical managers at AT&T. Apparently, the level of knowledge (i.e., expert power) played a more important role in the success of the technical managers versus the nontechnical managers. Second, McClelland (1985) concluded that although some need for power was necessary for leadership potential, successful leaders also have the ability to inhibit their manifestation of this need. Leaders who are relatively uninhibited in their need for power will act like a dictator; such individuals use power impulsively, to manipulate or control others, or to achieve at another's expense. Leaders with a high need for power but low activity inhibition may be successful in the short term, but their followers, as well as the remainder of the organization, may pay high costs for this success. Some of these costs may include perceptions by fellow members of the organization that they are untrustworthy, uncooperative, overly competitive, and looking out primarily for themselves.

Individuals vary in their motivation to manage, just as in their need for power. Miner (1974) described **motivation to manage** in the following terms:

- Maintaining good relationships with authority figures.
- Wanting to compete for recognition and advancement.
- Being active and assertive.
- Wanting to exercise influence over subordinates.
- Being visibly different from followers.
- Being willing to do routine administrative tasks.

Like McClelland, Miner also used a projective test to measure a person's motivation to manage. Miner's Sentence Completion Scale (MSCS) consists of a series of incomplete sentences dealing with the six components described above (e.g., "My relationship with my boss. . .). Respondents are asked to complete the sentences, which are then scored according to established criteria. The overall composite MSCS score (though not component scores) has consistently been found to predict leadership success in hierarchical or bureaucratic organizations (Miner, 1978). Thus, individuals who maintained respect for authority figures, wanted to be recognized, acted assertively, actively influenced subordinates, maintained "psychological distance" between themselves and their followers, and readily took on routine administrative tasks were more apt to be successful in bureaucratic organizations. However, Miner also claimed different qualities were needed in flatter, nonbureaucratic organizations, and his (1978) review of the MSCS supports this view.

Findings concerning both the need for power and the motivation to manage have several implications for leadership practitioners. First, not all individuals like being leaders. One reason may be that some have a relatively low need for power or motivation to manage. Because these scores are relatively stable and fairly difficult to change, leaders who do not enjoy their role may want to seek positions where they have few supervisory responsibilities.

Second, a high need for power or motivation to manage does not guarantee leadership success. The situation can play a crucial role in determining whether the need for power or the motivation to manage is related to leadership success. For example, McClelland and Boyatzis (1982) found the need for power to be related to leadership success for nontechnical managers only, and Miner (1978) found motivation to manage was related to leadership success only in hierarchical or bureaucratic organizations.

Third, in order to be successful in the long term, leaders may have to have both a high need for socialized power and a high level of activity inhibition. Leaders who impulsively exercise power merely to satisfy their own selfish needs will probably be ineffective in the long term.

Finally, it is important to remember that followers as well as leaders differ in the need for power, activity inhibition, and motivation to manage. Certain followers may have stronger needs or motives in this area. Leaders may need to behave differently toward these followers than they might toward followers having a low need for power or motivation to manage.

Power and the Leader-Follower Relationship

Several theories have examined how the nature of the relationship between leaders and followers affects the power and influence each can exert. Two of the more well-known theories that examine influence and counterinfluence between leaders and followers are Graen and Cashman's (1975) **vertical dyad linkage (VDL) theory** and Hollander's (1978) **social exchange theory**. In general, the VDL theory typically has been used to examine the different relationships among leaders and followers in formal organizations, whereas social exchange theory often is used to understand how power is related to the relationships that develop in informal, leaderless groups.

Vertical dyad linkage (VDL) theory. The vertical dyad linkage (VDL) theory was developed to describe two kinds of relationships that occur among leaders and followers, and how these relationships affect the types of power and influence tactics leaders use (Graen & Cashman, 1975). One type of relationship is distinguished by a high degree of mutual influence and attraction existing between the leader and a limited number of subordinates. These subordinates belong to the **in-group** and can be distinguished by their high degree of loyalty, commitment, and trust felt toward the leader. Leaders primarily use expert, referent, and reward power to influence members of the in-group. The other subordinates belong to the **out-group**, and leaders typically use reward, legitimate, and coercive power to influence them. Leaders have considerably more influence with in-group as opposed to out-group members. However, this greater degree of influence also has a price. If a leader uses legitimate or coercive power with in-group members, then she risks losing the high levels of loyalty and commitment they feel toward her.

Being a member of the in-group is related to several predictable outcomes. For example, in-group members receive higher performance ratings than do out-group members (Liden & Graen, 1980; Scandura, Green, & Novak, 1986). In addition, out-group members have higher levels of turnover than do in-group members (Ferris, 1985; Graen, Liden, & Hoel, 1982), and in-group members have more positive ratings of organizational climate than do out-group members (Kozlowski & Doherty, 1989).

Despite such empirical support for VDL theory, leadership practitioners need to be aware of several of its limitations. First, it is not clear how these two different relationships develop (Yukl, 1989). Some preliminary investigations have been accomplished (Duchon, Green, & Taber, 1986), but much more work needs to be done before we understand which factors affect group membership status. Second, it is not necessarily clear to all concerned just who actually is in the in-group and who is in the out-group; leaders and followers may have different perceptions of which followers belong in each group (Scandura, Graen, & Novak, 1986). Perhaps relationships between leaders and followers may be better depicted using some kind of continuous variable rather than a dichotomous one. Third, antagonism and jealousy may develop among followers in organizations with strong in-group and out-group distinctions, and the feelings may adversely affect organizational performance and effectiveness. Leaders probably should try to avoid developing differential relationships with subordinates and instead strive to make all members feel that they belong to the in-group. Incidentally, the latter point may be what makes charismatic leaders so unique; these leaders seem to have the capacity to expand the normally small in-group to include all of the members of their work unit or organization (Curphy, 1991). The ability of charismatic leaders to expand their in-group will be discussed in more detail later in this book.

Social exchange theory.   VDL theory has been investigated primarily in organizations or work units having formally appointed leaders. However, leaders often emerge informally even in groups having no appointed leader. Social exchange theory (Hollander, 1978) provides a useful explanation of this phenomenon. Social exchange theory uses a concept called **idiosyncrasy credits** to explain why certain individuals emerge as leaders among their peers, or in leaderless groups. Idiosyncrasy credits represent a sort of "psychological bank account" individuals build in the eyes of others through their conformity to group norms and competence in contributing to group goals. Individuals emerge as leaders and increase their potential to influence others by building their store of idiosyncrasy credits. For example, adolescent gang members gain more idiosyncrasy credits (and therefore more power and influence) by wearing gang colors, backing up other gang members during conflicts, and robbing others to get the gang money for alcohol and drugs.

Just as one has greater latitude of financial action when a bank account is sizable, leaders have greater latitude of action when they have a large store of idiosyncrasy credits. A leader's earned status and wealth of idiosyncrasy credits can be thought of as "venture capital" with which to take bold action. For example, a gang leader with plentiful idiosyncratic credits may risk attacking a strong, rival gang. If the attack is successful, the gang leader may wield even more power and influence. This phenomenon can also be seen in work settings, where the habitual violation of certain written or unwritten rules (e.g., haircut or dress codes) is tolerated because certain individuals have "earned' the right to break the rules by virtue of their extraordinary contributions. However, idiosyncratic credits can also be "spent" by violating group norms or through failure. If the gang had a policy of not associating with members of different races and the leader was discovered secretly dating someone from another race, then the leader may lose all of the idiosyncratic credits he might have earned.

Hollander (1978) has generalized the process of influence and counterinfluence among members in leaderless groups to describe the power and influence leaders have in formal organizations. He called this generalization of social exchange theory the **transactional approach to leadership**. The transactional approach to leadership has several fundamental tenets. First, the leader-follower relationship can be construed partly as an exchange of benefits. Thus, leaders give something to followers (often not tangible or monetary) and also get something from them in return. One of the most important benefits that can be exchanged is social approval. The leader's benefits often include status and the opportunity to exert influence and exercise authority. Some of the important but subtle benefits leaders provide to followers include structuring and directing their activities. This includes the leader's "definition of reality," that is, his analysis of the environmental pressures and opportunities the group faces.

Because of the contingencies of these mutual benefits, a sort of "psychological contact" exists between leaders and followers. In some cases, it literally may be a written contract (e.g., certain labor-management issues), but more often it is not. Whether formal or informal, however, the psychological contract involves the parties' understanding of their mutual rights and obligations, and dictates to a large extent the amount of power leaders can use to change the attitudes and behaviors of followers.

From this perspective, effective leadership exists when everyone perceives a fair exchange of benefits. If leaders receive benefits substantially disproportionate to their (perceived) contributions, however, followers may feel a sense of injustice. Followers may also feel a sense of inequity in the relationship if they perceive the leader as callous or indifferent to their interests. For example, GM autoworkers were extremely dissatisfied when they heard that Roger Smith, the company's CEO, had given himself a $2 million raise at the same time he was closing several major plants due to falling profits. Moreover, followers may feel frustrated if the leader makes mistakes, especially if the group suffers as a result of the leader's not listening to followers' input or advice. Any of these eventualities may prompt followers to redress perceived inequities in some way. In the corporate sector, this can include threats of work stoppage, industrial sabotage, or strikes. Followers in other sectors may use other sanctions. The most extreme is reported to have occurred during the Vietnam War, when there were a few accounts of American soldiers "fragging" (murdering) their own officers.

Concluding thoughts about VDL and social exchange theory.   Although both the VDL and social exchange theories are primarily descriptive in nature, they do provide new perspectives for understanding why some leaders exert more influence than others and why leaders often affect the attitudes, opinions, and behaviors of their followers differently. In addition to providing alternative perspectives for understanding power and influence, these two theories also provide helpful ideas for leadership practitioners. First, leadership practitioners may want to avoid developing in-group and out-group relationships among their followers. These relationships often foster an "us versus them" mentality, which may lead to decreased unit performance in the long run. Second, a leader may be able to wield more power and influence if he can get subordinates to accept his own rules and norms for the work group. If the followers' rules and norms about work differ substantially from the leader's, then the leader may be forced to use either legitimate or coercive power to influence followers. On the other hand, if leaders can get followers to buy into their rules and norms for the work unit, leaders may be better able to build idiosyncratic credits and thus rely primarily on referent power to influence subordinates. Similarly, by skillfully defining reality for followers, leaders can increase the likelihood followers will exert influence on each other to accomplish organizational goals. Third, leadership practitioners may increase their potential power if followers perceive that rewards are administered fairly and equitably.

Situational Factors Affecting Power

Although a coherent theory for explaining how or why situational factors affect power has yet to be developed, researchers have identified a number of situational factors that do affect a leader's or follower's ability to wield influence. These include things like symbols of accomplishment or expertise, office arrangements, clothing, and the presence or absence of crises. The following is a discussion of some of the situational factors that can affect the power a leader or a follower can exert in a particular leadership situation.

Something as seemingly trivial as the arrangement of furniture in an office can affect power relationships. One of the best examples of this comes from John Ehrlichman's (1982) book, *Witness to Power*. Ehrlichman described his first visit to J. Edgar Hoover's office at the Department of Justice. The legendary director of the FBI had long been one of the most powerful men in Washington, D.C., and as Ehrlichman's impressions reveal, Hoover took every opportunity to reinforce that image. Ehrlichman was first led through double doors into a room replete with plaques, citations, trophies, medals, and certificates jamming every wall. He was then led through a second room, similarly decorated, then into a third trophy room, and finally to a large but bare desk backed by several flags and still no J. Edgar Hoover. The guide opened a door behind the desk, and Ehrlichman went into a smaller office, which Hoover dominated from an impressive chair and desk that stood on a dais about six inches high. Erhlichman was instructed to take a seat on a lower couch, and Mr. Hoover peered down on Ehrlichman from his own loftier and intimidating place.

In addition to the factors just described, other aspects of office arrangements also can affect a leader's or follower's power. One factor is the shape of the table used for meetings. Individuals sitting at the ends of rectangular tables often wield more power, whereas circular tables facilitate communication and minimize status differentials. However, specific seating arrangements even at circular tables can affect participants' interactions; often individuals belonging to the same cliques and coalitions will sit next to each other. By sitting next to each other, members of the same coalition may exert more power as a collective group than they would sitting apart from each other. Also, having a private or more open office may not only reflect but also affect power differentials between people. Individuals with private offices can dictate to a greater degree when they want to interact with others by opening or closing their doors or by giving instructions about interruptions. Individuals with more open offices have much less power to control access to them.

Prominently displaying symbols like diplomas, awards, and titles also can increase one's power. This was shown in an experiment in a college setting where a guest lecturer to several different classes was introduced in a different way to each. To one group he was introduced as a student; to other groups he was introduced as a lecturer, senior lecturer, or professor, respectively. After the presentation, when he was no longer in the room, the class estimated his height. Interestingly, the same man was perceived by different groups as increasingly taller with each increase in academic status. The "professor" was remembered as being several inches taller than the "student!" (Wilson, 1968).

This finding demonstrates the generalized impact a seemingly minor matter like one's title can have on others. Another study points out more dramatically how dangerous it can be when followers are overly responsive to the *appearances* of title and authority. This other study took place in a medical setting and arose from concern among medical staff that nurses were responding mechanically to doctors' orders. A researcher made telephone calls to nurses' stations on numerous different medical wards. In each, he identified himself as a hospital physician and directed the nurse answering the phone to prescribe a particular medication for a patient on that ward. Many nurses complied with the request despite the fact it was against hospital policy to transmit prescriptions by phone. Many did so despite never even having talked to the particular "physician" before the call—and despite the fact that the prescribed medication was dangerously excessive, not to mention unauthorized. In fact, 95 percent of the nurses complied with the request made by the most easily falsifiable symbol of authority, a bare title (Cialdini, 1984) (also see Highlight 6–3).

Even choice of clothing can affect one's power and influence. Uniforms and other specialized clothing have long been associated with authority and status, including their use by the military, police, hospital staffs, clergy, and so on. In one experiment, people walking along a city sidewalk were stopped by someone dressed either in regular clothes or in the uniform of a security guard and told this: "You see that guy over there by the meter? He's overparked but doesn't have any change. Give him a dime!" Whereas fewer than half complied when the requestor was dressed in regular clothes, over 90 percent did when he was in uniform (Bickman, 1974). This same rationale is given for having personnel in certain occupations (e.g., airline crew members) wear uniforms. Besides more easily identifying them to others, the uniforms increase the likelihood that in emergency situations their instructions will be followed. Similarly, even the presence of something as trivial as tattoos can affect the amount of power wielded in a group. One of the authors of this text had a friend named Del who was a manager in an international book publishing company. Del was a former merchant marine whose forearms were adorned with tattoos. Del would often take off his suit coat and roll up his sleeves when meetings were not going his way, and he often exerted considerably more influence by merely exposing his tattoos to the rest of the group.

A final situational factor that can affect one's potential to influence others is the presence or absence of a crisis. Leaders usually can exert more power during a crisis than during periods of relative calm. Perhaps this is because during a crisis leaders are willing to draw on bases of power they normally forgo. For example, a leader who has developed close interpersonal relationships with

HIGHLIGHT 6–3

The Milgram Studies

One intriguing way to understand power, influence, and influence tactics is to read a synopsis of Stanley Milgram's classic work on obedience and to think about how this work relates to the concepts and theories discussed in the present chapter. Milgram's research explored how far people will go when directed by an authority figure to do something that might injure another person. More specifically, Milgram wanted to know what happens when the dictates of authority and the dictates of one's conscience seem incompatible.

The participants were men from the communities surrounding Yale University. They were led to believe they were helping in a study concerning the effect of punishment on learning; the study's legitimacy was certainly enhanced by being conducted on the Yale campus itself. Two subjects at a time participated in the study, one as a teacher and the other as learner. The roles apparently were assigned randomly. The teacher's task was to help the learner memorize a set of word pairs by providing electric shocks whenever the learner (who would be in an adjacent room) made a mistake.

A stern experimenter described procedures and showed participants the equipment for administering punishment. This "shock generator" looked ominous, with rows of switches, lights, and warnings labeled in 15-volt increments all the way to 450 volts. Various points along the array were marked with increasingly dire warnings such as *extreme intensity* and *danger: severe*. The switch at the highest level of shock simply was marked *XXX*. Every time the learner made a mistake, the teacher was ordered by the experimenter to administer the next higher level of electric shock.

In actuality, there was only one true subject in the experiment—the teacher. The learner was really a confederate of the experimenter. The supposed random assignment of participants to teacher and learner conditions had been rigged in advance. The real purpose of the experiment was to assess how much electric shock the teachers would administer to the learners in the face of the latter's increasingly adamant protestations to stop. This included numerous realistic cries of agony and complaints of a heart condition, all standardized, predetermined, tape-recorded messages delivered via the intercom from the learner's to the teacher's room. If the subject (i.e., the teacher) refused to deliver any further shocks, the experimenter prodded him with comments such as "The experiment requires that you go on," and "You have no other choice; you must go on."

Before Milgram conducted his experiment, he asked mental health professionals what proportion of the subjects would administer apparently dangerous levels of shock. The consensus was that only a negligible percentage would do so, perhaps 1 or 2 percent of the population. Milgram's actual results were dramatically inconsistent with what any of the experts had predicted. Fully 70 percent of the subjects carried through with their orders, albeit sometimes with great personal anguish, and delivered the maximum shock possible—450 volts!

Source: S. Milgram, "Behavioral Study of Obedience." *Journal of Abnormal and Social Psychology* 67, 1963, pp. 371–78.

followers generally uses her referent power to influence them. During crises or emergency situations, however, leaders may be more apt to draw on their legitimate and coercive bases of power to influence subordinates. That was precisely the finding in a study of bank managers' actions; the bank managers were more apt to use legitimate and coercive power during crises than during noncrisis situations (Mulder, de Jong, Koppelar, & Verhage, 1986). This same phenomenon is observable in many dramatizations. In the television series "Star Trek, the Next Generation," for example, Captain Picard normally uses his referent and expert power to influence subordinates. During emergencies, however, he will often rely on his legitimate and coercive power. Another factor may be that during crises followers are more willing to accept greater direction, control, and structure from leaders, whatever power base may be involved.

INFLUENCE TACTICS

Whereas power is the capacity or potential to influence others, influence tactics are the actual behaviors used by an agent to change the attitudes, opinions, or behaviors of a target person. Kipnis and his associates accomplished much of the early work on the types of influence tactics one person uses to influence another, and developed the Profile of Organizational Influence Strategies (POIS) to assess these behaviors (Kipnis & Schmidt, 1982). Several methodological problems, however, limit the usefulness of this instrument (Schriesheim & Hinkin, 1990). For example, influence tactics are evaluated only from the perspective of the influencing agent; the target's perceptions are ignored. Others, fortunately, have developed an alternative measure of influence tactics: the Influence Behavior Questionnaire, or IBQ (Yukl, Lepsinger, & Lucia, 1992). The IBQ is completed by both agents and targets, and appears to be a more valid instrument than the POIS. The following is a more detailed discussion of the tactics assessed by the IBQ.

Types of Influence Tactics

The IBQ is designed to assess nine types of influence tactics. **Rational persuasion** occurs when an agent uses logical arguments or factual evidence to influence others. Agents make **inspirational appeals** when they make a request or proposal designed to arouse enthusiasm or emotions in targets. **Consultation** occurs when agents ask targets to participate in planning an activity, and **ingratiation** occurs when the agent attempts to get you in a good mood before making a request. Agents use **personal appeals** when they ask another to do a favor out of friendship, whereas influencing a target through the exchange of favors is labeled **exchange**. **Coalition tactics** are different from consultation in that they are used when agents seek the aid or support of others to influence the target. Threats or persistent reminders used to influence targets are known as **pressure tactics**, and **legitimizing tactics** occur when agents make requests based on their position or authority.

Influence Tactics and Power

As alluded to throughout this chapter, a strong relationship exists between the powers possessed by agents and targets, and the type of influence tactic used by the agent to modify the attitudes, values, or behavior of a target. Because leaders with relatively high amounts of referent power have built up close relationships with followers, they may be more able to use a wide variety of influence tactics to modify the attitudes and behaviors of their followers. For example, leaders with a lot of referent power could use inspirational appeals, consultations, ingratiation, personal appeals, exchanges, and even coalition tactics to increase the amount of time a particular follower spends doing work-related activities. Note, however, that leaders with high referent power generally do not use legitimizing or pressure tactics to influence followers since by threatening followers leaders risk some loss of referent power. Leaders who have only coercive or legitimate power may be able to use only coalition, legitimizing, or pressure tactics to influence followers. In this case, coalition tactics are just pressure tactics one step removed, as these leaders can threaten other followers with disciplinary action if they do not persuade a fellow follower to change his attitudes or behavior.

Other factors also can affect the choice of influence tactics (Kipnis & Schmidt, 1985). People typically use hard tactics (i.e., the legitimizing or pressure tactics of the IBQ) when an influencer has the upper hand, when she anticipates resistance, or when the other person's behavior violates important norms. People typically use soft tactics (e.g., ingratiation) when they are at a disadvantage, when they expect resistance, or when they will personally benefit if the attempt is successful. People typically use rational tactics (i.e., the exchange and rational appeals tactics of the IBQ) when parties are relatively equal in power, when resistance is not anticipated, and when the benefits are organizational as well as personal.

Other studies, too, have shown that influence attempts based on factual, logical analyses are the most frequently reported method by which middle managers exert lateral influence (Keys, Case, Miller, Curran, & Jones, 1987) and upward influence (Case, Dosier, Murkison, & Keys, 1988). Other important components of successful influence of one's superiors included thorough preparation beforehand; involving others for support (i.e., coalition tactics); and persistence through a combination of approaches (Case, Dosier, Murkison, & Keys, 1988).

Findings about who uses different tactics, and when, provide interesting insights into the influence process. It is clear that one's influence tactic of choice depends on many factors, including intended outcomes and one's power relative to the target person. Whereas it may not be very surprising that people select influence tactics as a function of their power relationship with another person, it is striking that the relationship holds true so universally across different social domains. The relationship holds true for business executives, for parents and children, and for spouses. There is a strong tendency for people to resort to hard tactics whenever they have an advantage in clout if other tactics fail to get results (Kipnis & Schmidt, 1985). As the bank robber Willie Sutton once said, ''A gun and a smile are more effective than a smile by itself.'' This sentiment is apparently familiar to bank managers, too. The latter reported greater satisfaction in handling subordinates' poor performance when they were relatively more punishing (Green, Fairhurst, & Snavely, 1986).

Although hard tactics can be effective, relying on them can change the way we see others. This was demonstrated in an experiment wherein leaders' perceptions and evaluations of subordinates were assessed after they exercised different sorts of authority over the subordinates (Kipnis, 1984). Several hundred business students acted as managers of small work groups assembling model cars. Some of the students were told to act in an authoritarian manner, exercising complete control over the group's work; others were told to act as democratic leaders, letting group members participate fully in decisions about the work. As expected, authoritarian leaders used more hard tactics whereas democratic leaders influenced subordinates more through rational methods. More interesting was the finding that subordinates were evaluated by the two types of leaders in dramatically different ways even though the subordinates of both types did equally good work. Authoritarian leaders judged their subordinates as less motivated, less skilled, and less suited for promotion. Apparently, bosses who use hard tactics to control others' behavior tend not to attribute any resultant good performance to the subordinates themselves. Ironically, the act of using hard tactics leads to negative attributions about others, which, in turn, tend to corroborate the use of hard tactics in the first place.

Concluding Thoughts about Influence Tactics

In the above discussion, an implicit lesson for leaders is the value of being conscious of what influence tactics one uses and what effects are typically associated with each tactic. Knowledge of such effects can help a leader make better decisions about her manner of influencing others. It might also be helpful for leaders to think more carefully about why they believe a particular influence tactic might be effective. Research indicates that some reasons for selecting among various possible influence tactics lead to successful outcomes more frequently than others. More specifically, thinking an act would improve an employee's self-esteem or morale was frequently associated with successful influence attempts. On the other hand, choosing an influence tactic because it followed company policy and choosing one because it was a way to put a subordinate in his place were frequently mentioned as reasons for unsuccessful influence attempts (Dosier, Case, & Keys, 1988). In a nutshell, these results suggest that leaders should pay attention not only to the actual influence tactics they use—to *how* they are influencing others—but also to *why* they believe such methods are called for. It is consistent with these results to conclude that influence efforts intended to build others up more frequently lead to positive outcomes than influence efforts intended to put others down.

SUMMARY

This chapter has defined power as the capacity or potential to exert influence; influence tactics as the behaviors used by one person to modify the attitudes and behaviors of another; and influence as the degree of change in a person's attitudes, values, or behaviors as the result of another's influence tactic. Because power, influence, and influence tactics play such an important role in the leadership process, this chapter provides ideas to help leadership practitioners improve their effectiveness. Leadership practitioners can help themselves become more effective by reflecting on their leadership situation and considering the relative amounts of the five bases of social power both they and their followers possess. By reflecting on their bases of power, leadership practitioners can better understand how they can affect followers and how they can expand the amount of power they possess. In addition, the five bases of power also provide clues as to why subordinates are able to influence leaders and successfully resist leaders' influence attempts.

Leaders also may gain insight about why they may not enjoy their job by considering their own need for power or motivation to manage, or may better understand why some leaders exercise power selfishly by considering McClelland's concepts of personalized power and activity inhibition. Leaders can improve their effectiveness by finding ways to build their idiosyncratic credits and by not permitting in-group and out-group relationships to develop in their work unit. Furthermore, noting titles, clothing, office arrangements, or seating arrangements during meetings can give one hints about power differentials within the organization and ways to improve the perceptions others have of the leadership practitioner's own power.

Although power is an extremely important concept, having power is relatively meaningless unless a leader is willing to exercise it. The exercise of power occurs primarily through the influence tactics leaders and followers use to modify the attitudes and behaviors of each other. The types of influence tactics used seems to depend on the amount of different types of power possessed, the degree of resistance expected, and the rationale behind the different influence tactics. Because influence tactics designed to build up others are generally more successful than those that tear down others, leadership practitioners should always consider why they are using a particular influence attempt before they actually use it. By carefully considering the rationale behind the tactic, leaders may be able to avoid using pressure and legitimizing tactics and to find ways to influence followers that build them up rather than tear them down. Being able to use influence tactics that modify followers' attitudes and behaviors in the desired direction at the same time they build up followers' self-esteem and self-confidence should be a skill all leaders strive to master.

KEY TERMS AND CONCEPTS

power	social exchange theory
influence	in-group
influence tactics	out-group
expert power	idiosyncrasy credits
referent power	transactional approach to leadership
legitimate power	rational persuasion
reward power	inspirational appeals
coercive power	consultation
need for power	ingratiation
personalized power	personal appeals
socialized power	exchange
projective personality test	coalition tactics
motivation to manage	pressure tactics
vertical dyad linkage (VDL) theory	legitimizing tactics

DISCUSSION QUESTIONS

1. The following questions all pertain to the Milgram studies (Highlight 6–3):
   a. What bases of power were available to the experimenter, and what bases of power were available to the subjects?
   b. Do you think subjects with a low need for power would act differently from those subjects with a high need for power? What about subjects with differing levels of the motivation to manage?

  c. What situational factors contributed to the experimenter's power?
  d. What influence tactics did the experimenter use to change the behavior of the subjects, and how were these tactics related to the experimenter's power base?
  e. What actually was influenced? In other words, if influence is the change in another's attitudes, values, or behaviors as the result of an influence tactic, then what changes occurred in the subject as the result of the experimenter's influence tactics?
  f. Many people have criticized the Milgram study on ethical grounds. Assuming that some socially useful information was gained from the studies, do you believe this experiment could or should be replicated today?

2. Some definitions of leadership exclude reliance on formal authority or coercion (i.e., certain actions by a person in authority may "work" but should not be considered leadership). What are the pros and cons of such a view?

3. Does power, as Lord Acton suggested, tend to corrupt the power holder? If so, what are some of the ways it happens? Is it also possible subordinates are "corrupted" by a superior's power? How? Or even that superiors can be "corrupted" by a subordinate's power?

4. Some people say it dilutes a leader's authority if subordinates are allowed to give feedback to the leader concerning their perceptions of the leader's performance. Do you agree?

5. Is leadership just another word for influence? Can you think of some examples of influence that you would *not* consider leadership?

SUGGESTED READINGS

Clifford, C. *Counsel to the President.* New York: Random House, 1991.

Greiner, L. E., and V. E. Schein. *Power and Organization Development.* Reading, Mass.: Addison-Wesley, 1988.

McClelland, D. C. *Power: The Inner Experience.* New York: Irvington, 1975.

P A R T

II

FOCUS ON THE LEADER

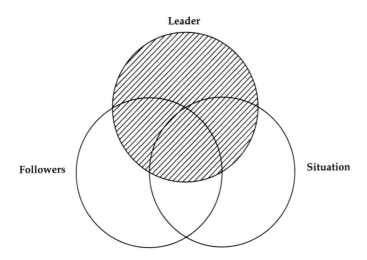

P art II focuses on the leader. The effectiveness of leadership, good or bad, is typically attributed to the leader much more than to the other elements of the model. Sometimes the leader is the only element of leadership we even think of. One great leader's views were clear enough about the relative importance of leaders and followers:

Men are nothing; it is the man who is everything. . . . It was not the Roman army that conquered Gaul, but Caesar; it was not the Carthaginian army that made Rome tremble in her gates, but Hannibal; it was not the Macedonian army that reached the Indus, but Alexander.

Napoleon

Because the leader plays such an important role in the leadership process, the next three chapters of this book review the research related to leaders' qualities, characteristics, and behaviors and, in turn, their contributions to leadership effectiveness and success. Chapter Seven reviews the evidence concerning the usefulness of using intelligence and personality traits to predict leadership effectiveness and success. Chapter Seven also provides several ideas on how to improve the observed relationships between intelligence, personality traits, and leadership success. Chapter Eight examines the relationships between leaders' values, attitudes, and preferences and leadership success and effectiveness. Chapter Nine reviews the research concerning leader behaviors and provides leadership practitioners with advice on how to improve their skills in order to enhance their own effectiveness.

Although the material in these three chapters is reviewed from the leader's perspective, it is important to remember that the followers also can vary considerably in the cognitive abilities, personality traits, attitudes, values, interests, preferences, and skills they possess, and these differences can have a substantial impact on the leadership process. For example, leaders probably will need to use a different set of influence tactics to successfully change the work behaviors of relatively skilled versus relatively unskilled followers. These differences in abilities, traits, values, and skills among leaders and followers, combined with the situational factors that can affect both parties, are what makes leadership often too difficult to study in its combined form. For this reason, we have chosen to break the leadership process down into component parts for analysis. Much like we use prisms to break down white light into its component parts, we can better understand leadership behaviors by examining the factors that affect the way leaders act. As seen in Figure II–1, there are a number of factors that influence leader behaviors, and the next three parts of this book are designed to provide fairly comprehensive explanations of the major components affecting the leadership process.

FIGURE II–1
The Leadership Prism

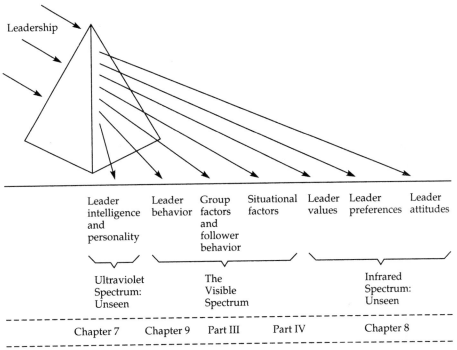

The complex and interrelated aspects of leadership can be analyzed separately. No aspect by itself is the whole, but we can understand the whole in helpful ways through such analysis.

Chapter Seven

Intelligence, Personality, and Leadership

INTRODUCTION

Perhaps the earliest theory of leadership was the **Great Man theory** (Stogdill, 1974). This theory, popular in the early 1900s, stated that leaders were fundamentally different from followers. More specifically, this theory was based on the premise that leaders were both more capable and possessed a different set of personality traits than followers. Although the Great Man theory generated a considerable amount of research, the general conclusion from it all was that leaders were not fundamentally different from followers. This lack of support for the Great Man theory was due primarily to the diversity of successful leaders. This diversity among successful leaders is evident in the following excerpt from sports commentator Howard Cosell's memoirs:

> Whom would you rather have dinner with—Pete Rozelle or Al Davis? If you had asked me that question several years ago, I wouldn't have hesitated. The answer is Rozelle. He is a charming, deferential man. He's got a sharp mind and an engaging sense of humor. The atmosphere is relaxed, the conversation convival, and he embraces you with the kind of warmth and attention that makes you feel like a special friend.
>
> Davis couldn't relax in a hot tub. He's always tense, charged up, his eyes working a room as if he were looking for snipers. And the talk is football, always football, whether it be on-the-field strategy, executive intrigue, or courtroom drama. The conversation is more often than not absorbing, but by the time the check is deposited on the table, you feel like you've just walked through the middle of Beirut during an air raid. You're shell-shocked. That's Davis's style. (Cosell, 1985, p. 82)

Both Pete Rozelle and Al Davis were extremely successful leaders in the National Football League, yet they were miles apart in personality and style. Although effective leaders can be quite diverse, the consensus among leadership researchers today is that there are characteristics or qualities leaders tend to share even if no two leaders will ever be mirror images of each other (also see Highlight 7-1).

In this chapter, we will examine whether intelligence and personality traits are among the qualities successful leaders tend to share. As an overview, this chapter first reviews the research regarding the relationship between intelligence and leadership. This section briefly describes some of the controversies surrounding intelligence, how intelligence is typically assessed, and whether intelligence is a useful predictor of leadership success. The next section in this chapter examines research concerning the relationships between various personality traits and leadership effectiveness. This section defines personality and personality traits, describes how personality traits are typically assessed, and provides an overview of the major findings concerning personality traits and leadership effectiveness. The last section in the chapter offers brief descriptions of the personality traits most related to leadership effectiveness or emergence.

INTELLIGENCE AND LEADERSHIP

What Is Intelligence?

"Perhaps no concept in the history of psychology has had or continues to have as great an impact on everyday life in the Western world as that of general intelligence" (Scarr, 1989, p. 75). Overwhelming evidence exists to support the notion that general intelligence plays a substantial role in human affairs (Hum-

---

HIGHLIGHT 7–1

Leadership Quotes, Chapter Seven

The question, ''Who ought to be boss?'' is like asking, ''Who ought to be the tenor in the quartet?'' Obviously, the man who can sing tenor.

Henry Ford

If the blind lead the blind, both shall fall into the ditch.

The Bible (Matt. 15:14)

A little learning is not a dangerous thing to one who does not mistake it for a great deal.

William Allen White

A little learning is a dangerous thing, but a lot of ignorance is just as bad.

Bob Edwards

If a man be gloomy, let him keep to himself. No one has a right to go croaking about society, or what is worse, looking as if he stifled grief.

Benjamin Disraeli

O wad some Power the giftie gie us
to see ourselves as others see us!

Robert Burns

The first method for estimating the intelligence of a ruler is to look at the men he has around him.

Machiavelli

---

phreys, 1984; Ree & Earles, 1992; Schmidt & Hunter, 1992). Still, intelligence and intelligence testing are highly controversial topics. Although controversies abound concerning a definition of intelligence, the number of separate or distinct abilities that may make up intelligence, the role of heredity and the environment in intelligence, the use of intelligence tests in public schools, and ethnic group differences in average intelligence test scores, we will bypass such controversies here. Our focus will be on the relationship between intelligence and leadership. (See Brody, 1992; Cronbach, 1984; Humphreys, 1984; and Linn, 1989 for more complete reviews of the controversies.)

We define **intelligence** as a person's all-around effectiveness in activities directed by thought (Cronbach, 1984). This definition suggests intelligence is a general, unitary ability. Although separate tests have been developed to assess different mental activities, scores on these tests tend to be highly correlated, implying a general intelligence factor underlying diverse, specific mental activities. Our definition also implies that intelligence is an unseen quality. It is not as easily measured as a person's height or weight and can only be inferred by observing behavior. However, it does not affect behavior equally across all situations. Some activities, such as relatively routine ones, may put less of a premium on intelligence than others where innovation or conceptualization may be required. Finally, we should point out that our definition of intelligence does *not* imply that intelligence is a fixed quantity. Although heredity plays a role, intelligence can be modified through education and experience (Cronbach, 1984; Humphreys, 1989).

Assessing Intelligence

Psychologists typically use tests to assess intelligence. Many different intelligence tests have been developed, partly because psychologists do not agree on a common definition of intelligence. Two of the more common are the Stanford-Binet and the Weschler Adult Intelligence Scale–Revised (WAIS–R). They are both administered individually, and both assess many of the same types of mental abilities such as vocabulary, spatial perception, memory, inductive reasoning, numerical reasoning, and reasoning by analogy.

Intelligence quotient (IQ) scores are calculated from the overall results for both the Stanford-Binet and the WAIS–R, and are often used as measures of general intelligence. The average American has an IQ of 100, and only 3 percent of the population have scores above 130, with an equal percentage below 70. Although some researchers have argued intelligence tests like the Stanford-Binet and WAIS–R primarily measure thinking in terms of white, middle-class values, there is overwhelming evidence showing IQ scores are useful predictors of a number of socially significant phenomena (Humphreys, 1984). General intelligence is often associated with level of education achieved, success in school, occupational choice, and performance within an occupation (Ree & Earles, 1992; Scarr, 1989; Schmidt & Hunter, 1992).

Implications for Leaders

Because intelligence is related to occupational choice and performance, a number of researchers have examined the relationship between intelligence and leadership effectiveness, success, or emergence. Most researchers have used the correlational approach described in Chapter Four to explore the relationship between intelligence and leadership. In many of these studies, researchers have administered intelligence tests to leaders and then collected data about the level of performance of the leaders' work units, the leaders' latest performance appraisal ratings, or the hierarchical levels leaders had achieved in the organization. For example, Bray, Campbell, and Grant (1974) and Bray and Howard (1983) reported that scores from intelligence tests administered up to 20 years earlier were positively related to managerial success in terms of promotions, organizational levels, and salaries at AT&T. Other researchers have administered intelligence tests to members of small, leaderless groups and then asked the group to perform a series of tasks. Group members would be asked to rate or rank order each other in terms of the leadership behaviors exhibited. Leadership researchers would then determine whether there is a positive correlation between intelligence test scores and leadership emergence ratings or rankings (i.e., are smarter people more likely to emerge as leaders?).

There have been 200 separate studies that have examined the relationship between intelligence and leadership effectiveness or emergence, and these studies have been the topic of major reviews by Stogdill (1948); Mann (1959); Ghiselli (1963); Stogdill (1974); Bray, Campbell, and Grant (1974); Cornwell (1983); Bray and Howard (1983); Lord, DeVader, and Allinger (1986); Bass (1990); and Fiedler (1992). Most of these reviews reported the relationship between intelligence and leadership to be in the $r = .3$ range. However, Lord, DeVader, and Allinger (1986) used advanced statistical techniques to estimate the true correlation between intelligence and leadership emergence to be $r = .5$. Thus, the 10 reviews listed above provide overwhelming support for the idea that leadership effectiveness or emergence is positively correlated with intelligence.

What do these findings mean to the leadership practitioner? First, it is important to note the correlation between intelligence and leadership emergence and effectiveness is far from perfect. The smartest people are not always the best leaders. Moreover, the magnitude of the correlation between intelligence and leadership effectiveness may depend on the situation. Intelligence may be a better predictor of success in certain leadership roles than in others. Intelligence alone is *not* a guarantee of leadership success.

Second, both Ghiselli (1963) and Stogdill (1974) noted that intelligence has a curvilinear relationship with leadership effectiveness. It is possible for leaders to be too smart; leaders who are substantially smarter than their followers may not be as effective as leaders who are just slightly smarter than their followers. When differences in intelligence between leader and followers are too great, communication can be impaired; a leader's intelligence can become an impediment to being understood by subordinates (Bass, 1990).

An alternative explanation for the curvilinear relationship between intelligence and leadership effectiveness may have to do with how stress affects leader-subordinate interactions. It may be that some studies in which more intelligent leaders were less effective primarily examined leadership challenges that were highly stressful. In that regard, Fiedler (1992) and Gibson (1992) found that smart, inexperienced leaders were less effective in stressful situations than less intelligent, experienced leaders. An example of this finding was clearly demonstrated in the movie *Platoon*. In one frantic scene, an American platoon is ambushed by the Vietcong, and an inexperienced, college-educated lieutenant calls for artillery support from friendly units. He calls in the wrong coordinates, however, and as a result artillery shells are dropped on his own platoon's, rather than the enemy's, position. The situation comes under control only after an experienced sergeant sizes up the situation and tells the artillery unit to cease firing.

PERSONALITY TRAITS AND LEADERSHIP

What Is Personality?

According to Robert Hogan (1991), the term **personality** has two quite different meanings. Sometimes it refers to the way a person is perceived by friends, family members, co-workers, or supervisors. This meaning of personality is derived from the observer's perspective and concerns a person's social reputation; it reflects an evaluation of one person in the eyes of others. Thus, when we say a person is stingy, aloof, or cold we are making evaluative judgments about that person's social reputation. The term *personality* also can have a somewhat different meaning. It can refer to the underlying, unseen structures and processes "inside" a person that explain why the person behaves in a characteristic manner. This meaning refers to one's private, inner nature, whereas the other meaning refers to a person's public reputation.

We will look at personality primarily as the structures and processes that cause a person to act in a characteristic manner (i.e., in terms of the second meaning above). Furthermore, although the various theoretical perspectives of personality (e.g., psychodynamic, humanistic, behavioral, trait, and phenomenological approaches) provide alternative explanations for the characteristic ways people behave, the next two sections of this chapter are devoted primarily to the **trait** approach (see Highlights 7–2 through 7–6). Most of the research addressing the relationship between personality and leadership effectiveness or emergence has been based on the trait approach, and that emphasis is appropriate here.

"Traits refer to recurring regularities or trends in a person's behavior" (R. Hogan, 1991, p. 875), and the trait approach to personality maintains that people behave the way they do because of the strengths of the traits they possess. For example, we would infer that a person scoring high on the trait of dependability would usually come to work on time, do a thorough job in completing work assignments, and never leave work early. We would infer a person scor-

---

HIGHLIGHT 7–2

Personality and the Presidency, I

Traits are unseen dispositions that can affect the way people act. Their existence can be inferred by a person's consistent pattern of behaviors. One way of examining a person's standing on the traits of achievement orientation and persistence is to examine his or her achievements and accomplishments over his or her life span. For example, consider the following leader's achievements and accomplishments, think about this person's standing on these two personality traits, and try to guess who this person might be:

Age 23: lost a job.

Age 23: was defeated in bid for state legislature.

Age 24: failed in business venture.

Age 25: was elected to legislature.

Age 26: sweetheart died.

Age 27: experienced several emotional problems.

Age 27: was defeated in bid to be speaker of the house.

Age 34: was defeated for nomination to Congress.

Age 37: was elected to Congress.

Age 39: lost renomination to Congress.

Age 40: was defeated in bid for land office.

Age 45: was defeated in bid for U.S. Senate.

Age 47: was defeated for nomination to be vice president.

Age 49: was defeated in bid for Senate a second time.

Age 51: was elected president of the United States.

The person was Abraham Lincoln.

---

ing low on the trait of dependability would frequently be late to work, often forget to turn in assignments, or call in sick frequently. Although traits cannot be seen, they can be inferred from consistent patterns of behavior.

The trait approach does not assume traits are the only causes of behavior. Rather, it maintains behavior reflects an interaction between a person's traits and various situational factors (see, for example, Highlight 7–3). Traits play a particularly important role in determining how people behave in novel, ambiguous, or what we might call "weak" situations. On the other hand, situations that are governed by clearly specified rules, demands, or organizational policies—"strong" situations—often minimize the effects traits have on behavior.

HIGHLIGHT 7–3

Personality and the Presidency, II

One way of determining the personality traits of presidents is to analyze their inaugural addresses, and researchers have found that those presidents whose speeches expressed greater needs for power and achievement tended to be the most innovative and dynamic. A similar approach has been used to study a president's psychological compatibility with the general populace and how that affected presidential leadership. Winter assessed achievement, affiliation, and power motives (which generally correspond to the achievement orientation, sociability, and dominance traits described in Table 7–1) in presidents and compared them with the levels of these needs in the American society at large during each presidency. He assessed motive strength in presidents by scoring achievement, affiliation, and power images in each president's first inaugural address. The strength of each motive in the broader American society was measured by analysis of the three themes in several common sorts of cultural documents (an approach that had been successfully used in previous research) including popular novels, children's readers, and hymns. Finally, Winter measured leader appeal (e.g., percentage of vote) and leader performance (e.g., ratings of greatness by historians).

In general, Winter found the congruence or match between a president's psychological motives and the society's had opposite relationships with leader appeal versus leader performance. Presidents were popular when their psychological profiles closely mirrored the predominant cultural psyche. Conversely, however, the most effective presidents were psychologically at variance with the national mood and character. One example is Abraham Lincoln, regarded as one of the two greatest presidents, who was elected in 1860 with only a minority of the popular vote. These findings of an inverse relationship between leader appeal and performance, which are inconsistent with much other leadership research, may be partly attributable to differences between the nature of effectiveness in national and world affairs, which occurs over years and may only be fully assessed decades later, and the nature of effectiveness on shorter-term leadership tasks.

Sources: D. G. Winter. "Leader Appeal, Leader Performance, and the Motive Profiles of Leaders and Followers: A Study of American Presidents and Elections. *Journal of Personality and Social Psychology* 52, 1987, pp. 196–202; and R. E. Donley and D. G. Winter. Measuring the Motives of Public Officials at a Distance: An Exploratory Study of American Presidents. *Behavioral Science* 15, 1970, pp. 227–36.

The following is an example of how a personality trait may exert greater or lesser influence on a person's behavior depending on the strength of the situation. Suppose someone has personality traits of high interpersonal aggressiveness, hostility, and impatience. How might such a person drive in traffic? The answer is, it depends somewhat on whether any particular traffic situation is

HIGHLIGHT 7–4

Personality and the Presidency, III

Simonton also has studied the effect of personality on presidential leadership. He studied the leadership styles of all the U.S. presidents. Using personality sketches abstracted verbatim from standard biographical sources, he had a set of judges independently rate each of the presidents on personality factors like intellectual brilliance, flexibility, power, achievement, affiliation, dominance, friendliness, and extroversion. Analysis of these ratings produced a set of five different presidential styles of leadership.

He also showed that these five styles were related to objective measures of presidential performance. Both the charismatic and creative styles were positively correlated with the number of significant acts passed during a president's time in office. Interestingly, both styles are also more likely targets of assassination attempts. Both the interpersonal and deliberative styles are less prone to experience Cabinet resignations. The creative president is more inclined than the charismatic to serve longer in the White House. On the other hand, the charismatic president is more likely than the creative president to promulgate executive orders. Interpersonal presidents have better relations with Congress than deliberative presidents, though deliberative presidents are less likely to see a scandal break out during their administration.

Here are the "best and worst" of 20th-century presidents on five stylistic dimensions

	Interpersonal	Charisma	Deliberative	Creative	Neurotic
High	Ford	FDR	McKinley Kennedy	FDR Nixon	LBJ
Low	Wilson Nixon	Coolidge	Truman	Taft	Reagan

Source: D. Simonton, Presidential Style: Personality, Biography, and Performance. *Journal of Personality and Social Psychology* 55, 1988, pp. 928–36.

weak or strong. Some situations, like waiting at a red light or being followed by a police car, are so strong most people will behave the same (i.e., they will wait until the light turns green or obey all traffic laws) whatever their personality traits may be. In weaker traffic situations, however, like driving behind a car going very slowly in the fast lane, we might expect the driver's behavior to reflect his personality traits to a much greater degree. The driver described above might be much more likely to curse out loud, honk the horn, or make unwelcome gestures to the car ahead when he finally passes it than another driver might who is lower on those same traits. Similarly, traits may have the greatest impact on leadership behavior in relatively weak situations.

Assessing Personality Traits

Although personality traits can be inferred by observing an individual's consistent patterns of behavior, personality traits are usually assessed using personality tests. As opposed to tests of maximal performance (e.g., intelligence tests), personality tests are designed to assess typical behavior (Campbell, Dunnette, Lawler, & Weick, 1970). There are basically two types of tests used to assess personality traits. One type, the **projective personality test**, was described in Chapter Six. The other type, the **objective personality test**, typically consists of a standard set of items such as adjectives, statements, or questions. Subjects are asked to indicate the extent to which certain adjectives, questions, or statements are descriptive of them. Usually, the strength of any trait is a function of the number and strength of the ratings for adjectives or items endorsed. Examples of adjective-based tests are the Adjective Check List (Gough & Heilbrun, 1987) and the Campbell Leadership Index (Campbell, 1991). Examples of other objective personality tests include the Hogan Personality Inventory (Hogan, 1986), the California Psychological Inventory (Gough, 1987), and the NEO-PI (Costa & McCrae, 1985).

Leadership researchers investigating the relationship between personality traits and leadership effectiveness or emergence generally use the same methods as those used to investigate the relationship between intelligence and leadership. Researchers typically examine either the relationships between leaders' personality traits and performance (as assessed by appraisal ratings or indices of work-unit performance) or relationships between members' personality traits and leadership emergence ratings or rankings in leaderless groups.

Personality Traits Associated with Leadership Effectiveness

Although no personality trait guarantees leadership success in all situations, some traits are more consistently related to leadership success than others. These are listed in Table 7–1, and described in greater detail below.

TABLE 7–1
Personality Traits Related to Leadership

Emergence and effectiveness
Dominance
Self-confidence
Achievement orientation
Dependability
Energy and activity level
Self-monitoring
Locus of control
Tolerance for ambiguity
Adjustment
Sociability
Agreeableness

Dominance. **Dominance**, which is conceptually similar to the need for power, has been consistently related to leadership success (Bass, 1990; Gough, 1988; Lord, DeVader, & Allinger, 1986; Stogdill, 1948, 1974). Individuals high in dominance like to be leaders, try to influence others, and work to establish and maintain control of the groups they are in. They tend to be confident, forceful, outspoken, and opinionated. Individuals low in dominance are more likely to be content in follower roles. They are often seen as meek, mild, modest, and unassuming. Bass (1990) pointed out that it is possible for some leaders to be too dominant; followers may be dissatisfied with leaders who are too bossy and maintain an "iron grip" on the work unit.

Self-confidence. **Self-confidence** is the degree to which individuals feel comfortable with their own judgment, abilities, or skills. Individuals with little self-confidence hesitate to take risks and feel uncomfortable relying on their own decisions. Research has shown that leaders with high self-confidence tend to be more successful than leaders with low self-confidence (Bass, 1990; Kaplan, 1986; Willner, 1984). However, leaders with too much self-confidence can be obstinate and may harbor unrealistic, inflated pictures of themselves.

Achievement orientation. Individuals high in **achievement orientation**, or the need for achievement, strive to successfully complete tasks and activities primarily for the satisfaction gained by accomplishing a challenging goal. These individuals tend to be hardworking, ambitious, and competitive. Individuals low in achievement orientation tend to be unambitious, complacent, and passive, and they may put forth relatively little effort to complete tasks unless they are promised some type of extrinsic reward. Not surprisingly,

HIGHLIGHT 7–5

Personality and the Presidency, IV: The Toughness of Harry Truman

Historians consider Harry Truman one of the greatest American presidents, and many older Americans consider him one of their favorites. However, he also was an unexpected president in two different ways. He first assumed the presidency when Franklin Delano Roosevelt died, and he won election to the presidency in his own right very unexpectedly in 1948. When Harry Truman defeated Thomas Dewey, the highly favored Republican candidate, it was the upset of the century. In the final weeks of the campaign, a poll of 50 political experts indicated every one of them predicted a GOP landslide (Clifford, 1991). You may have seen the famous pictures of Truman grinning and holding a newspaper with the premature and embarrassingly erroneous headline ''Dewey Defeats Truman.''

Clark Clifford, a key advisor to Truman during that campaign, and to numerous presidents since then, saw one reason for Truman's victory transcending all others—the man himself. Truman's tenacity and unwillingness to give up when few others held out any hope made the difference. This is one example of how personality made a significant difference in national leadership. Following are a few of Harry Truman's more famous quotations, which convey his toughness.

> *I told them I knew they had been making trouble for the previous commanders. I said: ''I didn't come over here to get along with you. You've got to get along with me. And if there are any of you who can't, speak up and I'll bust you right back.'' We got along.*

>> Captain Harry S. Truman
>> On taking command of a field
>> artillery battalion, 1918

> *If you need a friend in Washington, get a dog.*

> *A president who's any damn good at all makes enemies, makes a lot of them. I made a few myself and I wouldn't be without them.*

> *The buck stops here.*
> (a sign on his desk)

In December 1950, President Truman's daughter, Margaret, gave a public singing recital in Washington, which was unenthusiastically received by Paul Hume, the *Washington Post*'s music critic. He characterized her voice as having ''little size and fair quality,'' said she sang flat much of the time, and complained that there were ''few moments . . . when one can relax and feel confident that she will make her goal, which is the end of the song.''

HIGHLIGHT 7–5 *(concluded)*

Truman penned the following letter:

I have just read your lousy review buried in the back pages. You sound like a frustrated old man who never made a success, an eight-ulcer man on a four-ulcer job, and all four ulcers working. I have never met you, but if I do you'll need a new nose and plenty of beefsteak and perhaps a supporter below. Westbrook Pegler, a gutter-snipe, is a gentleman compared to you. You can take that as more of an insult than as a reflection on your ancestry.

This letter was made public and caused a considerable furor, but most Americans seem generally to have approved Truman's fatherly readiness to leap to his daughter's defense.

Source: Adapted from Clifton Fadiman, ed., *The Little, Brown Book of Anecdotes* (Boston: Little, Brown, 1985); and William Safir and Leonard Safir, eds., *Leadership* (New York: Simon & Schuster, 1990).

achievement orientation has been consistently associated with leadership success (Bass, 1990; Hall & Donnell, 1979; McClelland & Boyatzis, 1982). However, it may be possible for leaders to be too achievement-oriented. Leaders who are extremely achievement-oriented may have difficulty delegating tasks to subordinates.

Dependability.   Leaders high in **dependability** or conscientiousness tend to be conservative, careful, responsible, and reliable. They tend to have regular work habits, readily follow established rules, and meet their commitments. Individuals low in dependability tend to be impulsive, reckless, irresponsible, and thrill-seeking. Although dependability has been found to be positively related to job performance across a variety of jobs (Barrick & Mount, 1991; Tett, Jackson, & Rothstein, 1991) and with leadership emergence and effectiveness (Bass, 1990), individuals with extremely high scores may be hard to work with because of their rigidity and inflexibility.

Energy and activity level.   Leaders with high **energy and activity levels** are generally found to be more successful than leaders who do not exhibit a lot of energy or activity, and many good leaders are noted for their indefatigable constitutions (Bass, 1990; Bray, Campbell, & Grant, 1974; Bray & Howard, 1983). Leaders with high energy and activity levels work harder and produce greater output than associates with lower energy levels. For example, Bass (1990) described how several world-class leaders, such as Ataturk, Castro, or Lenin, could go for days on end with very little sleep or food. In addition to allowing leaders to accomplish more work, this high level of energy and activity may also be mirrored by their followers to some extent, thus indirectly affecting work-unit performance.

Self-monitoring.   As originally described by Snyder (1974), **high self-monitors** are particularly astute at picking up social and situational cues and adjusting their behavior accordingly. **Low self-monitors** are relatively insensitive to these cues, and their behavior is more unvarying and seemingly independent of interpersonal sensitivity or situational awareness. Zaccaro, Foti, and Kenny (1991) showed that high self-monitors were more likely to emerge as leaders in leaderless discussion groups than low self-monitors. However, it is important to remember that leadership emergence and effectiveness are *not* the same thing. Sometimes leaders who are low self-monitors may be effective, particularly if what is needed is a leader who will "stick to his guns" in order for the group, committee, or team to accomplish its goals (Hogan, R. T., Hogan, J., & Curphy, 1992).

Locus of control.   Rotter (1966) developed a self-assessment instrument to discriminate between people who feel their destiny is determined primarily by external forces, such as luck or fate (i.e., an **external locus of control**), and people who feel their destiny is largely determined by internal forces, such as abilities and skills (i.e., an **internal locus of control**). Mitchell, Smyser, and Weed (1975) reported that leaders with an internal locus of control were more likely to use reward, referent, and expert power to influence followers, whereas leaders with an external locus of control were more likely to influence followers using coercive power. Relatedly, Anderson and Schneier (1978) reviewed a number of studies that lend support to the idea that leaders who have an internal locus of control are more effective than leaders who have an external locus of control.

Tolerance for ambiguity.   People who have a high **tolerance for ambiguity** are relatively comfortable dealing with unstructured problems or uncertainty, whereas people with a low tolerance for ambiguity may become anxious when facing the same situations. Bass (1990); Bray, Campbell, and Grant (1974); and Stogdill, Goode, and Day (1964) all reported that tolerance for ambiguity was related to leadership emergence or effectiveness. Nevertheless, because the uncertainty surrounding different leadership positions tends to increase with organizational level, this trait may be more important for senior executives than for first-line supervisors (Bass, 1990).

Adjustment.   **Adjustment** refers to one's general emotional resilience and stability. Being well adjusted helps a person handle stress, frustration, conflict,

HIGHLIGHT 7–6

Is There a Military Mind?

To many, the word *leadership* is synonymous with military authority. It evokes images of uniforms, salutes, rank and insignia, and discipline. To some it suggests positive associations like the chain-of-command's clear lines of authority and responsibility, decisiveness, respect for authority, camaraderie, selfless commitment to a higher mission, and good discipline. Even individuals who never served in the military themselves may think of it as epitomizing good leaders and good leadership.

Others, however, do not have such a positive view. They may agree with Groucho Marx that military intelligence is a contradiction in terms. They may think of military leadership in mostly negative terms, promoting the sort of mindless inefficiency captured in this familiar soldier's adage:

If it moves, salute it.
If it doesn't move, pick it up.
If you can't pick it up, paint it!

What are military leaders really like? For approximately the past decade, all newly promoted generals in the U.S. Army have attended a special leadership development course at the Center for Creative Leadership. It included a significant emphasis on individual psychological feedback to the generals based on a comprehensive battery of psychological tests.

Psychologist David Campbell has extensively analyzed these test results, and his conclusions provide perhaps the best answers to questions about the psychological characteristics of military leaders. Campbell's analysis is based on a battery of psychological tests, including measures of intelligence, personality, and vocational preferences, as well as behavioral assessments based on performance during group exercises. It is a good example of how personality trait, ability, and preference measures all can be used in profiling commonalities among leaders in a particular sphere of activity.

Generals prove to be an extremely bright group, averaging at the 95th percentile of IQ for the general population. They scored higher, in fact, than a sample of corporate CEOs. In terms of personality, they are extremely dependable, socially mature, and alert to ethical and moral issues. They are more conventional (i.e., less innovative) in their approach to problem solving than other executive groups, but they still score right at the average for the overall population. In considering data from all sources, Campbell identified a common personality profile among the generals, which he termed The Aggressive Adventurer. This profile describes dominant, competitive, action-oriented, patriotic men drawn to physically adventurous activities.

Source: D. P. Campbell, "The Psychological Test Profiles of Brigadier Generals: Warmongers or Decisive Warriors?" Invited address presented to Division 14 of the American Psychological Association, New York, 1987.

and pressure adaptively and constructively. Research shows leaders who cope with stress well tend to be more effective (Bass, 1990; Bray, Campbell, & Grant, 1974; Fiedler, 1992; Gibson, 1992).

Sociability.   Individuals who are outgoing, expressive, humorous, and likely to initiate and sustain interactions with others are high in **sociability.** Individuals low in sociability tend to be interpersonally cautious, even somewhat withdrawn. Individuals who are outgoing and socially adept tend to exert greater influence in a group, and research has found this trait to be related to leadership emergence (Bass, 1990; Gough, 1988).

Agreeableness.   The trait of **agreeableness** indicates the extent to which individuals are trusting, cooperative, friendly, good-natured, and courteous. Agreeable people are easy to get along with, whereas those low on this trait tend to be moody, suspicious, aloof, intolerant, and relatively difficult to get along with. Researchers have found that leaders who show care, consideration, and trust toward subordinates are generally more effective than those who are less agreeable (Bass, 1990). Nevertheless, it is possible for leaders to be too agreeable. McClelland and Burnham (1976) reported that leaders with too high a need for affiliation, a related trait, were reluctant to use discipline when subordinates were disrupting group performance. They also tended to show favoritism when administering rewards.

Implications for Leaders

Most of the studies that have examined the relationship between intelligence and leadership also have examined the relationships between various personality traits and leadership effectiveness and emergence. Although many traits were positively correlated with leadership effectiveness and emergence, the magnitude of the correlations tended to be lower than those reported for intelligence and leadership emergence and effectiveness. Possessing certain personality traits does not guarantee leadership success (see Highlight 7–7 for further thoughts about this relationship).

What more should the practitioner understand about personality and leadership? Perhaps most important, leadership practitioners should gain an appreciation for the many ways in which leaders can differ. Few if any leaders have high scores on all of the traits found in Table 7–1. Instead, most leaders have some combination of high, medium, and low scores across those traits. Moreover, the leadership process becomes even more complicated when leaders' intelligence, values, preferences, and attitudes are added to the picture.

Second, practitioners need to realize that any trait's impact on behavior will vary with the situation. Some situations are fairly constrained, and the formal rules and policies governing behavior may play a larger role in determining a leader's behavior than the traits a leader possesses. Furthermore, situational factors also play a large role in determining which traits are important for leadership success. Depending on the leadership position, some of the traits found in Table 7–1 may be unrelated to leadership success.

Third, like leadership practitioners, followers also have varying levels of intelligence, personality traits, values, and attitudes. The attitudes, traits, and values possessed by followers also affect the ways in which leaders and followers interact. In many ways, it is somewhat surprising to find that *any* personality traits are related to leadership success, given the many ways that leaders, followers, and situations differ.

Fourth, leadership practitioners should spend some time reflecting on how situational demands and constraints as well as personality traits and intelligence affect the way they act. Through reflection, it may be possible to recognize the constraints that affect a leader's behavior and to find ways to modify the situation in order to minimize these constraints.

Finally, leadership practitioners should realize that it is relatively difficult to modify a person's personality. In all likelihood, a follower low in dependability or adjustment will not substantially change on these traits after a formal training program. Leaders may benefit by putting increased effort into selecting individuals with the traits needed to successfully perform a particular job than to try to significantly change someone (e.g., through training) who does not have the requisite traits. For example, it may be unrealistic to expect a disagreeable, unsociable receptionist to become an agreeable, sociable salesperson by sending him or her to a one-week sales course. Leadership practitioners may be able to have more success if they try to match their followers' abilities, skills, traits, and values with the demands of the positions within their work units. There also may be certain aspects of personality associated with leadership failure (see Highlight 7–8).

Is There a Leadership Trait?

Could there be a special **leadership trait?** Campbell (1977) hypothesized that such a trait may well exist but not be directly assessed by traditional measures of personality and intelligence. Both Curphy (1992b) and R. Hogan (1992) have speculated about the components underlying a leadership trait. Curphy (1992) hypothesized that good leaders have keen insight into the needs, wants, and expectations of their followers and have a good understanding of their leadership situation. Good leaders understand who holds power in the situation, how to build coalitions to overcome others' power bases, and how to circumvent situational constraints in order to get things done. However, just having a keen understanding of followers and the situation is not enough; leaders also

HIGHLIGHT 7-7

Individual Difference Variables, Leadership Emergence,
and Leadership Effectiveness

Although we have a pretty good idea which individual difference variables are related to leadership emergence, the findings regarding individual difference variables and leadership effectiveness tend to be less conclusive. After literally hundreds of research studies conducted over the past 80 years, we now know that people who are smarter, want to lead, are more outgoing, and who can adjust their behavior according to situational demands will tend to be seen as the leaders of informal social groups or rise to become captains of teams, leaders of volunteer committees, or presidents of sororities or fraternities. Nevertheless, research has also shown that being perceived to be smart, outgoing, and leaderlike by others does not necessarily mean that one will have highly satisfied subordinates, highly cohesive work groups, low turnover and absenteeism rates among followers, or success in achieving team or group goals. This implies that the traits of intelligence, dominance, sociability, and self-monitoring may be a necessary condition for leadership *emergence*, but possessing these traits is no guarantee that leaders will be *effective*.

Leadership research over the years indicates that there may be three reasons for the lack of consistent findings for personality traits and leadership effectiveness. First, the relationships between personality traits and leadership effectiveness will partly be a function of which effectiveness index is being examined. Leaders who are sociable may have higher organizational climate ratings but may also lead groups that fail to achieve group goals. Alternatively, leaders who are achievement-oriented may do a better job achieving group production goals but may not receive great organizational climate ratings. Second, research has also shown that most leadership effectiveness indices are affected by multiple leader, follower, and situational factors, and the relative importance of these factors varies substantially across situations. For example, consider how the differences in the followers, groups, tasks, and organizational and environmental factors affect the types of technical expertise and personality traits required by leaders of infantry troops in combat, coaches of high school gymnastics teams, heads of customer service units at department stores, and first-line supervisors on car assembly lines. Just as the leadership situations facing these four leaders differ, so do the characteristics needed for leadership success. Because the relative importance of the personality traits needed for leadership success varies substantially for each of these leaders, it is very difficult to find evidence that certain personality traits will be related to leadership effectiveness across *all* situations.

Third, Hogan, Hogan, and Curphy (1992) hypothesized that the inconsistent findings for the personality traits needed for effectiveness may be due to the fact that some leaders possess those traits necessary for leadership emergence but also possess certain personality flaws that prevent them from successfully building al-

HIGHLIGHT 7–7 *(concluded)*

liances or cohesive work units (i.e., prevent them from being effective). Because these leaders possess those personality traits needed to project a ''leadership image,'' they often do very well in interviews (i.e., they are seen as smart, outgoing, and wanting to lead by interviewers) and as a result, are often selected to fill leadership positions. However, Hogan, Hogan, and Curphy maintained that these personality flaws, or *dark-side* personality traits, would not be evident in the interview process but would manifest themselves only *after* these leaders had been on the job for several weeks. For example, some individuals who come across as outgoing, intelligent, and wanting to lead in the interview process may also tend to exploit their subordinates in order to further their own careers; however, this dark-side trait would be seen only after the leader had been in the job for some period of time. This personality flaw would make these leaders difficult to work for and would eventually result in lower climate and satisfaction ratings, high absenteeism and turnover rates, and perhaps outright revolt on the part of the followers.

Given that these dark-side traits are generally not assessed or evident in the selection process but will eventually result in leadership ineffectiveness and managerial derailment, what would a leadership researcher conclude if exploring the relationships between intelligence, dominance, sociability, and self-monitoring and leadership effectiveness? Essentially, a researcher would probably collect data that showed that some leaders who were outgoing and smart were highly effective (because they did not possess these personality flaws), whereas other leaders who were outgoing and smart were ineffective (because they possessed certain personality flaws that made them difficult to work with). Because this researcher would not know which of the leaders possessed the dark-side traits, he or she would erroneously conclude that the personality traits needed for leadership emergence were generally unrelated to leadership effectiveness. Although this would be the correct conclusion given the overall results, had the researcher been able to identify those leaders with and without dark-side traits, he or she may have concluded that those personality traits related to leadership emergence were also positively associated with leadership effectiveness *if those leaders possessing personality flaws were excluded from the study.* Thus, the hypothesis put forth by Hogan, Hogan, and Curphy maintains that if those individuals with dark-side traits could be identified and excluded from analysis, then the relationships between the personality traits needed for leadership emergence and leadership effectiveness may be much stronger than previously reported. Moreover, this hypothesis also maintains that organizational effectiveness could be improved if leaders' dark-side traits were assessed in the selection process.

Source: R. T. Hogan, J. Hogan, and G. J. Curphy. *The Necessary and Sufficient Traits for Leadership Effectiveness.* Manuscript submitted for publication, 1992.

HIGHLIGHT 7–8

Personality Traits and Flawed Leadership

Just as certain personality traits are generally related to leadership success, Hogan, Raskin, and Fazzini (1988) argued certain personality disorders are associated with leadership failure. These authors described three types of managers whose deficiencies may not be apparent when using personality tests or interviews, yet they may cost their organizations plenty in terms of time, morale, and resources by the time they are eventually discovered. The following is a brief overview of the three types of flawed leaders described by these authors.

The High Likeability Floater

High likeability floaters are exceedingly affiliative and agreeable but have rather low achievement scores. They are charming and congenial; they make great dinner companions and never argue, complain, or criticize. Because they are well liked and avoid offending anyone, they often rise steadily in their organizations. However, when they are placed in charge of a unit, little happens besides the maintenance of good morale. Because they have developed a network of loyal friends over the years, senior leaders often have a difficult time firing them when their incompetence is eventually discovered.

Hommes de Ressentiment

The model for the *hommes de ressentiment* leadership type is the legendary secret agent Kim Philby. Philby was a handsome, charming, bright, and highly effective man who steadily rose through the ranks of British intelligence to become in charge of the Soviet desk in Washington, D.C. Unfortunately, Philby also had a deep strain of resentment, smoldering hostility, and a strong desire for revenge. This eventually led to his becoming a double agent for the Soviet Union. The highly polished social skills and charm of *hommes de ressentiment* permit them to come across extremely well in interviews, yet they also may be the first to divulge organizational secrets to competitors.

Narcissists

Narcissism has been a topic of considerable concern in clinical psychology. Narcissism concerns one's feelings of entitlement and exemptions from social demands, feelings of omnipotence in controlling others, and an intolerance for criticism. Narcissists are concerned with self-enhancement and see others as extensions of themselves. They tend to take more credit than is due, are self-confident, and often are disproportionately influential in groups. Because they

---

HIGHLIGHT 7–8 *(concluded)*

are concerned only with themselves, they tend to exploit subordinates while currying favor with superiors. Narcissists are skilled communicators, persuasive, concerned with prestige and image, and particularly adept in social situations; however, these same qualities also help them get into positions where their personality flaws can cause considerable damage to the organization.

Source: R. T. Hogan, R. Raskin, and D. Fassini. "The Dark Side of Charisma." In K. E. Clark & M. B. Clark, eds., *Measures of Leadership* (West Orange, NJ: Leadership Library of America, 1989).

---

must be motivated to use their insight in order to accomplish various group or organizational goals. Curphy suggested that charismatic leaders may be those who have a good understanding of both their followers and the situation, and are motivated to use this knowledge to accomplish goals. Unfortunately, some charismatic leaders, such as Adolph Hitler and Jim Jones, have used these abilities for their own selfish ends.

Hogan's (1992) ideas about a leadership trait are fairly similar to those described by Curphy (1992). According to Hogan, effective leaders are those who can successfully build coalitions, and various personality traits may help leaders build alliances. By building coalitions, leaders can overcome obstacles to effective group performance. Another component of this coalition-building skill is the ability to think politically. Good leaders consider and correctly identify those who will be affected by decisions and actions and how they will be affected. Like a good strategist, good leaders incorporate such musings into their overall game plan for building coalitions in order to benefit their work unit. Good leaders also periodically reflect on the accuracy of their diagnoses and adjust their schema or body of knowledge regarding various members of the organization accordingly.

Although neither R. Hogan's (1992) nor Curphy's (1992a) views has been tested empirically, they do offer interesting ideas about the factors comprising a leadership trait. One reason neither has been studied more systematically is that measures do not exist to assess insight into situations and followers. Although some research in the social insight and empathy of leaders has been conducted, the measures used to assess empathy and social insight are generally poor and the research results disappointing (Bass, 1990). Nevertheless, recent research using low-fidelity simulations (Motowidlo, Dunnette, & Carter, 1989) may hold a key to future leadership-trait research. Low-fidelity simulations present respondents with a series of leadership situations. The respondents then indicate what actions they would take in each situation. Because respondents must make judgments about situational constraints, followers' motivations, expectations, and abilities, and how their actions will affect others in the situation, low-fidelity simulations could hold promise in future leadership-trait research.

The Heredity versus Environment Debate

Implicit in the Great Man theory described at the beginning of the chapter was the assumption that heredity was primarily responsible for the traits that distinguished leaders from followers. As the Great Man theory fell out of favor, so did the notion that heredity played a role in intelligence and personality. However, more recent studies of identical twins reared together and apart (i.e., adopted at birth) are revealing how important aspects of intelligence and personality are inherited (McGue & Bouchard, 1990; Tellegen et al., 1988; Willerman, 1979). This is *not* to say intelligence and personality are entirely due to heredity. On the contrary, the environment (i.e., upbringing) seems to play at least as large a role as genetic endowment. However, it is clear now that the Great Man theory was not all wrong; leadership success may be partly due to genetic endowment. Having the right educational and leadership experiences is extremely important to leadership success; however, having the right genes does not hurt either.

SUMMARY

This chapter overviewed research examining the relationships between intelligence, personality, and leadership success. Generally, more intelligent leaders are better leaders, but a large differential in the intellectual levels of a leader and followers may prove problematic. This may be because such leaders may have difficulty communicating effectively with followers. Another possible explanation is that intelligent, inexperienced leaders may not perform well under stress.

Like intelligence, many personality traits also have been found related to leadership success. Some of these include dominance, self-monitoring, locus of control, adjustment, tolerance for ambiguity, achievement orientation, dependability, energy and activity level, sociability, self-confidence, and agreeableness. Although these traits tend to be related to leadership effectiveness or emergence, the magnitude of the relationship depends to a large extent on the particular situation.

One way to be a more effective leader is to appreciate the many ways leaders and followers can differ. Because both intelligence and personality change only slowly, leadership practitioners may be able to improve the effectiveness of their group or work unit by selecting members with the intelligence and personality traits best suited for successful performance.

Some researchers have speculated about the existence of a leadership trait, but considerable research needs to be accomplished before that can be confirmed. Because personality is partly attributable to genetic factors as well as experience, evidence supporting the existence of a leadership trait may give at least partial credence to the notion that leaders are born, not made.

KEY TERMS AND CONCEPTS

Great Man theory

intelligence

personality trait

objective personality test

dominance

self-confidence

achievement orientation

dependability

energy and activity levels

high self-monitors

low self-monitors

external locus of control

internal locus of control

tolerance for ambiguity

adjustment

sociability

agreeableness

leadership trait

DISCUSSION QUESTIONS

1. Individuals may well be attracted to, selected for, or successful in leadership roles early in their lives and careers based on their ability and personality. But what happens over time and with experience? Do you think certain aspects of intelligence or personality also might change over time due to experience in leadership roles?

2. Compare the advantages and disadvantages of studying leader personality using case studies versus objective personality tests.

3. A theme of this book is that leaders will be more effective to the extent they can adapt their behavior to the needs of particular circumstances. Do you believe adjustment or adaptability in a leader is valuable? Is flexibility on some issues or aspects of behavior more important than others?

4. Do you think personality is a helpful dimension for understanding the effectiveness of political leaders? Does this question necessarily imply that successful political leaders have "good" personalities, and unsuccessful ones "bad" personalities? (Hint: explore this issue by considering both of the definitions of personality presented in the chapter.)

5. Do you think Abraham Lincoln could be elected president today? Why or why not?

6. Describe the situational factors that constrain or limit your behavior. Describe the situational factors that constrain or limit the effects intelligence or personality have on a leader's behavior.

SUGGESTED READINGS

Meir, G. *My Life*. New York: G. P. Putnam's Sons, 1975.

Phillips, D. T. *Lincoln on Leadership*. New York: Warner, 1992.

Chapter Eight

Values, Attitudes, Preferences, and Leadership

INTRODUCTION

Intelligence and certain personality traits are not the only individual difference variables related to leadership success. A leader's values, moral reasoning, attitudes, and preferences are also related to leadership success (see Highlight 8–1). This chapter reviews research concerning these additional individual difference variables and discusses implications for improving leadership success.

HIGHLIGHT 8–1

Leadership Quotes, Chapter Eight

Beware of the man who had no regard to his own reputation, since it is not likely he should have any for yours.

George Shelley

I have often thought that the best way to define a man's character would be to seek out the particular mental or moral attitude in which, when it came upon him, he felt himself most deeply and intensively active and alive. At such moments, there is a voice inside which speaks and says, "This is the real me."

William James

Only mediocrities rise to the top in a system that won't tolerate wave making.

Lawrence J. Peter

So near is a falsehood to truth that a wise man would do well not to trust himself on the narrow edge.

Cicero

Subordinates cannot be left to speculate as to the values of the organization. Top leadership must give forth clear and explicit signals, lest any confusion or uncertainty exist over what is and is not permissible conduct. To do otherwise allows informal and potentially subversive "codes of conduct" to be transmitted with a wink and a nod, and encourages an inferior ethical system based on "going along to get along" or the notion that "everybody's doing it."

Richard Thornburgh

Neither shall you allege the example of the many as an excuse for doing wrong.

The Bible (Exod. 23:2)

It's important that people know what you stand for. It's equally important that they know what you won't stand for.

Mary Waldrop

Like Chapter Seven, this chapter will describe the values, attitudes, and preferences from the leader's perspective. Nevertheless, just as followers can have a wide variety of intelligence levels and different standings on various personality traits, they also can have a wide variety of values, attitudes, and preferences. A leader can have two followers with above-average intelligence,

high achievement, high sociability, low self-monitoring, and low stress tolerance, yet have very different relationships with them because of their very different value systems. Leadership practitioners can gain a better appreciation of
themselves and others when they reflect about how human behavior is affected
by the complex interaction of intelligence, traits, values, attitudes, preferences,
and situational influences.

VALUES

What Are Values?

Values are "constructs representing generalized behaviors or states of affairs
that are considered by the individual to be important" (Gordon, 1975, p. 2).
Values play a fairly central role in one's overall psychological makeup and can
affect behavior in a variety of situations. In work settings, values can affect decisions about joining an organization, organizational commitment, relationships with co-workers, and decisions about leaving an organization (Boyatzis
& Skelly, 1989). It is important that leaders realize that individuals in the same
work unit can have considerably different values.

Some of the major values that may be considered important by individuals
in an organization are listed in Table 8-1. The instrumental values found in Table 8-1 refer to modes of behavior, and the terminal values refer to desired end
states (Rokeach, 1973). For example, some individuals value equality, freedom,
and having a comfortable life above all else; others may believe that family security and salvation are important goals to strive for. In terms of instrumental
values, such individuals may think that it is important always to act in an ambitious, capable, and honest manner, whereas others may think it is only important to be ambitious and capable. This difference is evident if one looks at the
instrumental values exhibited by Lee Iacocca and Michael Milken. Both Iacocca
and Milken were extremely successful in their respective businesses, yet
Milken was fined $600 million after he was convicted of numerous counts of
insider trading; Iacocca, on the other hand, is seen as a symbol of integrity in
the automotive industry. It would seem that, to Milken, being ambitious and
capable were much more important instrumental values than being honest. We
should add that the instrumental and terminal values in Table 8-1 are only a
few of those Rokeach has identified.

According to England and Lee (1974), values can affect leaders in six different
ways. First, values affect leaders' perceptions of situations and the problems at
hand. Leaders who are extremely ambitious may see a problem as an obstacle to
success, whereas leaders who are helpful may see a problem as an opportunity to
help a subordinate or another work unit. Second, leaders' values affect the solutions generated and the decisions reached about problems. If leaders believe be-

TABLE 8–1

People Vary in the Relative Importance They Place on Values Like the Following

Terminal Values	Instrumental Values
An exciting life	Being courageous
A sense of accomplishment	Being helpful
Family security	Being honest
Inner harmony	Being imaginative
Social recognition	Being logical
Friendship	Being responsible

Source: Adapted from M. Rokeach, *The Nature of Human Values* (New York: The Free Press, 1973).

ing courageous and standing up for one's beliefs are important, then they may be more likely to generate solutions or make decisions not considered politically correct in their organizations. Third, values play an extremely important role in interpersonal relationships; they influence how leaders perceive different individuals and groups. For example, leaders who value self-control may have a difficult time dealing with followers who are very emotionally demonstrative and, in turn, may choose to have fairly distant relationships with these followers. Fourth, values often influence leaders' perceptions of individual and organizational successes as well as the manner in which these successes are to be achieved. Leaders who primarily value being ambitious, independent, and imaginative may assess leadership effectiveness differently from leaders who value being helpful, logical, and cheerful. Fifth, values provide a basis for leaders to differentiate between "right" and "wrong," and between ethical and unethical behavior. Sixth, values also may affect the extent to which leaders accept or reject organizational pressures and goals. Leaders who place a premium on being obedient may never question the goals of the organization. However, leaders who believe being independent is important may often question and even actively resist the implementation of some organizational goals in their work units.

How Do Values Develop?

According to Massey (1979), each person's values reflect the contributions of diverse inputs including family, peers, the educational system, religion, the media, science and technology, geography, and current events (see Figure 8–1). Although one's values can change throughout one's life, they are relatively firmly established by young adulthood. Massey used the term **value programming** to highlight the extent to which forces outside the individual shape and mold per-

FIGURE 8–1
Some Influences on the Development of Personal Values

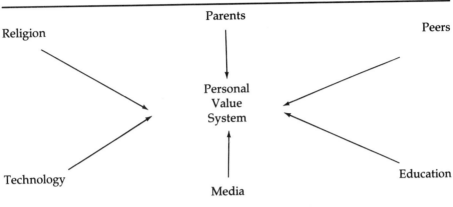

Source: Adapted from M. Massey, *The People Puzzle* (Reston, Va.: Reston, 1979).

sonal values. He analyzed changes in the value-programming inputs that characterized each of the decades since the 1920s and related them to dominant and distinctive values held among people who were value-programmed during those respective periods. For example, he said the monumental event of the 1930s, the Great Depression, programmed people growing up then to especially value economic security. People growing up in the 1960s, however, were value-programmed quite differently. Dramatic shifts and changes in American society occurred during the 1960s. There were violent social protests, experimentation with new lifestyles, and pervasive questioning of "establishment" values.

Boyatzis and Skelly (1989), Maccoby (1983), and Massey (1979) have all said that the pervasive influence of broad forces like these tend to create common value systems among people growing up at a particular time that distinguish them from people who grow up at different times. There are, of course, significant individual differences among people within any generational group, but these authors emphasized differences between groups. For example, people who grew up prior to World War II valued authority, job security, and stability; people who grew up in the 1960s valued participation, informality, and personal growth; and those who grew up in the 1980s valued competitiveness, entrepreneurialism, and cost-effectiveness. These authors attributed much of the misunderstanding between older leaders and younger followers to the fact that their basic value systems were formulated during quite different social and cultural conditions, and these analyses offer a helpful perspective for understanding how differences in values can add tension to the interaction between some leaders and followers.

Values, Moral Reasoning, and Leadership

Moral reasoning refers to the process leaders use to make decisions about ethical and unethical behaviors. Moral reasoning does not refer to the morality of individuals per se, but rather to the manner by which they solve moral problems. Values play a key role in the moral reasoning process, as value differences among individuals often result in different judgments regarding ethical and unethical behavior.

Leaders face ethical dilemmas at all levels, and the best leaders recognize and face them with a commitment to doing what is right, not just what is expedient. Of course, the phrase *doing what is right* sounds deceptively simple. Sometimes it will take great moral courage to do what is right, even when the right action seems clear. Other times, though, leaders face ethically complex issues that lack simple black-and-white answers. Whichever the case, leaders set a moral example to others that becomes the model for an entire group or organization, for good or bad. Leaders who themselves do not honor truth do not inspire it in others. Leaders mostly concerned with their own advancement do not inspire selflessness in others.

Both Gardner (1990) and Burns (1978) have stressed the centrality and importance of the moral dimension of leadership. Gardner said leaders ultimately must be judged on the basis of a framework of values, not just in terms of their effectiveness. He put the question of a leader's relations with his or her followers or constituents on the moral plane, arguing (with the philosopher Immanuel Kant) that leaders should always treat others as ends in themselves, not as objects or mere means to the leader's ends (which he said, by the way, does not necessarily imply that leaders need to be gentle in interpersonal demeanor or ''democratic'' in style). Burns (1978) took an even more extreme view regarding the moral dimension of leadership; he maintained that leaders who did not behave ethically did not demonstrate true leadership.

Implications for Leaders

Empirical studies of the ethical dimension of leadership have looked at the frequency or prevalence of unethical behaviors in the workplace, the relationship between values and leadership success, and factors affecting moral reasoning and ethical versus unethical behavior.

Studies exploring opinions about unethical behaviors or practices in the workplace have yielded fairly disturbing results. For example, a 1988 Harris poll reported that 89 percent of the 1,200 workers and managers surveyed believed it was important for leaders to be upright, honest, and ethical in their dealings. However, only 41 percent indicated their current supervisor had these characteristics. Another Harris poll conducted in 1989 reported that many individuals believed businesses would purposely sell unsafe products, risk employee health and safety, and harm the environment (see Figure 8–2). In

FIGURE 8–2
Perceptions of Unethical Business Practices

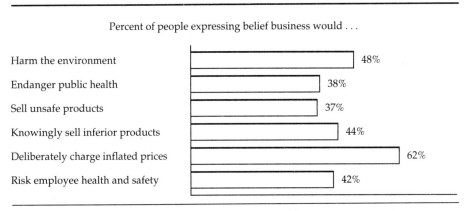

Percent of people expressing belief business would . . .

Harm the environment	48%
Endanger public health	38%
Sell unsafe products	37%
Knowingly sell inferior products	44%
Deliberately charge inflated prices	62%
Risk employee health and safety	42%

Source: Harris poll, reported in *Business Week*, May 29, 1989, p. 29.

addition, Pitt (1985) asked middle and senior managers in South Africa to rate the corruptness of various business practices and then indicate how frequently they believed colleagues and friends engaged in such acts. A representative finding was that although approximately 95 percent of the respondents said taking a large bribe was definitely wrong, they believed one third of their friends and colleagues would do so. Furthermore, even in the case of such a clearly corrupt act as bribery, only one third of the respondents said they believed legal action against the individual afterward would be appropriate. Among other things, data like these suggest ethical practices do not receive a high enough priority in many organizations.

Other studies also have examined how leaders' values are related to leadership style or success. Some have shown that men and women differ in the values they emphasize in moral reasoning; men are more concerned about equity and justice, whereas women show more care for others and social responsibility in their moral reasoning (Brockner & Adsit, 1986; Gilligan, 1982; Powell, Posner, & Schmidt, 1984). In addition, Schmidt and Posner (1986) reported that both public and private administrators were relatively more concerned with their obligations to their organizations than they were to society, and Weber (1989) reported that managers often used majority opinion rather than universal principles of justice when making decisions with ethical implications. Despite the cynicism that exists about the ethical practices of people in some leadership positions, managers with a strong sense of right and wrong do appear to be better leaders. Both Ghiselli (1968) and Gordon (1975) reported that leaders' personal values correlated positively with leadership effectiveness.

A final issue we will consider involves the role of both values and situational influences on moral reasoning. Several researchers have reported that individuals with strong value systems tend to behave more ethically, which at first may seem like a classic case of discovering the obvious. However, certain kinds of situations increased the likelihood of unethical behavior from people regardless of their value systems. Such situations tended to be highly competitive and unsupervised. Unethical behavior also was more likely to occur when there was no formal ethics policy governing behavior, when there was no threat of punishment for unethical behavior, or when unethical behavior actually was rewarded (Hegarty & Sims, 1978, 1979; Malinkowski & Smith, 1985; Trevino & Youngblood, 1990).

A slightly different question than behaving unethically oneself is that of tolerating unethical behavior in others. It seems that reporting or confronting individuals whose behavior violated ethical or organizational norms depends on at least two situational variables: the seriousness of the infraction and the emotional closeness of the violator (Curphy, Gibson, Macomber, Calhoun, Wilbanks, & Burger, 1992). Individuals appear less likely to ''blow the whistle'' on another's ethical infraction if the violation did not seem serious and if the offender was a close friend of the potential whistleblower. Finally, researchers have found that group decisions about ethical dilemmas can be at lower levels of moral reasoning than the decisions made by individual members if the leader of the group is a less principled moral reasoner himself or herself (Dukerich, Nichols, Elm, & Vollrath, 1990). This finding may have implications for what a group's collective morality may be when the leader himself or herself is relatively unprincipled.

These findings also have several other implications for leadership practitioners. Perhaps most important, leadership practitioners should expect to face a variety of ethical dilemmas during their careers. Additionally, values often are a source of interpersonal conflict. Although we sometimes say two people don't get along because of a ''personality conflict,'' often these conflicts are due to differences in value systems, not personality traits. Often, people on either side of an issue see *only* themselves and their own side as morally justifiable. Nonetheless, people holding seemingly (to themselves) antiethical values may still need to work together, and dealing with diverse and divergent values will be an increasingly common challenge for leaders. As noted earlier, interacting with individuals and groups holding divergent and conflicting values will be an inevitable fact of life for future leaders. This does not mean, however, that increased levels of interpersonal conflict are inevitable. Both leaders and followers might be well advised to minimize the conflict and tension often associated with value differences. Leaders in particular have a responsibility not to let their own personal values interfere with professional leader-subordinate relationships unless the conflicts pertain to issues clearly relevant to the work and the organization.

ATTITUDES

What Are Attitudes?

An **attitude** "refers to a general and enduring positive or negative feeling about some person, object, or issue" (Petty & Cacioppo, 1981, p. 7). Attitudes have three components: ideational, affective, and behavioral. The **ideational component** concerns *what* the attitude is about, and the **affective component** concerns the feelings one has about those ideas. For example, a leader may dislike the administrative aspects of her responsibilities. Her attitude has both a feeling dimension (she *detests* filling out seemingly endless forms) and a cognitive dimension (in this case, administrative tasks at work).

Attitudes also have a **behavioral component**, which means that attitudes dispose people to act in certain ways. For example, our leader above may tend to procrastinate on paperwork and underemphasize the importance of documentation and filling out forms properly. Students with positive attitudes about school tend to do more homework, turn in assignments on time, and ask more questions than students with negative attitudes about school. Similarly, workers with negative attitudes toward their employer are more likely to change jobs if given the opportunity. Like traits and values, however, attitudes do not *always* predict behavior. Fishbein and Azjen (1975) have shown that some attitudes are so general they tell us very little about how people actually act and that attitudes best predict behavior when they specifically pertain to relevant behaviors. For example, knowing only that a person has the attitude "democracy is good" will not help predict this person's vote in a presidential election. However, knowing this person has a strong attitude about a particular political candidate will be a more accurate predictor of his voting behavior. Attitudes do not always predict specific behavior because behavior is influenced by more factors than just attitudes. For example, a supervisor may be forced to terminate a subordinate's employment because of forced company downsizing despite having very positive attitudes about the person's work. Still, although many factors can affect a leader's behavior, a leader's attitudes can reveal useful insights about her approach to her role.

Attitudes share certain properties with values, but they are also different from values in fundamental ways. Both are unseen constructs that can affect behavior; both are inferred from one's behavior; and both are typically measured using paper-and-pencil measures. Nevertheless, values occupy a more central role in one's overall psychological makeup than attitudes do (Rokeach, 1973). Although the number of basic values anyone holds is relatively small, the number of attitudes anyone holds may be in the thousands, as they refer to diverse opinions about people, activities, or things. Despite these differences, values and attitudes are intimately linked: Values serve to organize our attitudes, and our attitudes are derived from and reflect our more basic values.

Leader Attitudes about Subordinates

A leader's interaction with subordinates depends in part on his or her implicit views of human nature. A leader's basic attitudes about what motivates others, about whether people generally can be trusted or not, and about the extent to which individuals can grow and develop all influence how a leader interacts with others in both overt and subtle ways. Several decades ago, Douglas McGregor (1966) explained different styles of managerial behavior on the basis of their implicit attitudes about human nature, and his work remains quite influential today. McGregor identified two contrasting sets of assumptions people make about human nature, calling these **Theory X** and **Theory Y**. These represent two different sets of attitudes, or belief systems, about ways to effectively influence subordinates. In the long run, any manager's approach to subordinates generally reflects such underlying assumptions and tendencies. Moreover, managers often are not consciously aware of their assumptions; they act as though their views are obviously true.

In the simplest sense, Theory X reflects a traditional and pessimistic view of others. Managers with this orientation rely heavily on coercive, external-control methods to motivate workers such as pay, disciplinary techniques, punishments, and threats. They assume people are not naturally industrious or motivated to work. Hence, it is the manager's job to minimize the harmful effects of workers' natural laziness and irresponsibility by closely overseeing their work and creating external incentives to do well and disincentives to avoid slacking off. Theory Y, on the other hand, reflects a view that most people are intrinsically motivated by their work. Rather than needing to be coaxed or coerced to work productively, such people value a sense of achievement, personal growth, pride in contributing to their organization, and respect for a job well done. Managers ascribing to a Theory Y attitude believe followers value the opportunity to take on tasks of greater responsibility and autonomy independent of whether there may be greater tangible rewards for doing so. The generally optimistic view of human nature implicit in Theory Y is reflected in a remark by former Supreme Court justice Tom Clark, who said, "I'm convinced that every boy, in his heart, would rather steal second base than an automobile."

Hall and Donnell (1979) reported findings of five separate studies involving over 12,000 managers that explored the relationship between managerial achievement and attitudes toward subordinates. Their criterion of managerial achievement was an objective index calculated on the basis of each manager's career progress in the context of chronological age and upward movement in an organizational hierarchy. These objective scores were transformed into standard scores that were the basis for categorizing three levels of managerial achievement—high, average, and low. The average-achieving group comprised essentially the middle two thirds of the distribution. Hall and Donnell compared the personal beliefs of high-, average-, and low-achieving managers and reasoned that managers with a Theory Y philosophy would better accomplish organizational objectives and better tap the potential of subordinates. Managers ascribing to a Theory X philosophy were predicted to restrict subordinate growth and limit organizational potential. In fact, managers who strongly subscribed to Theory X beliefs were far more likely to be in Hall and Donnell's low-achieving group.

Leader Attitudes about Themselves

We have seen that a leader's attitudes about others can have a substantial impact on his effectiveness. Another important factor in a leader's effectiveness concerns his attitudes about himself. The concept of self is one of the oldest and most central concepts in psychology. Some of the most important psychological concepts for understanding individuals are self-concept and self-esteem. Each of these deals with particular attitudes one has about oneself, and each plays a significant part in how we respond to events and to other people.

Self-concept is a construct from phenomenological personality theory (Kelly, 1955) and refers to the collection of attitudes we have about ourselves. One source of these attitudes involves the various experiences a person has had and the roles a person currently occupies, such as spouse, parent, supervisor, friend, athlete, or committee member. For example, if we asked the question ''Who are you?'' a particular leader might respond that she is a college-educated mother of two who is married and supervises 14 salespeople in a computer retail firm. **Self-esteem** refers to the overall positiveness or negativeness of a person's feelings about these experiences and roles. Individuals with high self-esteem generally see themselves in a positive light; individuals with low self-esteem generally see themselves in a negative light. Thus, if the leader above had high self-esteem, she may be likely to perceive that she is well loved by her children and husband and respected at work by her subordinates, peers, and superiors. Another way to think about self-esteem is in terms of the congruence or divergence between one's actual self and one's ideal self. In that sense, a person has high self-esteem if she perceives herself as being relatively close to the way she ideally would like to be; a person has low self-esteem if he perceives himself as being very unlike the way he ideally would like to be. Because self-esteem involves perceptions and feelings, it does not necessarily reflect an objective assessment of one's strengths and accomplishments. One can be extremely accomplished or hold a high position and yet have relatively low self-esteem. Let's return to our leader above, supposing her children consistently have been on the school honor role, she had just celebrated her 20th wedding anniversary, and she had received a bonus at work. Even in the face of such outward success, the person could have low self-esteem if she expected even more of herself.

Implications for Leaders

To briefly summarize the two foregoing sections, leaders can have positive or negative attitudes about themselves, and they can have positive or negative attitudes about others. An even simpler way of putting this is to say leaders can feel OK or not OK about themselves, and OK or not OK about others (Harris, 1967). These possibilities create four different attitudinal "positions." As seen in Figure 8–3, a leader's attitudes about himself or herself and others interact to produce four quite different leadership styles. Leaders who have a positive self-concept and ascribe to a Theory Y philosophy typically give and accept positive feedback, expect others to succeed, and give others autonomy in completing tasks. Leaders with a positive self-concept and a Theory X philosophy tend to be bossy, pushy, and impatient; they also generally take on a dictatorial leadership style. Leaders with a negative self-concept and a Theory Y philosophy may seem afraid to make decisions, unassertive, and self-blaming. Finally, leaders with a negative self-concept and a Theory X philosophy blame others for the work unit's problems, are pessimistic about the possibility of resolving personal or organizational problems, and generally promote feelings of hopelessness among followers.

PREFERENCES

Nearly 2 million people take the Myers-Briggs Type Indicator (MBTI) every year (Myers & McCaulley, 1985), which makes it one of the most popular psychological tests around (Thayer, 1988). It measures preferences (as characterized in Jungian theory), and it is often used in college-level leadership and adult education courses, in formal leadership training programs, in organizational personnel programs, and by consultants as a part of various organizational interventions. Moreover, numerous books and articles have been published about how the MBTI can be used to better understand oneself, co-workers, partners in intimate relationships, children, and educational or occupational preferences. Because of the overall popularity of the MBTI, we believe it is worthwhile to review the instrument in some detail.

The Nature of Preferences

Like values and attitudes, our **preferences** play a role in the way we approach tasks and interact with others. Preferences influence our choice of careers, ways of thinking, relationships, and work habits. Somewhat paradoxically, one reason preferences are important is precisely because it is so easy to forget about them. It is easy to forget how subjective and idosyncratic preferences re-

FIGURE 8–3

The Interactions between Attitudes toward Self and Attitudes toward Others

High self-esteem Respects others Self-confident Accepts positive feedback Gives positive feedback Expects others to succeed Nonjudgmental Nondefensive Seeks win-win solutions	High self-esteem Overbearing Bossy Highly evaluative of others Impatient Hostile Task-oriented
<div align="center">I'm OK/You're OK</div>	<div align="center">I'm OK/You're Not OK</div>
<div align="center">I'm Not OK/You're OK</div>	<div align="center">I'm Not OK/You're Not OK</div>
Low self-esteem Difficulty accepting positive feedback Unassertive Worrisome Assumes own fault	Low self-esteem Feelings of helplessness and hopelessness Blames others and world Nothing matters Expects to fail

ally are; we easily confuse our *preferences* with *the way things are, or ought to be.* For example, those who value being organized may prefer *everyone* to be organized. They may get annoyed when working with others who are less organized than they are. In other words, it is easy to let preferences affect judgments of others (e.g., people "should" be organized; therefore, not being well-organized is a deficiency). Many people are unaware of the extent to which their preferences shape their perceptions of reality.

According to Myers and McCaulley (1985), there are four basic preference dimensions in which people can differ. These four dimensions are **extraversion-introversion, sensing-intuition, thinking-feeling,** and **judging-perceiving.** The four dimensions are bipolar, meaning that individuals prefer being either, say, extroverted or introverted. (See Highlight 8–2 for a description of the four scales.) The predominant preference scores for each of the four dimensions are used to create one of 16 **psychological types.** For example, someone with high preferences for extroversion, sensing, thinking, and judging would be categorized as an ESTJ. Myers and McCaulley (1985) maintained that individuals within a particular type were more similar to each other than they were to individuals of a different type.

HIGHLIGHT 8–2

The Four Basic Preference Dimensions of the Myers-Briggs Type Indicator

Extraversion and introversion. Some people are naturally gregarious and outgoing. Their spontaneous sociability makes it easy for them to strike up conversations with anyone about almost anything. Not surprisingly, such extraverts have a breadth of interests and a large circle of acquaintances. Other people are more comfortable alone, or with just a few others. Introverts *can* interact effectively with others, but they are fundamentally both more reserved and more deliberate than extraverts. Of course, everyone needs to act in both extraverted and introverted ways at various times; however, some of us are more comfortable with one than the other.

Sensing and intuition. People who prefer their sensing mode like facts and details. People who rely on their intuition look for the big picture beyond particular facts or details. To sensors, the focus of information gathering concerns the real, the actual, the literal, the specific, and the present; to intuitors, information is most meaningful for its pattern, framework, figurative meaning, and future possibilities. Hence, sensing types tend to be practical and down-to-earth, and intuitive types tend to be innovative and conceptual (though sometimes impractical). Sensors and intuitors also differ in the manner they work. Sensors prefer orderly, rule-based activity; intuitors are more comfortable with their hunches and inspirations and prefer to be unconstrained by someone else's rules.

Thinking and feeling. Different people prefer to base decisions on different sorts of considerations. Thinkers approach decisions impersonally and objectively, with their ''heads,'' as it were. Thinking types adopt a relatively detached stance toward decisions and pay more attention to principles of general applicability. Feelers prefer to approach decisions personally and subjectively, with their ''hearts,'' as it were. Feeling types weigh heavily the impact of any decision on particular people. Feeling types value humaneness and social harmony; thinking types value fairness and firmness. Thinking types naturally analyze and criticize; feeling types naturally empathize and appreciate.

Judging and perceiving. Judgers like things being settled; they are decisive, methodical, and organized. Perceivers like to keep their options open; they are curious, spontaneous, and flexible. Perceivers prefer to collect as much information as possible before making a decision or a commitment; judgers like settling one thing and moving on to the next. Perceivers are very comfortable with the unplanned and unexpected; they adapt well to the unforeseen. Judgers are uncomfortable *unless* they have things planned and scheduled. Furthermore, they like *others* to have things well-organized, too. Perceivers are tolerant of others' differences and are open to new ideas and new ways of doing things. Judgers are decisive and frequently make their minds up quickly (though they may prejudge some things before they have all the facts).

Sources: I. Myers, (1980). *Gifts Differing* (Palo Alto, Calif.: Consulting Psychologists Press, 1980); and I. Myers, and M. H. McCaulley, (1985). *Manual: A Guide to the Development and Use of the Myers-Briggs Type Indicator* (Palo Alto, Calif.: Consulting Psychologists Press, 1985).

Implications for Leaders: Types and Preferences

As stated earlier, the preference scores for the four basic dimensions are combined to form 1 of 16 different types. Kroeger and Thuesen (1988) maintained that no one type was necessarily better than another in terms of leadership success and that each type had unique strengths and potential weaknesses. Although there appears to be little published evidence to support this claim, there is evidence to show that leaders are disproportionately represented by certain types far more than others. A majority of leaders preferred thinking and judging activities over feeling and perceiving activities. Leaders were more likely to be ISTJs, INTJs, ESTJs, or ENTJs than any of the other 12 types (McCaulley, 1988). We should add, however, that this finding may be more accurate a generalization for adults whose vocational choices and organizational socialization already are relatively well established. It may not be a valid generalization for leaders who are of college age or younger (Cummings, 1992).

Although more research is needed concerning how preferences affect leadership, it seems reasonable that awareness and appreciation of them can enhance any leader's effectiveness. In the following paragraphs, we will highlight several implications of preferences for leaders.

• *Knowing about preferences increases awareness of both your own and others' behavior.* Greater self-understanding reduces personal blind spots and helps one perceive leadership situations (including one's own behavior) more accurately. Leaders have a difficult time changing behavior if they are not aware of how they are acting, and some behaviors are difficult to change precisely because they have become so automatic. Knowledge of preferences can help leaders better understand their behavioral patterns at work and see how they might be able to avoid being a prisoner of their own preferences. It can also help leaders see others in new ways, with greater insight and tolerance.

• *Knowledge of preferences helps broaden one's behavioral repertoire, which is helpful because leaders face a great diversity of situations.* Sometimes leaders must inspire a group about a vision of the future; sometimes they just need to listen to someone else's ideas about how to do things differently. Sometimes leaders must take a stand that will displease and maybe hurt others; sometimes leaders need to make group morale a primary concern. Because different followers may have very different preferences, they may react very differently to a leader's behavior. Leaders may be more successful if they are able to adjust their behavior according to followers' preferences.

• *People with different preferences are often motivated in different ways.* There's a lot of truth to the saying "Different strokes for different folks." All leaders need to remember that followers with different preferences appreciate different things. For example, feelers hate impersonal treatment; perceivers like doing things their own way.

• *Working with people who have different preferences can be difficult.* Some difficulties with others at work are due to differences in preferences. For example, introverts may feel that an extravert they share an office with is obnoxious and loudmouthed; extraverts may become frustrated when they find out an introvert they are working with on a project had a great idea but did not mention it because no one asked him directly for his opinion. Understanding that office conflicts may be due to differences in preferences can give leadership practitioners some insight on how to resolve these conflicts.

• *Working with people who have different preferences can also be potentially more productive.* People say two heads are better than one, but that is not always true. If two heads have exactly the same thoughts, then one of them is redundant! In a sense, two people with different preferences provide greater differences of opinion and talent than do two people with exactly the same preferences. Lee Iacocca (1984) wrote about the importance of diverse interests and outlooks in organizations:

> By their very nature, financial analysts tend to be defensive, conservative, and pessimistic. On the other side of the fence are the guys in sales and marketing—aggressive, speculative, and optimistic. They're always saying, ''Let's do it,'' while the bean counters are always cautioning you on why you shouldn't do it. In any company you need both sides of the equation, because the natural tension between the two groups creates its own system of checks and balances. (p. 43)

Thinking Critically about the Myers-Briggs Type Indicator (MBTI)

Although the MBTI is an extremely popular and potentially useful instrument, leadership practitioners also need to be aware of its limitations and possible misuses. Although the four preference dimensions can provide useful insights about oneself and others, the concept of being a ''type'' is problematic. First of all, types do not appear to be stable over time. Some research indicates at least one letter in the four-letter type may change in half the people taking the test in as little as five weeks (McCarley & Carskadon, 1983; Myers & McCaulley, 1985). There also are data showing major developmental changes in distribution of types with age (Cummings, 1992). It is difficult to see how one should select individuals for teams or provide career guidance to others based on types if the types (or at least type scores) change, in some cases seemingly quickly. Second, types greatly oversimplify the complexities of human behavior. Individuals who share the same type but have dramatically different values, personality traits, or intelligence levels may act very differently in the same situation. Because behavior within a type may vary as greatly as behavior between types, the utility of any typing system must be called into question.

Perhaps the most serious problem of all in using typologies concerns the way they are sometimes misused. Unfortunately, some people become so enamored with simple systems of classifying human behavior that they begin to see *everything* through "type" glasses. Some people habitually categorize their friends, spouses, and co-workers into types. Knowledge of preferences should be a basis for appreciating the richness and diversity of behavior, and the capabilities in others and ourselves. It is not meant to be a system of categorization that overly simplifies our own and others' behavior by seemingly putting people into neat and tidy little boxes (i.e., types). Believing someone is a particular type (e.g., "He's an ISTJ") can become a sort of perceptual filter that keeps us from actually recognizing when that person is acting in a manner contrary to that type's characteristic style. Another misuse occurs when someone uses "knowledge" of type as an excuse or rationalization for his own counterproductive behaviors ("I know I'm talking on and on and dominating the conversation, but after all, I'm an extravert!"). Millions of people apparently believe the MBTI is a useful tool in enhancing awareness of self and others, but leadership practitioners need to understand that, like any tool, it can also be misused.

SUMMARY

This chapter reviews evidence regarding the relationships between values, attitudes, preferences, and leadership success. Values are constructs that represent general sets of behaviors or states of affairs that individuals consider to be important, and they play a central part of a leader's psychological makeup. Values are an important component of the moral reasoning process, which is the process people use to resolve moral or ethical dilemmas. This is important since leaders undoubtedly will face a variety of ethical dilemmas during their careers. Values also serve to organize attitudes, which are general and enduring positive or negative feelings about some person, object, or issue. People typically have only a few strongly held values, but they can have literally thousands of different attitudes. Although leaders can have a variety of attitudes, two sets of attitudes play particularly important roles in leadership behaviors. These include attitudes leaders have about themselves and attitudes leaders have about others.

Preferences also affect a leader's behavior. Preference tests require respondents to indicate what activities they like or dislike doing. The most popular preference test is the Myers-Briggs Type Indicator (MBTI), which measures a person's preferences on four major dimensions. Individuals' scores for these four dimensions are typically combined to define a psychological type. Although preferences can provide useful insights about leaders and followers, the validity of psychological types is less clear.

KEY TERMS

values	self-concept
value programming	self-esteem
moral reasoning	Myers-Briggs Type Indicator (MBTI)
attitude	preferences
ideational component	extraversion-introversion
affective component	sensing-intuition
behavioral component	thinking-feeling
Theory X	judging-perceiving
Theory Y	psychological types

DISCUSSION QUESTIONS

1. Do you think it always must be "lonely at the top" (or that if it is not, you are doing something wrong)?
2. How do you believe one's basic philosophy of human nature affects one's approach to leadership?
3. Identify several values you think might be the basis of conflict or misunderstanding between leaders and followers.
4. Can a leader's public and private morality be distinguished? Should they be?
5. Can a "bad" person be a "good" leader?
6. Do you think persons of every preference type can be effective leaders?

SUGGESTED READINGS

Gardner, J. *On Leadership*. New York: The Free Press, 1990.

Kroeger, O., and J. M. Thuesen. *Type Talk*. New York: Delacourte, 1988.

Lewis, H. *A Question of Values*. New York: Harper & Row, 1990.

Chapter Nine

Leadership Behaviors and Skills

INTRODUCTION

C hapters Seven and Eight examined relationships between leadership success and such individual difference variables as intelligence, personality traits, values, attitudes, and preferences. We observed, however, these individual difference variables only have a modest and indirect relationship with leadership effectiveness. These variables are hypothesized to have an effect on leaders' behaviors, which themselves have a more direct relationship to leadership success (see Highlight 9–1).

One advantage of looking at leaders in terms of behavior instead of personality is that behavior is often easier to measure; leadership behaviors can be observed, whereas personality traits, values, or intelligence must be inferred from behavior or measured with tests. Another advantage of looking at leader

---

HIGHLIGHT 9–1

Leadership Quotes, Chapter Nine

One of my favorite sayings is that in this company we stack every bit of criticism between two layers of praise. I think this is a more diplomatic, concerned approach.

Mary Kay Ash

Always be tactful and well mannered and teach your subordinates to be the same. Avoid excessive sharpness or harshness of voice, which usually indicates the man who has short-comings of his own to hide.

Field Marshall Erwin Rommel

Be willing to make decisions. That's the most important quality in a good leader. Don't fall victim to what I call the "ready-aim-aim-aim-aim syndrome." You must be willing to fire.

T. Boone Pickens

If I had to sum up in one word what makes a good manager, I'd say decisiveness. You can use the fanciest computers to gather the numbers, but in the end you have to set a timetable and act.

Lee Iacocca

A human being should be able to change a diaper, plan an invasion, butcher a hog, conn a ship, design a building, write a sonnet, balance accounts, build a wall, set a bone, comfort the dying, take orders, give orders, cooperate, act alone, pitch manure, solve equations, analyze a new problem, program a computer, cook a tasty meal, fight efficiently, die gallantly. Specialization is for insects.

Robert A. Heinlein, *The Note Book of Lazarus Long*

---

behavior is that many people are less defensive about and feel in more control of specific behaviors than they do about their personalities. To suggest someone needs to change his or her personality implies greater personal criticism than a suggestion that he or she needs to change his or her behavior. Furthermore, it seems a more manageable task to change a specific behavior (e.g., learn to express support and concern about others more frequently) than to change one's whole personality (e.g., develop an affable and agreeable personality). To say that leaders are people with certain kinds of personalities seems to exclude those who have different personalities from being leaders; but to say leaders need to *act* in certain ways is within everyone's reach. The focus on behaviors is based partly on the belief that leaders can be flexible in the way they behave whatever their personality.

Nevertheless, leaders with certain personality traits, values, attitudes, or preferences probably will find it easier to effectively perform some leadership behaviors than others. For example, leaders with high agreeableness (as defined in Chapter Seven) may find it relatively easy to show support and concern for followers but may also find it difficult to discipline followers. Leaders on a committee who are judgers and prefer planning out activities may have a difficult time learning to tolerate other team members who feel that plans tie them down (i.e., perceivers). Leaders can learn new behaviors, but it may take practice to develop ease and competence in performing them in new situations.

STUDIES OF LEADER BEHAVIOR

The Early Studies

As we have noted, the earliest data-based approaches to studying leaders emphasized their personality traits. The change in focus from the trait to the behavioral approach occurred for two primary reasons. The first involved a widespread overreaction to the conclusions of a comprehensive review of the trait research literature. Stogdill (1948) concluded in this review that certain individual difference variables do indeed appear related to leadership success. He also noted, however, that having particular personality traits was not a guarantee of success. Many other leadership researchers focused only on Stogdill's latter point and mistakenly concluded that traits were unrelated to leadership success.

A second factor in the shift from studying leader traits to studying leader behaviors involved a trend taking over the entire field of psychology. The whole discipline was undergoing a dramatic paradigm shift in the 1940s. Prior to the 1940s, psychologists were primarily interested in how behavior could be explained in terms of differences between people on certain stable, measurable dimensions (i.e., individual differences). During the 1940s and 1950s, however, the behavioral school in psychology was gaining ascendance. More emphasis was placed on how the situation (e.g., rewards and punishments) systematically affected overt behavior. Because of the disillusionment with the trait approach in general, the misunderstanding of Stogdill's work, and the paradigm shift away from traits and behaviors, leadership research in the 1940s and 1950s shifted away from traits and toward the study of leader behaviors.

Much of the initial leader behavior research was conducted at Ohio State University and the University of Michigan. Collectively, the Ohio State University studies developed a series of questionnaires to measure different leader behaviors in work settings. Hemphill (1949) began this development effort by collecting over 1,800 questionnaire items that described different types of leadership behaviors. These items were collapsed into 150 statements, and these statements were then used to develop a questionnaire called the **Leader Behavior Descrip-**

tion Questionnaire (LBDQ) (Hemphill & Coons, 1957). In order to obtain information about a particular leader's behavior, subordinates were asked to rate the extent to which their leader performed behaviors like the following:

He lets subordinates know when they've done a good job.

He sets clear expectations about performance.

He shows concern for subordinates as individuals.

He makes subordinates feel at ease.

In analyzing the questionnaires from thousands of subordinates, the statistical pattern of responses to all the different items indicated leaders could be described in terms of two primary dimensions of behavior called consideration and initiating structure (Fleishman, 1973; Halpin & Winer, 1957). **Consideration** refers to how much a leader is friendly and supportive toward subordinates. Leaders high in consideration engage in many different behaviors that show supportiveness and concern, such as speaking up for subordinates' interests, caring about their personal situations, and showing appreciation for their work. **Initiating structure** refers to how much a leader emphasizes meeting work goals and accomplishing the task. Leaders high in initiating structure engage in many different task-related behaviors, such as assigning deadlines, establishing performance standards, and monitoring performance levels.

The LBDQ was not the only leadership questionnaire developed by the Ohio State researchers. For example, the Supervisory Descriptive Behavior Questionnaire (SBDQ) measured the extent to which leaders in industrial settings exhibited consideration and initiating structure behaviors (Fleishman, 1972). The Leadership Opinion Questionnaire (LOQ) asked leaders to indicate the extent to which they believed different consideration and initiating behaviors were important to leadership success (Fleishman, 1989). The LBDQ-XII was developed to assess 10 other categories of leadership behaviors in addition to consideration and initiating structure (Stogdill, 1959). Some of the additional leadership behaviors assessed by the LBDQ-XII included acting as a representative for the group, being able to tolerate uncertainty, emphasizing production, and reconciling conflicting organizational demands.

Rather than trying to describe the variety of behaviors leaders exhibit in work settings, the objective of researchers at the University of Michigan was to identify leader behaviors that contributed to effective group performance (Likert, 1961). The Michigan researchers concluded that four categories of leadership behaviors are related to effective group performance: leader support, interaction facilitation, goal emphasis, and work facilitation (Bowers & Seashore, 1966).

Both goal emphasis and work facilitation are **job-centered dimensions** of behavior similar to the initiating structure behaviors described earlier. **Goal emphasis** behaviors are concerned with motivating subordinates to accomplish the task at hand, and **work facilitation** behaviors are concerned with clarifying roles, acquiring and allocating resources, and reconciling organizational conflicts. Leader support and interaction facilitation are **employee-centered dimensions** of behavior similar to the consideration dimension of the various Ohio State questionnaires. **Leader support** includes behaviors where the leader shows concern for his subordinates; **interaction facilitation** includes those behaviors where leaders act to smooth over and minimize conflicts among followers. Like researchers at Ohio State, those at the University of Michigan also developed a questionnaire, the Survey of Organizations, to assess the degree to which leaders exhibit these four dimensions of leadership behaviors (Bowers & Seashore, 1966).

Although the behaviors comprising the task-oriented and people-oriented leadership dimensions were similar across the two research programs, there was a fundamental difference in assumption underlying the work at the University of Michigan and Ohio State. Researchers at the University of Michigan considered job-centered and employee-centered behaviors to be at opposite ends of a single leadership behavior continuum. Leaders could manifest either strong employee or job-centered behaviors, but not both. On the other hand, researchers at Ohio State believed that consideration and initiating structure were independent continuums. Thus, leaders could be high in both initiating structure and consideration, low in both dimensions, or high in one and low in the other.

An assumption of both research programs was that certain behaviors could be identified that are universally associated with leadership success. In general, both groups reported that leaders exhibiting a high level of consideration or employee-centered behaviors typically had more satisfied subordinates. Leaders who exhibited high role and task clarification (i.e., initiating structure or job-centered) behaviors often had higher-performing work units if the group faced a relatively ambiguous or ill-defined task (Bass, 1990). At the same time, however, leaders whose behavior was highly autocratic (an aspect of initiating structure) were more likely to have relatively dissatisfied subordinates (Bass, 1990). Findings like these suggest that there is no universal set of leader behaviors associated with leadership success. Often the degree to which leaders need to exhibit task or people-oriented behaviors depends on the situation.

Recent Conceptualizations of Behaviors and Skills

A more recent and popular conceptualization of leadership is really an extension of the findings reported by the University of Michigan and Ohio State leadership researchers. The **Leadership Grid®** profiles leader behavior on two dimensions, called **concern for people** and **concern for production** (Blake & McCanse, 1991; Blake & Mouton, 1964). The word *concern* reflects how a leader's underlying assumptions about people at work and the importance of the "bottom line" affect leadership style. In that sense, then, the Leadership Grid

FIGURE 9–1

The Leadership Grid® Figure

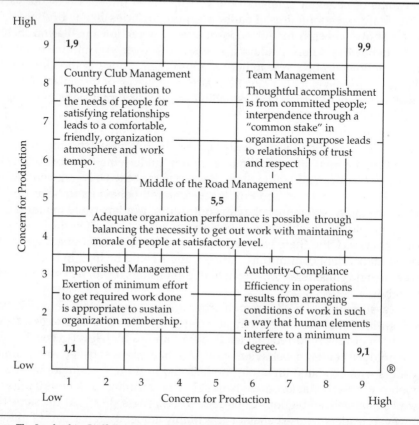

Source: The Leadership Grid® Figure from *Leadership Dilemmas—Grid Solutions,* by Robert R. Blake and Anne Adams McCanse. Houston: Gulf Publishing Company, p. 29. Copyright © 1991, by Scientific Methods, Inc. Reproduced by permission of the owners.

deals with more than just behavior. Nonetheless, it is included in this chapter because it is such a direct descendant of earlier behavioral studies.

As seen in Figure 9-1, leaders can get scores ranging from 1 to 9 on both concern for people and concern for production depending on their responses to a leadership questionnaire. These two scores are then plotted on the Leadership Grid, and the two score combinations represent different leadership orientations. Each orientation reflects a "unique set of assumptions for using power and authority to link people to production" (Blake & McCanse, 1991, p. 29). Amid the different leadership styles, the most effective leaders are claimed to have both high concern for people and high concern for production, and Leadership Grid training programs are designed to move leaders to a 9,9 leadership style. Whereas this objective seems intuitively appealing, we should note the evidence to support it comes primarily from Blake, Mouton, and their associates; little independent verification of the claim is available in the published literature. We also should remember those earlier studies of leader behavior suggesting no fixed set of leader behaviors are universally effective across all situations.

Three more recent conceptualizations of leadership behaviors are not prescriptive in the Leadership Grid sense but rather provide more extensive taxonomies of the different types of behaviors leaders perform. The Coaching Behavior Assessment System (CBAS) was designed to be used by observers to help them assess the frequency with which coaches exhibit different leadership behaviors (Curtis, Smith & Smoll, 1979). The CBAS consists of 12 behavior dimensions, including reinforcement, encouragement after mistakes, technical instruction after mistakes, punishment, and organization. Another leadership taxonomy involved an applied behavioral analysis framework for categorizing leaders' behaviors. **Applied behavioral analysis** is concerned with identifying the factors that preceded a particular behavior and identifying the rewards and punishments administered as a consequence of a particular behavior. Thus, several of the dimensions of the Operant Supervisory Taxonomy and Index (OSTI) categorized different leadership behaviors as antecedents, monitoring, or consequences of subordinates' behaviors (Komacki, 1986; Komacki, Zlotnick, & Jensen, 1986). In addition to these efforts, Yukl and his associates reviewed other taxonomies, developed a series of questionnaires, and collected data from thousands of leaders in order to develop a comprehensive taxonomy of 11 leadership behaviors. As seen in Table 9–1, some of the behaviors in this taxonomy include informing, planning and organizing, motivating, and managing conflict.

Assessment Instruments

One way to improve leadership effectiveness is to provide leadership practitioners with feedback regarding the frequency and skill with which they perform various types of leadership behaviors. Unfortunately, both the CBAS and OSTI are difficult to use in a practical sense, as both require a set of highly trained observers who need to watch leaders over a fairly lengthy period of time before their results could be used to provide meaningful feedback. However, Yukl, Wall, and Lepsinger (1989) developed the Managerial Practices Survey (MPS) to assess how important each of the 11 dimensions in Yukl's taxonomy were for success in a particular leadership position. In addition, the MPS could be used to assess the frequency or skill with which job incumbents exhibited behaviors associated with each of the 11 dimensions. The MPS can be a

TABLE 9–1
Yukl's Integrating Taxonomy of Managerial Behavior

Giving-Seeking Information

Informing	Disseminating needed or useful information
Clarifying	Communicating job responsibilities and expectations
Monitoring	Reviewing individual and organizational indices of performance

Making Decisions

Problem-solving	Identifying, analyzing, and solving work-related problems
Planning and organizing	Setting goals, building action plans, and coordinating activities
Consulting and delegating	Involving others in decisions and implementation

Influencing People

Motivating	Appealing to emotions, values, or logic or otherwise influencing desired action
Recognizing and rewarding	Praising and reinforcing performance

Building Relationships

Supporting	Acting friendly, considerate, and supportive both personally and careerwise
Networking	Developing contacts with others
Managing conflict and team building	Resolving conflict constructively and fostering teamwork

---

Source: Adapted from G. A. Yukl, *Leadership in Organizations*, 2nd ed. (Englewood Cliffs, N.J.: Prentice Hall, 1989).

very useful instrument for providing feedback to leaders, as it indicates which leadership dimensions are important for leadership success and indicates how frequently or how well leaders are performing these different types of behaviors.

Two other instruments that can provide useful feedback to leaders about their work behavior are Benchmarks (Lombardo & McCauley, 1989) and the Management Skills Profile (PDI, 1983). Although conceptually similar to the MPS, these two instruments differ in several important ways. First, both instruments provide feedback over a greater number of leadership dimensions than the MPS. Second, both Benchmarks and the Management Skills Profile provide **360-degree feedback**. In other words, superiors, peers, and subordinates complete Benchmarks or the Management Skills Profile for a target leader, and these ratings are compared to the leader's self-ratings. This feedback is typically much more powerful than self-ratings or subordinates' ratings alone, as it tells leaders how they are seen by different constituencies within the organization. The target leader described in Figure 9–2, for example, saw him-

FIGURE 9–2
Examples of 360-Degree Feedback from Benchmarks

Putting people at ease: Displays warmth and a good sense of humor.

Target person's percentile scores for various observer groups:

	0	25	50	75	100
Self					X
All observers		X			
Superiors		X			
Peers		X			
Subordinates		X			

Confronting Problem Subordinates: Acts decisively and with fairness when dealing with problem subordinates.

	0	25	50	75	100
Self				X	
All observers			X		
Superiors				X	
Peers				X	
Subordinates		X			

Source: M. M. Lombardo, & McCauley, C. D. *Benchmarks: A Guide to Its Development and Use* (Greensboro, N.C.: The Center for Creative Leadership, 1989). Used with permission.

self much more favorably than did others around him including his superior, peers, and subordinates. Leadership researchers would have a fairly distorted picture of his strengths and weaknesses if they relied only on this leader's self-report data. Finally, and perhaps most important, the *Benchmarks Developmental Guide* (Lombardo, Hutchinson, & Pryor, 1990) and the *Successful Manager's Handbook* (Davis, Hellervik, & Sheard, 1989) are two developmental guides that accompany Benchmarks and the Management Skills Profile, respectively. These guides provide managers with a number of practical suggestions as well as a list of different training courses that leaders may want to take in order to change the way they behave at work.

In summary, leadership practitioners can benefit from the leadership behavior research in several ways. First, the behavioral approach has served the important purpose of directing attention to identifying types of leadership behavior critical to success. Second, the behavioral approach allows leadership practitioners to focus on concrete and specific examples of leader behavior. This allows leadership practitioners to meaningfully compare one leader's behavior with another's and gives leadership practitioners more specific examples of how they may want to act in similar situations. Third, an outgrowth of the behavioral approach has been the development of various leadership behavior questionnaires. These questionnaires can be used to provide feedback to leadership practitioners, and the developmental guides that accompany some of the instruments can provide practitioners with valuable tips on how to improve.

HOW INDIVIDUAL DIFFERENCES AFFECT BEHAVIORS AND SKILLS

The behavioral taxonomies described above categorize leader behaviors into a number of different dimensions, and each of these dimensions consists of a set of relatively homogeneous behaviors. For example, the consulting and delegating dimension in Table 9–1 consists of those behaviors that pertain to getting subordinates actively involved in the decision-making process and delegating authority and responsibility to subordinates. It is important to note, however, that these taxonomies do not address the issue of how well a leader might perform those behaviors within a particular dimension. **Leadership skills** get around the purely descriptive aspect of leadership behavior taxonomies by adding an evaluative component to sets of related leadership behaviors. More specifically, leadership skills consist of three components, which include a well-defined body of knowledge, a set of related behaviors, and clear criteria of competent performance.

Perhaps leadership skills may be better understood by using an analogy from basketball. People differ considerably in their basketball skills; good basketball players know when to pass and when to shoot, and are adept at making lay-ups, shots from the field, and free throws. Knowing when to pass and when to shoot is an example of the knowledge component, and hitting lay-ups and free throws is an example of the behavioral component of skills. In addition, shooting percentages can be used as one type of criterion for evaluating basketball skills. Leadership skills, such as delegating, can be seen much the same way. Good leaders know when and to whom a particular task should be delegated (i.e., knowledge); they effectively communicate their expections concerning a delegated task (i.e., behavior); and they check to see whether the task was accomplished in a satisfactory manner (i.e., criteria).

Just as basketball skills can improve with practice, so too can leadership skills improve with practice. For example, shooting 200 free throws a day should improve a player's free-throw shooting percentages in games, and taking advantage of public-speaking opportunities can improve a leader's public-speaking skills. The degree of practice needed to develop proficiency in a skill will, of course, vary from person to person. Almost everyone can learn the skill of solving algebraic problems. However, people with relatively greater quantitative ability will learn how to solve more difficult algebraic problems, solve them faster, and be more likely to apply them in novel situations than people with weaker quantitative ability. Similarly, extroverted leaders with high self-confidence and high stress tolerance may benefit more from a relatively brief public-speaking course than introverted leaders with low self-confidence and low stress tolerance. This does not mean the latter cannot benefit from a public-speaking course, only that they may need to work longer at developing the skill than others. Thus, just as natural athleticism can make learning a new sport more or less difficult, so too can traits, cognitive abilities, values, or preferences help or hinder the development of a new leadership skill. Both initial individual differences and practice play important roles in the acquisition and development of leadership skills.

IMPLICATIONS FOR LEADERS AND FOLLOWERS: BASIC SKILLS FOR IMPROVING PERSONAL EFFECTIVENESS

Although there is a wide variety of leadership skills, some are more central and important than others. Some, such as public speaking, may be important to the success of senior-level executives but less important to first-line supervisors. Other skills seem consistently related to desirable outcomes (e.g., subordinates' level of satisfaction, work-unit performance, or organizational climate) regardless of role or organizational level. We will focus here on four basic leadership skills: communication, listening, being assertive, and giving feedback. We believe anyone who develops these basic interpersonal skills almost inherently increases her potential impact as a leader. In fact, anyone who develops these skills improves as a follower, too. That's why we describe them in the general sense as improving personal effectiveness. Developing them will help anyone function more effectively in the leadership process, whether fulfilling a leader role or a follower role at any particular time. In general, these basic leadership skills help establish and maintain constructive relationships with others. Additional skills useful to both leaders and followers will be covered in upcoming chapters. In general, however, since this book primarily concerns leadership, we usually will discuss the skills from the leader's perspective.

Communication

Bass (1990) defined communication effectiveness as the degree to which someone tells others something and ensures they understand what was said. Few skills are more vital to leadership. Studies show that good leaders communicate feelings and ideas, actively solicit new ideas from others, and effectively articulate arguments, advocate positions, and persuade others (Bennis &

"Baaahrrrrrimmmm stone-uh . . . !"

Nanus, 1985; Kanter, 1983; Parks, 1985). It seems likely the same can be said of good followers, though far less study has gone into that question. Moreover, the quality of a leader's communication is positively correlated with subordinate satisfaction (Klimoski & Haynes, 1980) as well as with productivity and quality of services rendered (Snyder & Morris, 1984). Effective communication skills are also important because they provide leaders and followers with greater access to information relevant to important organizational decisions (Fiechtner & Krayer, 1986).

A systems view of communication is depicted in Figure 9–3. Communication is best understood as a process beginning with an intention to exchange certain information with others. That intention eventually takes form in some particular expression, which may or may not adequately convey what was in-

FIGURE 9-3
A Systems View of Communication

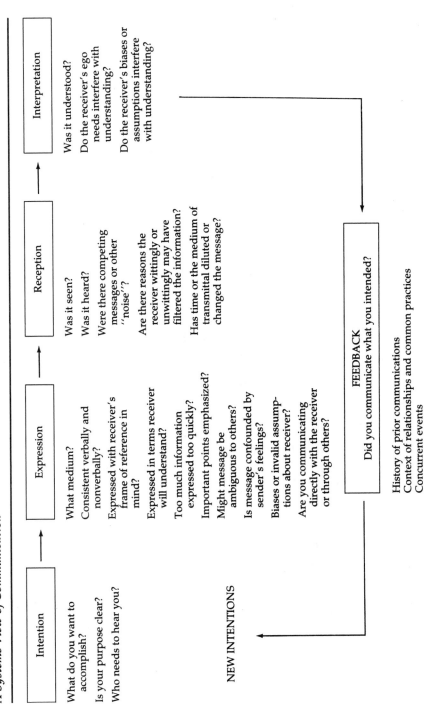

Intention	Expression	Reception	Interpretation

Intention → Expression → Reception → Interpretation

Intention

What do you want to accomplish?

Is your purpose clear?

Who needs to hear you?

Expression

What medium?

Consistent verbally and nonverbally?

Expressed with receiver's frame of reference in mind?

Expressed in terms receiver will understand?

Too much information expressed too quickly?

Important points emphasized?

Might message be ambiguous to others?

Is message confounded by sender's feelings?

Biases or invalid assumptions about receiver?

Are you communicating directly with the receiver or through others?

Reception

Was it seen?

Was it heard?

Were there competing messages or other "noise"?

Are there reasons the receiver wittingly or unwittingly may have filtered the information?

Has time or the medium of transmittal diluted or changed the message?

Interpretation

Was it understood?

Do the receiver's ego needs interfere with understanding?

Do the receiver's biases or assumptions interfere with understanding?

NEW INTENTIONS

FEEDBACK
Did you communicate what you intended?

History of prior communications
Context of relationships and common practices
Concurrent events

tended. The next stage is reception. Just as with a weak or garbled radio signal, or malfunctioning antenna, what is received is not always what was sent. Reception is followed by interpretation. If a driver asks, "Do I turn here?" and a passenger answers, "Right," did the passenger mean *yes* or *turn right*? Finally, it is not enough merely to receive and interpret information; their interpretations may or may not be consistent with what was intended at the outset. Therefore, it always helps to have a feedback loop to assess any communication's overall effectiveness.

We also can use the scheme in Figure 9–3 to think about the knowledge, behaviors, and criteria used to evaluate communication skills. Using this model, the knowledge component of communication skills concerns the intentions of the leader, knowing what medium is most effective, and knowing whether the message was heard and understood. The behavioral component of communication skills concerns the behaviors associated with communicating verbally and nonverbally. Feedback concerning whether or not the message was understood by the receiver comprises the evaluative component of communication skills. An important aspect regarding feedback is that it is an outcome of the previous steps in the communication process. In reality, the effectiveness of the communication process depends on the successful integration of all of the steps in the communication process. Effectiveness in just one step (e.g., speaking ability) is not enough. Successful communication needs to be judged in terms of the effective operation of the whole system.

The model also suggests a number of reasons why communication breakdowns might occur. For example, communication breakdowns can occur because the purpose of the message was unclear, the leader's or follower's verbal and nonverbal behaviors were inconsistent, the message was not heard by the receiver, or because someone may have misinterpreted another's message. Most people see themselves as effective communicators, and senders and receivers of messages often seem disposed to believe communication breakdowns are the other person's fault. Communication breakdowns often lead to blaming someone else for the problem, or "finger pointing" (see Figure 9–4). One way to avoid the finger pointing associated with communication breakdowns is to think of communication as a process, not as a set of discrete individual acts (i.e., giving instructions to someone). By using the communication model, leadership practitioners can minimize the conflict typically associated with communication breakdowns.

The model in Figure 9–3 can provide leadership practitioners with many ideas about how to improve communication skills. They can do so by (a) determining the purpose of their communication before speaking; (b) choosing an appropriate context and medium for the message; (c) sending clear signals; and (d) actively ensuring that others understand the message. The following is a more detailed discussion of some of the different ways in which leaders can improve their communication skills.

FIGURE 9–4
Breakdowns in Communication Sometimes Lead to Finger Pointing

Person A	Person B
"You weren't listening!"	"I only did what you told me to."
"That isn't what I said."	"Why didn't you say so?"
"You didn't follow directions."	"But you didn't seem serious."
"That isn't what you were supposed to do."	

Know what your purpose is.   One will communicate more effectively with others if one is clear about what one intends to communicate. By knowing his purpose, a leader or follower can better decide whether to communicate publicly or privately, orally or in writing, and so on. These decisions may seem trivial, but often the specific content of a message will be enhanced or diminished by how and where it is communicated.

Choose an appropriate context and medium.   There is a rule of thumb that says leaders should praise followers in public and punish them in private. It points out the importance of selecting physical and social settings that will enhance the effectiveness of any communication. If the leader has an office, for example, then how much of her communication with subordinates should occur in her office and how much in the followers' workplace?

Sometimes, of course, an office is the best place to talk. Even that decision, however, is not all a leader needs to consider. The arrangement of office furniture can enhance or interfere with effective communication. Informal, personal communications are enhanced when two people sit at a 90-degree angle and are relatively close to each other; more formal communication is enhanced when the follower remains standing when the leader is sitting or if the leader communicates across his desk to followers.

Additionally, a leader's communications often take place in a whole organizational context involving broader existing practices, policies, and procedures. Leaders need to take care that their words and deeds do not inadvertently undercut or contradict such broader organizational communications, including their own bosses. Organizational factors also help determine whether any particular communication is most appropriately expressed orally or in writing. Oral communication is the most immediate, the most personal, the most dynamic, and often the most impactive; it is ideal when communication needs to be two-way or when the personalized aspect is especially important. At the other extreme, a more permanent modality is probably most appropriate when the leader needs a record of the communication or when something needs to be expressed in a particular way to different people, at different times, in different settings.

Send clear signals.   Leaders and followers can enhance the clarity of their communications in several ways. First, it is helpful to be mindful of others' level of expertise, values, experiences, and expectations and how these characteristics affect their **frames of reference**. For example, the leader may brief a new organizational policy to followers, and they may come up with different interpretations of this policy based on different values and expectations. By being sensitive to followers' frames of reference and modifying messages accordingly, leaders can minimize communication breakdowns. Another way to clarify messages is to create a common frame of reference for followers before communicating a message. For example, consider the following passage:

> With hocked gems financing him, our hero bravely defied all scornful laughter that tried to prevent his scheme. "Your eyes deceive," he had said. "An egg, not a table correctly typifies this unexplored planet." Now, three sisters sought sturdy proof. Forging along, sometimes through calm vastness, yet more often over turbulent peaks and valleys, days became weeks as many doubters spread fearful rumors about the edge. At last, welcome winged creatures appeared signifying momentous success. (Sanford & Garrod, 1981)

Many are slow to recognize that the passage is about Christopher Columbus. Once the correct frame of reference is known, however, the previously confusing elements become sensible. Followers more readily understand new or ambiguous material when leaders paint a common frame of reference prior to introducing new material.

Another way to send clear signals is to use familiar terms, jargon, and concepts. This can serve to clarify and abbreviate messages when receivers are familiar with the terms. However, messages containing jargon can also be confusing to those receivers unfamiliar with those terms. For example, a freshman cadet at the United States Air Force Academy might say to another, "I hope we get an ONP this weekend, because after three GRs, a PCE, and a SAMI, I'll need it." Because the second cadet understands this organizational jargon, he or she would have no difficulty understanding what was said. However, a person unfamiliar with the Air Force Academy would not have the slightest idea what this conversation meant. Leaders should make sure followers understand any jargon they use—especially if the followers are relatively inexperienced. (In case you were wondering, the cadet said, "I hope we get a pass to go downtown this weekend, because after three academic tests, a military test, and a room inspection, I'll need it.)

Two other ways to improve the clarity of messages are to use unambiguous, concrete terms and to send congruent verbal and nonverbal signals. For example, a leader who tells a follower, "Your monthly sales were down 22 percent last month" will more effectively communicate her concerns and cause less follower defensiveness than a leader who states, "Your performance has been poor." Thus, the more specific the message, the less likely receivers will be confused over what it means. In addition, leaders will be more effective communicators if their nonverbal signals match the content of the message. Followers, like everyone, can get confused, and tend to believe nonverbal signals when leaders send mixed verbal and nonverbal messages (Remland, 1981). Similarly, followers may send mixed messages to leaders; communication goes both ways.

One particularly destructive form of incongruent verbal and nonverbal signals is sarcasm. It is not the anger of the message per se but rather the implicit message conveyed by dishonest words that drives a wedge in the trust between leaders and followers. It is *not* a wise idea for leaders to always share their transitory feelings with subordinates, but if the leader *is* going to share his or her feelings, it is important to do so in a congruent manner. Similarly, it can be just as unwise for followers to share transitory feelings with leaders; but if it's done, it's important for verbal and nonverbal behaviors to be congruent.

Actively ensure that others understand the message.   Leaders and followers can ensure that others understand their messages by practicing two-way communication and by paying attention to the others' emotional responses. Effective leaders and followers tend to actively engage in two-way communication (though this usually is more under the control of the leader than the follower). They can do so in many ways: by seeking feedback, by mingling in each other's work areas, and by being sincere about having an open-door policy (in the case of leaders) (Luthans & Larsen, 1986).

Although such steps appear to be straightforward, leaders typically believe they utilize two-way communication more frequently than their followers perceive them using it (Sadler & Hofstede, 1972). Leaders can get clues about the clarity of their messages by paying attention to the nonverbal signals sent by their followers. When followers' verbal and nonverbal messages seem to be incongruent, it may be because the message sent to them was unclear. For example, followers may look confused when they verbally acknowledge that they understand a particular task. In this case, leaders may find it useful to address the mixed signals directly in order to clear up such confusion.

Listening

Good leaders and followers recognize the value of two-way communication. Listening to others is just as important as expressing oneself clearly to them. People in leadership roles are only as good as the information they have, and much of their information comes from watching and listening to what goes on around them.

At first, it may seem strange to describe listening as a skill. Listening may seem like an automatic response to things being said, not something one practices to improve, like free throws. However, the best listeners are **active listeners**, not passive listeners (Davis, Hellervik, & Sheard, 1989). In passive listening, someone may be speaking but the receiver is not focused on understanding the speaker. Instead, the receiver may be thinking about the next thing he will say or how bored he is in listening to the speaker. In either case, the receiver is not paying attention to what the sender is saying. To truly get the fullest meaning out of what someone else says, one needs to practice active listening. Individuals who are listening actively exhibit a certain pattern of nonverbal behaviors, do not disrupt the sender's message, try to put the sender's message into their own words, and scan the sender for various nonverbal signals. Knowing what nonverbal signals to send and correctly interpreting the sender's nonverbal signals are the knowledge component of listening skills. One's nonverbal signals are the behavioral component, and how well one can paraphrase a sender's message makes up the evaluative component of listening skills.

In addition to helping one understand others better, active listening is a way to visibly demonstrate that one respects others. Often, people, particularly those with high self-monitoring scores, can sense when others are not truly paying attention to what they are saying. Followers will quickly decide it is not worth their time to give their leader information if they perceive they are not being listened to. Leaders may do the same. To avoid "turning off" others, leaders and followers can improve their active listening skills in a number of ways. Some of these tips include learning to (a) model nonverbal signals associated with active listening, (b) actively interpret the sender's message, (c) be aware of the sender's nonverbal behaviors, and (d) avoid becoming defensive. The following is a more detailed discussion of these four ways to improve active listening skills.

Demonstrate nonverbally that you are listening.   Make sure your nonverbal behaviors show that you have turned your attention entirely to the speaker. Many people mistakenly assume that listening is a one-way process. Although it seems plausible to think of information flowing only from the sender to the receiver, the essence of active listening is to see all communication, even listening, as a two-way process. Listeners show they are paying attention to the speaker with their own body movements. They put aside, both mentally and physically, other work they may have been engaged in. Individuals who are actively listening establish eye contact with the speaker, and they do not doodle, shoot rubber bands, or look away at other things. They show they are genuinely interested in what the speaker has to say.

Actively interpret the sender's message. The essence of active listening is trying to understand what the sender truly means. It is not enough merely to be (even if you could) a perfect human tape recorder. One must look for the meaning behind someone else's words. In the first place, this means one needs to keep one's mind open to the sender's ideas. This, in turn, implies not interrupting the speaker and not planning what to say while the speaker is delivering the message. In addition, good listeners withhold judgment about the sender's ideas until they have heard the entire message. This way, they avoid sending the message that their mind is made up and avoid jumping to conclusions about what the sender is going to say. Another reason to avoid sending a "closed-mind" message is that it may lead others to *not* bring up things one definitely needs to hear.

Another valuable way to actively interpret what the sender is saying is to **paraphrase** the sender's message. By putting the speaker's thoughts into their own words, leaders can better ensure that they fully understand what their followers are saying, and vice versa. The value of paraphrasing even a simple idea is apparent in the following dialogue:

Sarah:

Jim should never have become a teacher.

Fred:

You mean he doesn't like working with kids? Do you think he's too impatient?

Sarah:

No, neither of those things. I just think his tastes are so expensive he's frustrated with a teacher's salary.

In this example, Fred indicated what he thought Sarah meant, which prompted her to clarify her meaning. If he had merely said, "I know what you mean," Fred and Sarah mistakenly would have concluded they agreed when their ideas were really far apart. Paraphrasing also actively communicates your interest in what the other person is saying. Highlight 9–2 offers various "communication leads" that may help in paraphrasing others' messages to improve your listening skills.

Attending to the sender's nonverbal behavior. People should use all the tools at their disposal to understand what someone else is saying. This includes paraphrasing senders' messages, and being astute at picking up on senders' nonverbal signals. Much of the social meaning in messages is conveyed nonverbally, and when verbal and nonverbal signals conflict, people often tend to trust the nonverbal signals. Thus, no one can be an effective listener without paying attention to nonverbal signals. This requires listening to more than just the speaker's words themselves; it requires listening for feelings expressed via the speaker's loudness, tone of voice, and pace of speech as well as watching

---

HIGHLIGHT 9–2

Communication Leads for Paraphrasing and Assuring Mutual Understanding

From your point of view . . . .
It seems you . . . .
As you see it . . . .
You think . . . .
What I hear you saying is . . . .
Do you mean . . .?
I'm not sure I understand what you mean; is it . . .?
I get the impression . . . .
You appear to be feeling . . . .
Correct me if I'm wrong, but . . . .

---

the speaker's facial expressions, posture, gestures, and so on. These behaviors convey a wealth of information that is immensely richer in meaning than the purely verbal content of a message, just as it is richer to watch actors in a stage play rather than merely read their script (Robbins, 1989). Although there may not be any simple codebook of nonverbal cues with which one can decipher what a sender "really" feels, listeners should explore what senders are trying to say whenever the former sense mixed signals between a sender's verbal and nonverbal behaviors.

Avoid becoming defensive. Defensive behavior is most likely to occur when someone feels threatened (Gibb, 1961). Although it may seem natural to become defensive when criticized, defensiveness lessens a person's ability to constructively make use of the information. Acting defensively may also decrease followers' subsequent willingness to pass additional unpleasant information on to the leader or other followers, or even the leader's willingness to give feedback to followers. Defensiveness on the part of the leader can also hurt the entire team or organization, as it includes a tendency to place blame, categorize others as morally good or bad, and generally question others' motives. Such behaviors on a leader's part hardly build a positive work or team climate.

Leaders can reduce their defensiveness when listening to complaints by trying to put themselves in the other person's shoes. Leaders have an advantage if they can empathize with how they and their policies are seen by others; they can better change their behaviors and policies if they know how others perceive them. Leaders need to avoid the temptation to explain how the other person is wrong and should instead just try to understand how he perceives things. A useful warning sign that a leader may be behaving defensively (or perhaps closed-mindedly) is if he begins a conversation saying, "Yes, but. . . ."

Assertiveness

What is **assertive behavior**, and what are assertiveness skills? Basically, individuals exhibiting assertive behavior are able to stand up for their own rights (or their group's rights) in a way that also recognizes the concurrent right of others to do the same (see Highlight 9–3). Like the two skills already discussed, assertiveness skills also have knowledge, behavioral, and evaluative components. The behavioral component of assertiveness skills was mentioned already. It involves standing up for one's own or the group's rights in a constructive, nonhostile way. The knowledge component of assertiveness skills concerns knowing when and when not to behave assertively. People who are overly assertive may be perceived to be aggressive and often may "win the battle but lose the war." Finally, the evaluative component comes into play when individuals are successful (or unsuccessful) in standing up for their own or their group's rights, and in working in a continual effective manner with others.

Perhaps the best way to understand assertiveness is to distinguish it from two other styles people have for dealing with conflict: acquiescence (nonassertiveness) and aggression (Alberti & Emmons, 1974). **Acquiescence** is avoiding interpersonal conflict entirely either by giving up and giving in or by expressing one's needs in an apologetic, self-effacing way. Acquiescence is *not* synonymous with politeness or helpfulness, though it is sometimes rationalized as such. People who are acquiescent, or nonassertive, back down easily when challenged. By not speaking up for themselves, they abdicate power to others and, in the process, get trampled on. Besides the practical outcome of not attaining one's goals, an acquiescent style typically leads to many negative feelings such as guilt, resentment, and self-blame, as well as a low self-image. Sometimes people justify their nonassertiveness to themselves with the idea that acquiescing to others is being polite or helpful, but this often is just a rationalization.

Aggression, on the other hand, is an effort to attain objectives by attacking or hurting others. Aggressive people trample on others, and their aggressiveness can take such direct forms as threats, verbal attacks, physical intimidation, emotional outbursts, explosiveness, bullying, and hostility—and such indirect forms as nagging, passive-aggressive uncooperativeness, guilt arousal, and other behaviors that undermine an adversary's autonomy. It is important to understand that aggressiveness is not just an emotionally strong form of assertiveness. Aggressiveness tends to be reactive, and it tends to spring from feelings of vulnerability and a lack of self-confidence. Aggressive people inwardly

---

HIGHLIGHT 9-3

Assertiveness Questionnaire

- Do you let someone know when you think he or she is being unfair to you?
- Can you criticize someone else's ideas openly?
- Are you able to speak up in a meeting?
- Can you ask others for small favors or help?
- Is it easy for you to compliment others?
- Can you tell someone else you don't like what he or she is doing?
- When you are complimented, do you really accept the compliment without inwardly discounting it in your own mind?
- Can you look others in the eye when you talk to them?

If you could answer most of these questions affirmatively for most situations, then you do behave assertively.

Source: Adapted from R. E. Alberti, and M. L. Emmons, *Your Perfect Right* (San Luis Obispo, Calif.: Impact, 1974).

---

doubt their ability to resolve issues constructively through the give-and-take of direct confrontation between mutually respecting equals. Aggressiveness is a form of interpersonal manipulation in which one tries to put oneself in a "top-dog" role and others in a "bottom-dog" role (Shostrom, 1967). Additionally, aggressive people have difficulty expressing positive feelings.

Assertiveness is different from both acquiescence and aggression; it is not merely a compromise between them or a midpoint on a continuum. Assertiveness involves direct and frank statements of one's own goals and feelings, and a willingness to address the interests of others in the spirit of mutual problem solving and a belief that openness is preferable to secretiveness and hidden agendas. Assertiveness is the behavioral opposite of both acquiescence and aggression, as depicted in Figure 9-5. The qualitative differences between these three styles are like the differences between fleeing (acquiescence), fighting (aggression), and problem solving (assertiveness).

It may seem axiomatic that leaders need to behave assertively with subordinates. Sometimes, however, leaders also need to be assertive with their own bosses. Followers often need to be assertive with other followers and even with their leaders sometimes. For example, middle-level supervisors need to communicate performance expectations clearly and directly to subordinates, and they need to be strong advocates for their subordinates' interests with senior

FIGURE 9–5
Relationships between Assertiveness, Acquiescence, and Aggression

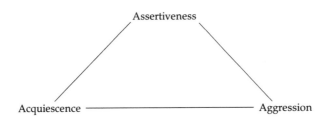

supervisors. Likewise, leaders sometimes need to give their own superiors bad news, and it is best to do so directly rather than hesitantly and guardedly. Followers may sometimes need to be assertive with a peer whose poor work habits are adversely impacting the work group. In addition, leaders sometimes need to be assertive with representatives of other power-holding or special-interest groups. For example, the leader of a community group seeking a new elementary school in a residential area may need to take a very assertive stand with local school board officials.

It is important to note that sometimes the hardest people to be assertive with are friends, family, and peers. Leaders who fail to be assertive with friends and peers run the risk of becoming victims of the Abilene paradox (see Highlight 9–4). The **Abilene paradox** (Harvey, 1974) occurs when someone suggests that the group engage in a particular activity or course of action, and no one in the group really wants to do the activity (including the person who made the suggestion). However, because of the false belief that everyone else in the group wants to do the activity, no one behaves assertively and voices an honest opinion about it. Only after the activity is over does anyone voice an opinion (and it is usually negative). For example, someone in your group of friends may suggest that the group go to a particular movie on a Friday night. No one in the group really wants to go, yet because of the false belief everyone else is interested, no one points out the movie is not supposed to be very good and the group should do something else instead. If group members' true opinions surface only *after* the movie, then the group has fallen victim to the Abilene paradox. Leaders can avoid the Abilene paradox by being assertive when suggestions about group decisions and activities are first made.

There are several things everyone can do to help themselves behave more assertively. These things include (*a*) using "I" statements, (*b*) speaking up for what you need, (*c*) learning to say no, (*d*) monitoring your inner dialogue, and (*e*) being persistent. The following is a more detailed discussion of these assertiveness tips.

HIGHLIGHT 9–4

The Abilene Paradox

That July afternoon in Coleman, Texas (population 5,607), was particularly hot—104 degrees according to the Rexall's thermometer. In addition, the wind was blowing fine-grained West Texas topsoil through the house. But the afternoon was still tolerable—even potentially enjoyable. A fan was stirring the air on the back porch; there was cold lemonade; and finally, there was entertainment. Dominoes. Perfect for the conditions. The game requires little more physical exertion than an occasional mumbled comment, "Shuffle 'em," and an unhurried movement of the arm to place the tiles in their appropriate positions on the table. All in all, it had the makings of an agreeable Sunday afternoon in Coleman. That is, until my father-in-law suddenly said, "Let's get in the car and go to Abilene and have dinner at the cafeteria."

I thought, "What, go to Abilene? Fifty-three miles? In this dust storm and heat? And in an unairconditioned 1958 Buick?"

But my wife chimed in with, "Sounds like a great idea. I'd like to go. How about you, Jerry?" Since my own preferences were obviously out of step with the rest, I replied, "Sounds good to me," and added, "I just hope your mother wants to go."

"Of course I want to go," said my mother-in-law. "I haven't been to Abilene in a long time."

So into the car and off to Abilene we went. My predictions were fulfilled. The heat was brutal. Perspiration had cemented a fine layer of dust to our skin by the time we arrived. The cafeteria's food could serve as a first-rate prop in an antacid commercial.

Some four hours and 106 miles later, we returned to Coleman, hot and exhausted. We silently sat in front of the fan for a long time. Then, to be sociable and to break the silence, I dishonestly said, "It was a great trip, wasn't it?"

No one spoke.

Finally, my mother-in-law said, with some irritation, "Well, to tell the truth, I really didn't enjoy it much and would rather have stayed here. I just went along because the three of you were so enthusiastic about going. I wouldn't have gone if you all hadn't pressured me into it."

I couldn't believe it. "What do you mean 'you all'?" I said. "Don't put me in the 'you all' group. I was delighted to be doing what we were doing. I didn't want to go. I only went to satisfy the rest of you. You're the culprits."

My wife looked shocked. "Don't call me a culprit. You and Daddy and Mama were the ones who wanted to go. I just went along to keep you happy. I would have had to be crazy to want to to out in heat like that."

Her father entered the conversation with one word. "Shee-it." He then expanded on what was already absolutely clear: "Listen, I never wanted to go to Abilene. I just thought you might be bored. You visit so seldom I wanted to be sure you enjoyed it. I would have preferred to play another game of dominoes and eat the leftovers in the icebox."

HIGHLIGHT 9–4 *(concluded)*

After the outburst of recrimination, we all sat back in silence. Here we were, four reasonably sensible people who—of our own volition—had just taken a 106-mile trip across a godforsaken desert in furnace-like heat and a dust storm to eat unpalatable food at a hole-in-the-wall cafeteria in Abilene, when none of us had really wanted to go. To be concise, we'd done just the opposite of what we wanted to do. The whole situation simply didn't make sense.

At least it didn't make sense at the time. But since that day in Coleman, I have observed, consulted with, and been a part of more than one organization that has been caught in the same situation. As a result, the organizations have either taken side trips or, occasionally, terminal journeys to Abilene, when Dallas or Houston or Tokyo was where they really wanted to go. And for most of those organizations, the negative consequences of such trips, measured in terms of both human misery and economic loss, have been much greater than for our little Abilene group.

I now call the tendency for groups to embark on excursions that no group member wants "the Abilene Paradox." Stated simply, when organizations blunder into the Abilene Paradox, they take actions in contradiction to what they really want to do and therefore defeat the very purpose they are trying to achieve. Business theorists typically believe that managing conflict is one of the greatest challenges faced by an organization, but a corollary of the Abilene Paradox states that the inability to manage agreement may be the major source of organization dysfunction.

Source: J. B. Harvey, "The Abilene Paradox: the Management of Agreement." *Organizational Dynamics* 3, 1974, pp. 63–80. Used with permission.

Use "I" statements.　Assertive people take responsibility for what they say. They are clear in their own minds and with others about what they believe and what they want. One of the easiest ways to do this is to use first-person pronouns when you speak. Highlight 9–5 provides examples of how to be more assertive by using first-person pronouns.

Speak up for what you need.　No one has all of the skills, knowledge, time, or resources needed to do all of the taskings assigned to their work group. Virtually everyone will need to ask superiors, peers, or subordinates for help at some time. Both effective leaders and effective followers ask for help from others when they need it. Highlight 9–5 also provides guidelines when making requests for help.

Learn to say no.　No one can be all things to all people, but it takes assertiveness to say no to others. Leaders, for example, may need to say no to their own

HIGHLIGHT 9–5

Tips for Being Assertive

Examples of Good and Bad ''I'' Statements

Bad: Some people may not like having to maintain those new forms.
Good: I don't think these new forms are any good. I don't think they're
        worth the effort.

Bad: Maybe that candidate doesn't have all the qualifications we're looking
        for.
Good: I think his academic record looks fine, but we agreed only to consider
        candidates with at least five years' experience. I think we should keep
        looking.

Tips for Speaking Up for What You Need

Do not apologize too much or justify yourself for needing help or assistance (e.g.,
''I just hate to ask you, and I normally wouldn't need to, but . . .'')

At the same time, giving a brief reason for your request often helps.

Be direct. Do not beat around the bush, hinting at what you need and hoping others get the message.

Do not play on someone's friendship.

Do not take a refusal personally.

Tips for Saying No

Keep your reply short and polite. Avoid a long, rambling justification.

Do not invent excuses.

Do not go overboard in apologizing because you cannot do it.

Be up front about your limitations and about options you *could* support.

Ask for time to consider it if you need to.

Source: Adapted in part from K. Back, and K. Back, *Assertiveness at Work* (London: McGraw-Hill, 1982).

superiors at times in order to stand up for their subordinates' or organization's rights and to keep from spreading themselves too thin and detracting from other priorities. Additionally, people who cannot (i.e., who *do not*) say no often build up a reservoir of negative emotions, such as those associated with feeling taken advantage of. Tips of assertively refusing to do something also can be found in Highlight 9–5.

Monitor your inner dialogue.   Most of us talk to ourselves, though not out loud. Such self-talk is natural and common, though not everyone is aware of how much it occurs or how powerful an influence on behavior it can be. Assertive people have self-talk that is positive and affirming. Nonassertive people have self-talk that is negative, doubtful, and questioning. Learning to say no is a good example of the role self-talk plays in assertiveness. Suppose that someone was asked to serve on a volunteer committee he simply does not have time for and that he *wants* to say no. In order to behave assertively, the person would need to talk to himself positively. He would need to ensure that he is not defeated by his own self-talk. It would hardly help the person's resolve, for example, to have an inner dialogue that says, "They'll think I'm selfish if I don't say yes," or "if they can make time for this committee, I should be able to make time for it, too." In learning to behave more assertively, therefore, it is necessary for leaders to become more aware of their own counterproductive self-talk, confront it, and change it.

Be persistent.   Assertive individuals stick to their guns without becoming irritated, angry, or loud. They persistently seek their objectives, whatever points or excuses another person may bring up as to why he cannot do what they ask. A good example of assertive persistence is in exchanging merchandise. Suppose someone purchased a shirt at a department store, wore it once, and then noticed the seam was poorly sewn. A person acting assertively might have an exchange much like that found in Highlight 9–6. An assertive person is similarly persistent in standing up for his own or his group's rights.

Feedback

Good feedback is essential to a subordinate's performance and development. Without feedback, a subordinate will not be able to tell whether she's doing a good job or whether or not her abrasiveness is turning people off and hurting her chances for promotion. And it's not just subordinates who need constructive feedback to learn and grow. Peers may seek feedback from peers, and leaders may seek feedback from subordinates. Besides fostering growth, effective supervisory feedback also plays a major role in building morale.

In many ways, the development of good feedback skills is an outgrowth of developing good communication, listening, and assertiveness skills. Giving good feedback depends on being clear about the purpose of the feedback and choosing an appropriate context and medium for giving it. Giving good feedback also depends on sending the proper nonverbal signals and trying to detect emotional signals from whoever may be receiving the feedback. In addition, giving good feedback depends on being somewhat assertive in providing it, even when it may be critical of a person's performance or behavior. Although feedback skills are related to communication, listening, and assertiveness

---

HIGHLIGHT 9-6

Example Exchange between a Buyer and a Clerk

Buyer:

I bought this shirt last week, and it's poorly made.

Clerk:

It looks like you've worn it. We don't exchange garments that already have been worn.

Buyer:

I understand that is your policy, but it's not that I don't like the shirt. It is obviously defective. I didn't know it had these defects when I wore it.

Clerk:

Maybe this seam came loose because of the way you wore it.

Buyer:

I didn't do anything unusual. It is defective. I want it exchanged.

Clerk:

I'm sorry, but you should have returned it earlier. We can't take it back now.

Buyer:

I understand your point, but I didn't get what I paid for. You need to return my money or give me a new shirt.

Clerk:

It's beyond my authority to do that. I don't make the policies, I just have to follow them.

Buyer:

I understand you don't think you have the authority to change the policy. But your boss does. Please tell her I'd like to see her right now.

---

skills, they are not the same thing. Someone may have good communication, listening, and assertiveness skills but poor feedback skills. Perhaps this distinction can be made clearer by examining the knowledge, behavior, and evaluative components of feedback skills.

The knowledge component of feedback concerns knowing when, where, and what feedback is to be given. For example, knowing when, where, and how to give positive feedback may be very different from knowing when, where, and how to give negative feedback. The behavioral component of feedback concerns how feedback actually is delivered (as contrasted with knowing how it should be delivered). Good feedback is specific, descriptive, direct, and helpful; poor feedback is often too "watered down" to be useful to the recipient. Finally, one way to evaluate feedback is to examine whether recipients actually modify their behavior accordingly after receiving it. Of course, this should not be the only way to evaluate feedback skills. Even when feedback is accurate in content and delivered skillfully, a recipient may fail to acknowledge it or do anything about it.

Although most leaders probably believe that feedback is an important skill, research has shown that leaders also believe they give more feedback than their subordinates think they do (Greller, 1980). There are many reasons leaders may be reluctant to give feeedback. Leaders may be reluctant to give positive feedback because of time pressures, doubts about the efficacy of feedback, or lack of feedback skills (Komacki, 1982). Sometimes supervisors are hesitant to use positive feedback because they believe subordinates may see it is politically manipulative, ingratiating, or insincere (Bass, 1990). Leaders also may give positive feedback infrequently if they rarely leave their desks, if their personal standards are too high, or if they believe good performance is expected and should not be recognized at all (Deep & Sussman, 1990). Other kinds of reasons may explain the failure to give negative feedback (Larson, 1986); this may be due to fears of disrupting leader-follower relations (Harrison, 1982) or fear of employee retaliation (Parsons, Herold, & Leatherwood, 1985).

Although there are a number of reasons leaders are hesitant to provide both positive and negative feedback, leaders need to keep in mind that followers, committee members, or team members will perform at a higher level if they are given accurate and frequent feedback. It is difficult to imagine how work-group or team performance could improve without feedback. Positive feedback is necessary to tell followers they should keep doing what they are doing well, and negative feedback is needed to give followers or team members ideas on how to change other behavior in order to improve their performance. Although accurate and frequent feedback is necessary, there are several other aspects of feedback that everyone can work on to improve their feedback skills. These other aspects of feedback include (a) making sure it's helpful, (b) being direct, (c) being specific, (d) being descriptive, (e) being timely, (f) being flexible, (g) giving both positive and negative feedback, and (h) avoiding blame and embarassment when giving feedback. Highlight 9–7 gives examples of each of these different aspects of feedback, and the following is a more complete description of ways leaders can improve their feedback skills.

Make It Helpful.   The purpose of feedback is to provide others with information they can use to change their behavior. Being clear about the intent and purpose is important because giving feedback sometimes can become emotional for both the person giving and the person receiving it. If the person giving

---

HIGHLIGHT 9–7

Tips for Improving Feedback Skills

Being Helpful

Do not: "I got better scores when I was going through this program than you just did."

Do: "This seems to be a difficult area for you. What can I do to help you master it better?"

Being Direct

Do not: "It's important that we all speak loud enough to be heard in meetings."

Do: "I had a difficult time hearing you in the meeting because you were speaking in such a soft voice."

Being Specific

Do not: "Since coming to work for us, your work has been good."

Do: "I really like the initiative and resourcefulness you showed in solving our scheduling problem."

Being Descriptive

Do not: "I'm getting tired of your rudeness and disinterest when others are talking."

Do: "You weren't looking at anyone else when they were talking, which gave the impression you were bored. Is that how you were feeling?"

Being Timely

Do not: "Joe, I think I need to tell you about an impression you made on me in the staff meeting last month."

Do: "Joe, do you have a minute? I was confused by something you said in the meeting this morning."

Being flexible

Do not: (while a person is crying, or while they are turning beet-red with clenched teeth in apparent anger) "There's another thing I want to tell you about your presentation yesterday . . . ."

Do: When a person's rising defenses or emotionality get in the way of their really listening, deal with those feelings first, or wait until later to finish your feedback. Do not continue giving information.

---

feedback is in an emotional state (e.g., angry), she may say things that make her temporarily feel better but that only alienate the receiver. In order to be helpful, individuals need to be clear and unemotional when giving feedback, and should give feedback only about behaviors actually under the other person's control.

People can improve the impact of the feedback they give when it is addressed to a specific individual. A common mistake in giving feedback is addressing it to "people at large" rather than to a specific individual. In this case, the individuals for whom the feedback was intended may not believe the feedback pertained to them. In order to maximize the impact of the feedback, people should try to provide it to specific individuals, not large groups.

Be specific. Feedback is most helpful when it specifies particular behaviors that are positive or negative. One of the best illustrations of the value of specific feedback is in compositions or term papers written for school. If someone turned in a draft of a paper to the instructor for constructive comments and the instructor's comments about the paper were "good start, but needs work in several areas," then the person would have a difficult time knowing just what to change or correct. More helpful feedback from the instructor would be specific comments like "This paragraph does not logically follow the preceding one" or "Cite an example here." The same is true of feedback in work situations. The more specifically leaders can point out which behaviors to change, the more clearly they let the other person know what to do.

Be descriptive. In giving feedback, it is good to stick to the facts as much as possible, being sure to distinguish them from inferences or attributions. A behavior description reports actions that others can see, about which there could be little question or disagreement. Such descriptions must be distinguished from inferences about someone else's feelings, attitudes, character, motives, or traits. It is a behavior description, for example, to say that Sally stood up and walked out of a meeting while someone else was talking. It is an inference, though, to say she walked out because she was angry. However, sometimes it is helpful to describe both the behavior itself as well as corresponding impressions when giving feedback. This is particularly true if the feedback giver believes the other person does not realize how the behavior negatively affects others' impressions.

Another reason to make feedback descriptive is to distinguish it from evaluation. When a person gives feedback based mostly on inferences, he often conveys evaluations of the "goodness" or "badness" of behavior as well. For example, saying "You were too shy" has a more negative connotation than saying "You had little to say." In the former case, the person's behavior was evaluated unfavorably, and by apparently subjective criteria. Yet evaluation is often an intrinsic part of a supervisor's responsibilities, and good performance feedback may necessitate conveying evaluative information to a subordinate. In such cases, leaders are better-off providing evaluative feedback when clear criteria for performance have been established. Filley and Pace (1976) described criteria that can be used to provide evaluative feedback; some are listed in Highlight 9-8.

HIGHLIGHT 9–8

Types of Criteria to Use for Evaluative Feedback

1. Compare behavior with others' measured performance. With this method, the subordinate's behavior is compared with that of her peers or co-workers; also called *norm-referenced appraisal*. For example, a subordinate may be told her counseling load is the lightest of all 10 counselors working at the center.

2. Compare behavior with an accepted standard. An example of this method would be where a counselor was told her workload was substantially below the standard of acceptable performance set at 30 cases per week. This is known as *criterion-referenced appraisal*.

3. Compare behavior with an a priori goal. With this method, the subordinate must participate in and agree with a goal. This is a form of criterion-referenced appraisal, with the subordinate's "ownership" and acceptance of the goal before the fact critical to the feedback procedure.

4. Compare behavior with past performance.

Source: Adapted from A. C. Filley, and L. A. Pace, "Making Judgments Descriptive." In J. E. Jones & J. W. Pfeiffer, eds. *The 1976 Annual Handbook for Group Facilitators* (La Jolla, Calif.: University Associates Press, 1976), pp. 128–31.

An issue related to impressions and evaluative feedback concerns the distinction between job-related (i.e., performance feedback) and more personal or discretionary feedback. Although leaders have a right to expect followers to listen to their performance feedback, that is not necessarily true concerning feedback about other behaviors. It may well be that sharing perceptions of the person's behavior could be very helpful to that person even when the behavior doesn't pertain specifically to his formal responsibilities; in such cases, however, it is the follower's choice whether to hear it or, if he hears it, whether to act on it or not.

Be timely.   Feedback usually is most effective when it is given soon after the behavior occurs. The context and relevant details of more recent events or behaviors are more readily available to everyone involved, thus facilitating more descriptive and helpful feedback.

Be flexible.   Although feedback is best when it is timely, sometimes waiting is preferable to giving feedback at the very earliest opportunity. In general, everyone should remember that the primary purpose of feedback is to be helpful. Feedback sessions should be scheduled with that in mind. For example, a subordinate's schedule may preclude conveniently giving him feedback right away, and it may not be appropriate to give him feedback when it will distract him from another more immediate and pressing task. Furthermore, it may not be constructive to give someone else feedback when the person receiving it is in a very emotional state (whether about the behavior in question or other matters entirely). Moreover, it is important to be attentive to the other person's emotional responses while giving feedback and to be ready to adjust one's own behavior accordingly.

A final important part of being flexible is to give feedback in manageable amounts. In giving feedback, one does not need to cover every single point at one time, as doing so would only overload the other person with information. Instead, anyone who needs to give a lot of feedback to someone else may want to spread out the feedback sessions and focus on covering only one or two points in each session.

Give positive as well as negative feedback.   Giving *both* positive and negative feedback is more helpful than giving only positive or negative feedback alone. Positive feedback tells the other person or the group only what they are doing right, and negative feedback tells the other person or group only what they are doing wrong. Providing both kinds of feedback is best.

Avoid blame or embarrassment.   Because the purpose of feedback is to give useful information to other people to help them develop, talking to them in a way merely intended (or likely) to demean or make them feel bad is not a helpful part of the development process. Followers tend to be more likely to believe feedback if it comes from leaders who have had the opportunity to observe the behavior and are perceived to be credible, competent, and trustworthy (Coye, 1982; Quaglieri & Carnazza, 1985; Stone, Guetal, & MacIntosh, 1984). Bass (1990) points out that followers will continue to seek feedback even if their leaders are not competent or trustworthy—though they will not seek it from their leaders. They will seek it from others they do trust, such as peers or other superiors.

SUMMARY

This chapter has reviewed the literature regarding leadership behaviors and skills. From a historical perspective, the initial interest in leadership behaviors was primarily due to psychology's shift in focus from traits to behaviors and due to misinterpretations of Stogdill's (1948) conclusions regarding leadership traits. Both Ohio State and the University of Michigan spearheaded much of the early leadership behavior research, and researchers at both institutions developed questionnaires designed to measure the frequency with which leaders engaged in task- or group-oriented behaviors. These studies generally demonstrated that, as with the trait research, there was not a universal set of leadership behaviors that would guarantee success in all situations. Again, situational demands often determined which leader behaviors were more effective than others.

More current research efforts concerning leadership behaviors have expanded on the taxonomies initially developed from the Ohio State and University of Michigan studies. These generally consist of a greater number of specific leadership behavior categories or dimensions. By having a greater number of leadership dimensions, leadership researchers, as well as practitioners, can more accurately describe the variety of behaviors leaders may exhibit. Moreover, some of the more recently developed leadership behavior questionnaires determine how important each of the dimensions is for leadership success and asks subordinates, peers, superiors, and leaders themselves to indicate how well or how frequently a leader manifests those behaviors crucial for success.

Finally, the last section of this chapter described the knowledge, behavioral, and evaluative components of communication, listening, assertiveness, and feedback skills, and what leadership practitioners—in both their leader and follower roles—could do to improve these skills. For example, communication skills can be improved by thinking about the purpose of a message before it is relayed, choosing the appropriate context and medium for the message, and creating a frame of reference for the message.

KEY TERMS

Leader Behavior Description Questionnaire (LBDQ)

consideration

initiating structure

job-centered dimensions

goal emphasis

work facilitation

employee-centered dimensions

leader support

interaction facilitation

Leadership Grid

concern for people

concern for production

applied behavioral analysis

360-degree feedback

leadership skills

frames of reference

active listeners

paraphrase

assertive behavior

acquiescence

aggression

Abilene paradox

DISCUSSION QUESTIONS

1. Do you think broad behavioral categories like "employee-centered" or "job-centered" are independent of personality traits or other individual differences?

2. What do you think are the advantages and disadvantages of 360-degree feedback to leaders?

3. Can you think of any good leaders who were poor communicators?

4. Is assertiveness a desirable quality in followers as well as in leaders?

SUGGESTED READINGS

Blake, R. R., and A. A. McCanse. *Leadership Dilemmas—Grid Solutions.* Houston, Tex.: Gulf, 1991.

Davis, B. L.; L. W. Hellervik; and J. L. Sheard. *The Successful Manager's Handbook.* Minneapolis, Minn.: Personnel Decisions Incorporated, 1989.

FOCUS ON THE FOLLOWERS

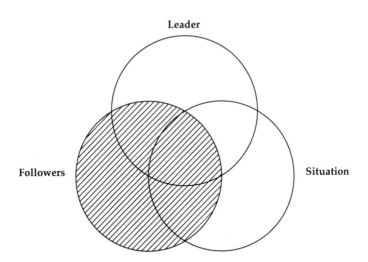

W e began Part II with Napoleon's belief that the individual leader is the crucial element of leadership. We should begin Part III, therefore, by qualifying that sentiment. Although the importance of good leaders cannot be denied, followers play an equally important—yet often overlooked—role in the success of any group or organization. It was not, after all, Napoleon by himself who won or lost battles; his soldiers played some part, too.

Organizational successes and failures often get unfairly attributed to leaders, although followers may have been the true reason for successes and failure (Meindl & Ehrlich, 1987). For example, when professional sports teams are doing well or poorly, the success or failure is often unfairly attributed to the coach. Coaches are often lauded for being the key to a team's successes and are often the first to be dismissed after an abyssmal season. However, a team loaded with talented players may have been successful regardless of the coach; conversely, a team with below-average players may be unsuccesful (at winning games) despite having a great coach. Thus, followers play a key role in the fate of an organization, but their contributions are often overlooked or erroneoueously attributed to leaders.

It is also important to remember that even when one is identified as a leader, the same person often holds a complementary follower role. Almost all leaders answer to someone else; school coaches answer to athletic directors, principals answer to school superintendents, managers answer to company presidents, sergeants answer to lieutenants, colonels answer to generals, and so on. Most individuals will spend more time as followers than as leaders, and it is not at all uncommon to switch between being a leader and being a follower several times over the course of a day.

Unfortunately, the follower role has been studied very little. Research efforts have focused instead on the characteristics associated with individuals in leadership roles; relatively little research has looked at what makes successful followers. Moreover, there does not appear to be a perfect and direct relationship between good followership and good leadership. Not all good leaders were necessarily good followers, and not all good followers become good leaders. The Center for Creative Leadership has used the term *derailment* to describe individuals who eventually fail as a leader despite performing well for a long time in followership and junior leadership roles (McCall & Lombardo, 1983). It might be that such individuals fail to reflect sufficiently on their followership experiences and on the potential lessons for their own development.

Some organizations believe followership is so important to leadership development that they make all members undergo a formalized followership experience prior to holding any type of leadership position. Staff at the U.S. Military Academy, for example, say the first step in developing leadership in new cadets is teaching them to be followers. Though it has been called the *West Point Thesis*, the view that able leaders emerge from the ranks of able followers certainly has applicability well beyond the military academies (Litzinger & Schaefer, 1982). It is also true that able followers may emerge from the ranks of able leaders. One position offering relatively little job security is that of coach of a professional athletic team; it is an interesting statistic that in 1991 there were 17 former National Football League head coaches working as assistant coaches in the NFL.

Because followers play a complementary role to leaders, and because follow-ership seems to play such an important role in leadership development, the next three chapters will focus on followers. Chapter Ten looks at followers from both an individual and a group perspective. Leaders need to be aware that fol-lowers vary in their levels of experience, referent power, intelligence, traits, self-concept, and preferences. These differences often affect how leaders inter-act with individual followers, and how followers interact with each other. Leaders also need to be able to analyze leadership situations by looking at the whole group as a level of analysis, not just individual followers. Chapter Eleven describes several different theories of motivation and how they can be used to enhance follower performance and satisfaction. Finally, Chapter Twelve is a continuation of Chapter Nine and provides ideas on how to im-prove leadership and followership skills. These skills deal primarily with effec-tive relationships with peers and superiors, and building technical compe-tence.

Chapter Ten

Followers, Groups, and Teams

INTRODUCTION

I n Chapter One, we noted how certain myths hinder our understanding of leadership. In a similar fashion, misconceptions about followers limit our understanding of followership. To a large extent, these misconceptions spring from conventions of language that promote a narrow and restrictive understanding of the term follower. *Webster's New Collegiate Dictionary* (1979) defines a follower as ''one in the service of another; one that follows the opinions or teachings of another; or one that imitates another.'' At first glance these defini-

223

tions may well seem reasonable. However, they imply that followers should do nothing until they receive explicit directions from a leader and then proceed to follow those directions in an unquestioning manner. Although sometimes the unquestioning and immediate execution of a leader's directions is important, in many other instances followers need to play a more proactive role in accomplishing a task. Moreover, the definitions above are static; they ignore the fact that individuals often play a variety of leadership and followership roles. These definitions of followership seem to imply a narrower view of the follower role than is actually constructive or realistic (see also Highlight 10-1).

If common definitions are misleading, then what is a good definition of followership? Because individuals are often both leaders and followers over the course of any day, one way to differentiate leadership from followership is to think about the roles rather than the individuals in different work groups. According to Kelley (1988), individuals who are effective in the **follower role** "have the vision to see both the forest and the trees, the social capacity to work well with others, the strength of character to flourish without heroic status, the moral and psychological balance to pursue personal and corporate goals at no cost to either, and, above all, the desire to participate in a team effort for the accomplishment of some greater purpose" (p. 107). Individuals successfully filling the **leader role** have the vision to set organizational and work group goals, the interpersonal skills to achieve consensus and develop enthusiasm in others, and a strong desire to lead (Kelley, 1988). Thus, Kelley's (1988) definitions of leader and follower roles take into account both the active nature of followership and the ease with which individuals slip in and out of leadership and followership roles.

Because leadership is not a one-way street, and most individuals are both leaders and followers, this chapter examines the leadership process by focusing on followers. More specifically, this chapter looks at followers from three different perspectives: the individual, the group, and the team. The individual perspective is important because leaders need to recognize differences in the education, experience, intelligence, personalities, and values of their followers. These characteristics often affect the nature of the relationship between leaders and individual followers.

The group perspective is also important. The group perspective examines how factors like group size, roles, norms, and cohesiveness can affect leader-follower relations. Looking at behavior from a group perspective also provides certain explanatory concepts that do not exist at the individual level, like why groups often take more extreme actions than individuals. The riots in Los Angeles after the acquittal of the policemen accused of beating Rodney King provide a vivid example of how groups influence individual behavior.

Finally, this chapter concludes with a discussion of teams. Teams and teamwork are becoming increasingly important in the production of goods and services. In a very real sense, the whole (i.e., the team) *can* be more than the sum of

---

HIGHLIGHT 10–1

Leadership Quotes, Chapter Ten

It does an organization no good when its leader refuses to share his leadership function with his lieutenants. The more centers of leadership you find in a company, the stronger it will become.

David Ogilvey

Commanders should be counseled, chiefly, by persons of known talents, by those who have made an art of war their particular study, and whose knowledge is derived from experience; from those who are present at the scene of action, who see the country, who see the enemy, who see the advantages that occasions offer, and who, like people embarked in the same ship, are sharers of the danger.

Lucius Aemilius Paulus, Roman consul who led
victorious campaign against the Macedonians

Trying to change individual and/or corporate behavior without addressing the larger organizational context is bound to disappoint. Sooner or later bureaucratic structures will consume even the most determined of collaborative processes. As Woody Allen once said, ''The lion and the lamb may lie down together, but the lamb won't get much sleep.'' What to do? Work on the lion as well as the lamb designing teamwork into the organization . . . . Although the Boston Celtics have won 16 championships, they have never had the league's leading scorer and never paid a player based on his individual statistics. The Celtics understand that virtually every aspect of basketball requires collaboration.

Robert W. Keidel

Snowflakes are one of nature's most fragile things, but just look at what they can do when they stick together.

Vesta M. Kelly

---

its parts (i.e., the individual followers). Improving followers' performance often requires understanding something about groups, not just understanding followers as a collection of individual subordinates.

FOLLOWERS AS INDIVIDUALS: REVISITING CHAPTERS ONE THROUGH NINE

Because leaders are often more visible than followers, the ways in which various leaders differ are often recognized more clearly than the ways various fol-

HAGAR

lowers differ (to leadership researchers, at least, if not to leadership practitioners). Moreover, because followers are often out of the limelight, it is not uncommon to think of followers as a group of fairly homogeneous or generic individuals. Relatively little of the leadership literature has examined how different follower characteristics affect the nature of leader-follower relationships, yet most leaders are constantly assessing their followers' individual characteristics and adjusting their own behavior accordingly. We think it will be helpful, therefore, to look briefly at followers in light of many of the concepts used to understand leaders as individuals. More specifically, this section uses an **individual perspective** to review how followers' education and experience, performance, power, intelligence, personality tratis, attitudes, values, preferences, and behaviors may affect the relationships among followers and between leaders and followers.

Follower Education and Experience

Followers vary tremendously in the relevant education and experiences they bring to their roles, and these differences can have a dramatic impact on the relationships among followers, and between leaders and followers. For example, as a junior officer in the U.S. Air Force, one of the authors of this book was responsible for managing the 20 enlisted and civilian personnel in a data processing office. The education and experience of these personnel ranged from "green" 18-year-olds to 55-year-old World War II veterans with master's degrees. Needless to say, these differences affected the nature of the relationships among the followers in the office and the manner in which the leader interacted with the various followers. The junior and inexperienced personnel needed almost constant guidance, coaching, and feedback, whereas the senior personnel needed only general guidance and periodic feedback in order to maintain high levels of performance. Moreover, the inexperienced personnel often looked up to and sought out the more senior personnel for guidance on how to improve their performance and for personal advice. Leaders will be more effective if they understand and appreciate their subordinates' backgrounds, training, education, and other relevant experiences.

It also will be important for leaders to understand certain trends in the sort of education and skills needed by followers. Workers today are better educated than ever before. One out of four workers between the ages of 25 and 64 is college educated, twice as many as 20 years ago; 85 percent have at least a high school education. Two implications of these facts for leadership are the greater number of options such workers have and the greater expectations they have concerning what a job should be like. A third implication for leadership involves a move away from the sort of control-oriented supervision of workers common when tasks were relatively routine, when power tended to be centralized in supervisors' hands, and innovation was discouraged (Naisbitt & Aburdene, 1990).

Although workers are better educated than ever, the need for continuing education and training on the job also will increase. One reason is that the technology of work is rapidly changing, and workers will be regularly updating their knowledge and skill bases to stay proficient with new task requirements. Alvin Toffler (1970) coined the term **future shock** 20 years ago to describe the accelerating rate of change in all aspects of our lives, and the increasing pace of technological change at work is no exception. As just one example, companies now recognize the competitive advantage of reducing the time it takes to get new products to customers (cycle time). General Electric has reduced the time it takes to produce customized circuits from three weeks to three days; Motorola has reduced the time it takes to make electronic pagers from three weeks to two hours (Naisbitt & Aburdene, 1990). Working in an environment of constant change takes a new kind of leadership and a new kind of followership. It will put a premium on what perhaps will be the most essential followership skill of the future: learning how to learn (Naisbitt & Aburdene, 1985).

Along with requirements to deal with the accelerating rate of technological change, essential follower skills also will change because of a pervasive trend to flatten organizational structures. Middle management is being reduced as much as 40 percent in some organizations (Naisbitt & Aburdene, 1985), and much of the authority previously reserved for that level is being delegated to followers.

Follower Power and Influence

Leaders need to bear in mind that they are not the sole possessors of power and influence in their work units; followers can wield considerable influence both with other followers and with the leader. Popular followers may be able to use referent power, and followers with high levels of education and experience may be able to use their expert power to influence other followers and the leader. However, followers in a leader's in-group may wield considerably more power and influence on the leader than followers in the out-group. Followers may even exercise coercive powers over leaders in certain situations. The practice of "fragging" certain leaders in Vietnam is an extreme example of this phenomenon: Leaders who were deemed to be dangerous or those who were perceived as not looking out for their subordinates would be subjected to having a hand grenade rolled into their tent. Leaders need to be cognizant of how these different bases of power and influence affect leader-follower and interfollower relationships.

Follower Behavior

Just as the Ohio State University leadership studies categorized leader behaviors into two broad dimensions, it may also be possible to categorize follower behaviors using a two-dimensional taxonomy. Kelly (1988) hypothesized that all follower behaviors could be broadly categorized in terms of (1) independent critical thinking and (2) activity level. Moreover, because behavior tends to be consistent over time, Kelley (1988) believed it was possible to use his two-dimensional taxonomy to categorize people as one of five types of followers (see Figure 10–1). **Sheep** are followers who do not play an active role in the organization and simply comply with any order or directive given to them. **Yes people** are active followers who readily carry out orders uncritically; they can be dangerous if their orders contradict societal standards of behavior or organizational policy. **Survivors** are followers who are rarely committed to workgroup goals but have learned to not make waves. Because they do not like to stick out, survivors tend to be mediocre performers and often clog the arteries of many organizations. **Alienated followers** are like festering wounds in their organizations; they are continuing sore spots who are more than happy to point out all the negative aspects of organizational goals, policies, and procedures (and overlook the positive apsects). Finally, **effective followers** play an active role in the organization but are not yes people; they reflect on company goals and policies, and are not hestitant to bring their concerns to their leaders. Although Kelley's (1988) two-dimensional taxonomy and categorization of followers has not been tested, his ideas are a creative and stimulating contribution to changing conceptions of followership.

Other Follower Characteristics

A variety of studies has shown that higher intelligence is associated with higher performance at work (Hunter & Hunter, 1984; Ree & Earles, 1992; Schmidt, Gast-Rosenberg, & Hunter, 1980). Also, research on followers' personal-

FIGURE 10–1
A Two-Dimensional Model of Follower Behavior

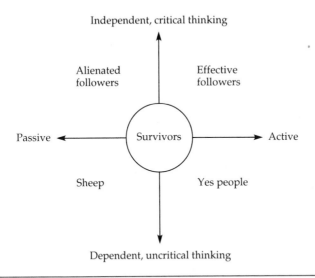

Source: Adapted from R. E. Kelley, "In Praise of Followers," *Harvard Business Review* 66, no. 6 (1988), pp. 142–48. Used with permission.

ity traits has shown that tolerance to stress, agreeableness, and dependability were related to performance in blue-collar jobs (Hogan, 1991; Tett, Jackson, & Rothstein, 1991).

Other research has suggested that a leader's effectiveness may well depend on the match between the leader's personality and the followers' personalities. This research specifically looked at the personality trait of locus of control. As described in Chapter Seven, locus of control involves a person's expectations about her ability to influence people and events around her. People who believe they are "masters of their own ship" are said to have an **internal locus of control;** people who believe they are (relatively speaking) "pawns of fate" are said to have an **external locus of control** (Rotter, 1966). A study of more than 1,000 employees of a public utility indicated that subordinates' locus of control influenced their preference for their supervisors' practices. Subordinates with an internal locus of control preferred a participatory management style, but subordinates with an external locus of control preferred a directive style (Mitchell, Smyser, & Weed, 1975). Other findings indicated that supervisors with an external locus of control provide more structure and guidance to subordinates than those with an internal locus (Durand & Nord, 1976). Taken together, these findings suggest that subordinataes with an external locus of control prefer the behaviors exhibited by leaders with an external locus of control.

We believe that even more research should be conducted on how leadership effectiveness is affected by follower personality traits, values, and preferences. We need to understand better how leader-follower and interfollower relationships are affected by characteristics like followers' tolerance to stress, agreeableness, dependability, dominance, and self-confidence. Similarly, some work-group conflicts can be understood as the result of differences in followers' values and preferences. For example, followers who are judgers (as assessed with the MBTI) may not like to work on projects with perceivers, as perceivers' relative disinclination to make decisions, plan, structure, and reach closure may frustrate judgers.

It also is advisable for leaders to be aware of several trends dealing with changes in follower motivation and values that will impact the leadership process. No longer can we assume—as perhaps we could 20 years ago—that workers feel loyal to their company or are primarily concerned with job security. Today, employees are far less committed to their organizations, especially when leadership is poor. They value balance between their work and personal lives, and seek more from work than just fair pay. This includes having work that is challenging and worthwhile, and having opportunities to be creative and develop personally on the job. They expect increased communication with management, participation in decisions that affect them, and flexibility in options afforded them (Mindell & Gorden, 1981; Naisbitt & Aburdene, 1990).

THE NATURE OF GROUPS

Understanding the unique characteristics that make individual followers "tick" is useful to leaders, but not enough. Leaders also need to understand how followers *as a group* represent something that cannot be understood solely in terms of their collective individual characteristics. While both leadership and followership often have been conceptualized in terms of characteristics of individuals, it is interesting to note that a recent unpublished survey of 35 current texts on organizational behavior found that in each one the chapter on leadership is in the section on group behavior, not in the section on individual behavior (Ginnett, 1992). Perhaps even more surprising, the concept of groups is sometimes omitted entirely from books on leadership. As stated earlier, the whole can be greater than the sum of its parts, and the **group perspective** looks at how different group characteristics can affect relationships both with the leader and among followers.

Perhaps we should begin by defining just what a group is. A **group** can be thought of as "two or more persons who are interacting with one another in such a manner that each person influences and is influenced by each other person'' (Shaw, 1981). Three aspects of this definition are particularly important to the study of leadership. First, this definition incorporates the concept of reciprocal influence between leaders and followers, an idea considerably different from the one-way nature of influence implicit in the dictionary's definition of followers. Second, group members interact and influence each other. Thus, people waiting at a bus stop would not constitute a group, as there generally is neither interaction nor influence between the various individuals. On the other hand, eight people meeting to plan a school bond election would constitute a group, as there probably would be a high level of mutual interaction among the attendees. Third, the definition does not constrain individuals to only one group. Everyone belongs to a number of different groups; an individual could be a member of various service, production, sports, religious, parent, and volunteer groups simultaneously.

It is important to realize that though people belong to many groups, just as they do to many organizations, groups and organizations are not the same thing (groups, of course, can exist within organizations). Organizations can be so large that most members do not know most of the other people in the organization. In such cases there is relatively little intermember interaction and reciprocal influence. Similarly, organizations typically are just too large and impersonal to have much effect on anyone's feelings, whereas groups are small and immediate enough to impact both feelings and self-image. People often tend to identify more with the groups they belong to than with the organizations they belong to; they are more psychologically ''invested'' in their groups. Also, certain important psychological needs (e.g., social contact) are better satisfied by groups than by organizations (see Chapter Eleven).

Perhaps an example will clarify the distinction between groups and organizations. Consider a church so large that it may fairly be described as an organization: so large that multiple services must be offered on Sunday mornings; so large that dozens of different study classes are offered each week; so large there are numerous different choirs and musical ensembles. In so large a church, the members hardly could be said to interact with or influence each other except on an occasional basis. Such size often presents both advantages and disadvantages to the membership. On the one hand, it makes possible a rich diversity of activities. On the other hand, such size can make the church itself (i.e., the overall organization) seem relatively impersonal. It may be difficult to identity with a large organization in other than name only (e.g., ''I belong to First Presbyterian Church''). In such cases many people identify more with particular groups within the church than with the church itself; it may be easier to *feel* a part of some smaller group such as the high school choir or a weekly study group.

Although groups play a pervasive role in society, in general people spend very little time thinking about the factors that affect group processes and intragroup relationships. Therefore, the rest of this section will describe some group characteristics that can affect both leaders and followers. Much of the research on groups goes well beyond the scope of this chapter (see Gibbard, Hartman & Mann, 1978; Shaw, 1981; Hackman, 1990), but six concepts are so basic to the group perspective that they deserve our attention. These six concepts are group size, stages of group development, roles, norms, communication, and cohesion.

Group Size

The size of any group has implications for both leaders and followers. First, leader emergence is partly a function of group size. The greater number of people in a large versus a small group will affect the probability that any individual is likely to emerge as leader. Second, as groups become larger, **cliques** are more likely to develop (Yukl, 1981). Cliques are subgroups of individuals who often share the same goals, values, and expectations. Because cliques generally wield more influence than individual members, they are likely to exert considerable influence—positively or negatively—on the larger group. Leaders need to identify and deal with cliques within their groups, as many intragroup conflicts are the results of cliques having different values, goals, and expectations.

Third, group size also can affect a leader's behavioral style. Leaders with a large **span of control** tend to be more directive, spend less time with individual subordinates, and use more impersonal approaches when influencing followers. Leaders with a small span of control tend to display more consideration and use more personal approaches when influencing followers (Badin, 1974; Goodstadt & Kipnis, 1970; Kipnis, Schmidt, & Wilkinson, 1980; Udell, 1967). Fourth, group size also affects group effectiveness. Whereas some researchers have suggested the optimal number of workers for any task is between five and seven (Bass, 1960; Indik, 1965), it probably is wise to avoid such a simple generalization. The answer to the question of appropriate group size seems to be "just big enough to get the job done." Obviously, the larger the group, the more likely it is that it will involve differentiated skills, values, perceptions, and abilities among its members. Also, there certainly will be more "people power" available to do the work as group size increases.

There are, however, limits to the benefits of size. Consider the question "If it takes one person two minutes to dig a 1-cubic-foot hole, how long will it take 20 people to dig the same size hole?" In all probability it will take the larger group considerably longer, especially if they all participate at the same time. Beyond the purely physical limitations of certain tasks, there also may be decreasing returns (on a per capita basis) as group size increases. This is true even when the efforts of all group members are combined on what is called an **additive task.** An additive task is one where the group's output simply involves the combination of individual outputs (Steiner, 1972). Such a case may be illustrated by the number of individuals needed to push a stalled truck from an intersection. One individual probably would not be enough—maybe not even two or three. At some point, though, as group size increases in this additive task, there will be enough combined force to move the truck. However, as the group size increases beyond that needed to move the truck, the individual contribution of each member will appear to decrease. Steiner (1972) suggested this may be due to **process loss** resulting from factors such as some members not pushing in the right direction. Process losses can be thought of as the inefficiencies created by more and more people working together.

Group size can affect group effectiveness in a number of other ways. As group size increases, the diminishing returns of larger work groups may be due to **social loafing** (Latané, Williams, & Hawkins, 1979). Social loafing refers to the phenomenon of reduced effort by people when they are not individually accountable for their work. Experiments across different sorts of tasks have tended to demonstrate greater effort when every individual's work is monitored than when many individuals' outputs are anonymously pooled into a collective product. Recent evidence, however, suggests the process may be considerably more complicated than initially thought (Porter, Bird & Wunder, 1991). The performance decrement may be affected more by the level of task complexity or the reward structure (e.g., cooperative vs. competitive) than by outcome attribution.

Sometimes, working in the presence of others may actually increase effort or productivity through a phenomenon called **social facilitation.** Social facilitation was first documented in classic experiments at the Hawthorne plant of the Western Electric Company (see Highlight 10–2). However, social facilitation is not limited to research situations. It refers to any time people increase their level of work due to the presence of others. Typically this occurs when the presence of others increases individual accountability for work, in contrast to other occasions when being in a group reinforces individual anonymity and social loafing (Zajonc, 1965).

As with social loafing, the social facilitation effect may be greater or lesser depending on several variables. If a task is fairly mundane, routine, or boring, the presence of others can indeed increase performance—at least in the short run. If a task is new, complex, or unfamiliar, however, task performance may be degraded by another's presence. This seems to be particularly true if the observer is a person of higher status or is in an evaluative role. These differences may be explained in terms of the way arousal level affects performance. On familiar or simple tasks, high arousal levels generally improve performance, but on new or complex tasks where arousal is already high, increasing arousal levels even further may impair performance. Because working in front of others tends to be arousing for most people, the effects of doing so will depend on the nature of the task (Zajonc, 1965).

HIGHLIGHT 10–2

Social Facilitation and the Hawthorne Effect

Social facilitation was first documented in experiments conducted at the Hawthorne plant of the Western Electric Company during the late 1920s and early 1930s. These classic studies were originally designed to evaluate the impact of different work environments (Mayo, 1933; Roethlisberger & Dickson, 1939). Among other things, researchers varied the levels of illumination in areas where workers were assembling electrical components and found production increased when lighting was increased. When lighting was subsequently decreased, however, production again increased. Faced with these rather confusing data, the researchers turned their attention from physical aspects of the work environment to its social aspects. As it turns out, one reason workers' production increased was simply because someone else (in this case, the researchers) had paid attention to them. The term **Hawthorne effect** is still used today to describe an artifactual change in behavior due merely to the fact a person or group is being studied.

Developmental Stages of Groups

Just as children go through different stages of development, so do groups. Tuckman's (1965) review of over 60 studies involving leaderless training, experimental, or therapeutic groups revealed that groups generally went through four distinct stages of development. The first stage, **forming,** was characterized by polite conversation, the gathering of superficial information about fellow members, and low trust. The group's rejection of emerging potential leaders with negative characteristics also took place during the forming stage. The second stage, **storming,** usually was marked by intragroup conflict, heightened emotional levels, and status differentiation as remaining contenders struggled to build alliances and fulfill the group's leadership role. The clear emergence of a leader and the development of group norms and cohesiveness were the key indicators of the **norming** stage of group development. Finally, groups reached the **performing** stage when group members played functional, interdependent roles that were focused on the performance of group tasks.

The four stages of group development identified by Tuckman (1965) are important for several reasons. First, people are in many more leaderless groups than they may realize. For example, many sports teams, committees, work groups, and clubs start out as leaderless teams. Team or club captains or committee spokespersons are likely to be the emergent leaders from their respective groups. On a larger scale, perhaps even many elected officials initially began their political careers as the emergent leaders of their cliques or groups, and were then able to convince the majority of the remaining members in their constituencies of their viability as candidates.

Another reason it is important to understand stages of group development deals with relationships between leadership behaviors and group cohesiveness and productivity. Some experts have maintained that leaders need to focus on consideration or group maintenance behaviors during the norming stage to improve group cohesiveness, and task behaviors during the performing stage in order to improve group productivity (Stogdill, 1972; Terborg, Castore, & DeNinno, 1975). They also have suggested leaders who reverse these behaviors during the norming and performing stages tend to have less cohesive and productive groups. Thus, being able to recognize stages of group development may enhance the likelihood that one will emerge as a leader as well as increase the cohesiveness and productivity of the group being led.

Group Roles

Group roles are the sets of expected behaviors associated with particular jobs or positions. Most people have multiple roles stemming from the various groups with which they are associated. In addition, it is not uncommon for someone to occupy numerous roles within the same group as situations change. Ginnett (1990) found that members of airline crews have varying roles over the course of a day. Although some behaviors were universally associated with certain roles, effective team members on these airline crews generally were more flexible in changing their behavior as other role demands changed. For example, whereas the captain of an airplane is responsible for the overall operation and decision making during a flight, flight attendants often take over responsibility for planning and carrying out the crew's social activities in the evening (i.e., when the flight is over). One captain in the study, however, continued to make *all* the crew's decisions, including their evening social plans; he was inflexible with regard to the role of decision maker. Not coincidentally, he was seen as a less effective leader—even during the actual flights—than more flexible captains.

Some roles, like positions on athletic teams, have meaning only in relatively specific contexts. Generally speaking, for example, one only plays a lineman's role during football games (admittedly, one might argue that at many schools being an intercollegiate athlete is a role that extends to aspects of student life outside sports). Other roles are more general in nature, including certain common ones that play a part in making any group work—or not work—well. Highlight 10–3 presents a vivid example of how powerful roles can be as determinants of behavior.

In Chapter Nine, leader behavior was characterized initially in terms of two broad functions. One deals with getting the task done **(task role),** and the other

---

HIGHLIGHT 10–3

The Stanford Prison Experiment

A fascinating demonstration of the power of roles occured when social psychologist Philip Zimbardo and his colleagues (1973) created a simulated prison environment at Stanford University. From a larger group of volunteers, two dozen male college students were randomly assigned to be either "prisoners" or "guards." The simulation was quite realistic, with actual cells constructed in the basement of one of the university buildings. The guards wore uniforms, and carried nightsticks and whistles; their eyes were covered by sunglasses. The prisoners were "arrested" at their homes by police cars replete with blazing sirens. They were handcuffed, frisked, blindfolded, and brought to the "jail." They were fingerprinted, given prisoner outfits, and assigned numbers by which they would henceforth be addressed.

It did not take long for the students' normal behavior to be overcome by the roles they were playing. The guards became more and more abusive with their power. They held prisoners accountable for strict adherence to arbitrary rules of prison life (which the guards themselves created), and seemed to enjoy punishing them for even minor infractions. They increasingly seemed to think of the prisoners—truly just other college students—as "bad" people. The emotional stress on the prisoners became profound, and just six days into the two-week episode the experiment was halted. This unexpected outcome basically occurred because participants' roles had become their reality. They were not just students role-playing guards and prisoners; to a disconcerting degree they became guards and prisoners.

What should people conclude from the Standford prison study? At an abstract level, the study dramatically points out how behavior is partly determined by social role. Additionally, it is clear how just being in the role of leader, especially to the extent it is attended by tangible and symbolic manifestations of power, can affect how leaders think and act toward followers. Still another lesson people might draw involves remembering the volunteers all had many different roles in life than those assigned to them in the study, though being a guard or prisoner was certainly the salient one for a period of time. Whereas everyone has many roles, the salience of one or another often depends on the situation, and a person's behavior changes as his or her role changes in a group.

Source: P. Zimbardo, C. Haney, W. Banks, and D. Jaffe. "The mind is a formidable jailer: A Pirandellian prison." *The New York Times Magazine* (April 8, 1973), pp. 38–60.

---

with supporting relationships within the work group **(relationship role)**. Similarly, roles in groups can be categorized in terms of task and relationship functions (see Table 10–1). Many of the roles in Table 10–1 are appropriate for followers, not just the official group leader; all of these different roles are part of the leadership process and all contribute to a group's overall effectiveness.

TABLE 10–1
Task and Relationship Roles in Groups

Task Roles

Initiating: Defining the problem, suggesting activities, assigning tasks.

Information Seeking: Asking questions, seeking relevant data or views.

Information Sharing: Providing data, offering opinions.

Summarizing: Reviewing and integrating others' points, checking for common understanding and readiness for action.

Evaluating: Assessing validity of assumptions, quality of information, reasonableness of recommendations.

Guiding: Keeping group on track.

Relationship Roles

Harmonizing: Resolving interpersonal conflicts, reducing tension.

Encouraging: Supporting and praising others, showing appreciation for others' contributions, being warm and friendly.

Gatekeeping: Assuring even participation by all group members, making sure that everyone has a chance to be heard and that no individual dominates.

Source: Adapted from K. D. Benne and P. Sheats, "Functional Roles of Group Members," *Journal of Social Issues* 4 (1948), pp. 41–49.

Moreover, it is important to recognize that the very distinction between task and relationship roles is somewhat arbitrary. It is sensible enough when looking at the short-term impact of any given behavior, but in another sense relationship roles *are* task roles. After all, task-oriented behavior may be adequate for accomplishing short-term objectives, but an appropriately cohesive and supportive group increases the potential for long-term effectiveness at future tasks as well as present tasks.

Although the roles in Table 10-1 generally contribute to a group's overall effectiveness, several types of problems can occur with group roles that can impede group performance. One type of role problem concerns the **dysfunctional roles,** listed in Table 10-2. The common denominator among these roles is how the person's behavior primarily serves selfish or egocentric purposes rather than group purposes.

Another role problem is **role conflict.** Role conflict involves receiving contradictory messages about expected behavior and can in turn adversely affect a person's emotional well-being and performance (Jamal, 1984).

Role conflict can occur in several different ways. Perhaps most common is receiving inconsistent signals about expected behavior from the same person. When the same person sends mixed signals, it is called **intrasender role conflict** ("I need this report back in five minutes, and it had better be perfect").

TABLE 10–2
Dysfunctional Roles

Dominating: Monopolizing group time, forcing views on others.
Blocking: Stubbornly obstructing and impeding group work, persistent negativism.
Attacking: Belittling others, creating a hostile or intimidating environment.
Distracting: Engaging in irrelevant behaviors, distracting others' attention.

Source: Adapted from K.D. Benne and P. Sheats, "Functional Roles of Group Members," *Journal of Social Issues* 4 (1948), pp. 41–49.

Intersender role conflict occurs when someone receives inconsistent signals from several others about expected behavior. Still another kind of role conflict is based on inconsistencies between different roles a person may have. Professional and family demands, for example, often create role conflicts. **Interrole conflict** occurs when someone is unable to perform all of his roles as well as he would like. A final type occurs when role expectations violate a person's values. This is known as **person-role conflict.** An example of person-role conflict might be when a store manager encourages a salesperson to mislead customers about the quality of the store's products when this behavior is inconsistent with the salesperson's values and beliefs.

A different sort of role problem is called **role ambiguity.** In role conflict, one receives clear messages about expectations, but the messages are not all congruent. With role ambiguity, the problem is lack of clarity about just what the expectations are (House, Schuler, & Levanoni, 1983; Rizzo, House, & Lirtzman, 1970). There may have been no role expectations established at all, or they may not have been clearly communicated. A person is experiencing role ambiguity if he or she wonders, "Just what am I supposed to be doing?" It is important for leaders to be able to minimize the degree to which dysfunctional roles, role conflict, and role ambiguity occur in their groups, as these problems have been found to have a negative impact on organizational commitment, job involvement, absenteeism, and satisfaction with co-workers and supervisors (Fisher & Gitelson, 1983).

Group Norms

Norms are the informal rules groups adopt to regulate and regularize group members' behaviors. Although norms are only infrequently written down or openly discussed, they nonetheless often have a powerful and consistent influence on behavior (Hackman, 1976). That is because most people are rather good at reading the social cues that inform them about existing norms. For example, most people easily discern the dress code in any new work environment without needing written guidance. People also are apt to notice when a norm is violated, even though they may have been unable to articulate the norm before its violation was apparent. For example, most students have expectations (norms) about creating extra work for other students. Imagine the reaction if a student in some class complained that not enough reading was being assigned each lesson or that the minimum length requirements for the term paper needed to be substantially raised.

Norms do not govern all behaviors, just those a group feels are important. Norms are more likely to be seen as important and apt to be enforced if they (a) facilitate group survival; (b) simplify, or make more predictable, what behavior is expected of group members; (c) help the group avoid embarrassing interpersonal problems; or (d) express the central values of the group and clarify what is distinctive about the group's identity (Feldman, 1984).

One irony about norms is that an outsider to a group often is able to learn more about norms than an insider. An outsider, not necessarily being subject to the norms himself, is more apt to notice them. In fact, the more "foreign" an observer is, the more likely the norms will be perceived. If a man is accustomed to wearing a tie to work, he is *less* likely to notice that men in another organization also wear ties to work, but *more* likely to note that the men in a third organization typically wear sweaters and sweatshirts around the office. Cadets at military academies so habitually address their military superiors as "Sir" or "Ma'am" that staff and faculty become almost unaware of it (except in its absence). Civilian visitors, however, are invariably taken aback by what often seems like unnatural formality.

It follows that one way to increase awareness of one's own group's norms is to observe norms in other groups. In a recent consulting project, one of the authors of this book was struck by the failure of the client organization to share certain information. The information the consulting team was seeking did not involve anything that might have adversely impacted the organization. On the contrary, sharing this particular information would have only helped the client organization. Nonetheless, the norm for the client organization was to be "guarded and secretive" with internal information. In reflecting on this situation, the consultants realized their own group's norm was quite different. The consulting team gladly and openly shared any and all information with each other. Prior to that incident, however, none of the consultants had ever thought about or could have articulated their own norm about sharing information because it was so second-nature to them.

Communication Networks in Groups

One way to determine a group's formal communication network is to examine the group's organizational chart. While the organizational chart may accurately depict the formal communication patterns within a group, often the pattern of actual interactions within a group may reveal a very different set of relationships. In reality, people may spend relatively little time communicating with those members they are connected to on the organizational chart and instead may spend considerably more time communicating with group members they are not directly linked to. Because the amount of time spent communicating affects the degree of mutual influence among group members, and because organizational charts may not accurately describe actual communication patterns within the group, using sociometric techniques is an alternative way to understand these influence processes (Moreno, 1955).

Sociometry is a two-stage process that involves the measurement of the acceptance or rejection of others in groups. The first stage asks individuals to indicate whom they go to for technical or personal advice, or to indicate whom they like, spend time interacting with, or avoid in the group. In the second stage, these individual responses are tabulated and the results are used to create a **sociogram.** As seen in Figure 10–2, sociograms provide a convenient way to summarize various sorts of group interactions and power relationships. Members holding more centralized positions in sociograms usually wield more influence in the group. Thus, leaders and followers may be better able to understand the dynamic processes within their groups by drawing sociograms of communication and influence networks.

In addition to sociograms, leaders and followers need to realize that office and seating arrangements often affect the degree of mutual interaction and reciprocal influence within groups. The most obvious example occurs when group members are geographically separated from each other, by being located either on different floors or in different buildings, cities, or even countries. However, the degree of mutual influence and reciprocal influence can be enhanced or impeded even when geographic separation is not an issue. For example, communication is usually increased when circular versus rectangular tables are used for meetings and when office doors are open or an open office arrangement is used (Stech, 1983). Although personality traits, values, experience, and interpersonal skills each play an important role, leaders and followers should also consider the role of physical space and office arrangements when interpreting the results of the sociograms for their groups or when trying to figure out how to exert more influence within their groups.

Group Cohesion

Group cohesion is the ''glue'' that keeps a group together. It is the sum of forces that attract members to a group, provide resistance to leaving it, and motivate them to be active in it. Highly cohesive groups interact with and influence each other more than do less-cohesive groups. Furthermore, a highly cohesive group may have lower absenteeism and lower turnover than a less-cohesive group, and low absenteeism and turnover often contribute to

FIGURE 10–2
Sociograms of an Eight-Person Work Group

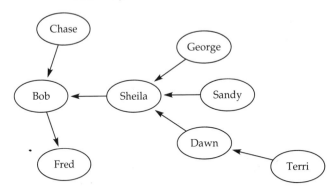

Whom do you seek technical advice from?

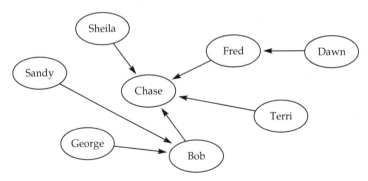

Whom do you seek personal advice from?

Read the arrows this way: (A) ──────▶ (B) means A seeks advice from B. Thus, in the bottom half of Figure 10-2. Dawn usually seeks personal advice from Fred, who in turn seeks personal advice from Chase.

higher group performance; higher performance can, in turn, contribute to even higher cohesion, thus resulting in an increasingly positive spiral.

However, greater cohesiveness does not always lead to higher performance. A highly cohesive but unskilled team is still an unskilled team, and such teams will often lose to a less cohesive but more skilled one. Additionally, a highly cohesive group may sometimes develop goals that are contrary to the larger organization's goals. For example, members of a highly cohesive research team at a particular college committed themselves to working on a problem that seemed inherently interesting to them. Their nearly zealous commitment to the project, however, effectively kept them from asking, or even allowing others to ask, if the research aligned itself well with the college's stated objectives. Their quite narrow and basic research effort deviated significantly from the college's expressed commitment to emphasize applied research. As a result, the college lost some substantial outside financial support.

Other problems also can occur in highly cohesive groups. Researchers (Alderfer, 1977; Ginnett, 1987) have found that some groups can become so cohesive they erect what amount to fences or boundaries between themselves and others. Such **"overbounding"** can block the use of outside resources that could make them more effective. Competitive product development teams can become so overbounded (often rationalized by security concerns or inordinate fears of "idea thieves") that they will not ask for help from willing and able staff within their own organizations.

One example of this problem was the failed mission to rescue U.S. embassy personnel held hostage in Iran during the Carter presidency. The rescue itself was a rather complicated mission involving many different sorts of U.S. military forces. Some of these forces included sea-based helicopters. The helicopters and their crews were carried on regular naval vessels, though most sailors on the vessels knew nothing of the secret mission. Senior personnel were so concerned that some sailor might "leak" information, and thus compromise the mission's secrecy, that maintenance crews aboard the ships were not directed to perform increased levels of maintenance on the helicopters immediately before the critical mission. Even if a helicopter was scheduled for significant maintenance within the next 50 hours of flight time (which would be exceeded in the rescue mission), crews were not told to perform the maintenance. According to knowledgeable sources, this practice did impact the performance of at least one of the failed helicopters, and thus the overall mission.

Janis (1982) discovered still another disadvantage of highly cohesive groups. He found that people in a highly cohesive group often become more concerned with striving for unanimity than in objectively appraising different courses of action. Janis labeled this phenomenon **groupthink** and believed it accounted for a number of historic fiascoes, including Pearl Harbor and the Bay of Pigs invasion. It may have played a role in the *Challenger* disaster, and it also occurs in other cohesive groups ranging from business meetings to air crews, and from therapy groups to school boards.

What is groupthink? Cohesive groups tend to evolve strong informal norms to preserve friendly internal relations. Preserving a comfortable, harmonious group environment becomes a "hidden agenda" that tends to suppress dissent, conflict, and critical thinking. Unwise decisions may result when concurrence-seeking among members overrides their willingness to express or

TABLE 10–3
Symptoms of Groupthink

- *An illusion of invulnerability,* which leads to unwarranted optimism and excessive risk taking by the group.

- *Unquestioned assumption of the group's morality* and therefore an absence of reflection on the ethical consequences of group action.

- *Collective rationalization* to discount negative information or warnings.

- *Stereotypes of the opposition* as evil, weak, or stupid.

- *Self-censorship* by group members from expressing ideas that deviate from the group consensus due to doubts about their validity or importance.

- *An illusion of unanimity* such that greater consensus is perceived than really exists.

- *Direct pressure on dissenting members,* which reinforces the norm that disagreement represents disloyalty to the group.

- *Mindguards,* who protect the group from adverse information.

Source: Adapted from I. L. Janis, *Groupthink,* 2nd ed. (Boston: Houghton Mifflin, 1982).

tolerate deviant points of view and think critically. Janis (1982) identified a number of symptoms of groupthink, which can be found in Table 10–3.

A policy-making or decision-making group displaying most of the symptoms in Table 10–3 runs a big risk of being ineffective. It may do a poor job of clarifying objectives, searching for relevant information, evaluating alternatives, assessing risks, and anticipating the need for contingency plans. Janis (1982) offered the following suggestions as ways of reducing groupthink and thus of improving the quality of a group's input to policies or decisions. First, leaders should encourage all group members to take on the role of critical evaluator. Everyone in the group needs to appreciate the importance of airing doubts and objections. This includes the leader's willingness to listen to criticisms of his or her own ideas. Second, leaders should create a climate of open inquiry through their own impartiality and objectivity. At the outset, leaders should refrain from stating personal preferences or expectations, which may bias group discussion. Third, the risk of groupthink can be reduced if independent groups are established to make recommendations on the same issue. Fourth, at least one member of the group should be assigned the role of devil's advocate, an assignment that should rotate from meeting to meeting.

One final problem with highly cohesive groups may be what Shephard (1991) has called **ollieism.** Ollieism, a variation of groupthink, occurs when illegal actions are taken by overly zealous and loyal subordinates who believe that what they are doing will please their leaders. It derives its name from the actions of Lieutenant Oliver North, who among other things admitted he lied to the U.S. Congress about his actions while working on the White House staff during the Iran-Contra affair. Shephard cites the slaying of Thomas à Becket by four of Henry II's knights and the Watergate break-in as other prime examples of ollieism. Ollieism differs from groupthink in that the subordinates' illegal actions usually occur without the explicit knowledge or consent of the leader. Nevertheless, Shephard points out that although the examples cited of ollieism were not officially sanctioned, the responsibility for them still falls squarely on the leader. It is the leader's responsibility to create an ethical climate within the group, and leaders who create highly cohesive yet unethical groups must bear the responsibility for the group's actions.

After reading about the uncertain relationships between group cohesion and performance, and the problems with overbounding, groupthink, and ollieism, one might think that cohesiveness should be something to avoid. Nothing, however, could be further from the truth. First of all, problems with overly cohesive groups occur relatively infrequently, and in general, leaders are probably better off thinking of ways to create and maintain highly cohesive teams than not to develop these teams out of concern for potential groupthink or overbounding situations. Second, perhaps the biggest argument for developing cohesive groups is to consider the alternative—groups with little or no cohesiveness. In the latter groups, followers would generally be dissatisfied with each other and the leader, commitment to accomplishing group and organizational goals may be reduced, intragroup communication may occur less frequently, and interdependent task performance may suffer (Robbins, 1986). Because of the problems associated with groups having low cohesiveness, leadership practitioners need to realize that developing functionally cohesive work groups is a goal they all should strive for.

In summary, the group perspective provides a complementary level of analysis to the individual perspective presented earlier in this chapter. A follower's behavior may be due to his or her values, traits, or experience (i.e., the individual perspective), or this behavior may be due to the followers' roles, the group norms, the group's stage of development, or the group's level of cohesiveness (i.e., the group perspective). Thus, the group perspective can also provide both leaders and followers with a number of explanations of why individuals in groups behave in certain ways. Moreover, the six group characteristics just described can give leaders and followers ideas about (a) factors that may be affecting their ability to influence other group members and (b) what to do to improve their level of influence in the group.

GROUPS VERSUS TEAMS: IS THERE A DIFFERENCE?

Virtually everyone has been involved in some group or other, often with the sort commonly called teams. But is there a difference between a group and a team? With *teams* and *teamwork* being the buzzwords of the 1990s, it is worth

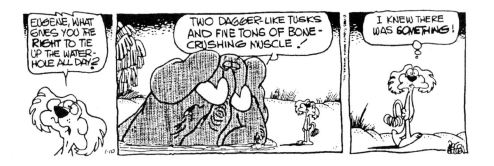

discussing the concept of teams and coordinated group work, or teamwork.

As described earlier in this chapter, two identifying characteristics of groups are mutual interaction and reciprocal influence. Members of teams also have mutual interaction and reciprocal influence, but we distinguish teams from groups in general in four other ways. First, teams generally have a stronger sense of identification among their members than groups do. Often, both team members and outsiders can readily identify who is and who is not on the team (athletic uniforms are one obvious example); identifying members of a group may be more difficult. Second, teams have common goals or tasks. These common goals may range from the development of a new product to an athletic league championship. Group members, on the other hand, may not have the same degree of consensus about goals as team members do. Group members may belong to the group for a variety of personal reasons, and these may clash with the group's stated objectives. (This phenomenon probably happens with teams, too, although perhaps not to the same extent.)

Third, task interdependence typically is greater with teams than with groups. For example, basketball players usually are unable to take a shot without other team members setting picks or passing the ball to them. On the other hand, group members often can contribute to goal accomplishment by working independently; the successful completion of their assigned tasks may not be contingent on other group members. Of course, task interdependence can vary greatly even across teams. Among athletic teams, for example, softball, football, soccer, and hockey teams have a high level of task interdependence whereas swimming, cross-country, and track teams have substantially lower levels of task interdependence. Fourth, team members often have more differentiated and specialized roles than group members. In the preceding section, we noted that group members often play a variety of roles within the group; however, team members often play a single, or primary, role on a team. Finally, it is important to bear in mind that the distinctions we have been high-lighting probably reflect only matters of degree. One might consider teams to be highly specialized groups.

Effective Team Characteristics and Team Building

Not only do teams vary in the extent to which they have specialized roles or task interdependence; teams also vary in their effectiveness. Virtually identical teams can be dramatically different in terms of success or failure (see Highlight 10–4). We must ask, therefore, what makes one team successful and another unsuccessful? Although this is an area only now being studied, exploratory work at the Center for Creative Leadership has tentatively identified several key characteristics for effective team performance (see Highlights 10–5 and 10–6 for still other perspectives on effective teams).

The Center for Creative Leadership's research with teams indicated that successful and unsuccessful teams could be differentiated on the basis of eight key characteristics, the first six of which are primarily concerned with task accomplishment (Hallam & Campbell, 1992). First, effective teams had a *clear mission* and *high performance standards.* Everyone on the team knew what the team was trying to achieve and how well he or she had to perform in order to achieve the team's mission. Second, leaders of successful teams often *took stock* of their equipment, training facilities and opportunities, and outside resources available to help the team. Leaders of effective teams spent a considerable amount of time *assessing the technical skills* of the team members. After taking stock of available resources and skills, good leaders would work to *secure those resources and equipment* necessary for team effectiveness. Moreover, leaders of effective teams would spend a considerable amount of time *planning* and *organizing* in order to make optimal use of available resources, to select new members with needed technical skills, or to improve needed technical skills of existing members.

The last two characteristics of effective teams were concerned with the group maintenance or interpersonal aspects of teams. Hallam and Campbell's (1992) research indicated that *high levels of communication* were often associated with effective teams. These authors believed this level of communication helped team members to stay focused on the mission and to take better advantage of the skills, knowledge, and resources available to the team. High levels of communication also helped to *minimize interpersonal conflicts* on the team, which often drained energy needed for team success and effectiveness.

The characteristics of effective teams identified in this research provide leadership practitioners with a number of ideas about how they may be able to increase the effectiveness of their work units or teams. Further ideas about how to develop effective teams are offered in the book *Groups that Work (and Those that Don't)* (Hackman, 1990). Based on his research, Hackman has developed a

---

HIGHLIGHT 10–4

Examples of Effective and Ineffective Teams

Most people can readily think up a number of examples of ineffective and effective teamwork. Consider the relative effectiveness of the teams depicted in the following two true stories:

> After an airline flight crew failed to get a "nose gear down and locked" indicator light to come on while making a landing approach into Miami, all three crew members became involved in trying to change the burned out indicator bulb in the cockpit. Nobody was flying the airplane and none of them were monitoring the flight of the L–1011 as it descended into the Everglades and crashed.

> The crew of a DC–10, after having lost all capability to control the airplane through flight controls, realized they needed all the help they could get. Captain Al Haynes discovered another experienced captain was traveling in the passenger cabin and invited him to come up to the cabin to help the regular crew out. Miraculously, their combined abilities enabled the crew—using techniques developed on the spot—to control the plane to within a few feet of the ground. Even though there were fatalities, over 100 people survived a nearly hopeless situation.

---

normative model of group effectiveness that identifies several characteristics critical to a team's effectiveness. An expanded revision of Hackman's normative model will be presented in Chapter Fifteen. For now, let us focus on that part of the model dealing with group or team design. The model, as modified by Ginnett (in press), posits four components that help any group get off to a good start, whatever its task. This is important because some groups' failures can be traced to having been set up inappropriately from the beginning. The four variables that need to be in place if a team is going to be able to work effectively and efficiently are the following:

1. *Task structure:* Does the team know what its task is? Is the task reasonably unambiguous and consistent with the mission of the team? Does the team have a meaningful piece of work, sufficient autonomy to perform it, and access to knowledge of its results?

2. *Group boundaries:* Is the collective membership of the team appropriate for the task to be performed? Are there too few or too many members? Do the members collectively have sufficient knowledge and skills to perform the work? In addition to task skills, does the team have sufficient maturity and interpersonal skills to be able to work together and resolve conflicts? Is there an appropriate amount of diversity on the team (e.g., members are not so similar that they do not have differing perspectives and experiences, and yet not so diverse that they cannot communicate or relate to one another)?

HIGHLIGHT 10–5

Followership in High Performing Teams

What distinguishes high-performing teams and organizations from more commonplace ones? That is a question the U.S. Navy has explored for many years
with the assistance of McBer and Company, a management consulting firm
(Whiteside, 1985).

A simple answer to the question is that good organizations have good leaders
and good followers. Just a collection of superstars, however, is not enough. This
became clear after the McBer researchers conducted more than 750 interviews
with ship captains and crews, administered and analyzed surveys, and examined
records from numerous different sorts of ships from aircraft carriers to subma-
rines. They found that what set ships with truly outstanding records of performance apart from others had a lot to do with how the followers on any given ship
functioned as a group.

One particularly important group of followers on any navy ship is its young
officers. They have significant responsibility but also can include some of the
youngest and least experienced individuals on the entire ship. It is important to
bear in mind that the navy's personnel assignment policies tended to equalize the
talent among young officers across the different ships. On an individual-by-
individual basis, then, one ship could not be judged much better than another, yet
some clearly performed much better than others. The following are some characteristics that distinguished followers on top-performing ships from their cohorts
on more average ones:

• *Cohesion.* The young officers on the best ships worked as a team. They interacted a lot in accomplishing their varied tasks, and they also interacted on a personal basis. Although they were not necessarily all friends, they worked effectively despite differences, and they appreciated each other's strengths. They
conveyed positive expectations about each other even in the midst of a competitive system of career advancement. Among average units, on the other hand,
there was more dysfunctional competition and much less mutual support. There
was less communication and less coordination.

• *Supporting Top Leadership.* On the best-performing ships, the young officers
adapted to and matched the leadership objectives and style of the ship's captain.
They knew and enthusiastically supported the captain's goals and philosophy,
showing none of the open criticism found among young officers on more mediocre ships. The best ships were characterized by congruence of leadership at all
levels.

• *Raising Issues with Top Leadership.* The superior ships were characterized by a
willingness among subordinates to ask questions, raise concerns, and bring both
good and bad news to their superiors.

• *Taking Initiative.* On the best ships, younger officers would take the initiative
to do what was necessasry without being told, including extra work beyond their

---

HIGHLIGHT 10–5 *(concluded)*

normally assigned duties. They also looked for better ways to accomplish their work. On more average ships, the younger officers tended to be satisfied with just doing their own specific jobs and with the status quo; they were resistant to change and to risk.
  • *Taking Personal Responsibility for Team Performance.* On the best ships, the young officers felt a personal responsibility for the performance of their respective work groups.

---

3. *Norms:* Does the team share an appropriate set of norms for working as a team? Norms can be acquired by the team in three ways: (*a*) They can be imported from the organization existing outside the team; (*b*) they can be instituted and reinforced by the leader or leaders of the team; or (*c*) they can be developed by the team itself as the situation demands. If the team is to have a strategy that works over time, then it must ensure that conflicting norms do not confuse team members. It also needs to regularly scan and review prevailing norms to ensure they support overall objectives.

4. *Authority:* Has the leader established a climate where her authority can be used in a flexible rather than rigid manner? Has she, at one end of the authority continuum, established sufficient competence to allow the group to comply when conditions demand (such as in emergencies)? Has she also established a climate such that any member of the team feels empowered to provide expert assistance when appropriate? Do team members feel comfortable in questioning the leader on decisions where there are no clear right answers? In short, have conditions been created where authority can shift to appropriately match the demands of the situation?

As noted above, many of these team design components may be imported from preexisting conditions in the organization within which the team is forming, from the industry in which the organization operates, or even from the environment in which the industry exists. To help team leaders consider these various levels, Hackman (1986) and Ginnett (in press) developed the concept of **organizational shells** (see Figure 10–3). Notice that the four critical factors for team design (task, boundaries, norms, and authority) are necessasry for the group to work effectively. In some cases, all the information about one of these critical factors may be input from the industry or organizational shell level. In these cases, the leader need do little else but affirm that condition. In other cases, there may be too little (or even inappropriate) input from the organizational level to allow the team to work effectively. In these cases, the leader

HIGHLIGHT 10–6

Women in Leadership, IV: Teamwork from an Astronaut's Perspective

Dr. Bonnie J. Dunbar is an American astronaut. She has flown on three space shuttle missions. We asked her to share a few personal reflections about the meaning of teamwork and followership to her as she was growing up as well as presently in her role in the space program. She wrote this during preparation for her flight in June 1992. She was payload commander for that space shuttle mission.

Above all, the success of a space flight depends upon teamwork: within the crew and between the ground controllers and the crew. Teamwork is a valued attribute among currently selected astronauts.

I was very fortunate as a young girl to have been exposed to that concept by my family. With four children and a multitude of chores to be performed, my mother and father impressed upon us our responsibilities within the family unit. Success of the farm (and our future) depended upon our contribution. As the oldest, I was expected to participate in all chores, including driving the tractor and "round-up" by horseback. There were no distinctions in these responsibilities between my brothers and me. Group experiences within the 4-H organization (showing steers, etc.) and playing on baseball, volleyball, and basketball teams reinforced the pride of sharing success together and consoling each other in defeat.

When I attended college, some of that team experience was missed. By virtue of my gender, I was considered an unwelcome minority by many in the engineering college. Therefore, I was never invited to the study groups or participated in group solution of the home work problems. Still, I found an outlet in group activities by belonging to Angel Flight (co-ed auxiliary to Air Force ROTC—I was elected Commander of 50 my junior year) and by continuing to play co-ed baseball. Ironically, my engineering classmates needed my athletic ability as first baseman on the playing field.

I was also supported by three very important individuals during this time: my father, my mother, and Chairman of the Ceramic Engineering Department, Dr. James I. Mueller. My parents always encouraged me to pursue my "dreams" and to be the best person I could be. The fact that I was the first in the family to attend college was a source of pride for them. That I ascribed to their principles of hard work, human compassion, and honesty was probably a souce of greater pride. They were proud of my selection as an astronaut but my father was more concerned that I not forget how to get manure on my boots.

In my professional life, the closest I have come to real group esprit de corps has come through my association with the Astronaut Office. Perhaps it was due to the concept of "class training," or the similarity of individuals involved, but I consider those I work with as also my closest friends. Our successes are really those of a family team that extends out to the engineers, managers, and administrative support in the Space Shuttle program.

I am now on my third NASA Space Shuttle crew. As Payload Commander I have tried to convey to the non-career payload specialists on my next flight the importance of being part of the crew . . . that we will share both the successes and the failures of the flight. It has been an interesting experience to assess others' ability to become "part of the team." I have seen what not being part of the team can do, and in a flight environment that can be highly risky. Not being a team member does more than cause internal friction within the crew; it can be hazardous.

HIGHLIGHT 10–6 *(concluded)*

So, what does being "part of the team" mean? It doesn't always mean being the smartest or the fastest. It does mean recognizing the big picture goal and the contribution that each individual brings to the whole. It may not mean being the life of the party, but it does mean being able to get along with people and to tread a fine line . . . knowing when to compromise and knowing when to stand firm. And, in an organization such as ours with competitive individuals used to being on top of the hill, it means knowing when to be a Chief and when to be an Indian. In the astronaut office, mission specialists rotate through technical jobs and different responsibilities during flights. Sometimes they are Indians instead of Chiefs. Those that perform best and appear to be well-regarded can do each equally well.

---

needs to modify the factors for team design. Ideally this is done during the formation process—the final shell before the team actually begins work.

These ideas may require a new way of thinking about the relationship between a leader and followers. In many organizational settings, leaders are as-

FIGURE 10–3
Organizational Shells

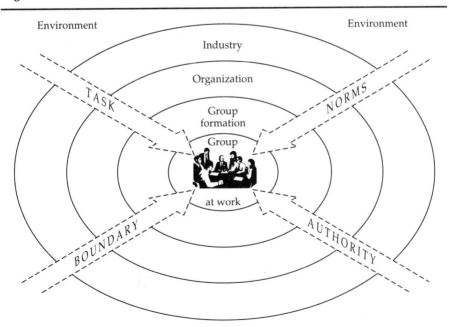

signed. Sometimes, however, the people who create conditions for improved group effectiveness are not the designated leaders at all; they may emerge from the ranks of followers. In fact, this model has been used to differentiate between effective and ineffective "self-managing work groups"—teams where the followers and leaders were the same people. Moreover, because the model is prescriptive, it also provides a number of suggestions about what ineffective work groups can do in order to be successful.

SUMMARY

The importance of followers seems, somewhat curiously, to have been dramatically undervalued. Followers usually play a key role in organizational successes and failures, yet these outcomes are often attributed solely to leaders. Followers have also been relatively unappreciated by leadership researchers; followers are either ignored completely or considered to be a relatively homogeneous group of individuals in most leadership research studies. Additionally, we have given too little attention to the fact many individuals, in larger organizations at least, are both followers and leaders at the same time. In an absolute sense, everyone has spent and will spend more time as a follower than as a leader, and spending time reflecting on follower experiences may be one important key to leadership success.

Because most people spend so much time as followers, and because followers play such an important role in organizational outcomes, this chapter reviewed followership from three different perspectives. First, the individual perspective showed that followers differ in as many ways as leaders do. This should hardly be surprising. Nevertheless, the myriad ways followers can differ from each other are often overlooked, and these differences can have a major impact on followers' behaviors.

Second, the group perspective showed that followers' behaviors can also be the result of factors somewhat independent of the individual characteristics of followers. Group factors that can affect followers' behaviors include group size, stages of group development, roles, norms, communication networks, and cohesion. Leadership practitioners should use these concepts to better understand followers' behaviors. Finally, leaders should also use a team perspective for understanding follower behavior and group performance. Leadership practitioners need to bear in mind how a team's sense of identity, common goals or tasks, level of task interdependence, and differentiated roles affect functional and dysfunctional follower behavior. Additionally, because effective teams have several readily identifiable characteristics, leadership practitioners may want to use the suggestions provided by Hackman (1990), Ginnett (1992), or Hallam and Campbell (1992) to develop more effective teams.

KEY TERMS AND CONCEPTS

follower role

leader role

individual perspective

future shock

sheep

yes people

survivors

alienated followers

effective followers

internal locus of control

external locus of control

group perspective

group

cliques

span of control

additive task

process loss

social loafing

social facilitation

Hawthorne effect

forming

storming

norming

performing

group roles

task role

relationship role

dysfunctional roles

role conflict

intrasender role conflict

intersender role conflict

interrole conflict

person-role conflict

role ambiguity

norms

sociometry

sociogram

group cohesion

overbounding

groupthink

ollieism

organizational shells

DISCUSSION QUESTIONS

1. Ted Turner, *Time* magazine's Man of the Year for 1991, has a plaque on his desk saying "Lead, follow, or get out of the way." Do you agree with that view? Discuss its implications in the context of leader and follower roles.

2. Not all group norms are positive or constructive from the leader's perspective. If a group holds counterproductive norms, what should the leader do?

3. Contrast groupthink with managing agreement (as exemplified in the Abilene paradox described in Chapter Nine). Do both phenomena reflect the same underlying dynamics?

4. What qualities do you think characterize the ideal follower? In what ways is this list different, if at all, from one characterizing the ideal leader?

5. Do traits, values, or preferences play a role in the groups people join? Do these individual difference variables influence the roles people play in groups?

SUGGESTED READINGS

Hackman, J. R., *Groups that Work (and Those that Don't)*. San Francisco: Jossey-Bass, 1990.

Bucholz, S., and T. Roth. *Creating the High-Performance Team*. New York: Wiley, 1987.

Isgar, T. *The Ten-Minute Team*. Boulder, Colo. Selvera Press, 1989.

"Well, guess I did it again, eh guys? Missed a field goal in the final seconds. But, hey, we're a team, right? Right, guys? . . . Guys?"

Chapter Eleven

Motivation, Satisfaction, and Performance

INTRODUCTION

M any people believe the most important quality of a good leader is the ability to motivate others to accomplish group tasks. The importance of motivation as a component of output is suggested in findings from diverse work groups that most people believe they could give as much as 15 percent or 20 percent more effort at work than they now do with no one, including their own bosses, recognizing any difference. Perhaps even more startling, these workers also believed they could give 15 percent or 20 percent *less* effort with no one noticing any difference (Kinlaw, 1991). Moreover, variation in the output of jobs varies significantly across leaders and followers. Hunter, Schmidt, and Judiesch (1990) estimated the top 15 percent of the workers for a particular job produced from 20 to 50 percent more output than the average worker, depending on the complexity of the job. What can leaders and followers do to enhance the motivation to perform?

HIGHLIGHT 11–1

Leadership Quotes, Chapter Eleven

The body of every organization is structured from four kinds of bones. There are the wishbones, who spend all their time wishing someone would do the work. Then there are the jawbones, who do all the talking, but little else. The knucklebones knock everything anybody else tries to do. Fortunately, in every organization there are also the backbones, who get under the load and do most of the work.

Leo Aikman, *On Bones*

Some players you pat their butts, some players you kick their butts, some players you leave alone.

Pete Rose

The first thing a young officer must do when he joins the Army is to fight a battle, and that battle is for the hearts of his men. If he wins that battle and subsequent similar ones, his men will follow him anywhere; if he loses it, he will never do any real good.

Viscount Montgomery of Alamein

Better debate a question without settling it than settle a question without debating it.

Joseph Joubert

There is no limit to the good one can do if he doesn't care who gets the credit.

George C. Marshall

Motivating others depends, most of all, on understanding others. Therefore, whereas motivation is an essential part of leadership, it is appropriate to include it in this part, which focuses on the followers. This chapter will examine links between leadership, satisfaction, motivation, and performance—four closely related concepts (see also Highlight 11–1).

DEFINING MOTIVATION, SATISFACTION, AND PERFORMANCE

Motivation, satisfaction, and performance seem clearly related. This seems evident enough in Highlight 11–2, for example, the case of Lori, who led her cheerleading team to a world championship. She seems to have *motivated* her team to work hard and thereby develop a high level of proficiency. In other

HIGHLIGHT 11–2

Women in Leadership, V: One Young Leader's Motivation

When Lori graduated from high school, she took a part-time position as coach of the cheerleading team she had just served with. There had been some opposition to offering Lori the job, since she was barely older than the present cheerleaders. However, the need for a coach was great; the school took pride in the caliber of its cheerleaders, and the previous coach had departed. Furthermore, Lori had been a superior cheerleader herself, and she was available for part-time work since she was a freshman at a nearby college.

Lori got the job, but it was not all roses. In some ways the concerns about her youth had been justified. It was more difficult for Lori to enforce certain standards (e.g., punctuality at practice) when the perception of some team members was that she hadn't followed all the rules herself when she was a cheerleader. Nonetheless, the confidence in this young woman proved justified. As a result of her dynamic leadership, technical skill, and demanding training, the team proved good enough to win the cheerleading competition at the state fair. It was even invited to go to the international cheerleading championships in Japan. Unfortunately, accepting the invitation seemed unlikely since the trip's total expenses would amount to over $50,000. Lori accepted the invitation, however, believing the team could raise the money. She personally organized numerous fund-raisers such as car raffles, candy sales, fashion shows, and so on. She won widespread community support and received significant donations from local businesses.

The team went to Japan . . . and placed first! Lori's team was best in the world.

Apply the various approaches to motivation covered in this chapter to Lori and the other members of her team. Which theories or models help explain Lori's level and persistence of effort? Which might help explain the motivation of the other members of the cheerleading team, a group little different from Lori in many ways?

words, she seems to have motivated her team to *perform* well. It also seems likely that the team took great pride (i.e., *satisfaction*) in winning the championship. But let's explore each of these concepts a bit more closely.

According to Kanfer (1990), **motivation** is anything that provides *direction, intensity,* and *persistence* to behavior. Another definition considers the term *motivation* a sort of shorthand to describe choosing an activity or task to engage in, establishing the level of effort to put forth on it, and determing the degree of persistence in it over time (Campbell & Pritchard, 1976). Like preferences and personality traits, motivation is not directly observable; it must be inferred from behavior. For example, if one person regularly assembles twice as many computers as any other person in his work group—assuming all have the same

FUNKY WINKERBEAN by Tom Batiuk

abilities, skills, and resources—then we likely would say this first person is more motivated than the others. We use the concept of motivation to explain differences we see among people in the energy and direction of their behavior.

Performance, on the other hand, concerns those behaviors directed toward the organization's mission or goals, or the products and services resulting from those behaviors. Thus, performance is synonomous with behavior. Performance differs from effectiveness, which generally involves making judgments about the adequacy of behavior with respect to certain criteria such as workgroup or organizational goals. Lori's team was motivated, performed those behaviors associated with team success, and would be judged to be effective (Campbell, McCloy, Oppler, & Sager, 1992). Performance is a broader concept than motivation. Factors such as intelligence, skill, and the availability of key resources can affect a person's behaviors toward accomplishing organizational goals (i.e., performance) even when the person is extremely motivated. For example, a salesperson may put considerable effort into establishing and maintaining sales contacts over a two-month period but still fail to make a single sale. In terms of the level and persistence of effort, the salesperson would be seen as highly motivated. However, if he made poor decisions about which contacts to maintain or lacked adequate computer resources to keep track of his clients, then much of his behavior would have been misdirected. Moreover, if sales volume were the criterion for evaluating performance, that individual would be judged to be ineffective. Thus, an adequate level of motivation may be a necessary but not sufficient condition of effective performance.

Job satisfaction is not how *hard* one works, or how *well* one works, but rather how much one *likes* a specific kind of work. In other words, job satisfaction deals with one's attitudes about work (Saal & Knight, 1988). Job satisfaction can be defined as a person's overall impression or evaluation of her job, and various polls over the past half century have consistently shown the vast majority of peo-

FIGURE 11–1

CWO Campbell Organizational Survey*: Organization Graph

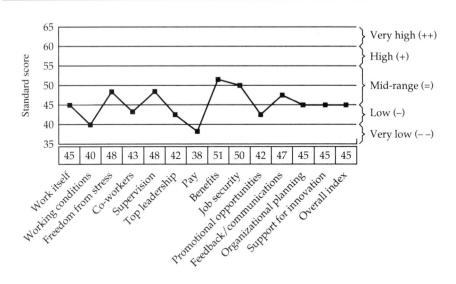

ple report liking their jobs (see Health, Education, & Welfare Task Force, 1973; Hoppock, 1935; Smith, Scott, & Hulin, 1977; or Staines & Quinn, 1979). Job satisfaction also refers to one's feelings about relatively specific aspects of the job. For example, an individual might have generally positive feelings about the job and feel especially good about pay and health benefits, but she may also think her boss is a poor supervisor. Questionnaires can measure both overall job satisfaction as well as that stemming from specific aspects of the job. Figure 11–1 provides an example of feedback from a job satisfaction questionnaire.

There are several practical reasons job satisfaction is an important concept for leaders to think about. According to Locke and Latham (1990), satisfied workers are more likely to continue working for an organization and are more likely than their co-workers to help others in it. Dissatisfied workers are more likely to be adversarial in their relations with leadership (e.g., file grievances) and engage in diverse other sorts of counterproductive behaviors (e.g., foster dissent).

Having now defined motivation, performance, and job satisfaction, we might briefly explore certain causal relationships among them. We have already noted how motivation does not always assure good performance. A leader may try to increase her followers' motivation, yet if they lack the necessary skills or resources to accomplish the group task, then increases in the level and persistence of effort will have a minimal effect on performance (Campbell, 1977; 1988). For example, no high school basketball team is likely to defeat the Chicago Bulls, however motivated the players may be. The players on the high school team simply lack the abilities and skills of the Bulls players. Higher motivation may only affect performance if followers already have the abilities, skills, and resources to get the job done. Leadership is more than motivating followers, and pep talks are not always enough.

The relationships between motivation and job satisfaction are a bit more straightforward—as a matter of fact, many theories of motivation are also theories of job satisfaction. The implicit link between satisfaction and motivation is that satisfaction often increases when people successfully accomplish a task, particularly when the task requires a lot of effort. For example, one person might feel very satisfied after successfully completing a marathon. One might also think performance is higher among more satisfied workers, but actually this is not always so (Iaffaldano & Muchinsky, 1985; Podsakoff & Williams, 1986). It is just not true that happy workers are necessarily those who spend the most time on behaviors directed toward organizational goals (i.e., the most productive ones) and that unhappy (i.e., dissatisfied) workers are always the poorest performers. It is entirely possible, for example, for poor performing workers to have a high level of job satisfaction (maybe because they are paid well yet do not have to work very hard, like Homer Simpson in the television show *The Simpsons*). It is also possible for dissatisfied workers to be relatively high performers (they may have a strong work ethic, or they may be trying to improve chances to get out of the current job). Despite the intuitive appeal of believing satisfied workers are also performing at higher levels, it may be that satisfaction has only an indirect effect on performance (Locke & Latham, 1990).[1] Nevertheless, having both satisfied *and* high performing followers is a goal all leaders should strive to achieve.

UNDERSTANDING AND INFLUENCING FOLLOWER MOTIVATION

Few topics of human behavior have been the subject of so many books and articles as that of motivation. So much has been written about motivation that a comprehensive review of the subject is beyond the scope of this book. This sec-

---

[1]Furthermore, there may even be a biological basis of satisfaction beyond anyone's direct control, leader or follower (see Highlight 11-3).

HIGHLIGHT 11–3

Does Job Satisfaction Have a Genetic Link?

Most people consider job satisfaction to be a function of the situation. For example, if workers are dissatisfied with their pay, working conditions, or health benefits, then leaders could work on improving these factors in order to increase workers' job satisfaction. However, a study of identical twins reared apart and together discovered that although situational factors played the most important role, genetic factors also affected subjects' reported levels of job satisfaction.

Evidence to support the findings can easily be found at work. If job satisfaction were purely a function of the situation, then an improvement in working conditions or pay levels would have a universal effect on all workers' satisfaction levels. However, even when "positive" changes are implemented, some workers will get excited, some will become angry, and others will not seem to care much either way. Because the situation is fairly constant, dispositional factors must play some role in the attitudinal differences between these workers. Therefore, leaders should always strive to increase followers' job satisfaction levels, but they also need to realize that some followers may be hard to please *no matter what the leader does.*

Source: Arvey, R.D.; T.J. Bouchard, Jr.; N.L. Segal; and L.M. Abraham. "Job satisfaction: Environmental and Genetic Components." *Journal of Applied Psychology* 74 (1989), pp. 187–92.

---

tion will, however, overview several major approaches to understanding work motivation, as well as address their implications for followers' satisfaction and performance. (See Kanfer, 1990; Campbell & Pritchard, 1976, for more comprehensive reviews.) It is important for leadership practitioners to become familiar with these major approaches, which offer a variety of perspectives and ideas for influencing followers' decisions to choose, exert effort, or resist an activity. Additionally, through such understanding, leadership practitioners may recognize that some motivation theories are more applicable in certain situations, or for producing certain outcomes, than others.

In this section we will discuss the key aspects of 10 different approaches to understanding motivation in a work or leadership context. We have organized the approaches into four broad categories: need theories, individual difference approaches, cognitive theories, and situational approaches. This categorization seems helpful for explanatory purposes, even though it is admittedly atheoretical.

Need Theories

The two major need theories include Maslow's (1954) hierarchy of needs and Alderfer's (1969) existence-relatedness-growth (ERG) theory. These two theo-

FIGURE 11–2
Maslow's Hierarchy of Needs

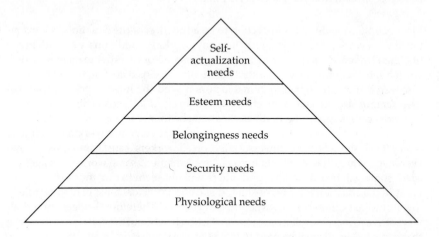

ries assume all people share a common set of basic needs. **Needs** refer to internal states of tension or arousal, or uncomfortable states of deficiency people are motivated to change (Kanfer, 1990).

Maslow's hierarchy of needs.   According to Maslow (1954), people are motivated to satisfy five basic sorts of needs. These include the need to survive physiologically, the need for security, the need for affiliation with other people, the need to feel self-esteem, and the need for self-actualization. Maslow's conceptualization of needs is usually represented by a triangle with the five levels of needs arranged in a hierarchy (see Figure 11–2) called, not surprisingly, the **hierarchy of needs.** According to Maslow, any person's behavior can be understood primarily as directed effort to satisfy one particular level of need in the hierarchy. Which level happens to be motivating one's behavior at any time depends on whether ''lower'' needs have been satisfied. According to Maslow, lower level needs must be satisfied before the next higher level would become salient in motivating behavior.

As an example, if Eric's salary were sufficient to meet his physiological needs, and his job security and retirement plan were sufficient to meet his security needs, neither of these two needs would serve to energize and direct his behavior. However, if he were in a secluded position on an assembly line and could not talk with others or be part of a close work group, he may still feel unfulfilled in his needs for affiliation and belongingness. This may cause him to put a lot of effort into forming friendships and socializing at work.

Maslow (1954) said higher-level needs like those for self-esteem or self-actualization would not become salient (even when unfulfilled) until lower needs were satisfied. Thus, a practical implication of his theory is that leaders may only be successful in motivating follower behavior by taking account of the follower's position on the need hierarchy. For example, it might be relatively inefficient to try to motivate our lonely assembly-line worker by appealing to how much pride he would take in a job well done (i.e., to his self-esteem); Maslow said only *after* one feels part of a social group will such motives become energizing. At all levels of the hierarchy, the leader should watch for mismatches between his motivational efforts and the followers' lowest unsatisfied needs.

ERG theory.   Alderfer's (1969) **existence-relatedness-growth (ERG) theory** has several similarities to Maslow's hierarchy of needs. In the terms of ERG theory, existence needs basically correspond to Maslow's physiological and security needs; relatedness needs are like Maslow's social and esteem needs; and growth needs are similar to the need for self-actualization. Beyond those similarities, however, are two important differences.

First, Alderfer (1969) reported that people sometimes try to satisfy more than one need at the same time. For example, even though a follower's existence needs may not be entirely satisfied, she may still be motivated to grow as a person. Second, he claimed frustration of a higher-level need can lead to efforts to satisfy a lower-level need. In other words, a follower who is continually frustrated in achieving some need might "regress" and exert effort to "satisfy" a lower need that already has been satisfied. For example, if the nature of work on an assembly line repeatedly frustrates Eric's need for relatedness with others, he may eventually stop trying to satisfy these needs at work and regress to demanding more pay—an existence need—and might, then, try to satisfy the relatedness need outside of work. Alderfer called this the **frustration-regression hypothesis.**

Concluding thoughts on need theories.   Although both Maslow's and Alderfer's need theories have played an important historical role in our understanding of motivation, they do have certain limitations. For one thing, neither theory makes specific predictions about what an individual will do to satisfy a particular need (Betz, 1984; Kanfer, 1990). In the example above, Eric may exert considerable effort to establish new friendships at work, try to make friends outside of work, or even spend a lot of money on a new car or stereo equipment (the frustration-regression hypothesis). The theories' lack of specificity and predictive power severely limits their practical applicability in organizational, school, or team settings. On the other hand, awareness of the general nature of the various sorts of basic human needs described in these two theories seems fundamentally useful to leaders.

Individual Differences in Motivation

Both Maslow's hierarchy of needs and Alderfer's ERG theory claimed that certain fundamental human needs exist in all people. A very different approach to understanding human motivation involves focusing on stable and consistent differences between people in the strength of certain motives. Two prominent examples of this approach focus, respectively, on the personality trait of achievement orientation and on how intrinsically motivating a particular task or activity is for any given person. These two approaches differ from the need theories in that individuals are believed to vary substantially in terms of achievement orientation and the activities and tasks people enjoy doing, whereas the need theories assume that all people are universally motivated by the same set of (three or five) needs.

Achievement orientation. Atkinson (1957) proposed that an individual's tendency to exert effort toward task accomplishment depended partly on the strength of her motive to achieve success, or, as Atkinson called it, on her **achievement orientation.** McClelland (1975) further developed Atkinson's ideas and said that individuals with a strong achievement orientation (or in McClelland's terms, a strong need for achievement) were competitive, liked taking responsibility for solving problems, and strived to accomplish socially acceptable endeavors and activities. These individuals also preferred tasks that provided immediate and ample feedback and were moderately difficult (i.e., tasks that required a considerable amount of effort but were accomplishable). Additionally, individuals with a strong need to achieve felt satisfied when they successfully solved work problems or accomplished job tasks (McClelland, 1975). Individuals with a relatively weak need to achieve were generally not as competitive, preferred easier tasks, and did not feel satisfied by solving problems or accomplishing assigned tasks. McClelland (1975) maintained that differences in achievement orientation were a primary reason people differed in the levels of effort they exerted to accomplish assignments, objectives, or goals.

Intrinsic motivation. Work behavior is motivated by both internal and external factors. In this section, we will focus on the former, although we also will examine how the two factors interact. We use the term **intrinsic motivation** to describe behavior seemingly motivated for its own sake, for the personal satisfaction and increased feelings of competence or control one gets from doing it. One activity may be intrinsically motivating for one person, and a quite different activity may be intrinsically motivating to someone else. Hobbies, for example, are almost by definition intrinsically motivating, yet they also reflect the diversity of human tastes for different activities. Stamp collecting may be highly intrinsically motivating to one person, yet it may be exceedingly boring to many others.

Deci (1975) observed that individuals often *voluntarily* put forth effort toward activities they enjoy doing. Since individuals already are engaging in such intrinsically motivating activities, one might wonder just what would result if extrinsic rewards were added to the intrinsic rewards. It might seem at first as though the behavior should be even further strengthened, that levels of effort and persistence would be even higher if external rewards were added to the internal rewards. Sometimes, though, that is not the case. Research has shown that providing people with external rewards or incentives when performing intrinsically motivating tasks may result in a decrease in the person's intrinsic motivation toward the tasks (Calder & Staw, 1975; Deci, 1972). Further study of this **overjustification effect** has shown that external rewards can result in a decrease in intrinsic motivation when they are perceived to be "controlling"; however, rewards seen as providing "informational" value (e.g., letting a person know how well he or she is doing) or those that are consistent with societal norms concerning pay and benefits typically do not result in a decrease in intrinsic motivation for the task (Deci, 1975; Fisher, 1973; Lepper, Greene, & Nisbett, 1973).

Concluding thoughts on individual differences in motivation.   Because people vary in their achievement orientation and in the tasks they find intrinsically motivating, one way to ensure that followers will exert the effort needed to accomplish group tasks is to select individuals who already have strong achievement motivation or who already are intrinsically motivated by the tasks necessary for goal accomplishment. Although McClelland (1985) has reported successfully training people to have higher achievement orientation scores, this can be a relatively expensive and inefficient process; putting more emphasis on selecting the right people for the job in the first place may be a preferable path for leaders to take.

It is also important to remember that sometimes using tangible incentives to increase effort may have deleterious effects. When rewards are perceived as controlling, they may serve to decrease one's intrinsic motivation toward an activity. Thus, leaders using rewards to increase effort levels need to emphasize the informational value of the rewards and minimize their controlling aspects. As rules of thumb, if the leader institutes a reward to "get someone to do it," then it is an attempt at control; if the leader provides rewards to demonstrate who is doing it well, then the reward provides information.

Finally, these two approaches help us understand why some people—but not all—exert considerable effort across a variety of work settings (in the case of individuals with high achievement orientation) or on certain tasks (in the case of individuals working on tasks that are intrinsically motivating to them) in the absence of any situational pressures or rewards.

FIGURE 11-3
Equity Theory Ratios

$$\frac{\text{Personal outcomes}}{\text{Personal inputs}} = \frac{\text{Reference group outcomes}}{\text{Reference group inputs}}$$

Cognitive Theories

The three cognitive theories we will describe here are concerned primarily with clarifying the conscious thought processes people use when deciding how hard or long to work toward some task or goal.

Equity theory.   As the name implies, **equity theory** emphasizes the motivational importance to followers of fair treatment by their leaders. It assumes that people value fairness in leader-follower exchange relationships (Kanfer, 1990). Followers are said to be most satisfied when they believe that what they put into an activity or job and what they get out of it are roughly equivalent to what others put into and get out of it (Adams, 1963; Vecchio, 1982). Equity theory proposes a very rational model for how followers assess these issues. Followers presumably reach decisions about equitable relationships by assigning values to the four elements in Figure 11-3 and then comparing the two ratios (Adams, 1963). In looking at the specific elements in each ratio, personal outcomes refer to what one is receiving for one's efforts, such as pay, job satisfaction, opportunity for advancement, and personal growth. Personal inputs refer to all those things one contributes to a job such as time, effort, knowledge, and skills.

A key aspect of equity theory is that Figure 11-3 contains *two* ratios. Judgments of equity are always based on comparison to some reference group. It is the *relationship* between *the two ratios* that is important in equity theory, not the absolute value of either one's own outcomes or inputs, or those of others, considered by themselves. What matters most is the comparison between one's own ratio and that of a reference group such as one's co-workers or workers holding similar jobs in other organizations. For example, there may be many people who make more money than a particular follower; they may also, however, work longer hours, have more skills, or have to live in undesirable geographic locations to do so. In other words, although their outcomes are greater, so are their inputs, and thus the ratios may still be equal; there is equity.

In essence, equity theory does not try to evaluate "equality of inputs" or "equality of outcomes." It is concerned with "fairness" of inputs relative to outcomes. The perception of inequity creates a state of tension and an inherent pressure for change. As long as there is general equality between the two ratios, there is no motivation (at least based on inequity) to change anything, and people are reasonably satisfied. If, however, the ratios are significantly differ-

---

HIGHLIGHT 11–4

Professional Athlete Salary Demands and Equity Theory

It can be difficult for anyone earning a modest income to understand an athlete's justification of demanding an increase from (say) $2 million to $3 million a year. One might argue that no one deserves that much money, much less for just playing a sport. However, the athlete's demands can be better understood by using an equity theory perspective. Whereas it may be difficult in any absolute way to assign the "right" salary level to athletic performance, it is possible to look at one athlete's salary and compare it to the salary and performance of another athlete. If, for example, one NFL quarterback earns a higher salary than another even when the latter has had several more productive years, then this inequity becomes grounds for the latter to demand more money. Additionally, this is precisely the argument presented during the contract negotiations for many professional athletes.

---

ent, a follower will be motivated to take action likely to restore the balance. Exactly what the follower will be motivated to do depends on the direction of the inequality. Adams (1965) suggested six ways people might restore balance: (*a*) changing their inputs; (*b*) changing their outcomes; (*c*) altering their self-perceptions; (*d*) altering their perceptions of their reference group; (*e*) changing their reference group; or, if all else fails, (*f*) leaving the situation. Thus, if a follower believed her ratio was lower than her co-worker's, she may reduce her level of effort or seek higher pay elsewhere. Research has shown that perceptions of underpayment generally resulted in actions in support of the model, but perceptions of overpayment did not. Instead of working harder in an overpayment condition (to make their own ratio more equitable), subjects often rationalized that they really deserved the higher pay (Campbell & Pritchard, 1976). An example of how equity theory might affect some salary negotiations is presented in Highlight 11–4.

Expectancy theory.   First described by Tolman (1932), **expectancy theory** has been modified for use in work settings (Vroom, 1964; Porter & Lawler, 1968; Lawler, 1973). It involves two fundamental assumptions: (*a*) Motivated performance is the result of conscious choice and (*b*) people will do what they believe will provide them the highest (or surest) rewards. Thus, expectancy theory, like equity theory, is a highly rational approach to understanding motivation. It assumes that people act in ways that maximize their expectations of attaining valued outcomes and that reliable predictions of behavior are possible if the factors that influence those expectations can be quantified. In this model, there are three such factors to be quantified. The first two are probability estimates (expectancies), and the third is a vector sum of predicted positive and negative outcomes.

The first probability estimate is the **effort-to-performance expectancy.** Like all probabilities, it ranges from no chance of the event occurring to an absolute certainty of it occurring; or, in decimal form, from 0.0 to 1.0. Here, the follower estimates the likelihood of performing the desired behavior adequately, assuming she puts forth the required effort. The second probability estimate is the **performance-to-outcome expectancy.** In this case, our follower estimates the likelihood of receiving a reward, given that she achieves the desired level of performance. This is a necessary step in the sequence since it is not uncommon for people actually to do good work yet not be rewarded for it (e.g., someone else may be the teacher's pet). Finally, the follower must determine the likely outcomes, assuming that the previous conditions have been met, and determine whether their weighted algebraic sum (**valence**) is sufficiently positive to be worth the time and effort. To put it more simply, expectancy theory says that people will be motivated to do a task if three conditions are met; (1) They *can* do the task, (2) they will be rewarded if they do it, and (3) they value the reward.

An example from student life might be helpful here. As seen in Figure 11-4, Amy Cook, a sophomore in college, is coming up on finals. She has a B in her required history course and is trying to determine how much effort to put into studying for the final exam. According to expectancy theory, Amy would first determine if long sessions of concerted study would enable her to obtain an A on the final (effort-to-performance expectancy). Secondly, she would have to determine if getting an A on the final would be sufficient to pull her overall grade up to an A in the course (performance-to-outcome expectancy). Finally, Amy would have to weigh the advantages of an A in the course (better GPA, improved chances for graduate school, jobs, etc.) relative to the disadvantages (stress, loss of free time, loss of sleep, etc.) (valences). Notice that if Amy did not believe that (*a*) long study sessions would help her to get an A on the final, (*b*) getting an A on the final would help her to get an A in the course, *or* (*c*) the benefits of getting an A on the final outweighed the costs, then Amy would choose not to exert effort, expend a high level of effort, or persist in studying for the final. All three components must have a relatively high probability or be favorably weighed in order for Amy to exert effort or persist in studying for her history final.

In terms of satisfaction, expectancy theory predicts that people will be most satisfied when they exert effort that maximizes their chances of gaining a valued reward and minimizes costs associated with exerting effort. In this case, Amy will be happiest when she exerts the minimal amount of effort needed to get an A on the final, given that this grade will get her an A in the course and lead to an outcome she values—a higher GPA. Research reviews have generally supported these predictions concerning satisfaction as well as those concerning the choice to exert effort (Campbell & Pritchard, 1976; Wanous, Keon, & Latack, 1983).

FIGURE 11–4
An Example of Expectancy Theory

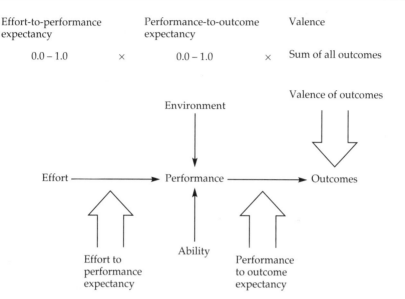

According to expectancy theory, Amy would first determine the probabilities of getting an A on her final exam depending on the amount of time she spent studying (effort-to-performance expectancies). Next, Amy would determine the probability of getting an A in the history course after getting an A on the final exam (performance-to-outcome expectancies). These probabilities would be affected by the strength of her grade going into the final exam and the relative amount of weight the final exam carried in the course. Finally, Amy would have to weigh the merits of the different outcomes (valences) before deciding how much effort to exert in studying for her final exam.

Goal setting. **Goal setting** is probably the most familiar and easiest formal system of motivation to use with followers. From the leader's perspective, it involves presenting followers with some future end state (a goal) and convincing them they can achieve it if they exert effort toward it. According to Locke and Latham (1990), goals are the most powerful determinants of task behaviors. Goals serve to direct attention, mobilize effort, help people develop strategies for goal achievement, and help people continue exerting effort until the goal is reached. That leads, in turn, to even higher goals (see Highlight 11–5).

Locke and Latham (1990) reported that nearly 400 studies across individuals, groups, and organizations in eight different countries have provided consis-

---

HIGHLIGHT 11–5

The High-Performance Cycle

According to Locke and Latham (1990), leaders can have both high-performing and highly satisfied workers by implementing the high-performance cycle in their work groups. Leaders start the high-performance cycle by first setting high expectations for followers and giving them specific, difficult goals to achieve. Specific, difficult goals will energize followers to develop task strategies, exert a certain level of effort, and persist on the task. Given this effort, followers will successfully accomplish the goal if they are committed to the goal, are given timely feedback, and have the necessary resources and abilities. Successful goal accomplishment leads to valued rewards, which in turn leads to increased job satisfaction and organzational commitment. Higher organizational commitment will allow leaders to set more difficult goals and to expect higher levels of performance and satisfaction from followers.

---

tent support for several aspects of goal setting. First, this research showed goals that were both *specific* and *difficult* resulted in consistently higher effort and performance when contrasted to "do your best" goals. Second, *goal commitment* is critical. Merely having goals is not enough. Although follower participation in setting goals is one way to increase commitment, goals set either by leaders unilaterally or through participation with followers can lead to necessary levels of commitment. Commitment to assigned goals was often as high as those goals followers helped to set, provided the leader was perceived to have legitimate authority, expressed confidence in followers, and provided clear standards for performance (Locke & Lathan, 1990). Third, followers exerted the greatest effort when goals were accompanied by feedback; followers getting goals or feedback alone generally exerted less effort.

Several other aspects of goal setting are also worth noting. First, goals can be set for any aspect of performance, be it reducing costs, improving the quality of services and products, increasing market share, or winning a league championship. Nevertheless, leaders need to ensure that they do not set conflicting goals, as followers can only exert so much effort over a given period of time. Second, determining just how challenging to make goals provides a bit of a dilemma for leaders. Successfully completed goals provide followers with a sense of job satisfaction, and easy goals are more likely to be completed than difficult goals. However, easily attainable goals result in lower levels of effort (and in turn, performance) than do more difficult goals. Locke and Latham (1990) suggested that leaders might motivate followers most effectively by setting moderately difficult goals, recognizing partial goal accomplishment, and making use of a continuous improvement philosophy by making goals incrementally more difficult (Imai, 1986).

Concluding thoughts on cognitive theories of motivation.   All three cognitive theories assume that people make rational, conscious decisions about what to put their energies into. Unfortunately (or fortunately?), human behavior does *not* always correspond to what rational analysis might predict. Motivation often is affected by nonrational or emotional considerations as well as rational ones; behavior does not follow a simple and logical formula. For example, followers may overestimate their own inputs and underestimate their reference group's inputs, causing errors in prediction from equity theory. Or, with our example from expectancy theory, it may be very logical for Amy to study 10 hours for her final, but she may decide nonetheless to "blow it off" and go to an end-of-year party instead. It is worth recalling our earlier discussion about how people always operate in both rational and emotional realms of behavior. Because people make choices to exert effort based on both rational and emotional considerations, predictions based on rational modeling alone are inexact. Still, they may be more helpful than no such modeling at all. Just because rational approaches do not reflect the full complexity of being human does not mean it would be wise for leaders to ignore the insights they offer.

Situational Approaches

These approaches place considerably more emphasis on how the situation affects motivation. In other words, these approaches emphasize the leader's role in changing various aspects of the situation in order to increase followers' motivational levels. The three theories that emphasize situational influences in motivation are Herzberg's two-factor theory, the job characteristics model, and the operant approach.

Herzberg's two-factor theory.   Herzberg (1964, 1966) developed the **two-factor theory** from a series of interviews he conducted with accountants and engineers. More specifically, he asked what satisfied them about their work and found that their answers usually could be sorted into five consistent categories. Furthermore, rather than assuming what dissatisfied people was always just the opposite of what satisfied them, he also specifically asked what dissatisfied people about their jobs. Surprisingly, the list of satisfiers and dissatisfiers represented entirely different aspects of work.

Herzberg labeled the factors that led to *satisfaction* at work **motivators,** and he labeled the factors that led to *dissatisfaction* at work **hygiene factors.** The most common motivators and hygiene factors can be found in Table 11–1. According to the two-factor theory, efforts directed toward improving hygiene factors will not increase followers' motivation. No matter how much leaders

TABLE 11–1
Motivators and Hygiene Factors of the Two-Factor Theory

Motivators	Hygiene Factors
Achievement	Supervision
Recognition	Working conditions
The work itself	Co-workers
Responsibility	Pay
Advancement and growth	Policies/procedures
	Job security

Source: Adapted from Herzberg, *Work and the Nature of Man* (Cleveland, Ohio: World Publishing, 1966).

improve working conditions, pay, or sick-leave policies, for example, followers *will not* exert any additional effort or persist any longer at a task. For example, followers will probably be no more motivated to do a dull and boring job merely by being given pleasant office furniture. On the other hand, followers may be asked to work in conditions so poor as to create dissatisfaction, which can distract them from constructive work.

Given limited resources on the leader's part, the key to increasing followers' effort levels according to two-factor theory is to just adequately satisfy the hygiene factors while maximizing the motivators for a particular job. It is important for working conditions to be adequate, but it is even more important (for enhancing motivation) to provide plenty of recognition, responsibility, and possibilities for advancement (see Figure 11–5). In the words of Fred Herzberg, "if you don't want people to have Mickey Mouse attitudes, then don't give them Mickey Mouse work" (unpublished comments).

Although the two-factor theory offers leaders ideas about how to, and how not to, bolster followers' motivation, it has received little empirical support beyond Herzberg's (1964) own results. In other words, it just may not be an accurate description of work motivation despite its apparent grounding in data. We present it here in part because it has become such a well-known approach to

FIGURE 11–5
Herzberg's Two-Factor Theory

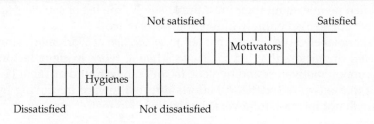

work motivation that the present account would appear incomplete to ignore it. The problem with two-factor theory, however, seems to lie in the very aspect that at first seemed its strength: the original data on which it was based. For one thing, as noted earlier, Herzberg developed his theory after interviewing only accountants and engineers, two groups who are hardly representative of workers in other lines of work or activity. Furthermore, his subjects typically attributed job satisfaction to their skill or effort yet blamed their dissatisfaction on circumstances beyond their control. This sounds suspiciously like the fundamental attribution error described earlier in this book. Despite such limitations, however, Landy (1985) concluded that the two-factor theory has provided helpful insight into what followers find satisfying and dissatisfying about work.

The job characteristics model.   According to the **job characteristics model,** jobs or tasks having certain kinds of characteristics provide inherently greater motivation and job satisfaction than others. Hackman and Oldham (1976, 1980) said that followers will work harder and be more satisfied if their tasks are meaningful, provide ample feedback, allow considerable latitude in deciding how to accomplish them, and require use of a variety of skills. The Hackman and Oldham model is based on five critical job characteristics: task identity, task significance, feedback, autonomy, and skill variety.

Note that while a job high in all these characteristics might seem intrinsically motivating, this model is not just another way of looking at intrinsic motivation. *Individuals* differ in their intrinsic motivation, whereas the job characteristics model says some *jobs* are, by their nature, more motivating and satisfying than others.

Actually, individual differences also play an important role in the job characteristics model. In this case the critical individual difference is called **growth-need strength,** which refers to the degree to which an individual is motivated by the need to fulfill herself (in Maslow's, 1954, terms, to increase one's self-esteem or self-actualization). Hackman and Oldham (1976, 1980) said that individuals with high growth-need strength especially desire jobs high on the five characteristics in the model; they are even more motivated and satisfied than others with such jobs, and even less motivated and satisfied than others with jobs very low on those characteristics. Thus, if leaders were to follow the tenets of the job characteristics model to increase followers' satisfaction and motivation, then they would hire followers with high growth-need strength, and they would restructure followers' jobs to have more favorable task characteristics.

Research has provided mixed support for the job characteristics model. The 28 studies reviewed by Loher, Noe, Moeller, and Fitzgerald (1985) provided evidence that strongly confirmed the satisfaction hypothesis. Other research, however, has called into question the satisfaction and motivation predictions of the model. There is even some evidence calling into question the presumed causal relationship between job satisfaction and job characteristics. While Hackman and Oldham (1976, 1980) presumed higher job satisfaction *resulted from* working in a job that had certain characteristics, other research indicated that people may, in fact, rate their job characteristics higher *as a result of* being satisfied in those jobs. For example, one study provided workers who had similar and equally satisfying jobs false satisfaction feedback. Those who were given higher job satisfaction feedback rated their job characteristics higher than workers given lower job feedback (Adler, Skov, & Salvemini, 1985). Moreover, Griffin, Welsh, and Moorhead (1981) reported that there was little evidence to show workers with favorable job characteristics and high growth-need strength actually exerted more effort or persisted at tasks longer than workers with less favorable job characteristics and lower growth-need strength. Despite these mixed findings, the job characteristics theory does provide an alternative perspective for improving followers' motivation levels and has been particularly useful in designing or redesigning jobs.

The operant approach.   The **operant approach** focuses on modifying rewards and punishments in order to change the direction, intensity, or persistence of *observable behavior.* It will help at the outset of this discussion to define several terms. A **reward** is any consequence that *increases* the likelihood that a particular behavior will be repeated. For example, if a student receives an A on a science project, then she will be more likely to work hard on the next science project. **Punishment** is the administration of an aversive stimulus or the withdrawal of something desirable, each of which *decreases* the likelihood a particular behavior will be repeated (Arvey & Ivancevich, 1980). Thus, if a child loses his allowance for talking back to his parents, then he will be less likely to do so again in the future. Both rewards and punishments can be administered in a contingent or noncontingent manner. **Contingent** rewards or punishments are administered as consequences of a particular behavior. Examples might include giving a runner a medal immediately after she won a race or grounding a teenage son after he comes home late. **Noncontingent** rewards and punishments are not associated with a particular behavior and might include receiving the same monthly paycheck even after working considerably less hard than the month before or getting a better parking slot because of seniority rather than performance. Rewards and punishments can also be administered using different schedules, such as those found in Table 11–2. Finally, behaviors that are not rewarded will eventually be eliminated through the process of **extinction.**

Research evidence has consistently shown that the operant approach is a very effective way of modifying followers' motivation and performance levels (Komacki, Zlotnick, & Jensen, 1986; Luthans & Kreitner, 1985; Pritchard, Hollenback, & DeLeo, 1980). Other evidence has shown that rewards were more strongly related to satisfaction and performance than was punishment (Lu-

TABLE 11–2
Schedules of Reinforcement

Continuous: When rewards are given every time a person manifests a specific response. An example would be giving a golfer praise every time he broke par.

Fixed ratio: When rewards are given after a certain number of responses occur. For example, a coach may give her players a reward every time they shoot 100 free throws before practice.

Fixed interval: When rewards are given after a fixed period of time has elapsed, such as a weekly or monthly paycheck.

Variable ratio: When rewards are administered on a variable basis, but on average after a certain number of responses have occurred. An example would be a worker who gets rewarded after successfully assembling as few as 10 or as many as 20 computers, but on average the worker receives reinforcement after an average of 15 computers have been assembled.

Variable interval: Similar to the variable ratio schedule, except in this case rewards are administered after an average amount of time has elapsed. A worker might get a reward after 3, 8, or 12 days of good work, but on average receives a reward once a week.

---

thans & Kreitner, 1985; Podsakoff, Todor, & Skov, 1982; Sims & Szilagyi, 1975), and that contingent rewards and punishments were more strongly related to satisfaction and performance than noncontingent rewards and punishments (Arvey, Davis, & Nelson, 1984; Pritchard, Hollenback, & DeLeo, 1980; Podsakoff & Todor, 1985).

Although these findings paint an encouraging picture of the practical utility of the operant approach, implementing it correctly in a work setting can be difficult (Saal & Knight, 1988). Using operant principles properly to improve followers' motivation and hence performance requires following several steps. First, leaders need to *clearly specify* what behaviors are important. Second, leaders need to determine if those behaviors are currently being punished, rewarded, or ignored. Believe it or not, sometimes followers are actually rewarded for behaviors that leaders are trying to extinguish and are punished for behaviors that leaders want to increase. For example, followers may get considerable positive attention from peers by talking back to the leader or by violating dress codes. Similarly, certain overly competitive employees may be promoted ahead of their peers (by walking over their backs, we might say), even when management's rhetoric extols the need for cooperation and teamwork. It also may be the case that leaders sometimes just ignore the very behaviors they would like to see strengthened. An example here would be if a leader consistently failed to provide rewards when followers produced high-quality products despite the leader's rhetoric always emphasizing the importance of quality.

Third, leaders need to find out what followers actually find rewarding and punishing. Leaders should *not* make the mistake of assuming that followers will find the same things rewarding and punishing as they do, nor should they assume that all followers will find the same things to be rewarding and punishing. What may be one follower's punishment may be another follower's reward. For example, some followers may dislike public attention and actually exert *less* effort after being publicly recognized; other followers may find public attention to be extremely rewarding. Fourth, leaders need to be wary of creating perceptions of inequity and decreasing intrinsic motivation when administering individually tailored rewards. Fifth, leaders should not limit themselves to administering organizationally sanctioned rewards and punishments. Using a bit of ingenuity, leaders can often come up with an array of potential rewards and punishments that are effective, inexpensive, and do not violate company policies. Finally, because the administration of noncontingent consequences has relatively little impact, leaders should administer rewards and punishments in a contingent manner whenever possible. An example of the positive results which can come from implementing the operant approach systematically is found in Highlight 11–6.

Concluding thoughts on situational approaches to motivation. The two-factor theory, the job characteristics model, and the operant approach all make one important point that is often overlooked in other theories of motivation: By changing the situation, leaders can enhance followers' motivation, performance, and satisfaction. Unfortunately, the same approaches tend to pay too little attention to the importance of needs, individual difference variables, and cognitive processes in the direction, intensity, and persistence of followers' behaviors (with the exception of growth-need strength in the job characteristics model). Perhaps the best strategy for leaders is to recognize that some motivational theories are more applicable to some situations than others, and to be flexible in the types of motivational interventions they use. However, leaders will only be able to adopt a flexible motivation intervention strategy if they become familiar with the strengths and weaknesses of the different theories and approaches. Just as a carpenter can more effectively build a house by using a variety of tools, a leader can be more effective by using a variety of motivational interventions to resolve work problems.

PUNISHMENT

In an ideal world, perhaps everyone would be dependable, achievement-oriented, and committed to the organization's goals. No one would ever break company rules or complain about working conditions, their co-workers, or having a boring job. But the fact is, leaders sometimes will need to deal with followers who are openly hostile or insubordinate, create conflicts among co-workers, do not work up to standards, break company policies and rules, or

---

HIGHLIGHT 11-6

Emery Air Freight

Emery Air Freight is one of the most successful examples of how leaders can change the direction, intensity, and persistence of followers' behaviors through the operant approach. Emery Air Freight discovered that it was using the full capacity of its air freight containers only 45 percent of the time and, because of the highly competitive nature of the air freight shipping business, wanted to reduce costs and increase profits by making better use of its air freight containers. The company initially had given employees detailed instructions on how to better use air freight containers. However, this intervention met with little success, and the senior executives at Emery Air Freight consequently decided to implement an operant motivational strategy.

Emery Air Freight's operant strategy consisted of several different steps. First, checklists for air freight container usage were developed. These checklists consisted of the specific behaviors or actions workers could take when preparing an air container for delivery. Second, workers recorded their performance on the checklists, which provided them with information on their own performance with respect to organizational goals. Third, supervisors were trained to provide positive reinforcement on a contingent basis, and in turn praised and rewarded workers for meeting goals or showing improvement over time. In terms of results, Emery Air Freight credited the operant strategy with $2 million in reduced costs after only three years.

---

abuse drugs and alcohol at work. There are several ways leaders can deal with such problem behaviors in followers. Of course, leaders can try to select only followers who are dependable, achievement-oriented, intrinsically motivated, and committed to the goals of the organization. Although sometimes this might be possible, it will more frequently be the case that leaders take over already intact work groups whose workers may vary dramatically on these factors. Alternatively, leaders can restructure jobs or provide rewards in order to increase the direction, intensity, and persistence of desired behaviors. However, some followers are so alienated that they are relatively insensitive to rewards or actions taken to increase their level of responsibility or autonomy. Sometimes leaders need to use punishment to control follower behavior.

Of all of the different aspects of leadership, few are as controversial as punishment. Some of the primary reasons for this controversy stem from myths surrounding the use of punsishment, as well as the lack of knowledge regarding the effects of punishment on followers' motivation, satisfaction, and performance. This section is designed to shed light on the punishment controversy by (*a*) addressing several myths about the use of punishment, (*b*) reviewing research findings concerning the relationships between punishment and various organizational variables, and (*c*) providing leadership practitioners with advice on how to properly administer punishment.

Myths Surrounding the Use of Punishment

We should begin by repeating the definition of punishment from the preceding section. Punishment is the administration of an aversive event or the withdrawal of a positive event or stimulus, which in turn *decreases* the likelihood a particular behavior will be repeated (Arvey & Ivancevich, 1980). Examples of punishment might include verbal reprimands, being moved to a less prestigious office, having pay docked, being fired, being made to run several laps around the athletic field, or losing eligibility for a sport entirely. There are three aspects of punishment especially worth noting. First, according to this definition, only those aversive events administered on a contingent basis are considered to be forms of punishment; aversive events administered on a noncontingent basis constitute harsh and abusive treatment, not punishment. Second, punishment appears to be in the "eye of the beholder"; aversive events that effectively change the direction, intensity, or persistence of one follower's behavior may have no effect on another's (Curphy, Gibson, Asiu, McCown, & Brown, 1992). Third, it is entirely possible some followers may find the administration of a noxious event or the removal of a positive event to be reinforcing. For example, it is not uncommon for some children to misbehave if that increases the attention they receive from parents, even if the latter's behavior outwardly may seem punishing to others. (To the children, some parental attention of any kind may be preferable to no attention.) Similarly, some followers may see the verbal reprimands and notoriety they receive by being insubordinate or violating company policies as forms of attention. Because these followers enjoy being the center of attention, they may find this notoriety rewarding. From an operant perspective, they may be even more likely to be insubordinate in the future.

We will examine four myths surrounding the use of punishment. Three of these myths were reviewed by Arvey and Ivancevich (1980) and included beliefs that the use of punishment resulted in undesirable emotional side effects on the part of the recipient, was unethical and inhumane, and never really eliminated the target response anyway. We will also discuss a fourth myth—that high levels of punishment can enhance group cohesiveness, not unlike the role initiation rites can play in elitist groups (Curphy et al., 1992).

B. F. Skinner (1938) first popularized the idea that punishment caused undesirable side effects. He based his conclusions on the unnatural behaviors manifested by rats and pigeons he punished in various learning experiments. Despite the dangers of generalizing from the behavior of these species to humans, a general impression seemed to develop that punishment was a relatively futile and often counterproductive tool to use to control human behavior. This seems so despite the fact that the reviews of research regarding the emotional effects of punishment on human subjects did not lend much support to Skinner's claim (Kazdin, 1975; Johnston, 1972; Solomon, 1964). In addition, Parke (1972) suggested that undesirable emotional side effects of punishment may occur only when punishment was administered indiscriminately or was particularly harsh.

With respect to the myth that punishment is unethical or inhumane, Arvey and Ivancevich (1980) maintained that there is an ethical distinction between "future-oriented" and "past-oriented" punishment. Future-oriented punishment may be effective in diminishing or eliminating undesirable behavior. It is future-oriented insofar as it ultimately helps improve the recipient's behavior. Retribution, or past-oriented punishment, on the other hand, is simply a type of payback for misdeeds. This sort of punishment may be more questionable ethically, especially when it is intended *only* as payback and not, say, as deterrent to others. Moreover, when considering the ethics of administering punishment one must also consider the ethics of *failing* to administer punishment. The costs of failing to punish a potentially harmful behavior, such as unsafe workplace practices, may far outweigh those associated with the punishment itself (Arvey & Ivancevich, 1980).

Skinner (1938, 1985), and more recently Campbell (1977) and Luthans (1989), claimed that punishment did not result in a permanent behavior change but instead only temporarily suppressed behavior. Evidence to support this claim was found by Huberman (1964), who reported that incarcerated prisoners had a recidivism rate of 85 percent. However, this high recidivism rate may be due to the fact that criminals may have received punishment primarily for retribution rather than for corrective purposes. A punisher who judiciously administers sanctions and provides advice on how to avoid punishment in the future perhaps could successfully eliminate undesirable behaviors on a more permanent basis (Arvey & Ivancevich, 1980).

A fourth myth about punishment seems based on the idea that group cohesiveness and esprit de corps is increased if a group is subjected to harsh treatment. This myth is sometimes used as a justification for the high levels of punishment associated with fraternity initiations or the initial socialization programs of the military (i.e., basic military training). For example, Roush (1991) and Blake and Potter (1992) stated that first-year cadets at the U.S. Naval and Coast Guard academies were subjected to harsh treatment to help them "circle the wagons" as well as help the institution "weed out" those first-year students who did not belong. Despite these institutional norms, cadets receiving harsh and noncontingent punishment had significantly lower group cohesiveness than cadets subjected to less severe levels of punishment (Blake & Potter, 1992).

Punishment, Satisfaction, and Performance

It appears that properly administered punishment does not cause undesirable emotional side effects, is not unethical, and may effectively suppress undesirable behavior. However, we also should ask what effect punishment has on followers' satisfaction and performance. Most people probably would predict that leaders who use punishment more frequently will probably have less satisfied and lower performing followers. Interestingly, this does not appear to be the case—at least when punishment is used appropriately. Let us look a little more closely at this issue.

Several researchers have looked at whether leaders who administer punishment on a contingent basis also administered rewards on a contingent basis. Generally, researchers have found that there is a moderate positive ralationship between leaders' contingent reward behaviors and contingent punishment behaviors (Arvey, Davis, & Nelson, 1984; Podsakoff &Todor, 1985; Strasser, Dailey, & Bateman, 1981). There also are consistently strong negative correlations found between leaders' contingent reward and noncontingent punishment behaviors. Thus, leaders meting out rewards on a contingent basis were also more likely to administer punishment only when followers behaved inappropriately or were not performing up to standards.

Keller and Szilagyi (1976, 1978) maintained that punishment can serve several constructive organizational purposes. They said it can help clarify roles and expectations, as well as reduce role ambiguity. Several other authors have found contingent punishment was either unrelated to or had a low positive relationship with followers' satisfaction with their supervisor ratings (Arvey, Davis, & Nelson, 1984; Podsakoff, Todor, Grover, & Huber, 1984). In other words, leaders who follow certain rules in administering punishment need not have dissatisfied subordinates. As a matter of fact, judicious and appropriate use of punishment by leaders may result in somewhat *higher* satisfaction of followers overall. These findings make sense when the entire work unit is considered; failing to use punishment when it seems called for in most followers' eyes may lead to perceptions of inequity, which may in turn lead to lower group cohesiveness and satisfaction. (Curphy et al., 1992; Dobbins & Russell, 1986).

With respect to followers' work behaviors, Arvey and Jones (1985) reported that punishment has generally been found to reduce absenteeism and tardiness rates. Nevertheless, the evidence about punishment's impact on performance appears mixed. Some authors report a strong positive relationship between punishment and performance (Beyer & Trice, 1984; Katz, Maccoby, Gurin, & Floor, 1951; Podsakoff & Todor, 1985; Schnake, 1986), whereas others found either no relationship between punishment and performance or a negative one (Curphy et al., 1992; Curtis, Smith, & Smoll, 1979).

Despite such mixed findings, there are several points about the relationship between punishment and performance findings still worth noting. First, the level of punishment as well as the manner in which it was administered across studies could have differed dramatically, and these factors could have affected the results. Second, of the studies reporting positive results, Schnake's (1986) experiment of the vicarious effects of punishment is by far the most provocative. Schnake hired college students for a temporary job, and after several hours at work, publically reduced the pay or threatened to reduce the pay of a confederate in the work group. As predicted, the more severe the punishment witnessed (either the threat of reduced pay or actual reduction of pay), the higher the subsequent performance of other work-group members.

Although these findings demonstrated that merely witnessing rather than receiving punishment could result in increased performance, these results should be interpreted with some caution. Because most of the individuals in the experiment did not know each other and had only been working together for several hours, there was probably not enough time for group cohesiveness or norms to develop. It is not at all clear whether members of cohesive groups or groups with strong norms would react the same way if they had observed another group member being punished (Curphy et al., 1992).

Third, of the studies reporting less favorable punishment-performance results, the Curtis, Smith, and Smoll (1979) study made an important point about the opportunities to punish. Curtis, Smith, and Smoll examined the relationships between Little League coaches' behaviors and their teams' win-loss records. They found coaches who punished more often had less successful teams. These coaches also, however, had less talented players and therefore had many more opportunities to use punishment. Coaches of successful teams had little if any reason to use punishment. Fourth, many behaviors that do get punished may not have a direct link to job performance. For example, being insubordinate, violating company dress codes, or arriving late to meetings are all punishable behaviors that may not be directly linked to solving work-related problems or producing goods or services.

Finally, almost all these studies implicitly assumed punishment enhanced performance (by correcting problem behaviors), but Curphy et al. (1992) were the only researchers who actually tested this assumption. Curphy et al. collected over 4,500 incidents of documented punishment and performance data from 40 identical organizations over a three-month period. (The punishment and performance data were collected monthly.) They found that low performance led to higher levels of punishment. Moreover, they found that inexperienced leaders administered almost twice as much punishment as experienced leaders. The authors hypothesized that inexperienced leaders used punishment (i.e., relied on their coercive power) more frequently because by being the newest arrivals to the organization, they lacked knowledge of the organizational norms, rules, and policies (i.e., expert power); had not yet established relationships with followers (i.e., referent power); and were severely limited in the rewards they could provide to followers (i.e., reward power).

In summary, the research evidence shows that punishment can lead to positive organizational outcomes if administered properly. When administered on a contingent basis, it may help increase job satisfaction; may decrease role ambiguity and absenteeism rates; and depending on the behaviors being punished, may have a positive effect on performance. However, administering intense levels of punishment in a noncontingent or capricious manner can have a devastating effect on the work unit. Group cohesiveness may suffer; followers are likely to become more dissatisfied and less apt to come to work; and they may perform at a lower level in the long term. Thus, learning how to properly administer punishment may be the key to maximizing the benefits associated with its use.

Administering Punishment

Usually, leaders administer punishment in order to rectify some type of behavioral or performance problem at work. However, not every behavior or performance problem is punished, and leaders probably weigh several different factors before deciding whether or not to administer punishment. Green and Mitchell (1979) maintained that leaders' decisions concerning punishment depended on whether leaders made internal or external attributions about a subordinate's substandard performance. Leaders making internal attributions were more likely to administer punishment; leaders making external attributions were more likely to blame the substandard performance on situational factors beyond the follower's control.

Attribution theory (Mitchell, Green, & Wood, 1981; Mitchell & Wood, 1980) maintains that leaders weigh three factors when making internal or external attributions about a follower's substandard performance. More specifically, leaders would be more likely to make an internal attribution about a follower's substandard performance (and administer punishment) if the follower had previously completed the task before, if other followers had successfully completed the task, and if the follower had successfully completed other tasks in the past. Moreover, Mitchell, Green, and Wood (1981) and Mitchell and Wood (1980) reported that leaders were biased toward making internal attributions about followers' poor performance (i.e., the fundamental attribution error) and thus more likely to use punishment to modify a follower's behavior.

Because leaders are biased toward making internal attributions about followers' substandard performance, leaders can administer punishment more effectively by being aware of this bias and getting as many facts as possible *before* deciding whether or not to administer punishment. Leaders also can improve the manner or skill with which they administer punishment by using tips provided by Arvey and Ivancevich (1980), who said punishment is administered most effectively when it focuses on the act, not the person. Followers probably cannot change their personalities, values, or preferences, but they can change their behaviors. By focusing on specific behaviors, leaders minimize the threat to followers' self-concepts. Also, punishment needs to be consistent across *both* behaviors and leaders; the same actions need to have the same consequences across work groups, or feelings of inequity and favoritism will pervade the organization. One way to increase the consistency in punishment is through the establishment of clearly specified organizational policies and procedures.

Administering punishment properly depends on effective two-way communication between the leader and follower. Leaders need to provide a clear rationale for punishment and indicate the consequences for unacceptable behavior in the future. Finally, leaders need to provide followers with guidance about how to improve. This guidance may entail role-modeling proper behaviors for followers, suggesting followers take additional training courses, or just giving followers accurate feedback about their behavior at work (Arvey & Ivancevich, 1980).

Overall, it may be the manner in which punishment is administered rather than the level of punishment that has the greatest effect on followers' satisfaction and performance. Leaders need to realize that they may be biased toward administering punishment to rectify followers' substandard performance, and the best way to get around this bias is to collect as much information as possible before deciding whether or not to punish. By collecting the facts, leaders will be better able to focus on the act, not the person, be able to administer a punishment consistent with company policy, provide the rationale for the punishment, and give guidance to followers on how to improve.

A final caution which leaders need to be aware of concerns the reinforcing or rewarding nature of punishment. As stated earlier in the discussion of the operant approach to motivation, behaviors that are rewarded are likely to be repeated. When leaders administer punishment and subsequently see improvement in a follower's behavior, the leader will be rewarded and be more apt to use punishment in the future. Over time, this may lead to an overreliance on punishment and an underemphasis of the other motivational strategies as the means for correcting performance problems. Again, by collecting as much information as possible and by carefully considering the applicability of goal setting, the operant approach, job characteristics theory, and so on to the problem, leaders may be able to successfully avoid having only one tool in their motivational tool kit.

SUMMARY

This chapter has provided a general overview of research concerning motivation, satisfaction, and performance. Motivation was defined as anything that provides direction, intensity, and persistsence to behavior. Although motivation is an important aspect of performance, performance and motivation are not the same thing. Performance involves the evaluation of behavior or of the goods/services produced. Performance is a broader concept than motivation, as abilities, skills, group norms, and the availability of resources can all affect followers' behaviors and, in turn, the leader's evaluation of those behaviors. Job satisfaction is a set of attitudes that people have about work. Although a majority of people are generally satisfied with their jobs, people often have varying levels of satisfaction for different aspect of their jobs, such as pay, working conditions, fringe benefits, supervisors, or co-workers.

Many of the various approaches to understanding motivation have distinct implications for increasing performance and satisfaction. Therefore, several different theories of motivation were reviewed in this chapter. The first two theories, Maslow's (1954) hierarchy of needs and Alderfer's (1969) ERG theory both assume that people are motivated to satisfy a set of universal needs. The next two theories examined motivation from an individual difference perspective; these primarily explain motivation in terms of a person's intrinsic motivation or achievement orientation. The next set of three theories examined motivation from a cognitive perspective. These theories assume that people make rational, conscious choices about the direction, intensity, and persistence of their behaviors, and generally engage in behaviors that maximize payoffs and minimize costs. The last three theories examined motivation from a situational perspective. Leadership practitioners likely will be more effective if they learn to recognize situations where various approaches, or the insights particular to them, may be differentially useful.

Because motivational strategies may not always produce desired behavior, this chapter also reviewed literature about punishment as a method of dealing with problem behavior. The chapter provided arguments and evidence concerning myths that punishment inevitably creates undesirable emotional side effects, is inhumane and unethical, only temporarily supresses behavior, and may be useful in building high levels of cohesiveness in newly formed groups. Moreover, the research evidence also showed that properly administered punishment could reduce role ambiguity and absenteeism and could have positive effects on job satisfaction and performance. Finally, this chapter provided advice on how to properly administer punishment, as well as a few cautions about its use. Although using punishment can be an effective way to change the direction, intensity, or persistence of followers' behaviors, leaders need to be aware that they may tend to be biased toward using punishment. Leaders should collect all the pertinent facts about a situation before acting and consider the applicability of alternative motivational strategies to punishment before deciding on a course of action.

KEY TERMS AND CONCEPTS

motivation

performance

job satisfaction

needs

hierarchy of needs

existence-relatedness-growth (ERG) theory

frustration-regression hypothesis

achievement orientation

intrinsic motivation

overjustification effect

equity theory

expectancy theory

effort-to-performance expectancy

performance-to-outcome expectancy

valence

goal setting

two-factor theory

motivators

hygiene factors

job characteristics model

growth-need strength

operant approach

reward

punishment

contingent

noncontingent

extinction

attribution theory

DISCUSSION QUESTIONS

1. Why do you think there are so many different theories or approaches to understanding motivation? Shouldn't it be possible to determine which one is best and just use it? Why or why not?

2. Many good leaders are thought of as good motivators. Select one you are personally familiar with and analyze that leader's motivational impact in terms of one of the theories or approaches presented in this chapter.

3. Select any group of followers you are personally familiar with. Analyze their different motivations in terms of the theories or approaches presented in this chapter.

4. Do you think most people have an implicit theory of human motivation that affects their attempts to motivate others (i.e., one they may be consciously unaware of but nonetheless seem to follow)? Characterize one or two individuals that come to mind, based on your inferences from each person's behavior.

5. What is your own view of what motivates people to work hard and perform well?

6. Is understanding different theories of motivation really important? Isn't it enough for a leader just to *be* a good motivator?

7. Think of two situations you're familiar with—one where you believe punishment was used appropriately, and another where you believe punishment was used inappropriately. What were some differences in those two situations in the way punishment was administered and in its effects?

8. Analyze your own willingness to use punishment to correct someone else's inappropriate behavior. Would you find it easy or difficult? What are some reasons people seem to differ this way?

SUGGESTED READINGS

Kerr, S. "On the Folly of Rewarding A While Hoping for B." *Academy of Management Journal* 18 (4) (1975, vol. 4), pp. 769–71.

Peters, T. J., and R. H. Waterman. *In Search of Excellence.* New York: Harper & Row, 1982.

Chapter Twelve

Leadership Skills II

INTRODUCTION

A s described in the introductions to Parts II and III, both leaders and followers make substantial contributions to the success of any organization, and many people play both leadership and followership roles over the course of a day. Given that the fate of an organization depends to a large extent on both leaders and followers, the ultimate success or failure of an organization may depend on how well its members perform their leadership and followership roles. However, performance in each role is a function of many factors, such as abilities, skills, motivation, adequate resources, group norms, morale, organizational regulations, and so on. Of these factors, individuals probably will find it easier to improve their skills than it is to change their personality, intelligence, or the norms of their work group. Because skills may be the easiest performance factor to change, this chapter provides advice on how to improve five skills that will help individuals become more effective in their leadership and followership roles (also see Highlight 12–1).

This chapter is designed to integrate much of the material described in Parts II and III, and is a continuation of material presented in Chapter Two (Making the Most of Your Leadership Experiences) and Chapter Nine (Implications for Leaders and Followers: Improving Four Skills Related to Personal Effectiveness). More specifically, this chapter provides practical advice on how to (a) build technical competence, (b) build effective relationships with superiors, (c) build effective relationships with peers, (d) correctly set goals, and (e) delegate effectively. By heeding the advice provided in this chapter, readers should be able to make greater contributions to the success of their organizations.

BUILDING TECHNICAL COMPETENCE

Technical competence concerns the knowledge and repertoire of behaviors one can bring to bear to successfully complete a task. For example, a highly skilled surgeon possesses vast knowledge of human anatomy and surgical techniques, and can perform an extensive set of highly practiced surgical procedures; a highly skilled volleyball player has a thorough understanding of the rules, tactics, and strategies of volleyball and can set, block, and serve effectively. Individuals usually acquire technical competence through formal education or training in specialized topics (i.e., law, medicine, accounting, welding, carpentry, etc.); on-the-job training; or experience (Yukl, 1989), and many studies have documented the importance of technical competence to a person's success and effectiveness as both a leader and a follower. This section describes why technical competence is important to followers and leaders; it also provides readers with ideas about how to increase their own technical competence.

There are many reasons why followers need to have a high level of technical competence. First, performance is often a function of technical competence (Borman, Hanson, Oppler & Pulakos, in press; Schmidt & Hunter, 1992). Relatedly, research has shown that technical expertise plays a key role in supervisors' performance appraisal ratings of subordinates (Borman, White, Pula-

---

HIGHLIGHT 12–1

Leadership Quotes, Chapter Twelve

There is no necessary connection between the desire to lead and the ability to lead, and even less to the ability to lead somewhere that will be to the advantage of the led. . . . Leadership is more likely to be assumed by the aggressive than by the able, and those who scramble to the top are more often motivated by their own inner torments than by any demand for their guidance.

Bergen Evans, *The Spoor of Spooks and Other Nonsense* (1954)

Good flutists learn from experience; unfortunately, so do bad flutists.

Anonymous

All rising to a great place is by a winding stair.

Francis Bacon

It is a characteristic of wisdom not to do desperate things.

Henry David Thoreau

We are building many splendid churches in this country, but we are not providing leaders to run them. I would rather have a wooden church with a splendid parson than a splendid church with a wooden parson.

Samuel Smith Drury

Study the big problems all the time, but never to skip a small task, for one of the simple duties may hold the key to the biggest problem.

John T. Faris

An acre of performance is worth the whole world of promise.

Clark Howell

---

kos & Oppler, 1991; J. Hogan, 1992b). Second, followers with high levels of technical competence have a lot of expert power, and at times can wield more influence in their groups than the leader does (Bugental, 1964; Farris, 1971). Third, individuals with high levels of technical competence may be more likely to be a member of a leader's in-group (Duchon, Green, & Taber, 1986). Relatedly, followers with high levels of technical competence are more likely to be delegated tasks and asked to participate in the decision-making process. Conversly, supervisors are more likely to use a close, directive leadership style when interacting with subordinates with poor technical skills (Dewhirst, Metts, & Ladd, 1987; Leana, 1987; Lowin & Craig, 1968; Rosen & Jerdee, 1977). Similarly, Blau (1968) noted that organizations with relatively high numbers of technically competent members tended to have a flatter organizational structure; organizations with relatively fewer qualified members tended to be more centralized and autocratic. Thus, if followers wish to earn greater rewards, exert more influence in their groups, and have greater say in the decision-making process, then they should do all they can to enhance their technical competence.

There are also many reasons why it benefits leaders to have high levels of technical competence. First, technical competence has been found to be consistently related to managerial promotion rates. Managers having higher levels of technical competence were much more likely to rise to the top managerial levels at AT&T than managers with lower levels of technical competence (Howard, 1986; Howard & Bray, 1989). Second, having a high level of technical competence is important because many leaders, particularly first-line supervisors, often spend considerable time training followers (Wexley & Latham, 1981). Perhaps nowhere is the importance of technical competence in training more readily apparent than in coaching; little is as frustrating as having a coach who knows less about the game than the team members. Third, leaders with high levels of technical competence seem to be able to reduce the level of role ambiguity and conflict in their groups (Podsakoff, Todor, & Schuler, 1983; Walker, 1976), and followers are generally more satisfied with leaders having high rather then average levels of technical competence (Bass, 1985; Penner, Malone, Coughlin, & Herz, 1973). Finally, leaders who have a high level of technical competence may be able to stimulate followers to think about problems and issues in new ways, which in turn has been found to be strongly related to followers' motivation to succeed and organizational climate ratings (Avolio & Bass, 1988; Curphy, 1991a). Given these findings for both leaders and followers, below is some practical advice for improving technical competence.

Determining How the Job Contributes to the Overall Mission

The first step in building technical competence is to determine how one's job contributes to the overall success of the organization. By taking this step, individuals can better determine what technical knowledge and which behaviors are most strongly related to job and organizational sucess. Next, people should evaluate their current level of technical skills by seeking verbal feedback from peers and superiors, reviewing past performance appraisal results, or reviewing objective performance data (i.e., golf scores, team statistics, the number of products rejected for poor quality, etc.). These actions will help individuals get a better handle on their own strengths and weaknesses, and in turn can help people assure any formal education or training program they pursue is best suited to meet their needs.

Becoming an Expert in the Job

Becoming an expert in one's primary field is often the springboard for further developmental opportunities. There are a number of ways in which individuals can become experts in their field, and these include enrolling in formalized education and training programs, watching others, asking questions, and teaching others. Attending pertinent education and training courses is one way to acquire technical skills, and many companies often pay the tuition and fees associated with these courses. Another way to increase expertise in one's field is by being a keen observer of human behavior. Individuals can learn a lot by observing how others handle work-coordination problems, achieve production goals, discipline team members, or develop team members with poor skills. Merely observing how others do things is not nearly as effective as observing *and* reflecting about how others do things, however. One method of reflection is trying to explain others' behaviors in terms of the concepts or theories described in this book. Observers should look for concepts that cast light on both variations and regularities in how others act and think about the reasons why a person might have acted a certain way. Additionally, observers can develop by trying to think of as many different criteria as possible for evaluating another person's actions.

It is also important to ask questions. Because everyone makes inferences regarding the motives, expectations, values, or rationale underlying another person's actions, it is vital to ask questions and seek information likely to verify the accuracy of one's inferences. By asking questions, observers can better understand why team practices are conducted in a particular way, what work procedures have been implemented in the past, or what really caused someone to quit a volunteer organization. Finally, perhaps nothing can help a person become a technical expert more than having to teach someone else about the equipment, procedures, strategies, problems, resources, and contacts associated with their job, club, sport, or activity. Teachers must have a thorough understanding of the job or position in order to effectively teach someone else. By seeking opportunities to teach others, individuals enhance their own technical expertise as well as that of others.

Seeking Opportunities to Broaden Experiences

Individuals can improve their technical competence by seeking opportunities to broaden their experiences. Just as a person should try to play a variety of positions in order to better appreciate the contributions of other team members, so should a person try to perform the tasks associated with the other positions in his or her work group in order to better appreciate how the work contributes to organizational success. Similarly, people should visit other parts of the organization in order to gain an understanding of its whole operation. Moreover, by working on team projects, people get a chance to interact with members of other work units and often get the opportunity to develop new skills. Additionally, volunteering to support school, political, or community activities is another way to increase one's organization and planning, public speaking, fund-raising, and public relations skills, all of which may be important aspects of technical competence for certain jobs.

BUILDING EFFECTIVE RELATIONSHIPS WITH SUPERIORS

As defined here, superiors are those individuals with relatively more power and authority than the other members of the group. Thus, superiors could be teachers, band directors, coaches, team captains, heads of committees, or first-line supervisors. Needless to say, there are a number of advantages to having a good working relationship with superiors. First, superiors and followers sharing the same values, approaches, and attitudes will experience less conflict, provide higher levels of mutual support, and be more satisfied with superior-follower relationships than superiors and followers having poor working relationships (Duchon, Green, & Taber, 1986; Porter, 1992). Relatedly, individuals having good superior-follower relationships are often in the superior's in-group and thus are more likely to have a say in the decision-making process, be delegated interesting tasks, and have the superior's support for career advancement (Yukl, 1989). Second, followers are often less satisfied with their supervisor and receive lower performance appraisal ratings when superior-follower relationships are poor (Pulakos & Wexley, 1983; Weiss, 1977).

Although the advantages of having a good working relationship with superiors seems clear, one might mistakenly think that followers have little, if any, say in the quality of the relationship. In other words, followers might believe their relationships with superiors are a matter of luck; either the follower has a "good" superior or a "bad" one, or the superior just happens to like or dislike the follower, and there is little if anything the follower can do about it. However, the quality of a working relationship is not determined solely by the superior, and effective subordinates do not limit themselves to a passive stance toward superiors. Effective subordinates have learned how to take active steps to strengthen the relationship and enhance the support they provide their superior and the organization (Gabarro & Kotter, 1980; Kelley, 1988).

Wherever a person is positioned in an organization, an important aspect of that person's work is to help his superior be successful, just as an important part of the superior's work is to help followers be successful. This does not mean that followers should become apple-polishers, play politics, or distort information just to make superiors look good. It does mean, however, that followers should think of their own and their superior's success as interdependent. It means that followers are players on their superior's team and should be evaluated on the basis of the team's success, not just their own. If the team succeeds, then both the coach and the team members should benefit; if the team fails, then the blame should fall on both the coach and the team members. Because team, club, or organizational outcomes depend to some extent on good superior-follower relationships, understanding how superiors view the world and adapting to superiors' styles are two things followers can do to increase the likelihood their actions will have positive results for themselves, their superiors, and their organizations (Gabarro & Kotter, 1980).

Understanding the Superior's World

There are a number of things followers can do to better understand their superior's world. First, they should try to get a handle on their superior's personal and organizational objectives. Loyalty and support are a two-way street, and just as a superior can help subordinates attain their personal goals most readily by knowing what they are, so can subordinates support their superior if they understand the superior's goals and objectives. Relatedly, knowing a superior's values, preferences, and personality can help followers better understand why superiors act the way they do and can give followers insights about how they might strengthen relationships with superiors.

Second, followers need to realize that superiors are not supermen or superwomen; superiors do not have all the answers, and they have both strengths and weaknesses. Subordinates can make a great contribution to the overall success of a team by recognizing and complementing a superior's weaknesses and understanding his constraints and limitations. For example, a highly successful management consultant might spend over 200 days a year conducting executive development workshops, providing organizational feedback to clients, or giving speeches at various public events. This same consultant, however, might not be skilled in designing and making effective visual aids for presentations, or she might dislike having to make her own travel and accommodation arrangements. A follower could make both the consultant and the consulting firm more successful through his own good organization and planning, attention to detail, computer graphics skills, and understanding that the consultant is most effective when she has at least a one-day break between engagements. A similar process can take place in other contexts, as when subordinates help orient and educate a newly assigned superior whose expertise and prior experience may have been in a different field or activity.

In an even more general sense, subordinates can enhance superior-follower relationships by keeping superiors informed about various activities in the work group or new developments or opportunities in the field. Few superiors like surprises, and any news should come from the person with responsibility for a particular area—especially if the news is potentially bad or concerns unfavorable developments. Followers wishing to develop good superior-follower relationships should never put their superior in the embarassing situation of having someone else know more about her terrain than she does (her own boss, for instance). As Kelley (1988) maintained, the best followers think critically and play an active role in their organizations, which means that followers should keep their superiors informed about critical information and pertinent opinions concerning organizational issues.

Adapting to the Superior's Style

Research has shown that some executives fail to get promoted (i.e., were derailed) because they are unable or unwilling to adapt to superiors with leadership styles different from their own (McCall & Lombardo, 1983). Followers need to keep in mind that it is *their* responsibility to adapt to their superior's style, not vice versa. For example, followers might prefer to interact with superiors face-to-face, but if their superior appreciates written memos, then written memos it should be. Similarly, a follower might be accustomed to informal interactions with superiors, but a new superior might prefer a more businesslike and formal style. Followers need to be flexible in adapting to their superiors' decision-making styles, problem-solving strategies, modes of communication, styles of interaction, and so on.

One way followers can better adapt to a superior's style is to clarify expectations about their role on the team, committee, or work group. Young workers often do not appreciate the difference between a job description and one's role in a job. A job description is a formalized statement of tasks and activities; a role describes the personal signature an incumbent gives to a job. For example, the job description of a high school athletic coach might specify such responsibilities as selecting and training a team or making decisions about lineups. Two different coaches, however, might accomplish those basic responsibilities in quite different ways. One might emphasize player development in the broadest sense, getting to know her players personally and using sports as a vehicle for their individual growth; another might see his role simply to produce the most winning team possible. Therefore, just because followers know what their job is does not mean their role is clear.

Although some superiors take the initiative to explicitly spell out the roles they expect subordinates to play, most do not. Usually it is the subordinate's task to discern his or her role. One way followers can do this is to make a list of major responsibilities and use it to guide a discussion with the superior about different ways the tasks might be accomplished and the relative priorities of the tasks. Relatedly, followers will also find it helpful to talk to others who have worked with a particular superior before.

Finally, followers interested in developing effective relationships with superiors need to be honest and dependable. Whatever other qualities or talents a subordinate might have, a lack of integrity is an absolutely fatal flaw. No one—superior, peer, or subordinate—wants to work with someone he cannot trust. After integrity, superiors value dependability. Superiors value workers who have reliable work habits, accomplish assigned tasks at the right time in the right order, and do what they promise (Kouzes & Posner, 1987).

BUILDING EFFECTIVE RELATIONSHIPS WITH PEERS

The phrase *influence without authority* (Cohen & Bradford, 1990) captures a key element of the work life of increasing numbers of individuals. More and more people are finding that their jobs require them to influence others despite having no formal authority over them. No man is an island, it is said, and perhaps no worker in today's organizations can survive on his or her own. Virtually everyone needs a co-worker's assistance or resources at one time or another. Along these lines, some researchers have maintained that one of the fundamental requirements of leadership effectiveness is the ability to build strong alliances with others, and groups of peers generally wield more influence (and can get more things done) than individuals working separately (R.T. Hogan, J. Hogan, & Curphy, 1992). Similarly, investing the time and effort to develop effective relationships with peers not only has immediate dividends but also can have long-term benefits if a peer ends up in a position of power in the future. Many times, leaders are selected from among the members of a group, committee, club, or team, and having previously spent time developing a friendly rather than an antagonistic relationship with other work group members will lay the groundwork for building effective relationships with superiors and becoming a member of superiors' in-groups. Given the benefits of strong relationships with peers, the following are a few ideas about how to establish and maintain good peer relationships.

Recognizing Common Interests and Goals

Although Chapters Seven through Eleven described a variety of ways people vary, one of the best ways to establish effective working relationships with peers is to acknowledge shared interests, values, goals, and expectations (Cohen & Bradford, 1990). In order to acknowledge shared aspirations and interests, however, one must know what peers' goals, values, and interests actually are. Establishing informal communication links is one of the best ways to discover common interests and values. To do so, one needs to be open and honest in communicating one's own needs, values, and goals, as well as being willing to acknowledge others' needs, aspirations, and interests. Little can destroy a relationship with peers more quickly than a person who is overly willing to share his own problems and beliefs but unwilling to listen to others' ideas about the same issues. Moreover, although some people believe that participating in social gatherings, parties, committee meetings, lunches, company sport teams, or community activities can be a waste of time, peers with considerable referent power often see such activities as opportunities to establish and improve relationships with others. Thus, an effective way to establish relationships with other members of a team, committee, or organization is to meet with them in contexts outside of normal working relationships.

Understanding Peers' Tasks, Problems, Rewards

Few things reinforce respect between co-workers better than understanding the nature of each other's work. Building a cooperative relationship with others depends, therefore, on knowing the sorts of tasks others perform in the organization. It also depends on understanding what their problems and rewards are. With the former, one of the best ways to establish strong relationships is by lending a hand whenever peers face personal or organizational problems. With the latter, it is especially important to remember that people tend to repeat those behaviors that are rewarded and are less likely to repeat behaviors that go unrewarded. A person's counterproductive or negative behaviors may be due less to his personal characteristics (e.g., "He is just uncooperative") than to the way his rewards are structured. For example, a teacher may be less likely to share successful classroom exercises with others if teachers are awarded merit pay on the basis of classroom effectiveness. To secure cooperation from others, it helps to know which situational factors reinforce both positive and negative behaviors in others (Cohen & Bradford, 1990). By better understanding the situation facing others, people can determine whether their own positive feedback (or lack thereof) is contributing or hindering the establishment of effective relationships with peers. People should not underestimate the power of their own sincere encouragement, thanks, and compliments in positively influencing the behavior of their colleagues.

Practicing a Theory Y Attitude

Another way to build effective working relationships with peers is to view them from a Theory Y perspective (see Chapter Eight). When a person assumes that others are competent, trustworthy, willing to cooperate if they can, and proud of their work, peers will look on that person in the same light. Even if one practices a Theory Y attitude, however, it may still be difficult to get along with a few co-workers. In such cases, it is easy to become preoccupied with their "bad" qualities. This should be resisted as much as possible. A vicious cycle can develop in which "enemies" put more and more energy into criticizing each other or making the other person look bad than into constructive work on the task at hand. The costs of severely strained relationships also can extend beyond the individual parties involved. Cliques, or sides, can develop among other co-workers as well, which can impair the larger group's effectiveness. The point here is not to overlook interpersonal problems, but rather to not let the problems get out of hand.

Practicing Theory Y does *not* mean looking at the world through rose-colored glasses, but it *does* mean recognizing someone else's strengths as well as weaknesses. Nevertheless, sometimes peers will be assigned to work on a task together when they don't get along with each other, and the advice "Practice a Theory Y attitude" may seem too idealistic. At such times, it is important to decide whether to focus energy first on improving the relationship (before addressing the task) or to focus it solely on the task (essentially ignoring the problem in the relationship).

Cohen and Bradford (1990) suggested several guidelines for resolving this problem. They said it is best to work on the task if there is little animosity between the parties; if success can be achieved despite existing animosities; if group norms inhibit openness; if success on the task will improve the feelings between the parties; if the other person handles directness poorly; or if *you* handle directness poorly. Conversely, they said it is best to work on the relationship if there is great animosity between the parties; if negative feelings make task success unlikely; if group norms favor openness; if feelings between the parties are not likely to improve even with success on the task; if the other person handles directness well; *and* if you handle directness well.

SETTING GOALS

The Roman philosopher Seneca wrote, "When a man does not know what harbor he is making for, no wind is the right wind." Setting goals and developing plans of action to attain them are important for individuals and for groups. For example, the purpose or goal is often the predominant norm in any group. Once group goals are agreed on, they serve to induce member compliance, act as a criterion for evaluating the leadership potential of group members, and are used as criteria for evaluating group performance (Bass, 1990).

Perhaps the most important step in accomplishing a personal or group goal is stating it right in the first place. The reason many people become frustrated with the outcomes of their New Year's resolutions is not because of any character flaw on their part (e.g., "I don't have any willpower"), but rather because their resolutions are so vague or unrealistic as to be unlikely to ever lead to demonstrable results. It *is* possible to keep New Year's resolutions, but one must set them intelligently. In a more general sense, some ways of writing goal statements increase the likelihood that someone will successfully achieve the desired goals. Goals should be specific and observable, attainable and challenging, based on top-to-bottom commitment, and designed to provide feedback to personnel about their progress toward them. The following is a more detailed discussion of each of these points.

Goals Should Be Specific and Observable

As described in Chapter Eleven, research provides strong support for the idea that specific goals lead to higher levels of effort and performance than general goals. General goals do not work as well because they often do not provide enough information regarding which particular behaviors are to be changed or when a clear end-state has been attained. This may be easiest to see with a personal example.

Assume that a student is not satisfied with her academic performance and wants to do something about it. She might set a very general goal, such as "I will do my best next year" or "I will do better in school next year." At first, such a goal may seem fine; after all, as long as she is motivated to do well, what more would be needed? However, on further thought you can see that "do my best" or "do better" are so ambiguous as to be unhelpful in directing her behavior and ultimately assessing her success. General goals have relatively little impact on energizing and directing immediate behavior, and they make it difficult to assess, in the end, whether someone has attained them or not. A better goal statement for this student would be, for example, to attain a B average or to get no deficient grades this semester. Specific goals like these make it easier to chart one's progress. A more business-oriented example might deal with improving productivity at work. Specific goal statements in this case might include a 20 percent increase in the number of products being produced by the work unit over the next three months or a 40 percent decrease in the number of products being returned by quality control next year.

The idea of having specific goals is closely related to that of having observable goals. It should be clear to everyone when the goal has or has not been reached. It is easy to say your goal is to go on a diet, but a much better goal is "to lose 10 pounds by March." Similarly, it is easy to say the team should do better next season, but a better goal is to say the team will win more than half of next season's games. It is important to note that specific, observable goals are also time limited. Without time limits for accomplishing goals, there would be little urgency associated with them. Neither would there be a finite point at which it is clear a person or group has or has not accomplished the goals. For example, it is better to set a goal of improving the next quarter's sales figures than just improving sales.

Goals Should Be Attainable but Challenging

Some people seem to treat goals as a sort of loyalty oath they must pass, as if it would be a break with one's ideals or be a reflection of insufficient motivation if any but the loftiest, highest goals were set for oneself or one's organization. Yet to be useful, goals must be realistic. The struggling high school student who sets a goal of getting into Harvard may be unrealistic; but it may be realistic to set a goal of getting into the local state university. A civil rights activist may *wish* to eliminate prejudice completely, but a more attainable goal might be to eliminate racial discrimination in the local housing project over the next five years. A track team is not likely to win every race, but it may be realistic to aim to win the league championship.

The corollary to the preceding point is that goals should also be challenging. If goals merely needed to be attainable, then there would be nothing wrong with setting goals so easy that accomplishing them would be virtually guaranteed. But Chapter Eleven showed that easy goals do not result in high levels of performance; higher levels of performance come about when goals stretch and inspire people toward doing more than they thought they could. Goals need to be challenging but attainable to get the best out of oneself and others.

Goals Require Commitment

There is nothing magical about having goals; having goals per se does not guarantee success. Unless supported by real human commitment, goal statements are mere words. Organizational goals are most likely to be achieved if there is commitment to them at both the top and bottom of the organization. Top leadership needs to make clear that it is willing to put its money where its mouth is. When top leadership sets goals, it should provide the resources workers need to achieve the goals and then should reward those who do. Subordinates often become committed to goals simply by seeing the sincere and enthusiastic commitment of top leadership to them. Another way to build subordinate acceptance and commitment to goals is to have subordinates participate in setting the goals in the first place. Research on the effects of goal setting demonstrates that worker acceptance and satisfaction tend to increase when workers are allowed to participate in setting goals (Erez, Earley, & Hulin, 1985; Locke, Latham, & Erez, 1987).

On the other hand, research is less conclusive about whether participation in goal setting actually increases performance or productivity. These mixed findings about participation and performance may be due to various qualities of the group and the leader. In terms of the group, groupthink may cause highly cohesive groups to commit to goals that are unrealistic and unachievable. Group members may not have realistically considered equipment or resource constraints, nor have the technical skills or abilities needed to successfully accomplish the goal. In addition, group members may not have any special enthusiasm for accomplishing a goal if the leader is perceived to have little expert power or is unsupportive, curt, or inept (House, 1984; Latham & Lee, 1986; Locke, Latham, & Erez, 1987). However, if leaders are perceived to be competent and supportive, then followers may have as much goal commitment as they would if they had participated in setting the goal. Thus, participation in goal setting often leads to higher levels of commitment and performance if the leader is perceived to be incompetent, but will not necessarily lead to commitment and performance over and above that when a competent leader assigns a goal. Again, these findings lend credence to the importance of technical competence in leadership effectiveness.

Goals Require Feedback

As described in Chapter Nine, one of the most effective ways to improve any kind of performance is to provide feedback about how closely a person's behavior matches some criterion, and some of the research reviewed in Chapter Eleven showed that performance was much higher when goals were accompanied by feedback than when either goals or feedback were used alone. Goals that are specific, observable, and time limited are conducive to ongoing assessment and performance-based feedback, and leaders and followers should strive to provide and/or seek feedback on a fairly regular basis. Moreover, people should seek feedback from a variety of sources or provide feedback using a variety of criteria. Often, different sources and criteria can paint very different pictures about goal progress, and people can get a better idea of the true level of their progress by examining the information provided and integrating it across the different sources and criteria (see Highlight 12–2).

DELEGATING

Although delegation is a relatively simple way for leaders to free themselves of time-consuming chores; provide followers with developmental opportunities; and increase the number of tasks accomplished by the work group, team, or committee, delegation is often an overlooked and underused management option (Bass, 1990; Leana, 1986). Delegation implies that one has been empowered by one's leader, boss, or coach to take responsibility for completing certain tasks or engaging in certain activities (Bass, 1990). Delegation gives the responsibility for decisions to those individuals most likely to be affected by or to implement the decision, and delegation is more concerned with autonomy, responsibility, and follower development than with participation (Leana, 1987).

Research has shown that leaders who delegate authority more frequently often have higher-performing businesses (Miller & Toulouse, 1986), but fol-

HIGHLIGHT 12–2

Seeking Feedback about Performance

There is no doubt that feedback helps people to improve their performance. A teacher who says "um" distressingly often during lectures might never know of his bad habit—and might never correct it—unless someone gives him feedback. The manager of a potato chip company's purchasing section will be more motivated to improve her information sharing with subordinates (which she thinks is pretty good) if she hears others rate it as poor. A quarterback improves his judgment by reviewing game films of plays that worked and plays that didn't work. Ironically, though, few people take advantage of readily available sources of feedback. Whereas it might seem that leaders are supposed to provide developmental feedback, the fact is some do and some don't; even if they do, the feedback may be infrequent and may not address all the areas important to followers (Greller, 1980). Good leaders and followers ask both peers and superiors for feedback rather than wait for it, and people usually find the more they and others talk openly about ways to do things better, the easier and more natural such conversations become.

lowers are not necessarily happier when their leaders frequently delegate tasks (Stogdill & Shartle, 1955). Bass (1990) maintained that the latter findings were due to subordinates who felt they were (*a*) not delegated the authority needed to accomplish delegated tasks, (*b*) monitored too closely, or (*c*) only delegated tasks leaders did not want to do. Nevertheless, Wilcox (1982) showed that leaders who delegated skillfully had more satisfied followers than leaders who did not delegate well. Because leaders who delegate skillfully often have more satisfied and higher-performing work groups, teams, or committees, the following suggestions from Taylor (1989) are provided to help leadership practitioners delegate more effectively and successfully. Taylor provided useful ideas about why delegating is important, common reasons for avoiding delegation, and principles of effective delegation.

Why Delegating Is Important

Delegation frees time for other activities.   The essence of leadership is achieving goals through others, not trying to accomplish them by oneself. Learning to think like a leader partly involves developing a frame of mind wherein one thinks in terms of the whole group's or organization's capabilities and not just one's own. This requires a new frame of reference for many individuals, especially those whose past successes resulted primarily from personal achievement in interpersonally competitive situations. Still, leaders typically have so many different responsibilities they invariably must delegate some of them to others.

It is not just the mere quantity of work that makes delegation necessary. There is a qualitative aspect, too. Because leaders determine what responsibilities will be delegated, the process is one by which leaders can assure that their time is allocated most judiciously to meet group needs. The leader's time is a precious commodity that should be invested wisely in those activities for which the leader is uniquely suited or situated to accomplish and that will provide the greatest long-term benefits to the group. What the leader *can* delegate, the leader *should* delegate.

Delegation develops followers.   Developing subordinates is one of the most important responsibilities any leader has, and delegating significant tasks to them is one of the best ways to support their growth. It does so by providing opportunities for initiative, problem solving, innovation, administration, and decision making. By providing practical experience in a controlled fashion, delegation allows subordinates the best training experience of all: learning by doing.

Delegation strengthens the organization.   Delegation is an important way to develop individual subordinates, but doing so also strengthens the entire organization. For one thing, an organization that uses delegation skillfully will be a motivating one to work in. Delegation sends an organizational signal that subordinates are trusted and their development is important. Moreover, skillful delegation inherently tends to increase the significance and satisfaction levels of most jobs, thus making subordinates' jobs better. Delegation also can be seen as a way of developing the entire organization, not just the individuals within it. To the extent that a whole organization systematically develops its personnel using delegation, its overall experience level, capability, and vitality increase. Finally, delegation stimulates innovation and generates fresh ideas and new approaches throughout the whole organization.

Common Reasons for Avoiding Delegation

Delegation takes too much time.   Delegation saves time for the leader in the long run, but it costs time for the leader in the short run. It takes time to train a subordinate to perform any new task, so many times it really does take less time for a leader to do the task herself than to put in the effort to train someone else to do it. When a task is a recurring or repetitive one, however, the long-term savings will make the additional effort in initial training worth it—both for the leader and for the subordinate.

Delegation is risky.   It can feel threatening to delegate a significant responsibility to another person because doing so reduces direct personal control over the work one will be judged by (Dewhirst, Metts, & Ladd, 1987). Delegation may be perceived as a career risk by staking one's own reputation on the motivation, skill, and performance of others. It is the essence of leadership, though, that the leader will be evaluated in part by the success of the entire team. Furthermore, delegation need not and should not involve a complete loss of control by the leader over work delegated to others. The leader has a responsibility to set performance expectations, ensure that the task is understood and accepted, provide training, and regularly monitor the status of all delegated tasks and responsibilities (Bass, 1990).

The job will not be done as well.   Often the leader can do many specific tasks or jobs better than anyone else. That is not surprising, as the leader is often the most experienced person in the group. This fact, however, can become an obstacle to delegation. The leader may rationalize not delegating a task to someone else because the follower lacks technical competence and the job would subsequently suffer (Dewhirst, Metts, & Ladd, 1987). However, this may only be true in the short term, and letting subordinates make a few mistakes is a necessary part of their development, just as it was for the leader at an earlier stage in her own development. Few things are likely to be so stifling to an organization as a leader's perfectionistic fear of any and all mistakes. When thinking about delegating tasks to others, leaders should remember what their own skill levels used to be, not what they are now. Leaders should assess subordinates' readiness to handle new responsibilities in terms of the former, not the latter.

The task is a desirable one.   A leader may resist delegating tasks that are a source of power or prestige. He may be quite willing to delegate relatively unimportant responsibilities but may balk at the prospect of delegating a significant one having high visibility (Bass, 1990; Dewhirst, Metts, & Ladd, 1987). The greater the importance and visibility of the delegated task, though, the greater will be the potential developmental gains for the subordinate. Furthermore, actions always speak louder than words, and nothing conveys trust more genuinely than a leader's willingness to delegate major responsibilities to subordinates.

Others are already too busy.   A leader may feel guilty about increasing a subordinate's already full workload. It is the leader's responsibility, though, to continually review the relative priority of all the tasks performed across the organization. Such a review might identify existing activities that could be eliminated, modified, or reassigned. A discussion with the subordinate about her workload and career goals would be a better basis for a decision than an arbitrary and unilateral determination by the leader that the subordinate could not handle more work. The new responsibility could well be something the subordinate wants and needs, and she might also have some helpful ideas about alternative ways to manage her present duties.

Principles of Effective Delegation

Decide what to delegate. The first step leaders should take when deciding what to delegate is to identify all of their present activities. This should include those functions regularly performed and decisions regularly made. Next, leaders should estimate the actual time spent on these activities. This can be done fairly easily by developing and maintaining a temporary log. After collecting this information, leaders need to assess whether each activity justifies the time they are spending on it. In all likelihood, at least some of the most time-consuming recurring activities should be delegated to others. This process will probably also identify some activities that could be done more efficiently (either by the leader or someone else) and other activities that provide so little benefit they could be eliminated completely.

Decide whom to delegate to. There might be one individual whose talent and experience makes her the logical best choice for any assignment. However, leaders must be careful not to overburden someone merely because that individual always happens to be the best worker. Additionally, leaders have a responsibility to balance developmental opportunities among all their followers. Leaders should look for ways to optimize, over a series of assignments, the growth of all subordinates by matching particular opportunities to their respective individual needs, skills, and goals.

Make the assignment clear and specific. As with setting goals, leaders delegating an assignment must be sure the subordinate understands just what the task involves and what is expected of him. Nevertheless, at times leaders provide too brief an explanation of the task to be delegated. A common communication error is overestimating one's own clarity, and in the case of delegation this can happen when the leader already knows the ins and outs of the particular task. Some of the essential steps or potential pitfalls in an assignment that seem self-evident to the leader may not be as obvious to someone who has never done the assignment before. Leaders should welcome questions and provide a complete explanation of the task. The time leaders invest during this initial training will pay dividends later on. When giving an assignment, leaders should ensure that they cover all of the points listed in Table 12–1.

Assign an objective, not a procedure. Indicate *what* is to be accomplished, not *how* the task is to be accomplished. End results are usually more important

TABLE 12–1
Points to Cover When Delegating a Task

- How does the task relate to organizational goals?
- When does the subordinate's responsibility for the task begin?
- How has the task been accomplished in the past?
- What problems were encountered with the task in the past?
- What sources of help are available?
- What unusual situations might arise in the future?
- What are the limits of the subordinate's authority?
- How will the leader monitor the task (e.g., provide feedback)?
- Finally, in covering the above points, always convey high confidence and expectations.

---

than the methods. It is helpful to demonstrate procedures that have worked before, but not to specify rigid methods to follow in the future. Leaders should not assume their ways always were and always will be best. Leaders need to be clear about the criteria by which success will be measured, but allowing subordinates to achieve it in their own ways will increase their satisfaction and encourage fresh ideas.

Allow autonomy, but monitor performance. Effective delegation is neither micromanagement of everything the subordinate does nor laissez-faire indifference toward the subordinate's performance. Leaders need to give subordinates a degree of autonomy (as well as time, resources, and authority) in carrying out their new responsibilities, and this includes the freedom to make certain kinds of mistakes. An organizational climate where mistakes are punished suppresses initiative and innovation. Furthermore, mistakes are important sources of development. Knowing this, one wise executive reassured a subordinate who expected to be fired for a gigantic mistake by saying, "Why should I fire you when I've just invested $100,000 in your development?" (McCall, Lombardo, & Morrison, 1988, p. 154).

Once a task has been delegated, even though the subordinate's training and development are continuing, the leader should be cautious about providing too much unsolicited advice or engaging in "rescue" activities. An exception would be when a subordinate's mistake would put significant organizational assets at risk. On the other hand, the leader needs to establish specific procedures for periodically reviewing the subordinate's performance of the delegated task. Leaders need to maintain good records of all the assignments they have delegated, including appropriate milestone and completion dates for each one.

Give credit, not blame.   Whenever leaders delegate, they must give subordinates *authority* along with responsibility. In the final analysis, however, leaders always remain fully responsible and accountable for any delegated task. If things should go wrong, then *leaders* should accept responsibility for failure fully and completely and never try to pass blame on to subordinates. On the other hand, if things go well, as they usually will, then leaders should give all the public credit to the subordinates. Also, when providing performance feedback privately to a subordinate, emphasize what went right rather than what went wrong. Leaders should not ignore errors in judgment or implementation, but they need not dwell on them, either. One helpful approach to performance feedback is called the **"sandwich" technique.** With this technique, negative feedback is placed in between two "pieces" of positive feedback. It affirms the subordinate's good work, puts the subordinate at least somewhat at ease, and keeps the ratio of positive and negative comments in balance. The idea of a sandwich, however, should not be taken too literally. There is nothing magical about two pieces of positive feedback for one piece of negative feedback. In fact, from the receiver's point of view the balance between positive and negative feedback may seem "about right" when the ratio is considerably higher than 2:1.

In summary, Taylor (1989) has provided useful insight about the importance of delegation as well as specific and helpful suggestions for delegating more effectively.

SUMMARY

This chapter, a continuation of the material in Chapters Two and Nine, has provided leaders and followers with ideas about how to improve five additional skills related to personal success and effectiveness. Of the five skills described in this chapter, perhaps none is more important than technical competence. Technical competence is critical because in many ways it plays an overarching role in building effective relationships with superiors and peers, setting goals, and delegation. For example, a follower will be more likely to be a member of a superior's in-group if he or she has a high level technical expertise. Moreover, by being a member of the in-group, such a follower will have a greater say in setting the goals of the group, team, or commmittee and will be more apt to be delegated highly visible and valued tasks and activities. Additionally, followers will have higher levels of commitment if goals are assigned by a competent leader, and peers will be more likely to seek technical advice or ask someone to be a member of a joint task force or committee if the person is recognized as being a technical expert. Given the benefits of technical competence, people should do all they can in terms of enrolling in training courses or on-the-job training programs, watching others and reflecting on what they see, asking questions, and seeking opportunities to broaden their experiences in order to enhance their levels of expertise.

Although technical skills are important, building effective relationships with superiors and peers are also skills that can enhance personal effectiveness. Followers can build effective relationships at work or on teams by better understanding superiors' and peers' values, goals, preferences, constraints, expectations, and weaknesses. One way to assess these characteristics in both superiors and peers is through informal conversations at social functions, such as church socials, office parties, committee luncheons, or company sports events. Followers can then use the information gathered at such functions to adjust their own behaviors and in turn establish and maintain strong relationships with others.

Finally, leadership practitioners can also become more effective if they learn how to set goals and delegate tasks correctly. Properly set goals (a) are specific, observable and time limited; (b) are attainable and challenging; (c) have high levels of leader and follower commitment; and (d) provide frequent feedback. Although delegation is a more elaborate procedure than goal setting, many of the steps of delegation parallel those of goal setting. For example, leaders who correctly use delegation determine what needs to be delegated to whom, ensure the delegated tasks are clear and specific, provide enough autonomy and guidance to get the task accomplished, periodically monitor performance and provide feedback, and take full responsibility for task accomplishment (which is not to say take credit).

KEY TERM AND CONCEPT

''sandwich'' technique

DISCUSSION QUESTIONS

1. How does the adage ''Friends come and go, but enemies accumulate'' apply to the material in this chapter?

2. What effect would group norms have on building effective relationships with peers and superiors?

3. How could one describe the delegation process using the interactional framework?

4. List three personal goals you have for the one-month, one-year, and five-year time frames. Can you state these in ways that meet the criteria for goal setting described in this chapter?

5. How do the five bases of power, idiosyncratic credits, and influence tactics (Chapter Six) relate to building effective relationships with superiors and peers?

6. How could one use the four preference dimensions of the Myers-Briggs Type Indicator (Chapter Eight) to help adapt to a superior's world?

SUGGESTED READINGS

Campbell, D. *If You Don't Know Where You're Going You'll Probably End Up Somewhere Else.* Allen, Tex.: Argus Communications, 1974.

Cohen, A. R., and D. L. Bradford. *Influence Without Authority.* New York: Wiley, 1990.

IV

FOCUS ON THE
SITUATION

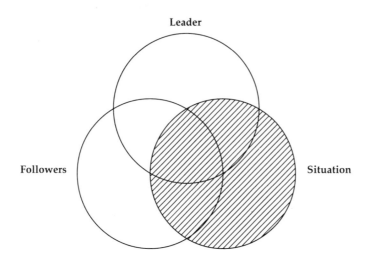

I n previous chapters we have noted how understanding leaders and followers is much more complicated than many people first think. For example, we examined how leaders' personality characteristics, behaviors, and attitudes affect the leadership process. Similarly, followers' attitudes, experience,
personality characteristics, and behaviors, as well as group size, norms, and
cohesiveness also affect the leadership process. Despite the complexities of

leaders and followers, perhaps no factor in the interactional framework is as complex as the situation. Not only do a variety of task, organizational, and environmental factors affect behavior but the relative salience or strength of these factors varies dramatically across people. What one person perceives to be the key situational factor affecting his or her behavior may be relatively unimportant to another person. Moreover, the relative importance of the situational factors also varies over time. Even in a soccer game between the same two teams, for example, the situation changes constantly over time: the lead changes, the time remaining in the game changes, weather conditions change, injuries might occur, and so on. Given the dynamic nature of situations, it is a misnomer to speak of "the" situation in reference to leadership.

Because of the complex and dynamic nature of situations and the substantial role perceptions play in the interpretation of situations, no one has been able to develop a comprehensive taxonomy describing all of the situational variables affecting a person's behavior. In all likelihood, no one ever will. Nevertheless, considerable research about situational influences on leadership has been accomplished. Leadership researchers have examined how different task, organizational, and environmental factors affect both leaders' and followers' behaviors, though most have examined only the effects of one or two situational variables on leaders' and followers' behavior. For example, a study might have examined the effects of task difficulty on subordinates' performance yet ignored how broader issues such as organizational policy or structure might also affect their performance. This is primarily due to the difficulty of studying the effects of organizational and environmental factors on behavior. As you might imagine, many of these factors, such as market conditions or crisis situations, do not easily lend themselves to realistic laboratory experiments where conditions can be controlled and their interactions analyzed. Nonetheless, several consistent findings have emerged. We will review these findings in this part.

Chapter Thirteen

Characteristics of the Situation

INTRODUCTION

T he appropriateness of a leader's behavior with a group of followers often makes sense only when you look at the situational context in which the behavior occurs. Whereas severely disciplining a follower might seem a poor way to lead, if the follower in question had just committed a safety violation endangering the lives of hundreds of people, then the leader's actions may be exactly right. In a similar fashion, the situation may be the primary reason why personality traits, experience, or cognitive abilities are related less consistently to leadership effectiveness than to leadership emergence (R.T. Hogan, J. Hogan, & Curphy, 1992; Yukl, 1989). Most leadership emergence studies have involved leaderless discussion groups, and for the most part the situation is pretty much the same across these studies. In studies of leadership effectiveness, however, the situation can and does vary drastically. The personality traits, values, cognitive abilities, or technical expertise needed to be an effective leader of a combat unit, chemical research-and-development division, computer sales company, or fast-food restaurant may vary considerably. Because the situations facing leaders of such groups may vary so much, it is hardly surprising that studies of leader characteristics have yielded fairly inconsistent results when looking at leadership effectiveness across jobs or situations. Thus, the importance of the situation in the leadership process should not be overlooked (also see Highlight 13–1).

Historically, some leadership researchers emphasized the importance of the situation in the leadership process in response to the Great Man theory of leadership. These researchers maintained that the situation, not someone's traits or abilities, plays the most important role in determing who emerges as a leader (Murphy, 1941; Person, 1928; Spiller, 1929). As support for the situational viewpoint, these researchers noted that great leaders typically emerged during economic crises, social upheavals, or revolutions; great leaders were generally not associated with periods of relative calm or quiet. For example, Schneider (1937) noted that the number of individuals identified as great military leaders in the British armed forces during any time period depended on how many conflicts the country was engaged in; the greater number of conflicts, the greater number of great military leaders. Moreover, researchers advocating the situational viewpoint believed leaders were made, not born, and that prior leadership experience helped forge effective leaders (Person, 1928). These early situational theories of leadership tended to be very popular in the United States, as they fit more closely with American ideals of equality and meritocracy, and ran counter to the genetic views of leadership that were more popular among European researchers at the time (Bass, 1990). (The fact many of these European researchers had aristocratic backgrounds probably had something to do with the popularity of the Great Man theory in Europe.)

More recent leadership theories have explored how situational factors affect leaders' behaviors. In **role theory,** for example, a leader's behavior was said to

---

HIGHLIGHT 13–1

Leadership Quotes, Chapter Thirteen

If you want to give a man credit, put it in writing. If you want to give him hell, do it on the phone.

Charles Beacham

A man may speak very well in The House of Commons, and fail very complete in The House of Lords. There are two distinct styles requisite.

Benjamin Disraeli

I claim not to have controlled events, but confess plainly that events have controlled me.

Abraham Lincoln

When you've exhausted all possibilities, remember this: you haven't!

Robert H. Schuller

The way of the superior is three-fold, but I am not equal to it. Virtuous, he is free from anxieties; wise, he is free from perplexities; bold, he is free from fear.

Confucius

The brain is a wonderful organ; it begins working the moment you get up in the morning and does not stop until you get to the office.

Robert Frost

---

depend on a leader's perceptions of several critical aspects of the situation: rules and regulations governing the job; role expectations of subordinates, peers, and superiors; the nature of the task; and feedback about subordinates' performance (Merton, 1957; Pfeffer & Salancik, 1975). Role theory clarified how these situational demands and constraints could cause role conflict and role ambiguity. Leaders may experience role conflict when subordinates and superiors have conflicting expectations about a leader's behavior or when company policies contradict how superiors expect tasks to be performed. A leader's ability to successfully resolve such conflicts may well determine leadership effectiveness (Tsui, 1984).

Another effort to incorporate situational variables into leadership theory was Hunt and Osborn's (1982) **multiple influence model.** Hunt and Osborn distinguished between microvariables (e.g., task characteristics) and macrovariables (e.g., the external environment) in the situation. Although most researchers looked at the effects tasks had on leader behaviors, Hunt and Osborn believed macrovariables had a pervasive influence on the ways leaders act. Both role theory and the multiple influence model highlight a major problem in addressing situational factors, which was noted previously: that situations can vary in countless ways. Because situations can vary in so many ways, it is helpful for leaders to have an abstract scheme for conceptualizing situations. This would be a step in knowing how to identify what may be most salient or critical to pay attention to in any particular instance.

One of the most basic abstractions is **situational levels.** The idea behind situational levels may best be conveyed with an example. Suppose someone asked you, "How are things going at work?" You might respond by commenting on the specific tasks you perform (e.g., "It is still pretty tough. I am under the gun for getting next year's budget prepared, and I have never done that before"). Or, you might respond by commenting on aspects of the overall organization (e.g., "It is really different. There are so many rules you have to follow. My old company was not like that at all"). Or, you might comment on factors affecting the organization itself (e.g., "I've been real worried about keeping my job— you know how many cutbacks there have been in our whole industry recently"). Each response deals with the situation, but each refers to a very different level of abstraction: the task level, the organizational level, and the environmental level. Each of these three levels provides a different perspective with which to examine the leadership process (see Figure 13–1).

These three levels certainly do not exhaust all the ways situations vary. Situations also differ in terms of physical variables like noise and temperature levels, workload demands, and the extent to which work groups interact with other groups. Organizations also have unique "corporate cultures," which define a context for leaderhip. And there are always even broader economic, social, legal, and technological aspects of situations within which the leadership process occurs. What, amid all this situational complexity, should leaders pay attention to? We will try to provide some insights into this question by looking at research pertaining to task, organizational, and environmental factors affecting the leadership process.

TASK CHARACTERISTICS

Given the variety of tasks people peform, it is natural for people to try to order and make sense of them. In thinking back across the many different tasks you have performed, you might categorize them as boring, challenging, dangerous, fun, interesting, and so on. However, labeling tasks is just a reaction to them and does not foster understanding about what aspects of any task may have caused a particular reaction. In looking at tasks, therefore, we want to get beyond subjective reactions to more objective ways of analyzing them.

FIGURE 13–1
An Expanded Leader-Follower-Situation Model

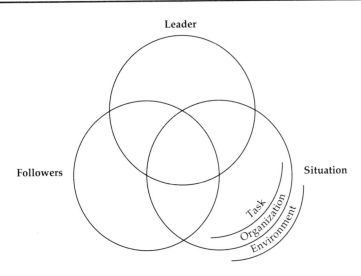

There are several objective ways to categorize tasks performed by leaders and followers. Tasks can be categorized according to their function, the skills or abilities needed to perform them, the equipment needed to perform them, and so on. We will present a scheme for analyzing tasks that, in part, was addressed earlier in the context of work motivation. In that case, tasks were described in terms of the relatively independent dimensions of skill variety, task identity, task significance, autonomy, and feedback. We will add to those two other dimensions: task structure and task interdependence. We will look at task structure first.

Task Structure

Perhaps the easiest way to explain **task structure** is by using an example demonstrating the difference between a structured and unstructured task. Assume the task to be accomplished is solving for x given the formula $3x + 2x = 15$. If that problem were given to a group of people who knew the fundamental rules of algebra, then everyone would arrive at the same answer. In this example there is a known procedure for accomplishing the task; there are rules governing how one goes about it; and, if people follow those rules, there is one result. These features characterize a *structured task.*

On the other hand, if the task is to resolve a morale problem on the team, committee, or work group, then there may be no clear-cut method for solving it. There are many different ways, perhaps none of which is obvious or necessarily best, for approaching a solution. It may even be that different observers would not see the problem in the same way; they may even have quite different ideas of what *morale* is. Solving a morale problem, therefore, exemplifies an *unstructured* task.

People vary in their preferences for or ability to handle structured versus unstructured tasks. With the Myers-Briggs Type Indicator (MBTI), for example, perceivers are believed to prefer unstructured situations, whereas judgers prefer activities that are planned and organized (Myers & McCaulley, 1985). Individuals with high tolerance for stress may handle ambiguous and unstructured tasks more easily than people with low tolerance for stress (Bass, 1990). Aside from these differences, however, we might ask whether there are any general rules for how leaders should interact with followers as a function of task structure. One consideration here is that while it is *easier* for a leader or coach to give instruction in structured tasks, it is not necessarily the most helpful thing to do.

We can see that by returning to the algebra problem described earlier. If a student had never seen such an algebra problem before, then it would be relatively easy for the teacher to teach the student the rules needed to solve the problem. Once any student has learned the procedure, however, he can solve similar problems on his own. Extending this to other situations, once a subordinate knows or understands a task, a supervisor's continuing instruction (i.e., initiating structure or directive behavior) may provide superfluous information and eventually become irritating (Ford, 1981; House & Dessler, 1974; Kerr & Jermier, 1978; Yukl, 1989). Subordinates *need* help when a task is unstructured, when they do not know what the desired outcome "looks like," and when they do not know how to achieve it. Anything a supervisor or leader can do to increase subordinates' ability to perform unstructured tasks is likely to increase their performance and job satisfaction (Siegall & Cummings, 1986). Paradoxically, though, unstructured tasks are by nature somewhat ill defined. Thus, they often are more difficult for leaders themselves to analyze and provide direction in accomplishing.

Skill Variety

Skill variety and the next four dimensions of tasks are all components of the job characteristics model (Hackman & Oldham, 1976, 1980) described in Chapter Eleven. Skill variety refers to the degree to which a job involves performing a variety of different activities or skills. For example, if an individual attaches the left taillight to a car on an automobile assembly line by mechanically screwing in the fasteners, there would be increased work but no increased skill variety if he subsequently stepped over the line to the other side to install the right taillight. Skill variety involves using different skills, whether mechanical, cognitive, or physical. We might also add that there is a qualitative dimension to skill variety. Whereas, in general, jobs requiring greater skill variety are more enjoyable than those requiring lesser skill variety, it also matters whether any particular individual personally values the skills she performs.

Although satisfaction may also depend on growth-need strength, typically jobs that require a low variety of skills are repetitive, monotonous, boring, and dissatisfying (Bass, 1990; Hackman & Oldham, 1980; House & Desslesr, 1974). And like structured tasks, tasks with low levels of skill variety make it easier for leaders to use directive behaviors but, because followers already know how to do the job, also make directive leadership behavior somewhat redundant (Howell & Dorfman, 1981, 1986; Kerr & Jermier, 1978; Kipnis, 1984). In such situations, leaders might try to restructure a subordinate's job in order to increase the number of (valued) skills needed. If that is not possible, then high levels of support and consideration for followers are helpful (Hackman & Oldham, 1980; House & Dessler, 1974).

Task Identity

Task identity refers to the degree to which a situation or task requires completion of a whole unit of work from beginning to end with a visible outcome. For example, if one works on an assembly line where circuit boards for compact disc (CD) players are being produced, and the task is to solder one wire to one electronic component and then pass the circuit board on to the next assembly worker, then this job would lack task identity. At the other extreme, if one assembled an entire CD player, perhaps involving 30 or 40 different tasks, then the perception of task identity would increase dramatically as one could readily see the final results of one's efforts. Furthermore, the job's skill variety (as discussed above) would increase as well.

Often, organizations redesign assembly lines in order to increase skill variety and task identity, and thereby increase job satisfaction and performance while decreasing absenteeism and turnover. Such changes, however, have important implications for leaders as well as for followers. Redesigning jobs to have greater skill variety and task identity for subordinates often places a higher premium on the leader's technical expertise; the leader may need greater technical competence herself in order to train or develop followers on a greater variety of tasks.

Task Significance

Task significance is the degree to which a job substantially impacts others' lives. Consider an individual whose task is to insert a bolt into a nut and tighten it down to a certain specification using a torque wrench. If that bolt is one of several that fasten a fender to other parts of an automobile body on an assembly line, then both skill variety and task identity would probably be very low. Moreover, if the assembly person leaves the entire bolt off, it may cause a squeak or a rattle, but probably would not cause the fender to fall off. In such a job, task significance would be quite low as well. However, if the worker tightens the only bolt securing a critical component of a brake assembly on the space shuttle, then skill variety and task identity would be exactly the same as for our fender installer. However, task significance would be substantially higher.

Autonomy

Autonomy is the degree to which a job provides an individual with some control over what he does and how he does it. Someone with considerable autonomy would have discretion in scheduling work and deciding the procedures used in accomplishing it. Autonomy often covaries with technical expertise, as workers with considerable expertise will be given more latitude, and those with few skills will be given more instruction and coaching when accomplishing tasks (Hersey & Blanchard, 1977, 1984). Moreover, responsibility and job satisfaction often increase when autonomy increases (Hackman & Oldham, 1980).

Feedback

The last task component in the job characteristics model is **feedback,** which refers to the degree to which a person accomplishing a task receives information about performance *from performing the task itself.* In this context feedback does not refer to feedback received from supervisors but rather to that intrinsic to the work activity itself. Driving a car is one example of feedback intrinsic to a task. If you are a skilled driver on a road with a number of twists and turns, then you get all the feedback you need about how well you are accomplishing the task merely by observing how the car responds to the inputs you make. This is feedback from the job itself as opposed to feedback from another person (who in this example would be a classic back seat driver). Extending this example to work or team settings, leaders sometimes may want to redesign tasks so that they (the tasks) provide more intrinsic feedback. Although this does not absolve the leader from giving periodic feedback about performance, it can help to free up some of the leader's time for other work-related activities. Additionally, leaders should understand that followers may eventually become dissatisfied if leaders provide high levels of feedback for tasks that already provide intrinsic feedback (House & Dessler, 1974; Howell & Dorfman, 1981; Kerr & Jermier, 1978).

Task Interdependence

Task interdependence concerns the degree to which tasks require coordination and synchronization in order for work groups or teams to accomplish desired goals. Task interdependence differs from autonomy in that workers or team members may be able to accomplish their tasks in an autonomous fashion, but the products of their efforts must be coordinated in order for the group or team to be successful. Tasks with high levels of interdependence place a premium on leaders' organizing and planning, directing, and communication skills (Curphy, 1991a, 1992, Galbraith, 1973). In one study, for example, coaches exhibiting high levels of initiating structure behaviors had better-performing teams for sports requiring relatively interdependent effort, such as football, hockey, lacrosse, rugby, basketball, and volleyball; the same leader behaviors were unrelated to team performance for sports requiring relatively independent effort, such as swimming, track, cross-country, golf, and baseball (Fry, Kerr, & Lee, 1986). Like task structure and skill variety, task interdependence can also dictate which leader behaviors will be effective in a particular situation.

In summary, these seven task dimensions provide a variety of ways in which to categorize or describe tasks. For example, ironing a shirt would probably have high task structure, autonomy, task identification, and feedback and low skill variety, task significance, and task interdependence. On the other hand, building your own home may garner high ratings on all seven dimensions. Still another familiar activity is evaluated on these dimensions in Highlight 13–2. These seven dimensions can provide leaders with insight about how their behavior and task assignments may either help or hinder followers' satisfaction and performance. At the same time, leaders should remember that these dimensions exist somewhat in the eye of the beholder. What one follower perceives as an unstructured task might be seen by another as fairly structured. As we have emphasized before, leaders should use their communication and listening skills to assure they understand subordinates' feelings and beliefs about tasks they perform.

ORGANIZATIONAL CHARACTERISTICS

As with tasks, there also are a variety of dimensions for conceptualizing the organizational level of situations. This section will address how level of authority, organizational structure, organizational design, lateral interdependence, and organizational culture affect leaders' and followers' behavior.

Level of Authority

Level of authority concerns one's hierarchical level in an organization. The types of behaviors most critical to leadership effectiveness can change substantially as one moves up an organizational ladder. First-line supervisors, lower level leaders, and coaches spend a considerable amount of time training followers, resolving work-unit or team-performance problems, scheduling practices or arranging work schedules, or implementing policies. Leaders at higher

---

HIGHLIGHT 13–2

Golf and the Task Factors of the Situation

Golf provides a convenient skill for illustrating the seven task factors described in this chapter. Golf provides a reasonable amount of *task structure,* as there are basic rules and procedures for properly hitting woods, long irons, short irons, and for putting.

Skill variety comes into play because golfers use a variety of skills and talents. These include deciding on a club, the method used to swing the club, how hard to swing them, what kind of equipment to use, where to target the ball, how to compensate for wind, when to putt, and so on.

Because one person does all of the driving, pitching, and putting and is solely responsible for his or her score, a round of golf has a high level of *task identity.*

Task significance may be a little more difficult to appreciate in this example. It may not be there at all unless one is a particularly poor golfer (where he or she endangers the lives of other people) or, in the case of the professional golfer, has a family who depends on his or her performance.

Autonomy is certainly present when playing golf. The golfer gets to decide when to do the ''work,'' how to do it, which clubs to use, and what strategies and tactics to use.

Feedback from the job is also apparent. Shortly after a golfer strikes the ball, she receives feedback on how well her swing worked. Whether it slices, hooks, or goes straight down the fairway are all bits of information that tell the golfer immediately how well her work is being accomplished.

Finally, golf generally lacks *task interdependence.* Golfers are not dependent on the other members in their foursome for their own score.

---

organizational levels have more autonomy and spend relatively more time setting policies, coordinating activities, and making staffing decisions (Blankenship & Miles, 1968; Luthans, Rosenkrantz, & Hennessey, 1985; Mintzberg, 1973; Page & Tornow, 1987). Moreover, leaders at higher organizational levels often perform a greater variety of activities and are more apt to use participation and delegation (Chitayat & Venezia, 1984; Kurke & Aldrich, 1983). A quite different aspect of how level of authority affects leadership is presented in Highlight 13–3.

Organizational Structure

Organizational structure refers to the way an organization's activities are coordinated and controlled, and represents another level of the situation in which leaders and followers must operate. Organizational structure is a conceptual or

---

HIGHLIGHT 13–3

Women in Leadership VI: The Glass Ceiling and the Wall

While the 1990s will be marked by increasing movement of women into leadership positions, it still is a fact that women occupy only a tiny percentage of the highest leadership positions. In Fortune 500 companies, for example, only 1 or 2 percent of the corporate officers are women. Researchers at the Center for Creative Leadership embarked on the Executive Woman Project to understand why (Morrison, White, & Van Velsor, 1987).

They studied 76 women executives in 25 companies who had reached the general management level or the one just below it. The average woman executive in the sample was 41 and married. More than half had at least one child, and the vast majority were white.

The researchers expected to find evidence of a "glass ceiling," an invisible barrier that keeps women from progressing higher than a certain level in their organizations *because they are women.* One reason the women in this particular sample were interesting was precisely because they had apparently "broken" the glass ceiling, thus entering the top 1 percent of the work force. These women had successfully confronted three different sorts of pressure throughout their careers, a greater challenge than their male counterparts faced. One pressure dealt with those from the job itself, and this was no different for women than for men. A second level of pressure, however, involved being a *female* executive, with attendant stresses such as being particularly visible, excessively scrutinized, and a role model for other women. Still a third level of pressure involved the demands of coordinating personal and professional life. It is still most people's expectation that women will take the greater responsibility in a family for managing the household and raising children. And beyond the sheer size of such demands, the roles of women in these two spheres of life are often at odds (e.g., being businesslike and efficient, maybe even "tough," at work yet intimate and nurturing at home).

The Center for Creative Leadership researchers described the "lessons for success" of this group of women who had broken through the glass ceiling. They also reported, however, a somewhat unexpected finding. Breaking through the glass ceiling only presented women executives with an even tougher obstacle. They "hit a wall" that kept them out of the very top positions. The researchers estimated only a handful of the women executives in their sample would enter the topmost echelon called senior management, and that none would become president of their corporation.

---

procedural reality, however, not a physical or tangible one. Typically, it is depicted in the form of a chart that clarifies formal authority relationships and patterns of communication within the organization. Most people take organizational structure for granted and fail to realize that structure is really just a tool for getting things done in organizations. Structure is not an end in itself, and different structures might exist for organizations performing similar work, each having unique advantages and disadvantages. There is nothing sacrosanct or permanent about any structure, and leaders may find having a basic understanding of organizational structure to be not only useful but imperative. Leaders may wish to design a structure to enhance the likelihood of attaining a desired outcome, or they may wish to change structure in order to meet future demands. There are a number of ways to describe organizational structures, but perhaps the simplest way is to think of structure in terms of complexity, formalization, and centralization.

Complexity.   Horizontal, vertical, and spatial elements make up organizational complexity. When looking at an organizational chart, **horizontal complexity** refers to the number of "boxes" at any particular organizational level. The greater the number of boxes at a given level, the greater the horizontal complexity. Typically, greater horizontal complexity is associated with more specialization within subunits and an increased likelihood for communication breakdowns between subunits. **Vertical complexity** refers to the number of hierarchical levels appearing on an organization chart. A vertically simple organization may only have two or three levels from the highest person to the lowest. A vertically complex organization, on the other hand, may have 10 or more. Vertical complexity can affect leadership by impacting other factors such as authority dynamics and communication networks. **Spatial complexity** describes geographical dispersion. An organization that has all of its people in one location is typically less spatially complex than an organization that is dispersed around the country or around the world. Obviously, spatial complexity makes it more difficult for leaders to have face-to-face communication with and personally administer rewards or provide support and encouragement to subordinates in geographically separated locations. Generally, all three of these elements are partly a function of organizational size. Bigger organizations are more likely to have more specialized subunits (horizontal complexity), a greater number of hierarchical levels (vertical complexity), and have subunits that are geographically dispersed (spatial complexity).

Formalization.   **Formalization** describes the degree of standarization in an organization. Organizations having written job descriptions and standardized operating procedures for each position have a high degree of formalization. The degree of formalization in an organization tends to vary with its size, just as complexity generally increases with size (Robbins, 1986). Formalization also varies with the nature of work performed. Manufacturing organizations, for example, tend to have fairly formalized structures, whereas research-and-development organizations tend to be less formalized. After all, how could there be a detailed job description for developing a nonexistent product or making a scientific discovery?

The degree of formalization in an organization poses both advantages and disadvantages for leaders and followers. Whereas formalizing procedures clarifies methods of operating and interacting, it also may constitute demands and constraints on leaders and followers. Leaders may be constrained in the way they communicate requests, order supplies, or reward or discipline subordinates (Hammer & Turk, 1987; Podsaskoff, 1982). If followers belong to a union, then union rules may dictate work hours, the amount of work accomplished per day, or who will be the first to be laid off (Hammer & Turk, 1987). Other aspects of the impact of formalization and other situational variables on leadership are presented in Highlights 13–4 and 13–5.

Centralization.   **Centralization** refers to the diffusion of decision making throughout an organization. An organization that allows decisions to be made by only one person is highly centralized. When decision making is dispersed to the lowest levels in the organization, the organization is very decentralized. Advantages of decentralized organizations include increased participation in the decision process and, consequently, greater acceptance and ownership of decision outcomes. These are both desirable outcomes. There are also, however, advantages to centralization, such as uniform policies and procedures (which can increase feelings of equity), and clearer coordination procedures (Bass, 1990). The task of balancing the degree of centralization necessary to achieve coordination and control, on the one hand, and gaining desirable participation and acceptance, on the other, is an ongoing challenge for the leader.

Organizational Design

In addition to being classified by their degree of complexity, formalization, and centralization, organizations can also be classified into several different kinds of **organizational design**. Three of the most common kinds of organizational designs include functional, product, and matrix organizations.

Functional.   Some organizations have their structures designed around certain important and continuing functions. For example, a manufacturing company with a **functional design** might have its organizational chart include one block for manufacturing, one for sales or marketing, one for research and development, and so on (see Figure 13–2). Advantages of functional organizations include efficient use of scarce resources, skill development for technical personnel, centralized decision making and control, and excellent coordination within each functional department. Disadvantages of functional organizations can include poor coordination across departments, slow responses to change, a piling up of decisions at the top of the hierarchy, and narrow or limited views by employees of overall organizational goals (Austin, Conlon &

HIGHLIGHT 13–4

Are There Substitutes for Leadership?

Are leaders always necessary? Or are certain kinds of leader behaviors, at least, sometimes unnecessary? Kerr and Jermier (1978) proposed that certain situational or follower characteristics may well effectively neutralize or substitute for leaders' task or relationship behaviors. *Neutralizers* are characteristics that reduce or limit the effectiveness of a leader's behaviors. *Substitutes* are characteristics that make a leader's behaviors redundant or unnecessary.

Kerr and Jermier (1978) developed the idea of **substitutes for leadership** after comparing the correlations between leadership behaviors and follower performance and satisfaction with correlations between various situational factors and follower performance and satisfaction. Those subordinate, task, and organizational characteristics having higher correlations with follower performance and satisfaction than the two leadership behaviors were subsequently identified as substitutes or neutralizers. The following are a few examples of the situational factors Kerr and Jermier found to substitute for or neutralize leaders' task or relationship behaviors:

- A subordinate's ability and experience may well substitute for task-oriented leader behavior. A subordinate's indifference toward rewards overall may neutralize both a leader's task and relationship behavior.

- Tasks that are routine or structured may substitute for task-oriented leader behavior, as can tasks that provide intrinsic feedback or are intrinsically satisfying.

- High levels of formalization in organizations may substitute for task-oriented leader behavior, and unbending rules and procedures may even neutralize the leader's task behavior. A cohesive work group may provide a substitute for both the leader's task and relationship behavior.

Source: Kerr, S., and J. M. Jermier. "Substitutes for Leadership: Their Meaning and Measurement." *Organizational Behavior and Human Performance* 22 (1978), pp. 375–403.

Daft, 1986). In organizations structured functionally, in other words, the very commonality within the various functional units can create problems. Functional groups can become so cohesive that they create rigid boundaries and dysfunctional competitiveness between themselves and other groups within the same organization.

Product. In an organization with a **product design,** the blocks on the organization chart define the various products or services that are delivered ultimtely to the consumer. One might consider an automobile organization such as General Motors, where there are the Buick, Oldsmobile, Chevrolet, Cadillac, and Pontiac divisions. These are identifiable products, and employees are assigned

HIGHLIGHT 13–5

A "Soap" Opera

Most of us have a preference for the type of organizational structure we would like to work in. Some people prefer formal structures, while others prefer almost no organizational structure at all. As we have noted, different structures enable certain behaviors better than others. When we mix preferences and structures, we can get some interesting and often humorous results. Such is the case in the following "soap" opera transmitted over an electronic mail network, where we find a man who would prefer a little personal attention in a system designed to apply the same rules to everyone. The setting is a London hotel that supplies free soap.

Dear Maid:
Please do not leave any more of those little bars of soap in my bathroom since I have brought my own bath-sized Dial. Please remove the 6 unopened little bars from the shelf under the medicine chest and another 3 in the shower soap dish. They are in my way.
Thank you, T. Brown

Dear Room 545:
I am not your regular maid. She will be back tomorrow from her day off. I took the 3 hotel soaps out of the shower soap dish as you requested. The 6 bars on your shelf I took out of your way and put on top of your Kleenex dispenser in case you should change your mind. This only leaves 3 bars I left today. My instructions from the management are to leave 3 soaps daily. I hope this is satisfactory.
Kathy, Relief Maid

Dear Maid:
I hope you are my regular maid. Apparently Kathy did not tell you about my note to her concerning the little bars of soap. When I got back to my room this evening I found you had added 3 little Camays to the shelf under my medicine cabinet. I am going to be here in the hotel for two weeks and have brought my own bath-sized Dial, so I won't need those 6 little Camays which are on the shelf. They are in my way when shaving, brushing teeth, etc. Please remove them.
T. Brown

Dear Mr. Brown:
My day off was last Wednesday so the relief maid left 3 hotel soaps which we are instructed by the management. I took the 6 soaps which were in your way on the shelf and put them in the soap dish where your Dial was. I put the Dial in the medicine cabinet for your convenience. I didn't remove the 3 complimentary soaps, which are always placed inside the medicine cabinet for all new check-ins, and which you did not object to when you checked in last Monday. Please let me know if I can be of further assistance.
Your regular maid, Dotty

Dear Mr. Brown:
The assistant manger, Mr. Kensedder, informed me this A.M. that you called him last evening and said you were unhappy with the maid service. I have assigned a new girl to your room. I hope you will accept my apologies for any past inconvenience. If you have any future complaints, please contact me so I can give it my personal attention. Call extention 1108 between 8 A.M. and 5 P.M. Thank you.
Elaine Carmen, Housekeeper

HIGHLIGHT 13–5 *(continued)*

Dear Miss Carmen:
    It is impossible to contact you by phone since I leave the hotel for business at 7:45 A.M. and don't get back before 5:30–6:00 P.M. The reason I called Mr. Kensedder last night was because you were off duty. I only asked Mr. Kensedder if he could do anything about those little bars of soap. The new maid you assigned me must have thought I was a new check in today, since she left another 3 bars of hotel soap in my medicine cabinet along with her regular delivery of 3 bars on the bathroom shelf. In just 5 days here I have accumulated 24 little bars of soap. Why are you doing this to me?
                                                                                      T. Brown

Dear Mr. Brown:
    Your maid, Kathy, has been instructed to stop delivering soap to your room and to remove the extra soaps. If I can be of further assistance please call extension 1108 between 8 A.M. and 5 P.M. Thank you.
                                                                    Elaine Carmen, Housekeeper

Dear Mr. Kensedder:
    My bath-sized Dial is missing. Every bar of soap was taken from my room including my own bath-sized Dial. I came in late last night and had to call the bellhop to bring me 4 little Cashmere Bouquets.
                                                                                      T. Brown

Dear Mr. Brown:
    I have informed our housekeeper, Elaine Carmen, of your soap problem. I cannot understand why there was no soap in your room since our maids are instructed to leave 3 bars of soap each time they service a room. The situation will be rectified immediately. Please accept my apologies for the inconvenience.
                                                                    M. L. Kensedder, Asst. Man.

Dear Mrs. Carmen:
    Who the hell left 54 little bars of Camay in my room? I came in last night and found 54 bars of soap. I don't want 54 little bars of Camay. I want my 1 damn bar of bath-sized Dial. Do you realize I have 54 bars of soap in here? All I want is my bath-sized Dial. Please give me back my bath-sized Dial.
                                                                                      T. Brown

Dear Mr. Brown:
    You complained of too much soap in your room so I had them removed. Then you complained to Mr. Kensedder that all your soap was missing so I personally returned them. The 24 Camays which had been taken and the 3 Camays you are supposed to receive daily. I don't know anything about the 4 Cashmere Bouquets. Obviously your maid, Kathy, did not know I had returned your soaps so she also brought 24 Camays plus the 3 daily Camays. I don't know where you got the idea this hotel issues bath-sized Dial. I was able to locate some bath-sized Ivory which I left in your room.
                                                                    Elaine Carmen, Housekeeper

HIGHLIGHT 13–5 *(concluded)*

Dear Mrs. Carmen:
    Just a short note to bring you up-to-date on my latest soap inventory. As of today I possess:
- on the shelf under medicine cabinet—18 Camay in 4 stacks of 4 and 1 stack of 2.
- on the Kleenex dispenser—11 Camay in 2 stacks of 4 and 1 stack of 3.
- on the bedroom dresser—1 stack of 3 Cashmere Bouquet, 1 stack of 4 hotel-size, bath-sized Ivory, and 8 Camay in 2 stacks of 4.
- in the medicine cabinet—14 Camay in 3 stacks of 4 and 1 stack of 2.
- in the shower soap dish—6 Camay, very moist.
- on the northeast corner of the tub—1 Cashmere Bouquet, slightly used.
- on the northwest corner of the tub—6 Camay in 2 stacks of 3.

Please ask Kathy when she services my room to make sure the stacks are neatly piled and dusted. Also, please advise her that stacks of more than 4 have a tendency to tip. May I suggest that my bedroom windowsill is not in use and will make an excellent spot for future soap deliveries. One more item, I have purchased another bar of bath-sized Dial which I am keeping in the hotel vault in order to avoid future misunderstandings.
                                                                            T. Brown

NOTE: The authors do not know of a published source for this episode. It was provided to the authors by an acquaintance who works for American Express, who received it herself over that company's electronic mail network. We were unsuccessful in locating any other source.

FIGURE 13–2
A Manufacturing Company with a Functional Design

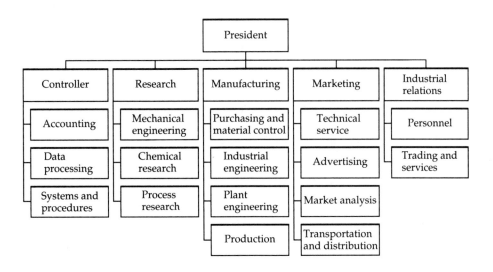

FIGURE 13–3
A Petroleum Company with a Product Design

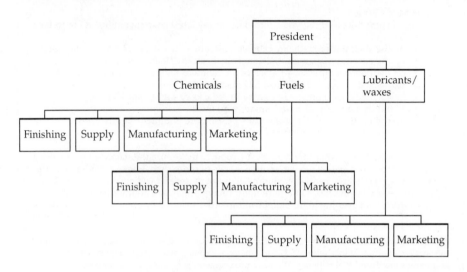

to these product groupings. A more generic product design is represented in Figure 13–3. A product organization design overcomes some of the problems associated with functional organizations, as a product organization has better coordination across functional skills, places a premium on organizational goals rather than functional goals, and has better control over diverse products or services. The disadvantages of product organizations include duplication of resources, less in-depth technical expertise, and weak coordination across different product groupings.

Matrix. The **matrix design** is a combination of the product and functional designs. In this design, products typically are arrayed across the top of the matrix and functions are arrayed down the side; thus, both product orientation and functional specialties are maintained (see Figure 13–4). In a matrix organization, there is a product manager for each product and one of her tasks is to obtain the resources necessary from the functional specialties as requirements demand. If the product will require the services of a computer software engineer, for example, then the product manager must acquire those services from the manager of the engineering function.

The greatest advantage of the matrix is efficient utilization of human resources. Imagine putting together a team to design a new product, and further suppose that a chemical engineer's services are among the team's needs. Also imagine, however, that the chemical engineer is required for only one month's work whereas the total product design phase encompasses a whole year. If our

FIGURE 13–4

A Manufacturing Company with a Matrix Design

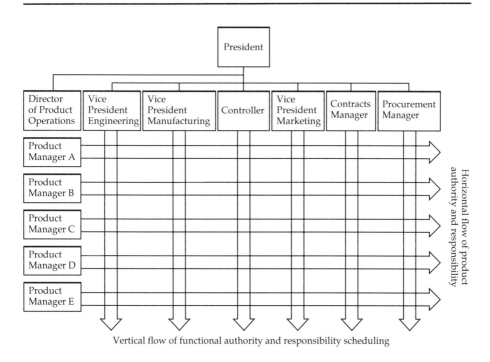

Vertical flow of functional authority and responsibility scheduling

imaginary organization were designed according to a product orientation, the product manager would have to hire a full-time chemical engineer despite needing her services for only one month. In a matrix organization, on the other hand, the chemical engineer could be assigned to the engineering division, and the various product managers could arrange to acquire her time on an as-needed basis. Such an arrangement can create scheduling nightmares, but it also results in more efficient utilization of unusual or scarce resources. Another advantage of the matrix design includes increased lateral communication and coordination.

The greatest disadvantage of the matrix design is that employees end up working for two bosses. Such a dual authority structure can create confusion and frustration. In the case above, the chemical engineer may have "professional loyalty" to the engineering group (which would dictate the highest quality engineering possible) and "profitability loyalty" to the product group (which would dictate the most cost-effective engineering). Our chemical engineer might very well experience conflict over which loyalty to serve first. Additionally, matrix designs can lead to conflict and disagreements over the use of shared resources, and time is lost through frequent meetings to resolve such issues. Thus, administrative costs are high in matrix organizations. Finally, matrix designs can work well only if managers see the "big picture" and do not adopt narrower functional or product perspectives.

Lateral Interdependence

The degree of **lateral interdependence** in an organization can also affect leaders' and followers' behaviors. Lateral interdependence concerns the degree of coordination or snychronization required between organizational units in order to accomplish work-group or organizational goals. Thus, lateral interdependence is similar to task interdependence but at a higher organizational level; lateral interdependence represents the degree to which a leader's work group is affected by the actions or activities of other subunits within the organization (Bass, 1990; Sayles, 1979). For example, a leader of a final assembly unit for personal computers will be very dependent on the activities of the power supply, cabinet, monitor, mother board, floppy drive, and hard drive manufacturing units in order to successfully meet production goals. On the other hand, the leader of a manufacturing unit that makes all of the products used to assemble backpacks has a much lower degree of lateral interdependence. As lateral interdependence increases, leaders usually spend more time building and maintaining contacts in other work units or on public relations activities (Hammer & Turk, 1987; Kaplan, 1986). Moreover, leaders are more likely to use rational persuasion as an influence tactic when the level of lateral interdependence is high (Kanter, 1982; Kaplan, 1986).

Organizational Culture and Climate

Although most people probably think of culture in terms of very large social groups, the concept also applies to organizations. **Organizational culture** has been defined as a system of shared backgrounds, norms, values, or beliefs among members of a group (Schein, 1985), and **organizational climate** concerns members' subjective reactions about the organization (Bass, 1990; Kozlowski & Doherty, 1989). These two concepts are distinct in that organizational climate is partly a function of or reaction to organizational culture; one's feelings or emotional reactions about an organization are probably affected by the degree to which a person shares the prevailing values, beliefs, and backgrounds of organizational members (Schneider, 1983). If a person does not share the same values or beliefs of the majority of members, then in all likelihood this person would have a fairly negative reaction about the organization overall. Thus, organizational climate (and indirectly organizational culture) is related to how well organizational members get along with each other (Bass, 1990; Kozlowski & Doherty, 1989). It is also important to note that organizational climate is narrower in scope but highly related to job satisfaction. Gener-

TABLE 13–1

Some Questions that Define Organizational Culture

- What can be talked about or not talked about?
- How do people wield power?
- How does one get ahead or stay out of trouble?
- What are the unwritten rules of the game?
- What are the organization's morality and ethics?
- What stories are told about the organization?

Source: Adapted from R. H. Kilmann and M. J. Saxton, *Organizational Cultures: Their Assessment and Change* (San Francisco: Jossey-Bass, 1983).

ally, organizational climate has more to do with nontask perceptions of work, such as feelings about co-workers or company policies, whereas job satisfaction usually also includes perceptions of workload and the nature of the tasks performed.

Just as there are many cultures across the world, there are a great number of different cultures across organizations. Members of many military organizations have different norms, background experiences, values, and beliefs, for example, from those of the faculty at many colleges. Similarly, the culture of an investment firm is very different from the culture of a research-and-development firm, a freight hauling company, or a college rugby team. Cultural differences can exist between different organizations even within any of these sectors. The culture of the U.S. Air Force is different from the culture of the U.S. Marine Corps, and Rutgers has a different culture than the University of Colorado even though they are both fine institutions of higher learning.

One of the more fascinating aspects of organizational culture is that it often takes an outsider to recognize it; organizational culture becomes so second nature to many organizational members that they are unaware of how it affects their behaviors and perceptions (Bass, 1990). Despite this transparency to organizational members, a fairly consistent set of dimensions can be used to differentiate between organizational cultures. For example, Kilmann and Saxton (1983) stated that organizational cultures can be differentiated based on members' responses to questions like those found in Table 13–1. Another way to understand an organization's culture is in terms of myths and stories, symbols, rituals, and language (Schein, 1985). A more detailed description of the four, key factors identified by Schein can be found in Highlight 13–6.

Here is an example of how stories contribute to organizational culture. A consultant was asked to help a plant that had been having morale and production problems for years. After talking with several individuals at the plant, the

HIGHLIGHT 13–6

Schein's Four Key Organizational Culture Factors

Myths and stories are the tales about the organization that are passed down over time and communicate a story of the organization's underlying values. Virtually any employee of Wal-Mart can tell you stories about Sam Walton and his behavior—how he rode around in his pickup truck, how he greeted people in the stores, and how he tended to "just show up" at different times. The Center for Creative Leadership has stories about its founder, H. Smith Richardson, who as a young man creatively used the mail to sell products. Sometimes stories and myths are transferred between organizations even though the truth may not lie wholly in either one. A story is told in AT&T about one of its founders and how he trudged miles and miles through a blizzard to repair a faulty component so that a woman living by herself in a rural community could get phone service. Interestingly enough, this same story is also told in MCI.

    Symbols and artifacts are objects that can be seen and noticed and that describe various aspects of the culture. In almost any building, for example, symbols and artifacts provide information about the organization's culture. For example, an organization may believe in egalitarian principles, and that might be reflected in virtually everyone having the same size office. Or there can be indications of opulence, which convey a very different message. Even signs might act as symbols or artifacts of underlying cultural values. At one university that believed students should have first priority for facilities, an interesting sign showed up occasionally to reinforce this value. It was not a road sign, but a sign appearing on computer monitors. When the university's main computer was being overused, the computer was programmed to identify nonstudent users, note the overload, and issue a warning to nonstudent users to sign off. This was a clear artifact, or symbol, underlying the priority placed on students at that school.

    Rituals are recurring events or activities that reflect important aspects of the underlying culture. An organization may have spectacular sales meetings for its top performers and spouses every two years. This ritual would be an indication of the value placed on high sales and meeting high quotas. Another kind of ritual is the retirement ceremony. Elaborate or modest retirement ceremonies may signal the importance an organization places on its people.

    Language concerns the jargon or idiosyncratic terms of an organization and can serve several different purposes relevant to culture. First, the mere fact that some know the language and some do not indicates who is in the culture and who is not. Second, language can also provide information about how people within a culture view others. Third, language can be used to help create a culture. A good example of the power of language in creating culture is in the words employees at Disneyland or Walt Disney World use in referring to themselves and park visitors. Employees—*all* employees, from the costumed Disney characters to

---

HIGHLIGHT 13–6 *(concluded)*

popcorn vendors—are told to think of themselves as members of a cast, and *never* to be out of character. Everything happening at the park is part of the "show," and those who paid admission to enter the park are not mere tourists, but rather "the audience." Virtually everyone who visits the Disney parks is impressed with the consistently friendly behavior of its staff, a reflection of the power of words in creating culture. (Of course, a strict and strongly enforced policy concerning courtesy toward park guests also helps.)

---

consultant believed he had located the problem. It seems everyone he talked to told him about "Sam," the plant manager. He was a giant of a man with a terrible temper. He had demolished unacceptable products with a sledgehammer, stood on the plant roof screaming at workers, and done countless other things sure to intimidate everyone around. The consultant decided he needed to go talk to this plant manager. When he did so, however, he met a very agreeable person named Paul. Sam, it seems, had been dead for nearly a decade, but his legacy lived on (Dumaine, 1990).

It is important for leaders to realize that they can play an active role in changing an organization's culture, not just be influenced by it (Bass, 1985; Kouzes & Posner, 1987; Schein, 1985; Tichy & Devanna, 1986). Leaders can change culture by attending to or ignoring particular issues, problems, or projects. They can modify culture through their reactions to crises, by rewarding new or different kinds of behavior, or by eliminating previous punishments or negative consequences for certain behaviors. Their general personnel policies send messages about the value of employees to the organization (e.g., cutting wages to avoid layoffs). They can use role modeling and self-sacrifice as a way to inspire or motivate others to work more vigorously or interact with each other differently. Finally, leaders can also change culture by the criteria they use to select or dismiss followers.

Changing an organization's culture, of course, takes time and effort, and sometimes it may be extremely difficult. This is especially true in very large organizations or those with strong cultures (see, for example, Highlight 13–7). New organizations, on the other hand, do not have the traditions, stories or myths, or established rites to the same extent that older companies do, and it may be easier for leaders to change culture in these organizations.

Why would a leader *want* to change an organization's culture? It all should depend on whether the culture is having a positive or negative impact on various desirable outcomes. We remember one organization with a very "polite" culture, an aspect that seemed very positive at first. There were never any po-

---

HIGHLIGHT 13–7

John Delorean and Counterculture at GM

One of the more interesting stories about organizational culture and the actions taken to change a culture concerns John DeLorean (Martin & Siehl, 1983). DeLorean was a senior executive at GM, an institution with a well-established culture. One of GM's key cultural values was showing *deference and respect to authority*. For example, subordinates were expected to meet out-of-town superiors at the airport, carry their bags, pay their hotel and meal bills, and chauffeur them around day and night. Additionally, the more senior the executive, the bigger the traveling party would be. Some employees were so eager to please their boss that a group of Chevrolet sales people had a refrigerator put in the hotel room of a visiting senior executive after they had learned he liked to have a few cold beers and to make a sandwich before going to bed. Unfortunately, the door to the suite was too small to accomodate the refrigerator, so the Chevrolet sales personnel went so far as to hire a crane to bring in and later remove the refrigerator through the windows of the suite. A second core value at GM was *communicating invisibilty by visible cues*. Ideal GM employees dressed identically, had the same office decor and layout, were "team players," and could easily fit in without drawing attention to themselves. The last key cultural value at GM was *loyalty to one's boss*. Loyalty to one's boss was clearly evident in the ritual of the retirement dinner, where a loyal subordinate was given the task of providing a detailed account of the retiree's steady rise through the corporation, counterpointed with allusions to the retiree's charming wife and family.

DeLorean took a number of actions to change the dominant culture at GM. First, DeLorean liked independence and dissent, and he modeled the behavior he wished others to emulate. He wore suits that stood out, and when appointed to head the Chevrolet division, he immediately changed the office furniture, carpeting, and decor and allowed executives to decorate their offices any way they wanted to "within reasonable limits." Second, because DeLorean believed that subordinates were more productive doing work than catering to superiors, he traveled by himself and did not greet his superiors at the airport, nor did he have his subordinates pick him up. Third, he changed the performance appraisal system within his division. Subordinates were to be rewarded on the basis of objective performance data, not subjective data that indicated a willingness to fit in. Although for a time DeLorean managed to maintain a delicate balance between culture and counterculture, his dissent was eventually met with disfavor, and he left GM to form a company of his own. Nevertheless, DeLorean's story provides several insights about the pervasiveness of organizational culture and the actions a leader might take to change culture.

---

tentially destructive emotional outbursts in the organization, and there was an apparent concern for other individuals' feelings in all interactions. However, a darker side of that culture gradually became apparent. When it was appropriate to give feedback for performance appraisals or employee development, supervisors were hesitant to raise negative aspects of behavior; they interpreted doing so as not being polite. And so the organization continued to be puzzled by employee behavior that tended not to improve; the organization was a victim of its own culture.

Leaders especially need to be sensitive to how their own "brilliant ideas" may adversely impact subtle but important aspects of organizational culture. What may appear to be a major technical innovation (and therefore seemingly desirable) may also be devastating to organizational culture. For example, for hundreds of years in England, coal was mined by teams of three persons each. In England, coal is layered in very narrow seams, most only a few feet high. In the past, the only practical means to get the coal out was to send the three-person teams of miners down into the mines to dig coal from the seam and then haul it to the surface on a tram. These mining teams had extremely high levels of group cohesiveness. A technological development called the long-wall method of coal extraction was to upset these close relationships, however. In the long-wall method, workers were arrayed all along an entire seam of coal rather than in distinct teams, and the method should have resulted in higher productivity among the miners. However, the breakdown of the work teams led to unexpected decreases in productivity, much higher levels of worker dissatisfaction, and even disruption of social life among the miners' families. Although the long-wall method was technically superior to the three-person mining team, the leaders of the coal-mining companies failed to consider the cultural consequences of this technological advancement (Emery & Trist, 1965).

After reading these examples, you may be asking whether it is better for leaders to create cultures that emphasize interpersonal relationships or organizational productivity. We can glean some insights into this question by looking at Mitchell's (1985) study of two groups of successful organizations. Mitchell compared two different groups of organizational cultures: those of organizations considered well managed; and those of organizations considered well liked by people working in the organization. The former group was comprised of the 62 organizations identified in *In Search of Excellence* (Peters & Waterman, 1982), and the latter group was comprised of firms identified in *The 100 Best Companies to Work for in America* (Levering, Moskowitz, & Katz, 1984).

Interestingly, there was relatively little overlap between the two lists. According to Mitchell, this lack of overlap was due primarily to differences between task- and relationship-oriented organizational cultures. Cultures in the well-liked organizations emphasized making employees feel they were part of a family, reducing social distance, and making the organization a pleasant one to work in. Cultures in the well-managed organizations, on the other hand, were much more manipulative. Those firms had cultures that valued people not for themselves but as instruments of productivity. Although which type of culture is best for an organization is still under debate, it is important to note that the 62 companies deemed excellently managed by Peters and Waterman did not provide any higher returns on investments than less-well-managed firms (Simpson & Ireland, 1987), and many of these 62 companies and cultures look considerably less excellent today.

An Afterthought on Organizational Issues for Students and Young Leaders

Let us conclude this section by adding an afterthought about what relevance it may have for students or others at the early stages of their careers, or at lower levels of leadership within their organizations. It is unlikely that such individuals will be asked soon to redesign their organization's structure or change its culture. The preceding sections were not intended as a how-to manual for changing culture. On the other hand, it has been our experience that younger colleagues sometimes develop biased impressions of leaders or have unrealistic expectations about decision making in organizations, based on their lack of familiarity with and appreciation for the sorts of organizational dynamics discussed in this section. In other words, one of the primary reasons for being familiar with such organizational variables is the context they provide for understanding the leadership process at your own level in the organization.

ENVIRONMENTAL CHARACTERISTICS

The last level of situational analysis concerns situational factors outside the task or organization that still affect the leadership process. These include technological, economic, political, social, and legal forces. For example, imagine how changing economic conditions, such as threats of layoffs from a recession or a hostile takeover, would affect leaders' and followers' behavior. These factors often create anxiety and therefore cause an increase in employees' security needs. They also tend to result in decreased training budgets for workers (Bass, 1990). Political changes also can have substantial impacts on leaders and followers. Just imagine, for example, how leaders' and followers' behaviors are changing in Eastern Europe as the various countries move from communist systems to private ownership of companies. Legal forces affecting Western organizations include those contributing to the growth of new industries (e.g., industrial waste disposal) or to personnel reductions in other industries due to changes in governmental rules and regulations (Ungson, James, & Spicer, 1985). Finally, technological advances are changing leader-follower relationships. For example, the advent of personal computers, fax machines, and the modem allow people to work at geographically dispersed locations.

Technology and Uncertainty

Technology affects the leadership process in other ways as well. For example, it might determine what design is best for an organization (Woodward, 1965). In environments of low **technological complexity,** workers play a large role and are able to modify their behavior depending on the situation. In environments of high technological complexity, there is a highly predictable work flow.

Examples of organizations in environments of low technological complexity are printing shops, tailor shops, or cabinet makers. In each case, the organization is well suited to meeting specific customer orders. One of the authors of this book recently encountered an organization fitting this mold in trying to find an oak wall unit that would meet his requirements for a stereo system. After much frustrating shopping and finding a number of mass-produced units that would *not* work, he found a shop that had a variety of different units. Some of these came close to what he needed, but even the closest was not quite right. After listening in detail to the requirements, the owner agreed he didn't have anything on the floor that would work. In the next breath, however, he said, "But if you can draw it, we can build it."

A higher level of technological complexity occurs when mass production is the focus and orders are filled from inventory. An example would be furniture purchased from large warehouse stores. As opposed to the individually crafted wall unit described above, most furniture is not specifically designed and built precisely to meet special customer needs. Instead, manufacturers produce large quantities of various pieces of furniture likely to adequately meet the tastes and needs of most customers.

The highest level of technological complexity occurs when a continuous process is mechanized from beginning to end. People don't play much of a role in such organizations at all except to monitor the process flow and detect problems. Oil refining operations, chemical production plants, and nuclear power plants are all examples of continuous process organizations. In such plants, people are merely observing and monitoring the processes and detecting anomalies that need to be corrected.

The significance of such a range of technological complexity is that different kinds of organizational structures or designs are best suited for different technological environments. An organization is most likely to be successful if the structure fits the technology. If the technological environment is one of moderately high complexity (like large furniture-manufacturing companies), a mechanistic or bureaucratic structure to the organization may be most appropriate. On the other hand, if the technological environment is one of low complexity (like the custom cabinetmaker or printer), setting up a rigid, bureaucratic structure will make it difficult for your organization to produce and "flex" as required by the different specific orders.

In addition to technology, the degree of **environmental uncertainty** also affects optimal organizational design. In stable environments where there is little change, a relatively formalized, centralized, and bureaucratic structure may be desirable. In turbulent environments, on the other hand, structures should be flexible enough to adapt to changing conditions (Burns & Stalker, 1961). In a similar fashion, flat, highly differentiated, and organic structures are most appropriate for very uncertain environments (Lawrence & Lorsch, 1967a, 1967b).

Crises

Another environmental variable that affects the leadership process is the presence or absence of **crises.** Some researchers believe crises play such an important part in charismastic leadership that certain leaders will purposely create crises in order to be perceived as being charismatic (Bass, 1985; Curphy, 1991; Roberts & Bradley, 1988). Furthermore, the behaviors associated with effective leadership during crises differ from those associated with noncrisis situations. During crises, followers are more likely to look to leaders to identify the problem as well as develop and implement a solution. Thus, work groups facing strong deadlines or crises generally expect their leaders to be more assertive, directive, and decisive (Mulder & Stemerding, 1963). Moreover, leaders are less apt to use participation or consultation during crises (Mulder, de Jong, Koppelaar, & Verhage, 1986; Pfeffer & Salancik, 1975). These findings make sense when contrasting emergency and nonemergency situations. For example, surgeons spend considerable time consulting with colleagues prior to conducting a difficult surgery. However, surgeons do not have time to consult with other specialists when a patient's heart has just stopped during surgery; the doctor must quickly diagnose the reason for the heart failure and coordinate the efforts of the surgical team for the patient to live. Similarly, coaches often spend considerable time consulting with other coaches and staff members when preparing for games, but during particularly close games, they may not even have the time to consult with their own staffs.

The Demands-Constraints-Choices Model

One theory of leadership that cuts across task, organizational, and environment levels of analysis is Stewart's (1967, 1976, 1982) demands-constraints-choices model. Using data collected from in-depth studies of managers using diaries, observations, and interviews, Stewart (1982) maintained that any leader's job could be described using three dimensions. **Demands** are role expectations set by superiors, deadlines, rules, regulations, policies, and so on. These are situational factors the leader simply must conform to in order to survive in the role. As might be expected, the demands on locally elected officials, fast-food restaurant managers, or first-line supervisors in a manufacturing plant can differ considerably.

Constraints differ from demands in that they are organizational or environmental factors that limit a leader's range of actions. For example, union contracts, governmental labor laws, available equipment and resources, personnel flexibility, market conditions, and technology all limit what a leader can or cannot do in response to a particular situation. Finally, **choices** are a leader's discretionary behaviors. In other words, choices are those opportunities or activities leaders freely choose; they might include the prioritization of unit goals or assignment of personnel to different teams.

Stewart's model has several important implications for leadership practitioners. First, the model provides a useful way to understand how the leadership process can differ across situations. For example, two positions may require the same type of technical expertise but may differ in terms of demands, constraints, and choices; the manager of a tire recycling plant may have the same technical expertise as an engineer working the company's research-and-development division, but the demands, constraints, and choices facing these two people may not be the same.

Stewart (1982) claimed that successful managers were those who quickly identified and worked to reduce the demands and constraints placed on them. This in turn helped to increase the latitude leaders had in determining unit strategies and objectives (i.e., choices). Thus, effective leaders were not those who adapted to the demands and constraints of the position but rather took an active role in reducing the amount of influence these factors had on them.

Although Stewart's ideas may seem intuitively appealing, her model does underestimate the importance of a leader's abilities, interpersonal skills, and technical expertise in determining leader effectiveness. For example, leaders with good interpersonal skills may be better able to persuade others to modify demands and constraints. Leaders with relatively poor interpersonal skills will have a much more difficult time generating enthusiasm in top management about the importance of new projects or convincing them about the need for additional resources for their work units. Therefore, we again must note the ultimate inadequacy of any approach to conceptualizing leadership that focuses too narrowly on just one element of the leader-follower-situation framework (in this case, too much on the situation.).

STRESS

This chapter has looked at how leader-follower interactions may be influenced by aspects of the situation at the task, organizational, and environmental levels. One important situational variable that cuts across all these levels is stress. Stress can be a huge factor in determining leadership success or failure, so we will examine it in some detail in this section.[1] The following subsections review what stress is, what its effects are, and how stress can affect a leader's ability to successfully lead a group.

---

[1]Highlight 13–8 describes one young leader's stress and how he dealt with it.

HIGHLIGHT 13–8

Taking Charge

A critical period for any leader often involves those first few moments and days of assuming command. It is a time when first impressions are formed and expectations are set. It is a crucial time for any leader in any situation, but can be a matter of life or death for a young leader in a combat situation. Here are one young officer's first reactions upon arriving in Southeast Asia to command a platoon.

> I was alone. That was my first sensation as a leader. The men were going about the morning's business—breaking out C rations, relieving themselves, shaving, brushing their teeth. They moved among each other comfortably, a word here, a smile there. I could hear snatches of conversation: "A good night's sleep . . ." "Only ninety days left." Occasionally a man would nod in my direction, or glance at me for a fleeting moment.
>
> I gathered up my belongings—weapon, web gear, and rucksack—and moved toward the command post. I needed a few minutes to gather my thoughts before I made my debut as a platoon leader. I knew it was going to be a tricky business.
>
> I had assumed that I would have a company commander nearby to give me my orders. But I had not even met him yet; I would not meet him for weeks. The fact was, I was totally on my own. What should I do? Whose advice could I ask? The platoon sergeant's? The squad leaders'? In time I would listen to their ideas and incorporate them with my own, but I could hardly begin my tour with "Well what do you think we ought to do, men?" No, I knew that the basic decisions were mine to make.
>
> The first few moments would be crucial. Obviously, I was the object of interest that morning. Everyone was wondering what the new Lieutenant would be like, and I would be telling them with my first words, my gestures, my demeanor, my eyes. I would have no grace period in which to learn my way around. This was a life and death environment. If I began with a blunder, my credibility as a leader would be shot, and so might some of the men.
>
> I decided to begin by giving my attention to tactics. In a military environment, everything is determined by tactical considerations. Where you sleep, when you sleep, where you go, what you do, and in whose company you do it—all are dictated by underlying tactical necessities. I would communicate my style of leadership through my tactical instructions.
>
> As I surveyed the soldiers, the nearby village, the distant rice paddies, the heavy undergrowth, the varied terrain, my mind raced back over the years of tactical training I had received. Conscious of the stares of the men, I hoped to appear composed as I fought back the panic of having to decide, both quickly and correctly.

Source: J. M. McDonough, *Platoon Leader* (San Francisco: Presidio Press, 1985), pp. 30–31. Reprinted with permission.

What Is Stress

Stress can be understood either as an independent or dependent variable. As a dependent variable, stress refers to a person's responses to a perceived threat, such as receiving a failing grade on a physics exam, arriving noticeably late to a meeting, or playing a sudden-death overtime period in hockey. On the other hand, stress can also be an independent variable. Researchers often manipulate the level of stress in subjects and observe how well subjects can perform relatively difficult or easy tasks.

We will define **stress** as the whole process by which we appraise and respond to events that challenge or threaten us (Myers, 1989). These responses usually include increased levels of emotional arousal and changes in physiological symptoms, such as increases in perspiration and heart rates, cholesterol levels, or blood pressure. Stress often occurs in situations that are overly complex, demanding, or unclear. **Stressors** are those specific characteristics in individuals, tasks, organizations, or the environment that pose some degree of threat or challenge to people (see Table 13–3). Although all the factors in Table 13–3 probably have an adverse impact on people, the degree of stress associated with each of them depends on one's overall level of stress tolerance and previous experience with the stressor in question (Benner, 1984). Similarly, it is important to realize that stress is in the eye of the beholder—what one person may see as challenging and potentially rewarding, another may see as threatening and distressful (McCauley, 1987; Staw, 1984).

Who do you think typically experiences greater stress—leaders or followers? In one sense, the answer is the same as that for much psychological research: it depends. The role of leader certainly can be quite stressful. Leaders face at least one major stressful event at least once a month (Ivancevich, Schweiger, & Ragan, 1986). Followers' stress levels, on the other hand, often depend on their leaders. Leaders can help followers cope with stress or, alternatively, actually increase their followers' stress levels. Many leaders recognize when followers are under a lot of stress and will give them time off, try to reduce their workload, or take other actions to help followers cope. On the other hand, about two out of three workers say their bosses play a bigger part in creating their stress than any other personal, organizational, or environmental factor (R. T. Hogan & Morrison, 1991; Shipper & Wilson, 1992). Similarly, McCormick and Powell (1988) reported that working for a tyrannical boss was the most frequently cited source of stress among workers. It is clear that leaders play a substantial role in how stressful their followers' work experience is, for good or ill.

The Effects of Stress

Stress can either facilitate or inhibit performance, depending on the situation. Too much stress can take a toll on individuals and organizations that includes decreased health and emotional well-being, reduced job performance, and decreased organizational effectiveness (see Highlight 13–9 for an example of how too much stress impaired one person's performance).

In order to understand the effects of stress, an analogy might be helpful. Kites need an optimal amount of wind to fly; they will not fly on windless days, and the string may break on a day that is too windy. You can think of stress as

TABLE 13–3
Job-Related Stressors

Individual Characteristics

Midcareer crises
Obsolescent skills
Dismissal or relocation of a close friend

Job Characteristics

Job insecurity
Time pressures
Role conflict and ambiguity
Work overload
Crowding
Noise
Task interdependence
Competitive work
Repetitive work
Inadequate feedback about performance

Organizational Characteristics

Pay or promotion inequities
Excessive formalization or centralization
Work relocation
Ambiguous goals
Lateral interdependence
Poor relations with boss or colleagues
Unskilled subordinates
Type of organizational design
Organizational culture

Environmental Characteristics

Union demands and constraints
Market conditions
Labor laws, grievances, and lawsuits
Crises
Societal or political changes
Family demands

Source: Modified from A. P. Brief, R. S. Schuler, and M. Van Sell, *Managing Job Stress* (Boston: Little, Brown, 1981).

like the wind for a kite: There is a certain level that is optimal, neither too little nor too much. Another analogy is your car. Just as an automobile engine operates optimally within a certain range of revolutions per minute (RPM), most people function best at certain levels of stress. A certain amount of stress or arousal is helpful in increasing motivation and performance, but too much stress can be counterproductive. For example, it is common and probably help-

---

HIGHLIGHT 13–9

Stress on a TV Game Show

The television game show "Wheel of Fortune" pits contestants against each other in trying to identify common sayings. By spinning a wheel, contestants determine varying dollar amounts to be added to their potential winnings.

The game is similar to the game of Hangman you may have played as a child. It begins with spaces indicating the number of words in a saying and the number of letters in each word. One player spins the wheel, which determines prize money, and then guesses a letter. If the letter appears somewhere in the saying then the player spins the wheel again, guesses another letter, and so on. The letters are "filled in" as they are correctly identified. A player may try to guess the saying after naming a correct letter.

If a player names a letter that does not appear in the saying, then that prize money is not added to the contestant's potential winnings, and play moves on to another contestant.

One day a contestant was playing for over $50,000 to solve the puzzle below. Perhaps because of the stress of being on television and playing for so much money, the contestant could not accurately name a letter for one of the four remaining spaces. Most people, not experiencing such stress, easily solve the problem. Can you? For the answer, see the bottom of the box.

$$T \ H \ E \qquad T \ H \ R \ I \ \_ \ \_$$
$$O \ F \qquad \_ \ I \ \_ \ T \ O \ R \ Y$$
$$A \ N \ D \qquad T \ H \ E$$
$$A \ G \ O \ N \ Y \qquad O \ F$$
$$D \ E \ F \ E \ A \ T$$

Answer: The Thrill of Victory and the Agony of Defeat

---

ful to feel a little anxiety before giving a speech, but being too nervous can destroy one's effectiveness.

The optimal level of stress depends on a number of factors. One is the level of physical activity actually demanded by the task. Another is the perceived difficulty of the task. Performance often suffers when difficult tasks are performed under stressful situations. For example, think how one's performance might differ when learning to first drive a car with an instructor who is quiet and reserved rather than one who yells a lot. Chances are, performance will be much better with the first instructor than with the latter.

*"... Then it's agreed. As a crowd, we'll be subdued in
innings one through seven, then suddenly become a factor
in innings eight and nine ..."*

Tribune Media Services

It is important to note that task difficulty is gererally a function of experience; the more experience one has with a task, the less difficult it becomes. Thus, the more driving experience one has, the easier the task becomes. Moreover, not only do people cope with stress more readily when performing easier tasks; people often need higher levels of stress for performing them optimally. One underlying purpose behind any type of practice, be it football, marching band, soccer, or drama, is to reduce task difficulty and help members or players to perform at an even higher level when faced with the stress of key performances and games.

Although stress can have positive effects, research has focused on the negative implications of too much stress on health and work. In terms of health, stress has been linked to heart disease (Friedman & Ulmer, 1984); immune system deficiencies (Pomerleau & Rodin, 1986); and the growth rates of tumors (Justice, 1985). In terms of work behaviors, both Latack (1986) and Quayle (1983) reported that work-related stress has caused a dramatic increase in drug and alcohol use in the workplace, and Jamal (1984) found that stress was positively related to absenteeism, intentions to quit, and turnover. Relatedly, Quayle (1983) and Albrecht (1979) estimated the economic impact of stress to companies in the Unites States to be somewhere between $70 and $150 billion annually. Stress can also affect the decision-making process. Although leaders need to act decisively in stressful situations (i.e., crises), they may not make good decisions under stress (Fiedler, 1992; Gibson, 1992; Mulder, de Jong, Koppelaar, & Verhage, 1986). According to Weschler (1955) and Tjosvold (1985), people make poor decisions when under stress because they revert to their intuition rather than thinking rationally about problems.

Leaders and Stress: Cognitive Resources Theory

As you might recall from Chapter Seven, leader intelligence is one of the best single predictors of leadership effectiveness, although the relationship between intelligence and effectiveness is far from perfect. Recent research suggests that stress plays a key role in determining just how a leader's intelligence affects his effectiveness. It may be that leaders act one way in normal circumstances and quite differently when under stress. That would be consistent with other findings that stress affects behavior in various ways. Simon (1987), for example, stated that lying was much more often the result of panic than of purposeful scheming. Because people may have different "stress" and "normal" behavior patterns, Fiedler and Garcia(1987) developed the cognitive resources theory (CRT) as an explanation for the different relationships between leaders' intelligence and experience levels and group performance in stressful versus nonstressful conditions.

Before delving into CRT in depth, it will help first to define several of the theory's key concepts. Certainly one of these is intelligence. Fiedler and Garcia (1987) defined intelligence in much the same way it was defined in Chapter Seven. Intelligence is one's all-around effectiveness in activities directed by thought and is typically measured using standardized intelligence tests. Another key concept is experience, which represents the habitual behavior patterns, overlearned knowledge, and skills acquired for effectively dealing with task-related problems. Although experience is often gained under stressful and unpleasant conditions, experience also provides a "crash plan" to revert back to when under stress (Fiedler, 1992). For most of the CRT studies, experience has been defined as time in the job or organization. A third key concept is stress. Stress is often defined as the result of conflicts with superiors or the apprehension associated with performance evaluation (Gibson, 1992). This interpersonal stress is believed to be emotionally disturbing and can divert attention from problem-solving activities (Sarason, 1986). In sum, cognitive resource theory provides a conceptual scheme for explaining how leader behavior changes depending on perceived stress levels to impact group performance.

Cognitive resources theory makes two major predictions with respect to intelligence, experience, stress, and group performance. First, because experienced leaders have a greater repertoire of behaviors to fall back on, leaders with greater experience but lower intelligence are hypothesized to have higher performing groups under conditions of high stress. Leaders' experience levels can interfere with performance under low-stress conditions, however. That leads to the second hypothesis. Because experience leads to habitual behavior patterns, leaders with high levels of experience will have a tendency to use old solutions to problems when creative solutions are called for (Fiedler, 1992). Thus, leaders with higher levels of intelligence but less experience should not be constrained by previously acquired behavior patterns and will have higher-performing groups under low-stress conditions. In other words, experience is helpful when one is under stress but is often a hindrance to performance in the absence of stress.

These two major predictions of CRT can be readily seen in everyday life. For the most part, it is not the most intelligent but the most experienced members of sporting teams, marching bands, acting troops, or volunteer organizations who are selected to be leaders. These leaders are often chosen because other members recognize their ability to perform well under the high levels of stress associated with sporting events and public performances. In addition, research with combat troops, firefighters, and students has provided reasonably strong support for the two major tenets of CRT (Fiedler & Garcia, 1987; Fiedler, 1992; Gibson, 1992).

Despite this initial empirical support, one problem with CRT concerns the apparent dichotomy between intelligence and experience. Fiedler and Garcia's (1987) initial investigations of CRT did not examine the possibility that leaders could be both intelligent and experienced. Subsequent research by Gibson (1992) showed not only that many leaders were both intelligent and experienced, but also that these leaders would fall back on their experience in stressful situations and use their intelligence to solve group problems in less stressful situations.

SITUATIONAL ENGINEERING

One of the most important points this chapter can make concerns the idea of situational engineering. Although leaders' and followers' behaviors are affected by task, organizational, and environmental factors, all too often leaders and followers completely overlook how changing the situation can help them to change their behavior. Just as a dieter can better stick to a diet by identifying bad eating habits and limiting food cues, so can a leader or follower become more effective by identifying problem areas and restructuring the situation so that these problems become easier to overcome.

Say, for example, a leader attended a leadership development program and received feedback that he did not interact enough with his subordinates. This leader might set a goal and may genuinely make an attempt to increase the level of interaction with his followers. Because his typical day is hectic and he manages a work group with a high level of lateral interdependence, however, situational demands may more or less force him to revert to his old behaviors. This leader would be likely to realize more success if he *also* restructured the situation in order to facilitate the accomplishment of this goal.

He could, for example, delegate more activities to subordinates. This would give the leader more opportunities to interact with followers (by mutually setting performance goals and monitoring progress), and it would give the leader more time to engage in other activities. Moreover, the leader could project a more approachable and friendly attitude by rearranging office furniture, keeping his door open as much as possible, and building specific times into his daily schedule to "manage by wandering around."

There are a variety of ways in which leaders and followers can change the task, organizational, and environmental factors affecting their behaviors and attitudes. By asking questions and listening effectively, leaders may be able to redesign work using the suggestions from Hackman and Oldham's (1980) job characteristics model or Herzberg's (1966) two-factor theory in order to improve followers' satisfaction and productivity levels. Similarly, leaders might discover ways to adjust followers' workloads, responsibilities, or levels of task interdependence; rearrange office layouts; establish new or different policies or procedures; or modify reporting relationships and appraisal systems (Yukl, 1989). More senior leaders might be able to change the organization itself or work to influence changes in the environment. Perhaps the most important point regarding situational engineering is to get leaders and followers to understand that the situation is not set in concrete, and to think about how they can change the situation in order for everyone to be more satisfied and productive.

SUMMARY

The situation may well be the most complex factor in the leader-follower-situation framework. Moreover, situations vary not only in complexity but also in strength. Situational factors can play such a pervasive role that they can effectively minimize the effects of personality traits, intelligence, values, and preferences on leaders' and followers' behaviors, attitudes, and relationships. Given the dynamic nature of leadership situations, finding fairly consistent results is a highly encouraging accomplishment for leadership researchers.

As an organizing framework, this chapter reviewed some of the consistent findings regarding the role of task, organizational, and environmental factors in the leadership process. In terms of task factors, leaders need to be aware of how task interdependence and feedback, skill variety, autonomy, and task structure can affect both their own and their followers' behaviors, and how they might change these factors in order to improve followers' satisfaction and performance. Research also has shown that organizational factors, such as lateral interdependence, structure, design, and culture play major roles in determining why certain communication problems and conflicts might exist, how work is accomplished, and why some people may be more satisfied in the organization than others. Finally, factors in the environment, such as legal, political, or economic forces can also affect leaders' and followers' behaviors. Sometimes these may effectively wipe out any changes a leader may make to improve productivity or satisfaction among work-group members.

Stress is one consequence of many of the situational factors leaders and followers face. In work settings, stress is often a function of boring, repetitive work, ambiguous tasks, role conflicts, time pressures, or uncertain job security. Stress generally is related to increased incidence of heart disease, weakened immune systems, and tumor growth rates as well as increased turnover, absenteeism, and drug and alcohol use among workers. One effective way of reducing stress and improving followers' satisfaction and performance is through situational engineering. Situational engineering involves changing various aspects of the task, organizational, or even environmental factors affecting workers in order to achieve more positive work outcomes.

KEY TERMS AND CONCEPTS

role theory	horizontal complexity
multiple influence model	vertical complexity
situational levels	spatial complexity
task structure	formalization
skill variety	substitutes for leadership
task identity	centralization
task significance	organizational design
autonomy	cognitive resource theory
feedback	situational engineering
task interdependence	functional design
level of authority	product design
organizational structure	matrix design

lateral interdependence environmental uncertainty

organizational culture crises

organizational climate demands

myths and stories constraints

symbols and artifacts choices

rituals stress

language stressors

technological complexity

DISCUSSION QUESTIONS

1. The term *bureaucratic* has a pejorative connotation to most people. Can you think of any positive aspects of a bureacracy?

2. Think of a crisis situation you are familiar with involving a group, team, organization, or country, and analyze it in terms of the leader-follower-situation framework. For example, were the followers "looking for" a certain kind of behavior from the leader? Did the situation "demand" it? Did the situation, in fact, contribute to a particular leader's emergence?

3. Do you see stress affecting some leaders the way cognitive resource theory says it does? Have you seen any situations where, under stress, a leader's intelligence became a disadvantage?

SUGGESTED READINGS

Deal, T. E., and A. A. Kennedy, *Corporate Cultures.* Reading, Mass.: Addison-Wesley, 1982.

Morrison, A. M.; R. P. White; and E. Van Velsor, *Breaking the Glass Ceiling; Can Women Reach the Top of America's Largest Corporations?* Reading, Mass.: Addison-Wesley, 1987.

Chapter Fourteen

Leadership Skills III

INTRODUCTION

L ike Chapters Nine and Twelve, this chapter provides further advice and reviews relevant research about improving your leadership, followership, and personal effectiveness. More specifically, this chapter provides ideas on how you can improve your skills in conducting meetings; encouraging creativity; managing conflict and negotiating; managing stress; and diagnosing performance problems in individuals, groups, and organizations. In addition to self-improvement, these skills also provide different perspectives for understanding various group or organizational issues. There are many ways one might explain, for example, the low satisfaction among members of a work group. It could be due to poor information exchanges as the result of poorly planned meetings, unresolved conflict among the group members, heightened stress, or the leader's misdiagnosis of a performance problem, which in turn caused the team to fail to achieve a goal. Thus, like the skills described in the earlier chapters, the five skills that will be discussed in this chapter provide multiple perspectives for examining the leadership process (also see Highlight 14–1).

CONDUCTING MEETINGS

Meetings are a fact of organizational life. It is difficult to imagine a leader who could (or should) avoid them, particularly when groups, committees, or teams have high levels of task or lateral interdependence. Well-planned and well-led meetings are a valuable mechanism for accomplishing diverse goals and are an important way of exchanging information and keeping open lines of communication within and between work groups or volunteer organizations (Bass, 1990; O'Reilly, 1977). Although meetings have many advantages, they also cost time and money. The annual cost of meetings in the corporate sector alone may well be in the billions of dollars. Furthermore, unnecessary or inefficient meetings can be frustrating and are often a source of dissatisfaction for participants. Given the investment of time and energy meetings require, leaders have a responsibility to make them as productive as possible. Guth and Shaw (1980) provided seven helpful tips for running meetings, which follow.

Perhaps the most important step in conducting a meeting is to take the time to *determine whether or not a meeting is really necessary*. If you are evaluating whether or not to have a meeting, assess what it can accomplish. Only have a meeting if the potential benefits outweigh the costs. As part of this process, get the opinions of the other participants beforehand if that is possible. Moreover, if meetings are regularly scheduled, then you should have significant business

---

HIGHLIGHT 14–1

Leadership Quotes, Chapter Fourteen

The best way to have a good idea is to have a lot of ideas.

Dr. Linus Pauling

The Chinese use two brush strokes to write the word crisis. *One brush stroke stands for danger, the other for opportunity. In a crisis, be aware of the danger—but recognize the opportunity.*

Richard M. Nixon

Creativeness often consists of merely turning up what is already there. Did you know that right and left shoes were thought up only a little more than a century ago?

Bernice Fitz-Gibbon

Creativity is so delicate a flower that praise tends to make it bloom, while discouragement often nips it in the bud. Any of us will put out more and better ideas if our efforts are appreciated.

Alex F. Osborn

Creative minds always have been known to survive any kind of bad training.

Anna Freud

Genius, in truth, means little more than the faculty of perceiving in an unhabitual way.

William James

He who has a why to live for can bear with almost any how.

Nietzsche

For all your days prepare, and meet them ever alike: When you are the anvil, bear; when you are the hammer, strike.

Edwin Markham

---

to conduct in each meeting. If not, then these meetings should probably be scheduled less frequently.

Once you have decided that a meeting is necessary, you should then *list your objectives for the meeting and develop a plan for attaining them* in an orderly manner. Prioritize what you hope to accomplish at the meeting. It is often helpful to indicate approximately how much time will be spent on each agenda item. Finally, get the agenda and issues to be covered to the participants well in advance; also let them know who else will be attending.

Besides an agenda, a meeting is often more effective if leaders also provide the other participants with *pertinent reports or support materials well in advance.* Passing out materials and waiting for people to read them at the meeting itself wastes valuable time. Most people will come prepared, having read relevant material beforehand, if you have given it to them, and almost everyone will resent making a meeting longer than necessary doing work that could and should have been done earlier. In a similar vein, prepare well in advance for any presentations you will make. If you did not provide reports before the meeting, then it is often helpful to provide an outline of your presentation for others to take notes on. Finally, of course, be sure the information you pass out is accurate.

Another way to maximize the benefits of meetings is to *pick a time and place as convenient as possible for all participants.* Besides maximizing attendance, this will also keep key participants from being distracted with thoughts of other pressing issues. Similarly, choose a place that is convenient for the participants and suitable for the nature of the meeting. Be sure to consider whether you need such things as a table for the meeting (that has adequate seating); a blackboard, an overhead projector, or similar audiovisual aids; coffee or other refreshments; and directions on how to find the meeting place. And start on time; waiting for stragglers is unfair to those who were punctual, and it sends the wrong signal about the seriousness of the meeting. Also plan and announce a time limit on the meeting beforehand and stick to it.

Once the meeting gets started, is it important for leaders to *stick to the agenda.* It is easy for groups to get sidetracked by tangential issues or good-natured storytelling. Although you should try to keep a cooperative and comfortable climate in the meeting, it is better to err on the side of being organized and businesslike than being lax and laissez-faire. If items were important enough to put on the agenda, they are important enough to get to in the time allotted for the meeting.

Leaders have a responsibility to *encourage participation;* everyone at the meeting should have an opportunity to be heard and should feel some ownership in the meeting's outcome. In some cases, you may need to solicit participation from quieter participants at the meeting, as these members often make valuable contributions to the group when given the chance. Furthermore, ensuring that the quieter members participate will also help you to avoid interpreting someone's quietness as implied consent or agreement. By the same token, you sometimes may need to curtail the participation of more verbal and outspoken participants. You can do this respectfully by merely indicating that the group has a good idea of their position and that it would be useful also to hear from some others. You also help encourage relevant participation by providing interim summaries of the group's discussion.

During a meeting, the points of discussion and various decisions or actions taken may seem clear to you. However, do not trust your memory to preserve them all. *Take minutes for the record* so you and others can reconstruct what the participants were thinking and why you did or did not take some action. Record decisions and actions to be taken, including *who* will be responsible for doing it and *when* it is supposed to be accomplished. Such records are also very useful for preparing future meeting agendas.

By following the preceding simple steps, both leaders and followers are likely to get much more out of their meetings as well as appear well organized and effective.

ENCOURAGING CREATIVITY

Sometimes the problems we face are just like problems we have faced before. At those times it is usually most efficient to solve these problems with formulas or procedures that have worked in the past. Some schoolwork consists of learning the correct solutions for various well-defined sorts of problems. Some math problems, for example, just require applying certain basic formulas to new number sets. Other tasks can be prepared for to a degree but also may present unexpected elements. Preparing for a soccer game consists to a large extent of anticipating various situations and practicing the tasks required to effectively meet them. Commanding large military forces in wartime is facilitated by having practiced "war games" in realistic simulations. The Israeli Defense Forces, for example, prepare for war based on the concept that the most predictable element of battle is its unpredictability; commanders are trained to be innovative and resourceful, and to take advantage of unanticipated situations (Gal, 1986). Success in sports, business, and war often depends on both routinized preparation and the ability to adapt to unexpected changes.

Because organizations face a myriad of supply, customer-service, production, and coordination problems on a daily basis, successful individuals and organizations are those that on a daily basis can generate and implement new and useful ideas. The leader's own creativity certainly can be helpful in that regard. However, it may be even more important for the leader to be able to stimulate creativity in others (Keller, 1989). That can begin with an appreciation of what creativity is and the psychological and organizational factors that block or stifle creativity. In the latter case, creativity can be impeded by perceptual blocks (e.g., failing to see that one thing can be used as something else) and emotional blocks (e.g., fear of failure). Additionally, part of the leader's challenge is appreciating the nature of group interaction and organizational dynamics in the creative process. For example, creativity can be impeded by uncooperativeness and mistrust among co-workers.

What Is Creativity?

Before describing the factors that can facilitate or impede creativity, it is necessary to first define what creativity is. According to Cronbach (1984), **creativity** or **divergent thinking** is one's adeptness in making fresh observations and ideas. Creativity is the ability to see something in a new way. When Newton ''discovered'' gravity, for example, his great insight was recognizing an essential similarity between a falling apple and the orbiting moon (Koestler, 1964). The inventor of Velcro got his idea while picking countless thistles out of his socks; he realized the same principle producing his frustration might be translated into a useful fastener. The inventor of 3M's Post-It notes was frustrated about bookmarks in his church hymnal continually sliding out of place and saw a solution in a low-tack adhesive discovered by a fellow 3M scientist. To the latter scientist, the low-tack glue represented a failure since he had been trying to develop a new superglue. To the Post-It inventor, however, it was a step toward a bookmark that would attach to a page and come off without damaging the printing. All these insights involved looking at one thing and seeing something else. Thus, creativity is the ability to look at things from new and different perspectives. However, these novel ideas must be accompanied by some level of critical thinking or evaluation, as novel ideas in and of themselves may not be very helpful in solving a problem. Moreover, it is important to note that creativity seems to be specific to certain fields and subfields: Most composers are not architects, and most writers are not mathematicians (Cronbach, 1984).

Two of the more interesting questions surrounding creativity and divergent thinking concern the role of intelligence and the assessment of creative ability. Guilford (1967) said that divergent thinking was related to intelligence but still a separate ability. Barron and Harrington (1981) maintained that intelligence was a necessary but not a sufficient condition for creativity. Some level of intelligence seems necessary for creativity, but having a high level of intelligence is no guarantee that someone will be creative. Figure 14–1 provides a depiction of this proposed relationship between intelligence and creativity.

In addition, actually assessing creativity is no simple matter. Tests of creativity or divergent thinking are very different from tests that assess convergent thinking. Tests of **convergent thinking** usually have a single best answer, whereas tests of creativity or divergent thinking have many possible answers (see Table 14–1). Moreover, because creativity is field-specific, it is not clear whether generating as many uses for a common object as possible is at all related to creativity in painting, sculpting, writing music, or solving technical production problems. Relatedly, people often differ considerably in terms of judging the relative creativity of different responses. Unlike convergent tests, for example, there is no set answer or standard for determining whether the title for a short story is truly creative.

FIGURE 14–1

Hypothesized Relationship between Intelligence and Creativity

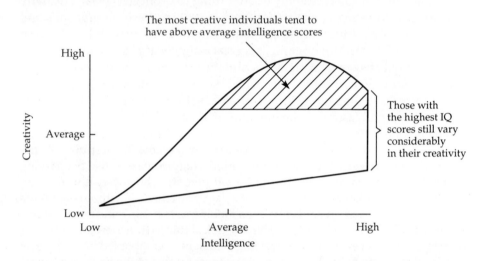

Although creativity may be difficult to measure, it does seem related to how people act. Children with high creativity test scores tend to be expansive and spontaneous, whereas less creative children tend to be more cautious and insecure (Wallach & Kogan, 1965). Adults seen as creative tend to gravitate into certain occupations, such as music, art, drama, or architecture (D. P. Campbell, Hyne, & Nilsen, 1992). Nevertheless, people vary considerably in creativity within any occupation. For example, peers characterized creative female mathematicians as being rebellious and nonconforming, having unconventional

TABLE 14–1

Typical Tests of Divergent Thinking

- *Product improvement.*Individuals are given a drawing of a typical household product and are asked to modify the drawing in any way that would improve the usefulness of the product.

- *Unusual uses.* These tests ask individuals to come up with as many uses for common products, such as paper clips or bricks, as possible.

- *Clever plot titles.* In these tests, people are given a short story to read and are asked to come up with a clever title.

Source: Adapted from L. J. Cronbach, *Essentials of Psychological Testing,* 4th ed. (San Francisco: Harper & Row, 1984).

thought processes, and being thorough and patient in research. Less creative female mathematicians were characterized by their peers as grasping others' ideas quickly, favoring conservative values, and having an active and well-organized mind (Helson, 1971). Creativity has also been found to be related to leadership effectiveness, although the strength of this relationship varies depending on level of authority. Rusmore (1984) and Rusmore and Baker (1987) showed that general intelligence was more highly related to lower-level managers' success and that creativity was more important for upper-level managers' success.

The Components of Creativity

So far we have discussed creativity as a unitary ability. However, research suggests that creativity is made up of three components: *expertise, imaginative thinking,* and *intrinsic motivation* (Kohn, 1987; Sternberg, 1985). Expertise is very important to creativity as it provides an extensive knowledge base from which to generate and critically evaluate solutions to problems. Imaginative thinking is what we traditionally view as creativity; these skills help people see things in new ways or recognize novel patterns or connections. Finally, people will often be the most creative when they are intrinsically interested in or feel challenged by the subject matter or problem itself (Amabile & Hennessey, 1988). Creative people are more likely to focus attention on solving the problem at hand, not on the need to meet deadlines, make money, or impress others.

The story of Chester Carlson provides a good example of how technical expertise, imaginative thinking skills, and intrinsic motivation play important roles in developing a creative and useful solution to a problem. Chester Carlson invented the photocopy duplicating process, which revolutionized office work. Duplicating machines are relied on so much today that most people probably assume the invention was met with instant acceptance. That was not the case, however. Most people do not realize that it was 22 years from the time Carlson got the idea to the time his product became commercially available—or that refining and "selling" his concept was an uphill battle primarily because of the existence of carbon paper. (With carbon paper, people thought, why would you need anything else?) His solution for making copies of documents was certainly imaginative, but it was also derived from his considerable technical expertise. Moreover, his persistence in developing and persuading others of the potential of his process is a testament to the importance of intrinsic motivation in creativity.

Creative thinking is not an entirely rational or conscious process. Many times we do our most imaginative thinking unconsciously; people often gain sudden insights to an old problem out of the blue. There are interesting anecdotal accounts of how different creative thinkers recognized and even harnessed these unconscious processes. Einstein, for example, once remarked that he got his best ideas in the morning when he was shaving. The great inventor Thomas Edison reportedly developed a technique to awaken himself and capture the typically unusual imagery and mental activity occurring as one falls asleep. These thinkers recognized the mind's fertility during its "resting" periods. Einstein's and Edison's receptivity to ideas emerging from their nonlogical mental processes was surely an important part of their genius. They were able to harness their unconscious rather than censor it, as many of us may do by suppressing or discounting mental activity that seems purposeless, nonsensical, or threatening.

Blocks to Creativity

Having an understanding of the three components of creativity can foster insight about the conditions that can hinder or facilitate creativity. One block or hindrance to creativity is a lack of technical expertise. People with little technical expertise will be limited in their ability to generate novel solutions to problems or to see opportunities for improvement. On the other hand, Fiedler's (1992) work in cognitive resource theory (CRT) indicated that having a high level of technical expertise and experience also can hinder the generation of novel solutions. Fiedler (1992) maintained that individuals with lower levels of intelligence but higher levels of experience will often try to resolve new problems in old ways. These past solutions to novel problems are often less than optimal and can impede the creative thought process. Thus, technical expertise can be a two-edged sword: It is a necessary condition for generating creative solutions to problems, but leaders need also to be aware that technical expertise can make them or their followers all too ready to impose old solutions to new problems.

Imaginative thinking skills and idea generation can be hindered if people believe that their ideas will be evaluated. Amabile's (1983, 1987) experiments showed that students who were told their projects were to be judged by experts produced less creative projects than students who were not told their projects would be judged. A similar sort of phenomenon can occur in groups. Even when a group knows its work must ultimately be evaluated, there is a pronounced tendency for members to be evaluative and judgmental too early in the solution-generation process. This tends to reduce the number of creative solutions generated, perhaps because of a generally shared belief in the value of critical thinking (and in some groups the norm seems to be the more criticism the better) and of subjecting ideas to intense scrutiny and evaluation. When members of a group judge ideas as soon as they are offered, two dysfunctional things can happen. People in the group may censor themselves (i.e., not share all their ideas with the group), as even mild rejection or criticism has a significant dampening effect (Prince, 1972), or they may prematurely reject others' ideas through negativistic focus on an idea's flaws rather than its possibilities.

Other potential blocks to creativity concern intrinsic versus extrinsic motivation and autonomy. Research has found that people tend to generate more creative solutions when they are told to focus on the intrinsic motivation for generating solutions (i.e., the pleasure of solving the task itself) rather than focusing on the extrinsic motivation for generating solutions (i.e., public recognition or pay) (Amabile, 1985; Amabile & Hennessey, 1988). Relatedly, leaders having less autonomy and freedom to make decisions, a lower sense of control, and less freedom from constraints were often judged to be less creative (Amabile & Gryskiewicz, 1987).

Steps for Improving Creativity

There are several things leaders can do to increase their own and their followers' creativity. Some of these facilitating factors have already been discussed and include assuring adequate levels of technical expertise, delaying and minimizing the evaluation or judgment of solutions, focusing on the intrinsic motivation of the task, removing unnecessary constraints on followers, and giving followers more latitude in making decisions. One popular technique for stimulating creative thinking in groups is called **brainstorming** (see Highlight 14–2).

An additional thing leaders can do to enhance creativity is to *see things in new ways*, or to look at problems from as many perspectives as possible. This is, though, easier said than done. It can be difficult to see novel uses for things we are very familiar with, or to see such in novel ways. Psychologists call this kind of mental block **functional fixedness** (Duncker, 1945). Creative thinking depends on overcoming the functional fixedness associated with the rigid and stereotyped perceptions we have of the things around us.

One way to see things differently is to think in terms of analogies. Thinking in terms of analogies is a practical extension of Cronbach's (1984) definition of creativity—making fresh observations, or seeing one thing as something else. In this case, the active search for analogies is the essence of the problem-solving method. In fact, finding analogies is the foundation of a commercial creative-problem-solving approach called **Synectics** (W.J.J. Gordon, 1961). An actual example of use of analogies in a Synectics problem-solving group concerned designing a new roofing material that would adjust its color to the season, turning white in the summer to reflect heat and black in the winter to absorb heat. The group's first task was to find an analogy in nature, and it thought of fishes whose colors change to match their surroundings. The mechanism for such changes in fish is the movement of tiny compartments of pigments closer to or farther away from the skin's surface, thus changing its color. After some discussion, the group designed a black roof impregnated with little white plastic

---

HIGHLIGHT 14–2

Steps for Enhancing Creativity through Brainstorming

Brainstorming is a technique designed to enhance the creative potential of any group trying to solve a problem. Leaders should use the following rules when conducting a brainstorming session:

1. *Groups should consist of five to seven people:* Less than five limits the number of ideas generated, but more than seven often can make the session unwieldy. It may be more important to carefully decide who should attend a session than how many people should attend.

2. *Everybody should be given the chance to contribute.* The first phase of brainstorming is idea generation, and members should be encouraged to spontaneously contribute ideas as soon as they get them.

3. *No criticism is allowed during the idea generation phase.* This helps to clearly separate the activities of imaginative thinking and idea production from idea evaluation.

4. *Freewheeling and outlandish ideas should be encouraged.* With some modification, these ideas may be eventually adopted.

5. *"Piggybacking" off others' ideas should be encouraged.* Combining ideas or extending others' ideas often results in better solutions.

6. *The greater the quantity and variety of ideas, the better.* The more ideas generated, the greater the probability a good solution will be found.

7. *Ideas should be recorded.* Ideally, ideas should be recorded on a blackboard or butcher paper so that members can review all of the ideas generated.

8. After all of the ideas have been generated, *each idea should be evaluated* in terms of pros and cons, costs and benefits, feasibility, and so on. Choosing the final solution often depends on the results of these analyses.

Source: A. F. Osborn, *Applied Imagination* (New York: Scribner's, 1963).

---

balls which would expand when it is hot, making the roof lighter, and contract when it is cold, making the roof darker (W.J.J. Gordon, 1961).

Another way to see things differently is to try putting an idea or problem into a picture rather than into words. Feelings or relationships that have eluded verbal description may come out in a drawing, bringing fresh insights to an issue. An example of this is in the following cartoon, which is one professor's response when asked to draw his frustrations with the nature of college education today.

In addition to getting followers to see problems from as many perspectives as possible, a leader can also *use her power constructively to enhance creativity.* As noted earlier, groups may suppress creative thinking by being overly critical or by passing judgment during the solution-generation stage. This effect may be even more pronounced when strong authority relationships and status differ-

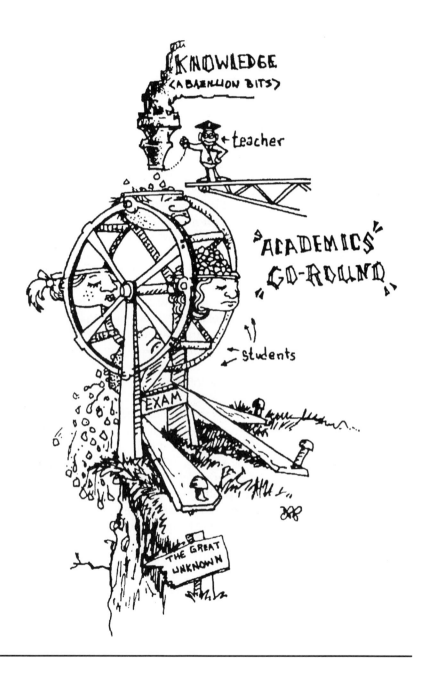

ences are present. Group members may be reluctant to take the risk of raising a "crazy" idea when superiors are present, especially if the leader is generally perceived as unreceptive to new ideas, or they may be reluctant to offer the idea if they believe others in the group will take potshots at it in front of the leader. Leaders who wish to create a favorable climate for fostering creativity need to use their power to encourage the open expression of ideas and to suppress uncooperative or aggressive reactions (overt or covert) between group members. Further, leaders can use their power to encourage creativity by rewarding successes, not by punishing mistakes.

Leaders can also use their power to delegate authority and responsibility, relax followers' constraints, and empower followers to take risks. By taking these steps, leaders can help followers to build idiosyncratic credits, which in turn will encourage them to take risks and to be more creative (see Chapter Six). Along these same lines, the entire climate of an organization can be either more or less conducive to creative thinking, differences that may be due to the use of power within the organization. In an insightful turn of the familiar adage "power corrupts," Kanter (1982) noted how powerlessness also corrupts. She pointed out how managers who feel powerless in an organization may spend more energy guarding their territory than collaborating with others in productive action. The need to actively support followers' creativity may be especially important for leaders in bureaucratic organizations, as such organizations tend to be so inflexible, formalized, and centralized as to make many people in them feel relatively powerless.

Leaders can enhance creativity by *forming diverse problem-solving groups.* Group members with similar experiences, values, and preferences will be less likely to create a wide variety of solutions and more apt to agree on a solution prematurely than more diverse groups. Thus, selecting people for a group or committee with a variety of experiences, values, and preferences should increase the creativity of the group, although these differences may also increase the level of conflict within the group and make it more difficult for the leader to get consensus on a final solution. One technique for increasing group diversity and, in turn, creativity in problem-solving groups involves the use of the four preference dimensions of the MBTI (Myers & McCaulley, 1985) (see Chapter Eight). Actual evidence to support this specific approach appears scanty (Thayer, 1988), but perhaps preferences only assume significance after certain other conditions for group creativity already have been met. For example, diversity cannot make up for an absence of technical expertise. Although the MBTI dimensions may be useful in selecting diverse groups, this instrument should only be used after ensuring that all potential members have high levels of technical expertise. Choosing members based solely on MBTI preferences ignores the crucial role that technical expertise plays in creativity. Still other aspects of the relationship between creativity and leadership are described in Highlights 14–3 and 14–4.

MANAGING CONFLICT AND NEGOTIATING

We read or hear every day in the news about various types of negotiations. Nations often negotiate with each other over land or fishing rights, trade agreements, or diplomatic relations. Land developers often negotiate with city councils for variances on local zoning laws for their projects. Businesses often spend considerable time negotiating employee salaries and fringe benefits with labor unions. In a similar fashion, negotiations go on every day about matters ranging from high school athletic schedules to where a new office copying machine will be located. In one sense, all these negotiations, big or small, are similar. In every case, representatives from different groups meet to resolve some sort of conflict. Conflict is an inevitable fact of life and an inevitable fact of leadership. Researchers have found that first-line supervisors and middle-level managers can spend more than 25 percent of their time dealing with conflict (Thomas & Schmidt, 1976), and resolving conflicts has been found to be an important factor in leadership effectiveness (Morse & Wagner, 1978). In fact, successfully resolving conflicts is so important that it is a central theme in some of the literature about organizations (Brown, 1983; Ouchi, 1981; Peters & Waterman, 1982). Moreover, successfully resolving conflicts will become an increasingly important skill as leadership and management practice moves away from authoritarian directives and toward cooperative approaches emphasizing rational persuasion, collaboration, compromise, and solutions of mutual gain.

What Is Conflict?

There are times in life when we confront values worth fighting for. This is one such time.
George Bush (before the allied attack on Iraq)   *Time*, January 21, 1991.

Should the Americans become embroiled, we will make them swim in their own blood.
Saddam Hussein (before the allied attack on Iraq)   *Time*, January 21, 1991.

Conflict occurs when two opposing parties have interests or goals that appear to be incompatible (Robbins, 1986). There are a variety of sources of conflict in team, committee, work-group, and organizational settings. For example, conflict can occur when group or team members (*a*) have strong differences in values, beliefs, or goals; (*b*) have high levels of task or lateral interdependence; (*c*) are competing for scarce resources or rewards; (*d*) are under high levels of stress; or (*e*) face uncertain or incompatible demands (i.e., role ambiguity and role conflict) (Yukl, 1989). Conflict can also occur when leaders act in a manner inconsistent with the vision and goals they have articulated for the organization (Kets de Vries & Miller, 1984). Of these factors contributing to the level of conflict within or between groups, teams, or committees, probably the most important source of conflict is the lack of communication between parties (Thomas & Schmidt, 1976). Because many conflicts are the result of misunder-

HIGHLIGHT 14–3

Managing Creativity

R. T. Hogan and Morrison (in press) maintained that people who are seen as more creative tend to have several distinguishing personality characteristics. In general, creative people are more open to information and experience, have high energy, can be personally assertive and even domineering, react emotionally to events, are impulsive, are more interested in music and art than in hunting and sports, and finally are very motivated to prove themselves (i.e., are concerned with personal adequacy). Thus, creative people tend to be independent, willful, impractical, unconcerned with money, idealistic, and nonconforming. Given that these tendencies may not make them ideal followers, the interesting question raised by Hogan and Morrison is, How does one lead or manage creative individuals?

This question becomes even more interesting when considering the personality traits of successful leaders or managers. As discussed in Chapter Seven, successful leaders tend to be intelligent, dominant, conscientious, stable, calm, goal-oriented, outgoing, and somewhat conventional. Thus, one might think that the personalities of creative followers and successful leaders might be the source of considerable conflict and make them natural enemies in organizational settings. Because many organizations depend on creativity to grow and prosper, being able to successfully lead creative individuals may be a crucial aspect of success for these organizations.

Given that creative people already possess technical expertise, imaginative thinking skills, and intrinsic motivation, Hogan and Morrison suggested that leaders take the following steps to successfully lead creative followers:

1. *Set goals.* Because creative people value freedom and independence, this step will be best accomplished if leaders use a high level of participation in the goal-setting process. Leaders should ask followers what they can accomplish in a particular time frame.

2. *Provide adequate resources.* Followers will be much more creative if they have the proper equipment to work with, as they can devote their time to resolving the problem rather than spending time finding the equipment to get the job done.

3. *Reduce time pressures, but keep followers on track.* Try to set realistic milestones when setting goals, and make organizational rewards contingent on reaching these milestones. Moreover, leaders need to be well organized to acquire necessary resources and to keep the project on track.

4. *Consider nonmonetary as well as monetary rewards.* Creative people often gain satisfaction from resolving the problem at hand, not from monetary rewards. Thus, feedback should be aimed at enhancing their feelings of personal adequacy. Monetary rewards perceived to be controlling may decrease rather than increase motivation toward the task.

HIGHLIGHT 14–3 *(concluded)*

5. *Recognize that creativity is evolutionary, not revolutionary.* Although followers can create truly novel products (such as the Xerox machine), often the key to creativity is continuous product improvement. Making next year's product faster, lighter, cheaper, or more efficient requires minor modifications that can, over time, culminate in major revolutions. Thus, it may be helpful if leaders think of creativity more in terms of small innovations, not major breakthroughs.

Source: R. T. Hogan and J. Morrison, "Managing Creativity." ed. A. Montouri. *Create & Be Free: Essays in Honor of Frank Barron* (Amsterdam: J. C. Gieben, in press).

---

standings and communication breakdowns, leaders can minimize the level of conflict within and between groups by improving their communication and listening skills as well as spending time networking with others (Yukl, 1989).

Before reviewing specific negotiation tips and conflict-resolution strategies, it is necessary to describe several aspects of conflict that can have an impact on the resolution process. First, the "size" of an issue ("bigger" issues are more difficult to resolve), the extent to which parties define the problem egocentrically (how much they have personally invested in the problem), and the existence of hidden agendas (unstated but important concerns or objectives) can all affect the conflict resolution process. Second, seeing a conflict situation in **win/lose** or either/or terms restricts the (perceived) possible outcomes to either total satisfaction or total frustration. A similar but less extreme variant is to see a situation in zero-sum terms. A **zero-sum situation** is one in which intermediate degrees of satisfaction are possible (i.e., not either/or), but wherein increases in one party's satisfaction inherently decrease the other party's satisfaction, and vice versa. Still another variant can be when parties perceive a conflict as unresolvable. In such cases neither party gains at the expense of the other, but each continues to perceive the other as an obstacle to satisfaction (Thomas, 1976).

Is Conflict Always Bad?

So far, we have described conflict as an inherently negative aspect of any group, team, committee, or organization. This certainly was the prevailing view of conflict among researchers during the 1930s and 40s, and it probably also represents the way many people are raised today (i.e., most people have a strong value of minimizing or avoiding conflict). Today, researchers studying group effectiveness have come to a different conclusion. Some level of conflict may be helpful in order to bolster innovation and performance (Robbins, 1986). Conflict that enhances group productivity is viewed as useful, and conflict that

HIGHLIGHT 14-4

The Creative Genius of Walt Disney

Walt Disney's creative genius has imprinted our cultural landscape with characters and stories more familiar to many people than their neighbors. Read through this brief description of his life and career, and as you do so think about what different factors contributed to his effectiveness as a creative leader. Do you think he practiced the principles of managing creativity described in Highlight 14-3?

Disney built a major studio that produced motion picture masterpieces like *Snow White* and *Fantasia*. Throughout his career, he pioneered technical innovations that set new standards for the industry. These innovations included introducing sound and color to cartoons, inventing special cameras to create new effects in films, and developing sophisticated robotics. He changed the nature of amusement parks in America with Disneyland and Walt Disney World. In fact, these parks are so visionary they've been required study at many schools of architecture. Far more than "fun places," they are serious experiments in urban design, testing radical ideas for solving the problems facing our cities.

For example, the Magic Kingdom at Walt Disney World is really a small city built on top of a huge service-and-utility tunneled infrastructure. The entire park was designed from the start with a quiet and efficient monorail system for mass transit. The area is unique, probably in the world, for setting nearly one third of its acreage aside for conservation of natural habitat. It is, in sum, a city built with people in mind and a plan for the future. Disney originally intended that EPCOT be a test bed of concepts of planning and living that would always be 25 years ahead of its time and always evolving (EPCOT stands for Experimental Prototype Community of Tomorrow). Walt Disney, who once experimented with drawings that move, became a designer of communities for the 21st century (P. Blake, 1972, 1973).

What kind of a person was Walt Disney? What enabled him to accomplish all this? Certainly his creativity and resourcefulness were apparent early in his life. He was a cartoonist for his school paper, and while serving overseas as an ambulance driver during World War I (he was too young for actual military duty), he built a small business selling souvenir German helmets that appeared to have weathered rough combat. (He actually used new helmets painted to look old and used. A partner pounded dents in the helmets and shot holes in them; they even got human hair from a barber to put in the holes!) (Miller, 1956).

Disney always was committed to making his product the best, from souvenir war helmets to his films. He continuously experimented with new ways of doing things, innovating new technologies to produce the effects he wanted. In the 1930s, he had his special effects staffs make slow-motion pictures of bubbles popping, smoke blowing, and balls bouncing to improve their animation of such actions. He developed rigorous training programs for his animation staffs to help them draw more lifelike cartoons, like learning to blur fast-moving figures. And he had an uncanny sense of timing. For example, Disney profited from the emer-

---

HIGHLIGHT 14-4 *(concluded)*

gence of sound and color in live-action film by seeing their potential application to animated subjects sooner and more clearly than others. He acquired exclusive rights to the Technicolor process because he showed commitment to the new technique when other cartoon producers were skeptical (Thomas, 1976).

Disney had a genius for spotting talent, and he surrounded himself with other creative people, even eccentric ones. After he found them, though, he was a taskmaster. At work, he was all business, not what you might call a people person. He did not like dealing with others' personal problems, and he had a well-known temper. One of Disney's biographers wrote the following:

> He was incapable of small talk. His employees learned not to engage him in the banter that animators used as relief from the tedium of drawing. His mind was too involved with the problems of the moment—a storyline that defied solution; a cartoon that failed to evoke laughs at the preview; an overdue check from Columbia Pictures that threatened next week's payroll. His workers learned not to be offended if he passed them in the hallway without a word; they knew that he was preoccupied with a studio problem. (Thomas, 1976, p. 111).

Disney also had a sixth sense about what would appeal broadly to the American culture, young and old. He trusted his intuition and judgment to an extraordinary degree, and took great risks with his studio to back them up. Furthermore, he made sure that every project had his personal stamp on it, including such details as what voices to use for the various characters. He was unique in Hollywood for the close personal supervison he gave his work. Walt Disney's name on a film meant it had received his individual touch (Thomas, 1976).

---

hinders group performance is viewed as counterproductive (Robbins, 1986). Various possible positive and negative effects of conflict are listed in Table 14-2.

Along these lines, researchers have found that conflict can cause a radical change in political power (Bass, 1985; Weber, 1947; Willner, 1984), as well as dramatic changes in organizational structure and design, group cohesiveness, and group or organizational effectiveness (Roberts & Bradley, 1988; Kanter, 1983). Nevertheless, it is important to realize that this current conceptualization of conflict is still somewhat limited in scope. For example, increasing the level of conflict within a group or team may enhance immediate performance but may also have a disastrous effect on organizational climate and turnover. As described in Chapter Four, leaders may be evaluated in terms of many criteria, only one of which is group performance. Thus, leaders should probably use criteria such as turnover and absenteeism rates and followers' satisfaction or organizational climate ratings in addition to measures of group performance

Tribune Media Services

TABLE 14–2
Possible Effects of Conflict

Possible Positive Effects of Conflict	Possible Negative Effects of Conflict
Increased effort	Reduced productivity
Feelings get aired	Decreased communication
Better understanding of others	Negative feelings
Impetus for change	Stress
Better decision making	Poorer decision making
Key issues surfaced	Decreased cooperation
Critical thinking stimulated	Political backstabbing

when trying to determine whether conflict is good or bad. Leaders are cautioned against using group performance alone, as these indices may not reveal the overall effects of conflict on the group or team.

Negotiation Tips

Given that conflicts can have detrimental effects, and that a leader's effectiveness depends to some extent on his or her skills in managing conflict with and between groups or teams, the following negotiation tips are provided. For the most part, the negotiation tips are steps all leaders should consider when trying to resolve conflicts. These tips, from Fisher and Ury (1981), include taking the time to prepare for a negotiating session; keeping the people and problems separate; focusing on issues, not positions; and seeking win-win outcomes.

To successfully resolve conflicts, leaders may need to *spend considerable time preparing for a negotiating session.* Leaders should anticipate each side's key concerns and issues, attitudes, possible negotiating strategies, and goals. Fisher and Ury (1981) also advise negotiators to *separate the people from the problem.* Because all negotiations involve substantive issues *and* relationships between negotiators, it is easy for these parts to become entangled. When that happens, parties may inadvertently treat the people and the problem as though they were the same. For example, a group of teachers angry that their salary has not been raised for the fourth year in a row may direct their personal bitterness toward the school board president. However, reactions such as these are usually a mistake, as the decision may be out of the other party's hands, and personally attacking the other party often only serves to make the conflict even more difficult to resolve.

There are several things leaders can do to separate the people from the problem. First, leaders should not let their fears color their perceptions of each side's intentions. It is easy to attribute negative qualities to others when one feels threatened. Similarly, it does no good to blame the other side for one's own problems (Blake, Shepard, & Mouton, 1964). Even if it is justified, it is still usually counterproductive. Another thing leaders can do to separate the people from the problem is to communicate clearly. Earlier in this text, we suggested techniques for active listening. Those guidelines are especially helpful in negotiating and resolving conflicts.

Another of Fisher and Ury's (1981) main points is to *focus on interests, not positions.* Focusing on interests depends on understanding the difference between interests and positions. Here is one example. Say Raoul had the same reserved seats to the local symphony every season for several years and that he was just notified he will no longer get his usual tickets. Feeling irate, he goes to the ticket office to complain. One approach he could take would be to demand the same seats he has always had; this would be his *position.* A different approach would be to find alternative seats that are just as satisfactory as his old seats had been; this would be his *interest.* In negotiating, it is much more constructive to satisfy interests than to fight over positions. Furthermore, it is important to focus on both your counterpart's interests (not position) as well as your own interests (not position).

Finally, winning a negotiation at your counterpart's expense is likely to be only a short-term gain. Leaders should attempt to work out a resolution by looking at long-term rather than short-term goals, and they should try to build a working relationship that will endure and be mutually trusting and beneficial beyond the present negotiation. Along these lines, leaders should always seek **win-win** outcomes, which try to satisfy both sides' needs and continuing interests. This often takes creative problem solving to find new options that provide gains for both sides. Realistically, however, not all situations may be conducive to seeking win-win outcomes (see Highlight 14–5).

Conflict Resolution Strategies

In addition to spending time understanding and clarifying positions, separating people from the problem, and focusing on interests, there are five strategies or approaches leaders can use to resolve conflicts. Perhaps the best way to differentiate between these five strategies is to think of conflict resolution in terms of two independent dimensions: cooperativeness/uncooperativeness and assertiveness/unassertiveness (see Figure 14–2). Parties in conflict do vary in their commitment to satisfy the other's concerns, but they also vary in the extent to which they assertively stand up for their own concerns (Thomas, 1976). Thus, conflict resolution can be understood in terms of how cooperative or uncooperative the parties are *and* how assertive or unassertive they are.

Using this two-dimension scheme, Thomas (1976) described five general approaches to managing conflict:

1. **Competition** reflects a desire to achieve one's own ends at the expense of someone else. This is domination, also known as a win-lose orientation.

2. **Accommodation** reflects a mirror-image of competition, entirely giving in to someone else's concerns without making any effort to achieve one's own ends. This is a tactic of appeasement.

3. **Sharing** is an approach that represents a compromise between domination and appeasement. Both parties give up something, yet both parties get something. Both parties are moderately, but incompletely, satisfied.

4. **Collaboration** reflects an effort to fully satisfy both parties. This is a problem-solving approach that requires the integration of each party's concerns.

5. **Avoidance** involves indifference to the concerns of both parties. It reflects a withdrawal from or neglect of any party's interests.

HIGHLIGHT 14–5

How to Swim with Sharks

It is dangerous to swim with sharks, but not all sharks are found in the water. Some people may behave like sharks, and a best-selling book for executives written a few years ago took its title from that theme. However, an article appeared in the journal *Perspectives in Biology and Medicine* nearly two decades ago claiming to be a translated version of an essay written in France more than a century earlier for sponge divers (Cousteau, 1973). The essay notes that while no one *wants* to swim with sharks, it is an occupational hazard for certain people. For those who must swim with sharks, it can be essential to follow certain rules. See if you think the following rules for interacting with the sharks of the sea serve as useful analogies for interacting with the sharks of everyday life.

> *Rule 1: Assume any unidentified fish is a shark.* Just because a fish may be acting in a docile manner does not mean it is not a shark. The real test is how it will act when blood is in the water.

> *Rule 2: Don't bleed.* Bleeding will prompt even more aggressive behavior and the involvement of even more sharks. Of course, it is not easy to keep from bleeding when injured. Those who cannot do so are advised not to swim with sharks at all.

> *Rule 3: Confront aggression quickly.* Sharks usually give warning before attacking a swimmer. Swimmers should watch for indications an attack is imminent and take prompt counteraction. A blow to the nose is often appropriate since it shows you understand the shark's intentions and will respond in kind. It is particularly dangerous to behave in an ingratiating manner toward sharks. People who once held this erroneous view often can be identified by a missing limb.

> *Rule 4: Get out of the water if anyone starts bleeding.* Previously docile sharks may begin attacking if blood is in the water. Their behavior can become so irrational, even including attacking themselves, that it is safest to remove yourself entirely from the situation.

> *Rule 5: Create dissension among the attackers.* Sharks are self-centered and rarely act in an organized fashion with other sharks. This significantly reduces the risk of swimming with sharks. Every now and then, however, sharks may launch a coordinated attack. The best strategy then is to create internal dissension among them since they already are quite prone to it; often sharks will fight among themselves over trivial or minor things. By the time their internal conflict is settled, sharks often have forgotten about their organized attack.

> *Rule 6: Never divert a shark attack toward another swimmer.* Please observe this final item of swimming etiquette.

Does one of these approaches seem clearly a better method than the other to you? Each of them does, at least, reflect certain culturally valued modes of behavior (Thomas, 1977). For example, the esteem many people hold for athletic, business, and military heroes reflects our cultural valuation of competition. Valuation of a pragmatic approach to settling problems is reflected in the com-

FIGURE 14–2

Five Conflict-Handling Orientations, Plotted According to Party's Desire to Satisfy Own and Other's Concerns

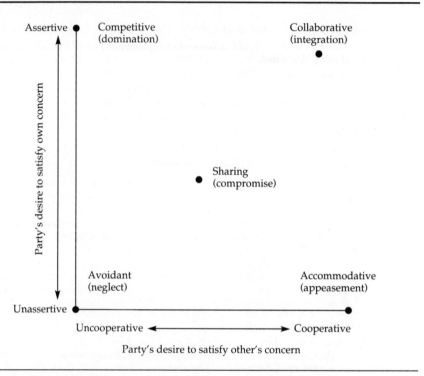

Source: Thomas, K. W. "Conflict and Conflict Management." In *Handbook of Industrial and Organizational Psychology,* ed. M. D. Dunnette. Chicago: Rand McNally, 1976. Used by permission of Marvin D. Dunnette.

promising approach. Cultural values of unselfishness, kindness, and generosity are reflected in accommodation, and even avoidance has roots in philosophies that emphasize caution, diplomacy, and turning away from worldly concerns. These cultural roots to each of the approaches to managing conflict suggest that no single one is likely to be the right one all the time. There probably are circumstances when each of the modes of conflict resolution can be appropriate. Rather than seeking to find some single best approach to managing conflict, it may be wisest to appreciate the relative advantages and disadvantages of all approaches, and the circumstances when each may be most appropriate. A summary of experienced leaders' recommendations for when to use each strategy is presented in Table 14–3 (Thomas, 1977).

TABLE 14–3
Situations in Which to Use the Five Approaches to Conflict

Competing

1. When quick, decisive action is vital (e.g., emergencies).
2. On important issues where unpopular actions need implementing (e.g., cost cutting, enforcing unpopular rules, discipline).
3. On issues vital to company welfare when you know you're right.
4. Against people who take advantage of noncompetitive behavior.

Collaborating

1. To find an integrative solution when both sets of concerns are too important to be compromised.
2. When your objective is to learn.
3. To merge insights from people with different perspectives.
4. To gain commitment by incorporating concerns into a consensus.
5. To work through feelings that have interfered with a relationship.

Compromising

1. When goals are important, but not worth the effort or potential disruption of more assertive modes.
2. When opponents with equal power are committed to mutually exclusive goals.
3. To achieve temporary settlements to complex issues.
4. To arrive at expedient solutions under time pressure.
5. As a backup when collaboration or competition is unsuccessful.

Avoiding

1. When an issue is trivial, or more important issues are pressing.
2. When you perceive no chance of satisfying your concerns.
3. When potential disruption outweighs the benefits of resolution.
4. To let people cool down and regain perspective.
5. When gathering information supersedes immediate decision.
6. When others can resolve the conflict more effectively.
7. When issues seem tangential or symptomatic of other issues.

Accommodating

1. When you find you are wrong—to allow a better position to be heard, to learn, and to show your reasonableness.
2. When issues are more important to others than yourself—to satisfy others and maintain co-operation.
3. To build social credits for later issues.
4. To minimize loss when you are outmatched and losing.
5. When harmony and stability are especially important.
6. To allow subordinates to develop by learning from mistakes.

Source: K. W. Thomas, "Toward Multidimensional Values in Teaching: The Example of Conflict Management," *Academy of Management Review* 2, no. 3, (1977), pp. 484–490. Used with permission.

MANAGING STRESS

As discussed in Chapter Thirteen, too much stress can take a toll on individuals and their organizations. For individuals, the toll can be in terms of their health, mental and emotional well-being, job performance, or interpersonal relationships. For organizations, the toll includes decreased productivity and increased employee absenteeism, turnover, and medical costs. It stands to reason, then, that leaders in any activity should know something about stress. Leaders should understand the nature of stress because the leadership role itself can be stressful and because leaders' stress can impair the performance and well-being of followers. To prevent stress from becoming so excessive that it takes a toll in some important dimension of your own or your followers' lives, the following rules and practices for effective stress management are provided.

One of the most important steps in managing stress is to *monitor your own and your followers' stress levels.* Although this seems straighforward, a seemingly paradoxical fact about stress is that it often takes a toll without one's conscious awareness. A person experiencing excessive stress might manifest various symptoms apparent to everyone but him- or herself. For that reason, it is useful to develop the habit of regularly attending to some of the warning signs that your stress level may be getting too high. Some of the warning signs of stress are in Table 14–4. If you answered yes to any of these questions, then your own or your followers' stress levels may be getting too high and it would probably be a good idea to put some of the following stress management strategies into practice right away. On the other hand, answering some of the questions affirmatively does not necessarily mean your stress level is too high. There could, for example, be some other physiological explanation.

Monitoring your stress will reduce the chances that it will build to an unhealthy level before you take action, but monitoring is not enough. Leaders also need to *identify what is causing the stress.* It may seem at first that the causes of stress always will be obvious, but that is not true. Sometimes the problems are clear enough even if the solutions are not (e.g., family finances, or working in a job with a high workload and lots of deadlines). Other times, however, it may be difficult to identify the root problem. For example, a coach may attribute his anger to the losing record of his team, not recognizing that a bigger cause of his emotional distress may be the problems he is having at home with his teenage son. A worker may feel frustrated because her boss overloads her with work, not realizing that her own unassertiveness keeps her from expressing her feelings to her boss. Problem solving can be applied constructively to managing stress, but only if the problem is identified properly in the first place. Once the problem is identified, then a plan for minimizing stress or the effects of the stressor can be developed.

Practicing a healthy lifestyle is one of the best ways to minimize stress. There are no substitutes for balanced nutrition, regular exercise, adequate sleep, ab-

TABLE 14–4
Stress Symptoms

- Are you behaving "unlike" yourself?
- Has your mood become negative, hostile, or depressed?
- Do you have difficulty sleeping?
- Are you defensive or touchy?
- Are your relationships suffering?
- Have you made more mistakes or bad decisions lately?
- Have you lost interest in normally enjoyable activities?
- Are you using alcohol or other drugs?
- Do you seem to have little energy?
- Do you worry a lot?
- Are you nervous much of the time?
- Have you been undereating or overeating?
- Have you had an increase in headaches or back pains?

This checklist can also be used to help determine the level of stress in followers.

stention from tobacco products, and drinking only moderate amounts of alcohol (if at all) as keys to a healthy life. A long-term study of the lifestyles of nearly 7,000 adults confirmed these as independent factors contributing to wellness and the absence of stress symptoms (Wiley & Camacho, 1980). Insufficient sleep saps energy, interferes with alertness and judgment, increases irritability, and lowers resistance to illness. Exercise, besides being a valuable part of any long-term health strategy, is also an excellent way to reduce tension.

Although physical exercise is a good relaxation technique, sometimes you will need to relax but not have an opportunity to get a workout. Having practiced other relaxation techniques will come in handy when the situation prevents strenuous exercise. Also, of course, some people simply prefer alternate relaxation techniques to exercise. *Deep-breathing techniques, progressive muscle relaxation,* and *thinking of calming words and images* can be powerful on-the-spot calming techniques to reduce arousal level. They are applicable in stressful situations ranging from job interviews to sports. The effectiveness of these techniques is somewhat a matter of personal preference, and no single one is best for all purposes or all people.

Another powerful antidote to stress is having a *network of close and supportive relationships* with others (Berkman & Syme, 1979). People who have close ties to others through marriage, church membership, or other groups tend to be healthier than those with weaker social ties. Also, social supports of various kinds (e.g., the supportiveness of one's spouse, one's co-workers, or boss) can buffer the impact of job stress (Cummings, 1990; Jayaratne, Himle, & Chess, 1988), and unit cohesion is believed to be a critical element of soldiers' ability to withstand even the extreme physical and psychological stresses of combat (West Point Associates, 1988). Leaders can play a constructive role in developing mutual supportiveness and cohesiveness among subordinates, and their own open and frank communication with subordinates is especially important when a situation is ambiguous as well as stressful.

As we noted earlier, the stressfulness of any event depends partly on the way one interprets it, not just on the event itself. For example, a poor grade on an examination may be more stressful for one student than for another, just as a rebuke from a boss may be more stressful for one worker than for another. This is partly due, of course, to the fact individuals "invest" themselves in activities to different degrees because they value different things. A problem in an area of heavy personal investment is more stressful than one in an area of little personal investment. It goes deeper than that, however. Managing stress effectively depends on *keeping things in perspective.* This is difficult for some people because they have a style of interpreting events that aggravates their felt stress.

Individuals who have relatively complex self-concepts, as measured by the number of different ways they describe or see themselves, are less susceptible to common stress-related complaints than are people with lesser degrees of "self-complexity" (Linville, 1987). Take, for example, someone who has suffered a setback at work, such as having lost out to a colleague for a desired promotion. Someone low in self-complexity (e.g., a person whose self-concept is defined solely in terms of professional success) could be devastated by the event. Low self-complexity implies a lack of resilience to threats to one's ego. Consider, on the other hand, someone with high self-complexity facing the same setback. The person could understandably feel disappointed and perhaps dejected about work, but if she were high in self-complexity, then the event's impact would be buffered by the existence of relatively uncontaminated areas of positive self-image. For example, she might base her feelings of professional success on more criteria than just getting (or not getting) a promotion. Other criteria, such as being highly respected by peers, may be even more important bases for her feelings of professional success. Furthermore, other dimensions of her life (e.g., her leadership in the local Democratic party, support to her family, etc.) may provide more areas of positive self-image.

Unfortunately, because there are no shortcuts to developing self-complexity, it is not really a viable stress management strategy. There are other cognitive approaches to stress management, however, that can produce more immediate results. These approaches have the common goal of changing a person's self-talk about stressful events. One of the simplest of these to apply is called the **A-B-C model** (Ellis & Harper, 1975; Steinmetz, Blankenship, Brown, Hall, & Miller, 1980).

To appreciate the usefulness of the A-B-C model, it is helpful to consider the chain of events that precedes feelings of stress. Sometimes people think of this as a two-step sequence. Something *external* happens (i.e., a stressful event), and then something *internal* follows (i.e., symptoms of stress). We can depict the sequence like this:

A. Triggering Event
(e.g., knocking your boss's coffee onto his lap)

C. Feelings and Behaviors
(e.g., anxiety, fear, embarrassment, perspiration)

In other words, many people think their feelings and behaviors result directly from external events. Such a view, however, leaves out the critical role played by our thoughts, or self-talk. The actual sequence looks like this:

A. Triggering Event
(knocking your boss's coffee onto his lap)

B. Your Thinking
("He must think I'm a real jerk.")

C. Feelings and Behaviors
(anxiety, fear, embarrassment, perspiration)

From this perspective you can see the causal role played by inner dialogue, or self-talk, in contributing to feelings of stress. Such inner dialogue can be rational or irrational, constructive or destructive—and which it will be is under the individual's control. People gain considerable freedom from stress when they realize that by changing their own self-talk they can control their emotional responses to events around them. Consider a different sequence for our scenario:

A. Triggering Event
(knocking your boss's coffee onto his lap)

B. Your Thinking
("Darn it! But it was just an accident.")

C. Feelings and Behavior
(apologizing and helping clean up)

Thus, a particular incident can be interpreted in several different ways, some likely to increase feelings of stress and distress, and others likely to maintain self-esteem and positive coping. You will become better at coping with stress as you practice listening to your inner dialogue and changing destructive self-talk to constructive self-talk. Even this is not a simple change to make, however. Changing self-talk is more difficult than you might think, especially in emotionalized situations. Because self-talk is covert, spontaneous, fleeting, and reflexive (McKay, Davis, & Fanning, 1981), it, like any bad habit, can be difficult to change. Nevertheless, precisely because self-talk *is* just a habit, you can change it.

Finally, leaders need to recognize their role in their followers' stress levels. A leader in a stressful situation who is visibly manifesting some of the symptoms found in Table 14–3 is not going to set much of an example for followers. On the contrary, because followers look to leaders for guidance and support, these behaviors and symptoms could become contagious and may serve to increase followers' stress levels. Leaders need to recognize the importance of role modeling in reducing (or increasing) followers' stress levels. Leaders also need to make sure their style of interacting with subordinates does not make the leaders ''stress carriers.''

DIAGNOSING PERFORMANCE PROBLEMS IN INDIVIDUALS, GROUPS, AND ORGANIZATIONS

One way to integrate many of the topics covered in Parts I through IV is to discuss how they can impact individual, group, and organizational performance. The model in Figure 14–3 provides a framework for these topics and is a modification of models developed by J.P. Campbell (1977) and J.P. Campbell, McCloy, Oppler, and Sager (in press). We hypothesize that performance (i.e., those behaviors directed toward accomplished or satisfied goals) is a function of abilities, skills, task understanding, choice to perform, level of effort and persistence, resources, group factors, and organizational and environmental factors. As a multiplicative rather than compensatory model, a deficit in any one component should result in a substantial decrement in performance that cannot easily be made up by increasing other components. Like the example described earlier of the high school basketball team playing the Chicago Bulls, exerting more effort will not always compensate for lacking the abilities or skills needed for performance.

The model provides general guidance about the actions leaders can take to improve follower, group, or organizational performance. The model also indi-

FIGURE 14–3
A Model of Performance

Performance = f(Abilities × Skills × Task understanding

$\times$ Choice to perform × Level of effort and persistence

$\times$ Necessary resources × Group factors

$\times$ Organizational and environmental factors)

cates how certain leader actions actually may disrupt performance. Primarily, though, we offer the model as a tool to show how ideas from several preceding chapters all play a part in performance.

Abilities

Abilities include such individual difference variables as athleticism, intelligence, and creativity, and are characteristics that are relatively difficult to change with training. In other words, abilities represent raw talent. For example, it would probably be impossible to take a person off the street and train him to be as good a hockey player as Wayne Gretzky or Mario Lemieux, just as it would be very difficult to train people to have extremely high levels of intelligence or creativity. Because abilities are relatively insensitve to training interventions, sending people who lack the required abilities to more training or motivating them to work harder will have relatively little effect on performance. Instead, performance deficits in this area can be more easily resolved by selecting those individuals with the abilities needed for performance.

Skills

As discussed in Chapter Nine, skills consist of a well-defined body of knowledge, a set of related behaviors, and clear criteria of competent performance. Individuals or groups often have the abilities but lack the necessary skills to perform at a high level. Such is the case with many athletic teams or musical groups at the beginning of a season or when a work group gets a new set of equipment or responsibility for tasks they have no previous experience with. Skills are very amenable to training, and leaders with high levels of technical expertise may perform the training themselves, see that it is obtained in other ways on the job, or send their people to training programs in order to improve followers' skill levels.

Task Understanding

Performance problems often occur because individuals or groups do not understand what they are supposed to do. There are many instances where talented, skilled groups accomplished the wrong objective because of miscommunication or sat idly by waiting for instructions that never arrived. Leaders can minimize the effects of communication breakdowns on performance by improving their own communcation and listening skills. Leaders must do more than communicate clearly; they must ensure that their messages are fully understood.

Choice to Perform

Sometimes people will choose not to perform a task even when they have the necessary abilities, skills, and task understanding. If this occurs, leaders should first try to learn why. For example, the task may involve risks the leader is unaware of. Another possibility, of course, is that motivation is low. If this is the case, leaders should replace nonperformers with others who are more intrinsically interested in the task or more achievement-oriented. Leaders could also increase followers' choice to perform by setting goals, restructuring rewards to encourage performance, making the paths between effort-to-performance and performance-to-reward clearer, or redesigning the task to increase skill variety, autonomy, or feedback. If all these interventions fail, and the tasks to be performed are reasonable, then leaders may need to use punishment as a sanction for choosing not to perform.

Level of Effort and Persistence

Sometimes individuals or groups just seem to run out of steam. If this happens, then leaders need to communicate with followers to find out why their effort has dropped off. They may find that more periodic feedback is all that is needed to increase the level of effort or return effort to prior levels. Other interventions to enhance the level of effort and persistence include selecting followers who are intrinsically motivated by the task, setting longer-term goals, changing rewards to promote long-term rather than short-term effort, and redesigning the job to provide greater responsibility, autonomy, task significance, or task identity.

Necessary Resources

Performance also can be limited when followers lack the resources needed to get the job done. These may include equipment, computers, supplies, or even time, money, and additional manpower. Effective two-way communication is a key aspect of determining what followers need. Beyond that, leaders need good relationships with suppliers and some means of influence or exchange for securing resources.

Group Factors

Factors such as norms and cohesiveness can affect both individual and group performance. For example, leaders may run into situations where the group is not very cohesive or where the group has a low performance norm. In either case, leaders may need to create **superordinate goals** in order to increase group cohesiveness and performance. Superordinate goals are those that are achievable only when *all* group members exert effort; individual effort alone will not result in goal achievement. Moreover, group cohesiveness and performance might also be enhanced by deemphasizing individual rewards and promoting group rewards. Group norms can also be changed by changing the group's membership or composition.

Organizational and Environmental Factors

Leaders, particularly those in more senior positions, need to consider how the design, structure, or culture of the organization affects individual, group, and organizational performance. There are limits, however, to how much even the most senior or high-ranking leaders can change these factors. Particularly with regard to environmental factors, perhaps the best leaders can do is recognize how they can affect individual, group, or organizational performance. By recognizing that political, legal, and social factors sometimes may be the primary factors affecting performance, leaders can at least avoid taking actions based on a misdiagnosis of the problem, which may, in fact, turn out to be detrimental to performance in the long term.

Concluding Comments on the Diagnostic Model

In summary, this model provides an integrative framework for many of the topics affecting performance previously reviewed in this text. It reviews some of the factors that affect performance and suggests ideas for rectifying performance problems. It should be emphasized, however, that this model concerns only follower, group, or organizational performance. Leaders need to be mindful that there are other desirable outcomes, too, such as organizational climate and job satisfaction, and that actions designed to increase performance (especially just in the short term) may adversely impact these other desirable outcomes.

SUMMARY

This chapter was designed to improve your skills in five areas related to leadership and followership effectiveness. Because both leaders and followers often organize meetings, the first section in this chapter provided specific advice on how you can make meetings more effective. The second section in this chapter reviewed some of the pertinent literature concerning creativity. Creativity was defined as the ability to make fresh observations or to see things in new ways, and technical expertise, imaginative thinking skills, and intrinsic motivation are all important components of creativity. These three components of creativity provided leaders with several suggestions on how to improve their own and their followers' creativity.

Another important skill in leadership effectiveness is managing conflict both within and between groups. Many conflicts are resolved through negotiation, and leaders can improve their negotiation skills by better understanding the values and assumptions of the parties in conflict; focusing on interests, not positions; and seeking win-win outcomes. Beyond these negotiation tips, leaders may also use one of the five strategies discussed in this chapter, which include competing, collaborating, compromising, avoiding, or accommodating. Each of these five strategies has advantages and disadvantages, and the relative utility of each strategy often depends on the situation.

Because excessive stress has important health and organizational implications, managing stress is also an important skill for leaders and followers to have. Perhaps the most important step in managing stress is learning to monitor both your own and your followers' stress levels. If stress symptoms are detected, then leaders need to try to pinpoint the cause of the excessive stress. Some stressors, such as a death in the family, may be beyond the leader's control. However, other stressors, such as excessive workloads or role conflict, may be well within the leader's capability to change. Moreover, leaders need to realize that they may be the primary source of their followers' excessive stress. In any case, leaders or followers under excessive levels of stress may be able to cope more successfully if they practice a healthier lifestyle, build support groups, learn to relax, and keep things in perspective.

Finally, this chapter provided a model of individual, group, and organizational performance that integrates many of the topics reviewed in Parts I through IV. This model hypothesized that performance was a function of abilities, skills, task understanding, choice to perform, level and persistence of effort, necessary resources, group factors, and organizational and environmental factors. This is a multiplicative rather than a compensatory model, and deficits in one performance factor cannot be made up easily by increases in other factors. By describing performance this way, the model provides leaders several alternatives for improving individual, group, or organizational performance. Nevertheless, leaders need to remember that performance is only one of the factors related to effectiveness. Leaders ought to weigh the ramifications of their actions on climate, satisfaction, and group cohesiveness before taking action to correct any performance problem.

KEY TERMS AND CONCEPTS

creativity

divergent thinking

convergent thinking

functional fixedness

Synectics

brainstorming

conflict

win-lose

zero-sum situation

win-win

competition

accommodation

sharing

collaboration

avoidance

A-B-C model

superordinate goals

DISCUSSION QUESTIONS

1. We usually think of creativity as a characteristic of individuals, but might some organizations be more creative than others? What factors do you think might affect an organization's level of creativity?

2. Can you think of any examples where leaders used conflict constructively in a group or organization? Can you think of other examples where the conflict in a group was very counterproductive? What was different in these situations?

3. Describe taking a different perspective about something stressful in your own life in terms of the A-B-C model.

4. Do you think life today is more stressful than it was 100 years ago? 500 years ago? What makes you think so? Is stress a greater concern for leaders today than it was 100 years ago?

SUGGESTED READINGS

Walton, R. E. *Managing Conflict*. Reading, Mass.: Addison-Wesley, 1987.

Adams, J. L. *The Care and Feeding of Ideas*. Reading, Mass.: Addison-Wesley, 1986.

P A R T

V

PUTTING IT ALL TOGETHER

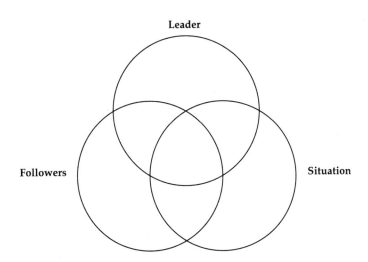

I n Parts II through IV, we purposely focused in each part on a specific aspect of the leader-follower-situation model. By following this strategy, we could give readers a better understanding of the complexity of the leadership process. Yet there are limitations to such an approach, too. Although the interactional framework gives us a variety of lenses with which to view the leadership process, the images provided by each lens paint a somewhat incomplete picture. With the leadership process, the whole is greater than the sum of its parts. In other words, although it is important to understand how situational factors such as the task, organization, and environment affect the leadership process, a more complete picture is gained when we also look at how the characteristics and behaviors of the leader, the technical expertise and values of the followers, and the norms and level of cohesiveness of the team or group interact with these situational factors. Because the leadership process may be best understood when all three components of the interactional framework are taken into account, the last three chapters in this text review some of the more comprehensive theories of leadership.

More specifically, Chapter Fifteen provides a description of four of the more comprehensive and well-known contingency theories of leadership, which include the normative decision model (Vroom & Yetton, 1973); the situational leadership theory (SLT) (Hersey & Blanchard, 1977, 1982); the contingency model (Fiedler, 1967); and path-goal theory (House & Dessler, 1974). Chapter Fifteen also critically reviews the research evidence relating to these four theories or models of leadership. Chapter Sixteen describes and critically reviews the research concerning two of the more recent conceptualizations of leadership, which include the group effectiveness model (Ginnett, 1992; Hackman, 1990) and transformational or charismatic leadership. In addition, discussions of how the six theories or models described in these two chapters fit into the interactional framework are provided. Chapter Seventeen also provides an integrated review of the interactional framework, but does so in a manner different than Chapters Fifteen and Sixteen. Just as stress was used as a topic to cut across the task, organizational, and environmental factors of the situation, so do aspects of the "quality movement" cut across the three components of the interactional framework. Thus, Chapter Seventeen provides an overview of the quality movement, looks at a few of the tools and techniques used by leaders and followers in organizations trying to improve quality, and critically addresses some of the questions being asked about the quality movement.

Finally, given the comprehensive nature of the latter theories, some might argue that readers would have gained a better appreciation of the complexity of the leadership process if these more comprehensive theories had appeared earlier in the text. Although there are some merits to this argument, we believe readers will be better able to think critically about these theories *after* having achieved a fuller understanding of the individual components of the interactional framework. By having an appreciation of the myriad of leader, follower, and situational factors that can affect the leadership process, readers will more readily recognize the advantages and limitations of the theories described in this part.

Chapter Fifteen

Contingency Theories of Leadership

INTRODUCTION

T his chapter reviews four of the more well-known contingency theories of leadership. These four theories are generally more comprehensive than those previously discussed in this text, as all four address certain aspects of the leader, the followers, and the situation. These four theories also share several other similarities. First, because they are theories rather than someone's personal opinions, these four models have been the focus of a considerable amount of empirical research over the years. Second, these theories implicitly assume that leaders are able to accurately diagnose or assess key aspects of the followers and the leadership situation. Third, with the exception of the contingency model (Fiedler, 1967), leaders are assumed to be able to act in a flexible manner. In other words, leaders can and should change their behaviors as situational and follower characteristics change. Fourth, a correct match between situational and follower characteristics and leaders' behaviors is assumed to have a positive effect on group or organizational outcomes. Thus, these theories maintain that leadership effectiveness is maximized when leaders correctly make their behaviors *contingent* on certain situational and follower characteristics. Because of these similarities, Chemers (1984) argued that these four theories were more similar than they were different. He said they differed primarily in terms of the types of situational and follower characteristics that various leader behaviors should be contingent on (also see Highlight 15–1 for some different perspectives on theories and leadership).

THE NORMATIVE DECISION MODEL

Obviously, in some situations leaders can delegate decisions to subordinates or should ask subordinates for relevant information before making a decision. In other situations, such as emergencies or crises, leaders may need to make a decision with little, if any, input from subordinates. The level of input subordinates have in the decision-making process can and does vary substantially depending on the issue at hand, followers' level of technical expertise, or the presence or absence of a crisis. Although the level of participation varies due to various leader, follower, and situational factors, Vroom and Yetton (1973) maintained that leaders could often improve group performance by using an optimal amount of participation in the decision-making process. Thus, the normative decision model is directed solely at determining how much input subordinates should have in the decision-making process. Precisely because the normative decision model is limited only to decision making and is not a grand, all-encompassing theory, it is a good model with which to begin the chapter.

HIGHLIGHT 15–1

Leadership Quotes, Chapter Fifteen

The real world is a messy place—yet, even a messy place can (should?) be attacked systematically.

Alex Cornell

Although people object when a scientific analysis traces their behavior to external conditions and thus deprives them of credit and the chance to be admired, they seldom object when the same analysis absolves them of blame.

B. F. Skinner

There is to me something profoundly affecting in large masses of men following the lead of those who do not believe in men.

Walt Whitman

Disraeli cynically expressed the dilemma when he said: "I must follow the people. Am I not their leader?" He might have added: "I must lead the people. Am I not their servant?"

Edward L. Bernays

Men are marked out from the moment of birth to rule or be ruled.

Aristotle

To act is easy; to think is hard.

Goethe

It is a capital mistake to theorize before one has data.

Sir Arthur Conan Doyle

Irrationally held truths may be more harmful than reasoned errors.

Thomas Huxley

Levels of Participation

Like the other theories in this chapter, the **normative decision model** (Vroom & Yetton, 1973) was designed to improve some aspects of leadership effectiveness. In this case, Vroom and Yetton explored how various leader, follower, and situational factors affect the degree of subordinates' participation in the

TABLE 15–1

Levels of Participation in the Normative Decision Model

Autocratic Processes

AI: The leader solves the problem or makes the decision by him- or herself using the information available at the time.

AII: The leader obtains any necessary information from followers, then decides on a solution to the problem herself. She may or may not tell followers the purpose of her questions or give information about the problem or decision she is working on. The input provided by them is clearly in response to her request for specific information. They do not play a role in the definition of the problem or in generating or evaluating alternative solutions.

Consultative Processes

CI: The leader shares the problem with the relevant followers individually, getting their ideas and suggestions without bringing them together as a group. Then *he* makes a decision. This decision may or may not reflect the followers' influence.

CII: The leader shares the problem with her followers in a group meeting. In this meeting, she obtains their ideas and suggestions. Then she makes the decision, which may or may not reflect the followers' influence.

Group Process

GII: The leader shares the problem with his followers as a group. Together they generate and evaluate alternatives and attempt to reach agreement (consensus) on a solution. The leader's role is much like that of a chairman, coordinating the discussion, keeping it focused on the problem, and making sure that the critical issues are discussed. He can provide the group with information or ideas that he has, but he does not try to "press" them to adopt "his" solution. Moreover, leaders adopting this level of participation are willing to accept and implement any solution that has the support of the entire group.

Source: Adapted from V. H. Vroom and P. W. Yetton, *Leadership and Decision Making* (Pittsburgh: University of Pittsburgh Press, 1973).

decision-making process and, in turn, group performance. To determine which situational and follower factors affect the level of participation and group performance, Vroom and Yetton first investigated the decision-making processes leaders use in group settings. They discovered a continuum of decision-making processes ranging from completely autocratic (labeled "AI") to completely democratic, where all member of the group have equal participation (labeled "GII"). These processes are listed in Table 15–1.

Decision Quality and Acceptance

After establishing a continuum of decision processes, Vroom and Yetton (1973) established criteria to evaluate the adequacy of the decisions made—criteria they believed would be credible to leaders and equally applicable across the five levels of participation. Although a wide variety of criteria could be used, Vroom and Yetton believed decision quality and decision acceptance were the two most important criteria for judging the adequacy of a decision.

Decision quality means simply that if the decision has a rational or objectively determinable "better or worse" alternative, the leader should select the better alternative. Vroom and Yetton (1973) intended quality in their model to apply when the decision could result in an objectively or measurably better outcome for the group or organization. In the "for-profit" sector, this criterion can be assessed in several ways, but perhaps the easiest to understand is, Would the decision show up on the balance sheet? In this case, a high-quality (or, conversely, low-quality) decision would have a direct and measurable impact on the organization's bottom line. In the public sector, one might determine if there was a quality component to a decision by asking, " Will one alternative have a greater cost saving than the other?" or "Does this decision improve services to the client?" Although it may seem that leaders should always choose the alternative with the highest decision quality, this is not always the case. Often, leaders are confronted with equally good (or bad) alternatives. At other times, the issue in question is fairly trivial, rendering the quality of the decision relatively unimportant.

Decision acceptance implies that followers accept the decision as if it were their own and do not merely comply with the decision. Acceptance of the decision outcome by the followers may be critical, particularly if it is the followers who will bear principle responsibility for implementing the decision. With such acceptance, there will be no need for superiors to monitor compliance, which can be a continuing and time-consuming activity (and virtually impossible in some circumstances, such as with a geographically dispersed sales staff).

As with quality, acceptance of a decision is not always critical for implementation. For example, most organizations have an accounting form that employees use to obtain reimbursement for travel expenses. Suppose a company's chief financial officer has decided to change the format of the form for reimbursing travel expenses and has had the new forms printed and distributed throughout the company. Further, she has sent out a notice that effective June 1, the old forms will no longer be accepted for reimbursement—only claims made using the new forms will be processed and paid. Assuming the new form has no gross errors, problems, or omissions, our CFO really has no concern with acceptance as defined here. If people want to be reimbursed for their travel expenses, then they will use the new form. This decision, in essence, implements itself.

On the other hand, leaders sometimes assume that they do not need to worry about acceptance because they have so much power over their followers that overt rejection of a decision is not likely to occur. A corporate CEO is not apt to see a junior accountant stand up and openly challenge the CEO's decision to implement a new policy, even though the young accountant may not "buy in" to the new policy at all. Because followers generally do not openly object to the decisions made by leaders with this much power, these leaders often mistakenly assume that their decisions have been accepted and will be fully implemented. This is a rather naive view of what really goes on in organizations. Just because the junior subordinate does not publicly voice his opposition does not mean he will rush right out and wholeheartedly implement the decision. In fact, the junior accountant has a lot more time to destructively undermine the policy than the CEO does to check to ensure it is being carried out to the letter of the law.

The Decision Tree

Having settled on quality and acceptance as the two principle criteria for effective decisions, Vroom and Yetton then developed a normative decision model. (A normative model is one based on what "ought" to happen rather than describing what does happen.) They also developed a set of questions to protect quality and acceptance by eliminating decision processes that would be "wrong" or inappropriate. Generally, these questions concern the problem itself, the amount of pertinent information possessed by the leader and followers, and various situational factors.

In order to make it easier for leaders to determine how much participation subordinates should have to optimize decision quality and acceptance, Vroom and Yetton (1973) incorporated these questions into a decision tree (see Figure 15-1). To use the decision tree, one starts at the left by stating the problem and then proceeds through the model from left to right. Every time a box is encountered, the question associated with that box must be answered with either a yes or no response. Eventually, all paths lead to a set of decision processes that, if used, will lead to a decision that protects both quality and acceptance.

Having reached a set of feasible alternatives that meet the desirable criteria for quality and acceptance among followers, the leader may then wish to consider additional criteria. One very practical consideration is the amount of time available. If time is critical, then the leader should select the alternative in the feasible set that is farthest to the *left*, again noting that the feasible set is arranged from AI through GII. It generally takes less time to make and implement autocratic decisions than it does to make consultative or group decisions. Nevertheless, it is important to note that the first step is to protect quality and acceptance (by using the model). Only *after* arriving at an appropriate set of outcomes should leaders consider time in the decision-making process. This tenet is sometimes neglected in the workplace by leaders who overemphasize time as a criterion. Obviously, there are some situations where time is absolutely critical, as in life-or-death emergencies. But too often, leaders ask for a decision to be made as if the situation were an emergency when, in reality, they (the leaders, not the situation) are creating the time pressure. Despite such be-

FIGURE 15–1
Vroom and Yetton's Leadership Decision Tree

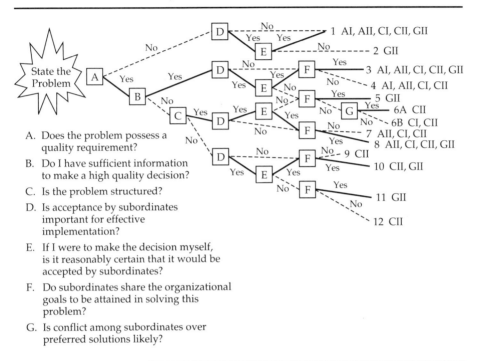

A. Does the problem possess a quality requirement?

B. Do I have sufficient information to make a high quality decision?

C. Is the problem structured?

D. Is acceptance by subordinates important for effective implementation?

E. If I were to make the decision myself, is it reasonably certain that it would be accepted by subordinates?

F. Do subordinates share the organizational goals to be attained in solving this problem?

G. Is conflict among subordinates over preferred solutions likely?

Source: Adapted from Vroom and Yetton, *Leadership and Decision Making* (Pittsburgh: University of Pittsburgh Press, 1973). Used with permission.

havior, it is difficult to imagine a leader who would knowingly prefer a fast decision that lacks both quality and acceptance among the implementors than one that is of high quality and acceptable to followers but that takes more time.

Another important consideration is follower development. Again, after quality and acceptance have been considered using the decision tree, and if the leader has determined that time is not a critical element, she may wish to follow a decision process more apt to allow followers to develop their own decision-making skills. This can be achieved by using the decision tree and then selecting the alternative within the feasible set that is farthest to the *right*. As was the case above, the arrangement of processes from AI to GII provides an increasing amount of follower development by moving from autocratic to group decisions.

Finally, if neither time nor follower development is a concern and multiple options are available in the feasible set of alternatives, the leader may select a

FIGURE 15–2

Factors from the Normative Decision Model and the Interactional Framework

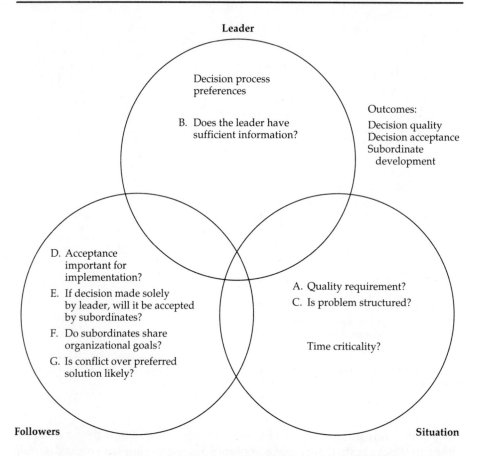

style that best meets his or her needs. This may be the process with which they are most comfortable (''I'm a CII kind of guy''), or it may be a process in which they would like to develop more skill.

Concluding Thoughts about the Normative Decision Model

Having looked at this model in some detail, we will now look at it from the perspective of the leader-follower-situation (L-F-S) framework. To do this, we have used the different decision processes and the questions from the decision tree to illustrate different components in the L-F-S model (see Figure 15–2). Several issues become apparent in this depiction. First, for ease of presentation we have placed each question or factor solely within one circle or another. Nevertheless, one could argue that some of the questions could or should be placed in another part of the model. For example, the question ''Do I have sufficient information to make a high-quality decision?'' is placed in the leader block. It might be argued, however, that no leader could answer this question without some knowledge of the situation. Strictly speaking, therefore, perhaps this question should be placed in the intersection between the leader and the situation. Nonetheless, in keeping with our theme that leadership involves interactions among all three elements, it seems sufficient at this point to illustrate them in their cleanest (if not purest) state.

A second issue also becomes apparent when the normative decision model is viewed through the L-F-S framework. Notice how the Vroom and Yetton (1973) model shifts focus away from the leader toward both the situation and, to an even greater degree, the followers. There are no questions about the leader's personality, motivations, values, or attitudes. In fact, the leader's preference is considered only after higher-priority factors have been considered. The only underlying assumption is that the leader is interested in implementing a high-quality decision (when quality is an issue) that is acceptable to followers (when acceptance is critical to implementation). Given that assumption and a willingness to consider aspects of the situation and aspects of the followers, the leader's behavior can be channeled into more effective decision-making processes.

A third issue is that the L-F-S framework organizes concepts in a familiar conceptual structure. This is an advantage even for a theory with as limited a focus as the normative decision model (i.e., decision making); it will be even more helpful later as we consider more complex theories.

Finally, because the normative decision model is a *leadership theory* rather than Vroom and Yetton's personal opinions, a number of empirical studies have investigated the model's efficacy. Research conducted by Field (1982) and Vroom and Jago (1974, 1988) provided strong support for the model, as these studies showed that leaders were much more likely to make effective or successful decisions when they followed its tenets than when they ignored them. Nevertheless, although leaders may be more apt to make more effective decisions when using the model, there is no evidence to show that these leaders are more effective overall than leaders not using the model (Miner, 1975). The latter findings again point out that both the leadership process and leadership effectiveness are complex phenomema; being a good decision maker is not enough to be a good leader (although it certainly helps). Other problems with the model are that it views decision making as taking place at a single point in time (Yukl, 1989); assumes that leaders are equally skilled at using all five decision procedures (Yukl & Van Fleet, 1992); and assumes that some of the prescriptions of the model may not be the best for a given situation. For example, the normative decision model prescribes that leaders use a GII decision process if conflict may occur over a decision, but leaders may be more effective if they instead make an AI decision and avoid intragroup conflict (Couch & Yetton, 1987). Despite these problems, the normative model is one of the best supported of the four major contingency theories of leadership, and leaders would be wise to consider using the model when making decisions.

THE SITUATIONAL LEADERSHIP THEORY

It seems fairly obvious that leaders do not interact with all followers in the same manner. For example, a leader may give general guidelines or goals to her highly competent and motivated followers but spend considerable time coaching, directing, and training her unskilled and unmotivated followers. Or leaders may provide relatively little praise and assurances to followers with high self-confidence but high amounts of support to followers with low self-confidence. Although leaders often have different interactional styles when dealing with individual followers, is there an optimum way for leaders to adjust their behavior with different followers and thereby increase their likelihood of success? And if there is, then what factors should the leader base his behavior on—the follower's intelligence? Personality traits? Values? Preferences? Technical competence? Hersey and Blanchard (1969, 1977, 1982) developed **situational leadership theory** *(SLT)* to answer these two important leadership questions.

Leader Behaviors

Situational leadership theory has evolved over time. Its roots are in the Ohio State studies, in which the two broad categories of leader behaviors, initiating structure and consideration, were initially identified (see Chapter Nine). As SLT evolved, so did the labels (but not the content) for the two leadership behavior categories. Initiating structure changed to **task behaviors,** which were defined as the extent to which the leader spells out the responsibilities of an individual or group. Task behaviors include telling people what to do, how to do it, when to do it, and who is to do it. Similarly, consideration changed to **relationship behaviors,** or how much the leader engages in two-way communication. Relationship behaviors include listening, encouraging, facilitating, clarifying, and giving socioemotional support.

As noted in Chapter Nine, there was little evidence to show these two categories of leader behavior were consistently related to leadership success. As with traits, the relative effectiveness of these two behavior dimensions often depended on the situation. Hersey and Blanchard proposed (1969, 1977, 1982) a model to explain why leadership effectiveness varied across these two behavior dimensions and situations. First, they arrayed the two orthogonal dimensions as in the Ohio State studies and then divided each of them into high and low segments (see Figure 15-3). According to Hersey and Blanchard, depicting the two leadership dimensions this way indicated that certain combinations of task and relationship behaviors may be more effective in some situations than in others. For example, in some situations high levels of task but low levels of relationship behaviors were effective; in other situations, just the opposite was true. So far, however, we have not considered the key follower or situational characteristics with which these combinations of task and relationship behaviors were most effective. Hersey and Blanchard stated that these four combinations of task and relationship behaviors would increase leadership effectiveness if they were made contingent on the maturity level of the individual follower.

Maturity of the Follower

Follower maturity is comprised of two components: job maturity and psychological maturity. **Job maturity** is the amount of *task-relevant* knowledge, experience, skill, and ability that the follower possesses. In a sense, job maturity is much the same as technical expertise. **Psychological maturity** is the follower's self-confidence, commitment, motivation, and self-respect *relative to the task* at hand. Notice that both of these elements of maturity are meaningful only with regard to a particular task. Someone with a medical degree and years of experience as a surgeon might be rated as extremely mature at performing open-heart surgery. That same person might have virtually no job or psychological maturity for the tasks of designing and building a house, piloting a hot-air balloon, or counseling a suicidal patient. It is impossible to assess either job or psychological maturity if the task is unknown. Similarly, because most of us perform multiple tasks, there is no universal level of maturity. Both job and psychological maturity vary according to the task at hand.

Prescriptions of the Theory

Now that the key contingency factor, follower maturity, has been identified, let us move on to another aspect of the figure—combining follower maturity levels with the four combinations of leader behaviors described earlier. The horizontal bar or arrow in Figure 15-3 depicts follower maturity as increasing from *right to left* (not in the direction we are used to seeing). There are four segments along this continuum, ranging from M1 (the least mature) to M4 (the most mature). Along this continuum, however, the assessment of follower maturity can be fairly subjective. A follower who possesses high levels of both job and psychological maturity relative to the task would clearly fall in the M4 category, just as a follower with neither job nor psychological maturity would fall in M1. The discriminating factors for categories M2 and M3 are less clear, however.

FIGURE 15–3
The SLT Prescriptions for the Most Appropriate Leader Behaviors
Based on Follower Maturity

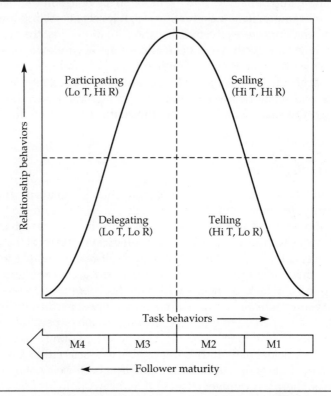

Source: Hersey, P. & K. H. Blanchard. *Management of Organizational Behavior: Utilizing Human Resources.*
4th ed. (Englewood Cliffs, N.J.: Prentice Hall, 1982), p. 152. Adapted by permission of Prentice Hall.

To complete the model, Hersey and Blanchard (1982) added a curved line that represents the leadership behavior that will most likely be effective given a particular level of follower maturity. In order to use SLT, leaders should first assess the maturity level (M1–M4) of the follower relative to the task to be accomplished. Next, a vertical line should be drawn from the center of the maturity level up to the point where it intersects with the curved line in Figure 15–3. The quadrant in which this intersection occurs represents the level of task and relationship behavior that has the best chance of producing successful outcomes. For example, imagine you are a fire chief and have under your command a search-and-rescue team. One of the team members is needed to rescue a backpacker who has fallen in the mountains, and you have selected a particular follower to accomplish the task. What leadership behavior should you exhibit? Assuming this is a responsible and psychologically mature follower who has both substantial training and experience in this type of rescue, you would assess his maturity level as M4. A vertical line from M4 would intersect the curved line in the quadrant where both low task and low relationship behaviors by the leader are most apt to be successful. As the leader, you should exhibit a low level of task and relationship behaviors and delegate this task to the follower. On the other hand, you may have a brand-new member of the fire department who still has to learn the ins and outs of firefighting. Because this particular follower has low job and psychological maturity (M1), SLT maintains that the leader should use a high level of task and a low level of relationship behaviors when initially dealing with this follower.

Hersey and Blanchard suggest one further step leaders may wish to consider. The model described above helps the leader select the most appropriate behavior given the current level of follower maturity. However, there may be cases when the leader would like to see the followers increase their level of maturity. Because more mature followers are generally more effective than less mature followers, leaders may wish to implement a series of **developmental interventions** to help boost follower maturity levels. The process would begin by first assessing the follower's current level of maturity and then determining the leader behavior that best suits that follower in that task. Instead of using the behavior prescribed by SLT, however, the leader would select the next higher leadership behavior. Another way of thinking about this would be for the leader to select the behavior pattern that would fit the follower if that follower were one level higher in maturity. This intervention is designed to help followers in their maturity development, hence its name (see Highlight 15-2, on developmental interventions).

Concluding Thoughts about the Situational Leadership Theory

In Figure 15-4, we can see how the factors in SLT fit within the L-F-S framework. In comparison to the Vroom and Yetton model, there are fewer factors to be considered in each of the three elements. The only situational consideration is knowledge of the task, and the only two follower factors are job and psychological maturity. On the other hand, the theory goes well beyond decision making, which was the sole domain of the normative decision model. In fact, Hersey and Blanchard have suggested that their model can even be extended to other applications, such as parenting.

Situational leadership theory is usually appealing to students and practitioners because of its commonsense approach as well as its ease of understanding. Unfortunately, there is little research to support the predictions of SLT in the workplace (Vecchio, 1987; Yukl & Van Fleet, 1992). Moreover, follower maturity is poorly defined (Graeff, 1983), and the model provides inadequate ra-

---

HIGHLIGHT 15–2

A Developmental Intervention Using SLT

Dianne is a resident assistant in charge of a number of students in a university dorm. One particular sophomore, Michael, has volunteered to work on projects in the past but never seems to take the initiative to get started on his own. Michael seems to wait until Dianne gives him explicit direction, approval, and encouragement before he will get started. Michael can do a good job, but he seems to be unwilling to start without some convincing that it is alright and making explicit the steps to be taken. Dianne has assessed Michael's maturity level as M2, but she would like to see him develop, both in task maturity and in psychological maturity. The behavior most likely to fit Michael's current maturity level is *selling* or high task, high relationship. But Dianne has decided to implement a developental intervention to help Michael raise his maturity level. Dianne can be most helpful in this intervention by moving up one level to *participating* or low task, high relationship. By reducing the amount of task instructions and direction while encouraging Michael to lay out a plan on his own and supporting his steps in the right direction, Dianne is most apt to help Michael become an M3 follower. This does not mean the work will get done most efficiently, however. Just as we saw in the Vroom and Yetton model earlier, if part of the leader's job is development of followers, then time may be a reasonable and necessary trade-off for short-term efficiency.

---

tionale or sufficiently specific guidance about *why* or *how* particular levels of task and relationship behaviors correspond to each of the follower maturity levels (Yukl, 1989). Furthermore, Hersey and Blanchard have simply defined leadership effectiveness as those leader behaviors that match the prescriptions of SLT. They have not presented any evidence that leaders who behave according to the model's prescriptions actually have higher unit performance indices, better performing or more satisfied subordinates, or a more favorable organizational climate (Vecchio, 1987). Nevertheless, even with these shortcomings, SLT is a useful way to get leaders to think about how leadership effectiveness may depend somewhat on being flexible with different subordinates, not on acting the same way toward them all.

THE CONTINGENCY MODEL

Although leaders may be able to change their behaviors toward individual subordinates, leaders also have dominant behavioral tendencies. Some leaders may be generally more supportive and relationship-oriented, whereas others

FIGURE 15–4

Factors from the Situational Leadership Theory and the Interactional Framework

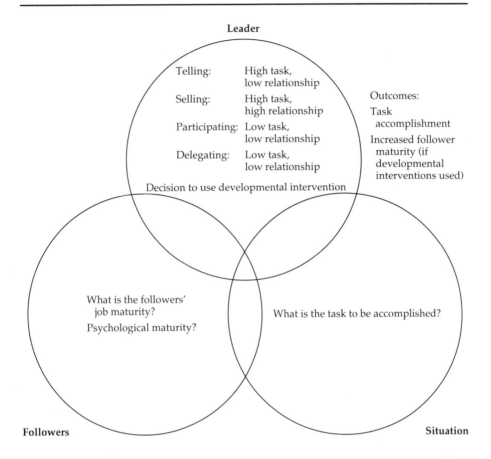

may be more concerned with task or goal accomplishment. The contingency model (Fiedler, 1967) recognizes that leaders have these general behavioral tendencies and specifies situations where certain leaders (or behavioral dispositions) may be more effective than others.

Fiedler's (1967) **contingency model** of leadership is probably the earliest and most well-known contingency theory, and is often perceived by students to be almost the opposite of SLT. In comparing the contingency model to SLT, SLT emphasizes flexibility in leader behaviors, whereas the contingency model maintains that leaders are much more consistent (and consequently less flexible) in their behavior. Situational leadership theory maintains that leaders who *correctly base their behaviors* on follower maturity will be more effective, whereas the contingency model suggests that leader effectiveness is primarily determined by *selecting the right kind of leader for a certain situation or changing the situation* to fit the particular leader's style. Another way to say this is that leadership effectiveness depends on both the leader's style and the favorableness of the leadership situation. Some leaders are better than others in some situations but less effective in other situations. To understand contingency theory, therefore, we need to look first at the critical characteristics of the leader and then at the critical aspects of the situation.

The Least Preferred Co-Worker Scale

In order to determine a leader's general style or tendency, Fiedler developed an instrument called the **least preferred co-worker (LPC) scale**. The scale instructs a leader to think of the single individual with whom he has had the greatest difficulty working (i.e., the least preferred co-worker) and then to describe that individual in terms of a series of bipolar adjectives (e.g., friendly–unfriendly, boring–interesting, sincere–insincere). Those ratings are then converted into a numerical score.

In thinking about such a procedure, many people assume that the score is determined primarily by the characteristics of whatever particular individual the leader happened to identify as his least preferred co-worker. In the context of contingency theory, however, it is important to understand that the score is thought to *represent something about the leader, not the specific individual the leader evaluated.*

The current interpretation of these scores is that they identify a leader's motivation hierarchy (Fiedler, 1978). Based on their LPC scores, leaders are categorized into two groups: low LPC leaders and high LPC leaders. In terms of their motivation hierarchy, **low LPC leaders** are primarily motivated by the task, which means that these leaders primarily gain satisfaction from task accomplishment. Thus, their dominant behavioral tendencies are similar to the initiating structure behavior described in the Ohio State research or the task behavior of SLT. However, if tasks are being accomplished in an acceptable manner, then low LPC leaders will move to their secondary level of motivation, which is forming and maintaining relationships with followers. Thus, low LPC leaders will focus on improving their relationships with followers *after* they are assured that assigned tasks are being satisfactorily accomplished. As soon as tasks are no longer being accomplished in an acceptable manner, however, low LPC leaders will refocus their efforts on task accomplishment and persist with these efforts until task accomplishment is back on track.

In terms of motivation hierarchy, **high LPC leaders** are primarily motivated by relationships, which means that these leaders are primarily satisfied by establishing and maintaining close interpersonal relationships. Thus, their dominant behavioral tendencies are similar to the consideration behaviors described in the Ohio State research or the relationship behaviors in SLT. If high LPC

FIGURE 15–5
Motivational Hierarchies for Low and High LPC Leaders

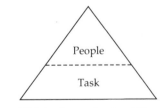

Low LPC Leader motivational hierarchy

High LPC Leader motivational hierarchy

leaders have established good relationships with their followers, then they will move to their secondary level of motivation, which is task accomplishment. As soon as leader-follower relations are jeopardized, however, high LPC leaders will cease working on tasks and refocus their efforts on improving relationships with followers.

It may help to think in terms of an analogy with a motivational theory we discussed in Chapter Eleven—Maslow's hierarchy of needs. You can think of the LPC scale as identifying two different sorts of leaders with their respective motivational hierarchies depicted in Figure 15–5. As with Maslow's hierarchy of needs, lower-level needs must be satisfied first. Low LPC leaders will move ''up'' to satisfying relationship needs when they are assured the task is being satisfactorily accomplished. High LPC leaders will move ''up'' to emphasizing task accomplishment when they have established good relationships with their followers.

Because all tests have some level of imprecision, Fiedler (1978) suggested that the LPC scale cannot accurately identify the motivation hierarchy for those individuals with certain intermediate scores. Research by Kennedy (1982) suggests an alternative view. Kennedy has shown that individuals within the intermediate range of LPC scale scores may more easily or readily switch between being task- or relationship-oriented leaders than those individuals with more extreme scale scores. They may be equally satisfied by working on the task or establishing relationships with followers.

Situational Favorability

The other critical variable in the contingency model is **situation favorability,** which is the amount of control the leader has over the followers. Presumably, the more control a leader has over followers, the more favorable the situation is, at least from the leader's perspective. Fiedler included three subelements in situation favorability. These were leader-member relations, task structure, and position power.

Leader-member relations is the most powerful of the three subelements in determining overall situation favorability. It involves the extent to which relationships between the leader and followers are generally cooperative and friendly or antagonistic and difficult. Leaders who rate leader-member relations as high would feel they had the support of their followers and could rely on their loyalty.

Task structure is second in potency in determining overall situation favorability and is similar to that described in Chapter Thirteen. Here the leader would objectively determine task structure by assessing whether there were detailed descriptions of work products, standard operating procedures, or objective indicators of how well the task is being accomplished. The more one could answer these questions affirmatively, the higher the structure of the task.

Position power is the weakest of the three elements of situation favorability. Position power is similar to legitimate power described in Chapter Six, and leaders who have titles of authority or rank, the authority to administer rewards and punishments, and the legitimacy to conduct follower performance appraisals have greater position power than leaders who lack them.

The relative weights of these three subelements, when added together, can be used to create a continuum of situational favorability. When using the contingency model, leaders are first asked to rate items that measure the strength of leader-member relations, the degree of task structure, and their level of position power. These ratings are then weighted and combined to determine an overall level of situational favorability facing the leader (Fiedler & Chemers, 1982). Any particular situation's favorability can then be plotted on a continuum Fiedler divided into octants representing distinctly different levels of situational favorability. The relative weighting scheme for the subelements and how they make up each of the eight octants can be seen in Figure 15–6.

You can see that the octants of situation favorability range from 1 (highly favorable) to 8 (very unfavorable). The highest levels of situational favorability occur when leader-member relations are good, the task is structured, and position power is high. The lowest levels of situational favorability occur when there are high levels of leader-member conflict, the task is unstructured or unclear, and the leader does not have the power to reward or punish subordinates. Moreover, the relative weighting of the three subelements can easily be

FIGURE 15–6

Contingency Model Octant Structure for Determining Situation Favorability

High ⟵	Overall situation favorability							Low

Leader-member relations	Good				Poor			
Task structure	Structured		Unstructured		Structured		Unstructured	
Position power	High	Low	High	Low	High	Low	High	Low
Octant	1	2	3	4	5	6	7	8

seen by their order of precedence in Figure 15–6, with leader-member relations appearing first, followed by task structure and then position power. For example, because leader-member relations carries so much weight, it is impossible for leaders with good leader-member relations to have anything worse than moderate situational favorability, regardless of their task structure or position power. In other words, leaders with good leader-member relations will be in a situation that has situational favorability no worse than octant 4; leaders with poor leader-member relations will be facing a leadership situation with situational favorability being no better than octant 5.

Prescriptions of the Model

Fiedler and his associates have conducted numerous studies to determine how different leaders (as described by their LPC scores) have performed in different situations (as described in terms of situational favorability). Figure 15–7 describes which type of leader (high or low LPC) Fiedler found to be most effective, given different levels of situation favorability. The solid dark line represents the relative effectiveness of a low LPC leader, and the dashed line represents the relative effectiveness of a high LPC leader. It is obvious from the way the two lines cross and recross that there is some interaction between the leader's style and the overall situation favorability. If the situation favorability is moderate (octants 4, 5, 6, or 7), then those groups led by leaders concerned with establishing and maintaining relationships (high LPC leaders) seem to do best. However, if the situation is either very unfavorable (octant 8) or highly favorable (octants 1, 2, or 3), then those groups led by the task-motivated (low LPC) leaders seem to do best.

Fiedler suggested that leaders will try to satisfy their primary motivation when faced with unfavorable or moderately favorable situations. This means

FIGURE 15–7
Leader Effectiveness Based on the Contingency between
Leader LPC Score and Situation Favorability

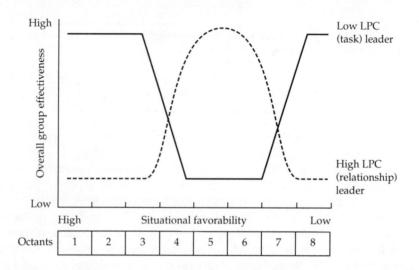

that low LPC leaders will concentrate on the task and high LPC leaders will concentrate on relationships when faced with these two levels of situational favorability. Nevertheless, leaders facing highly favorable situations know that their primary motivations will be satisfied and thus will move to their secondary motivational state. This means that *leaders will behave according to their secondary motivational state only when faced with highly favorable situations* (see Highlight 15-3, High and Low LPC Leaders and the Contingency Model).

There are several interesting implications of Fiedler's (1967) model worthy of additional comment. Because leaders develop their distinctive motivation hierarchies and dominant behavior tendencies through a lifetime of experiences, Fiedler believed these hierarchies and tendencies would be difficult to change through training. Fiedler maintained it was naive to believe that sending someone to a relatively brief leadership training program could substantially alter any leader's personality or typical way of acting in leadership situations; after all, such tendencies had been developed over many years of experience. Instead of trying to change the leader, Fiedler concluded, training would be more effective if it showed leaders how to recognize and change key situational characteristics to better fit their personal motivational hierarchies and behavioral tendencies. Thus, according to Fiedler, the content of leadership training should emphasize situational engineering rather than behavioral flexibility in leaders. Relatedly, organizations could become more effective if they matched the characteristics of

---

HIGHLIGHT 15–3

High and Low LPC Leaders and the Contingency Model

Suppose we had two leaders, Tom Low (a low LPC or task motivated leader) and Brenda High (a high LPC or relationship motivated leader). In unfavorable situations, Tom will be motivated by his primary level and will thus exhibit *task behaviors*. In similar situations, Brenda will also be motivated by her primary level and as a result will exhibit *relationship behaviors*. Fiedler found that in unfavorable situations, task behavior will help the group to be more effective, so Tom's behavior would better match the requirements of the situation. Group effectiveness would not be aided by Brenda's relationship behavior in this situation.

Moving to situations with moderate favorability, both Tom and Brenda are still motivated by their primary motivations, so their behaviors will be precisely the same as described: Tom will exhibit task behaviors and Brenda will exhibit relationship behaviors. Because the situation has changed, however, group effectiveness no longer requires task behavior. Instead, the combination of situational variables leads to a condition where a leader's relationship behaviors will make the greatest contribution to group effectiveness. Hence, Brenda will be the most effective leader in situations of moderate favorability.

In highly favorable situations, the explanation provided by Fiedler gets more complex. When leaders find themselves in highly favorable situations, they no longer have to be concerned about their primary motivations being satisfied (they already are). *In highly favorable situations, leaders switch to satisfying their secondary motivations.* Because Tom's secondary motivation is to establish and maintain relationships, in highly favorable situations he will exhibit relationship behaviors. Similarly Brenda will also be motivated by her secondary motivation, so she would manifest task behaviors in highly favorable situations. Fiedler believed that leaders who manifested relationship behaviors in highly favorable situations helped groups to be more effective. In this case, Tom is giving the group what they need to be more effective.

---

the leader (in this case LPC scores) with the demands of the situation (i.e., situational favorability) than if they tried to change the leader to fit the situation. These suggestions imply that high or low LPC leaders in mismatched situations should either change the situation or move to jobs that better match their motivational hierachies and behavorial patterns. Although the idea of fitting the characteristics of the leader to the demands of the situation is very similar to earlier suggestions made about improving the usefulness of personality traits (Chapter Seven) in leadership selection, the suggestions for leadership training are almost the opposite of those put forth by the other theories in this chapter.

FIGURE 15–8
Factors from Fiedler's Contingency Theory and the Interactional Framework

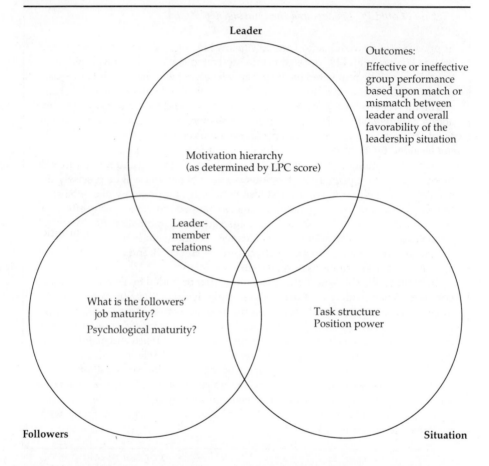

Concluding Thoughts about the Contingency Model

Before reviewing the empirical evidence, perhaps a clearer understanding of the contingency model can be attained by examining it through the L-F-S framework. As seen in Figure 15–8, task structure is a function of the situation and LPC scores are a function of the leader. Because position power is not a characteristic of the leader but of the situation the leader finds him- or herself in, it is included in the situational circle. Leader-member relations is a joint function of the leader and the followers; thus, it best belongs in the overlapping intersection of the leader and follower circles.

As opposed to the dearth of evidence for Hersey and Blanchard's (1969, 1982) situational theory, Fiedler and his fellow researchers have provided considerable evidence that the predictions of the model are empirically valid, particularly in laboratory settings (Fiedler, 1978; Fiedler & Chemers, 1982; Peters, Hartke, & Pohlmann, 1985; Strube & Garcia, 1981). However, a review of the studies conducted in field settings yielded only mixed support for the model (Peters, Hartke, & Pohlmann, 1985). Moreover, researchers have criticized the model for the uncertainties surrounding the meaning of LPC scores (Kennedy, 1982; Rice, 1978; Schriesheim & Kerr, 1977); the interpretation of situational favorability (Jago & Ragan, 1986a, 1986b); and the relationships between LPC scores and situational favorability (Jago & Ragan, 1986a, 1986b; Vecchio, 1983).

Recent research by Ayman and Chemers (1991) may provide a partial explanation for why some studies failed to support certain hypotheses of the contingency model. These researchers assessed leaders' motivational hierarchies (via LPC scores) and situational favorability levels as well as leaders' standing on the trait of self-monitoring (as described in Chapter Seven). Ayman and Chemers found that those leaders who were low in self-monitoring performed poorly when there was not a match between their LPC scores and situational favorability. However, in the same mismatches between LPC score and situation favorability, high self-monitors performed significantly better than the model predicted. Apparently, those leaders who were good at reading social cues from their followers and modifying their behavior according to those cues had higher-performing groups, even when the leaders' motivational hierarchies did not match the needs of the situation. Thus, Fiedler's explanation of behavior determinism may be less applicable to high self-monitors than it is to low self-monitors.

The latter finding by Ayman and Chemers (1991) makes an important point that concerns all four of the theories in this chapter. Even though the contingency theories are more comprehensive than any of the other leadership models or theories previously described in this text, even these four theories are still extremely limited with respect to the myriad of leader, follower, and situational factors that affect the leadership process. For example, none of the theories really consider the variety of leadership traits found to be related to leadership effectiveness (like self-monitoring); the leader's and followers' values, attitudes, and preferences; the cohesiveness, norms, or size of the group; or the task, organizational design and culture, or environmental factors that can affect the leadership process. Because many of the latter variables can and do vary in field settings (and often have a greater effect on the leadership process than the variables considered by the theories described in this chapter), finding any support for these theories outside controlled laboratory experiments is fairly remarkable. Thus, although many of the criticisms of Fiedler's contingency model remain unanswered, the theory has been thoroughly tested in laboratory settings and has found some degree of empirical support in field settings. Furthermore, like any good theory, the contingency model has stimulated considerable research, and even if this research did not always lend support to the model, the findings still contributed to our knowledge of the leadership process.

THE PATH–GOAL THEORY

Perhaps the most sophisticated (and comprehensive) of the four contingency models is **path-goal theory.** The underlying mechanism of path-goal theory is not particularly new or complicated. In fact, we discussed the "engine" of path-goal theory when we described expectancy theory in Chapter Eleven. You may recall that expectancy theory was a cognitive theory of motivation where people calculated effort-to-performance probabilities (If I study for 12 hours what is the probability I will get an A on the final exam?), performance-to-outcome probabilities (If I get an A on the final what is the probability of getting an A in the course?), and assigned valences or values to outcome (How much do I value a higher GPA?). Theoretically at least, people were assumed to make these calculations on a rational basis, and the theory could be used to predict what tasks people will put their energies into, given some finite number of options.

Path-goal theory uses the same basic assumptions of expectancy theory. At the most fundamental level, the effective leader will provide or ensure the availability of valued rewards for followers (the "goal") and then help them find the best way of getting there (the "path"). Along the way, the effective leader will help the followers identify and remove roadblocks, and avoid dead ends; the leader will also provide emotional support as needed. These "task" and "relationship" leadership actions essentially involve increasing followers' probability estimates for effort-to-performance and performance-to-reward expectancies. In other words, the leader's actions should strengthen followers' beliefs that if they exert a certain level of effort then they will be more likely to accomplish a task, and if they accomplish the task then they will be more likely to achieve some valued outcome.

Although not very complicated in its basic concept, the model added more variables and interactions over time. Evans (1970) is credited with the first version of path-goal theory, but we will focus on a later version developed by House and Dessler (1974). Their conceptual scheme is ideally suited to the L-F-S framework because they described three classes of vairables, which include leader behaviors, followers, and the situation. We will examine each of these in turn.

Leader Behaviors

The four types of leader behavior in path-goal theory can be seen in Table 15–2. Like SLT, path-goal theory assumes that leaders not only may use varying styles with different subordinates but might very well use differing styles with

TABLE 15–2
The Four Leader Behaviors of Path-Goal Theory

Directive Leadership. These leader behaviors are very similar to the task behaviors from SLT. They include telling the followers what they are expected to do, how to do it, when it is to be done, and how their work fits in with the work of others. This behavior would also include setting schedules, establishing norms, and providing expectations that followers will adhere to established procedure and regulations.

Supportive leadership. Supportive leadership behaviors include courteous and friendly interactions, expressing genuine concern for the followers' well-being and individual needs, and remaining open and approachable to followers. These behaviors, which are very similar to the relationship behaviors in SLT, also are marked by attention to the competing demands of treating followers equally while recognizing status differentials between the leader and the followers.

Participative leadership. Participative leaders engage in the behaviors that mark the consultative and group behaviors described by Vroom and Yetton (1973). As such, they tend to share work problems with followers; solicit their suggestions, concerns, and recommendations; and weigh these inputs in the decision-making process.

Achievement-oriented leadership. Leaders exhibiting these would be seen as both demanding and supporting in interactions with their followers. In the first place, they would set very challenging goals for group and follower behavior, continually seek ways to improve performance en route, and expect the followers to always perform at their highest levels. But they would support these behaviors by exhibiting a high degree of ongoing confidence that subordinates *can* put forth the necessary effort; *will* achieve the desired results; and, even further, *will* assume even more responsibility in the future.

---

the same subordinates in different situations. Path-goal theory suggests that depending on the followers and the situation, these different leader behaviors can increase followers' acceptance of the leader, enhance their level of satisfaction, and raise their expectations that effort will result in effective performance, which in turn will lead to valued rewards.

The Followers

Path-goal theory contains two groups of follower variables. The first relates to the *satisfaction of followers,* and the second relates to the *followers' perception of their own abilities* relative to the task to be accomplished. In terms of followers' satisfaction, path-goal theory suggests that leader behaviors will be acceptable to the followers to the degree followers see the leader's behavior as either an immediate source of satisfaction or as directly instrumental in achieving future satisfaction. In other words, followers will actively support a leader as long as they view the leader's actions as a means for increasing their own levels of satisfaction. However, there is only so much a leader can do to increase followers' satisfaction levels, as satisfaction also depends on characteristics of the followers themselves.

A frequently cited example of how followers' characteristics influence the impact of leader behaviors on followers' levels of satisfaction involves the trait of

FIGURE 15–9

Interaction between Followers' Locus of Control Scores
and Leader Behavior in Decision Making

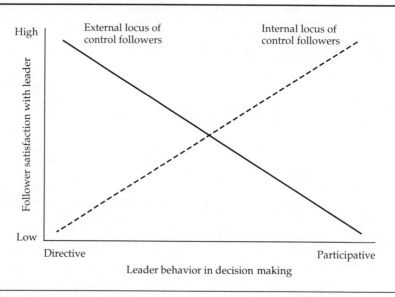

Source: Adapted from T. R. Mitchell, C. M. Smyser, and S. E. Weed, "Locus of Control: Supervision and Work Satisfaction," *Academy of Management Journal* 18 (1975), pp. 623–30.

locus of control (as described in Chapter Seven). Mitchell, Smyser, and Weed (1975) found that follower satisfaction was not directly related to the degree of participative behaviors manifest by the leader (i.e., followers with highly paritcipative leaders were not any more satisfied than followers with more autocratic leaders). However, when followers' locus of control scores were taken into account, a contingency relationship was discovered. As can be seen in Figure 15–9, internal-locus-of-control followers, who believed outcomes were a result of their own decisions, were much more satisfied with leaders who exhibited participative behaviors than they were with leaders who were directive. Conversely, external locus of control followers were more satisfied with directive leader behaviors than they were with participative leader behaviors.

Followers' perceptions of their own skills and abilities to perform particular tasks can also affect the impact of certain leader behaviors. Followers who believe they are perfectly capable of performing a task are not as apt to be motivated by, or as willing to accept, a directive leader as they would a leader who exhibits participative behaviors. Using the same rationale as for locus of control, one can predict the oposite relationship for followers who do not percieive thay have sufficient abilities to perform the task. Once again, the acceptability of the leader and the motivation to perform are in part determined by followers' characteristics. Thus, path-goal theory suggests that both leader behaviors and follower characteristics are important in determining outcomes.

The Situation

Path-goal theory considers three situational factors that impact or moderate the effects of leader behavior on follower attitudes and behaviors. These include *the task, the formal authority system,* and *the primary work group.* Each of these three factors has been described earlier in this text, and each can influence the leadership situation in one of three ways. These three factors can serve as an independent motivational factor, a constraint on the behavior of followers (which may be either positive or negative in outcome), or as a reward. For example, it may be recalled from Chapter Thirteen that the task itself could be motivational (if it involved a high level of skill variety and task significance), constraining (if it had a high level of task interdependence), or delegated as a reward (if it had a high level of autonomy).

However, it should also be increasingly apparent that these variables can often affect the impact of various leader behaviors. For example, if the task is very structured and routine, the formal authority system has constrained followers' behaviors, and the work group has established clear norms for performance, then leaders would be serving a redundant purpose by manifesting directive or achievement-oriented behaviors. These prescriptions are similar to some of those noted in substitutes for leadership theory (Kerr & Jermier, 1978), as everything the follower needs in order to understand the effort-to-performance and performance-to-reward links is provided by the situation. Thus, redundant leader behaviors might be interpreted by followers as either a complete lack of understanding or empathy by the leader, or an attempt by the leader to exert excessive control. Neither of these interpretations is likely to enhance the leader's acceptance by followers or increase their motivation.

Although we have already described how follower characteristics and situational characteristics can impact leader behaviors, path-goal theory also maintains that follower and situational variables can impact each other. In other words, situational variables, such as the task performed, can also impact the influence of followers' skills, abilities, or personality traits on folllowers' satisfaction. Although this seems to make perfect sense, hopefully you are beginning to see how complicated path-goal theory can be when one starts considering how situational variables, follower characteristics, and leader behaviors interact in the leadership process. Because these interactions can become extremely complicated and are beyond the scope of this text, readers who wish to learn more about the intricacies of path-goal theory are encouraged to read House and Dessler (1974).

FIGURE 15–10
Examples of Applying Path-Goal Theory

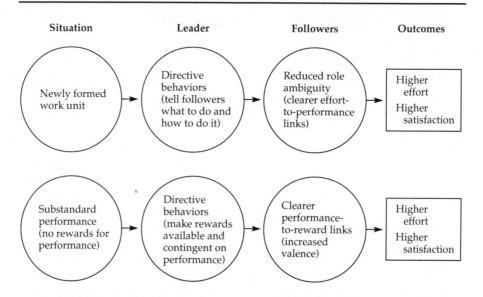

Prescriptions of the Theory

In general, path-goal theory maintains that leaders should first assess the situation and select a leadership behavior appropriate to situational demands. By manifesting the appropriate behaviors, leaders can increase followers' effort-to-performance expectancies, performance-to-reward expectancies, or valences of the outcomes. These increased expectancies and valences will improve subordinates' effort levels and the rewards attained, which in turn will increase subordinates' satisfaction and performance levels and the acceptance of their leaders. Perhaps the easiest way to explain this fairly complicated process is through the use of an example. Suppose we have a set of followers who are in a newly created work unit and do not have a clear understanding of the requirements of their positions. In other words, the followers have a reasonably high level of role ambiguity. According to path-goal theory, leaders should exhibit a high degree of directive behaviors in order to reduce the role ambiguity of their followers. The effort-to-performance link will become clearer when leaders tell followers what to do and how to do it in ambiguous situations, which in turn will cause followers to exert higher effort levels. Because role ambiguity is assumed to be unpleasant, these directive leader behaviors and higher effort levels should eventually result in higher satisfaction levels among followers. Figure 15–10 provides a graphic representation of this process. Similarly, leaders may look at the leadership situation and note that followers' per-

FIGURE 15–11
Factors from Path-Goal Theory and the Interactional Framework

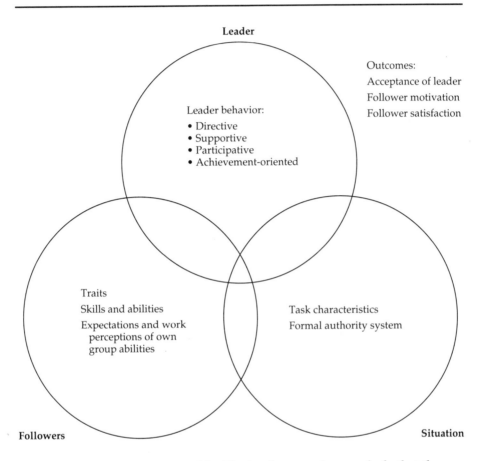

formance levels are not acceptable. The leader may also conclude that the current situation offers few, if any, incentives for increased performance. In this case, the leader may use directive behaviors to increase the value of the rewards (or valence), which in turn will increase followers' effort levels and performance.

Concluding Thoughts about the Path-Goal Theory

Before getting into the research surrounding path-goal theory, it may be useful to examine the theory using the L-F-S framework. As seen in Figure 15–11, the components of path-goal theory fit quite nicely into the L-F-S model. The four leader behaviors fit squarely in the leader circle, the characteristics of the followers fit into the follower circle, and the task and formal authority system fit into the situation circle. Of all the components of path-goal theory, the only "mismatch" with the L-F-S model deals with the primary work group. The norms, cohesiveness, size, and stage of development of groups is considered to be part of the follower function in the L-F-S model but is part of the situation function in path-goal theory. In that regard, we hasten to note we use the L-F-S framework primarily for heuristic purposes. Ultimately, the concepts described in these four theories are sufficiently complex and ambiguous that there probably is no "right" answer to any single depiction.

In terms of research, the path-goal theory has received only mixed support to date (Schriesheim & DeNisi, 1981; Schriesheim & Kerr, 1977; Yukl, 1989). Although many of these mixed findings may be due to the fact that the path-goal theory excludes many of the variables found to impact the leadership process, thay may also be due to problems with the theory. Yukl (1989) maintained that most of these criticisms deal with the methodology used to study path-goal theory and the limitations of expectancy theory (as noted in Chapter Eleven). Moreover, the path-goal theory assumes that the only way to increase performance is to increase followers' motivation levels. The theory ignores the roles leaders play in selecting talented followers, building their skill levels through training, and redesigning their work (Yukl & Van Fleet, 1992).

Nonetheless, path-goal theory is useful for illustrating two points. First, as noted by Yukl (1989), "path-goal theory has already made a contribution to the study of leadership by providing a conceptual framework to guide researchers in identifying potentially relevant situational moderator variables" (p. 104). Path-goal theory also illustrates that as models become more complicated, they may be more useful to researchers and less appealing to practitioners. Our experience is that pragmatically oriented students and in-place leaders want to take something from a model that is understandable and can be applied in their work situation right away. This does not mean they prefer simplicity to validity—they generally appreciate the complexity of the leadership process. But neither do they want a model that is so complex as to be indecipherable.

SUMMARY

This chapter is designed to provide an overview of four of the more well-known contingency theories of leadership, which include the normative decision model (Vroom & Yetton, 1973), the situational leadership model (Hersey & Blanchard, 1984), the contingency model (Fiedler, 1967), and the path-goal theory (House & Dessler, 1974). All four models are fairly similar in that they specify that leaders should make their behaviors contingent on certain aspects of the followers or the situation in order to improve leadership effectiveness. In addition, all four theories implicitly assume that leaders can accurately assess key follower and situational factors. However, based on the material in Chapter Two about perception, it is entirely possible that two leaders in the same situation may reach very different conclusions about followers' level of knowledge, maturity, the strength of leader-follower relationships, the degree of task structure, or the level of role ambiguity being experienced by followers. These differences in perception could lead these two leaders to reach different conclusions about the situation, which may in turn cause them to take very different actions in response to the situation. Furthermore, these actions may be in accordance or in conflict with the prescriptions of any of these four theories, and leaders whose perceptions may have caused them to act in a manner not prescribed by a particular model may be an underlying reason why these four theories have reported conflicting findings, particularly in field settings.

Another reason why these theories have generally found mixed support in field settings concerns the fact that they are all fairly limited in scope. Many of the factors that affect leader and follower behaviors in work group, team, or volunteer committee settings are not present in laboratory studies but often play a substantial role in field studies. For example, none of the models take into acoount how levels of stress, organizational culture and climate, working conditions, technology, economic conditions, or type of organizational design affect the leadership process. Nevertheless, the four contingency theories have been the subject of considerable research, and even if only mixed support for the models has been found, this research has succeeded in adding to our body of knowledge about leadership and has given us a more sophisticated understanding of the leadership process.

KEY TERMS AND CONCEPTS

normative decision model

decision quality

decision acceptance

situational leadership theory (SLT)

task behaviors

relationship behaviors

job maturity

psychological maturity

developmental interventions

contingency model

least preferred co-worker (LPC) scale

low LPC leaders

high LPC leaders

situational favorability

path-goal theory

DISCUSSION QUESTIONS

1. Given the description of the leadership situation facing the airplane crash survivors described in Chapter One, how would the Vroom-Yetton model, situational leadership theory, the contingency model, and path-goal theory prescribe how a leader should act?

2. Given the leadership situation in the social services agency described in Chapter Five, how would situational leadership theory, the contingency model, and path-goal theory prescribe how the leader should act?

3. Can leaders be flexible in how they interact with others? Is this a function of any of the traits described in Chapter Seven?

4. What perspectives do the theories in this chapter offer concerning the question of whether leadership develops through experience?

SUGGESTED READINGS

Fiedler, F. E., and M. M. Chemers. *Improving Leadership Effectiveness: The Leader Match Concept*. 2nd ed. New York: Wiley, 1982.

Hersey, P., and K. H. Blanchard. *The Management of Organizational Behavior*. 4th ed. Englewood Cliffs, N.J.: Prentice Hall, 1984.

Chapter Sixteen

Current Topics in
Leadership Research

INTRODUCTION

If you think about all of the research reviewed in the first 15 chapters in this text, then you will probabably agree that we know quite a bit about the leadership process. Nevertheless, what we do not know about the leadership process far outweighs what we do know. Because much about the leadership process remains to be discovered, and because of the intrinsic interest of the topic, there has been an explosion of leadership research over the past 20 years. For example, the first comprehensive listing of leadership research cited approximately 3,500 leadership studies (Stogdill, 1974), but the most recent edition listed over 8,000 references (Bass, 1990). Some of this more recent research has

---

HIGHLIGHT 16–1

Leadership Quotes, Chapter Sixteen

Setting an example is not the main means of influencing another, it is the only means.

Albert Einstein

A prime function of a leader is to keep hope alive.

John W. Gardner

Nothing great was ever achieved without enthusiasm.

Ralph Waldo Emerson

I am tired of dealing with a lot of prima donnas. By God, you tell that bunch that if they can't get together and stop quarreling like children, I will tell the Prime Minister to get someone else to run this damn war.

General Dwight D. Eisenhower

The beatings will continue until morale improves.

Sign on an executive's desk

---

tried to answer the questions raised by some of the earliest leadership research-ers, such as what roles individual difference variables play in leadership effec-tiveness, how leaders and followers influence each other, or how situational variables affect the leadership process. However, other research has focused on answering a number of new leadership questions, and this chapter reviews the research surrounding two of these newer questions (also see Highlight 16–1 for other kinds of ideas about leadership).

More specifically, given the recent interest in self-managed work groups and teams (Hackman, 1990; Manz, 1986; Wall, Kemp, Jackson, & Clegg, 1986; Yukl & Van Fleet, 1992), the first section in this chapter details a model of group effectiveness developed by Hackman (1990) and Ginnett (1992). Although many of the components of this model have been described earlier in this text, the specific hypotheses about how these components affect group effective-ness make this model quite unique. The second section reviews what we cur-rently know about transformational or charismatic leadership. This section provides a brief historical review of the research on charismatic leadership, de-tails the unique characteristics of charismatic leadership, and describes one of the more well-known theories of charismatic or transformational leadership. It is important to note the two leadership topics reviewed in this chapter are fairly comprehensive, as they generally take into account a far greater number of leader, follower, and situational factors than any of the other leadership theories described in this text.

THE GROUP EFFECTIVENESS MODEL

Since we have emphasized that leadership is a group function and have suggested that one measure of leadership effectiveness may be whether the group achieves its objectives, it is reasonable to examine a model specifically designed to help groups perform more effectively: the **group effectiveness model.** Another way to think of this model is as a mechanism to first identify what a group needs to be effective, and then point the leader either toward the roadblocks that are hindering the group or toward ways to make the group even more effective than it already is. This approach is similar to McGrath's (1964) description of leadership, which suggested that the leader's main job was to determine what needs the group was faced with and then take care of them.

We have mentioned this model of group effectiveness briefly before, but now we will explore it in greater detail. The original model was developed by Hackman and has been the basis for much research on groups and teams over the last 20 years (Hackman, 1990). The model presented here includes modifications by Ginnett and represents an example of a leadership model that is guiding ongoing research. A complete illustration of the model will be shown later. Because of its complexity, it is easier to understand by starting with a few simpler illustrations.

At the most basic level, this model (see Figure 16–1) resembles a systems theory approach with inputs on the left (i.e., individual, group, and organizational factors), processes or throughputs in the center (i.e., what one can tell about the group by actually observing group members at work), and outputs on the right (i.e., how well the group did in accomplishing its objectives). We will examine each of these stages. However, we will proceed through the model in reverse order—looking at outputs first, then the process stage, then inputs.

Outputs

What do we mean by **outputs**? Quite simply, outputs are the results of the group's work. For example, a football team scores 24 points. A production team produces 24 valves in a day. A tank crew hits 24 targets on an artillery range. Such raw data, however, are insufficient for assessing group effectiveness. How do we know if a group's output is good? How do we know if a group is effective? Even though it was possible for the three different teams mentioned above to measure some aspect of their work, these measurements are not very helpful in determining their effectiveness, either in an absolute sense

FIGURE 16–1
Systems View of Group Leadership Model

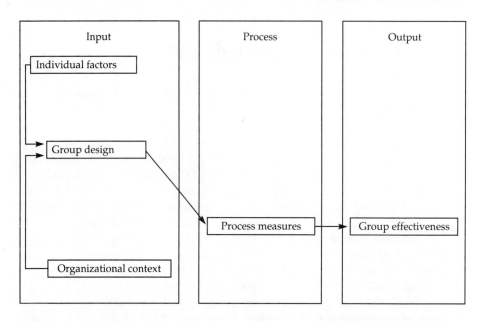

or in a relative sense. For comparison and research purposes, it is desirable to have some measures of group effectiveness that can be applied across groups and tasks. Hackman (1990) argued that a group is effective if (*a*) the team's productive output (goods, services, decisions) meets the standards of quantity, quality, and timeliness of the people who use it; (*b*) the group process that occurs while the group is performing its task enhances the ability of the members to work together as a team in the future; and (*c*) the group experience enhances the growth and personal well-being of the individuals who comprise the team.

Process

It should be obvious why leaders should be concerned with the outputs listed in the preceding section. After all, if a group does not "produce" (output), then it could not be considered effective. But what is *process*? And why should a leader care about it? Actually, there are several reasons a leader might want to pay attention to the group's process—how it goes about its work.

Some groups may have such a limited number of products that the leader can ill afford to wait until the product is delivered to assess its acceptability to the client. For example, a team whose task is to build one (and only one) satellite to be launched into orbit will have no second chances. There will be no op-

FIGURE 16–2
Process Measures of Effectiveness

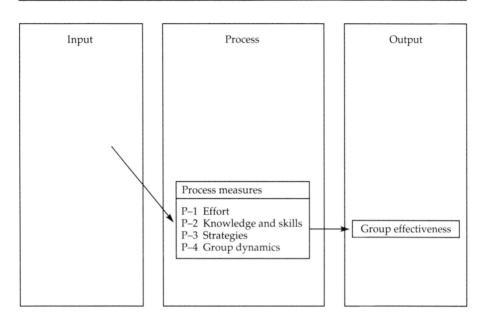

portunity to correct any problem once the satellite is launched. Therefore, it may be desirable for the leader of such a team to assess his team's work *while it is working* rather than after the satellite is launched. Other kinds of teams have such high standards for routine work that there simply are not enough critical indicators in the end product to determine effectiveness from outcome measures. As an example of this situation, a team operating a nuclear power plant is surrounded by so many technical backup systems that it may be difficult to determine team effectiveness by looking at "safe operation" as a measurement criterion. But we have evidence that all teams in nuclear power plants do not operate equally well (Chernobyl and Three Mile Island are but two examples). It would seem helpful to be able to assess real teams "in process" rather than learn of group problems only following disastrous outcomes. Even leaders of noncritical teams might like to be able to routinely monitor their teams for evidence of effective or ineffective processes. The way groups go about their work can provide some very useful information to the leader.

Let us focus for a moment on the block containing the four **process measures** of effectiveness in Figure 16–2. These four process measures of effectiveness provide criteria by which we can examine the ways in which groups work. If a team is to perform effectively, it must (*a*) work hard enough; (*b*) have sufficient knowledge and skills to perform the task; (*c*) have an appropriate strategy to accomplish its work (or ways to approach the task at hand); and (*d*) have constructive and positive group dynamics among its members. (The phrase *group dynamics* refers to interactions among group members, including such aspects as how they communicate with other, express feelings toward each other, and deal with conflict with each other.) These are identified by the labels *P–1* through *P–4* (*P* stands for process) in Figure 16–2.

What should the leader do if she discovers a problem with one of these four process measures? Paradoxically, the answer is *not* to focus her attention on that process per se. While the four process measures are fairly good *diagnostic* measures for a group's ultimate effectiveness, they are, unfortunately, not particularly good leverage points for *fixing* the problem. An analogy from medicine would be a doctor who diagnoses the symptoms of an infection (a fever) but who then treats the symptoms rather than attacking the true underlying cause (a nail in the patient's foot). Similarly at the group level, rather than trying to correct a lack of effort being applied to the task at hand (perhaps a motivation problem), the team leader would be better advised to discover the underlying problem and fix that than to assume that a motivational speech to the group will do the job. This is not to imply that groups cannot benefit from process help. It merely suggests that the leader should ensure that there are not underlying problems (at the input level) that should be fixed first.

Inputs

In a manufacturing plant, inputs are the raw materials that are processed into products for sale. Similarly in group situations, inputs are what is available for groups as they go about their work. There is a variety of levels of inputs, ranging from the individual level to the environmental level. Some of the inputs provide little opportunity for the leader to influence or alter—they are merely givens. Leaders are often put in charge of teams with little or no control over the environment, industry, or even the organizational conditions. There are other inputs, however, that the leader can impact to create the conditions for effective group work.

Figure 16–3 shows the multiple levels in the **input stage** of the model. Note that there are input factors at the individual and organizational levels and that both of these levels affect the group design level. Also note that there is a **leverage point** [*I*(ndividual) *1–4*, *G*(roup) *1–4*, and *O*(rganization) *1–4*] corresponding to each of the four process measures of effectiveness (*P–1* through *P–4*). The meaning and importance of these leverage points will be clearer if we look at a few specific examples. As described earlier, let us assume we have observed a group and discovered that its members are just not working very hard. They seem to be uninterested in the task, frequently wandering off or not even showing up for work. We would diagnose this at the process level as a problem of effort (*P–1*). Rather than just encouraging them to work harder (or threaten-

FIGURE 16–3
Input Stage for the Group Leadership Model

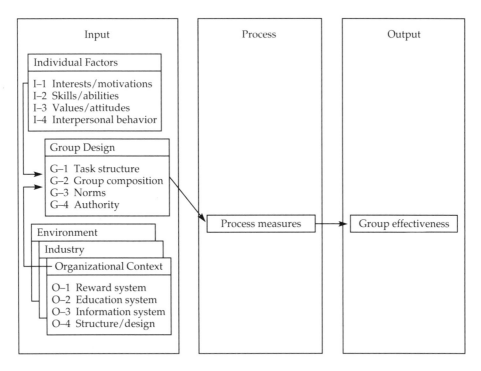

ing them), we should first look at the input level to see if there is some underlying problem.

The individual level (*I–1*, corresponding to a *P–1* diagnosis) suggests that we look at the interests and motivations of the individual team members. These are referred to as **individual factors** in the model. If we have built a team to perform a mechanical assembly task but the individuals assigned have little or no interest in mechanical work, and instead prefer the performing arts, they may have little interest in contributing much effort to the team task. Here, selection of personnel using instruments such as the Cambell Interest and Skills Survey may help our team's effort level from an individual perspective (D. P. Campbell, Hyne, & Nilsen, 1992).

Next let us look at inputs in the **organizational context.** While it may seem logical to move to the group-level inputs next, it may be useful to point out again that this model emphasizes the way groups are influenced by both individual and organizational level inputs (note the direction of the arrows "leading into" the group design stage in Figure 16–3). Therefore, we will look at the organizational level next. At the organizational level (*0–1*), the model suggests that we should examine the reward system that may be impacting the team. If the individuals have no incentive provided by the organization for putting forth effort, they might not be very inclined to work hard, or at all. Similarly, the reward system may be solely structured to reward individual performance. Such a reward structure would be inconsistent with designs for a team task where interdependence and cooperation among members is often an underlying premise. If a professional basketball organization provides rewards for players based only on individual points scored, with no bonuses for team performance (games won or making the playoffs), you can expect little passing, setting picks for teammates, and so on.

Both the individual and organizational level variables contribute to the group's ability to perform the task. But there can also be problems at the **group design** level. Here (G-1), a poorly designed task is hypothesized to be unmotivating. (The job characteristics model for designing intrinsically rewarding work was discussed in a previous chapter.) If a job is meaningless, lacks sufficient autonomy, or provides no knowledge of results, we would not expect to see followers putting forth much effort.

Using the model, we found key leverage points at various levels of the input stage that would impact the way the group went about its work (group process). In the example cited, we diagnosed a process-level problem with effort (P-1), so we examined the 1-level variables at the individual, organizational, and group levels for input stage problems. By the way, the concept of leverage point does not imply that *only* factors at corresponding "numbers" should be considered. For example, a group's effort might be affected by other variables such as group norms (G-3), values, attitudes (I-3), and so on. The model predicts *most likely* problem areas.

Before moving to the leadership component, let us examine a recent addition to the model: the process measure of group dynamics (G-4). Consider the following two examples:

Surgical team

A surgical team comprised of highly experienced members is involved in a surgical procedure that each member has participated in numerous times before. During one portion of the procedure, the surgeon asks for a particular instrument. The scrub nurse looks across the table at the assistant with a questioning gaze and then hands the surgeon the instrument he requested. Recognizing the instrument he has been handed (and asked for) is not correct for the current procedure, he throws it down on the table and curses at the scrub nurse. All members of the surgical team take a half-step back from the table and all casual conversation stops. No one offers any further voluntary assistance to the surgeon.

Commercial airline crew

A commercial airline crew is making a routine approach into an uncrowded airport on a clear day. The captain is flying and has declared a visual approach. His final approach to the runway is not good, which greatly complicates the plane's landing, and the landing is poor. After taxiing to the gate, the captain and his entire crew debrief (discuss) the poor approach, and the team members talk about what they could have done individually and collectively to help the captain avoid or improve a poor approach in the future. The captain thanks the members for their help and encourages them to consider how they could implement their suggestions in other situations.

Obviously, the group dynamics are very different in these two cases. In the first example, the surgeon's behavior, coupled with his status, created a condition inappropriate for effective teamwork. The airline captain in the second example, even though not performing the task well, created a group environment where the team was much more likely to perform well in the future. In both of these cases, we would have observed unusual (one negative and one positive) group dynamics while the group was at work. These are examples of the authority dynamics at the G–4 level.

Again returning to the model for determining points of leverage, we would check the I–4 variable at the individual level to determine if the group members involved had adequate interpersonal skills to interact appropriately. At the organizational level, the 0–4 variable would suggest we check organizational components to determine if the design or structure inhibits effective group work. Finally, at the group design level, the G–4 variable would have us examine authority dynamics created between the leader and the followers. Authority dynamics describe the various ways the group members relate and respond to authority. It is at the group level that the followers have opportunities to relate directly with the team's authority figure, the team leader. The intricacies of how these various authority dynamics can play themselves out in a group's life are more complex than this chapter warrants. Suffice it to say that there is a range of authority relationships that can be created, ranging from autocratic to laissez-faire.

It would be simple if leaders could identify and specify in advance the ideal type of authority for them and their groups, and then work toward that objective. However, groups seldom can operate effectively under one fixed type of authority over time. The leader might prefer to use his or her favorite style, and the followers might also have an inherent preference for one type of authority or another; but if the group is to be effective, then the authority dynamics they are operating with should complement the demands of the situation. Since situations often change over time, so should the authority dynamics of the team. This idea is very similar to a point made earlier in the book—that effective leaders tend to use all five sources of leader power.

In research on the behavior of leaders in forming their teams, Ginnett (in press) found that highly effective leaders used a variety of authority dynamics in the first few minutes of the group's life. This does not mean that each highly effective leader used a single style that was different from the others (i.e., other leaders). It does mean that each one of the effective leaders used a variety of authority styles. At one point in the first meeting of the group, the leader would behave directively, which enabled him to establish his competence and hence his legitimate authority. At another time, he would engage the group in a very participative activity and actively seek participation from each member of the team. By modeling a range of authority behaviors in the early stages of the group's life, the effective leaders laid the groundwork for continuing expectations of shifting authority as the situational demands changed.

Prescriptions of the Model

Having examined two examples of how this model uses group process measures to guide the search for critical input variables (or key leverage points) at the individual, organizational, and group design levels, we are ready to move on to the job of the leader. Following McGrath's (1964) view of the leader's role (the leader's main job is to identify and help satisfy group needs), and using the group effectiveness model, it is possible to identify constructive approaches for the leader to pursue. As described in Chapter Ten, what leaders do depends on where a group is in its development. Ideally, leaders will have the opportunity to assume their leadership role at the very beginning of a group's life. Understanding the model and working at both the individual and organizational levels first, the leader is then in the best position to design the team for effective work. This is a luxury few leaders get, however. If a leader takes over the reins of an in-place group, then she should (1) examine the group at work to determine if the process measures indicate potential problems, (2) back up to the appropriate level in the input stage to identify problems that may need to be corrected or redesigned, and (3) take appropriate action.

If the leader finds that the input variables at the individual, organizational, and group levels are contributing positively to group effectiveness (i.e., the design portion of the leader's job has been taken care of), then she can turn her attention to the coaching level. Coaching is the ongoing work done with the team at the process level to continue to find ways to improve an already well-designed team. Given our individualistic culture, we have identified many teams in organizations that are apparently well designed and supported at the input level, but that have had no training or experience in the concept of teamwork. There are times when effective teamwork is based on very different concepts than effective individual work. For example, for a *team* to do well, the individuals comprising the team must sometimes *not* maximize their *individual* effort. Referred to as subsystem nonoptimization, this concept is at first not intuitively obvious to many people. Nevertheless, consider the example of a high school football team that has an extremely fast running back and some very good (but considerably slower) blocking linemen. Often, team members are told they all need to do their absolute best if the team is going to do well. If our

FIGURE 16–4

A Model for Leadership and Group Effectiveness

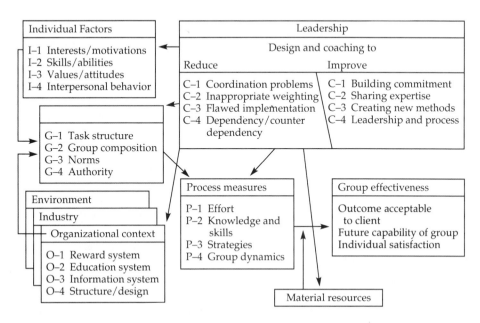

running back does his absolute best on a sweep around the end, then he will run as fast as he can. By doing so, he will leave his blocking linemen behind. The team is not likely to gain much yardage on such a play, and the linemen and the back, who have done their individual best, are apt to learn an important experiential lesson about teamwork. Most important, after several such disastrous plays, all of the team members may be inclined to demonstrate poor team process (lower effort, poor strategy, poor use of knowledge, and poor group dynamics represented by intrateam strife). Assuming that all the input stage variables are satisfactorily in place, ongoing coaching may now be appropriate. The coach would get better results if he worked out a better coordination plan between the back and the linemen. In this case, the fast running back needs to slow down (i.e., not perform maximally) to give the slower but excellent blockers a chance to do their work. After they have been given a chance to contribute to the play, the back will have a much better chance to then excel individually, and so will the team as a whole.

We are now in a position to add leadership to the model (see Figure 16–4). It has been shown that leaders can influence group effectiveness by designing or redesigning input stage variables at the individual, organizational, and group design levels. They can also improve group performance through ongoing coaching at various stages, but particularly while the group is actually performing its task. These "midcourse corrections" should not only improve the group outcomes but should also help to avoid many of the group-generated problems that can cause less-than-optimal group performance (Steiner, 1972).

Concluding Thoughts about the Group Effectiveness Model

It is important to point out the one remaining box for **material resources.** Note that this is a physical requirement, not an issue for the design or coaching of the team itself. But even if a group is well designed and has access to superior-quality ongoing coaching, without adequate physical resources it is not likely to do well on the output level.

Also, this model has been presented as if it were a machine (e.g., if P-2 breaks, check I-2, O-2, and G-2). As with other models of leadership or other human systems, however, nothing is that simple. There are obviously other variables that impact team and group effectiveness. There are also complex interactions between the variables described even in this model. But we have considerable evidence that the model can be useful for understanding groups (Hackman, 1990) and, in light of the relationship between groups and leadership, we are now using it as a model guiding further leadership research (Ginnett & Austin, 1992). One strength of the model clearly is the number of specific, testable hypotheses it suggests. The model has also been adopted by several organizations attempting to improve their leadership effectiveness, but insufficient time has passed and insufficient data collected to determine its ultimate utility to leaders.

Let us integrate the variables from this model into our L-F-S framework (see Figure 16–5). Clearly, the variables of importance fall into the arenas of the followers and of the situation. Notice that the characteristics of the leader play little role because the leader's job is to work on what is *not* being provided for the group in order for it to perform its task.

TRANSFORMATIONAL OR CHARISMATIC LEADERSHIP

Hopefully, after reading this far in the text you will have a better appreciation of the myriad of leader, follower, and situational factors that affect the leadership process. Still, when most people are asked to think about leadership, they often think about those political, religious, military, and business leaders whose personal magnetism, spellbinding powers, and heroic qualities have unusually strong effects on followers, societies, or organizations. These leaders might include Alexander the Great, Jesus Christ, Joan of Arc, Mahatma Gandhi,

FIGURE 16–5
*Factors from the Normative Model of Group Effectiveness
and the Interactional Framework*

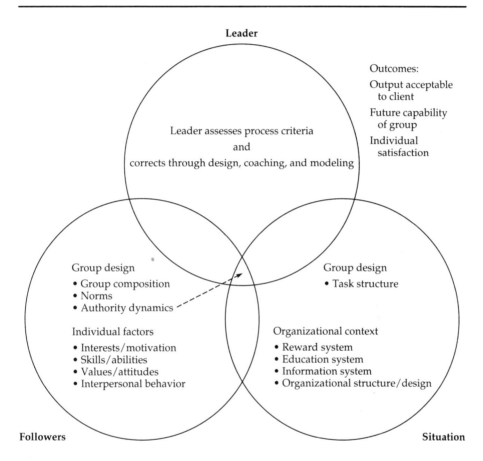

Adolph Hitler, Winston Churchill, the Ayatollah Khomeini, John Kennedy, Martin Luther King, Jr., Lee Iacocca, or Norman Schwartzkopf (see Highlight 16–2). Although these leaders differ in a number of important ways, one distinct characteristic or quality they all share is charisma. Charismatic leaders are able to build particularly strong emotional attachments with followers, and in turn followers put fourth greater effort to meet organizational or societal challenges.

Even though many people conjure up images of charismatic leaders when thinking about leadership, oddly enough the systematic investigation of charismatic leadership is relatively new. This section reviews the findings of both the past and the more recent charismatic leadership research efforts. As an

HIGHLIGHT 16–2

The Humility of Gandhi

Ghandi was one of the great leaders in world history. No less an intellect than Albert Einstein wrote this of him: "Generations to come, it may be, will scarce believe that such a one as this ever in flesh and blood walked upon this earth." Viscount Louis Mountbatten, the last Viceroy of India, compared him to the Buddha and to Christ. As a young journalist, William L. Shirer chronicled Gandhi's rebellion against British colonialism in India and described his first meeting with Gandhi. In reading it, think about what aspects of Gandhi's personality, behavior, and vision made him so charismatic a leader.

> Gandhi was squatting on the floor in the corner of the verandah, spinning. He greeted me warmly, with a smile that lit up his face and made his lively eyes twinkle. The welcome was so disarming, his manner so friendly and radiant, that my nervousness evaporated before I could say a word. . . .
>
> As our talk began I tried to take in not only what Gandi was saying but how he looked. I had seen many photographs of him but I was nevertheless somewhat surprised at his actual appearance. His face at first glance did not convey at all the stature of the man, his obvious greatness. It was not one you would have especially noticed in a crowd. It struck me as not ugly, as some had said—indeed it radiated a certain beauty—but it was not uncommon either. Age—he was 61—and fasting, and Indian sun and the strain of years in prison, of long, hard, nervous work, had obviously taken their toll, turned the nose down, widened it at the nostrils, sunk in his mouth just a little so that the lower lip protruded, and teeth were missing—I could see only two. His hair was closely cropped, giving an effect of baldness. His large ears spread out, rabbit-like. His gray eyes lit up and sharpened when they peered at you through his steel-rimmed spectacles and then they softened when he lapsed, as he frequently did, into a mood of almost puckish humor. I was almost taken back by the gaiety in them. This was a man inwardly secure, who, despite the burdens he carried, the hardships he had endured, could chuckle at man's foibles, including his own.
>
> He seemed terribly frail, all skin and bones, though I knew that this appearance was deceptive, for he kept to a frugal but carefully planned diet that kept him fit, and for exercise he walked four or five miles each morning at a pace so brisk, as I would learn later when he invited me to accompany him, that I, at 27 and in fair shape from skiing and hiking in the alps below Vienna, could scarcely keep up. Over his skin and bones was a loosely wrapped dhoti, and in the chilliness of a north Indian winter he draped a coarsely spun white shawl over his bony shoulders. His skinny legs were bare, his feet in wooden sandals.
>
> As he began to talk, his voice seemed high-pitched, but his words were spoken slowly and deliberately and with emphasis when he seemed intent on stressing a point, and gradually, as he warmed up, the tone lowered. His slightly accented English flowed rhythmically, like a poet's at times, and always, except for an occasional homespun cliché, it was concise, homely, forceful.
>
> For so towering a figure, his humble manner at first almost disconcerted me. Most of the political greats I had brushed up against in Europe and at home had seemed intent on impressing you with the forcefulness of their personalities and the boldness of their minds, not being bashful at all in hiding their immense egos. But here was the most gentle and unassuming of men, speaking softly and kindly, without egotism, without the slightest pretense of trying to impress his rather awed listener.

HIGHLIGHT 16–2 *(concluded)*

How could so humble a man, I wondered, spinning away with his nimble fingers on a crude wheel as he talked, have begun almost single-handedly to rock the foundations of the British Empire, aroused a third of a billion people to rebellion against foreign rule, and taught them the technique of a new revolutionary method—nonviolent civil disobedience—against which Western guns and Eastern lathis were proving of not much worth. That was what I had come to India to find out.

Source: W. L. Shirer, *Gandi* (New York: Simon & Schuster, 1979), pp. 27–29. Reprinted with permission.

---

overview, this section (*a*) provides a brief historical review of the charismatic leadership research; (*b*) describes the distinguishing characteristics of charismatic leadership; (*c*) reviews one of the more popular charismatic or transformational leadership theories; and (*d*) asks whether charismatic leadership is always good, and whether it is possible to train leaders to be charismatic.

Charismatic Leadership: A Historical Review

Although psychologists played a major role in the development of all of the leadership theories described in this text, they did not play a role in charismatic leadership research until only 15 years ago. Instead, most of the charismatic leadership research from the 1920s to the 1970s was accomplished by historians, political scientists, and sociologists. Of this early research, probably the single most important work was written by Weber (1947). Weber was a sociologist primarily interested in the forces of authority in society and how these forces changed over time. Weber maintained that societies could be identified in terms of one of three types of authority systems: traditional, legal-rational, and charismatic.

In the **traditional authority system,** the traditions and unwritten laws of the society dictate who has authority and how this authority can be used. The transfer of authority in such systems is based on traditions such as the passing of power to the firstborn son of a king after a king dies. Although fairly uncommon today, historically the traditional authority system has been quite widespread. A more prevalent authority system today is the **legal-rational authority system.** Authority in the legal-rational system derives from society's belief in the laws that govern it. In this system, a person possesses authority not because of tradition or his or her special qualties, but because of the laws that govern the position occupied. A distinctive characteristic of legal-rational system is the bureaucracy, which exists solely to enforce existing laws and to maintain stability in society.

The basis of authority in the **charismatic authority system** comes from society's belief in the exemplary characteristics of the leader. Charismatic leaders are thought to possess "superhuan" qualties or powers of divine origin, which set them apart from ordinary men. The locus of authority in this system rests with the individual possessing these unusual qualities; it is not associated with the traditions, beliefs, or laws of a society.

According to Weber, charismatic individuals come from the margins of society and emerge as leaders during times of great social crisis. These leaders serve to focus society on both the problems it faces and on the revolutionary solutions proposed by the leader. Thus, charismatic authority systems are usually the result of a revolution against traditional or legal-rational authority systems. Although these revolutions are associated with a high degree of identification, attachment, and emotional appeal for the charismatic leader, charismatic authority systems tend to be short-lived. Charismatic leaders must project the image of success in order for followers to continue believing they possess superhuman qualities. Any failures to accomplish the proposed changes to society will cause followers to question the divine qualities of the leader and, in turn, seriously erode the leader's authority.

A number of historians, political scientists, and sociologists have commented on various aspects of Weber's conceptualization of charismatic authority systems. Of all of these comments, however, probably the biggest controversy surrounding Weber's theory concerns the locus of charismatic leadership. Is charisma primarily the result of the situation or social context facing the leader, the leader's extraordinary qualities, or the strong relationships between charismatic leaders and followers? A number of authors argued that charismatic movements could not take place unless the society was in a crisis (Blau, 1963; Chinoy, 1961; Wolpe, 1968). Along these lines, Friedland (1964), Gerth and Mills (1946), and Kanter (1972) argued that before a leader with extraordinary qualities would be perceived as charismatic, the social situation must be such that followers recognize the relevance of the leader's qualities.

Other authors have argued that charismatic leadership is primarily a function of the leader's extraordinary qualities, not the situation. According to Tucker (1968), these qualities include having extraordinary powers of vision, the rhetorical skills to communicate this vision, a sense of mission, high self-confidence and intelligence, and high expectations for followers. Dow's (1969) review of a number of historical crises lends support to this argument, as he reported that a number of crises were resolved using noncharismatic solutions. Thus, according to Dow's findings, a leader's qualities were the key to charismatic leadership, as a crisis alone was not enough for charismatic leader emergence.

Finally, several authors have argued that the litmus test for charismatic leadership does not depend on the leader's qualities or the presence of a crisis, but rather on followers' reactions to their leader (Clark, 1972; Deveraux, 1955; Downton, 1973; Marcus, 1961; Shils, 1965). According to this argument, charisma is attributed only to those leaders who can develop particularly strong emotional attachments with followers. Leaders with extraordinary qualities who fail to develop these strong emotional bonds are not charismatic leaders.

As you will see shortly, many of these early questions and arguments have strong parallels to the questions currently being raised about charismatic leadership. Researchers are still studying how much charismatic leadership is a function of the situation, the qualities of the leader, the relationships certain leaders have with followers, or some combination of these three perspectives.

What Are the Characteristics of Charismatic Leadership?

Many of the political scientists, historians, and sociologists conducting the early charismatic leadership research identified a number of characteristics that differentiated world, society, cultural, and religious charismatic and noncharismatic leaders. More recently, these characteristics were elaborated on by a number of leadership researchers, including Berlew (1974), House (1977), Bass (1985), and Conger and Kanungo (1988). The following is a synthesis of these more recent ideas concerning the characteristics of charismatic leadership. As seen in Figure 16–6, the unique characteristics of charismatic leadership fit in nicely with the leader-follower-situation framework used throughout this text.

Leader characteristics.   Like their earlier counterparts, some researchers have recently argued that the leader's personal qualities are the key to charismatic leadership (Boal & Bryson, 1987; C. W. Hill, 1984, Kets de Vries, 1977; Sashkin, 1988; Zeleznik, 1974). Although we do not believe the leader's qualities are the key to charismatic leadership, we do acknowledge several common threads in the behavior and style of charismatic leaders. We believe charismatic leaders are distinguished by their vision, their rhetorical skills, their ability to build a particular kind of image in the hearts and minds of their followers, and their personalized style of leadership.

Vision.   Leadership is inherently future-oriented. It involves helping a group move from here to there. Leaders differ, however, in how they define or perceive the *here* and *there*. For some, the voyage between here and there is relatively routine, like driving on a familiar road. Others, however, see the need to chart a new course toward unexplored territory. Such leaders perceive fundamental discrepancies between the ways things are and the way things can (or should) be. They recognize the shortcomings of a present order and offer an imaginative vision to overcome them. In Conger's (1989) words, they "see beyond current realities" (see Highlight 16–3).

FIGURE 16–6
Factors Pertaining to Charismatic Leadership and the Interactional Framework

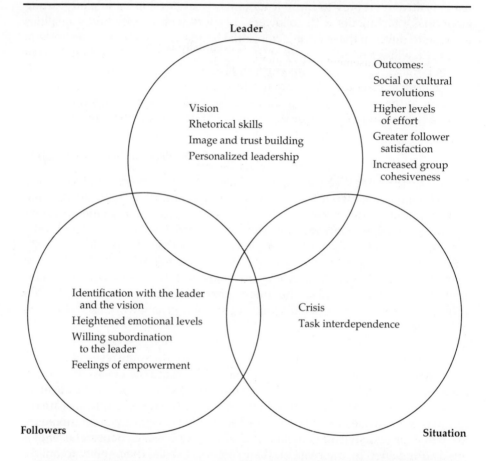

Several additional aspects of vision are worth elaborating on. First, both Bennis and Nanus (1985) and Tichy and Devanna (1986) reported that the leader's vision of the future is often a collaborative effort; the genius of the leader is his or her ability to synthesize seemingly disparate issues and problems and develop a vision that ties all of these concerns together. Second, Berlew (1974, 1992) maintained that the charismatic leader's vision had both a stimulating and a unifying effect on followers' efforts. As seen in Figure 16–7, these two effects often result in higher performance levels on the part of followers. Third, Berlew (1974) also maintained that for a charismatic leader's vision to arouse followers' emotions, the vision should be articulated verbally only. Visions often lose their emotional appeal (and consequently result in lower follower commitment to the vision) when they are written or posted.

HIGHLIGHT 16–3

The Visions of Walt Disney and Mary Kay Ash

Walt Disney's motivation to create what eventually became Disneyland grew from visits to amusement parks with his own daughters. He observed the parks' run-down squalor, litter, and unfriendly employees, and the boredom of the parents. Furthermore, he sensed a need among tourists for something to *see* when they visited Hollywood. In a 1948 memo, he sketched out plans for what he tentatively called Mickey Mouse Park:

> The Main Village, which includes the Railroad Station, is built around a village green or informal park. In the park will be benches, a bandstand, drinking fountain, trees and shrubs. It will be a place for people to sit and rest; mothers and grandmothers can watch over small children at play. I want it to be very relaxing, cool and inviting. (Thomas, 1976, p. 218)

Mary Kay Ash, the founder of Mary Kay cosmetics, had a vision based on the emerging needs of women in the 1960s and 1970s. Women's liberation had begun, and new opportunities for women were needed. Mary Kay offered women an appealing career (beauty consultant, not salesperson!) they could pursue in their homes.

Source: J. A. Conger, *The Charismatic Leader* (San Francisco: Jossey-Bass, 1989), and B. Thomas, *Walt Disney* (New York: Simon & Schuster, 1976).

Rhetorical skills. Charismatic leaders have vision, but they are also especially gifted in sharing their vision. As discussed earlier, charismatic leaders have superb rhetorical skills that heighten followers' emotional levels and inspire them to embrace the vision. Charismatic leaders stir dissatisfaction with the present while they build support for their picture of a new future. It should be no surprise, then, that rhetorical skills are one of the most important tools in charismatic leadership. Although the leader's message is important, so is the way it is communicated.

Conger (1989) described some of the rhetorical techniques used by charismatic leaders. Charismatic leaders make extensive use of metaphors, analogies, and stories rather than abstract and colorless rational discourse to make their points. Moreover, these stories and metaphors can be particularly effective when they invoke potent cultural symbols and elicit strong emotions. Charismatic leaders are adept at tailoring their language to particular groups, thereby better engaging them mentally and emotionally. Many charismatic religious and political leaders effectively use speech techniques like repetition, rhythm, balance, and alliteration to strengthen the impact of their messages. Adolph Hitler mastered techniques so well that his speeches can have a hypno-

FIGURE 16–7
A Leader's Vision of the Future Can Help Groups Accomplish More

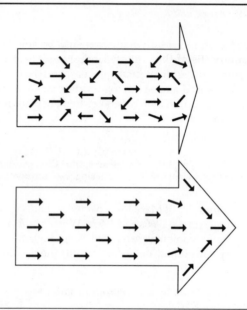

Source: Adapted from P. M. Serge, *The Fifth Discipline* (New York: Doubleday, 1990).

tizing power even to people who do not understand German (Willner, 1984). Similarly, many people consider Martin Luther King, Jr.'s "I Have a Dream" speech one of the most moving speeches they have ever heard. Note his use of different speech techniques and his masterful evocation of patriotic and cultural themes in the excerpt presented in Highlight 16–4.

Image and trust-building.   Charismatic leaders build trust in their leadership and the attainability of their goals through seemingly unshakable self-confidence, strength of moral conviction, personal example and sacrifice, and unconventional tactics or behavior (House, 1977; Conger, 1989). They are perceived to have unusual insight and ability, typically are more experienced and knowledgeable than their followers, and act in a manner consistent with their vision. Creating an *appearance* of success, however, can be as important as the factual record (House, 1977). Whereas charismatic leaders build support by showing commitment to followers' needs over self-interest, some are not beyond taking credit for others' accomplishments or exaggerating their expertise (Conger, 1989). Some charismatic political leaders have conveyed an impression of profound intellect merely by using a good memory to impress others (Willner, 1984).

HIGHLIGHT 16–4

"I Have a Dream"

This will be the day when all of God's children will be able to sing with new meaning—"my country 'tis of thee, sweet land of liberty, of thee I sing; land where my fathers died, land of the pilgrim's pride; from every mountain side, let freedom ring"—and if America is to be a great nation, this must become true. So let freedom ring from the prodigious hilltops of New Hampshire. Let freedom ring from the mighty mountains of New York. Let freedom ring from the snow-capped Rockies of Colorado. Let freedom ring from the curvaceous slopes of California. But not only that. Let freedom ring from Stone Mountain of Georgia. Let freedom ring from Lookout Mountain of Tennessee. Let freedom ring from every hill and molehill of Mississippi, from every mountainside, let freedom ring. And when we allow freedom to ring, when we let it ring from every village and every hamlet, from every state and every city, we will be able to speed up that day when all of God's children—black and white men, Jews and Gentiles, Protestants and Catholics—will be able to join hands and to sing in the words of the old Negro spiritual: "Free at last, free at last; thank God Almighty, we are free at last."

Source: Martin Luther King, Jr., "I Have a Dream."

Personalized leadership.   One of the most important aspects of charismatic leadership is the personal nature of the leader's power. It is intensely relational, even when the leader occupies a formal organizational role. Charismatic leadership involves emotionalized relationships with followers. This does not mean that charismatic leaders are necessarily friendly with their followers, just that followers of charismatic leaders become relatively dependent on the leader's personal approval for their own self-worth. Thus, doing well in the eyes of a charismatic leader can be tremendously uplifting, but letting a charismatic leader down can be psychologically devastating (Conger, 1989).

It is this personalized style that seems to be responsible for the feelings of empowerment notable among followers of charismatic leaders, and it has two important components. First, charismatic leaders tend to be emotionally expressive, especially through such nonverbal channels as their eye contact, posture, movement, gestures, tone of voice, and facial expressions (Bass, 1990). It is partly through their nonverbal behaviors that some people are perceived to have a "magnetic" personality. Second, charismatic leaders empower followers by building their self-efficacy. They can do this by giving followers tasks that lead to successively greater success experiences and heightened self-confidence, by persuading followers of their capabilities, by creating an environment of heightened excitement and positive emotions, and by their own role modeling as a visible symbol of the group's purpose (Conger, 1989).

Follower characteristics.   If charismatic leadership were defined solely by individual characteristics, then it would be relatively easy to identify those individuals with good visioning, rhetorical, and impression management skills and place them in leadership positions. Although these three leadership skills may help an individual to be seen as charismatic, charismatic leadership is probably more a function of the followers' reactions to a leader than of the leader's personal characteristics. For example, a leader may possess a vision of the future, have good rhetorical skills, and engage in impression management, but if a follower does not buy in to the leader's vision or become emotionally attached to the leader, then the leader will not be perceived to be charismatic. Nevertheless, followers who believe in the leader's vision and respond with heightened emotional levels will perceive the leader to be charismatic. *Thus,* **charisma** *is in the eyes and heart of the beholder—it is a particularly strong emotional reaction to, identification with, and belief in some leaders by some followers.* It is important to note that many of the more popular conceptualizations of charisma and charismatic leadership also define charisma in a similar fashion (Bass, 1985; Conger & Kanungo, 1988; House, 1977; Howell, 1988; Willner, 1984). By defining charisma as a reaction followers have toward leaders, it seems reasonable to turn our attention to the four unique characteristics of these reactions.

Identification with the leader and the vision.   Two of the effects House (1977) associated with charismatic leadership included a strong affection for the leader and a similarity of follower beliefs with those of the leader. These effects describe a sort of bonding or identification with the leader personally, and a parallel psychological investment to a goal or activity (a "cause") bigger than oneself. Followers' identities or self-concepts become defined in terms of the leader. Being like the leader, or approved by the leader, becomes an important part of one's self-worth. Effects like these go well beyond what might be expected from the typical contractual or exchange relationships between most supervisors and subordinates.

Heightened emotional levels.   House (1977) also maintained that followers of charismatic leaders had heightened emotional levels. Charismatic leaders stir followers' feelings, perhaps more literally than many people suppose; experimental studies have confirmed greater physiological arousal among subjects listening to inspirational speeches than to travel lectures (Steele, 1977; A. J. Stewart & Winger, 1976). Moreover, House (1977) and Bass (1985) have maintained that this heightened emotional state resulted in increased efforts being devoted to accomplishing the vision, which in turn resulted in increased performance levels.

Willing subordination to the leader.   Three other effects of charismatic leadership identified by House (1977) included unquestioning acceptance of the leader by followers; willing obedience to the leader; and trust in the correctness of the leader's beliefs. Whereas the preceding factor dealt with followers' emotional and psychological closeness to the leader, this factor involves their deference to his or her authority. Charismatic leaders are often imbued with superhuman qualities, and as a result followers seem to naturally and willingly submit to what appears to be the leader's natural authority and superiority. Because followers volitionally submit to a charismatic leader's authority, Willner (1984) used the term **spellbinders** to describe the group of charismatic political leaders she studied who were larger than life in the minds of their followers.

Feelings of empowerment.   The final effect of charismatic leadership noted by House (1977) included heightened expectations by followers of themselves. Followers of charismatic leaders are moved to expect more of themselves, and they work harder to achieve these higher goals. Somewhat paradoxically, then, followers feel stronger and more powerful at the very same time they willingly subordinate themselves to the charismatic leader. Charismatic leaders are able to make their followers feel more powerful without any diminution or threat to their own status. These feelings of empowerment, when combined with heightened emotional levels and a leader's vision of the future, may result in increases in organizational, group, or team performance or significant social change.

Situational characteristics.   Some authors have recently asserted that certain leader skills and behaviors are a necessary but not sufficient condition for charismatic leadership. Instead, Bradley (1987), Roberts and Bradley (1988), and Westley and Mintzberg (1988) have argued that situational factors, not personal qualities, determine whether a leader will be perceived to be charismatic. These authors have shown that individuals possessing the qualities of charismatic leaders were perceived to be charismatic only when facing certain types of situations. Because the situation may play an important role in the attribution of charisma, the following is a brief description of two of the situational factors believed to affect charismatic leadership.

Crises.   Although a number of situational characteristics may affect whether or not a leader is perceived to be charismatic, probably the most important of these factors is the presence or absence of a crisis. Followers who are content with the status quo will not be ready or willing to devote a great amount of effort to change an organization or a society. On the other hand, if enough followers are discontented with the rules, values, or laws of their society or are concerned whether or not their company will survive the next fiscal year, then the society or organization will be facing a crisis. Generally, followers in these situations are "charisma hungry"—they are looking for a leader to alleviate or resolve these crises (Madsen & Snow, 1983; Trice & Beyer, 1986). Because the presence of a crisis has such a facilitating effect on charismatic leader emergence, Avolio and Bass (1988), Boal and Bryson (1987), and Kets de Vries (1977) all maintained that some leaders may purposely create crises in order to be perceived as charismatic.

Task interdependence.   One other situational characteristic that may affect followers' perceptions of charisma is the level of interdependent effort required to accomplish committee, team, or work-group tasks. It may be easier for individuals to be seen as charismatic leaders when the tasks performed require a high level of interdependent effort. Because team sports such as soccer, basketball, football, and hockey often require self-sacrifice, extra effort, and cooperation among team members for success, coaches of these teams may be more likely to be perceived as charismatic than coaches of sports with low levels of interdependent effort.

Concluding Thoughts about the Characteristics of Charismatic Leadership. Several final points about the characteristics of charismatic leadership need to be made before we discuss Bass's (1985) theory of transformational and transactional leadership. First, although we defined charisma as a quality attributed to certain leaders based on the relationships they share with followers, charismatic leadership is most fully understood when we also consider how leader and situational factors affect this attribution process. The special relationships charismatic leaders share with followers do not happen by accident; rather, they are often the result of interaction between followers' needs, leader qualities, and the presence of a crisis. Second, it seems unlikely that all the characteristics of charismatic leadership need to be present before charisma is attributed to a leader. For example, some leaders may have the ability to develop particularly strong relationships with followers in the absence of a vision or a crisis. Relatedly, if high task and high relationship leaders (a 9,9 leader) also develop strong emotional bonds with followers, then is charisma nothing more than being a 9,9 leader (see Figure 9–1)? The bottom line for charisma seems to be the relationships certain leaders share with followers, and there may be a variety of ways in which these relationships can develop.

Third, given that there are a number of ways to develop strong emotional attachments with followers, one important question is whether it is possible to attribute charisma to an individual based solely on her position or celebrity status (Etzioni, 1961; Hollander, 1978; Bass, 1990). Some individuals in positions of high public visibility and esteem—such as film stars, musicians, athletes, television evangelists, and politicians—can develop (even cultivate) charismatic images among their fans and admirers. In these cases, it is helpful to recognize that charismatic leadership is a two-way street. Not only do followers develop strong emotional bonds with leaders, but leaders also develop strong emotional bonds with followers and are concerned with follower development (Burns, 1978). It is difficult to see how the one-way communication channels of radio and television can foster these two-way relationships or enhance follower growth. Thus, although we sometimes view certain individuals as charismatic based on media manipulation and hype, this is not charismatic leadership in the truest sense.

Fourth, it is important to remember that charismatic leadership does not happen overnight; it takes time for the strong emotional bonds between charismatic leaders and followers to develop. Relatedly, these bonds do not only form on the world stage, but they can also be seen on the smaller stages of leadership. For example, charismatic leaders exist in such commonplace environments as college campuses and military training squadrons. Students identify some professors as more charismatic than others (Labak, 1973), and cadets identify certain military superiors as more inspirational than others (Adams, Prince, Instone, & Rice, 1984; Clover, 1990; Curphy, 1991a). Thus, charismatic leadership is not the exclusive charter of world, societal, or religious leaders but can occur in any type of group, team, or organizational setting (see Highlight 16–5).

Bass's (1985) Theory of Transformational and Transactional Leadership

Although the previous section described a number of the more recent conceptualizations of charismatic leadership, probably the most well-known and researched is Bass's (1985) **theory of transformational and transactional leadership.** Bass believed that transformational leaders possessed those charismatic leader characteristics described earlier; he used subordinates' perceptions or reactions to determine whether or not a leader was transformational. Thus, transformational leaders possess good visioning, rhetorical, and impression management skills, and they use these skills to develop strong emotional bonds with followers. According to Bass, transactional leaders do not possess these leader characteristics, nor are they able to develop strong emotional bonds with followers or inspire followers to do more than they thought they could. Instead, transactional leaders were believed to motivate followers by setting goals and promising rewards for desired performance.

HIGHLIGHT 16–5

Women in Leadership, VII: Charisma on the "Small" Stage

Dr. Jodi Kassover-Taylor is the director of the Colorado Springs branch of the Center for Creative Leadership (CCL). She has been extremely successful in that role and is regarded by most who know her as a charismatic leader. We asked her to reflect on her own development as a leader, her feelings about how she is perceived by others, and her vision for her organization.

Charisma and leadership are words that describe a person's impact on others: describing results of behavior rather than motivation or intent. I doubt if anyone plans to grow up to become a charismatic leader. One is a charismatic leader as a result of who one is and what one is about. So I am always surprised when people refer to me as a charismatic leader. Since I feel rather ordinary myself, I am left with the question "What is it about me, or anyone for that matter, that causes them to appear to others as a charismatic leader?"

Growing up in a small West Texas town in the middle of oil and wheat country, life was very stable for me. Both my parents worked, so expectations of achievement and hard work seemed perfectly normal. Additionally, people have always described me as a person with restless energy and focus. By the age of nine, I was reading a book a day. By the age of 14, I had my first job working in a factory. As a senior in high school I worked two after-school jobs while continuing to be an honor student and a student body officer, wrote a column for the school newspaper, served on both the annual and school magazine staffs. Again, that all seemed quite ordinary to me.

A fascination with people was another theme in my early life. My grandmother always drove my handicapped aunt downtown each Saturday afternoon to park on the main street and watch the people shopping. I often joined them and developed a lifelong curiosity about the differences among people.

Always propelled by a strong future orientation, by the age of 13 I was worried about what I would be when I grew up, so I read the encyclopedia of occupations. When I discovered "psychologist," it immediately connected with my interest in people and I began focusing on that career, completing my Ph.D. by the age of 24. My background in psychology, with its emphasis on people, combined with my strong need to create, has led me to organizational settings. By combining focus, energy, interest in people, and the need to create, I have been able to facilitate an organizational structure that enables people to grow and allows us collectively to make the world a better place. This sense of mission, personal growth, and commitment to the team, in turn gives us new energy, focus, and vision to be more creative so that the end result is an upward spiral. It's that upward spiral that leadership is all about.

Perhaps *upward spiral* is the best term to describe what has happened at CCL Colorado Springs over the last five years. When I became director (part-time) in 1987, we had no full-time employees and were conducting only 13 courses a year. We did, however, have a solid basis formed by CCL's reputation and a viable product. My mission for the branch was to build on that basis so we could leverage our impact on organizations. We wanted to "really make a difference" in organizations by working with a "critical mass" of people in the organization, not just one or two people at a time as we do in our public courses. At the same time, we also focused our energies on working with senior executives. I wanted the image of CCL, Colorado Springs, and the mountains to be inextricably linked whenever people from anywhere in the world thought of senior leadership. To achieve that vision, I set out to hire the best people I could find in the area of leadership training and build them into a team and an intellectual community. We could achieve our vision only if we practiced what we preached—by being a high-functioning team, constantly searching for new ideas about leadership and looking for ways to share them.

HIGHLIGHT 16–5 *(concluded)*

So far, we are succeeding (although you are never complete when trying to achieve a vision). Our revenues have increased 825 percent over the last five years (which means we can help support some of the Center's research since we are a not-for-profit organization), our staff has grown from 0 to 32 in five years, and we have embarked on an ambitious building project to create our own training campus. This building will then enable us to fulfill our mission even better, as we can offer more courses, have more space for research, and then impact more people. We are in that delicious stage of the life cycle of an organization when we believe anything is possible.

Again, it is that upward spiral. Today, with a strong high-functioning team, we have even more leverage to build toward that vision of using our knowledge and research to make the world a better place by tapping the leadership potential in everyone we work with.

The Multifactor Leadership Questionnaire. Like the "initiating structure" and "consideration" behaviors described in Chapter Nine, Bass hypothesized that transformational and transactional leadership comprised two independent leadership dimensions. Thus, individuals could be high transformational but low transactional leaders, low transformational and low transactional leaders, and so on. Bass developed a questionnaire, known as the **Multifactor Leadership Questionnaire (MLQ),** to assess the extent to which leaders exhibited transformational or transactional leadership and the extent to which followers were satisfied with their leader and believed their leader was effective. Before going into the research findings, however, we will describe the various factors comprising transformational and transactional leadership assessed by the MLQ.

Although the original version of MLQ has undergone a number of modifications over the past eight years, the MLQ basically assesses three transformational and two transactional leadership factors (Curphy, 1991a). The three factors in transformational leadership are charisma, individualized consideration, and intellectual stimulation. The charisma factor on the MLQ assesses followers' emotional reactions toward their leader. For example, items on the charisma factor ask subordinates to indicate the extent to which they are proud to be associated with their leader, the extent to which their leader generates enthusiasm, and the extent to which their leader is seen as a symbol of success. These follower reactions were believed to be the result of the leader's vision of the future, high self-confidence, use of impression management techniques, and rhetorical skills. The individualized consideration factor concerns the extent to which leaders treat followers as individuals and how much of a mentoring orientation leaders have for followers. Items on this factor ask followers to indicate how much their leader gives them personal attention, coaching, personal advice, and opportunities to develop. The last transformational leadership factor is intellectual stimulation. Intellectual stimulation concerns the leader's vision and those behaviors that increase followers' understanding of the problems they face. Transformational leaders use intellectual stimulation to point out the problems in the current situation and to contrast them with their vision of the future.

The MLQ also assesses two transactional leadership factors: contingent reward and management-by-exception. The contingent reward factor concerns the extent to which leaders set goals, make rewards contingent on performance, obtain necessary resources, and provide rewards when performance goals have been met. Avolio and Bass (1987, 1988) maintained that contingent reward behaviors could have positive effects on follower satisfaction and performance levels, but they also stated that these behaviors were often underutilized because of time constraints, a lack of leader skills, and a disbelief among leaders that rewards could boost performance. Management-by-exception makes up the other component of transactional leadership, and this factor occurs when a leader interacts with followers only when standards for performance are not being met. Moreover, because these leaders interact with followers only during times of substandard performance, these interventions often consist of negative feedback or punishment.

Research results using the MLQ.   As stated earlier, Bass's theory of transformational and transactional leadership has generated a considerable amount of research. Curphy's (1991a) comprehensive review of this literature showed that most of these studies consisted of administering the MLQ to followers and examining the relationships among the MLQ factors or the relationships between the MLQ factors and followers' satisfaction and leader effectiveness ratings, leaders' promotion rates, or leaders' performance appraisal ratings. In general, Curphy reported that these studies showed the two dimensions of the MLQ, transformational and transactional leadership, were not independent dimensions of leadership. Instead, these two dimensions were highly related; leaders getting high ratings on one dimension tended to get high ratings on the other dimension and vice versa. These research studies also showed that both the transformational factors and the contingent reward factor of transactional leadership were strongly related to followers' satisfaction and leader effectiveness ratings. The relationships between these leadership factors and leaders' promotion rates and performance appraisal ratings were much lower, however.

In addition to reviewing the previous research, Curphy (1991a, 1992a) also conducted several studies at the U.S. Air Force Academy that helped to shed additional light on Bass's theory. Curphy's studies were conducted over a two-year period; used much bigger sample sizes than previously reported (over

11,500 cadets rated 160 officer leaders); and used unit performance indices, attrition rates, and organizational climate ratings for leadership effectiveness criteria. Like the previous researchers, Curphy also reported that transformational and transactional leadership were not independent but rather were highly interrelated. He also reported both the transformational leadership and contingent reward factors had strong positive correlations with organizational climate ratings.

Curphy's findings regarding unit performance indices are especially interesting. Curphy found that transformational and contingent reward leadership had no effect on unit performance indices requiring *independent effort* but had strong positive effects on those unit performance indices requiring *interdependent effort*. Moreover, the relationships between those unit performance indices requiring interdependent effort and these leadership factors got stronger over time. Thus, there may be a time lag before one can see the effects of transformational and contingent reward leadership and performance. Leaders may first have to concentrate on selling their vision, setting goals, developing strong attachments with followers, and administering rewards before they will see any differences in the performance of their work group or team.

In summary, the theory of transformational and transactional leadership has helped to advance our leadership knowledge well beyond the mere listing of the leader, follower, and situational charateristics of charismatic leadership presented in the previous section. Bass has provided researchers with a number of empirically testable hypotheses about transformational or charismatic leadership and developed an instrument for collecting data to verify or refute these hypotheses. His theory has generated a considerable amount of research over the past eight years. Based on this research, we now know that tranformational leaders may also use a number of contingent reward behaviors to motivate followers. Additionally, we know that leaders getting high transformational and contingent reward ratings have more satisfied followers and have work groups or teams with better organizational climates. Nevertheless, we also know that transformational leaders may be well liked by their subordinates but may not rise in their organizations any faster than nontransformational leaders. The latter findings may be due to the fact that unit performance indices requiring independent effort may be relatively insensitive to a leader's actions (Curphy, 1991a, 1992a) or that superiors may base promotion recommendations and performance appraisals more on technical expertise than on the relationships leaders have with followers (J. Hogan, 1992b). Nevertheless, transformational leaders whose performance appraisal ratings or promotion recommendations are based on how well their groups accomplish interdependent tasks may be promoted more quickly, given Curphy's research results. Although Curphy (1991, 1992); Yukl (1989); and Yukl and Van Fleet (1992) have described a number of methodological concerns with Bass's theory that have yet to be resolved, the theory has been very successful in advancing what we know about charismatic or transformational leadership and the effects this type of leadership has on various leadership effectiveness criteria.

Are Charismatic Leaders Always Good?

Just as charismatic leaders can be seductive, the very topic of charismatic leadership can be seductive, too. It is all too easy in reading about the personal magnetism, vision, and empowering style of charismatics to conclude that they are the "best" leaders and that theirs is a style all leaders should emulate. It is worth reminding ourselves, therefore, that not all charismatic leaders are necessarily good leaders. Precisely because charismatic leaders' effects can be more emotional than rational, many observers have warned of the dangers charismastic leaders can pose.

Followers of charismatic leaders can be so zealous as to be blind, a bit like the children who followed the Pied Piper of Hamelin (Newman, 1983) (also see Highlights 16–6 and 16–7). At their best, charismatic leaders can positively transform and empower their followers, and researchers have reported that some charismatic U.S. presidents, social leaders, and organizational leaders were the underlying cause of many positive social and organizational changes (House, Spangler, & Woycke, 1991; House, Woycke, & Fodor, 1988; Tichy & Devanna, 1986; Westley & Mintzberg, 1988; Willner, 1984). However, at their worst, charismatic leaders emotionally manipulate followers and create dysfunctional dependencies for their own self-aggrandizement; they can even wreak havoc on the rest of the world (e.g., Alexander the Great, Genghis Khan, Attila the Hun, or Adolph Hitler). A tragic example of the negative aspects of charismatic leadership was the Jim Jones cult that self-exterminated in the Jonestown massacre (Conway & Siegelman, 1979). Virtually all of the 912 who died there voluntarily drank from large vats of a flavored drink containing cyanide after Jones said they all must commit "mass suicide for the glory of socialism." As described in Chapter Six, part of that seemingly bizarre behavior probably had been conditioned by Jones' extensive use of punishment as a control technique, but there seems to be little question that he also had a charismatic impact on the group.

Several researchers have offered explanations for why some charismatic leaders have either tremendously positive or negative effects on followers, organizations, societies, or the world order. Both Kets de Vries (1977) and Zaleznik (1974) maintained that there are two types of charismatic leaders, one type being psychologically "healthy" and the other type being psychologically "unhealthy." Zaleznik (1974) posited that healthy charismatic leaders have well-developed inner lives and had healthy and significant relationships with their mothers. Because unhealthy leaders are typically overattached to their

HIGHLIGHT 16–6

The Seduction of Charisma

Susceptibility to influence by a charismatic leader can pose its own dangers, as the following story by James Thurber illustrates.

The Owl Who Was God

Once upon a starless midnight there was an owl who sat on the branch of an oak tree. Two ground moles tried to slip quietly by, unnoticed. "You!" said the owl. "Who?" they quavered in fear and astonishment, for they could not believe it was possible for anyone to see them in that thick darkness. "You two!" said the owl. The moles hurried away and told the other creatures of the field and forest that the owl was the greatest and wisest of all animals because he could see in the dark and because he could answer any question. "I'll see about that," said a secretary bird, and he called on the owl one night when it was again very dark. "How many claws am I holding up?" said the secretary bird. "Two," said the owl, and that was right. "Can you give me another expression for 'that is to say' or 'namely'?" asked the secretary bird. "To wit," said the owl. "Why does a lover call on his love?" asked the secretary bird. "To woo," said the owl.

The secretary bird hastened back to the other creatures and reported that the owl was indeed the greatest and wisest animal in the world because he could see in the dark and because he could answer any question. "Can he see in the daytime, too?" asked a red fox. "Yes," echoed a dormouse and a French poodle. "Can he see in the daytime, too?" All the other creatures laughed loudly at this silly question, and they set upon the red fox and his friends and drove them out of the region. Then they sent a messenger to the owl and asked him to be their leader.

When the owl appeared among the animals it was high noon and the sun was shining brightly. He walked very slowly, which gave him an appearance of great dignity, and he peered about him with large staring eyes, which gave him an air of tremendous importance. "He's God!" screamed a Plymouth Rock hen. And the others took up the cry "He's God!" So they followed him wherever he went and when he began to bump into things they began to bump into things, too. Finally he came to a concrete highway and he started up the middle of it and all the other creatures followed him. Presently a hawk, who was acting as outrider, observed a truck coming toward them at fifty miles an hour, and he reported to the secretary bird and the secretary bird reported to the owl. "There's danger ahead," said the secretary bird. "To wit?" said the owl. The secretary bird told him. "Aren't you afraid?" he asked. "Who?" said the owl calmly, for he could not see the truck. "He's God!" cried all the creatures again, and they were still crying "He's God!" when the truck hit them and ran them down. Some of the animals were merely injured, but most of them, including the owl, were killed.

Moral: You can fool too many of the people too much of the time.

Source: J. Thurber, *Fables for Our Time* (New York: Harper & Brothers, 1940), p. 35. Reprinted with permission of Rosemary Thurber.

mothers, they have not resolved their inner conflicts and foster similar overdependent relationships in their followers. Kets de Vries added that unhealthy charismatic leaders are particularly dangerous, as such leaders often have the ability to turn their internal fantasies of power and control into social and physical reality.

HIGHLIGHT 16–7

Marjoe Gortner

At the age of 4, Marjoe Gortner preached at tent revival meetings, billed as "The World's Youngest Ordained Minister." He was well prepared for it, having been coached in dramatic techniques including the right way to shout "Glory" into a microphone. His sermons (with titles such as "Heading for the Last Roundup") were memorized down to each pause and gesture. Gortner's role, in his own view, was to be a sort of conductor, orchestrating and engineering the group frenzy. Cynically recalling his manipulations, Gortner said, "It's the same as at a rock and roll concert . . . You have an opening number with a strong entrance; then you go through a lot of the old standards, building up to your hit song at the end" (Conway & Siegelman, 1979, p.48). Was Marjoe a charismatic leader? In one sense, because he was able to get followers to form strong emotional bonds with him and to trust in the correctness of his religious beliefs, Marjoe would probably be considered a charismatic leader using our definition of charisma. However, in another sense, Marjoe would not be considered a charismatic leader. According to Burns (1978), charismatic or transformational leaders also develop strong emotional bonds and are concerned with the development of their followers. Because Marjoe was interested only in developing relationships with followers for his own personal gain and self-aggrandizement, he would not be considered a transformational leader according to Burns's definition.

Source: F. Conway and J. Siegelman, *Snapping* (New York: Delta, 1979).

More recently, Howell (1988) maintained that there are both socialized and personalized charismatic leaders. Socialized charismastic leaders express goals that are follower driven and work to develop followers into leaders. Personalized charismatic leaders pursue leader-driven goals and promote feelings of obedience, dependency, and submission in followers. The differences between these two types of leaders, however, may be due to their values, not their personalities. Martin Luther King, Jr., and Adolph Hitler may have shared certain similarities in ability and personality, and these similarities may have played a major role in allowing them to develop strong emotional bonds with followers and to articulate their visions of the future. However, no one would argue that these two leaders shared the same value systems. Thus, the differences between positive and negative charismatic leaders may be due to differences in value systems; negative charismatic leaders only may be interested in their own self-aggrandizement and power, whereas positive charismatic leaders are primarily motivated to improve their followers, organizations, or societies (see Highlight 16–8).

Training and Selecting Charismatic Leaders

Given the potential positive benefits of transformational or charismatic leadership, two important questions that remain to be answered concern whether it is possible to train or select charismatic leaders. Although little research has been done in either of these areas, Howell and Frost (1988) have conducted a laboratory experiment that sheds some light on this question. Howell and Frost trained several actresses to exhibit charismatic, directive, or relationship-oriented behaviors as leaders of four-person work groups. For example, actresses exhibiting charismatic behaviors acted confidently and dynamically, expressed high confidence in followers, set high performance expectations, and empathized with the needs of followers. The four-person work groups of charismatic leaders performed at higher levels and had greater levels of satisfaction than the four-person work groups having a directive or relationship-oriented leader. Although some have used these findings to argue that it is possible to train leaders to be more charismatic (Avolio & Gibbons, 1988; Bass, 1988; Conger & Kanungo, 1988), this conclusion seems somewhat premature. Because Howell and Frost did not train a leader to exhibit *both* high task and high relationship behaviors, it is uncertain whether the followers of charismatic leaders would have any higher performance or satisfaction levels than followers of 9,9 leaders (Curphy, 1991a; Yukl, 1989).

Perhaps the best way to think about whether it is possible to train leaders to be more charismatic is to go back and review the leader, follower, and situational characteristics of charismastic leadership. Certainly, one could train leaders to recognize and restructure those situational factors facilitating charismatic leader emergence. However, it may be relatively difficult to train leaders to improve the follower factors, as the strong emotional attachments followers develop with charismatic leaders will depend as much on followers' needs and expectations as on the leader's visioning, rhetorical, and impression management skills (though some leaders—unscrupulous ones in particular—probably select certain causes to champion precisely because they sense particularly strong needs on the part of potential followers). Furthermore, while it may be possible to train leaders to improve their visioning, impression management, and rhetorical skills, leaders who have lower intelligence, creativity, dominance, and achievement-oriented scores—and who are low self-monitors and unsociable—may not obtain much benefit from this training. The idea that anyone can become more charismatic through appropriate training may be a bit naive and certainly remains to be demonstrated.

A final comment concerning charismatic leadership involves personnel selection, often thought of as the flip side of training. Some people may argue that if leaders cannot be trained to be more charismatic, then we should focus effort toward selecting leaders with the individual difference characteristics associated with charismatic leadership and placing them in leadership positions.

HIGHLIGHT 16–8

The Destruction of Alexander the Great

Just as some charismatic leaders can have significant positive changes on an organization, society, or nation, so can others have an equally strong negative effect on organizations or societies. The story of Alexander the Great provides an excellent example of a famous charismatic leader whose actions and activities were focused solely on his own self-aggrandizement. The following are some of the distinctive accomplishments and characteristics of Alexander the Great.

• *His accomplishments:* Alexander the Great was born in 356 B.C., and 35 years later he had managed to conquer most of the known world. Based in Macedonia (in the southern peninsula of Greece), Alexander's campaigns allowed him to rule lands in Turkey, Lebanon, Israel, Egypt, Syria, Iraq, Iran, Pakistan, Afghanistan, and India.

• *His vision:* Quite simply, Alexander's vision was to rule the world. He viewed his campaign as a Homerian epic and wanted to guarantee himself a place in history.

• *His intellect:* Alexander was an incisive strategist and a brilliant tactician. For example, because the massive Persian fleet was powered by rowers (who needed food and water to power the ships), Alexander correctly assumed that the Persian fleet would be rendered useless if their home ports were captured. Moreover, he learned from his battles and sieges, and applied this knowledge in future battles.

• *His concern for his followers and personal example:* Alexander was a man of tireless energy and an absolutely fearless warrior. He showed a complete disregard for danger in battle—he was often at the front lines leading his troops into the thick of the battle. Because of his leadership style, Alexander had been wounded by swords, spears, darts, stones, clubs, and catapult missles over the course of his campaigning. Nevertheless, he showed a great deal of compassion toward his troops. He granted many of his troops leave and canceled all of their debts. He made sure they had enough food, visited the wounded after each battle, and conducted elaborate military funerals for his fallen comrades.

• *His excellent rhetorical and dramatic skills:* Alexander was formally schooled in debate and epic poetry by Aristotle. He spoke in a forceful, dramatic style and had the gift of being able to tailor his messages to the situation at hand. Alexander was also very theatrical; he feigned sleep immediately before the battle of Gaugamela. Similarly, when rumors about his wounding and death began circulating among his troops after a particularly fierce battle, he stayed within his tent for three days, allowing the rumors to reach a fever pitch. He waited until he was the subject of concern of all of his troops before he assuaged their fears.

• *He understood the importance of success:* He constantly excelled at war, as he knew failures would cause his troops to question his "supernatural" powers.

HIGHLIGHT 16–8 *(concluded)*

• *The destruction:* Although Alexander conquered much of the known world at the time, to what end did this destruction serve? He did not formally develop his troops, nor did he advance Greek society beyond supplying it with the spoils of his campaigns. The destruction of Alexander's campaigns served only to secure his own place in history—he did not create a new and better society for the Macedonians or for the people whose lands he conquered.

Source: J. Keegan, *The Mask of Command* (New York: Penguin Press, 1988).

Unfortunately, there are two difficulties with this strategy. First, we know very little about the personality traits that differentiate charismatic from noncharismatic leaders. Although House, Spangler, and Woycke (1991); House, Woycke, and Fodor (1988); and Ross and Offermann (1991) have done some preliminary work in this regard, much more research needs to be accomplished before we can say we have identified those traits consistently associated with charismatic leadership. Second, the selection of charismatic leaders is particularly difficult because charisma exists in the eyes of the beholders. In most cases, this means charisma is in the eyes of the followers, yet followers hardly ever play a role in the selection process (in organizations, at least). Again, much more research is needed before we can say with any confidence that we can select or train charismatic leaders.

Concluding Thoughts about Transformational or Charismastic Leadership

Certainly the early research conducted by historians, sociologists, and political scientists provided the springboard for many of the questions currently being asked about transformational leadership in organizational settings. Although there is considerable work yet to be accomplished, we know a lot more about charismatic leadership today than we knew about the topic 15 years ago. For example, we have a pretty good idea of the distinguishing leader, follower, and situational characteristics of charismatic leadership, and we know that charismatic leadership can occur in any team, group, or organizational setting. We also know that charismatic leaders can have stronger effects on some leadership effectiveness criteria than others and that values may play a key role determining whether charismatic leaders have positive or disruptive effects on a group or organization. We also suspect that training and selecting charismatic leaders may be very difficult. Future research efforts must better identify the individual difference variables related to charismatic leadership and determine whether or not charismatic leadership behaviors are amenable to training.

SUMMARY

Although there is considerable research currently being conducted on a variety of leadership topics, this chapter reviews research concerning only the group effectiveness model of leadership and the literature pertaining to transformational or charismatic leadership. By encompassing a wide variety of leader, follower, and situational factors, these two perspectives on leadership are among the most comprehensive of any discussed in this book.

The group effectiveness model posited that group effectiveness can best be understood in terms of inputs, processes, and outcomes. The input level consists of the intelligence, skills, personality traits, and values of the followers; the design of the group; and various organizational and environmental factors. The process level concerns the way in which groups get tasks accomplished, and the output level concerns whether or not customers are satisfied with the group's product and whether followers are satisfied to be members of the group. By identifying certain process problems in groups, leaders can use the model to diagnose appropriate "leverage points" for action at the individual, group design, or organizational levels, or for coaching at the process level. Although this model is relatively new, the research that has been accomplished has shown initial support for this conceptualization of factors affecting group effectiveness.

Although the topic of transformational or charismatic leadership has been of interest to sociologists, historians, and political scientists over the years, it has only recently been investigated by organizational researchers. In the past 15 years, organizational researchers have been able to identify distinctive leader, follower, and situational characteristics of charismatic leadership. Moreover, researchers using Bass's MLQ have shown that there are many transformational leaders in organizational settings who often have very positive effects on their followers. These effects include more positive attitudes toward work and their organizations, and on unit performance indices requiring interdependent effort. Nevertheless, some charismatic or transformational leaders can be disruptive to organizations, particularly if the leader's vision is in conflict with the goals of the organization or if the leader is only developing strong emotional bonds with followers for their own (i.e., the leader's) selfish ends. Finally, because charisma is an attribution followers confer to certain leaders, it may be difficult to select or train leaders to be charismatic. We may be able to "improve the odds" somewhat by providing appropriate training to individuals with the requisite individual difference characteristics, but whether followers will perceive these individuals as charismatic will depend to a large extent on their own needs and expectations. Therefore, considerably more research is needed before we fully understand the charismatic leadership process and can accurately predict who will be perceived as charismatic in group, team, or organizational settings.

KEY TERMS AND CONCEPTS

group effectiveness model

outputs

process measures

inputs

leverage point

individual factors

organizational context

group design

material resources

traditional authority system

legal-rational authority system

charismatic authority system

charisma

spellbinders

theory of transformational and transactional leadership

Multifactor Leadership Questionnaire (MLQ)

DISCUSSION QUESTIONS

1. How do the tenets of the group effectiveness model compare with the components of team performance described in Chapter Ten?

2. How do the tenets of the group effectiveness model compare to the model of performance provided in Chapter Fourteen? What differences do you see between these two models?

3. Would the model of group effectiveness be equally applicable to groups led by charismatic versus noncharismatic leaders? What components of the model would be most affected by these two types of leaders?

4. Who, to you, are the most charismatic leaders in the United States today? In the world? How do they differ from noncharismatic national or world leaders?

5. President Bush had some of the highest and lowest presidential approval ratings ever reported for modern U.S. presidents. Do you think most people percieved President Bush to be a charismatic leader during his times of highest ratings (i.e., during Operation Desert Storm)? If so, what role do you think the situation played in people's perceptions of President Bush as a charismatic or noncharismatic leader?

SUGGESTED READINGS

Bass, B. M. *Leadership and Performance beyond Expectations.* New York: Free Press, 1985.

Conger, J. A., and R. N. Kanungo. *Charismatic Leadership: The Elusive Factor in Organizational Effectiveness.* San Francisco: Jossey-Bass, 1988.

Hackman, J. R. *Groups that Work (and Those that Don't).* San Francisco: Jossey-Bass, 1990.

Keegan, J. *The Mask of Command.* New York: Penguin, 1988.

Chapter Seventeen

From Qualities of Leaders to Leaders of Quality

INTRODUCTION

O ver the past decade, a philosophy of leadership and management frequently referred to as Total Quality (TQ) has gained increasing acceptance in both corporate and government circles. At least this is true in the United States. Elsewhere in the world, most notably in Japan, TQ has been the standard for nearly half a century. Strictly speaking, TQ is not a theory of leadership. However, it is an approach that merits consideration, even though it has not received much attention by academicians so far. Furthermore, it is an approach that integrates many concepts from throughout this book, and thus it serves as a fitting subject for the concluding chapter.

The essence of the TQ movement is that certain organizational principles and practices are essential to delivering high-quality goods and services. This, in turn, is essential to long-term success. Those principles and practices must be part of an organization's fabric and lifeblood, not simply a cosmetic embellishment or inspirational rhetoric to overlay actual operating procedures.

A commitment to quality purportedly involves a new way of organizational life. It demands, therefore, a new approach to leadership. More and more of today's organizational leaders are finding their roles shaped by the ideas and methods of the TQ approach. In one sense, then, we might well say the discipline of leadership has moved from studying the qualities of leaders to studying leaders of quality. (see Highlight 17–1 for further thoughts about leadership and quality).

A BRIEF HISTORY OF THE QUALITY REVOLUTION

In 1946, Japan was a defeated nation. Today, it boasts one of the strongest economies in the world. For years after World War II, Americans thought Japanese-manufactured products were inferior. Today, Japanese products have a well-deserved reputation for consistently high quality. What accounts for such a remarkable turnaround? It is ironic that Japan's recovery occurred in part because Japanese business leaders took seriously the teachings of certain American management consultants when, by and large, American business leaders did not. Even more ironically, many of the procedures associated with the quality movement were developed during World War II to further the American war effort. Techniques that had been developed by an enemy to mass-produce wartime weapons and material became the foundation of Japanese economic recovery.

One of the several individuals who have played a seminal role in TQ is W. Edwards Deming. With a Ph.D. in mathematical physics from Yale, Deming may seem an unlikely person to become a sought-after management consultant. His mathematical expertise, however, led him to focus on applied statistics and the developing field of quality control. Today, Deming is perhaps best known for his "Fourteen Points," a sort of Ten Commandments of TQ (see Table 17–1).

Another leader in the TQ movement has been J. M. Juran. Juran was one of

---

HIGHLIGHT 17–1

Leadership Quotes, Chapter Seventeen

The man who would lift others must be uplifted himself, and he who would command others must learn to obey.

Charles K. Ober

Work is love made visible.
And if you cannot work with love but only with distaste, it is better that you should leave your work and sit at the gate of the temple and take alms of those who work with joy.
For if you bake bread with indifference, you bake a bitter bread that feeds but half a man's hunger.

Kahlil Gibran

Ask not what your country can do for you. Ask what you can do for your country.

John F. Kennedy

Quality is not a thing. It is an event.

Robert M. Pirsig

Be a yardstick of quality. Some people aren't used to an environment where excellence is expected.

Steve Jobs

We are born for cooperation, as are the feet, the hands, the eyelids, and the upper and lower jaws.

Marcus Aurelius Antoniuus

The definition of total quality is simple: It is a leadership philosophy which creates throughout the entire enterprise a working environment which inspires trust, teamwork, and the quest for continuous, measurable improvement.

John M. Loh

The secret of success is constancy of purpose.

Benjamin Disraeli

---

the first to call attention to the real nature of the economic revolution occurring in Japan in the decades after World War II. Most American businesspeople believed that the Japanese competitive advantage was in offering goods of lower price, but Juran said their real advantage was offering goods of higher quality (Juran, 1967).

TABLE 17–1
Deming's 14 Points

1. *Constancy of purpose.* An organization must be clear about its fundamental purpose in order to provide quality goods and services over time. Without such clarity and constancy of purpose, leaders often base decisions on expediencies, sacrificing quality for short-term benefits.

2. *Adopt the new philosophy.* Quality cannot be achieved piecemeal. These 14 points represent an integrated philosophy that must be implemented throughout an entire organization.

3. *Cease reliance on mass inspection to assure quality.* Mass inspection implies that unacceptable, defective work is expected. It is better to build quality into processes than to inspect at the end to eliminate mistakes.

4. *End the practice of awarding business largely on the basis of price.* Offering goods and services of continuously improving quality depends on having long-term, trusting relationships with suppliers similarly committed to quality. It is self-defeating to award business to whatever supplier at any particular moment happens to offer the "lowest bid."

5. *Improve constantly.* Continuous improvement occurs through systematic efforts to model and measure key processes.

6. *Institute training.* The key to improving quality is understanding the statistical variability of critical processes. This requires extensive training at all levels.

7. *Institute leadership.* It takes leadership to change the coercive and dysfunctionally competitive paradigm by which most organizations operate.

8. *Drive out fear.* Leadership and management practices that suppress initiative, innovation, and cooperation among workers are counterquality.

9. *Break down barriers between departments.* There needs to be coordinated work across departments based on shared understanding and mutual support of customer needs.

10. *Eliminate slogans, exhortations, and targets for the work force.* These mistakenly imply improvement comes primarily through extra effort by individual workers rather than through improvements to a whole system. They focus attention at the wrong level, and often create adversarial relationships in the process.

11. *Eliminate numerical goals and quotas.* Focusing on numerical goals and quotas emphasizes end goals rather than processes, and can lead to counterquality "square filling."

12. *Remove barriers to pride of workmanship.* The vast majority of people want to take pride in their work. Sometimes, however, organizational systems rob workers of their pride of workmanship. One way is simply through a toleration of sub-quality work by management. Another is through competitive appraisal systems which numerically compare one worker's contributions with another's.

13. *Institute a vigorous program of education and self-improvement.* The pride people take in work comes in part through their own continued growth, and organizations should provide opportunities for continuous development and self-improvement to all members.

14. *Involve everyone in the transformation.* Everyone in every organization has the capability to improve the processes he or she is responsible for.

Source: A. Gabor, *The Man Who Discovered Quality* (New York: Random House, 1990), pp. 19–30.

By the 1980s, many American businesspeople were visiting Japan to better understand how to improve their own companies' operations. The postwar American business strategy of stressing immediate financial results above all else was proving shortsighted (Aguayo, 1990). In some ways, the problem boiled down to simple things. For example, Aguayo tells of buying a telephone made by ITT, which at the time was among the top 10 companies on the Fortune 500 list. The phone had a 90-day warranty, and it broke on the 91st day he owned it. While many American companies reported impressive financial results, their products simply lacked quality.

Gradually, however, American companies, too, learned to pay attention to quality. Companies like Ford, Motorola, Xerox, Milliken, and Cadillac described major turnarounds after adopting TQ. TQ is not even limited to the manufacturing world. The entire U.S. federal government officially adopted TQ in the 1980s, though it has taken years for it to become implemented throughout all departments. In sum, by certain early indicators, the TQ movement seems to have changed many organizations' ways of doing business, and thus the nature of leadership, in both the private and the public sectors.

QUALITY IN PERSPECTIVE

What Is Quality?

Quality is difficult to define, but people claim to know it when they see it. Quality of service is poor when a restaurant's food arrives tardy and tepid at your table. Quality of product is poor when the interior trim on your automobile falls off. Quality of government is low when information provided in response to tax queries has a 25 percent error rate (Aguayo, 1990). Yet for many years, quality of product or service did not seem to be a criterion of success to many U. S. organizations. In the corporate sector, for example, criteria such as increased market share and increased profits through selling cheaper products were emphasized more than quality. Although quality can seem difficult to define, Juran (1989) said there are two essential aspects to a definition of quality: goods or services that meet customer needs, and goods or services that are free from defects.

A problem in understanding what TQ is all about is that most people, it seems, have learned to think of quality as an economic trade-off: Quality may be desirable, but it is thought to cost more. One of the fundamental tenets of the TQ perspective, however, is that quality actually costs less. There are several reasons for this belief. For one thing, quality products are said to actually cost less to produce; quality service costs less to offer. Quality is a matter of **customer satisfaction,** and systematically incorporating customer feedback into product design while also increasing the uniformity of production processes will cost less in the long run. It may be helpful in this regard to distinguish between a product's quality and the number of features it has. Quality is not defined by how many features a product has. A high-priced car (with more features such as power seats, automatic temperature control, etc.) is not necessarily of higher quality than an inexpensive car (with fewer features). The key is how well the car—or any product or service—meets the customer's needs.

Another reason quality costs less, according to TQ proponents, is that word of inferior products or services gets around faster than word of quality products or services; dissatisfied customers talk more about their dissatisfaction than satisfied customers talk about their satisfaction (Aguayo, 1990). It is nearly impossible and extraordinarily expensive to try to offset the firsthand complaints of dissatisfied customers with expensive advertising campaigns.

There is one other important aspect of quality: the intangible contribution of a worker's pride to the quality of his or her work. A worker who takes pride in his or her work, who gets intrinsic satisfaction from doing a good job, is more likely to produce high-quality results. And what makes some workers take pride in their work when others do not? Many of us have been conditioned to think it is just the way some workers are; some take pride in their work while others do not. Another fundamental tenet of the TQ movement, however, is that most workers *want* to do a good job. Quality of work is poor in many organizations not because of "bad" or "unmotivated" workers, but because the organizational cultures and systems they work within stifle employee pride and initiative. Quality work depends less on having "good" workers than it does on an organizational culture wherein pride in workmanship is nurtured and reinforced. Put differently, the TQ approach *assumes* that workers are intrinsically motivated to do good work if given a chance. For many organizations, therefore, a commitment to quality involves culture change. And needless to say, the responsibility for changing an organization's culture belongs to its leadership.

Quality Is Achieved through Culture Change

Organizations adopting TQ principles and practices almost invariably undergo cultural changes. We are particularly concerned here with those aspects of an organization's culture dealing with leadership and followership—with the whole pattern of organizational norms involving communication patterns, authority relationships, decision-making processes, and so on. The more traditional an organization was before adopting TQ principles and practices, the more radical the culture change will seem to be. Some major differences between the leadership culture in traditional organizations and TQ organizations are listed in Table 17–2. It should be noted, however, that many actual organizations may be difficult to classify as purely one type or the other. Most organizations probably fall somewhere in between.

TABLE 17–2

Contrasting Traditional and Quality Orientations to Leadership in Organizations

Traditional	Quality
Theory X	Theory Y
Bossing	Coaching
Extrinsic motivation	Intrinsic motivation
Authoritarian	Participating
Control	Empowerment
Reactive followers	Active followers
Restricted communication	Open communication
Short-term	Long-term
Centralized	Decentralized
Bureaucracy	More ad hoc groups
Structure	Process
Reward individuals	Reward teams
Competition	Cooperation

Some of these changes have to do with the nature and quality of the relationship between leaders and followers. The TQ perspective is an embodiment of Theory Y assumptions about human nature. Implementing TQ programs can be likened to an investment in subordinates through greater use of participative decision making and greater emphasis on subordinate development through education and training programs. Correspondingly, the leader's role becomes one of coach more than boss, and emphasis is placed on empowering subordinates rather than controlling them.

Consistent with this emphasis on empowerment, the TQ organization is characterized by reduced centralized control overall. Organizational structure is deemphasized, and cross-functional ad hoc work groups are a major mechanism for seeking ever better methods of meeting long-term organizational objectives. Communication is relatively open, both laterally and vertically. Workers are encouraged to use their expertise and creativity in developing better ways to accomplish their work. All this enhances organizational responsiveness to a dynamic social, economic, and technological environment, but it also contributes to another important outcome: It makes work more intrinsically motivating by increasing worker autonomy.

Another factor that makes the TQ work environment a motivating one to work in is the nature of co-worker relations. Cooperation rather than competition among workers is emphasized. One important way this is accomplished is by rewarding teams rather than individuals. Rewards pitting one member against another can be particularly devisive and organizationally dysfunctional. A corporate culture of individualism—a sort of ''survival of the fittest'' in organizations—is giving way to a corporate culture emphasizing the group or team.

Hopefully, these examples suggest how the norms of a TQ culture would be thought of as an interdependent whole. It should not go unnoticed how emphasis on teams rather than individuals is particularly compatible with cooperative instead of competitive practices; how a leader who makes Theory X assumptions may not function well in a participative structure and a person who makes Theory Y assumptions may not function best in an authoritarian, hierarchical environment; how more open communication is compatible with decentralized authority; and how empowerment increases intrinsic motivation (see Highlight 17-2 for how similar ideas are applicable in athletics). Put another way, implementing TQ in any organization must be a *systemic* process. It must involve the whole organizational system, top to bottom. Appropriate styles of leadership and followership are defined by the TQ culture, not left to individual choice. Implementing TQ takes leaders who can articulate a vision, change organizational culture, and empower others. These were, you will recall, important themes in Chapter Sixteen's discussion of charisma and transformational leadership.

Quality Is Achieved through Continuous Process Improvement

Implementing TQ must be systemic, but it also must be *systematic*. If any single idea is central to TQ, it is that of **continuous process improvement.** Continuous process improvement, in turn, depends on methodical approaches at all organizational levels to data collection, problem solving, and decision making. In that sense, TQ is a management system as well as a leadership philosophy. As part of this management system, there are numerous analytical tools that practitioners of TQ become thoroughly familiar with. They range from relatively simple tools to sophisticated techniques like the design of experiments and statistical process control. Since these techniques generally apply to the managerial aspects of TQ, they are beyond the scope of this book. It is essential, however, to appreciate the meaning of continuous process improvement.

Each of those three words is important, but let's begin with the idea of process. Processes are the ways things are done. The way you shave or put on makeup is a process. The way orders are taken in a crowded fast-food restaurant is a process. The way teachers present material to students, integrated circuits are installed in computers, the right amount of corn flakes is put into cereal boxes, and time is allocated to different stories on the evening news are processes. Processes are important because most of the opportunity for improving any product or service involves improving its component processes.

This is not the traditional way of thinking. The traditional view has been that improvement comes by exhorting workers to do more or better work. The traditional view is that workers need to improve within a system that is assumed to remain constant. The TQ perspective, however, is that the greatest opportunity for improvement—some estimate as much as 85 percent—involves working *on* the system (i.e., on its processes) rather than *in* the system (i.e., on the workers).

Therefore, whereas the first key word is process, the second key word is improvement. The processes for producing or delivering goods and services can always be improved, and it always pays to improve them. The term *improvement* also implies that there is a goal or target toward which the process is directed. It is nearly impossible to improve a process if customer needs have not been identified. Finally, improvements in processes should be made continuously. TQ puts faith in the cumulative power over time of continued small improvements ("kaizen"). All the analytical tools and techniques—and the emphasis on decentralization, teams, cooperation, participation, and empowerment—collectively contribute to continuous process improvement.

Putting It All Together

In some ways, there are few new ideas in TQ. In another sense, however, the systematic integration of all these ideas is very new. One way of depicting this integration emphasizes the balance of TQ's cultural and behavioral aspects with its analytical aspects. The particular concepts on either side of the scale in Figure 17-1 have been around for some time, but TQ combines them in a distinctive approach to organizational leadership. In large part, TQ involves cooperative systematic reflection about what works and what does not work in producing desired results and creating the kind of organization where those behaviors are encouraged.

PROBLEM SOLVING: A KEY TQ SKILL

Three previous chapters in this book dealt with specific leadership and followership skills. Problem solving is a skill that easily could have been addressed in any one of those chapters. Putting it in this chapter in no way implies that proponents of TQ are the only people to have emphasized the importance of problem solving, or that it can be effectively implemented independent of the other skills (e.g., effective communication). Obviously that is not true. On the other hand, the TQ culture of empowerment, participation, teamwork, cooperation, decentralization, systematic change, and process improvement places particular importance on the role of followers as well as leaders as problem solvers. Therefore, we decided to include problem solving—the final leader-

HIGHLIGHT 17–2 *(concluded)*

lows. I wanted them executing the sound offensive and defensive principles we taught in practice.''

There's no pillow as soft as a clear conscience

''To me success isn't outscoring someone, it's the peace of mind that comes from self-satisfaction in knowing you did your best. That's something each individual must determine for himself. You can fool others but you can't fool yourself.''

''Many people are surprised to learn that in 27 years at UCLA, I never once talked about winning. Instead I would tell my players before games, 'When it's over, I want your head up. And there's only one way your head can be up, that's for you to know, not me, that you gave the best effort of which you're capable. If you do that, then the score doesn't really matter, although I have a feeling that if you do that, the score will be to your liking.' I honestly, deeply believe that in not stressing winning as such, we won more than we would have if I'd stressed outscoring opponents.''

Why do so many people dread adversity,
when it's only through adversity that we grow stronger?

''There's no great fun, satisfaction, or joy derived from doing something that's easy. Failure is never fatal, but failure to change might be.''

''Your strength as an individual depends on, and will be in direct proportion to, how you react to both praise and criticism. If you become too concerned about either, the effect on you is certain to be adverse.''

The main ingredient of stardom

''I always taught players that the main ingredient of stardom is the rest of the team. It's amazing how much can be accomplished if no one cares who gets the credit. That's why I was as concerned with a player's character as I was with his ability.''

''While it may be possible to reach the top of one's profession on sheer ability, it is impossible to stay there without hard work and character. One's character may be quite different from one's reputation.''

''Your character is what your really are. Your reputation is only what others think you are. I made a determined effort to evaluate character. I looked for young men who would play the game hard, but clean, and who would always be trying to improve themselves to help the team. Then, if their ability warranted it, the championships would take care of themselves.''

Source: Reprinted with permission of the Panhandle Eastern Corporation.

FIGURE 17–1
Three Aspects of Total Quality

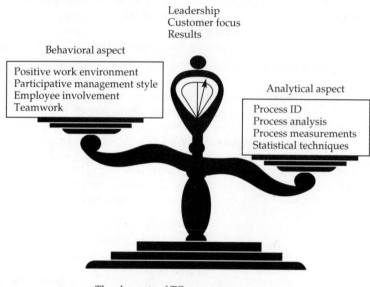

- The elements of TQ are not new
- Ideally, TQ is like a diet of good food and exercise

ship skill in the book—in this chapter on Total Quality. The following are some steps to follow in solving problems in TQ organizations, highlighting a few of the basic TQ tools.

Identifying Problems or Opportunities for Improvement

The first step in problem solving is to state the problem so that everyone involved in developing a solution has an informed and common appreciation and understanding of the task. This is a critical stage in problem solving and will take time and probably group discussion. It is dangerous to assume that everyone (or anyone!) knows at the outset what the problem is. A hurried or premature definition of the problem (e.g., as a result of groupthink) may lead to considerable frustration and wasted effort. In counseling and advising, for example, a significant portion of the work with a client is devoted to clarifying the problem. A student may seek help at the school counseling center to improve his study skills because he is spending what seems to be plenty of time studying yet is still doing poorly on examinations. A little discussion, however, may reveal that he is having difficulty concentrating on schoolwork because of problems at home. If the counselor had moved immediately to developing the client's study skills, the real cause of his difficulties would have gone un-treated, and the client might have become even more pessimistic about his abil-ities and the possibility that others can help him. Or consider the case of a po-lice chief who is concerned about the few volunteers willing to serve on a citizen's advisory committee to her department. There are many problems she might identify here, such as citizen apathy or poor publicity concerning the need and importance of the committee. The real problem, however, might be her own reputation for rarely listening to or heeding recommendations made by similar advisory committees in the past. If the chief were to take the time to explore and clarify the problem at the outset, then she *could* discover this im-portant fact and take steps to solve the *real* problem (her own behavior). If, on the other hand, she pressed ahead aggressively, trusting her own appraisal of the problem, then nothing likely would change.

The reason it helps to take time to define a problem carefully is that some-times people mistake symptoms for causes. In the case of the student, his poor studying was a symptom of another cause (family difficulties), not the cause of his poor grades. In the case of the police chief, lack of citizen participation on the advisory committee was a symptom of a problem, not the problem itself. If a plan addresses a symptom rather than the causes of a problem, the desired results will not be attained. It also is important during this stage to avoid scape-goating or blaming individuals or groups for the problem, which may just en-gender defensiveness and reduce creative thinking. This is a stage where con-flict resolution techniques and negotiating skills can be very important. Finally, the statement of a problem should not imply that any particular solution is the correct one.

As an application of these considerations, let us consider two pairs of prob-lem statements that a teacher might present to his class as a first step in ad-dressing what he considers to be an unsatisfactory situation. These samples of dialogue touch on many aspects of communication, listening, and feedback skills addressed earlier in this book. Here, however, our focus is on differences in defining problems. In each case, the second statement is the one more likely to lead to constructive problem solving.

A: I don't think you care enough about this course. No one is ever prepared. What do I have to do to get you to put in more time on your homework?
B: What things are interfering with you doing well in this course?

A: Your test grades are too low. I'm going to cancel the field trip unless they im-prove. Do you have any questions?
B: I'm concerned about your test scores. They're lower than I expected them to be, and I'm not sure what's going on. What do you think the problem is?

Another aspect of this first stage of problem solving involves identifying those factors that, when corrected, are likely to have the greatest impact on improving an unsatisfactory situation. Since there are almost always more problems or opportunities for improvement than time or energy to devote to them all, it is crucial to identify those whose solutions offer the greatest potential payoff. A useful concept here is known as the **Pareto principle.** It states that about 80 percent of the problems in any system are the result of about 20 percent of the causes. In school, for example, most of the discipline problems are caused by a minority of the students. Of all the errors people make on income tax returns, just a few kinds of errors (e.g., forgetting to sign them) account for a disproportionately high percentage of returned forms. We would expect about 20 percent of the total mechanical problems in a city bus fleet to account for about 80 percent of the fleet's downtime. The Pareto principle can be used to focus problem-solving efforts on those causes that have the greatest overall impact.

Analyzing the Causes

Once a problem is identified, the next step is to analyze its causes. Analysis of a problem's causes should precede a search for its solutions. Two helpful tools for identifying the key elements affecting a problem situation are the **cause-and-effect diagram** (also called the "fishbone" diagram because of its shape, or the Ishikawa diagram after the person who developed it) and **force field analysis.** The cause-and-effect diagram uses a graphic approach to depict systematically the root causes of a problem, the relationships between different causes, and potentially a prioritization of which causes are most important (see Figure 17–2).

Force field analysis (see Figure 17–3) also uses a graphic approach, this time to depict the opposing forces that tend to perpetuate a present state of affairs. It is a way of depicting any stable situation in terms of dynamic balance, or equilibrium, between those forces that tend to press toward movement in one direction and those other forces that tend to restrain movement in that direction. So long as the net sum of all those forces is zero, no movement occurs. When a change is desirable, force field analysis can be used to identify the best way to upset the balance between "positive" and "negative" forces so that a different equilibrium can be reached.

Developing Alternative Solutions

Several ideas from Chapter Fourteen are relevant here (e.g., brainstorming), as is the importance of solutions meeting criteria for quality and acceptance. A procedure called **Nominal Group Technique (NGT)** (Delbecq, Van de Ven, & Gustafson, 1975) is another way to generate a lot of ideas pertinent to a problem. This procedure is similar to brainstorming in that it is an idea-generating activity conducted in a group setting. With NGT, however, group members write down ideas on individual slips of paper, which are later transferred to a blackboard or flipchart for the entire group to work with.

FIGURE 17–2
A Cause-and-Effect Diagram

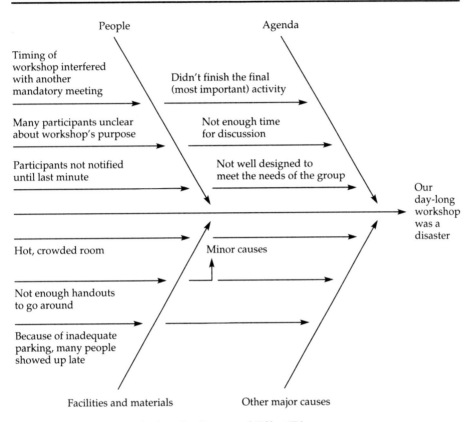

Using the Cause-and-Effect Diagram

1. Write the problem situation inside a box with a long arrow leading to it. The arrow represents the sum of all the various influences which contribute to the problem or opportunity for improvement.

2. Decide what the problem's major causes are and write these in boxes which diagonally join the main arrow.

3. Use brainstorming to identify minor causes which influence each of the respective major causes. Write these on separate horizontal arrows joining the appropriate major diagonal arrows. You can use other arrows to depict how one minor cause leads to another minor cause.

4. The resulting analysis can be used to identify potential solutions.

FIGURE 17–3
Force Field Analysis

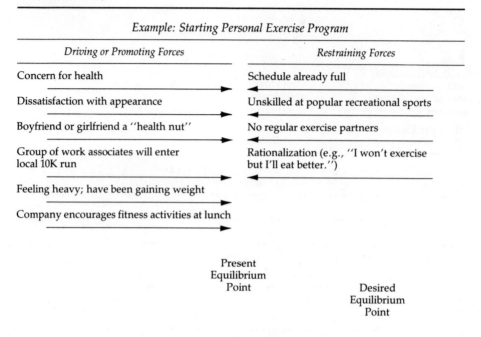

Example: Starting Personal Exercise Program

Driving or Promoting Forces	*Restraining Forces*
Concern for health	Schedule already full
Dissatisfaction with appearance	Unskilled at popular recreational sports
Boyfriend or girlfriend a ''health nut''	No regular exercise partners
Group of work associates will enter local 10K run	Rationalization (e.g., ''I won't exercise but I'll eat better.'')
Feeling heavy; have been gaining weight	
Company encourages fitness activities at lunch	

Present
Equilibrium
Point

Desired
Equilibrium
Point

Using Force Field Analysis

1. State the present situation and the desired situation.

2. Illustrate the present equilibrium in terms of a vertical line represented by the convergence of two sets of arrows. Arrows pointing to the right will represent desired change and arrows pointing to the left will represent forces restraining desired change.

3. Use brainstorming to identify the forces promoting and restraining desired change.

4. Evaluate each force in terms of both the impact of changing it and the ease of changing it.

5. Starting with the most easily changed and high impact forces, develop strategies to reduce restraining forces and increase promoting forces.

Selecting and Implementing the Best Solution

The first solution one thinks of is not necessarily the best solution, even if everyone involved finds it acceptable. It is better to select a solution on the basis of established criteria. These include such questions as the following: Have the advantages and disadvantages of all possible solutions been considered? Have all the possible solutions been evaluated in terms of their respective impacts on the whole organization, not just a particular team or department? Is the information needed to make a good decision among the alternatives available?

Assessing the Impact of the Solution

One should not assume that just by going through the preceding steps that the actions implemented will solve the problem. The solution's continuing impact must be assessed, preferably in terms of measurable criteria of success that all parties involved can agree on.

UNANSWERED QUESTIONS ABOUT TOTAL QUALITY

Is Total Quality a Theory?

As we noted at the beginning of this section, TQ is not a theory of leadership. Most often, it is presented as an approach to be followed rather than an idea to be tested. If we think of a theory of leadership as the articulation of hypothesized conditional relationships between leader variables, follower variables, and situational variables, then TQ is not a theory. Anyone who has studied behavior in organizations knows how complex the interactions are among relevant variables, and TQ's basic ideas may seem simplistic in comparison.

Nor has TQ evolved, like theories are supposed to, through hypothesis testing with appropriate controls and interpretation of empirical results. Little research on TQ per se has been reported in relevant scholarly journals. In fact, unlike theories of leadership developed in academic settings and validated through the scientific method, TQ developed in manufacturing settings and was validated in proponents' eyes through the economic successes of companies that had adopted it. But that does not constitute proof of TQ's validity as a conceptual system any more than the economic success of a religious cult validates its theology.

Is Total Quality a Religion?

In fact, TQ strikes some observers as quite like a religion. For one thing, TQ typically is presented in a take-it-or-leave-it manner. Sometimes it is presented as an indivisible body of principles and practices to be adopted or ignored, but not to be critically evaluated or refined. For another thing, there is a quality rather like adoration that seems to characterize proponents' attitudes toward the founders of TQ. It is quite common in TQ literature, in fact, for its seminal thinkers to be referred to as "gurus." They seem to be regarded by many "believers" with nothing short of awe, and questioning the gurus' "revealed wisdom" is seen to be "heresy." We had just this point in mind when previously we likened Deming's "Fourteen Points" to the Ten Commandments. In writing about the increasing movement of TQ to college campuses, G. Keller (1992) expressed concern about the "born-again evangelism" of some TQ proponents.

This is not to say that everyone using TQ feels reverence toward its early thinkers. Clearly that is not the case. Nonetheless, many presentations of TQ have this tone, which may be one reason some scholars (especially in the fields of leadership, organizational behavior, and management) have viewed TQ with at least a little disdain. Advocates of TQ sometimes seem more evangelistic than scientific.

Related to this is the fact that larger and larger numbers of "salesmen" or consultants are making TQ education and training a huge commercial enterprise. The "selling" of TQ seems similarly inconsistent with rigorous, objective, empirical, evaluation of its tenets. Sometimes the intellectual depth and substance of an idea seems inversely proportional to the number of people trying to make money out of it.

Is Total Quality a Fad?

This question is related to the preceding one but emphasizes more how short-lived the current interest in TQ will be. Many other leadership and management fads have had bright but brief heydays, and some believe that Total Quality will fade away just like others have. Probably it is still too soon to answer this question, but TQ's half-century history in Japan and decade-long history of increasing momentum in the United States suggest it may be here to stay.

On the other hand, TQ principles and practices may well survive and flourish at the same time everyone becomes less conscious of TQ as a specialized approach to organizational effectiveness. One could well argue, in fact, that the surest sign of TQ's future success would be if its principles and practices became widespread yet were no longer designated by capital letters and acronyms.

Does Total Quality Work?

How short-lived or long-lived the TQ approach proves to be will depend on results in those organizations that have attempted to implement its principles and procedures. Does implementing TQ make a difference? Some accounts of dramatic company turnarounds make TQ appear to be a panacea, but other accounts tell a different story.

A recent article in *The Economist* described "the cracks in quality" (April 18, 1992). In a survey of 500 American companies, for example, only a third saw TQ as contributing significantly to their competitiveness. Many TQ programs that began with fanfare and high hopes have been discontinued because of lack of results. A factor that seems to distinguish companies in which TQ succeeds versus those in which it fails is the extent to which TQ truly becomes the organization's "way of doing business." One study is cited that found firms whose TQ programs succeeded were twice as likely to have empowered workers by flattening the organizational structure and pushing responsibility for quality to the lowest levels of the organization. Perhaps one conclusion we can reach from such findings is that TQ failures, where they have occurred, seem attributable more to poor implementation than to a basic fallacy in TQ concepts.

One of the very few attempts to systematically evaluate TQ's impact was recently reported by the General Accounting Office (1990) in a report called "Management Practices: U.S. Companies Improve Performance through Quality Efforts." The report was based on surveys, interviews, and other studies of performance in 20 companies that had received high scores competing for the Malcolm Baldridge National Quality Award. While specific practices varied considerably across the companies, there was a common and generalized commitment to the principles of TQ as described in this chapter. The overall conclusion of the GAO was that these companies' commitment to and successful implementation of TQ principles truly did lead to higher corporate performance. We also should note, however, that this represents a relatively biased sample of companies—only those that received high scores on the Baldridge criteria. A fair and complete verdict also should consider those other, more numerous, companies that were less successful in implementing TQ.

In fact, even looking at just the extremely biased group of companies that have *won* the Baldridge Award—a highly respected and valued accomplishment—presents a mixed picture of the impact of TQ on an organization. Putting too much emphasis on winning the award per se can, ironically, devastate a company at the very time it seems to be excelling according to the Baldridge criteria (Main, 1991). Gabor (1990) described the rocky road of several Baldridge-winning companies even after they had won the award.

Does Total Quality Imply There Is a Recipe for Leadership?

Over time, theories of leadership have become increasingly contingent in nature (Jago, 1982). The "Great Man" view of leadership was based on the idea that good leaders share a common set of personality traits, but today the importance of any given personality trait is understood to depend partly on both follower and situational variables. Similarly, our understanding of leader behavior has changed from a universalist to a contingent view. Previously, some leader behaviors were considered always right. Today, however, the effectiveness of any given leader behavior tends to be viewed as contingent on the circumstances.

Total Quality seems to be flying in the face of these trends since it seems to prescribe a certain leadership approach as always right. In a way, though, maybe the TQ approach to leadership is still consistent with these trends. In fact, Glasser (1990) points out that some styles that may appear very autocratic and demanding (such as Jaime Escalante's approach to teaching as depicted in the film *Stand and Deliver*) are at their heart very caring and compassionate, and thus consistent with total quality. In that vein, TQ is not just a new name for Theory Y (see Chapter Eight). TQ's emphasis on empowering workers involves more than viewing them positively, trusting them, creating a supportive climate, and so on. TQ involves an emphasis on task as well as relationship. TQ stresses accountability and high performance by everyone in the organization holding themselves accountable to rigorous efforts to measure and improve work effectiveness.

There also is a way in which TQ is *not* claimed to be a universalist approach. The behavior of leaders in a TQ organization does occur in a particular situation—an organizational culture wherein certain kinds of relationships and activities are explicitly valued. To put it differently, perhaps the leadership style appropriate to a TQ organization is *not* claimed to be universally right, just right in the TQ culture. Perhaps even TQ's Theory Y perspective toward followers (though it is more than just that) is less universal than it may seem at first. Maybe Theory Y assumptions just happen to be most applicable to current demographic realities of the work force, especially in those service and manufacturing industries that depend on and attract better-educated, more self-managing workers.

Thus, TQ concepts do not necessarily contradict the contingent relationships that theoretically exist across the broad range of leader, follower, and situational variables. Some of these theoretical relationships, however, may be simply irrelevant to the practical realities of organizations in which TQ is implemented. Total Quality may not be a theory of leadership, but neither does it proffer a simplistic recipe of leadership. At its root, Total Quality may be seen as an *application* of complex ideas about human relationships and organizational functioning. How well specific organizations implement the spirit of these ideas and principles, how much difference this makes in those organizations' operations and products, and whether increasing numbers of organizations try to nurture leadership styles consistent with the TQ approach are three remaining unanswered questions.

SUMMARY

Total Quality refers to a set of principles and procedures said to be necessary for the production and delivery of high-quality goods and services. Many people credit the dramatic economic recovery in Japan after World War II to this approach, and many organizations around the world are following suit. Organizations that have adopted TQ typically undergo a significant cultural change—or attempt to—including a new approach to leadership and management. Despite the passionate commitment of TQ's proponents, however, relatively little data exist to demonstrate its overall impact, let alone the specific mechanisms of its impact. For now, therefore, it is safest to say that there are still many unanswered questions about TQ.

KEY TERMS AND CONCEPTS

quality
customer satisfaction
continuous process improvement
Pareto principle

cause-and-effect diagram
force field analysis
Nominal Group Technique (NGT)

DISCUSSION QUESTIONS

1. Do you think it is useful to contrast traditional and TQ approaches to leadership? Do you believe one is "better" than the other?
2. Discuss whether TQ is or is not a theory of leadership.
3. How have your own views of effective leadership changed?
4. What aspect of your own leadership do you most wish to develop?
5. What aspect of your own followership do you most wish to develop?
6. Compare and contrast the ideas and methods of TQ with the model for diagnosing subordinate performance problems presented in Chapter Fourteen.

SUGGESTED READINGS

Aguayo, R. *Dr. Deming—the American Who Taught the Japanese about Quality.* New York: Carol Publishing Group, 1990.

Gabor, A. *The Man Who Discovered Quality.* New York: Random House, 1990.

Glasser, W. *The Quality School.* New York: Harper & Row, 1990.

Senge, P. M. *The Fifth Discipline.* New York: Doubleday, 1990.

References

Adams, J.; H. T. Prince; D. Instone; and R. W. Rice. "West Point: Critical Incidents of Leadership." *Armed Forces and Society* 10 (1984), pp. 597–611.

Adams, J. L. *Conceptual Blockbusting.* New York: W. W. Norton, 1979.

Adams, J. S. "Toward an Understanding of Inequity." *Journal of Abnormal and Social Psychology* 67 (1963), pp. 422–36.

Adams, J. S. "Inequity in Social Exchange." In *Advances in Experimental Social Psychology.* ed. L. Berkowitz. Vol. 2. New York: Academic Press, 1965, pp. 267–96.

Adler, S.; R. B. Skov; and N. J. Salvemini. "Job Characteristics and Job Satisfaction: When Cause Becomes Consequences." *Organizational Behavior and Human Decision Processes* 35 (1985), pp. 266–78.

Adler, S., and H. M. Weiss. "Criterion Aggregation in Personality Research: A Demonstration Looking at Self-Esteem and Goal Setting." *Human Performance* 1, no. 2 (1988), pp. 99–109.

Aguayo, R. *Dr. Deming: The Man Who Taught the Japanese about Quality.* New York: Carol Publishing Group, 1990.

Alberti, R. E., and M. L. Emmons. *Your Perfect Right.* San Luis Obispo, Calif.: Impact, 1974.

Albrecht, K. *Stress and the Manager.* Englewood Cliffs, N.J.: Prentice Hall, 1979.

Alderfer, C. P. "An Empirical Test of a New Theory of Human Needs." *Organizational Behavior and Human Performance* 4 (1969), pp. 142–75.

————. "Group and Intergroup Relations." In *Improving Life at Work,* ed. J. R. Hackman and J. L. Suttle. Santa Monica, Calif.: Goodyear, 1977.

Aldrich, H. E. *Organizations and Environments.* Englewood Cliffs, N.J.: Prentice Hall, 1979.

Allen, T. H. "Situational Management Roles: A Conceptual Model." *Dissertation Abstracts International* 42, no. 2A (1981), p. 465.

Amabile, T. M. *The Social Psychology of Creativity.* New York: Springer-Verlag, 1983.

————. "Motivation and Creativity: Effects of Motivation Orientation on Creative Writers." *Journal of Personal and Social Psychology,* 48 (1985), pp. 393–99.

_____. "The Motivation to be Creative." In *Frontiers in Creativity: Beyond the Basics*, ed. S. Isaksen. Buffalo, N.Y.: Bearly Limited, 1987.

Amabile, T. M., and S. S. Gryskiewicz. "Creativity in the R&D Laboratory." Greensboro, N.C.: Center for Creative Leadership, (Tech Report No. 30), 1987.

Amabile, T. M., and B. A. Hennessey. "The Motivation for Creativity in Children." In *Achievement and Motivation: A Social-Developmental Perspective*, ed. A. K. Boggiano and T. Pittman. New York: Cambridge University Press, 1988.

Anastasi, A. *Psychological Testing*. 5th ed. New York: Macmillian, 1982.

Anderson, C. R., and C. E. Schneier. "Locus of Control, Leader Behavior, and Leader Performance among Management Students." *Academy of Management Journal* 21 (1978), pp. 690–98.

Andrews, P. H. "Performance, Self-Esteem and Perceptions of Leadership Emergence: A Comparative Study of Men and Women." *Western Journal of Speech Communication* 48 (1984), pp. 1–13.

Andrews, R. L., and R. Soder. "Principal Leadership and Student Achievement." *Educational Leadership* 44 (1987), pp. 9–11.

Argyris, C. *Increasing Leadership Effectiveness*. New York: Wiley, 1976.

Arvey, R. D.; T. J. Bouchard Jr.; N. L. Segal; and L. M. Abraham. "Job Satisfaction: Environmental and Genetic Components." *Journal of Applied Psychology* 74 (1989), pp. 187–92.

Arvey, R. D.; G. A. Davis; and S. M. Nelson. "Use of Discipline in an Organization: A Field Study." *Journal of Applied Psychology* 69 (1984), pp. 448–60.

Arvey, R. D., and J.M. Ivancevich. "Punishment in Organizations: A Review, Propositions, and Research Suggestions." *Academy of Management Review* 5 (1980), pp. 123–32.

Arvey, R. D., and A. P. Jones. "The Use of Discipline in Organizational Settings; A Framework for Future Research." In *Research in Organizational Behavior*, ed. L. L. Cummings and B. M. Staw, vol. 7. Greenwich, Conn.: JAI, 1985, pp. 367–408.

Astin, H. S., and C. Leland. *Women of Influence, Women of Vision*. San Francisco: Jossey-Bass, 1991.

Atkinson, J. W. "Motivational Determinants of Risk Taking Behavior." *Psychological Review* 64 (1957), pp. 359–72.

Austin, J. S.; E. J. Conlon; and R. L. Daft. "Organizing for Effectiveness: A Guide to Using Structural Design for Mission Accomplishment." (LMDC-TR-84-3-0). Maxwell AFB, Ala.: Leadership and Management Development Center, Air University, 1986.

Avolio, B. J., and B. M. Bass. "Charisma and Beyond." In *Emerging Leadership Vistas*, ed. J. G. Hunt, B. R. Baliga, H. P. Dachler, and C. A. Schriesheim. Lexington, Mass.: D. C. Heath, 1987.

_____. "Transformational Leadership, Charisma, and Beyond." In *Emerging Leadership Vistas*, ed. J. G. Hunt, B. R. Baliga, and C. A. Schriesheim. Lexington. Mass.: D. C. Health, 1988.

Avolio, B. J., and T. C. Gibbons. "Developing Transformational Leaders: A Life Span Approach." In *Charismatic Leadership: The Elusive Factor in Organizational Effectiveness*, ed. J. A. Conger and R. N. Kanungo. San Francisco: Jossey-Bass, 1988.

Ayman, R., and M. M. Chemers. "The Effect of Leadership Match on Subordinate Satisfaction in Mexican Organizations: Some Moderating Influences of Self-Monitoring." *Applied Psychology: An International Review* 40, no. 3 (1991), pp. 299–314.

Back, K., and K. Back. *Assertiveness at Work*. London: McGraw-Hill, 1982.

Badin, I. J. "Some Moderator Influences on Relationships between Consideration, Initiating Structure, and Organizational Criteria." *Journal of Applied Psychology* 59 (1974), pp. 380–82.

Bales, R. F. "Task Roles and Social Roles in Problem-Solving Groups." In *Readings in Social Psychology*, ed. E. E. Maccoby, T. M. Newcomb, and E. L. Hartley. New York: Holt, 1958.

Baltzell, E. D. *Puritan Boston and Quaker Philadelphia*. New York: The Free Press, 1980.

Barnes, F. "Mistakes New Presidents Make." *Reader's Digest* (January 1989), p. 43.

Barrick, M. R. and M. K. Mount. "The Big Five Personality Dimensions and Job Performance: A Meta-analysis." *Personnel Psychology* 44 (1991), pp. 1–26.

Barron, F., and D. M. Harrington. "Creativity, Intelligence, and Personality." *Annual Review of Psychology* 32 (1981), 439–76.

Bass, B. M. *Leadership, Psychology, and Organizational Behavior*. New York: Harper, 1960.

_____. *Leadership and Performance Beyond Expectations*. New York: The Free Press, 1985.

_____. "Evolving Perspectives of Charismatic Leadership." In *Charismatic Leadership: The Elusive Factor in Organizational Effectiveness*, ed. J. A. Conger and R. N. Kanungo. San Francisco: Jossey-Bass, 1988.

_____. *Bass and Stogdill's Handbook of Leadership*. 3rd ed. New York: Free Press, 1990.

Bass, B. M., and F. J. Yammarino. *Long-term Forecasting of Transformational Leadership and Its Effects among Naval Officers: Some Preliminary Findings*. (Technical Report No. ONR-TR-2). Arlington, Va.: Office of Naval Research, 1988.

Benne, K. D., and P. Sheats. "Functional Roles of Group Members." *Journal of Social Issues* 4 (1948), pp. 41–49.

Benner, P. E. *Stress and Satisfaction on the Job*. New York: Praeger, 1984.

Bennis, W. G. *On Becoming a Leader.* Reading, Mass.: Addison-Wesley, 1989.

Bennis, W. G. "Leadership Theory and Administrative Behavior: The Problem of Authority." *Administrative Science Quarterly* 4 (1959).

Bennis, W. G., and B. Nanus. *Leaders: The Strategies for Taking Charge.* New York: Harper & Row, 1985.

Berkman, L., and S. L. Syme. "Social Networks, Host Resistance, and Mortality: A Nine-Year Follow-up Study of Alameda County Residents." *American Journal of Epidemiology* 109 (1979), pp. 186–204.

Berlew, D. E. "Leadership and Organizational Excitement." In *Organizational Psychology: A Book of Readings,* ed. D. A. Kolb, I. M. Rubin, and J. M. McIntyre. 2nd ed. Englewood Cliffs, N.J.: Prentice-Hall, 1974.

_____. "Leadership and Empowerment." Workshop presented at the Seventh Annual Society for Industrial and Organizational Psychologists Convention, Montreal, May 1992.

Berry, J. K. "Linking Management Development to Business Strategies." *Training and Development Journal,* August 1990, pp. 20–22.

Betz, E. L. "Two Tests of Maslow's Theory of Need Fulfilment." *Journal of Vocational Behavior,* 24 (1984), pp. 204–20.

Beyer, J. M., and H. M. Trice. "A Field Study in the Use and Perceived Effects of Discipline in Controlling Work Performance." *Academy of Management Journal* 27 (1984), pp. 743–64.

Bickman, L. "The Social Power of a Uniform." *Journal of Applied Social Psychology* (1974), pp. 47–61.

Blake, P. "Walt Disney World: No Mere Amusement Park." *The Architectural Forum* 136, no. 5 (1972), 24–40.

_____. "The Lessons of the Parks." In *The Art of Walt Disney: From Mickey Mouse to the Magic Kingdom,* ed. C. Finch. New York: Harry N. Abrams, 1973, pp. 423–49.

Blake, R. J., and E. H. Potter III. "Novice Leaders, Novice Behaviors, and Strong Culture: Promoting Leadership Change Beyond the Classroom." In *Impact of Leadership,* ed. K. E. Clark, M. B. Clark, and D. P. Campbell. Greensboro, N. C.: The Center for Creative Leadership, 1992.

Blake, R. R., and A. A. McCanse. *Leadership Dilemmas—Grid Solutions.* Houston, Tex.: Gulf, 1991.

Blake, R. R., and J. S. Mouton. *The Managerial Grid.* Houston, Tex.: Gulf, 1964.

_____. *The Managerial Grid III.* Houston, Tex.: Gulf, 1985.

Blake, R. R.; H. A. Shepard; and J. S. Mouton, *Managing Intergroup Conflict in Industry.* Houston, Tex.: Gulf, 1964.

Blank, T. O. "What High School Leaders Think of Leadership." *High School Journal* 63 (1986), pp. 207-13.

Blankenship, L. V., and R. E. Miles. "Organizational Structure and Managerial Decision Behavior." *Administrative Science Quarterly* 13 (1968), pp. 106–20.

Blau, P. M. "Critical Remarks on Weber's Theory of Authority." *American Political Science Review* 57, no. 2 (1963), pp. 305–15.

Blau, P. M. "The Hierachy of Authority in Organizations." *American Journal of Sociology* 73 (1968), pp. 453–67.

Blum, R. E.; J. A. Butler; and N. L. Olson. "Leadership for Excellence: Research-based Training for Principals." *Educational Leadership*, 45, no. 1 (1987), pp. 25–29.

Boal, K. M., and J. M. Bryson. "Charismatic Leadership: A Phenomenal and Structural Approach." In *Emerging Leadership Vistas*, ed. J. G. Hunt, B. R. Baliga, H. P. Dachler, and C. A. Schriesheim. Lexington, Mass.: Heath Company.

Borman, W. C.; M. A. Hanson; S. H. Oppler; and E. D. Pulakos. "The Role of Early Supervisory Experience in Supervisor Performance." *Journal of Applied Psychology* (in press).

Borman, W. C.; L. A. White; E. D. Pulakos; and S. A. Oppler. "Models Evaluating the Effects of Rated Ability, Knowledge, Proficiency, Temperament, Awards, and Problem Behavior on Supervisor Ratings." *Journal of Applied Psychology* 76 (1991), pp. 863–72.

Bottger, P. C. "Expertise and Air Time as Bases of Actual and Perceived Influence in Problem-Solving Groups." *Journal of Applied Psychology* 69 (1984), pp. 214–21.

Bowers, D. G., and S. E. Seashore. "Predicting Organizational Effectiveness with a Four Factor Theory of Leadership." *Administrative Science Quarterly* 11 (1966), pp. 238–63.

Boyatzis. R. E., and F. R. Skelly. "The Impact of Changing Values on Organizational Life." In *Organizational Behavior Readings*, ed. D. A. Kolb, I. M. Rubin, and J. Osland. 5th ed. Englewood Cliffs, N.J.: Prentice Hall, 1991, pp. 1–16.

Bradley, R. T. *Charisma and Social Power: A Study of Love and Power, Wholeness and Transformation.* New York: Paragon, 1987.

Brandt, R. "On Leadership and Student Achievement: A Conversation with Richard Andrews." *Educational Leadership* 45, no. 1 (1987), pp. 9–16.

Bray, D. W., and A. Howard. "The AT&T Longitudinal Study of Managers." In *Longitudinal Studies of Adult Psychological Development*, ed. K. W. Schaiel. New York: Guilford, 1983.

Bray, D. W.; R. J. Campbell; and D. L. Grant. *Formative Years in Business: A Long-term AT&T Study of Managerial Lives.* New York: Wiley-Interscience, 1974.

Brief, A. P.; R. S. Schuler; and M. Van Sell. *Managing Job Stress.* Boston: Little, Brown, 1981.

Brockner, J., and L. Adsit. "The Moderating Impact of Sex on the Equity-Satisfaction Relationship." *Journel of Applied Psychology* 71 (1986), pp. 585–90.

Brody, N. *Intelligence.* San Diego: Academic Press, 1992.

Brown, L. D. *Managing Conflict at Organizational Interfaces.* Reading, Mass.: Addison-Wesley, 1983.

Bugental, D. E. "A Study of Attempted and Successful Social Influence in Small Groups as a Function of Goal-Relevant Skills," *Dissertation Abstracts* 25 (1964), p. 660.

Burke, M. J., and R. R. Day. "A Cumulative Study of the Effectiveness of Managerial Training." *Journal of Applied Psychology* 71 (1986), pp. 242–45.

Burke, P. J. "The Development of Task and Socio-Emotional Role Differentiation." *Socieometry* 30 (1967), pp. 379–92.

Burns, J. M. *Leadership.* New York: Harper & Row, 1978.

Burns, T., and G. M. Stalker. *The Management of Innovation.* London: Tavistock, 1961.

Calder, B. J. and B. M. Staw. "Self-Perception of Intrinsic and Extrinsic Motivation." *Journal of Personality and Social Psychology* 31 (1975), pp. 599–605.

Campbell, D. P. *Handbook for the Strong Vocational Interest Blank.* Stanford, Calif.: Stanford University Press, 1971.

———. "The Psychological Test Profiles of Brigadier Generals: Warmongers or Decisive Warriors?" Invited address presented to Division 14 of the American Psychological Association, New York, 1987.

———. *Campbell Leadership Index Manual.* Minneapolis: National Computer Systems, 1991.

Campbell, D. P.; S. Hyne; and D. L. Nilsen. *Campbell Interests and Skills Survey Manual.* Minneapolis: National Computer Systems, 1992.

Campbell, J. P. "The Cutting Edge of Leadership: An Overview." In *Leadership: The Cutting Edge,* ed. J. G. Hunt and L. L. Larson. Carbondale, Ill.: Southern Illinois University Press, 1977.

———. "Training design for performance improvement." In *Productivity in Organizations: New Perspectives from Industrial and Organizational Psychology,* ed. J. P. Campbell, R. J. Campbell, and Associates. San Francisco: Jossey-Bass, 1988, pp. 177–216.

Campbell, J. P.; M. D. Dunnette; E. E. Lawler; and K. E. Weick. *Managerial Behavior, Performance, and Effectiveness.* New York: MacGraw-Hill, 1970.

Campbell, J. P.; R. A. McCloy; S. H. Oppler; and C. E. Sager. "A Theory of Performance." In *Frontiers in Industrial/Organizational Psychology and Personnel Selection,* ed. N. Schmitt and W. C. Borman. San Francisco: Jossey-Bass, 1993, pp. 35–70.

Campbell, J. P., and R. D. Pritchard. "Motivation Theory in Industrial and Organizational Psychology." In *Handbook of Industrial and Organizational Psychology*, ed. M. D. Dunnette. Chicago: Rand McNally, 1976, pp. 60–130.

Case, T.; L. Dosier; G. Murkison; and B. Keys. "How Managers Influence Superiors: A Study of Upward Influence Tactics." *Leadership and Organization Development Journal* 9 (4), (1988), pp. 4, 25–31.

Charters, W. W., and N. J. Pitner. "The Application of the Management Behavior Survey to the Measurement of Principle Leadership Behaviors." *Education and Psychological Measurement*, 46 (1986), pp. 811–25.

Chemers, M. M. "The Social, Organizational, and Cultural Contest of Effective Leadership." In *Leadership: Multidisciplinary Perspectives*, ed. B. Kellerman. Englewood Cliffs, N.J.: Prentice Hall, 1984.

Chinoy, E. *Society*. New York: Random House, 1961.

Chitayat, G., and I. Venezia. "Determinants of Management Styles in Business and Nonbusiness Organizations." *Journal of Applied Psychology* 69 (1984), pp. 437–47.

Cialdini, R. B. *Influence*. New York: William Morrow, 1984.

Clark, B. R. "The Organizational Saga in Higher Education." *Administrative Science Quarterly* 17 (1972), pp. 178–84.

Cleveland, H. *The Knowledge Executive: Leadership in an Information Society*. New York: Dutton, 1985.

Clover, W. H. "Transformational Leaders: Team Performance Leadership Ratings and Firsthand Impressions." In *Measures of Leadership*, ed. K.E. Clark and M. B. Clark. West Orange, N. J.: Leadership Library of America, 1990.

————. "At TRW, Executive Training Contributes to Quality." *The Human Resources Professional* (Winter 1991), pp. 16–20.

Clutterbuck, D. "How Much Does Success Depend upon a Helping Hand from Above?" *International Management* 37 (1982), pp. 17–19.

Cohen, A. R., and D. L. Bradford. *Influence without Authority*. New York: Wiley, 1990.

Conger, J. A. *The Charismatic Leader*. San Francisco: Jossey-Bass, 1989.

Conger, J. A., and R. N. Kanungo. *Charismatic Leadership: The Elusive Factor in Organizational Effectiveness*. San Francisco: Jossey-Bass, 1988.

Conway, F., and J. Siegelman. *Snapping*. New York: Delta, 1979.

Cornwell, J. M. "A Meta-Analysis of Selected Trait Research in the Leadership Literature." Paper presented at the Southeastern Psychological Association, Atlanta, Ga., 1983.

Cosell, H. *I Never Played the Game*. New York: William Morrow, 1985.

Costa, P. T., Jr., and R. R. McCrae. *The NEO Personality Inventory.* Odessa, Fla.: Psychological Assessment Resources, 1985.

Couch, A., and P. W. Yetton. "Manager Behavior, Leadership Style, and Subordinate Performance: An Empirical Extension of the Vroom-Yetton Conflict Rule." *Organizational Behavior and Human Decision Processes* 39 (1987), pp. 384–96.

Cousteau, V. "How to Swim with Sharks: A Primer." *Perspectives in Biology and Medicine* (summer 1973), pp. 525–28.

Coye, R. W. "Subordinate Responses to Ineffective Leadership." *Dissertation Abstracts International* 43, 6A (1982), p. 2070.

Cronbach, L. J. *Essentials of Psychological Testing.* 4th ed. San Francisco: Harper & Row, 1984.

Cronshaw, S. F., and R. J. Ellis. "A Process Investigation of Self-Monitoring and Leader Emergence." Paper presented at the Academy of Management Annual Meeting, San Francisco, 1990.

Csikszentmihalyi, M. *Flow: The Psychology of Optimal Experience.* New York: Harper & Row, 1990.

Cummings, R. C. "Job Stress and the Buffering Effect of Supervisory Support." *Group and Organization Studies* 15, no. 1, pp. 92–104.

Cummings, W, H. "Age Group Differences and Estimated Frequencies of the MBTI Types: Proposed Changes." *Proceedings of the Psychology in the Department of Defense Thirteenth Symposium,* U. S. Air Force Academy, Colo., April 1992.

Curphy. G. J. "Transformational, Charismatic, and Transactional Leadership: A Literature Review." Unpublished manuscript, University of Minnesota, Department of Psychology, Minneapolis, 1990.

———. "An empirical investigation of Bass' (1985) theory of transformational and transactional leadership." Ph.D. dissertation, University of Minnesota, 1991a.

———. "Some closing remarks about the use of self-and other-ratings of personality and behaviors." In *Multirater assessment systems: What we've learned,* chair M. D. Dunnette. Symposium conducted at the 99th American Psychological Association Convention, San Francisco, August 1991b.

———. "The Effects of Transformational and Transactional Leadership on Organizational Climate, Attrition, and Performance." In *Impact of Leadership,* ed. K. E. Clark, M. B. Clark, and D. P. Campbell. Greensboro, N.C.: Center for Creative Leadership, 1992a.

———. "Using Low Fidelity Simulations to Predict Future Leadership Success." In *Selections in Leadership: Some New Research Directions,* chair R. T. Hogan. Symposium conducted at the 13th Biennial Psychology in the DoD Conference, United States Air Force Academy, 1992b.

Curphy, G. J.; F. W. Gibson; B. W. Asiu; C. P. McCown; and C. Brown. "A Field Study of the Causal Relationships between Organizational Performance, Punishment, and Justice," Submitted for publication, 1992.

Curphy, G. J.; F. W. Gibson; G. Macomber; C. Calhoun; L. A. Wilbanks; and M. J. Burger. "A Field Study of Situational Variables Affecting Adherence to Formal Organizational Ethics Policies." Submitted for publication, 1992.

Curtis, B.; R. E. Smith; and F. L. Smoll. "Scrutinizing the Skipper: A Study of Behaviors in the Dugout." *Journal of Applied Psychology* 64 (1979), pp. 391–400.

Davis, B. L.; L. W. Hellervik; and J. L. Sheard. *Successful Manager's Handbook.* 3rd ed. Minneapolis: Personnel Decisions, 1989.

Davis, R. C. *The Fundamentals of Top Management.* New York: Harper, 1942.

DeBolt, J. W.; A. E. Liska; and B. R. Weng, "Replications of Associations between Internal Locus of Control and Leadership in Small Groups." *Psychological Reports* 38 (1976), p. 470.

Deci, E. L. "Effects of Contingent and Noncontingent Rewards and Controls on Intrinsic Motivation." *Organizational Behavior and Human Performance* 22 (1972), pp. 113–20.

_____. *Intrinsic Motivation.* New York: Plenum, 1975.

_____. *The Psychology of Self-Determination.* Lexington, Mass.: Lexington Books, 1980.

Deci, E. L., and R. M. Ryan. "The Support of Autonomy and the Control of Behavior." *Journal of Personality and Social Psychology* 53 (1987), pp. 1024–37.

Decker, P. J. "Social Learning Theory and Leadership." *Journal of Management* 5 (1986), pp. 46–58.

Deep, S., and L. Sussman. *Smart Moves.* Reading, Mass.: Addison-Wesley, 1990.

Delbecq, A. L.; A. H. Van de Ven; and D. H. Gustafson. *Group Techniques for Program Planning: A Guide to Nominal and Delphi Processes.* Glenview, Ill.: Scott, Foresman, 1975.

Deveraux, G. "Charismatic Leadership and Crisis." In *Psychoanalysis and the Social Sciences,* ed. W. Muensterberger and S. Axelrod. New York: International University Press, 1955.

Dewhirst, H. D.; V. Metts; and R. T. Ladd. "Exploring the Delegation Decision: Managerial Responses to Multiple Contingencies." Paper presented at the Academy of Management Convention, New Orleans, 1987.

Dobbins, G. H., and J. M. Russell. "The Biasing Effects of Subordinate Likeableness on Leaders' Responses to Poor Performance." *Personnel Psychology* 39 (1986), pp. 759–77.

Donley, R. E., and D. G. Winter. "Measuring the Motives of Public Officials at a Distance: An Exploratory Study of American Presidents." *Behavioral Science* 15 (1970), pp. 227–36.

Donno, D. "Introduction." In *The Prince and Selected Discourses: Machiavelli,* ed. and trans. D. Donno. New York: Bantam, 1966.

Dosier, L.; T. Case; and B.Keys. "How Managers Influence Subordinates: An Empirical Study of Downward Influence Tactics. *Leadership and Organization Development Journal* 9, no. 5 (1988), pp. 22–31.

Dow, T. E. "The Theory of Charisma." *Sociological Quarterly* 10 (1969), pp. 306–18.

Downton, J. V. *Rebel Leadership: Commitment and Charisma in the Revolutionary Process.* New York: Free Press, 1973.

Duchon, D.; S. G. Green; and T. D. Taber. "Vertical Dyad Linkage: A Longitudinal Assessment of Antecedents, Measures, and Consequences." *Journal of Applied Psychology* 71 (1986), pp. 56–60.

Dukerich, J. M.; M. L. Nichols; D. R. Elm; and D. A. Vollrath. "Moral Reasoning in Groups: Leaders Make a Difference," *Human Relations* 43 (1990), pp. 473–93.

Dumaine, B. "Creating a New Company Culture." *Fortune.* 121, no. 2 (1990), pp. 127–131.

Duncker, K. "On Problem Solving." *Psychological Monographs* 58, no. 5, Whole No. 270.

Durand, D. E., and W. R. Nord. "Perceived Leader Behavior as a Function of Personality Characteristics of Supervisors and Subordinates." *Academy of Management Journal* 19 (1976), pp. 427–38.

Eden, D., and A. B. Shani. "Pygmalion Goes to Boot Camp: Expectancy, Leadership, and Trainee Performance." *Journal of Applied Psychology* 67 (1982), pp. 194–99.

Edwards, B. *Drawing on the Right Side of the Brain.* Los Angeles, Calif.: J. P. Tarcher, 1979.

_____. *Drawing on the Artist Within.* New York: Simon & Schuster, 1986.

Ehrlichman, J. *Witness to Power.* New York: Simon & Schuster, 1982.

Einstein, A. *On Education. Ideas and Opinions.* New York: Bonaza Books, 1954.

Ellis, A., and R. Harper. *A New Guide to Rational Living.* Englewood Cliffs, N.J.: Prentice Hall, 1975.

Ellis, R. J.; R. S. Adamson; G. Deszca; and T. F. Cawsey. "Self-Monitoring and Leadership Emergence." *Small Group Behavior* 19 (1988), pp. 312–24.

Emery, F. E., and E. L. Trist. "The Causal Texture of Organizational Environments." *Human Relations* 18 (1965), pp. 21–32.

_____. *Towards a Social Ecology.* London: Plenum, 1973.

England, G. W., and R. Lee. "The Relationship between Managerial Values and Managerial Success in the Unites States, Japan, India, and Australia." *Journal of Applied Psychology* 59 (1974), 411–419.

Erez, M.; P. C. Earley; and C. L. Hulin. "The Impact of Participation on Goal Acceptance and Performance: A Two-Step Model." *Academy of Management Journal* (1985), pp. 359–72.

Etzioni, A. *A Comparative Analysis of Complex Organizations.* New York: Free Press, 1961.

Evans, M. G. "The Effects of Supervisory Behavior on the Path-Goal Relationship." *Organizational Behavior and Human Performance* 5 (1970), pp. 277–98.

Fadiman, C. *The Little, Brown Book of Anecdotes.* Boston: Little, Brown, 1985.

Farris, G. F. "Colleagues' Roles and Innovation in Scientific Teams." (Working paper No. 552–71). Cambridge, Mass.: Alfred P. Sloan School of Management, M.I.T., 1971.

Feldman, D. C. "The Development and Enforcement of Group Norms," *Academy of Management Review,* January 1984, pp. 47–53.

Ferris. G. R. "Role of Leadership in the Employee Withdrawal Process: A Constructive Replication." *Journal of Applied Psychology* 70 (1985), pp. 777–81.

Fiechtner, B., and J. J. Krayer, "Variations in Dogmatism and Leader-Supplied Information: Determinants of Perceived Behavior in Task-Oriented Groups." *Group and Organizational Studies* 11 (1986), 403–18.

Fiedler, F. E. *A Theory of Leadership Effectiveness.* New York: McGraw-Hill, 1967.

————. "The Contingency Model and the Dynamics of the Leadership Process. In *Advances in Experimental Social Psychology,* ed. L. Berkowitz. New York: Academic Press, 1978.

————. "The Effect and Meaning of Leadership Experience: A Review of Research and a Preliminary Model." In *Impact of Leadership,* ed. K. E. Clark, M. B. Clark, and D. P. Campbell. Greensboro, N.C.: Center for Creative Leadership, 1992.

Fiedler, F. E., and M. M. Chemers. *Improving Leadership Effectiveness: The Leader Match Concept.* 2nd Ed. New York: Wiley, 1982.

Fiedler, F. E., and J. E. Garcia. *New Approaches to Leadership: Cognitive Resources and Organizational Performance.* New York: Wiley, 1987.

Field, R. H. G. "A Test of the Vroom-Yetton Normative Model of Leadership." *Journal of Applied Psychology* 67 (1982), 523–32.

Filley, A. C., and L. A. Pace. "Making Judgments Descriptive." In *The 1976 Annual Handbook for Group Facilitators,* ed. J. E. Jones and J. W. Pfeiffer. La Jolla, Calif.: University Associates Press, 1976.

Fishbein, M., and I. Azjen. *Belief, Attitude, Intention, and Behavior: An Introduction to Theory and Research.* Reading, Mass.: Addison-Wesley, 1975.

Fisher, C. D. "The Effects of Personal Control, Competence, and Extrinsic Reward Systems on Intrinsic Motivation." *Organizational Behavior and Human Performance* 21 (1978), pp. 273–288.

Fisher, C. D., and R. Gitleson. "A Meta-Analysis of the Correlates of Role Conflict and Ambiguity." *Journal of Applied Psychology* 68 (1983), pp. 320–33.

Fisher, R., and W. Ury. *Getting to Yes.* Houghton Mifflin, 1981.

Flanagan, J. C. "Defining the Requirements of the Executive's Job." *Personnel* 28, no. 1 (1951), pp. 28–35.

Fleishman, E. A. *Examiner's Manual for the Supervisory Behavior Description Questionnaire.* Washington, D.C.: Management Research Institute, 1972.

_____. "Twenty Years of Consideration and Structure." In *Current Developments in the Study of Leadership,* ed. E. A. Fleishman and J. G. Hunt. Carbondale, Ill.: Southern Illinois University Press, 1973.

_____. *Examiner's Manual for the Leadership Opinion Questionnaire.* rev. ed. Chicago: Science Research Associates, 1989.

Fodor, E. "Motive Pattern as an Influence on Leadership in Small Groups." Paper presented at the meeting of the American Psychological Association, New York, August 1987.

Folkman, S., and R. S. Lazarus. "An Analysis of Coping in a Middle-Aged Community Sample." *Journal of Health and Social Behavior* 21 (1980), pp. 219–39.

Ford, J. D. "Departmental Context and Formal Structure as Constraints on Leader Behavior." *Academy of Management Journal* 24 (1981), pp. 274–88.

Foushee, H. C. "Dyads and Triads at 35,000 Feet: Factors Affecting Group Process and Aircrew Performance." *American Psychologist* 39 (1984), pp. 885–93.

French, J., and B. H. Raven. "The Bases of Social Power." In *Studies of Social Power,* ed. D. Cartwright. Ann Arbor, Mich.: Institute for Social Research, 1959.

Friedland, W. H. "For a Sociological Concept of Charisma." *Social Forces* no. 1 (1964), pp. 18–26.

Freud, S. *Group Psychology and the Analysis of the Ego,* trans. J. Strachey. 2nd ed. The standard edition of the complete psychological works of Sigmund Freud, Vol. 2. London: Hogarth Institute for Psycho-analysis.

Friedman, M., and D. Ulmer. *Treating Type A Behavior—and Your Heart.* New York: Knopf, 1984.

Fry, L. W.; S. Kerr; and C. Lee. "Effects of Different Leader Behaviors under Different Levels of Task Interdependence." *Human Relations* 39 (1986), pp. 1067–82.

Gabarro, J. J., and J. P. Kotter. "Managing Your Boss." *Harvard Business Review* 58, no. 1 (1980), pp. 92–100.

Gabor, A. *The Man Who Discovered Quality.* New York: Penguin, 1990.

Gabrenya, W. K., and R. M. Arkin. "Self-Monitoring Scale: Factor Structure and Correlates." *Personality and Social Psychology Bulletin* 6 (1980), pp. 12–22.

Gal, R. *A Portrait of the Israeli Soldier.* New York: Greenwood Press, 1986.

Galbraith, J. *Designing Complex Organizations.* Menlo Park, Calif.: Addison-Wesley, 1973.

Gardner, J. W. "The Antileadership Vaccine." Essay in the Carnegie Corporation of New York annual report, 1965.

———. The Tasks of Leadership. (Leadership paper No. 2). Washington, D.C.: Independent Sector, 1986.

———. *On Leadership.* New York: Free Press, 1990.

Garforth, F. I. de la P. "War Office Selection Boards." *Occupational Psychology* 19 (1945), pp. 97–108.

Gaugler, B. B.; D. B. Rosenthal; G. C. Thornton III; and C. Bentson. "Meta-Analysis of Assessment Center Validity." *Journal of Applied Psychology* 72 (1987), pp. 493–511.

General Accounting Office. "Management Practices—U.S. Companies Improve Performance through Quality Efforts," (1990).

Gerth, H. H., and C. W. Mills. *Max Weber: Essays in Sociology.* New York: Oxford University Press, 1946.

Ghiselli, E. E. "Intelligence and Managerial Success." *Psychological Reports* 12 (1963), pp. 898.

———. "Interaction of Traits and Motivational Factors in the Determination of the Success of Managers." *Journal of Applied Psychology* 52 (1968), pp. 480–83.

Gibb, C. A. "Leadership." In *The Handbook of Social Psychology,* ed. G. Lindzey and E. Aronson. 2nd ed., vol. 4. Reading, Mass.: Addison-Wesley, 1968, pp. 205–82.

Gibb, J. R. "Defensive Communication." *Journal of Communication,* XIII no. 3 (1961), pp. 141–48.

Gibbard, G. S.; J. J. Hartman; and R. D. Mann. *Analysis of Groups: Contribution to the Theory, Research, and Practice.* San Francisco: Jossey-Bass, 1974.

Gibble, J. L., and J. D. Lawrence. "Peer Coaching for Principals." *Educational Leadership* 45 (1987), pp. 72–73.

Gibson, F. W. "A Taxonomy of Leader Abilities and Their Influence on Group Performance as a Function of Interpersonal Stress." In *Impact of Leadership,* ed. K. E. Clark, M. B. Clark, and D. P. Campbell. Greensboro, N.C.: Center for Creative Leadership, 1992.

Gilligan, C. *In a Different Voice.* Cambridge, Mass.: Harvard University Press, 1982.

Ginnett, R. C. "The Formation Process of Airline Flight Crews." *Proceedings of the Fourth International Symposium on Aviation Psychology*. Columbus, Ohio, 1987.

———. "Cockpit Crew Effectiveness from the Inside Out: A Micro-Analysis Leading to Macro Considerations." *Proceedings of the Eleventh Psychology in the Department of Defense Symposium*. Colorado Springs, Colo., 1988.

———. "Behavioral Characteristics of Effective Crew Leaders." *Human Error Avoidance Techniques: Proceedings of the Second Conference*. Herndon, Va.: Society of Automotive Engineers, 1989.

———. "Airline Cockpit Crew." In *Groups that Work (and Those that Don't)*, ed. J. Richard Hackman. San Francisco: Jossey-Bass, 1990.

———. "Crews as groups: Their Formation and their leadership," In *Cockpit Resource Management*, ed. E. Wiener; B. Kanki; and R. Helmreich, Orlando, Fla.: Academic Press (in press).

———. "Effectiveness Begins Early: The Leadership Role in the Formation of Intra-Organizational Task Groups." (unpublished manuscript, 1992).

Glasser, W. *The Quality School*. New York: Harper & Row, 1990.

Goldstein, I. L. *Training in Organizations: Needs Assessments, Development, and Evaluation*. 2nd ed. Monterey, Calif.: Brooks/ Cole, 1986.

Goodstadt, B. E., and L. A. Hjelle. "Power to the Powerless: Locus of Control and the Use of Power." *Journal of Personality and Social Psychology* 27 (1973), pp. 190–96.

Goodstadt, B. E., and D. Kipnis. "Situational Influences on the Use of Power." *Journal of Applied Psychology* 54 (1970), pp. 201–07.

Gordon, L. V. *Measurement of Interpersonal Values*. Chicago: Science Research Associates, 1975.

Gordon, W. J. J. *Synectics*. New York: Harper & Row, 1961.

Gough, H. G. "A Leadership Index on the California Psychological Inventory." *Journal of Counseling Psychology* 16, (1969), pp. 283–89.

———. "A Managerial Potential Scale for the California Psychology Inventory." *Journal of Applied Psychology* 69 (1984), pp. 233–40.

———. *Administrator's Guide for the California Psychological Inventory*. Palo Alto, Calif. Consulting Psychologists Press, 1987.

———. "Testing for Leadership with the California Psychological Inventory." In *Measures of Leadership*, ed. K. E. Clark and M. B. Clark. West Orange, N.J.: Leadership Library of America, 1989.

Gough, H. G., and A. B. Heilbrun, Jr. *The Adjective Check List Manual*. Palo Alto, Calif.: Consulting Pyschologists Press, 1983.

Graeff, C. L. "The Situational Judgement Theory: A Critical Review." *Academy of Management Journal* 8 (1983), pp. 285–96.

Graen, G. B., and J. F. Cashman. "A Role-Making Model of Leadership in Formal Organizations: A Developmental Approach." In *Leadership Frontiers*, ed. J. G. Hunt and L. L. Larson. Kent, Ohio: Kent State University Press, 1975.

Graen, G. B.; R. C. Linden; and W. Hoel. "Role of Leadership in the Employee Withdrawal Process." *Journal of Applied Psychology* 67 (1982), pp. 868–72.

Green, S. G.; G. T. Fairhurst; and B. K. Snavely. "Chains of Poor Performance and Supervisory Control." *Organizational Behavior and Human Decision Processes* 38 (1986), pp. 7–27.

Green, S. G., and T. R. Mitchell. "Attributional Processes of Leaders in Leader-Member Interactions." *Organizational Behavior and Human Performances* 23 (1979), pp. 429–58.

Greller, M. M. "Evaluation of Feedback Sources as a Function of Role and Organizational Development." *Journal of Applied Psychology* 65 (1980), pp. 24–27.

Griffin, R. W.; A. Welsh; and G. Moorehead. "Perceived Task Characteristics and Employee Performance: A Literature Review." *Academy of Management Review* 6 (1981), pp. 655–64.

Guilford, J. P. *The Nature of Human Intelligence.* New York: McGraw-Hill, 1967.

Guion, R. M. "Personnel Assessment, Selection, and Placement." In *Handbook of Industrial and Organizational Psychology*, ed. M. D. Dunnette and L. M. Hough. Vol. 2, Palo Alto, Calif.: Consulting Psychologists Press, Inc., 1991, pp. 327–98.

Guion, R. M., and R. F. Gotter. "Validity of Personality Measures in Personnel Selection." *Personnel Psychology* 18 (1965), pp. 135–64.

Guth, C. K., and S. S. Shaw. *How to Put on Dynamic Meetings.* Reston, Va.: Reston, 1980.

Hackman, J. R. "Group Influences on Individuals." In *Handbook of Industrial and Organizational Psychology*, ed. M. D. Dunnette. Chicago: Rand NcNally, 1976.

————. "Group Level Issues in the Design and Training of Cockpit Crews." In *Proceedings of the NASA/MAC Workshop on Cockpit Resource Management*, ed. H. H. Orlady and H. C. Foushee. Moffett Field, Calif.: NASA Ames Research Center, 1986.

Hackman, J. R. *Groups that Work (and Those that Don't).* San Francisco: Jossey-Bass, 1990.

Hackman, J. R., and G. R. Oldham. "Motivation through the Design of Work: Test of a Theory." *Organizational Behavior and Human Performance* 16 (1976), pp. 250–79.

————. *Work Redesign.* Reading, Mass.: Addison-Wesley, 1980.

Hall, J., S. M. Donnell. "Managerial Achievement: The Personal Side of Behavioral Theory." *Human Relations* 32 (1979), pp. 77–101.

Hallam, G. L., and D. P. Campbell. "Selecting Team Members? Start with a Theory of Team Effectiveness." Paper presented at the seventh annual meeting of the Society of Industrial/Organizational Psychologists, Montreal, Canada, May 1992.

Halpin, A. W., and B. J. Winer. "A Factorial Study of the Leader Behavior Descriptions." In *Leader Behavior: It's Description and Measurement*, ed. R. M. Stogdill and A. E. Coons. Columbus, Ohio: Ohio State University, Bureau of Business Research, 1957.

Hamburger, K. E. "Leadershp in Combat." Unpublished report, Deaprtment of History, U.S. Military Academy, 1984.

Hammer, T. H., and J. Turk. "Organizational Determinants of Leader Behavior and Authority." *Journal of Applied Psychology* 71 (1987), pp. 674–82.

Haney, C.; C. Banks; and P. G. Zimbardo. "Interpersonal Dynamics in a Simulated Prison." *International Journal of Criminology and Penology*, 1 (1973), pp. 69–97.

Hansen, J. C., and D. P. Campbell. *Manual for the Strong Interest Inventory*, 4th ed. Stanford, Calif.: Stanford University Press, 1985.

Harris, T. A. *I'm OK—You're OK: A Practical Guide to Transactional Analysis*. New York: Harper & Row, 1967.

Harrison, E. L. "Training Supervisors to Discipline Effectively." *Training and Development Journal* 36, no. 11 (1982), pp. 111–13.

Hart, M. H. *The 100: A Ranking of the Most Influential Persons in History*. New York: Hart, 1978.

Harvey, J. B. "The Abilene Paradox: The Management of Agreement." *Organizational Dynamics* 3 (1974), pp. 63–80.

Health, Education, and Welfare Task Force. *Work in America*. Cambridge, Mass.: MIT Press, 1973.

Hegarty, W. H., and H. P. Sims. "Some Determinants of Unethical Decision Behavior: An Experiment." *Journal of Applied Psychology* 63 (1978), pp. 451–57.

————. "Organizational Philosophy, Policies, and Objectives Related to Unethical Decision Behavior: A Laboratory Experiment." *Journal of Applied Psychology* 64 (1979), pp. 331–38.

Heller, T., and J. Van Til. "Leadership and Followership: Some Summary Propositions." *Journal of Applied Behavioral Science* 18, 405–14.

Helson, R. "Women Mathematicians and Creative Personality." *Journal of Consulting and Clinical Psychology* 36 (1971), pp. 210–20.

Hemphill, J. K. "The Leader and His Group." *Journal of Educational Research* 28 (1949), pp. 225–29, 245–46.

Hemphill, J. K. and A. E. Coons. "Development of the Leader Behavior Description Questionnaire." In *Leader Behavior: Its Description and Measurement*, ed. R. M. Stogdill and A. E. Coons. Columbus, Ohio: Ohio State University, Bureau of Business Research, 1957.

Hersey, P. and K. H. Blanchard. "Life Cycle Theory of Leadership." *Training and Development Journal* 23 (1969), pp. 26–34.

_____. *Management of Organizational Behavior: Utilizing Human Resources.* 3rd ed. Englewood Cliffs, N.J.: Prentice Hall, 1977.

_____. *Management of Organizational Behavior: Utilizing Human Resources.* 4th ed. Englewood Cliffs, N.J.: Prentice Hall, 1982.

Herzberg, F. "The Motivation-Hygiene Concept and Problems of Manpower." *Personnel Administrator* 27 (1964), pp. 3–7.

Herzberg, F. *Work and the Nature of Man.* Cleveland, Ohio: World Publishing, 1966.

Hill, C. W. "Leadership and Symbolic Authority in Psychoanalysis." In *Multidisciplnary Perspectives,* ed. B. Kellerman. Englewood Cliffs, N.J.: Prentice Hall, 1984.

Hill, N. "Self Esteem: The Key to Effective Leadership." *Administrative Management* 38, no. 8 (1976), p. 24.

Hill, R. "The Business Leader with the Shakespearean Touch." *International Management* 40, no. 9, (1985), pp. 71–76.

Hinkin, T. R., and C. A. Schriesheim. "Development and Application of New Scales to Measure the French and Raven (1959) Bases of Social Power." *Journal of Applied Psychology* 74 (1989), pp. 561–67.

_____. "Relationships between Subordinate Perceptions of Supervisory Influence Tactics and Attributed Bases of Supervisory Power." *Human Relations* 43 (1990), pp. 221–37.

Hogan, J. "The Mask of Integrity." Paper presented at the 13th Biennial Psychology in the Department of Defense Symposium, Unites States Air Force Academy, Colo., 1992a.

_____. "The View from Below." In *The Future of Leadership Selection,* chair, R. T. Hogan. Symposium conducted at the 13th Biennial Psychology in the DoD Conference, United States Air Force Academy, 1992b.

Hogan, R. T. *Hogan Personality Inventory Manual.* Minneapolis: National Computer Systems, 1986.

_____. "Personality and Personality Measurement." In *Handbook of Industrial and Organizational Psychology,* ed. M. D. Dunnette and L. M. Hough. Vol. 2, Palo Alto, Calif.: Consulting Psychologists Press, Inc. 1991, pp. 873–919.

Hogan, R. T., and A. M. Morrison. "The Psychology of Managerial Incompetence." Paper presented at a joint American Psychological Association–National Institute of Occupational Safety and Health conference, Washington, D.C., October 1991.

Hogan, R. T., and J. Morrison. "Managing Creativity," In *Create to Be Free: Essays in Honor of Frank Barron*, ed. A. Montouri. Amsterdam: J. C. Gieben, in press.

Hogan, R. T., J. Morrison, and G. J. Curphy. *The Necessary and Sufficient Traits for Leadership Effectiveness*. Manuscript submitted for publication.

Hogan, R. T.; R. Raskin; and D. Fazzini. "The Dark Side of Charisma." In *Measures of Leadership*, ed. K. E. Clark and M. B. Clark. West Orange, N.J.: Leadership Library of America, 1989.

Hollander, E. P. *Leadership Dynamics: A Practical Guide to Effective Relationships*. New York: Free Press, 1978.

————. "Leadership and Power." In Handbook of Social Psychology. ed. G. Lindzey and E. Aronson. 3rd ed., vol. 2. New York: Random House, 1985.

Hollander, E. P., and J. W. Julian. "Contemporary Trends in the Analysis of Leadership Processes." *Psychological Bulletin* 71 (1969), pp. 387–91.

Hollander, E. P., and L. R. Offermann. "Power and Leadership in Organizations." *American Psychologist* 45 (1990), pp. 179–89.

Holloman, C. R. "Leadership and Headship: There Is a Difference." *Personal Administration* 31, no. 4 (1968), pp. 38–44.

Hoppock, R. *Job Satisfaction*. New York: Harper, 1935.

House, R. J. "A 1976 Theory of Charismatic Leadership." In *Leadership: The Cutting Edge*, ed. J. G. Hunt and L. L. Larson. Carbondale, Ill.: Southern Illinois University Press, 1977.

————. "Power in Organizations: A Social Psychological Perspective." Unpublished manuscript, University of Toronto, Toronto, Canada, 1984.

House, R. J., and G. Dressler. "The Path-Goal Theory of Leadership: Some Post-hoc and A Priori Tests." In *Contingency Approaches to Leadership*, ed. J. G. Hunt and L. L. Larson. Carbondale, Ill.: Southern Illinois University Press, 1974.

House, R. J.; R. S. Schuler; and E. Levanoni. "Role Conflict and Ambiguity Scales: Reality or Artifact?" *Journal of Applied Psychology* 68 (1983), pp. 334–37.

House, R. J.; W. D. Spangler; and J. Woycke. "Personality and Charisma in the U.S. Presidency: A Psychological Theory of Leadership Effectiveness." *Administrative Science Quarterly* 36 (1991), pp. 364–96.

House, R. J.; J. Woycke; and E. M. Fodor. "Charismatic and Noncharismatic Leaders: Differences in Behavior and Effectiveness." In *Charismatic Leadership: The Elusive Factor in Organizational Effectiveness*, ed. J. A. Conger and R. N. Kanungo. San Francisco: Jossey-Bass, 1988, pp. 98–121.

House, R. J. and T. R. Mitchell. "Path-Goal Theory of Leadership." *Contemporary Business* 3 (Fall 1974), pp. 81–98.

Howard, A. "College Experiences and Managerial Performance." *Journal of Applied Psychology* 71 (1986), pp. 530–52.

Howard, A. and D. W. Bray. "Predictors of Managerial Success Over Long Periods of Time." In *Measures of Leadership*, ed. M. B. Clark and K. E. Clark. West Orange, N.J.: Leadership Library of America, 1989.

Howell, J. M. "Two Faces of Charisma: Socialized and Personalized Leadership in Organizations." In *Charismatic Leadership: The Elusive Factor in Organizational Effectiveness*, ed. J. A. Conger and R. N. Kanungo. San Francisco: Jossey-Bass, 1988.

Howell, J. M., and P. Frost. "A Laboratory Study of Charismatic Leadership." *Organizational Behavior and Human Decision Processes* 43 (1988), pp. 243–69.

Howell, J. P., and P. W. Dorfman, "Substitutes for Leadership: Test of a Construct." *Academy of Management Journal* 24 (1981), pp. 714–28.

———. "Leadership and Substitutes for Leadership among Professional and Nonprofessional Workers." *Journal of Applied Behavioral Science* 22, (1986), pp. 29–46.

Huberman, J. "Discipline without Punishment." *Harvard Business Review*, July-August 1964, p. 62.

Hughes, R. L., and R. LaScala. *Helper Effectiveness Learning Program*. Chicago: Instructional Dynamics, Inc., 1977.

Humphreys, L. G. "General Intelligence." In *Perspectives on Bias in Mental Testing*, ed. C. R. Reynolds and R. T. Brown. New York: Plenum, 1984, pp. 221-47.

———. "Intelligence: Three Kinds of Instability and Their Consequences for Policy." In *Intelligence: Measurement, Theory, and Public Policy*, ed. R. L. Linn. Chicago: University of Illinois Press, 1989, pp. 193–216.

Hunt, D. M., and C. Michael. "Mentorship: A Career Training and Development Tool. *Academy of Management Review* 8, no. 3 (1983), pp. 475–85.

Hunt, J. G., and R. N. Osborn. "Toward a Macro-oriented Model of Leadership: An Odyssey." In *Leadership: Beyond Establishment Views*, ed. J. G. Hunt, U. Sekaran, and C. A. Schriesheim. Carbondale, Ill.: Southern Illinois University Press, 1982, pp. 196–221.

Hunter, J. E., and R. F. Hunter. "Validity and Utility of Alternative Predictors of Job Performance." *Psychological Bulletin* 96 (1984), pp. 72–98.

Hunter, J. E.; F. L. Schmidt; and M. K. Judiesch. "Individual Differences in Output Variability as a Function of Job Complexity." *Journal of Applied Psychology* 74 (1990), pp. 28–42.

Iacocca, L., with W. Novack. *Iacocca; An Autobiography*. New York: Bantam, 1984.

Iaffaldano, M. T., and P. M. Muchinsky. "Job Satisfaction and Job Performance: A Meta-Analysis." *Psychological Bulletin* 97 (1985), pp. 251–273.

Imai, M. *Kaizen: The Key to Japan's Competitive Success.* New York: Random House, 1986.

Indik, B. P. "Organizational Size and Member Participation: Some Empirical Tests of Alternative Explanations." *Human Relations* 18 (1965), pp. 339–50.

Instone, D.; B. R. Major; and B. B. Bunker. "Gender, Self-Confidence, and Social Influence Strategies: An Organizational Simulation." *Journal of Personality and Social Psychology* 44 (1983), pp. 322–33.

Ivancevich, J. M.; D. M. Schweiger; and J. W. Ragan. "Employee Stress, Health, and Attitudes: A Comparison of American, Indian, and Japanese Managers." Paper presented at the Academy of Management convention, Chicago, 1986.

Jago, A. G. "Leadership: Perspectives in Theory and Research." *Management Science* 28 (1982), pp. 315–36.

Jago, A. G., and J. W. Ragan. "The Trouble with LEADER MATCH Is that It Doesn't Match Fiedler's Contingency Model." *Journal of Applied Psychology* 71 (1986a), pp. 555–59.

———. "Some Assumptions Are More Troubling than Others: Rejoinder to Chemers and Fiedler." *Journal of Applied Psychology* 71 (1986b), pp. 564–65.

Jamal, M. "Job Stress and Job Performance Controversy: An Empirical Assessment." *Organizational Behavior and Human Performance* 33 (1984), pp. 1–21.

Janda, K. F. "Towards the Explication of the Concept of Leadership in Terms of the Concept of Power." *Human Relations,* 13 (1960), pp. 345–63.

Janis, I. L. *Groupthink.* 2nd ed. Boston: Houghton Mifflin, 1982.

Jaques, E. "Assessing Creative Leaders." In *Proceedings of the Creativity and Innovation Symposium,* National Defense University, ed. V. E. Hendrix, D. B. Chapla, and W. Mizzle. Washington, D.C., 1985, pp. 145–56.

Jayaratne, S.; D. Himle; and W. A. Chess. "Dealing with Work Stress and Strain: Is the Perception of Support More Important than Its use?" *Journal of Applied Behavioral Science* 24, no. 2 (1988), pp. 191–202.

Johnson, A. L.; F. Luthans; and H. W. Hennessey. "The Role of Locus of Control in Leader Influence Behavior." *Personal Psychology* 37 (1984), pp. 61–75.

Johnson, J. C. and M. D. Dunnette. "Validity and Test-Retest Stability of the Nash Managerial Effectiveness Scale on the Revised Form of the Strong Vocational Interest Blank." *Personnel Psychology* (1968), pp. 283–93.

Johnston, J. M. "Punishment of Human Behavior." *American Psychologist* 27 (1972), pp. 1033–54.

Jones, E. E. "Interpreting Interpersonal Behavior: The Effects of Expectancies." *Science* 234 (1986), pp. 41–46.

Jones, J. E. "Criteria of Effective Goal-Setting: The Spiro Model." In *The 1972 Annual Handbook for Group Facilitators*, ed. J. E. Jones and J. W. Pfeiffer. La Jolla, Calif.: University of Associates Press, 1972, pp. 133–34.

Jung, C. G. *Psychological Types*, trans. R. F. C. Hall. Princeton, N.J.: Princeton University Press, 1971.

Juran, J. M. "The QC Circle Phenomenon." *Industrial Quality Control*, January 1967, pp. 329–36.

_____. *Juran on Leadership for Quality*. New York: Free Press, 1989.

Justice, A. "Review of the Effects of Stress on Cancer in Laboratory Animals: Importance of Time of Stress Application and Type of Tumor." *Psychological Bulletin* 98 (1985), pp. 108–38.

Kanfer, R. "Motivation Theory in Industrial and Organizational Psychology." In *Handbook of Industrial and Organizational Psychology*, ed. M. D. Dunnette and L. M. Hough. Vol. 1. Palo Alto, Calif.: Consulting Psychologists Press, 1990, pp. 75–170.

Kanter, R. M. *Commitment and Community*. Cambridge, Mass.: Harvard University Press, 1972.

_____. "Dilemmas of Managing Participation." *Organizational Dynamics* 11, no. 1 (1982), pp. 5–27.

_____. *The Change Masters*. New York: Simon & Schuster, 1983.

Kaplan, R. E. "The Warp and Woof of the General Manager's Job." In *Facilitating Work Effectiveness*, ed. B. Schneider and D. Schoorman. Lexington, Mass.: Lexington Books, 1986.

Karp, D. A., and W. C. Yoels. *Symbols, Selves, and Society*. New York: Lippincott, 1979.

Katz, D.; N. Maccoby; G. Gurin; and L. G. Floor. *Productivity, Supervision, and Morale Among Railroad Workers*. Ann Arbor, Mich.: University of Michigan, Survey Research Center, Institute of Social Research, 1951.

Katzell, R. A., and R. A. Guzzo. "Psychological Approaches to Productivity Improvement." *American Psychologist* 38 (1983), pp. 468–72.

Kazdin, A. E. *Behavior Modification in Applied Settings*. Homewood, Ill.: Dorsey, 1975.

Keller, G. "Increasing Quality on Campus." *Change* 24, no. 3 (1992), pp. 48–51.

Keller, R. T. *Toward a Contingency Theory of Leader Behavior and Creative versus Incremental Innovative Outcomes in Research and Development Project Groups: Report on the First Wave of Data*. Bethlehem, Penn.: Lehigh University, Center for Innovative Management, 1989.

Keller, R. T., and A. D. Szilagyi. "Employee Reactions for Leader Reward Behavior." *Academy of Management Journal* 19 (1976), pp. 619–27.

————. "A Longitudinal Study of Leader Reward Behavior, Subordinate Expectancies, and Satisfaction." *Personnel Psychology* 11 (1978), pp. 119–29.

Kelley, R. E. "In Praise of Followers." *Harvard Business Review* 66, no. 6 (1988), pp. 142–48.

Kelly, G. *The Psychology of Personal Constructs.* New York: W. W. Norton, 1955.

Kennedy, J. K. "Middle LPC Leaders and the Contingency Model of Leader Effectiveness." *Organizational Behavior and Human Performance* 30 (1982), pp. 1–14.

Kerr, S., and J. M. Jermier. "Substitutes for Leadership: Their Meaning and Measurement." *Organizational Behavior and Human Performance* 22 (1978), pp. 375–403.

Kets de Vries, M. F. R. "Crises Leadership and the Paranoid Potential: An Organizational Perspective." *Bulletin of the Menninger Clinic* 41 (1977), pp. 349–65.

Kets de Vries, M. F. R., and D. Miller. "Managers Can Drive Their Subordinates Mad." In *The Irrational Executive: Psychoanalytic Explorations in Management,* ed. M. F. R. Kets de Vries. New York: International Universities Press, 1984.

Keys, B.; T. Case; T. Miller; K. E. Curran; and C. Jones. "Lateral Influence Tactics in Organizations." *International Journal of Management* 4 (1987), pp. 425–37.

Kilmann, R. H. and M. J. Saxton. *Organizational Cultures: Their Assessment and Change.* San Francisco: Jossey-Bass, 1983.

Kipnis, D. "Technology, Power, and Control." *Research in the Sociology of Organizations* 3 (1984a), pp. 125–56.

————. "The View from the Top." *Psychology Today* 18, no. 12 (1984b), pp. 30–36.

Kipnis, D., and S. M. Schmidt. *Profiles of Organizational Strategies.* (Form M). San Diego, Calif.: University Associates, 1982.

————. "The Language of Persuasion." *Psychology Today* 19, no. 4 (1985), pp. 40–46.

Kipnis, D.; S. M. Schmidt; and I. Wilkinson. "Intraorganizational Influence Tactics: Explorations in Getting One's Way." *Journal of Applied Psychology* 65 (1980), pp. 440–52.

Kirkpatrick, D. L. "Evaluation of Training." In *Training and Development Handbook,* ed. R. L. Craig and L. R. Bittel. New York: McGraw-Hill, 1967.

Klein, S. B. *Learning.* 2nd ed. New York: McGraw-Hill, 1991.

Klimoski, R. J., and N. J. Hayes. "Leader Behavior and Subordinate Motivation." *Personnel Psychology* 33 (1980), pp. 543–55.

Koestler, A. *The Act of Creation.* New York: Macmillan, 1964.

Kohn, A. "It's Hard to Get Left Out of a Pair." *Psychology Today,* October 1987, pp. 53–57.

Kojimoto, C. "The Kids-Eye View of Effective Principals." *Educational Leadership,* September 1987, pp 69–74.

Kolb. D. *Experiential Learning: Experience as the Source of Learning and Development.* Englewood Cliffs, N.J.: Prentice-Hall, 1983.

Komacki, J. L. "Why We Don't Reinforce: The Issues." *Journal of Organizational Behavior Management* 4, no. 3–4 (1982), pp. 97–100.

———. "Toward Effective Supervision: An Operant Analysis and Comparison of Managers at Work." *Journal of Applied Psychology* 71 (1986), pp. 270–79.

Komacki, J. L.; S. Zlotnick; and M. Jensen. "Development of an Operant-based Taxonomy and Observational Index on Supervisory Behavior." *Journal of Applied Psychology* 71 (1986), pp. 260–69.

Kotter, J. P. "Power and Influence: Beyond Formal Authority." *Macmillan Executive Summary Program,* September 1985, pp. 1–8.

Kouzes, J. M., and B. Z. Posner. *The Leadership Challenge: How to Get Extraordinary Things Done in Organizations.* San Francisco: Jossey-Bass, 1987.

Kozlowski, S. W. J. and M. L. Doherty. "Integration of Climate and Leadership: Examination of a Neglected Issue." *Journal of Applied Psychology* 74 (1989), pp. 546–53.

Kraiger, K.; J. K. Ford; and E. Salas. *Integration of Cognitive, Behavioral, and Affective Theories of Learning into New Methods of Training Evaluation.* Manuscript submitted for publication.

Kroeger, O., and J. M. Thuesen. *Type Talk.* New York: Delacourt, 1988.

Kuhn, T. *The Structure of Scientific Revolutions.* Chicago: The University of Chicago Press, 1962,

Kurke, L. B., and H. E. Aldrich. "Mintzberg Was Right! A Replication and Extension of 'The Nature of Managerial Work.' " *Management Science* 29 (1983), pp. 975–84.

Labak, A. S. "The Study of Charismatic College Teachers." *Dissertation Abstracts International* 34 (1973), pp. 1258B.

Landy, F. J. *Psychology of Work Behavior.* 3rd ed. Homewood, Ill.: Dorsey, 1985.

Larson, J. R., Jr. "Supervisors' Performance Feedback to Subordinates: The Impact of Subordinate Performance Valence and Outcome Dependence." *Organizational Behavior and Human Decision Processes* 37 (1986), pp. 391–408.

Latack, J. C. "Coping with Job Stress: Measures and Future Directions for Scale Development." *Journal of Applied Psychology* 71 (1986), pp. 377–85.

Latane, B.; K. Williams; and S. Harkins. "Social Loafing." *Psychology Today* 13, no. 4 (1979), p. 104.

Latham, G. P., and T. W. Lee. "Goal Setting." In *Generalizing from Laboratory to Field Settings,* ed. E. A. Locke. Lexington, Mass.: Lexington Books, 1986.

Lawler, E. E. III. *Motivation in Work Organizations.* Pacific Grove, Calif.: Brooks/Cole, 1973.

Lawrence, P. R., and J. W. Lorsch. "Differentiation and Integration in Complex Organizations." *Administrative Science Quarterly* 12 (1967a), pp. 1–47.

————. *Organization and Environment.* Boston: Harvard University, 1967b.

————. *Organization and Environment: Managing Differentiation and Integration.* Homewood, Ill.: Irwin, 1969.

Lazarsfeld, P. F. "The American Soldier: An Expository Review." *Public Opinion Quarterly* 13 (1949), pp. 377–404.

Lazarus, R. S., and S. Folkman. *Stress, Appraisal, and Coping.* New York: Springer.

Leana, C. R. "Predictors and Consequences of Delegation." *Academy of Management Journal* 29 (1986), pp. 754–74.

————. "Power Relinquishment vs. Power Sharing: Theoretical Clarification and Empirical Comparison of Delegation and Participation." *Journal of Applied Psychology* 72 (1987), pp. 228–33.

Lee, David B. "War Gaming: Thinking for the Future." *Airpower Journal* 3 (1990), pp. 40–51.

Lepper, M. R.; D. Greene; and R. E. Nisbett. "Undermining Children's Intrinsic Interests with Extrinsic Rewards: A Test of the 'Overjustification' Hypothesis." *Journal of Personality and Social Psychology* 28 (1973), pp. 128–37.

Levering, R., M. Moskowitz, and M. Katz. *The 100 Best Companies to Work for in America.* Reading, Mass.: Addison-Wesley, 1984.

Levy, J. "Right Brain, Left Brain: Fact and Fiction." *Psychology Today,* May 1985, pp 38–44.

Liden, R. C., and G. B. Graen. "Generalizability of the Vertical Dyad Linkage Model of Leadership." *Academy of Management Journal* 23 (1980), pp. 451–65.

Likert, R. *New Patterns of Management.* New York: McGraw-Hill, 1961.

Litzinger, W., and T. Schaefer. "Leadership through Followership." *Business Horizons,* 25, no. 5 (1982), pp. 78–81.

Linn, R. L., ed. *Intelligence: Measurement, Theory, and Public Policy.* Chicago: University of Illinois Press, 1989.

Linville, P. W. "Self-Complexity as a Cognitive Buffer Against Stress-Related Illness and Depression. *Journal of Personality and Social Psychology* 52, no. 4 (1987), pp. 663–76.

Lippitt, R. "The Changing Leader-Follower Relationships of the 1980s." *Journal of Applied Behavioral Science* 18 (1982), pp. 395–403.

Locke, E. A. and G. P. Latham. *Goal Setting: A Motivational Technique that Works.* Englewood Cliffs, N.J.: Prentice Hall, 1984.

_____. "Work Motivation and Satisfaction: Light at the End of the Tunnel." *Psychological Science* 1 (1990), pp. 240–46.

Locke, E. A.; G. P. Latham; and M. Erez. "3-way Interactive Presentation and Discussion; A Unique Approach to Resolving Scientific Disputes; Designing Crucial Experiments." Papers presented at the Society of Industrial and Organizational Psychology Convention, Atlanta, Ga., 1987.

Locke, E. A.; S. J. Motowidlo; and P. Bobko. "Using Self-Efficacy Theory to Resolve the Conflict between Goal-Setting Theory and Expectancy Theory in Organizational Behavior and Industrial/Organizational Psychology." *Journal of Social and Clinical Psychology* 4 (1986), pp. 328–38.

Loher, B. T.; R. A. Noe; N. L. Moeller; and M. P. Fitzgerald. "A Meta-Analysis of the Relation of Job Characteristics to Job Satisfaction." *Journal of Applied Psychology* 70 (1985), pp. 280–89.

Lombardo, M. M., and R. W. Eichinger. *Eighty-eight Assignments for Development in Place: Enhancing the Developmental Challenge of Existing Jobs.* Greensboro, N.C.: Center for Creative Leadership, 1989.

Lombardo, M.M.; E. Hutchinson; and T. D. Pryor. *Benchmarks Development Guide.* Greensboro, N.C.: Center for Creative Leadership, 1990.

Lombardo, M. M. and C. D. McCauley. *Benchmarks: A Guide to Its Development and Use.* Greensboro, N.C.: Center for Creative Leadership, 1989.

Lombardo, M. M.; M. N. Ruderman; and C. D. McCauley. "Explorations of Success and Derailment in Upper-Level Management Positions." Paper presented at meeting of the Academy of Management, New York, 1987.

Lord, R. G.; C. L. DeVader; G. M. Allinger. "A Meta-Analysis of the Relationship between Personality Traits and Leadership Perceptions: An Application of Validity Generalization Procedures." *Journal of Applied Psychology* 71 (1986), pp. 402–10.

Lowin, A., and J. R. Craig. "The Influence of Level of Performance on Managerial Style: An Experimental Object-Lesson in the Ambiguity of Correlational Data." *Organizational Behavior and Human Performance* 3 (1968), pp. 68–106.

Lundin, S. C., and L. C. Lancaster. "Beyond Leadership . . . The Importance of Followership." *The Futurist*, May-June 1990, pp. 18–22.

Luthans, F. 1989. *Organizational Behavior.* 5th ed. San Francisco: McGraw-Hill, 1992.

Luthans, F., and R. Kreitner. *Organizational Behavior Modification and Beyond: An Operant and Social Learning Approach.* Glenview, Ill.: Scott, Foresman, 1985.

Luthans, F., and J. K. Larsen. "How Managers Really Communicate." *Human Relations* 39 (1986), pp. 161–78.

Luthans, F.; S. A. Rosenkrantz; and H. W. Hennessey. "What Do Successful Managers Really Do? An Observational Study of Managerial Activites." *Journal of Applied Behavioral Science* 21 (1985), pp. 255–70.

Lytle, C. F., ed. *Leaves of Gold*. Williamsport, Pa.: Coslett, 1948.

Maccoby, M. "Management: Leadership and the Work Ethic." *Modern Office Procedures* 28, no. 5 (1983), pp. 14, 16, 18.

MacKenzie, R. A. "The Management Process in 3-D." *Harvard Business Review* 47, no. 6 (1969), pp. 80–87.

Macrorie, K. *20 Teachers*. Oxford: Oxford University Press, 1984.

Madsen, D., and P. G. Snow. "The Dispersion of Charisma." *Comparative Political Studies* 16, no. 3 (1983), pp. 337–62.

Mahoney, T. A.; T. H. Jerdee; and S. I. Carroll. "The Job(s) of Management." *Industrial Relations* 4 (1965), pp. 97–110.

Main, J. "Is the Baldridge Overblown?" *Fortune*, July 1, 1991, pp. 62–65.

Malinkowski, C. I., and C. P. Smith. "Moral Reasoning and Moral Conduct: An Investigation Prompted by Kohlberg's Theory." *Journal of Personality and Social Psychology* 49 (1985), pp. 1016–27.

Mann, F. C. "Toward an Understanding of the Leadership Role in a Formal Organization." In *Leadership and Productivity*, ed. R. Dubin. San Francisco: Chandler, 1965.

Mann, R. D. "A Review of the Relationships between Personality and Performance in Small Groups." *Psychological Bulletin* 56 (1959), pp. 241–70.

Manz, C. C. "Self-Leadership: Toward an Expanded Theory of Self-Influence Processes in Organizations." *Academy of Management Review* 11 (1986), pp. 585–600.

Marcus, J. T. "Transcendence and Charisma." *The Western Political Quarterly* 16 (1961), pp. 236–41.

Margerison, C. J. "Action Learning and Excellence in Management Development." *Journal of Management Development* 7, no. 5 (1988), pp. 43–53.

Martin, J., and C. Siehl. "Organizational Culture and Counterculture: An Uneasy Symbiosis." *Organizational Dynamics* 11, no. 2 (1983), pp. 52–64.

Martinko, M. J. and W. L. Gardner. "Beyond Structured Observation: Methodological Issues and New Directions." *Academy of Management Review* 10 (1985), pp. 676–95.

Maslow, A. H. *Motivation and Personality*. New York: Harper & Row, 1954.

Massey, M. *The People Puzzle: Understanding Yourself and Others*. Reston, Va.: Reston, 1979.

Mayer, R. E. *Thinking, Problem Solving, Cognition*. New York: W. H. Freeman, 1983.

Mayo, E. *The Human Problems of an Industrial Civilization*. New York: Macmillan, 1933.

McCall, M. W., Jr., and M. M. Lombardo. "Using Simulation for Leadership and Management Research: Through the Looking Glass." *Management Science* 28 (1982), pp. 533–49.

_____. "Off the Track: Why and How Successful Executives Get Derailed." (Tech. Rep. No. 21). Greensboro, N.C.: Center for Creative Leadership, 1983.

McCall, M. W.; M. M. Lombardo; and A. M. Morrison. *The Lessons of Experience: How Successful Executives Develop on the Job.* Lexington, Mass.: Lexington Books, 1988.

McCarley, N., and T. G. Carskadon. "Test-Retest Reliabilities of Scales and Subscales of the Myers-Briggs Type Indicator and of Criteria for Clinical Interpretive Hypotheses Involving Them." *Research in Psychological Type* 6 (1983), pp. 24–36.

McCauley, C. D. "Stress and the Eye of the Beholder." *Issues & Observations* 7, no. 3 (1987), pp. 1–16.

McCaulley, M. H. "The Myers-Briggs Type Indicator and Leadership." In *Measures of Leadership*, ed. K. E. Clark and M. B. Clark. Greensboro, N.C.: Center for Creative Leadership, 1988.

McClelland, D. C. *Power: The Inner Experience.* New York: Irvington (distributed by Halstead Press), 1975.

_____. *Human Motivation.* Glenview, Ill.: Scott, Foresman, 1985.

McClelland, D. C., and R. E. Boyatzis. "Leadership Motive Pattern and Long-Term Success in Management." *Journal of Applied Psychology* 67 (1982), pp. 737–43.

McClelland, D. C., and D. H. Burnham. "Power Is the Great Motivator." *Harvard Business Review*, 54, no. 2 (1976), pp. 100–10.

McCormick, J. and B. Powell. "Management for the 1990s." *Newsweek*, April 1988, pp. 47–48.

McGrath, J. E. *Leadership Behavior: Some Requirements for Leadership Training.* Washington, DC: Office of Career Development, U. S. Civil Service Commission, 1964.

McGregor, D. *Leadership and Motivation.* Cambridge, Mass.: MIT Press, 1966.

McGue, M., and T. J. Bouchard, Jr. "Genetic and Environmental Determinants of Information Processing and Special Mental Abilities: A Twin Analysis." In *Advances in the Psychology of Human Intelligence*, ed. R. J. Sternberg. Hillsdale, N.J.: Erlbaum, 1989, pp. 7–45.

McKay, M.; M. Davis; and P. Fanning. *Thoughts & Feelings: The Art of Cognitive Stress Intervention.* Richmond, Calif.: New Harbinger, 1981.

Meindl, J. R., and S. B. Ehrlich. "The Romance of Leadership and the Evaluation of Organizational Performance." *Academy of Management Journal* 30 (1987), pp. 90–109.

Meindl, J. R.; S. B. Ehrlich; and J. M. Dukerich. "The Romance of Leadership." *Administrative Science Quarterly* 30 (1985), pp. 78–102.

Merton, R. K. *Social Theory and Social Structure.* New York: Free Press, 1957.

———. "The Social Nature of Leadership." *American Journal of Nursing,* 69 (1969), pp. 2614–18.

Michener, H. A., and M. R. Burt. "Use of Social Influence under Varying Conditions of Legitimacy." *Journal of Personality and Social Psychology* 32 (1975), pp. 398–407.

Milgram, S. "Behavioral Study of Obedience." *Journal of Abnormal and Social Psychology* 67 (1963), pp. 371–78.

Miller, D. D. *The Story of Walt Disney.* New York: Henry Holt, 1956.

Miller, D., and J. M. Toulouse. "Strategy, Structure, CEO Personality and Performance in Small Firms." *American Journal of Small Business,* Winter 1986, pp. 47–62.

Mindell, M., and W. Gorden. *Employee Values in a Changing Society: An AMA Management Briefing.* New York: American Management Associations, 1981.

Miner, J. B. "Student Attitudes toward Bureaucratic Role Prescriptions and the Prospects for Managerial Shortages." *Personnel Psychology* 27 (1974), pp. 605–13.

———. "The Uncertain Future of the Leadership Concept: An Overview." In *Leadership Frontiers,* ed. J. G. Hunt and L. L. Larson. Kent, Ohio: Kent State University, 1975.

———. "Twenty Years of Research on Role Motivation Theory of Managerial Effectiveness." *Personnel Psychology* 31 (1978), pp. 739–60.

Mintzberg, H. *The Nature of Managerial Work.* New York: Harper & Row, 1973.

———. "If You're Not Serving Bill or Barbara, Then You're Not Serving Leadership." In *Leadership: Beyond Establishment Views,* ed. J. G. Hunt, U. Sekaran, and C. A. Schriesheim. Carbondale, Ill.: Southern Illinois University Press, 1982.

Mitchell, T. R. "Review of *In Search of Excellence* versus *The 100 Best Companies to Work for in America:* A Question of Perspective and Values." *Academy of Management Review* 10 (1985), pp. 350–55.

Mitchell, T. R., S. G. Green; and R. E. Wood, "An Attributional Model of Leadership and the Poor Performing Subordinate: Development and Validation." In *Research in Organizational Behavior,* ed B. M. Staw and L. L. Cummings. Greenwich, Conn.: JAI, 1981, pp. 197–234.

Mitchell, R. R.; C. M. Smyser; and S. E. Weed. "Locus of Control: Supervision and Work Satisfaction." *Academy of Management Journal.* 18 1975, pp. 623–30.

Mitchell, T. R., and R. E. Wood. "Supervisors' Responses to Subordinate Poor Performance: A Test of an Attributional Model. *Organizational Behavior and Human Performance* 25 (1980), pp. 123–38.

Moore, L. I. "The FMI: Dimensions of Follower Maturity." *Group and Organizational Studies* 1 (1976), pp. 203–22.

Morabito, M. A., and B. L. Dilla. "Leadership Development of USAF Aircraft Maintenance Officers." Presented at the 27th Annual Meeting of the Military Testing Association, San Diego, Calif., October 1985.

Moreno, J. L. *Sociodrama: A Method of Analysis for Social Conflicts.* Beacon, N.Y.: Beacon House, 1955.

Morrison, A. M.; R. P. White; and E. Van Velsor. *Breaking the Glass Ceiling.* Reading, Mass.: Addison-Wesley, 1987.

Morse, J. J. and F. R. Wagner. "Measuring the Process of Managerial Effectiveness." *Academy of Management Journal* 21 (1978), pp. 23–35.

Motowidlo, S. J.; M. D. Dunnette; and G. W. Carter. "An Alternative Selection Procedure: The Low-Fidelity Simulation." *Journal of Applied Psychology* 75 (1990), pp. 640–47.

Mowday, R. T. "Leader Characteristics, Self-Confidence, and Methods of Upward Influence in Organizational Decision Situations." *Academy of Management Journal* 22, no. 4 (1979), pp 709–25.

Mulder, M., and A. Stemerding. "Threat, Attraction to Group, and Need for Strong Leadership." *Human Relations* 16 (1963), pp. 317–34.

Mulder, M.; R. D. de Jong; L. Koppelar; and J. Verhage. "Power, Situation, and Leaders' Effectiveness: An Organizational Study." *Journal of Applied Psychology* 71 (1986), pp. 566–70.

Munson, C. E. "Style and Structure in Supervision." *Journal of Education for Social Work* 17 (1981), pp. 65–72.

Murphy, A. J. "A Study of the Leadership Process." *American Sociological Review* 6 (1941), pp. 674–87.

Murray, H. A. and D. W. MacKinnon. "Assessment of OSS Personnel." *Journal of Consulting Psychology* 10 (1946), pp. 76–80.

Mussen, P. H. and L. W. Porter, "Personal Motivations and Self-Conceptions Associated with Effectiveness and Ineffectiveness in Emergent Groups." *Journal of Abnormal and Social Psychology* 59 (1959), pp. 23–27.

Myers, D. G. *Psychology.* 2nd ed. New York: Worth, 1989.

Myers, I. *Gifts Differing.* Palo Alto, Calif.: Consulting Psychologists Press, 1980.

Myers, I. B., and M. H. McCaulley. *Manual: A Guide to the Development and Use of the Myers-Briggs Type Indicator.* Palo Alto, Calif.: Consulting Psychologists Press, 1985.

Naisbitt, J., and P. Aburdene. *Re-inventing the Corporation.* New York: Warner Books, 1985.

_____. *Megatrends 2000.* New York: William Morrow, 1990.

Nash, A. N. "Vocational Interests of Effective Managers: A Review of the Literature." *Personnel Psychology* 18 (1965), pp. 21–37.

―――. "Development of a SVIB Key for Selecting Managers." *Journal of Applied Psychology* 50 (1966), pp. 250–54.

Newman, R. G. "Thoughts on Superstars of Charisma: Pipers in Our Midst." *American Journal of Orthopsychiatry* 53 (1983), pp. 201–08.

Neilsen, E. H., and J. Gypen. "The Subordinate's Predicament." *Harvard Business Review* 57, no. 5 (1979), pp. 133–43.

Nierenberg, G. I. *The Art of Creative Thinking.* New York: Simon & Schuster, 1982.

Nilsen, D. L. "Using Observer Judgments for Selection." In *The Future of Leadership Selection,* chair, R. L. Hughes. Symposium conducted at the 13th Biennial Psychology in the DoD Conference, U.S. Air Force Academy, April 1992.

Nixon, R. M. *Leaders.* New York: Warner Books, 1982.

Nystrom, P. C. "Comparing Beliefs of Line and Technostructure Managers." *Academy of Management Journal* 29 (1986), pp. 812–19.

O'Reilly, C. A. "Supervisors and Peers as Information Sources, Group Supportiveness, and Individual Decision-Making Performance." *Journal of Applied Psychology* 62 (1977), pp. 632–35.

Osborn, A. F. *Applied Imagination.* New York: Scribner's, 1963.

Ouchi, W. G. *How American Business Can Meet the Japanese Challenge.* Reading, Mass.: Addison-Wesley, 1981.

Page, R. C. and W. W. Tornow. "Managerial Job Analysis: Are We Any Further Along?" Paper presented at a meeting of the Society of Industrial Organizational Psychology, Atlanta, Ga., 1987.

Parke, R. D. "Some Effects of Punishment on Children's Behavior." In *The Young Child: Reviews of Research,* ed. W. W. Hartup. Vol 2. Washington, D.C.: National Association for the Education of Young Children, 1972.

Parks, M. R. "Interpersonal Communication and the Quest for Personal Competence." In *Handbook of Interpersonal Communication,* ed. M. L. Knapp and G. R. Miller. Beverly Hills, Calif.: Sage, 1985.

Parsons, C. K.; D. M. Herold; and M. L. Leatherwood. "Turnover during Initial Employment: A Longitudinal Study of the Role of Causal Attributions." *Journal of Applied Psychology* 70 (1985), pp. 337–41.

Pearson, C. S. *The Hero Within.* San Francisco: Harper-Collins, 1986.

Penner, D. D.; D. M. Malone; T. M. Coughlin; and J. A. Herz. *Satisfaction with U.S. Army Leadership.* U.S. Army War College, Leadership Monograph Series, no. 2, 1973.

Perkins, D. N. "Thinking Frames." *Educational Leadership* 43 (1986), pp. 4–10.

Person, H. S. "Leadership as a Response to Environment." *Educational Record Supplement* no. 6 (1928), pp. 9, 10–21.

Personnel Decisions, Inc. *Successful Managers Handbook: Development Suggestions for Today's Managers.* Minneapolis: Author, 1983.

Personnel Decisions, Inc. *The Management Skills Profile.* Minneapolis: Author, 1983.

Peter, L., and R. Hull. *The Peter Principle.* New York: Morrow, 1969.

Peters, L. H.; D. D. Hartke; and J. T. Pohlmann. "Fiedler's Contingency Theory of Leadership: An Application of the Meta-Analytic Procedures of Schmidt and Hunter." *Psychological Bulletin* 97 (1985), pp. 274–85.

Peters, T. J. and R. H. Waterman. *In Search of Excellence.* New York: Harper & Row, 1982.

Petty, R. E., and J. T. Cacioppo. *Attitudes and Persuasion: Classic and Contemporary Approaches.* Dubuque, Iowa: Wm. C. Brown, 1981.

Pfeffer, J. "The Ambiguity of Leadership." In *Leadership: Where Else Can We Go?*, ed. M. W. McCall, Jr., and M. M. Lombardo. Durham, N.C.: Duke University Press, 1977.

Pfeffer, J., and G. R. Salancik. "Determinants of Supervisory Behavior: A Role Set Analysis." *Human Relations* 28 (1975), 139–54.

Pitt, L. F. "Managerial Attitudes Towards Corruption: A Pilot Study." *South African Journal of Business Management* 16 (1985), pp. 27–30.

Podsakoff, P.M. "Determinants of a Supervisor's Use of Rewards and Punishments: A Literature Review and Suggestions for Future Research." *Organizational Behavior and Human Performance* 29 1982, pp. 58–83.

Podsakoff, P. M., and L. J. Williams. "The relationship between Job Performance and Job Satisfaction." In *Generalizing from Laboratory to Field Setting*, ed. E. A. Locke. Lexington, Mass.: Lexington, 1986.

Podsakoff, P. M., and C. A. Schriesheim. Field Studies of French and Raven's Bases of Power: Critique, Reanalysis, and Suggestions for Future Research." *Psychological Bulletin* 97 (1985), pp. 387–411.

Podsakoff, P. M., and W. D. Todor. "Relationships between Leader Reward and Punishment Behavior and Group Process and Productivity." *Journal of Management* 11 (1985), pp. 55–73.

Podsakoff, P. M.; W. D. Todor; R. A. Grover; and V. L. Huber. "Situational Moderators of Leader Reward and Punishment Behaviors: Fact or Fiction?" *Organizational Behavior and Human Performance* 34 (1984), pp. 21–63.

Podsakoff, P. M.; W. D. Todor; and R. S. Schuler. "Leadership Expertise as a Moderator of the Effects of Instrumental and Supportive Leader Behaviors." *Journal of Management* 9 (1983), pp. 173–85.

Podsakoff, P. M.; W. D. Todor; and R. Skov. "Effects of Leader Contingent and Noncontingent Reward and Punishment Behaviors on Subordinate Performance and Satisfaction." *Academy of Management Journal.* 25 (1982), pp. 810–25.

Polanyi, M. *Personal Knowledge.* Chicago: University of Chicago Press, 1962.

Pomerleau, O. F., and J. Rodin. "Behavioral Medicine and Health Psychology." In *Handbook of Psychotherapy and Behavior Change,* ed. S. L. Garfield and A. E. Bergin. 3rd ed. New York: Wiley, 1986.

Porter, D. A. "Student Course Critiques: A Case Study in Total Quality in the Classroom." *Proceedings of the 13th Biennial Psychology in DoD Conference,* U.S. Air Force Academy, Colo., 1992, pp. 26–30.

Porter, L. W., and E. E. Lawler, III. *Managerial Attitudes and Performance.* Homewood, Ill.: Dorsey, 1968.

Porter, D. B.; M. Bird; and A. Wunder. "Competition, Cooperation, Satisfaction, and the Performance of Complex Tasks among Air Force Cadets." *Current Psychology Research and Reviews* 9, no. 4 (1991), pp. 347–54.

Posner, B. Z., and J. M. Kouzes. "Leadership Practices: An Alternative to the Psychological Perspective." In *Measures of Leadership,* ed. K. E. Clark and M. B. Clark. West Orange, N.J.: Leadership Library of America, 1990, pp. 205–15.

Posner, B. Z., and W. H. Schmidt. "Values and the American Manager: An Update." *California Management Review* 3 (1984), pp. 206–16.

Powell, G. N.; B. Z. Posner; and W. H. Schmidt. "Sex Effects on Managerial Value Systems." *Human Relations* 37 (1984), pp. 909–21.

Prince, G. M. "Creative Meetings through Power Sharing." *Harvard Business Review* 50, no. 4 (1972), pp. 47–54.

Pritchard, R. D.; J. Hollenback; P. J. DeLeo. "The Effects of Continuous and Partial Schedules of Reinforcement of Effort, Performance, and Satisfaction." *Organizational Behavior and Human Performance* 25 (1980), pp. 336–53.

Pritchard, R. D.; D. W. Leonard; C. W. VonBergen; and R. J. Kirk. "The Effects of Varying Schedules of Reinforcement on Human Task Performance." *Organizational Behavior and Human Performance* 16 (1976), pp. 205–30.

Pryer, M. W., and M. K. DiStefano. "Perceptions of Leadership Behavior, Job Satisfaction, and Internal-External Control Across Three Nursing Levels." *Nursing Review* 20 (1971), pp. 534–37.

Pulakos, E. D., and K. N. Wexley. "The Relationship among Perceptual Similarity, Sex, and Performance Ratings in Manager-Subordinate Dyads." *Academy of Management Journal* 26 (1983), pp. 129–39.

Quaglieri, P. L., and J. P. Carnazza. "Critical Inferences and the Multidimensionality of Feedback." *Canadian Journal of Behavioral Science* 17 (1985), pp. 284–93.

Quayle, D. "American Productivity: The Devastating Effect of Alcoholism and Drug Use." *American Psychologist* 38 (1983), pp. 454–58.

Rath, G. J., and K. S. Stoyanoff. "Understanding and Improving Communication Effectiveness." In *The 1982 Annual for Facilitators, Trainers, and Consultants,* ed. J. W. Pfeiffer and L. D. Goodstein. San Diego, Calif.: University Associates, 1982.

Read, P. P. *Alive.* New York: J. B. Lippincott, 1974.

Reason, J., and K. Mycielska. *Absent-Minded? The Psychology of Mental Lapses and Everyday Errors.* Englewood Cliffs, N.J.: Prentice Hall, 1982, p. 183.

Ree, M. J., and J. A. Earles. "Intelligance Is the Best Predictor of Job Performance." *Current Directions in Psychological Science* 1, no. 3 (1992), pp. 86–89.

Remland, M. S. "Developing Leadership Skills in Nonverbal Communication: A Situational Perspective." *Journal of Business Communication* 18, no. 3 (1981), pp. 17–29.

Reykowski, J. "Social Motivation." *Annual Review of Psychology* 33 (1982), pp. 123–54.

Rice, R. W. "Construct Validity of the Least Preferred Co-worker Score." *Psychological Bulletin* 85 (1978), pp. 1199–1237.

Rizzo, J. R.; R. J. House; and S. I. Lirtzman. "Role Conflict and Ambiguity in Complex Organizations." *Administrative Science Quarterly* 15 (1970), pp. 150–63.

Roach, C. F., and O. Behling. "Functionalism: Basis for an Alternate Approach to the Study of Leadership." In *Leaders and Managers: International Perspectives on Managerial Behavior and Leadership,* ed. J. G. Hunt, D. M. Hosking, C. A. Schriesheim, and R. Stewart. Elmsford, N.Y.: Pergamon, 1984.

Robbins, S. P. *Organizational Behavior: Concepts, Controversies, and Applications.* Englewood Cliffs, N.J.: Prentice Hall, 1986.

_____. *Training in Interpersonal Skills.* Englewood Cliffs, N.J.: Prentice Hall, 1989.

Roberts, N. C., and R. T. Bradley. "Limits of Charisma." In *Charismatic Leadership: The Elusive Factor in Organizational Effectiveness,* ed. J. A. Conger and R. N. Kanungo. San Francisco: Jossey-Bass, 1988, pp. 253–75.

Roethlisberger, F. J.; and W. J. Dickson. *Management and the Worker: An account of a Research Program Conducted by the Western Electric Company, Hawthorne Works, Chicago.* Cambridge, Mass.: Harvard University Press, 1939.

Rogers, C., and R. E. Farson. "Active Listening." In *Organizational Psychology,* ed. D. A. Kolb, I. M. Rubin, and J. M. McIntyre. Englewood Cliffs, N.J.: Prentice Hall, 1984, pp. 255–66.

Rokeach, M. *The Nature of Human Values.* New York: Free Press, 1973.

Rorabaugh, W. J. *Berkeley at War.* New York: Oxford University Press, 1989.

Rosen, B., and T. H. Jerdee. "Influence of Subordinate Characteristics on Trust and Use of Participative Decision Strategies in a Management Simulation." *Journal of Applied Psychology* 59, (1977), pp. 9–14.

Rosenbach, W. E. "Mentoring: A Gateway to Leader Development." In *Contemporary Issues in Leadership*, ed. W. E. Rosenbach and R. L. Taylor. 2nd ed. Boulder, Colo.: Westview, 1989, pp. 139–48.

Ross, S. M., and L. R. Offermann. "Transformational Leaders: Measurement of Personality Attributes and Work Group Performance." Paper presented at the Sixth Annual Society for Industrial and Organizational Psychologists Convention, St. Louis, Mo., April 1991.

Rotter, J. B. "Generalized Expectancies for Internal versus External Control of Reinforcement." *Psychological Monographs* 80, Whole No. 609, 1966.

Roush, P. E. "The Myers-Briggs Type Indicator and Perceptions of Leadership Effectiveness." Paper presented at the Center for Creative Leadership's Impact of Leadership Conference, Colorado Springs, Colo., July 1991.

Rusmore, J. T. *Executive Performance and Intellectual Ability in Organizational Levels.* San Jose, Calif.: San Jose State University, Advanced Human Systems Institution, 1984.

Rusmore, J. T. and H. Baker. "Executive Performance in Four Organizational Levels and Two Kinds of Intellectual Ability." Paper presented at Society of Industrial and Organizational Psychology Convention, Atlanta, Ga., 1987.

Rutan, J. S., and C. A. Rice. "The Charismatic Leader: Asset or Liability?" *Psychotherapy: Theory, Research, and Practice* 18 (1981), pp. 487–92.

Ryan, E. M.; V. Mims; and R. Koestner. "Relation of Reward Contingency and Interpersonal Context to Intrinsic Motivation: A Review and Test Using Cognitive Evaluation Theory." *Journal of Personality and Social Psychology* 45 (1983), pp. 736–50.

Saal, F. E., and P. A. Knight. *Industrial Organizational Psychology: Science and Practice.* Belmont, Calif.: Brooks/Cole, 1988.

Sadler, P. J., and G. H. Hofstede. "Leadership Styles: Preferences and Perceptions of Employees of an International Company in Different Countries." *Mens en Onderneming* 26 (1972), pp. 43–63.

Safire, W., and L. Safir, eds. *Leadership.* New York: Simon & Schuster, 1990.

Sales, C. A.; E. Levanoni; and D. H. Saleh. "Satisfaction and Stress as a Function of Job Orientation, Style of Supervision, and the Nature of the Task." *Engineering Management International* 2 (1984), pp. 145–53.

Sanford, A., and S. Garrod. *Understanding Written Language.* New York: Wiley, 1981.

Sarason, I. "Stress, Anxiety, and Cognitive Interference: Reactions to Stress." *Journal of Personality and Social Psychology* 46 (1986), pp. 929–39.

Sashkin, M. *A Manager's Guide to Performance Management.* New York: American Management Association Publications Division, 1986.

_____. "A New Vision of Leadership." *Journal of Management Development* 6, no. 4 (1987), pp. 19–28.

_____. "The Visionary Leader." In *Charismatic Leadership: The Elusive Factor in Organizational Effectiveness,* ed. J. A. Conger and R. N. Kanungo. San Francisco: Jossey-Bass, 1988.

Sashkin, M., and G. Huddle. "Recruit Top Principals." *School Administrator* 45, no. 2 (1988), pp. 8–15.

Sayles, L. *Leadership: What Effective Managers Really Do . . . and How They Do It.* New York: McGraw-Hill, 1979.

Scandura, T. A.; G. B. Graen; and M. A. Novak. "When Managers Decide Not to Decide Autocratically: An Investigation of Leader-Member Exchange and Decision Influence." *Journal of Applied Psychology* 71 (1986), pp. 579–84.

Scarr, S. "Protecting General Intelligence: Constructs and Consequences for Interventions." In *Intelligence: Measurement, Theory, and Public Policy,* ed. R. L. Linn. Chicago: University of Illinois Press, 1989.

Schein, E. H. *Organizational Culture and Leadership: A Dynamic View.* San Francisco: Jossey-Bass, 1985.

Schmidt, F. L.; I. Gast-Rosenberg; and J. E. Hunter. "Validity Generalization Results for Computer Programmers." *Journal of Applied Psychology* 65 (1980), pp. 643–61.

Schmidt, F. L., and J. E. Hunter. "Development of a Causal Model of Job Performance." *Current Directions in Psychological Science* 1, no. 3 (1992), pp. 89–92.

Schmidt, W. H., and B. Z. Posner. "Values and Expectations of Federal Service Executives." *Public Administration Review* 46 (1986), pp. 447–54.

Schnake, M. E. "Vicarious Punishment in a Work Setting." *Journal of Applied Psychology* 71 (1986), pp. 343–45.

Schneider, B. "Interactional Psychology and Organizational Behavior," In *Research in Organizational Behavior,* ed. L. L. Cummings and B. M. Staw. New York: Praeger, 1983, pp. 106–128.

Schneider, J. "The Cultural Situation as a Condition for the Condition of Fame." *American Sociology Review* 2, (1937), pp. 480–91.

Schriesheim, C. A., and A. S. DeNisi. "Task Dimensions as Moderators of the Effects of Instrumental Leadership: A Two Sample Replicated Test of Path-Goal Leadership Theory." *Journal of Applied Psychology* 66 (1981), pp. 589–97.

Schriesheim, C. A., and T. R. Hinkin. "Influence Tactics Used by Subordinates: A Theoretical and Empirical Analysis and Refinement of the Kipnis, Schmidt, and Wilkinson Subscales." *Journal of Applied Psychology* 75 (1990), pp. 246–57.

Schriesheim, C. A., and S. Kerr. "Theories and Measures of Leadership: A Critical Appraisal of Current and Future Directions." In *Leadership: The Cutting Edge*, ed. J. G. Hunt and L. L. Larson. Carbondale, Ill.: Southern Illinois University Press, 1977.

Schriesheim, C. A.; R. T. Mowday; and R. M. Stogdill. "Crucial Dimensions in Leader-Group Interactions." In *Cross-Currents in Leadership*, ed. J. G. Hunt and L. L. Larsen. Carbondale, Ill.: Southern Illinois University Press, 1979.

Seldes, G., ed. *The Great Quotations*. Seacaucus, N.J.: Citadel, 1983.

Senge, P. M. *The Fifth Discipline*. New York: Doubleday, 1990.

Shaver, K. G. *Principles of Social Psychology*. 2nd ed. Hillsdale, N.J.: Erlbaum, 1985.

Shaw, M. *Group Dynamics: The Psychology of Small Group Dynamics*. 3rd ed. New York: McGraw-Hill, 1981.

Shephard, J. E. "Thomas Becket, Ollie North, and You." *Military Review* 71, no. 5 (1991), pp. 20–33.

Shils, E. "Charisma, Order, and Status." *American Sociological Review* 30 (1965), 199–213.

Shipper, F., and C. L. Wilson. "The Impact of Managerial Behaviors on Group Performance, Stress, and Commitment." In *Impact of Leadership*, ed. K. E. Clark, M. B. Clark, D. P. Campbell. Greensboro, N.C.: Center for Creative Leadership, 1992.

Shostrom, E. L. *Man, the Manipulator*. New York: Bantam, 1967.

Siegall, M., and L. L. Cummings. "Task Role Ambiguity, Satisfaction, and the Moderating Effect of Task Instruction Source." *Human Relations* 39 (1986), pp. 1017–32.

Simon, H. A. "Making Management Decisions: The Role of Intuition and Emotion." *Academy of Management Executive* 1 (1987), pp. 57–64.

Simoneit, M. *Grundriss de Charakterologischen Diagnostik*. Leipzig: Teubner, 1944.

Simonton, D. "Creativity and Leadership: Convergence and Divergence." In *National Defense University, Proceedings of the Creativity and Innovation Symposium*, ed. V. E. Hendrix, D. B. Chapla, and W. Mizzelle. Washington, D. C., 1985, pp. 157–70.

————. "Presidential Style: Personality, Biography, and Performance." *Journal of Personality and Social Psychology* 55 (1988), pp. 928–36.

Simpson, W. G., and T. C. Ireland. "Managerial Excellence and Shareholder Returns." *American Association of Individual Investors Journal* 9 (1987), pp. 4–8.

Sims, H. P., and A. D. Szilagyi. "Leader Reward Behavior and Subordinate Satisfaction and Performance." *Organizational Behavior and Human Performance* 14 (1975), pp. 426–38.

Skinner, B. F. *The Behavior of Organisms.* New York: Appleton-Century-Crofts, 1938.

———. *Walden Two.* New York: MacMillan, 1948.

Slovic, P., and B. Fischoff. "On the Psychology of Experimental Surprises." *Journal of Experimental Social Psychology* 22 (1977), pp. 544–51.

Smith, F. J.; K. D. Scott; and C. L. Hulin. "Trends in Job-Related Attitudes in Managerial and Professional Employees." *Academy of Management Journal* 20 (1977), pp. 454–60.

Smith, J. E.; K. P. Carson; and R. A. Alexander. "Leadership: It Can Make a Difference." *Academy of Management Journal* 27 (1984), pp. 765–76.

Smith, M. J. *When I Say No I Feel Guilty.* New York: Dial, 1975.

Smith, P. C. "Behaviors, Results, and Organizational Effectiveness: The Problem of Criteria." In Handbook of Industrial and Organizational Psychology, ed. M. D. Dunnette. Chicago: Rand, 1976.

Snyder, M. "Self-Monitoring of Expressive Behavior." *Journal of Personality and Social Psychology* 30 (1974), pp. 526–37.

Snyder, R. A., and J. H. Morris. "Organizational Communication and Performance." *Journal of Applied Psychology* 69 (1984), pp. 461–65.

Solomon, R. L. "Punishment." *American Psychologist* 19 (1964), pp. 239–53.

Sperry, R. W. "Some Effects of Disconnecting the Cerebral Hemispheres." *Science* 217 (1968), pp. 1223–26.

Spiller, G. "The Dynamics of Greatness." *Sociological Review* 21 (1929), pp. 218–32.

Spitzberg, I. J. "Paths of Inquiry into Leadership." *Liberal Education* 73, no. 2 (1987), pp. 24–28.

Springer, S.; and G. Deutsch. *Left Brain, Right Brain.* San Francisco: W. H. Freeman, 1981.

Stahl, M. J. "Achievement, Power, and Managerical Motivation: Selecting Managerial Talent with the Job Choice Exercise." *Personnel Psychology* 36 (1983), pp. 775–89.

Staines, G. L., and R. P. Quinn. "American Workers Evaluate the Quality of Their Jobs." *Monthly Labor Review* 102, no. 1 (1979), pp. 3–12.

Staw, B. M. "Organizational Behavior: A Review and Reformulation of the Field's Outcome Variables." *Annual Review of Psychology* 35 (1984), pp. 627–66.

Stech, E. L. *Leadership Communication.* Chicago: Nelson-Hall, 1983.

Steele, R. S. "Power Motivation, Activation, and Inspirational Speeches." *Journal of Personality* 45 (1977), pp. 53–64.

Steiner, I. D. *Group Process and Productivity.* New York: Academic Press, 1972.

Steinmetz, J.; J. Blankenship; L. Brown; D. Hall; and G. Miller. *Managing Stress before It Manages You.* Palto Alto, Calif.: Bull, 1980.

Sternberg, R. J. *Beyond IQ: A Triarchic Theory of Human Intelligence.* New York: Cambridge University Press, 1985.

Stewart, A. J. and D. G. Winter. "Arousal of the Power Motive in Women." *Journal of Consulting and Clinical Psychology* 44 (1976), pp. 495–96.

Stewart, R. *Managers and Their Jobs.* London: MacMillian, 1967.

————. *Contrasts in Management.* Maidenhead, Berkshire, England: McGraw-Hill UK, 1976.

————. *Choices for the Manager: A guide to Understanding Managerial Work.* Englewood Cliffs, N.J.: Prentice Hall, 1982.

Stogdill, R. M. "Personal Factors Associated with Leadership: A Review of the Literature." *Journal of Psychology* 25 (1948), pp. 35–71.

————. *Individual Behavior and Group Achievement.* New York: Oxford University Press, 1959.

————. "Group Productivity, Drive, and Cohesiveness." *Organizational Behavior and Human Performance* 8 (1972), pp. 26–43.

————. *Handbook of Leadership.* 1st ed. New York: Free Press, 1974.

Stogdill, R. M.; O. S. Goode; and D. R. Day. "The Leader Behavior of Presidents of Labor Unions." *Personnel Psychology* 17 (1964), pp. 49–57.

Stogdill, R. M., and C. L. Shartle. *Methods in the Study of Adminstrative Performance.* Columbus, Ohio: Ohio State University, Bureau of Business Research, 1955.

Stone, D. L.; H. G. Gueutal; and B. MacIntosh. "The Effects of Feedback Sequence and Expertise of Rater of Percveived Feedback Accuracy." *Personnel Psychology* 37 (1984), pp. 487–506.

Strasser, S.; R. C. Dailey; and T. S. Bateman. "Attitudinal Moderators and Effects of Leaders' Punitive Behavior." *Psychological Reports* 49 (1981), pp. 695–98.

Strickland, B. R. "Internal-External Expectancies and Health-Related Behaviors." *Journal of Consulting and Clinical Psychology* 46 (1978), pp. 1192–1211.

Strube, M. J., and J. E. Garcia. "A Meta-Analytic Investigation of Fiedler's Contingency Model of Leadership Effectiveness." *Psychological Bulletin* 90 (1981), pp. 307–21.

Sutton, C. D., and R. W. Woodman. "Pygmalion Goes to Work: The Effects of Supervisor Expectations in the Retail Setting." *Journal of Applied Psychology* 74 (1989), pp. 943–50.

Swets, J. A.; and R. A. Bjork. "Enhancing Human Performance: An Evaluation of "New Age" Techniques Considered by the U. S. Army." *Psychological Science* 1, no. 2 (1990), pp. 85–96.

Taylor, H. L. *Delegate: The Key to Successful Management.* New York: Warner Books, 1989.

Tellegen, A.; D. T. Lykken; T. J. Bouchard, Jr.; K. J. Wilcox; N. L. Segal; and S. Rich. "Personality Similarity in Twins Reared Apart and Together." *Journal of Personality and Social Psychology* 54 (1988), pp. 1031–39.

Terborg, J. R.; C. H. Castore; and J. A. DeNinno. "A Longitudinal Field Investigation of the Impact of Group Composition on Group Performance and Cohesion." Paper presented at the meeting of the Midwestern Psychological Association, Chicago, 1975.

Tett, R. P.; D. N. Jackson; and M. Rothstein. "Personality Measures as Predictors of Job Performance: A Meta-Analytic Review." *Personnel Psychology* 44 (1991), pp. 703–42.

Thayer, P. W. "The Myers-Briggs Type Indicator and Enhancing Human Performance." Report prepared for the Committee on Techniques for the Enhancement of Human Performance of the National Academy of Sciences, 1988.

Thomas, B. *Walt Disney.* New York: Simon and Schuster, 1976.

Thomas, K. W. "Conflict and Conflict Management." In *Handbook of Industrial and Organizational Psychology,* ed. M. D. Dunnette. Chicago: Rand McNally, 1976.

_____. "Toward Multidimensional Values in Teaching: The Example of Conflict Management." *Academy of Management Review* 2, no. 3 (1977), pp. 484–90.

Thomas, K. W.; and W. H. Schmidt. "A Survey of Managerial Interests with Respect to Conflict." *Academy of Management Journal* 19 (1976), pp. 315–18.

Tichy, N. M., and M. A. Devanna. *The Transformational Leader.* New York: Wiley, 1986.

Tjosvold, D. "Stress Dosage for Problem Solvers." *Working Smart,* August 1985, p. 5.

Toffler, A. *Future Shock.* New York: Random House, 1970.

Tolman, E. C. *Purposeful Behavior in Animals and Men.* New York: Appleton-Century-Crofts, 1932.

Trevino, L. K., and S. A. Youngblood. "Bad Apples in Bad Barrels: A Causal Analysis of Ethical Decision-Making Behavior." *Journal of Applied Psychology* 75 (1990), pp. 378–85.

Trice, H. M. and J. M. Beyer. "Charisma and Its Routinization in Two Social Movement Organizations." In *Research in Organizational Behavior,* ed. B. M. Staw and L. L. Cummings. Vol. 8. Greenwich, Conn.: JAI, 1986.

Trist, E. L., and K. W. Bamforth. "Some Social and Psychological Consequences of the Longwall Method of Coal Getting." *Human Relations* 4 (1951), pp. 1–38.

Tsui, A. "A Role Set Analysis of Managerial Reputation." *Organizational Behavior and Human Performance* 34 (1984), pp. 64–96.

Tucker, R. C. "The Theory of Charismatic Leadership." *Daedalus* 97 (1968), pp. 731–56.

Tuckman, B. W. "Developmental Sequence in Small Groups." *Psychological Bulletin* 63 (1965), pp. 384–99.

Udell, J. G. "An Empirical Test of Hypotheses Relating to Span of Control." *Administrative Science Quarterly* 12 (1967), pp. 420–39.

Uecker, M. E. and B. L. Dilla. "Mentoring as a Leadership Development Tool in the United States Air Force." *Proceedings of the 26th Annual Meeting of the Military Testing Association*, Munich, Germany, 1985, pp. 423–28.

Ungson, G. R.; C. James; and B. H. Spicer. "The Effects of Regulatory Agencies on Organizations in Wood Products and High Technology/Electronics Organizations." *Academy of Management Journal* 28 (1985), pp. 426–45.

Urwick, L. F. *Notes on the Theory of Organization.* New York: American Management Association, 1952.

Vecchio, R. P. "Predicting Worker Performance in Inequitable Settings." *Academy of Management Review* 7 (1982), pp. 103–10.

————. "Assessing the Validity of Fiedler's Contingency Model of Leadership Effectiveness: A Closer Look at Strube and Garcia." *Psychological Bulletin* 93 (1983), pp. 404–08.

————. "Situational Leadership Theory: An Examination of a Prescriptive Theory." *Journal of Applied Psychology* 72 (1987), pp. 444–51.

Vroom, V. H. *Work and Motivation.* New York: Wiley, 1964.

Vroom, V. H., and A. G. Jago. "Leadership and Decision Making: A Revised Normative Model. Paper presented at the Academy of Management Convention, Boston, Mass., 1974.

————. *The New Theory of Leadership: Managing Participation in Organizations.* Englewood Cliffs, N.J.: Prentice Hall, 1988.

Vroom, V. H., and P. W. Yetton. *Leadership and Decision Making.* Pittsburgh: University of Pittsburgh Press, 1973.

Wainer, H. A., and I. M. Rubin. "Motivation of Research and Development Entrepreneurs: Determinants of Company Success." *Journal of Applied Psychology* 53 (1969), pp. 178–84.

Wakabayashi, M., and G. B. Graen. "The Japanese Career Progress Study: A Seven-Year Follow-up." *Journal of Applied Psychology* 69 (1984), pp. 603–14.

Wakin, M. M. "Ethics of Leadership." In *Military Leadership*, ed. J. H. Buck and L. J. Korb. Beverly Hills, Calif.: Sage, 1981.

Walker, T. G. "Leader Selection and Behavior in Small Political Groups." *Small Group Behavior* 7 (1976), pp. 363–68.

Wall, T. D.; N. J. Kemp; P. R. Jackson; and C. W. Clegg. "Outcomes of Autonomous Work Groups: A Long-Term Field Experiment." *Academy of Management Journal* 29 (1986), pp. 280–304.

Wallach, M. A., and N. Kogan. *Modes of Thinking in Young Children.* New York: Holt, Rinehart & Winston, 1965.

Wallas, G. *The Art of Thought.* New York: Harcourt Brace Jovanovich, 1926.

Wanous, J. P.; T. L. Keon; and J. C. Latack. "Expectancy Theory and Occupational/Organizational Choices: A Review and Test." *Organizational Behavior and Human Performance* 32 (1983), pp 66–86.

Weber, J. "Managers' Moral Meaning: An Exploratory Look at Managers' Responses to the Moral Dilemmas." *Proceedings of the Academy of Management Convention,* Washington, D.C., 1989, pp. 333–37.

Weber, M. *The Theory of Social and Economic Organization,* ed. and trans. A. M. Henderson and T. Parsons. (Original work published in 1923). New York: The Free Press.

Weber, M. *The Theory of Social and Economic Organization,* ed. Talcott Parsons; trans. A. M. Henderson and T. Parsons. New York: Free Press, 1964.

Weschler, D. *Weschler Adult Intelligence Scale: Manual.* New York: Psychological Corporation, 1955.

Weiss, H. M. "Subordinate Imitation of Supervisor Behavior: The Role of Modeling in Organizational Socialization." *Organizational Behavior and Human Performance* 19 (1977), pp. 89–105.

West Point Associates, the Department of Behavioral Sciences and Leadership, United States Military Academy. *Leadership in Organizations.* Garden City Park, N.Y.: Avery, 1988.

Westley, F. R., and H. Mintzberg. "Profiles of Strategic Vision: Levesque and Iacocca." In *Charismatic Leadership: The Elusive Factor in Organizational Effectiveness,* ed. J. A. Conger and R. N. Kanungo. San Francisco: Jossey-Bass, 1988.

Wexley, K. N., and G. P. Latham. *Developing and Training Human Resources in Organizations.* Glenview, Ill.: Scott, Foresman, 1981.

Whitely, W.: T. W. Dougherty; and G. F. Dreher. "The Relationship of Mentoring and Socioeconomic Origin to Managers' and Professionals' Early Career Progress." *Proceedings, Academy of Management,* Anaheim, Calif., 1988, pp. 58–62.

Whiteside, D. E. *Command Excellence: What It Takes to Be the Best!* Department of the Navy, Washington, D.C.: Leadership Division, Naval Military Personnel Command, 1985.

Wilcox, W. H. "Assistant Superintendents' Perceptions of the Effectiveness of the Superintendent, Job Satisfaction, and Satisfaction with the Superintendent's Supervisory Skills." Ph. D. dissertation, University of Missouri, Columbia, Mo., 1982.

Wiley, J., and T. Camacho. "Life-Style and Future Health: Evidence from the Alameda County Study." *Preventive Medicine* 9 (1980), pp. 1–21.

Willerman, L. *The Psychology of Individual and Group Differences.* San Francisco: W. H. Freeman, 1979.

Willner, A. R. *The Spellbinders: Charismatic Political Leadership.* New Haven, Conn.: Yale University Press, 1984.

Wilson, J. A., and N. S. Elman. "Organizational Benefits of Mentoring." *Academy of Management Executive* 4 (1990), pp. 88–93.

Wilson, P. R. "The Perceptual Distortion of Height as a Function of Ascribed Academic Status." *Journal of Social Psychology* 74 (1968), pp. 97–102.

Winter, D. G. "Leader Appeal, Leader Performance, and the Motive Profiles of Leaders and Followers: A Study of American Presidents and Elections." *Journal of Personality and Social Psychology* 52 (1987), pp. 196–202.

Wolpe, H. "A Critical Analysis of Some Aspects of Charisma." *The Sociological Review* 16 (1968), pp. 305–18.

Wood, G. "The Knew-It-All-Along Effect." *Journal of Experimental Psychology: Human Perception and Performance* 4 (1979), pp. 345–53.

Woodward, J. *Industrial Organization.* London: Oxford University Press, 1965.

Yukl, G. A. *Leadership in Organizations.* 1st ed. Englewood Cliffs, N.J.: Prentice Hall, 1981.

_____. *Leadership in Organizations.* 2nd ed. Englewood Cliffs, N.J.: Prentice Hall, 1989.

Yukl, G. A., and C. M. Falbe. "Importance of Different Power Sources in Downward and Lateral Relations." *Journal of Applied Psychology* 76 (1991), pp. 416–23.

Yukl, G. A.; R. Lepsinger; and T. Lucia. "Preliminary Report on the Development and Validation of the Influence Behavior Questionnaire." In *Impact of Leadership,* ed. K. E. Clark, M. B. Clark, and D. P. Campbell. Greensboro, N.C.: Center for Creative Leadership, 1992.

Yukl, G. A., and D. D. Van Fleet. "Cross-Situational Multi-Method Research on Military Leader Effectiveness." *Organizational Behavior and Human Performance* 30 (1982), pp. 87–108.

_____. "Theory and Research on Leadership in Organizations." In Handbook of Industrial & Organizational Psychology, ed. M. D. Dunnette and L. M. Hough. Vol. 3. Palo Alto, Calif.: Consulting Psychologists Press, 1992. pp. 1–51.

Yukl, G. A.; S. Wall; and R. Lepsinger. "Preliminary Report on Validation of the Managerial Practices Survey." In *Measures of Leadership,* ed K. E. Clark and M. B. Clark. Greensboro, N.C.: Center for Creative Leadership, 1989.

Zaccaro, S. J.; R. J. Foti; and D. A. Kenny. "Self-Monitoring and Trait-Based Variance in Leadership: An Investigation of Leader Flexibility across Multiple Group Situations." *Journal of Applied Psychology* 76 (1991), pp. 308–15.

Zajonc, R. "Social Facilitation," *Science* 149 (1965), pp. 269–74.

Zaleznik, A. "Charismatic and Consensus Leaders: A Psychological Comparison." *Bulletin of the Menninger Clinic* 38 (1974), pp. 222–38.

———. "The Leadership Gap." *The Washington Quarterly* 6, no. 1 (1983), pp. 32–39.

Zey, M. G. *The Mentor Connection.* Homewood, Ill.: Dow Jones-Irwin, 1984.

Zimbardo, P.; C. Haney; W. Banks; and D. Jafe. "The Mind Is a Formidable Jailer: A Pirandellian Prison." *The New York Times Magazine,* April 8, 1973, pp. 38–60.

Name Index

Subject Index